# IRELAND 2008

**Featuring 1,000 Hotels & Guesthouses** as well as details on **Golfing, Angling, Conference, Spa & Leisure Facilities** and extensive **Touring Maps**

**IRISH HOTELS FEDERATION**
**13 Northbrook Road, Dublin 6, Ireland**
**Telephone +353 1 497 6459 Fax: +353 1 497 4613**

When dialling Ireland from abroad, please use the following codes:
Republic of Ireland: 00 353 + local code (drop the 0).
Northern Ireland: 00 44 + local code (drop the 0).
If dialling Northern Ireland directly from the Republic of Ireland replace the prefix code 028 with the code 048.

**The Irish Hotels Federation does not accept any responsibility for errors, omissions or any information whatsoever in the Guide and members and users of the Guide are requested to consult page 11 hereof for further information.**



Design & Database published by NeoGen, www.neogen.ie - First Print

GUINNESS

*" come & discover the undiscovered "*

*" enjoy the spectacular scenic contrasts "*

*" step into a world of history & culture "*



**Contents**



**Illustrated Guide to Hotels and Guesthouses**



**Activities**

*" take a journey through time in no time at all "*

## REGIONS

Begin by selecting the **Region(s)** you wish to visit. This guide divides into **4 separate Regions – Ireland West, Ireland South, Dublin & Ireland East, Northern Ireland** – and they are represented in that order.

## COUNTIES

Within each Region, Counties are presented alphabetically.

## LOCATIONS – CITIES, TOWNS, VILLAGES

Within Counties, Locations are also presented alphabetically, see **Index to Locations** on Pages 12 & 13.

### HOTELS & GUESTHOUSES

Within Locations, Hotels and Guesthouses are also presented in alphabetical order, see **Index of Hotels and Guesthouses** on Pages 495 to 512.

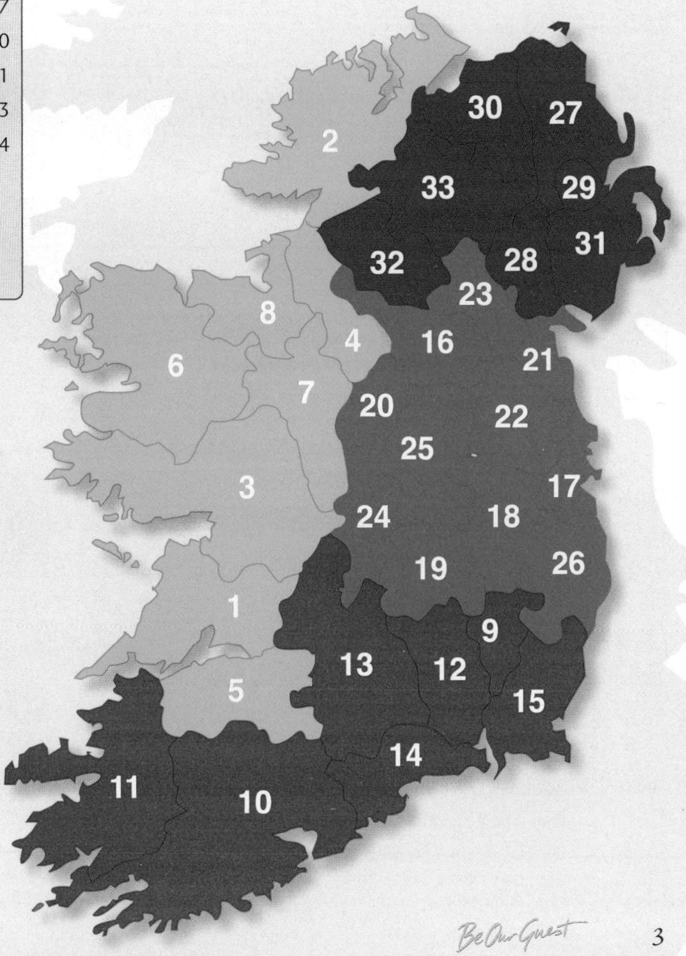

## FACILITIES - KEY TO SYMBOLS

- Total Number of Bedrooms, All En Suite unless otherwise stated
- Total Number of Bedrooms Without Bath/Shower & Toilet
- Lift/Elevator
- Can be Booked Through Travel Agent / Tourist Office and Commission Paid
- Child Friendly
- Garden for Visitors' Use
- Leisure Facilities
- Horse Riding/Pony Trekking On Site or Nearby
- Golf Course On Site
- Angling on Site or Nearby
- Car Parking
- Facilities for Pets
- Price Reduction for Senior Citizens excl. July/August and Subject to Availability
- Tea/Coffee Making Facilities in Bedroom
- Restaurant
- Wine Licence
- Licensed to Sell All Alcoholic Drink
- Internet Access
- Air Conditioning (Other than Conference Area)
- Guide Dogs Welcome

1. Accessible to Ambulant People Capable of Climbing Flights of Steps with a Maximum Height Between Landings of 1.8 Metres.
2. Accessible to Ambulant People with Mobility Impairments but Capable of Climbing Three Steps.
3. Accessible to Wheelchair Users Including those who can Transfer Unaided to and from the Wheelchair.
4. Accessible to All Wheelchair Users Including those Requiring Assistance to Transfer to and from the Wheelchair e.g. Carer/Partner.

## ACTIVITY SECTIONS

*Green symbols Illustrated below denote that the hotel or guesthouse is included in a particular Activity Section. Detailed information on these Activities is shown on pages: 397 to 475*

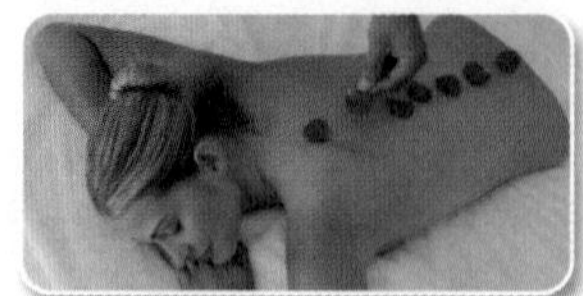

GUINNESS

# SAMPLE ENTRY



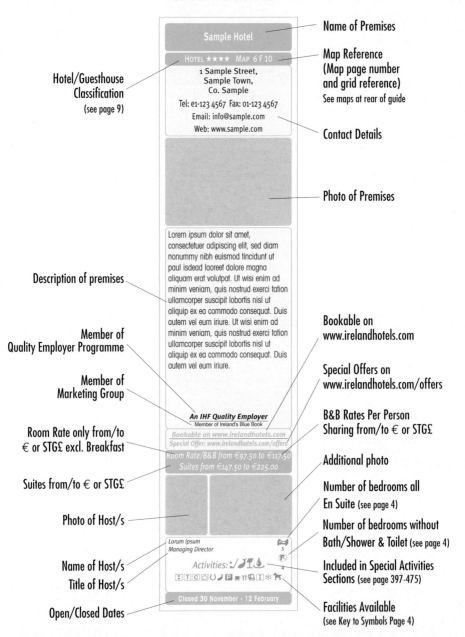

Closed 30 November - 12 February

Name of Premises

Map Reference (Map page number and grid reference)
See maps at rear of guide

Hotel/Guesthouse Classification (see page 9)

Contact Details

Photo of Premises

Description of premises

Sample Hotel
HOTEL ★★★★ MAP 6 F 10
1 Sample Street,
Sample Town,
Co. Sample
Tel: 01-123 4567 Fax: 01-123 4567
Email: info@sample.com
Web: www.sample.com
Lorem ipsum dolor sit amet, consectetuer adipiscing elit, sed diam nonummy nibh euismod tincidunt ut paul isdead laoreet dolore magna aliquam erat volutpat. Ut wisi enim ad minim veniam, quis nostrud exerci tation ullamcorper suscipit lobortis nisl ut aliquip ex ea commodo consequat. Duis autem vel eum iriure. Ut wisi enim ad minim veniam, quis nostrud exerci tation ullamcorper suscipit lobortis nisl ut aliquip ex ea commodo consequat. Duis autem vel eum iriure.
An IHF Quality Employer
Member of Ireland's Blue Book

Bookable on www.irelandhotels.com

Special Offer: www.irelandhotels.com/offers
Room Rate/B&B from €97.50 to €117.50
Suites from €147.50 to €225.00
Lorum Ipsum
Managing Director

Member of Quality Employer Programme

Special Offers on www.irelandhotels.com/offers

Member of Marketing Group

B&B Rates Per Person Sharing from/to € or STG£

Room Rate only from/to € or STG£ excl. Breakfast

Additional photo

Suites from/to € or STG£

Number of bedrooms all En Suite (see page 4)

Photo of Host/s

Number of bedrooms without Bath/Shower & Toilet (see page 4)

Name of Host/s

Included in Special Activities Sections (see page 397-475)

Title of Host/s

Open/Closed Dates

Facilities Available (see Key to Symbols Page 4)

**It is essential that when booking your accommodation you request the "Be Our Guest 2008" Rate**

Our Guide features a broad selection of Irish Hotels and Guesthouses, from ultra modern buildings to stately Country Houses, luxurious Castles and old-world Inns. The majority of these Hotels and Guesthouses are members of the Irish Hotels Federation or the Northern Ireland Hotels Federation and we hope that the illustrations and descriptions of these premises and the amenities they offer will help you to choose the most suitable premises for your holiday.

All of the Hotels and Guesthouses featured in the Guide at the time of going to print (10th October 2007) have been registered or are in the process of applying for registration by Fáilte Ireland or by the Northern Ireland Tourist Board, in accordance with the Statutory Registration Regulations which they administer.

## B&B, ROOM AND SUITE RATES*

The only rates featured in this publication relate to either **a Bed & Breakfast Per Person Sharing, a Room Rate only or a Suite Rate**. These are **Guideline Rates**, please ensure that you contact the premises to vertify the rates applicable to your reservation. **Supplements may be payable for suites (see below) or superior/de luxe rooms. Also, where single or double/twin bedded rooms are occupied by one person, a supplement may be payable. Correspondingly, if more than two persons share a family room, special reduced rates may be arranged.**

***The definition of a Suite or Half Suite, broadly speaking, is:** The bedroom area must be either separate from the living area or clearly defined by an obvious divide i.e. a door or arch or different floor coverings e.g. carpet, tiles or wooden flooring. Please contact each premises to ascertain the exact definition of their suite(s).

**Per Person Sharing:** relates to the cost of Bed & Full Breakfast per Person per Night, on the basis of two persons occupying a Standard Double/Twin Bedded Room, most having private bath/shower.

**Room Rate:** relates to the cost of a Standard Room per Night. There may be a restriction on the number of persons allowed to share the room. It is advisable to check this when making your reservation.

**Suites:** relates to the cost of a Suite per Night. There may be a restriction on the number of persons allowed to share the suite. It is advisable to check this when making your reservation.

**The rates range from minimum to maximum and are those generally in operation throughout the year, but may not apply during special occasions such as Public Holiday Weekends, Christmas and New Year, International Events, Major Festivals and Sporting Fixtures, or on such other occasions as individual premises may decide.**

Rates are inclusive of Value Added Taxes at current (2007) rates and Services Charges (if any).
In the case of Hotels and Guesthouses in the Republic of Ireland, rates are quoted in **€ (Euro)**, whereas in Northern Ireland rates are quoted in **STG£**.

SPECIAL OFFERS
Many of the Hotels & Guesthouses featured in this guide offer great special offers. For more information visit **www.irelandhotels.com/offers**

## OPENING DATES FOR PREMISES UNDER CONSTRUCTION OR REFURBISHMENT

Some of the premises featured in the guide were not open at the guide print date (10th October 2007). The planned date of opening as supplied by these premises is displayed on the premises photograph.

# EXPLANATION OF CLASSIFICATION (STAR RATING) SCHEME

## REPUBLIC OF IRELAND

A mandatory **Hotel and Guesthouse Classification Scheme** has been developed by Fáilte Ireland, in conjunction with the Irish Hotels Federation (IHF), which was introduced during 2007. This new classification scheme will be in place for 2008.

**Hotels are rated from 1 Star to 5 Stars and Guesthouses are rated from 1 Star to 4 Stars. The stars are indicated on each entry under the Name of the Hotel or Guesthouse.**

**If the star rating is not shown**, this means that the premises is perhaps undergoing a period of renovation or refurbishment and is awaiting its assessment for grading or, it was a late addition to the guide and missed the deadline for the inspection process. Where this is the case, the premises should be contacted directly for a classification update.

**"Built to a 1/2/3/4/5 star specification": This is shown in the first line of description where premises are Under Construction** and not yet opened at the time of going to print, but are due to open during 2008

**or**

**where premises have not yet been registered by Fáilte Ireland.** This means that, although not yet formally inspected for their star grading, the premises has been built to the standards set out in the classification criteria and it is expected to reach this standard during the inspection visit.

As the new classification system is mandatory for all premises in the Republic of Ireland, their classification details must be displayed as outlined above.

The new classification criteria for each grade can be viewed and downloaded from **http://www.failteireland.ie/developing-enterprises/quality---standards/classification-scheme.aspx**

Please refer to Page 4 for the Explanation of Facilities/Key to Symbols shown at the end of each entry in order to review the services and facilities offered by individual premises. Further details of facilities and services available in each premises can be viewed on **www.discoverireland.ie**

## NORTHERN IRELAND

All premises listed in the Northern Ireland section of this guide have been awarded their classification by Northern Ireland Tourist Board – please see page 28 for contact details.

## RESERVATIONS

Courtesy Onward Reservations

If you are moving around the country, the premises in which you are staying will be delighted to help you select your next accommodation from the Be Our Guest Guide and make your reservation.

The following are other ways in which a booking can be made:

1. Advance enquiries and reservations may be made directly to the premises by phone, fax, e-mail or letter and details of the reservation should be confirmed by both parties. A deposit should be forwarded if requested.

2. Book your accommodation online at:

*Irelandhotels.com features all premises listed in the Be Our Guest Guide.*

**www.irelandhotels.com**

3. Some of the hotels and guesthouses in the Guide participate in a Central Reservations system which may be indicated in their entry.

4. Travel Agent - your travel agent will normally make a booking on your behalf without extra charge where the premises pays travel agents' commission (this is indicated by the symbol [T] in the Guide). In other cases, agents will usually charge a small fee to cover the cost of telephone calls and administration.

5. Some local tourist information offices listed in this guide (see pages 24-26) operate an enquiry and booking service and will make an accommodation reservation on your behalf.

## COMPLAINTS

Should there be cause for complaint, the matter should be brought to the notice of the Management of the premises in the first instance. Failing satisfaction, the matter should be referred to the Tourist Information Office concerned (see list on pages 24-26) or Fáilte Ireland, Baggot Street Bridge, Dublin 2. In the case of Northern Ireland premises, complaints should be addressed to the Customer Relations Section, Northern Ireland Tourist Board, 59 North Street, Belfast BT1 1NB.

## ERRORS AND OMISSIONS

The information contained in the accommodation section has been supplied by individual premises. While reasonable care has been taken in compiling the information supplied and ensuring its accuracy and compliance with consumer protection laws, the Irish Hotels Federation cannot accept any responsibility for any errors, omissions or misinformation regarding accommodation, facilities, prices, services, classification or any other information whatsoever in the Guide and shall have no liability whatsoever and howsoever arising to any person for any loss, whether direct, indirect, economic or consequential, or damages, actions, proceedings, costs, claims, expenses or demands arising therefrom. The listing of any premises in this guide is not and should not be taken as a recommendation from the IHF or a representation that the premises will be suitable for your purposes.

## THINK ABOUT INSURANCE

We strongly advise you to take out an insurance policy against accidents, cancellations, delays, loss of property and medical expenses. Such travel and holiday insurance policies are available quite cheaply and are worth every penny for peace of mind alone.

## CANCELLATIONS

Should it be necessary to amend or cancel your reservation, please advise the premises immediately, as there may be a cancellation penalty. Please establish, when making a reservation, what cancellation policy applies.

# INDEX TO LOCATIONS

***Annette Devine***
***President, Irish Hotels Federation***

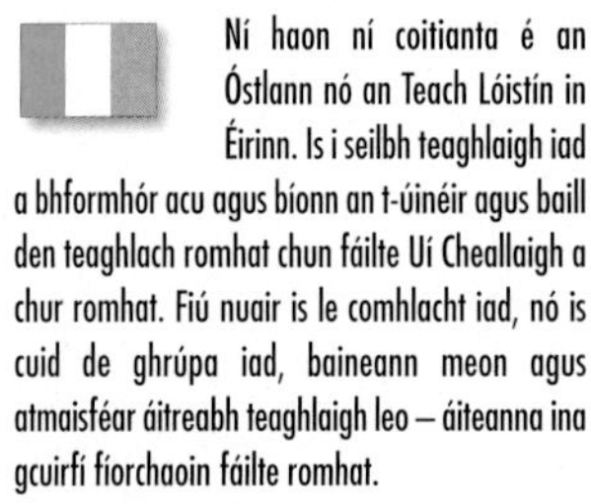

Ní haon ní coitianta é an Óstlann nó an Teach Lóistín in Éirinn. Is i seilbh teaghlaigh iad a bhformhór acu agus bíonn an t-úinéir agus baill den teaghlach romhat chun fáilte Uí Cheallaigh a chur romhat. Fiú nuair is le comhlacht iad, nó is cuid de ghrúpa iad, baineann meon agus atmaisféar áitreabh teaghlaigh leo – áiteanna ina gcuirfí fíorchaoin fáilte romhat.

Rud ar leith is ea an óstlann in Éirinn agus is dócha ná a mhalairt go bhfeidhmíonn sí mar lárionad sóisialta don phobal. Cuireann an óstlann i bhfad níos mó ná leaba agus béile ar fáil - is lárionad sóisialta,a siamsaíochta, gnó agus pobail ar fheabhas í chomh maith agus gach aon áis faoin spéir aici, a chuireann bia, lóistín, imeachtaí spóirt, áiseanna siamsíochta agus só agus tarraingtí nach iad ar fáil.

Agus tú ag taisteal timpeall na tíre gheobhaidh tú amach go mbeidh "Bí i d'Aoi Againn" an-áisiúil agus an chéad suíomh eile á roghnú agat. Is mian le hóstlannaithe agus le lucht tithe lóistín na hÉireann fáilte a chur romhat agus a bheith in ann a dheimhniú go mbainfidh tú sult as do sheal in Éirinn. Tá súil againn go bhfanfaidh tú linn agus go mbainfidh tú leas as an treoir seo chun do rogha óstlann nó teach lóistin a aimsiú, i dtreo is go mbeimid in ann a rá leat go pearsanta -

Hotels and Guesthouses in Ireland are very special. The majority are family owned with the proprietor and members of the family there to welcome guests and to extend to them renowned Irish hospitality. Even when they are owned by a company, or are part of a group, they still retain the character and ambience of a family premises - a place where you will be truly welcome.

The Irish hotel is unique, in that more often than not, it acts as a social centre for the community. Hotels offer a lot more than just a bed and a meal - they are fully fledged social, leisure, business and community centres with every imaginable facility and amenity, providing food, accommodation, sports, leisure facilities, entertainment and other attractions.

If you are moving around the country, you'll find that "Be Our Guest" is an invaluable help in choosing your next location.

Ireland's hoteliers and guesthouse owners want to welcome you and want to play their part in ensuring that your stay in Ireland is a happy one. We hope that you will stay with us and that you will use this guide to select the hotel or guesthouse of your choice, so that we can personally invite you to -

Les hôtels et les pensions en Irlande sont d'un caractère particulier. Ils sont très souvent gérés par le propriétaire et des membres de sa famille, présents pour accueillir les visiteurs et leur faire découvrir la célèbre hospitalité irlandaise. Même s'ils appartiennent à une entreprise ou font partie d'un groupe de sociétés, ils possèdent toujours ce caractère et cette ambiance des lieux familiaux - un endroit où vous serez sincèrement bien accueillis.

L'hôtel irlandais est unique en ce qu'il joue très souvent le rôle de centre social pour la communauté. Les hôtels offrent beaucoup plus qu'un lit et un repas - ce sont, pour la communauté, de véritables centres sociaux, de loisirs et d'affaires, équipés de toutes les infrastructures et installations imaginables. Ils vous proposent le gîte et le couvert, mais aussi activités sportives et de loisir, divertissements et autres attractions.

Si vous voyagez dans le pays, vous trouverez que le guide "Be Our Guest" est d'une aide précieuse pour vous aider à choisir votre prochaine destination.

Les hôteliers et les propriétaires de pensions irlandais veulent vous accueillir et être là pour vous assurer un séjour agréable en Irlande. Nous espérons que vous resterez avec nous et que vous utiliserez ce guide pour sélectionner l'hôtel ou la pension de votre choix, afin que nous ayons le plaisir de vous compter parmi nos visiteurs -

Be Our Guest

Die Hotels und Pensionen in Irland sind von ganz besonderer Art. Zum größten Teil handelt es sich dabei um private Familienbetriebe, in denen der Besitzer und die Familienmitglieder ihre Gäste mit der vielgerühmten irischen Gastfreundschaft willkommen heißen. Aber auch wenn sich diese Häuser in Unternehmensbesitz befinden oder einer Kette angehören, strahlen sie dennoch den Charakter und die Atmosphäre von Familienbetrieben aus - ein Ort, an dem Sie immer herzlich willkommen sind.

Hotels in Irland sind einzig in ihrer Art und dienen oftmals als Mittelpunkt geselliger Treffen. Hotels haben viel mehr zu bieten als nur ein Bett und eine Mahlzeit - sie sind Gesellschafts-, Freizeit-, Geschäfts- und öffentlicher Treffpunkt mit allen nur erdenklichen Einrichtungen und Annehmlichkeiten, angefangen bei Essen, Unterkunft, Sport und Freizeitmöglichkeiten bis zur Unterhaltung und anderen Anziehungspunkten.

Auf Ihren Reisen im Land werden Sie feststellen, daß Ihnen der "Be Our Guest"-Führer eine wertvolle Hilfe bei der Suche nach der nächstgelegenen Unterkunft leistet.

Irlands Hotel und Pensionsbesitzer heißen Sie gerne willkommen und möchten ihren Anteil dazu beitragen, daß Ihnen Ihr Aufenthalt in Irland in angenehmer Erinnerung bleibt. Wir hoffen, daß Sie uns besuchen werden und diesen Führer bei der Auswahl Ihres Hotels oder Ihrer Pension zu Rate ziehen, so daß wir Sie persönlich willkommen heißen können -

*Be Our Guest*

Los hoteles y las pensiones en Irlanda son muy especiales. La mayoría son propiedades familiares habitadas por el mismo propietario junto a los miembros de su familia que se encuentran predispuestos a dar la bienvenida a los huéspedes y, de este modo, contribuir a ampliar su reconocida hospitalidad irlandesa. Incluso si pertecen a una compañía o forman parte de un grupo, siempre mantendrán el carácter y ambiente de las propiedades familiares, un lugar donde siempre serás bienvenido de corazón.

El hotel irlandés es único y se comporta bastante a menudo como el mismo centro social de la comunidad. Estos hoteles ofrecen algo más que una cama y comida, rebozan de centros sociales comunitarios de ocio y negocios con una amplia gama de servicios inimaginables. Ofrece comida, alojamiento, deportes, actividades de ocio, entretenimiento y todo tipo de atracciones.

Si te encuentras viajando por nuestro país, te darás cuenta que la ayuda que te ofrece "Be Our Guest", a la hora de elegir tu próximo destino, no tiene precio. Los hoteleros y propietarios de pensiones de Irlanda quieren darte la bienvenida y quieren contribuir a que tu estancia en Irlanda sea una estancia feliz. Esperamos que te quedes con nosotros y que utilices esta guía para elegir el hotel o pensión que tú elijas y para que nosotros podamos invitarte personalmente a ser nuestro invitado, el invitado de -

*Be Our Guest*

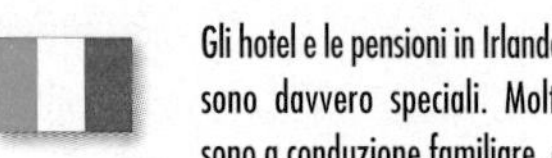

Gli hotel e le pensioni in Irlanda sono davvero speciali. Molti sono a conduzione familiare, e gli ospiti vengono accolti dai proprietari e le loro famiglie secondo le famose tradizioni di ospitalità irlandesi. Il calore e l'ambiente intimo e accogliente si ritrovano persino negli hotel delle grandi compagnie e catene alberghiere: avrete sempre la sensazione di essere ospiti graditi.

Una caratteristica unica degli hotel irlandesi è che, molto spesso, fungono anche da centro di aggregazione della comunità. Gli alberghi offrono molto di più di un letto e dei pasti: sono centri per socializzare, divertirsi, fare affari e vivere la dimensione locale. Qui si può trovare ogni attrezzatura e comfort immaginabile: ristoranti, alloggi, impianti sportivi, attività ricreative, divertimento e tante altre attrazioni.

Se prevedete molti spostamenti, scoprirete in "Be Our Guest" uno strumento di valore inestimabile per la scelta delle prossime mete. Gli albergatori e i proprietari delle pensioni irlandesi vi aspettano per darvi il benvenuto e fare la loro parte per rendere piacevole il vostro soggiorno in Irlanda. Ci auguriamo che vogliate viaggiare con noi, usando la nostra guida per scegliere un hotel o una pensione di vostro gusto, così da potervi invitare personalmente a -

*Be Our Guest*

To assist visitors with mobility impairment, the following 4 symbols are shown on entries in the Republic of Ireland for those hotels and guesthouses which have been certified by Fáilte Ireland.

## Validated Accessible Scheme (VAS)

**Category 1**
Accessible to ambulant people capable of climbing flights of steps with a maximum height between landings of 1.8 metres.

**Category 2**
Accessible to ambulant people with mobility impairments but capable of climbing three steps.

**Category 3**
Accessible to wheelchair users including those who can transfer unaidedto and from the wheelchair.

**Category 4**
Accessible to all wheelchair users including those requiring assistance to transfer to and from the wheelchair e.g. carer / partner

These symbols are also explained on page 4 and you will find them amongst the grey symbols at the end of relevant premises.

As this is a recent scheme more premises will be approved during 2007, so it is always worthwhile enquiring directly with the hotel and guesthouse. A large number of premises who have not yet been approved under the new scheme at the time of going to print, were approved under a previous scheme and will therefore have good access for the disabled.

**Republic of Ireland -** Should you require further information on access, please contact Fáilte Ireland, Baggot Street Bridge, Dublin 2. Tel: +353 1 602 4000 Fax: +353 1 602 4100.

**Northern Ireland -** No official approval system is currently in place. Therfore, we would advise that you contact the Hotel or Guesthouse directly in order to confirm the status of their accessibility for disabled persons.

Further information may also be available from: Northern Ireland Tourist Board, 59 North Street, Belfast, BT1 1NB, Tel: +44 28 9023 1221 Fax: +44 28 9024 0960 or Disability Action Northern Ireland, Tel: +44 28 9029 7880 Fax: +44 28 9029 7881 Email: hq@disabilityaction.org

## LANGUAGE

Irish (Gaelic) and English are the two official languages of the Republic of Ireland and street and road signs are all bilingual. In Gaeltacht areas Irish is spoken daily, however English is spoken by everyone. In Northern Ireland, English is the official language. The Irish Language, Gaelic, is also taught in many schools, and summer schools. Ulster Scots, spoken in Northern Ireland, is on the increase and is being taught to those who are keen to explore another facet of their national identity.

## CURRENCY

The Euro is the local currency of the Republic of Ireland. One Euro consists of 100 cent. Notes are €5, €10, €20, €50, €100, €200 and €500. Coins are 1c, 2c, 5c, 10c, 20c, 50c, €1 and €2.

In Northern Ireland (as in the rest of the United Kingdom), Sterling is the local currency. Stg£1 consists of 100 pence. The notes consist of £5, £10, £20, £50 and £100. The coins are 1p, 2p, 5p, 10p, 20p, 50p, £1 & £2.

The Currencies of the Republic of Ireland and Northern Ireland are not interchangeable.

## REGULATIONS FOR UNDER 21 YEAR OLDS IN BARS

In the Republic of Ireland the Liquor Licensing Hours provide that persons under the age of 18 are not allowed in the bar areas of licensed premises (including hotels and guesthouses) after 9.00 p.m. (10.00 p.m. May to September)

Persons aged 18 – 21 are required to produce evidence of age in order to be allowed enter or remain in the bar area of licensed premises (including hotels) after 9.00 pm. The acceptable evidence of age may be one of the following: Garda Age Card, a Passport or Identity Card of a EU Member State, a Driver's Licence.

## EMERGENCY NUMBERS

In case of emergency, please ring 999 & 112.

## PROHIBITION ON SMOKING

In order to combat the damage to health caused by tobacco smoke and to provide an environment of smoke free air, the Government of the Republic of Ireland introduced, early in 2004, a total ban on smoking in the workplace (indoors). This means that smoking is not permitted in all enclosed areas of hotels and guesthouses with the exception of hotel and guesthouse bedrooms. However the proprietor is not legally obliged to offer any smoking bedrooms and may choose to provide a totally smoke-free environment.

## DRIVING

Visitors should be in possession of either; a valid full national driving licence, or an international driving permit issued abroad. These are readily available from motoring organisations in the country of origin. If planning to bring your car to Ireland, advise your insurance company before travelling.

Driving in Ireland is on the left and seat belts must be worn at all times in the front and the back of the vehicle; likewise, motorcyclists and their passengers must wear helmets. There are very strict laws on drinking and driving and the best advise is simply 'don't drink and drive'.

In both the Republic of Ireland and Northern Ireland, speed limits are 50kmph/30mph in built-up urban areas, 100kmph/60mph on the open road and 120kmph/75mph on the motorway.

In the Republic of Ireland, the majority of signposts denoting distance are now in kilometres and speed limits are denoted in kilometres per hour. All signposts and place names are displayed bilingually in both Irish (Gaelic) and English.

In Northern Ireland, all signposts and speed limits are in miles and place names are displayed in the English language.

*Driving Associations within Ireland include:*

The Automobile Association (AA), Tel: 01 617 9999 or visit www.aaireland.ie and the RAC Motoring Services, Tel: 01 412 5500 or visit www.rac.ie.

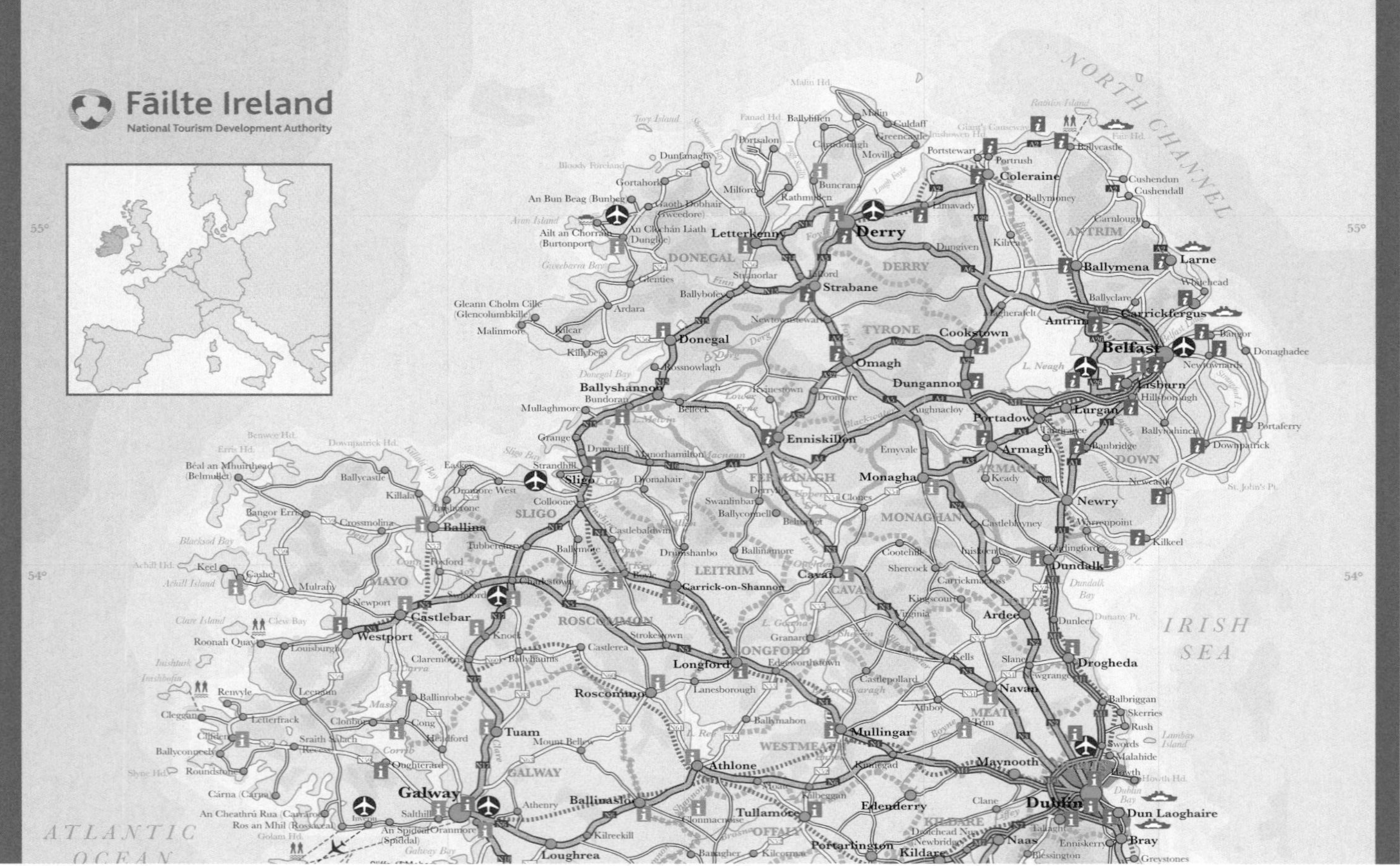

Fāilte Ireland
National Tourism Development Authority
NORTH CHANNEL
IRISH SEA
ATLANTIC OCEAN
10°
9°
8°
7°
6°
55°
54°
DONEGAL
DERRY
ANTRIM
TYRONE
FERMANAGH
ARMAGH
DOWN
MONAGHAN
CAVAN
LEITRIM
SLIGO
MAYO
ROSCOMMON
LONGFORD
WESTMEATH
MEATH
LOUTH
GALWAY
OFFALY
KILDARE
Derry
Belfast
Coleraine
Ballymena
Larne
Carrickfergus
Antrim
Lisburn
Lurgan
Portadown
Armagh
Newry
Dundalk
Drogheda
Navan
Dublin
Dun Laoghaire
Bray
Naas
Kildare
Maynooth
Mullingar
Athlone
Tullamore
Portarlington
Edenderry
Longford
Roscommon
Carrick-on-Shannon
Cavan
Monaghan
Enniskillen
Omagh
Dungannon
Cookstown
Strabane
Letterkenny
Donegal
Ballyshannon
Sligo
Ballina
Castlebar
Westport
Tuam
Galway
Ballinasloe
Loughrea
Ardee
Bundoran
Mullaghmore
Killybegs
Ardara
Glenties
Dunfanaghy
Buncrana
Moville
Limavady
Portrush
Portstewart
Ballycastle
Cushendun
Cushendall
Bangor
Donaghadee
Newtownards
Portaferry
Downpatrick
Kilkeel
Warrenpoint
Banbridge
Keady
Castleblayney
Carrickmacross
Kells
Trim
Slane
Balbriggan
Skerries
Rush
Swords
Malahide
Howth
Greystones
Enniskerry
Blessington
Clane
Athboy
Castlepollard
Edgeworthstown
Granard
Lanesborough
Strokestown
Castlerea
Boyle
Ballymote
Tubbercurry
Charlestown
Swinford
Knock
Ballyhaunis
Claremorris
Ballinrobe
Cong
Headford
Oughterard
Clifden
Roundstone
Cleggan
Letterfrack
Renvyle
Leenaun
Louisburgh
Newport
Mulranny
Keel
Crossmolina
Killala
Ballycastle
Enniscrone
Easkey
Strandhill
Collooney
Dromahair
Manorhamilton
Drumshanbo
Ballinamore
Ballyconnell
Swanlinbar
Belturbet
Clones
Cootehill
Shercock
Kingscourt
Virginia
Emyvale
Aughnacloy
Irvinestown
Belleek
Rossnowlagh
Ballybofey
Stranorlar
Lifford
Newtownstewart
Dungiven
Kilrea
Ballymoney
Carnlough
Ballyclare
Whitehead
Magherafelt
Tandragee
Hillsborough
Ballynahinch
Newcastle
Carlingford
Dunleer
Oranmore
Salthill
Athenry
Kilreekill
Mount Bellew
Kilbeggan
Moate
Clonmacnoise
Banagher
Kilcormac
Ballymahon
Kinnegad
Newbridge
Tallaght
Gortahork
Milford
Rathmullan
Ramelton
Portsalon
Ballyliffen
Malin
Culdaff
Greencastle
Carndonagh
An Bun Beag (Bunbeg)
Gaoth Dobhair (Gweedore)
Ailt an Chorráin (Burtonport)
An Clochán Liath (Dungloe)
Gleann Cholm Cille (Glencolumbkille)
Malinmore
Kilcar
Béal an Mhuirthead (Belmullet)
Bangor Erris
An Spidéal (Spiddal)
An Cheathrú Rua (Carraroe)
Ros an Mhíl (Rossaveal)
Cárna (Carna)
Ballyconneely
Malin Hd.
Fanad Hd.
Bloody Foreland
Tory Island
Aran Island
Gweebarra Bay
Donegal Bay
Sligo Bay
Killala Bay
Blacksod Bay
Clew Bay
Clare Island
Achill Island
Achill Hd.
Erris Hd.
Benwee Hd.
Downpatrick Hd.
Inishturk
Inishbofin
Slyne Hd.
Galway Bay
Dundalk Bay
Dunany Pt.
Dublin Bay
Howth Hd.
Lambay Island
St. John's Pt.
Strangford L.
Belfast Lough
L. Neagh
Lough Foyle
Lough Swilly
Rathlin Island
Fair Hd.
Giant's Causeway
Inishowen Hd.
L. Melvin
L. Gill
L. Corrib
L. Mask
L. Conn
L. Ree
L. Gowna
Lower Erne
Upper Erne
Shannon

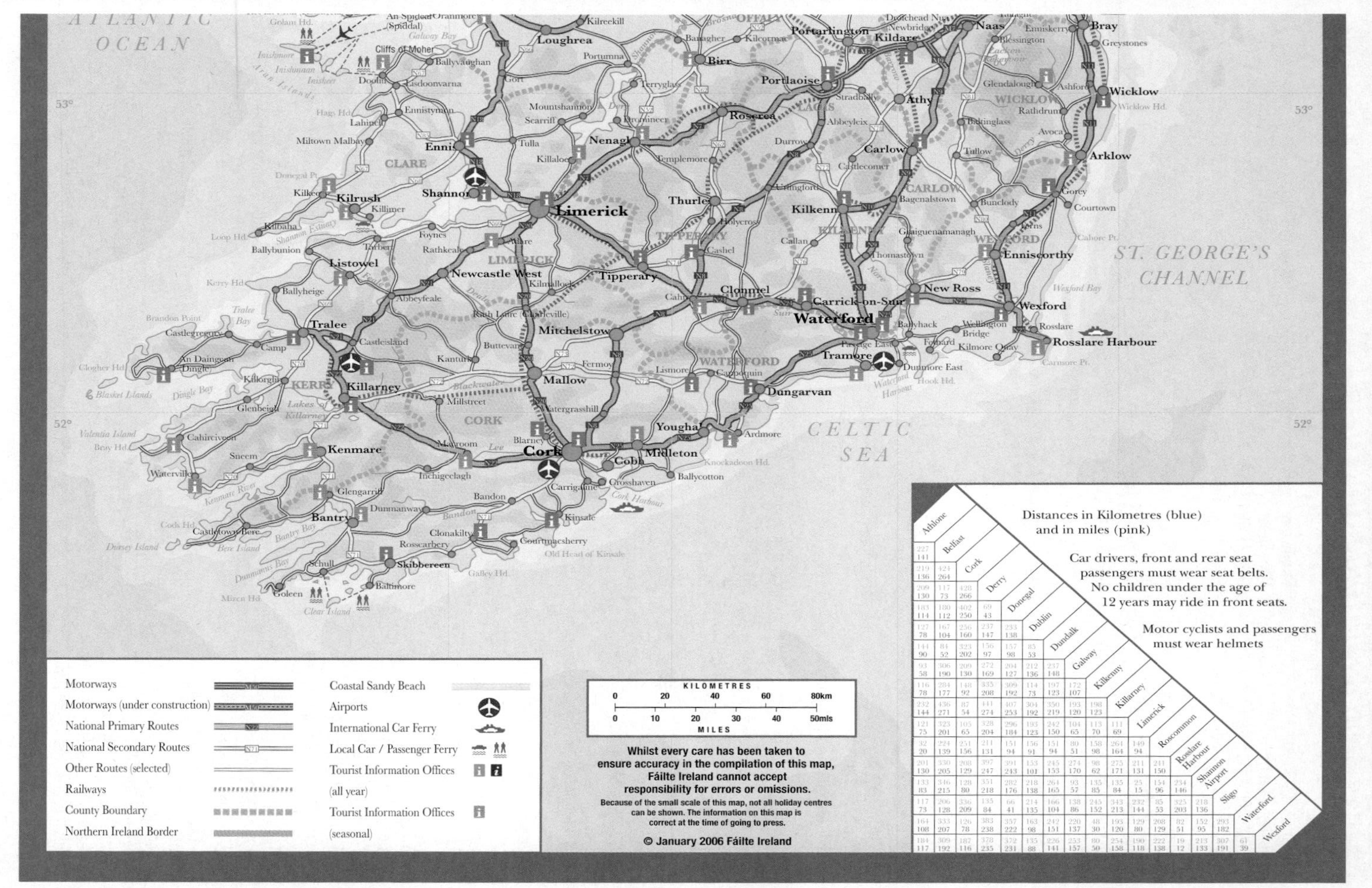


| | Athlone | Belfast | Cork | Derry | Donegal | Dublin | Dundalk | Galway | Kilkenny | Killarney | Limerick | Roscommon | Rosslare Harbour | Shannon Airport | Sligo | Waterford |
|---|---|---|---|---|---|---|---|---|---|---|---|---|---|---|---|---|
| Belfast | 227 / 141 | | | | | | | | | | | | | | | |
| Cork | 219 / 136 | 424 / 264 | | | | | | | | | | | | | | |
| Derry | 209 / 130 | 117 / 73 | 428 / 266 | | | | | | | | | | | | | |
| Donegal | 183 / 114 | 180 / 112 | 402 / 250 | 69 / 43 | | | | | | | | | | | | |
| Dublin | 127 / 78 | 167 / 104 | 256 / 160 | 237 / 147 | 233 / 138 | | | | | | | | | | | |
| Dundalk | 144 / 90 | 84 / 52 | 323 / 202 | 156 / 97 | 157 / 98 | 85 / 53 | | | | | | | | | | |
| Galway | 93 / 58 | 306 / 190 | 209 / 130 | 272 / 169 | 204 / 127 | 212 / 136 | 237 / 148 | | | | | | | | | |
| Kilkenny | 116 / 78 | 284 / 177 | 148 / 92 | 335 / 208 | 309 / 192 | 114 / 73 | 197 / 123 | 172 / 107 | | | | | | | | |
| Killarney | 232 / 144 | 436 / 271 | 87 / 54 | 441 / 274 | 407 / 253 | 304 / 192 | 350 / 219 | 193 / 120 | 198 / 123 | | | | | | | |
| Limerick | 121 / 75 | 323 / 201 | 105 / 65 | 328 / 204 | 296 / 184 | 193 / 123 | 242 / 150 | 104 / 65 | 113 / 70 | 111 / 69 | | | | | | |
| Roscommon | 32 / 20 | 224 / 139 | 251 / 156 | 211 / 131 | 151 / 94 | 156 / 91 | 151 / 94 | 80 / 51 | 158 / 98 | 261 / 164 | 149 / 94 | | | | | |
| Rosslare Harbour | 201 / 130 | 330 / 205 | 208 / 129 | 397 / 247 | 391 / 243 | 153 / 101 | 245 / 153 | 274 / 170 | 98 / 62 | 275 / 171 | 211 / 131 | 241 / 150 | | | | |
| Shannon Airport | 133 / 83 | 346 / 215 | 128 / 80 | 351 / 218 | 282 / 176 | 218 / 138 | 264 / 165 | 93 / 57 | 135 / 85 | 135 / 84 | 25 / 15 | 154 / 96 | 234 / 146 | | | |
| Sligo | 117 / 73 | 206 / 128 | 336 / 209 | 135 / 84 | 66 / 41 | 214 / 135 | 166 / 104 | 138 / 86 | 245 / 152 | 343 / 213 | 232 / 144 | 85 / 53 | 325 / 203 | 218 / 136 | | |
| Waterford | 164 / 108 | 333 / 207 | 126 / 78 | 383 / 238 | 357 / 222 | 163 / 98 | 242 / 151 | 220 / 137 | 48 / 30 | 193 / 120 | 129 / 80 | 208 / 129 | 82 / 51 | 152 / 95 | 293 / 182 | |
| Wexford | 184 / 117 | 309 / 192 | 187 / 116 | 378 / 235 | 372 / 231 | 135 / 88 | 226 / 141 | 253 / 157 | 80 / 50 | 254 / 158 | 190 / 118 | 222 / 138 | 19 / 12 | 213 / 133 | 307 / 191 | 61 / 39 |

**Adare**
The Heritage Centre
Tel: 1800 200 541
www.discoverireland.ie/shannon

**Antrim**
16 High Street
Tel: 028-9442 8331
Email: info@antrim.gov.uk

**Aran Islands**
Oifig Fáilte, Kilronan
Inis Mór, Co. Na Gaillimhe
Tel: 099-61263
Fax: 099-61420
www.discoverireland.ie/west

**Armagh**
40 English Street
Tel: 028-3752 1800
Email: ticreception@armagh.gov.uk

**Ballycastle**
7 Mary Street
Tel: 028-2076 2024
Email: tourism@moyle-council.org

**Ballymena**
76 Church Road
Tel: 028-2563 8494
Email:
tourist.information@ballymena.gov.uk

**Ballymoney**
Ballymoney Town Hall,
1 Townhead Street, Ballymoney
Tel: 028-2766 0230

**Banbridge**
200 Newry Road
Tel: 028-4062 3322
Email: tic@banbridge.gov.uk

**Bangor**
34 Quay Street
Tel: 028-9127 0069
Email: tic@northdown.gov.uk

**Belfast**
47 Donegall Place
Tel: 028-9024 6609
Email: info@belfastvisitor.com
Also George Best, Belfast City Airport Arrivals Hall & Belfast International Airport Arrivals Hall

**Bundoran**
Main Street
Tel: 071-984 1350
Email: bundoran@failteireland.ie

**Carlow**
Tullow Street
Tel: 059-913 1554
Fax: 059-917 0776

**Carrickfergus**
Museum & Civic Centre, Antrim Street
Tel: 028-9335 8049
Email: touristinfo@carrickfergus.org

**Clonakilty**
Ashe Street
Tel: 023-33226
Email: clonakiltytio@eircom.net

**Coleraine**
Railway Road
Tel: 028-7034 4723
Email: colerainetic@btconnect.com

**Cookstown**
The Burnavon, Burn Road
Tel: 028-8676 9949
Email: tic@cookstown.gov.uk

**Cork City**
Grand Parade
Tel: 021-425 5100
Fax: 021-425 5199
Email: corkkerryinfo@failteireland.ie

**Derry**
44 Foyle Street
Tel: 028-7126 7284
Email: info@derryvisitor.com

**Dingle**
The Quay
Tel: 066-915 1188
Fax: 066-915 1270
Email: dingletio@eircom.net

**Donegal Town**
The Quay
Tel: 074-972 1148
Fax: 074-972 2762
Email: donegal@failteireland.ie

**Downpatrick**
St. Patrick's Centre, 53A Market Street
Tel: 028-4461 2233
Email: downpatrick.tic@downdc.gov.uk

**Dublin**
**Dublin City**
Suffolk Street
O'Connell Street
Baggot Street
**Dublin Airport**
Arrivals Hall
**Dun Laoghaire**
Ferryport

For information and reservations please visit www.visitdublin.com or contact Dublin Reservations Freephone
Tel: 1800 363 626

**Dungannon / Killymaddy**
100, Ballygawley Road (off A4)
Tel: 028-8772 8651
Email:
killymaddy.reception@dungannon.gov.uk

**Dundalk**
Jocelyn Street
Tel: 042-933 5484
Fax: 042-933 8070
Email: dundalk@failteireland.ie

**Dungarvan**
The Courthouse
Tel: 058-41741

**Ennis**
Arthur's Row
Reservations Tel: 1800 200 541
www.discoverireland.ie/shannon

**Enniskillen**
Wellington Road
Tel: 028-6632 3110
Email: tic@fermanagh.gov.uk

**Galway**
Aras Fáilte, Forster Street
Galway City
Tel: 091-537700
Fax: 091-537733
Email: irelandwestinfo@failteireland.ie
www.discoverireland.ie/west

**Giant's Causeway**
Causeway Road, Bushmills
Tel: 028-2073 1855
Email: info@giantscausewaycentre.com

**Hillsborough**
The Square
Tel: 028-9268 9717
Email: tic.hillsborough@lisburn.gov.uk

**Kildare Town**
Heritage Centre
Tel: 045-521240

**Kilkeel**
28 Bridge Street
Tel: 028-4176 2525
Email: kdakilkeel@hotmail.com

**Kilkenny**
Shee Alms House
Tel: 056-775 1500
Fax: 056-776 3955

**Killarney**
Beech Road
Tel: 064-31633
Fax: 064-34506
Email: corkkerryinfo@failteireland.ie

**Kinsale**
Pier Road
Tel: 021-477 2234
Email: kinsaletio@eircom.net

**Larne**
Narrow Gauge Road
Tel: 028-2826 0088
Email: larnetourism@btconnect.com

**Letterkenny**
Neil T Blaney Road
Tel: 074-912 1160
Fax: 074-912 5180
Email: letterkenny@failteireland.ie

**Limavady**
7 Connell Street
Tel: 028-7776 0307
Email: tourism@limavady.gov.uk

**Limerick City**
Arthur's Quay
Reservations Tel: 1800 200 541
www.discoverireland.ie/shannon

**Lisburn**
Lisburn Square
Tel: 028-9266 0038
Email: tic.lisburn@lisburn.gov.uk

**Magherafelt**
The Bridwell, 6 Church Street
Tel: 028-7963 1510
Email:
thebridewell@magherafelt.gov.uk

**Mullingar**
Tel: 044-934 8650
Fax: 044-934 0413
Email:
eastandmidlandsinfo@failteireland.ie

**Newcastle (Co. Down)**
10-14 Central Promenade
Tel: 028-4372 2222
Email: newcastle.tic@downdc.gov.uk

**Newgrange**
Bru na Boinne Tourist Office
Donore, Co. Meath
Tel: 041-988 0305
Email: brunaboinne@failteireland.ie

**Newry City**
Bagenal's Castle, Castle Street, Newry
Tel: 028-3031 3170
Email:
newrytic@newryandmourne.gov.uk

**Newtownards**
31 Regent Street
Tel: 028-9182 6846
Email: tourism@ards-council.gov.uk

**Omagh**
Strale Arts Centre, Townhall Square,
Omagh
Tel: 028-8224 7831
Email: marian.hilley@omagh.gov.uk

**Oranmore**
Co. Galway
Tel: 091 790811
Fax: 091 790187
Email: oranmore@iol.ie

**Oughterard**
Main Street, Oughterard, Co. Galway
Tel: 091 552808
Fax: 091 552811
Email: info@oughterardbegins.com
www.connemarabegins.com

**Shannon Airport**
Arrivals Hall
Reservations Tel: 1800 200 541
www.discoverireland.ie/shannon

**Skibbereen**
North Street
Tel: 028-21766
Fax: 028-21353
Email: skibbereen@failteireland.ie

**Sligo**
Temple Street
Tel: 071-916 1201
Fax: 071-916 0360
Email: northwestinfo@failteireland.ie

**Strabane**
Alley Arts & Conference Centre,
1A Railway Street,
Strabane
Tel: 028-7138 4444
Email: tic@strabanedc.com

**Tralee**
Ashe Memorial Hall
Tel: 066-712 1288
Fax: 066-712 1700
Email: traleetio@eircom.net

**Waterford City**
The Quay
Tel: 051-875823
Fax: 051-877388
Email: southeastinfo@failteireland.ie

**Westport**
James Street, Westport
Co. Mayo
Tel: 098-25711
Fax: 098-26709
Email: westport@failteireland.ie
www.discoverireland.ie/west

**Wexford**
Crescent Quay
Tel: 053-9123111
Fax: 053-9141743

**Wicklow**
Fitzwilliam Square
Tel: 0404-69117
Fax: 0404-69118

# *Ireland's Welcoming Tourist Information Network*

# YOUR GATEWAY

## to the Holiday Regions of Ireland

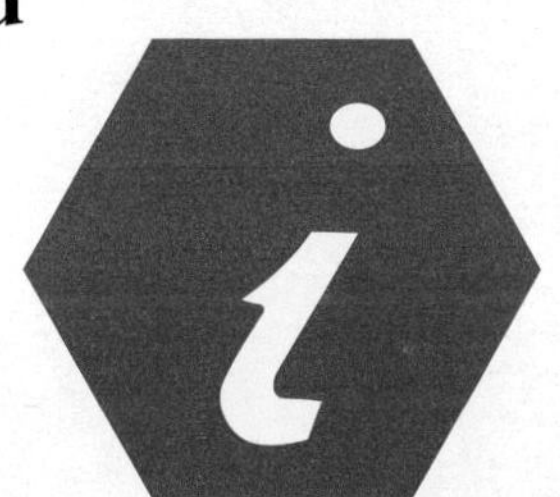

Visit our Tourist Information Offices for detailed information on what to see and do and what's on. Avail of the popular and convenient accommodation booking service.

## For your convenience we provide

- Instant confirmed accommodation booking service
- Guide books for sale
- Local and National Information
- Maps – local and national
- Stamps and postcards
- Itinerary and Route planning service
- Display and sale of local craft items
- Souvenirs and gifts

## Be sure to follow the Shamrock

Look for the Shamrock sign on all accommodation. It is your assurance that this premises provide accommodation which is inspected and whose standards are fully registered by agencies supervised by Fáilte Ireland.

# FÁILTE IRELAND

## NATIONAL TOURISM DEVELOPMENT AUTHORITY

**www.discoverireland.ie**

**IRELAND**
**Dublin**
Fáilte Ireland,
Baggot Street Bridge, Dublin 2
Tel: 01 - 602 4000
Fax: 01 - 602 4100

**NORTHERN IRELAND**
**Belfast**
Fáilte Ireland,
53 Castle Street, Belfast BT1 1GH
Tel: 028 - 9026 5500
Fax: 028 - 9026 5515

**Derry**
Fáilte Ireland,
44 Foyle Street, Derry BT48 6AT
Tel: 028 - 7136 9501
Fax: 028 - 7136 9501

**If dialling Northern Ireland directly from the Republic of Ireland the code 048 followed by the telephone number is sufficient.*

## NORTHERN IRELAND TOURIST BOARD

**www.discovernorthernireland.com**

**Belfast**
Northern Ireland Tourist Board,
59 North Street, Belfast BT1 1NB
Tel: 028 - 9023 1221
Fax: 028 - 9024 0960

**Dublin**
Northern Ireland Tourist Board,
16 Nassau Street, Dublin 2
Tel: 01 - 679 1977
Fax: 01 - 679 1863

## TOURISM IRELAND – EUROPE

**www.discoverireland.com**

**Austria**
Tourism Ireland,
Libellenweg 1, A-1140 Vienna
Tel: 0501 59 60 00
Email: info.at@tourismireland.com
Web: www.discoverireland.com

**Belgium/Luxembourg**
Tourism Ireland,
Avenue Louise 327, Louizalaan,
1050 Brussels
Tel: 02 - 275 0171
Email: info.be@tourismireland.com
Web: www.ireland-tourism.be

**Britain-London**
Tourism Ireland, Nations House,
103 Wigmore Street, London WIU 1QS
Tel: 0800-039 7000 (Call Centre)
Email: info.gb@tourismireland.com
Web: www.discoverireland.com

**Britain-Glasgow**
Tourism Ireland,
James Miller House,
98 West George Street, (7th Floor),
Glasgow G2 1PJ
Tel: 0800 - 039 7000
Email: infoglasgow@tourismireland.com
Web: www.discoverireland.com

**France**
Tourisme Irlandais,
33 Rue de Miromesnil,
75008 Paris
Tel: 01 - 70 20 00 20
Email: info.fr@tourismireland.com
Web: www.irlande-tourisme.fr

**Germany**
Tourism Ireland,
Gutleutstrasse 32, D-60329
Frankfurt am Main
Tel: 069 668 00950
Email: info.de@tourismireland.com
Web: www.entdeckeirland.de

**Italy**
Turismo Irlandese,
Piazza Cantore 4,
20123 Milano
Tel: 02 - 4829 6060
Email:
informazioni@tourismireland.com
Web: www.discoverireland.com/it

**The Netherlands**
Tourism Ireland,
Spuistraat 104,
1012 VA Amsterdam
Tel: 020 - 504 0689
Email: info@ierland.nl
Web: www.ierland.nl

**Nordic Region**
Tourism Ireland,
Nyhavn 16, (3rd Floor),
DK 1051 Copenhagen K,
Denmark
Tel: 80 60 15 18
Email: info.nordic@tourismireland.com
Web: www.discoverireland.com

Finland Tel: 0800 41 969
Norway Tel: 800 35 018
Sweden Tel: 02 0015 9101

**Spain**
Tourism Ireland,
Paseo de la Castellana 46,
3a Planta, 28046
Madrid
Tel: 91-745 6420
Email: info.sp@tourismireland.com
Web: www.turismodeirlanda.com

**Switzerland**
Tourism Ireland,
Hindergartenstrasse 36,
CH-8447 Dachsen
Tel: 044-210 4153
Email: info.ch@tourismireland.com
Web: www.discoverireland.com

## TOURISM IRELAND – REST OF THE WORLD

**www.discoverireland.com**

**Australia**
Tourism Ireland,
Level 5, 36 Carrington Street,
Sydney, NSW 2000
Tel: 02 - 9299 6177
Email: info@tourismireland.com.au
Web: www.discoverireland.com.au

**New Zealand**
Tourism Ireland,
Level 7, Citibank Building,
23 Customs St. East, Auckland 1010
Tel: 09 - 977 2255
Email: tourism@ireland.com.nz
Web: www.discoverireland.com.nz

**Canada**
Tourism Ireland,
2 Bloor St. West, Suite 3403
Toronto, M4W 3E2
Tel: 1800 - 223 6470
Email: info.ca@tourismireland.com
Web: www.discoverireland.com

**USA**
Tourism Ireland,
345 Park Avenue, New York NY 10154
Tel: 1800-223 6470
Email: info.us@tourismireland.com
Web: www.discoverireland.com

**China**
Tourism Ireland,
Suite 728, Shanghai Centre,
1376 Nanjing Road West,
Shanghai 200040
Tel: 021 6279 8788
Fax: 021 6279 8799
Email: sli@tourismireland.com
Web: www.discoverireland.com

**India**
Grants Building Annexure,
Office No. 46, 1st Floor,
Near Strand Cinema, Colaba
Mumbai 400 005
Tel: 22 3296 1624 / 3296 1725
Fax: 22 2287 6355
Email: infoindia@tourismireland.com
Web: www.discoverireland.com

**Japan**
Tourism Ireland,
International Place, 26-3, Sanei-cho,
Shinjuku-ku,
Tokyo 160-0008
Tel: 03 5367 6525
Email: kasano@aviareps.com
Web: www.discoverireland.com

**South Africa**
Tourism Ireland,
c/o Development Promotions
Everite House, Level 7,
20 De Korte Street,
Braamfontein 2001, Gauteng
Tel: 011 - 339 48 65
Email: tourismireland@dpgsa.co.za
Web: www.discoverireland.com

The wonderful, diverse country of Ireland is divided into four regions each with its own charm, attractions and appealing characteristics. They are Ireland West, Ireland South, Dublin & Ireland East and Northern Ireland. Together, they form a very special island, full to bursting with dramatic landscapes, idyllic lakes, beaches, cosmopolitan towns and vibrant city life. Most of all, Ireland's regions are renowned for their rich cultural heritage, historical treasures and warm hospitality.

Discover a spectacular rural landscape of rich colour, an enchanted countryside dotted with reminders of a colourful past, a coastline etched out by the mighty Atlantic, great activities, ancient sites and city lights. Experience the renowned welcome for yourself.

Access has never been easier, either through the major ports or via airports. Many local airports offer an increasing range of flights to the UK, Europe and even the USA, making it easier than ever to reach this wonderful island. Internal flights from Dublin make reaching other parts of the country straightforward.

## OUR REGIONS

**Ireland West** covers the mighty Atlantic coastline from the northernmost tip of Donegal right down to Limerick, an unspoiled and pristine countryside proudly maintaining the traditions and cultures of yesteryear.

Discover food as fresh as the air in picturesque **Ireland South** encompassing the South East with Cork and Kerry. From farmers markets and pub grub, to restaurants and fine dining, the South is fast acquiring a reputation as Ireland's gourmet region.

**Dublin & Ireland East** incorporates the capital city as well as the East Coast and Midlands. Dublin itself is a fascinating city, energetic and youthful with a compelling mix of history, culture, architecture, pubs and shopping. The surrounding region offers so much for the visitor to see and do, all within easy reach.

The six counties of **Northern Ireland** are just waiting to be explored, and welcome visitors with an enticing combination of history, culture, magnificent landscapes and vibrant festivals.

Small enough for easy travelling, yet full of contrasts and contradictions, Ireland is waiting here for you.

For Detailed Maps of this Region See Pages 477-492

Each Hotel or Guesthouse has a Map Reference to these detailed maps under their photograph.

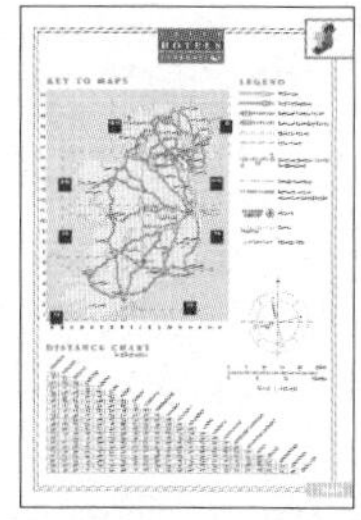

See page 477 for map with access points and driving distances

The Green Carpet is out and ready for you ... in Ireland's Western Regions

Ireland's Western Regions are a beautiful part of a magical island. Come to Ireland's North West, West and Shannon Regions and discover a special place, rich in history and wild in spirit.

This is the Ireland made famous in poetry, song and film. It's the essence of Ireland and the part you can't miss if you want to see the real country. Come to the Western Regions where the best of the past mingles effortlessly with a pulsating, contemporary present. The magic is all in the blend.

The scenery might be just the beginning, but what a way to start! A dramatic Atlantic coastline running from Donegal to Clare. Towering cliffs contrast with golden sandy beaches; the Cliffs of Moher, Keem Bay and Black Head. Inland, nature offers lakes and mountains, the splendour of Connemara, the fragile beauty of the Burren and a series of beautiful National Parks.

No matter when you visit you'll find a festival in full swing somewhere. It could be traditional music at the Willie Clancy Festival, match making in Lisdoonvarna, Arts or Oysters in Galway, perhaps a Salmon Festival in Ballina or the time honoured Mary from Dungloe. Learn to play the Bodhran on the Aran Islands, play music in Sligo or try out one of the many summer schools scattered throughout the region.

We have so many places to visit and attractions to see. Ancient castles, forts and abbeys; sea life centres, waterworlds, folk parks, museums, show-caves, steam-trains, pet-farms, island and dolphin-watching boat trips, island safaris, river boat tours and much more. Some are world famous - Bunratty, Dun Aenghus, Cong and the Quiet Man Cottage. A host of others are just waiting to be discovered, by you.

It's a playground for sports - on dry land or in the water. Over 80 golf links and parkland courses compete for attention, so golfers will be in their element. Challenge yourself on some of the top courses in the country, and be pleasantly surprised at the green fees. Fishermen find their utopia. Casting a line in Ballina, The Salmon Capital, is almost a rite of passage for the game fisherman. The Great Western Lakes teem with trout and coarse fishermen will find healthy fishing waters all around the region. The best sea angling waters in the country tempt everyone from the novice to the expert. Watch out for competitions throughout the year to test yourself against the best.

The geography of the region lends itself perfectly to walking trails and paths. Beaches, woodland, mountains, drumlin and lakeland compete for attention. Marked long distance walks criss-cross the country and many towns and communities have their own shorter walks for visitors to enjoy. Take only pictures, leave only footprints.

Sailors plot courses through picturesque islands, and a growing supply of visitor moorings and marinas. The great river Shannon offers idyllic cruising waters with delightful stop off villages and pubs along the banks. Wind surfers, snorkellers, surfers, body boarders, canoeists and swimmers can take their choice of a hundred beaches, many with EU Blue Flag status. Deep sea divers revel in pristine waters of perfect clarity. It's no wonder the West is known as the Adventure Capital of Ireland.

Don't feel obliged to take part, try some spectator sports. Come horse racing and join in the fun at the big Galway race festival or at one of the smaller traditional racecourses. It's the heart of real Ireland. Go to the dogs at a greyhound track or catch a rugby match. The West is home to the mighty red army of Munster and Connaught Rugby Teams.

The West is the home of traditional music and melodies spill from pubs and sessions every night of the week. Music is an intrinsic part of the culture and spontaneous singing or playing are part of every event all year around. Festivals abound and visitors are enthusiastically welcomed into the celebrations.

Don't forget our cities and towns. Sligo, Galway and Limerick are great centres for shopping, dining and nightlife. They're full of character, colour and life and they're just waiting here for you.

*Wherever you visit, you'll always remember the West.*

## GUINNESS CALENDAR OF EVENTS

**June**
Guinness Castlebar Blues Festival, Castlebar, Co. Mayo

**July**
Ballina Arts Festival, Ballina, Co. Mayo
Galway Arts Festival, Galway City
Willie Clancy Summer School, Milltown Malbay, Co. Clare

**July/August**
Ballyshannon Traditional and Folk Music Festival, Co. Donegal
Buncrana Festival, Buncrana, Co. Donegal
Fleadh Cheoil na hEireann, Letterkenny, Co. Donegal
Guinness Galway Racing Festival, Galway City

**September/October**
Guinness Clarenbridge Oyster Festival, Clarenbridge, Co. Galway
Guinness Galway International Oyster Festival, Galway City
Ballinasloe International Horse Fair & Festival, Ballinasloe, Co. Galway

## Ballyvaughan

### Ballyvaughan Lodge

GUESTHOUSE ★★★ MAP 6 F 10

Ballyvaughan,
Co. Clare

Tel: 065-707 7292 Fax: 065-707 7287
Email: ballyvau@iol.ie
Web: www.ballyvaughanlodge.com

Located in the heart of Ballyvaughan, a small fishing village overlooking Galway Bay. A custom built modern guesthouse, dedicated to the comfort and relaxation of our guests. Each room is en suite having TV, direct dial phone, tea/coffee making facilities, etc. Allow us to plan your carefree days in the most unspoilt natural environment imaginable, The Burren, including Neolithic caves, sea fishing, hill walking, cycling, Cliffs of Moher and the Aran Islands.

*B&B from €35.00 to €45.00*

*Pauline Burke*
*Owner*

11

**Closed 25 - 26 December**

### Burren Coast Hotel & Holiday Complex

HOTEL MAP 6 F 10

Coast Road,
Ballyvaughan,
Co. Clare

Tel: 065-708 3000 Fax: 065-708 3001
Email: info@burrencoast.ie
Web: www.burrencoast.ie

Built to a 4**** specification. This stylish comfortable retreat opened July 2007. Built and furnished to the highest standards it offers luxurious accommodation with spectacular views across the harbour. Delicious fresh locally sourced food is served in the Hazelwood Restaurant & we also offer an excellent menu daily in our bar The Limestone Inn. The Burren coast is the perfect base from which to explore the Burren and beyond. Spa due to open in Spring 2008. Please enquire about Facilities for Persons with Mobility Impairment.

Member of Atlantis Holiday Group

*B&B from €50.00 to €125.00*
*Suites from €150.00 to €250.00*

*John Broderick*
*General Manager*

20

**Open All Year**

### Gregans Castle Hotel

HOTEL ★★★★ MAP 6 F 10

The Burren,
Ballyvaughan,
Co. Clare

Tel: 065-707 7005 Fax: 065-707 7111
Email: stay@gregans.ie
Web: www.gregans.ie

Family-run 4 star, luxurious retreat. Set among the rugged unspoilt beauty of the Burren hills. Overlooking Galway Bay. Extensive gardens, country house comforts and turf fires. Fresh, organic local food. Individually decorated bedrooms. Georgina Campbell's Hideaway of The Year 2007. Swimming, hill walking, horse riding, day trips to Aran Islands. Cliffs of Moher. Golf at Lahinch, Gort and Doonbeg. Situated halfway between Kerry and Conemara. 1 hour from both Shannon and Galway airports. Book online at www.gregans.ie

***An IHF Quality Employer***

Member of Ireland's Blue Book

*Bookable on www.irelandhotels.com*

*B&B from €97.50 to €117.50*
*Suites from €147.50 to €225.00*

*Simon Haden*
*Managing Director*

21

**Closed 30 November - 12 February**



B&B Rates are per Person Sharing per Night incl. Breakfast. or Room Rates are per Room per Night - See also Page 8

## Hyland's Burren Hotel

HOTEL ★★★ MAP 6 F 10

Ballyvaughan,
Co. Clare

Tel: 065-707 7037 Fax: 065-707 7131
Email: hylandsburren@eircom.net
Web: www.hylandsburren.com

Hyland's Burren Hotel is a charming hotel, dating back to the 18th century and now tastefully modernised. It is located in the picturesque village of Ballyvaughan, nestling in the unique Burren landscape of County Clare. Experience bygone charm with the best of modern facilities, open turf fires, informal bars and restaurants specialising in the finest local seafood. An ideal base for golfing and walking enthusiasts and truly an artist's haven. Also closed during November. A member of Signature Park Hotels.

***An IHF Quality Employer***

Member of Irish Country Hotels

*Bookable on www.irelandhotels.com*
*Special Offer: www.irelandhotels.com/offers*

*B&B from €50.00 to €80.00*

*Tony McDermott*
*Managing Director*

29

Closed 05 - 30 January

## Rusheen Lodge

GUESTHOUSE ★★★★ MAP 6 F 10

Ballyvaughan,
Co. Clare

Tel: 065-707 7092 Fax: 065-707 7152
Email: rusheen@iol.ie
Web: www.rusheenlodge.com

Rusheen Lodge is a 4****, AA ♦♦♦♦♦, RAC ♦♦♦♦♦ luxury guesthouse nestling in the Burren Mountains, providing elegant, tastefully designed en suite bedrooms, suites, dining room and residents' lounge, ensuring a comfortable and relaxing stay. Previous winner Good Food Guide (2006), Jameson Guide (2001) and RAC "Guesthouse of the Year". RAC Sparkling Diamond and Warm Welcome Award. Ideally located for touring the Shannon region, Aran Islands and Connemara. Non-smoking.

*Bookable on www.irelandhotels.com*

*B&B from €45.00 to €50.00*
*Suites from €130.00 to €190.00*

*Karen McGann*
*Proprietor*

9

Closed 18 November - 02 February

B&B Rates are per Person Sharing per Night incl. Breakfast.
or Room Rates are per Room per Night - **See also Page 8**

## Bunratty

### Bunratty Castle Hotel & Angsana Spa

HOTEL ★★★ MAP 6 G 7

Bunratty,
Co. Clare

Tel: 061-478700 Fax: 061-364891

Email: info@bunrattycastlehotel.com

Web: www.bunrattycastlehotel.com

Bunratty Castle Hotel Leisure Club and Luxury Spa is a luxury hotel situated 8km from Shannon Airport, in the centre of Bunratty Village, overlooking the historic Bunratty Castle. You will discover excellent furnishings and superb facilities that create a haven of relaxation, enabling you to begin your day rested and rejuvenated. Experience sheer indulgence in our Angsana Spa where our Thai therapists offer a wide range of holistic treatments that will rejuvenate your body and soul.

Member of Blarney Group Hotels

Bookable on www.irelandhotels.com
Special Offer: www.irelandhotels.com/offers

B&B from €75.00 to €90.00
Suites from €260.00 to €300.00

*Lee Gregson*
*General Manager*

144

Activities:

Closed 24 - 26 December

### Bunratty Grove

GUESTHOUSE ★★★ MAP 6 G 7

Castle Road (Low Road),
Bunratty,
Co. Clare

Tel: 061-369579 Fax: 061-369561

Email: bunrattygrove@eircom.net

Web: http://homepage.eircom.net/~bunrattygrove

Bunratty Grove is a purpose built luxurious guesthouse. This guesthouse is located within 3 minutes drive of Bunratty Castle and Folk Park and is 10 minutes from Shannon Airport. Fishing, golfing and historical interests are within a short distance. Ideally located for tourists arriving or departing Shannon Airport. Bookings for Bunratty and Knappogue Banquets taken on request. All rooms en suite with multi-channel TV, hairdryer, tea/coffee facilities and direct dial phone.

B&B from €35.00 to €40.00

*Joe & Maura Brodie*
*Proprietors*

6

Closed 01 December - 28 January

### Bunratty Manor Hotel

HOTEL ★★★ MAP 6 G 7

Bunratty,
Co. Clare

Tel: 061-707984 Fax: 061-360588

Email: bunrattymanor@eircom.net

Web: www.bunrattymanor.ie

Bunratty Manor is a "home from home" style relaxed intimate family-run hotel renowned for friendliness and hospitality. Just two minutes walk from the mediaeval banquets of Bunratty Castle and Folk Park, it serves as an ideal touring base for the Cliffs of Moher, The Burren and numerous championship golf courses. Our intimate restaurant has a delicately selective menu with locally sourced seafood and meats. It is very popular locally so booking is strongly advised. All rooms have been tastefully redecorated. Come and enjoy the unequalled warmth of Bunratty Manor.

B&B from €75.00 to €88.00
Suites from €189.00 to €210.00

*Fiona & Noel Wallace*
*Owners*

20

Activities:

Closed 24 December - 06 January



B&B Rates are per Person Sharing per Night incl. Breakfast.
or Room Rates are per Room per Night - See also Page 8

## Aran View House Hotel & Restaurant

HOTEL ★★★ MAP 5 E 9

Coast Road,
Doolin,
Co. Clare

Tel: 065-707 4061 Fax: 065-707 4540

Email: bookings@aranview.com

Web: www.aranview.com

A Georgian house built in 1736, it has a unique position commanding panoramic views of the Aran Islands, the Burren region and the Cliffs of Moher. Situated on 100 acres of farmland, Aran View echoes spaciousness, comfort and atmosphere in its restaurant and bar. Menus are based on the best of local produce, fish being a speciality. All rooms with private bathroom, colour TV and direct dial phone. Visitors are assured of a warm and embracing welcome at the Aran View House Hotel.

*B&B from €55.00 to €80.00*
*Suites from €140.00 to €180.00*

*Theresa & John Linnane*
*Proprietors*

19

*Activities:*

Closed 29 October - 01 May

## Ballinalacken Castle Country House & Restaurant

HOTEL ★★★ MAP 5 E 9

Coast Road,
Doolin,
Co. Clare

Tel: 065-707 4025 Fax: 065-707 4025

Email: ballinalackencastle@eircom.net

Web: www.ballinalackencastle.com

A romantic peaceful oasis steeped in history and ambience offering the most spectacular views of the Cliffs of Moher, Aran Islands, Atlantic Ocean and Connemara Hills. Built in 1840 as the home of Lord O'Brien. Family members radiate a warm friendly welcome. Peat and log fires add to the cosy atmosphere. Ideal base for exploring Clare. Recommended by Egon Ronay, Michelin, Fodor, Frommer, Charming Hotels of Ireland, New York Times, Washington Post and London Times. The restaurant with its great views has many culinary delights and specialises in local seafood.

*Bookable on www.irelandhotels.com*
*Special Offer: www.irelandhotels.com/offers*

*B&B from €65.00 to €80.00*
*Suites from €160.00 to €200.00*

*Mary & Denis O'Callaghan*
*Proprietors*

12

*Activities:*

Closed 01 November - 15 April

## Ballyvara House

GUESTHOUSE ★★★★ MAP 5 E 9

Ballyvara,
Doolin,
Co. Clare

Tel: 065-707 4467 Fax: 065-707 4868

Email: info@ballyvarahouse.ie

Web: www.ballyvarahouse.ie

Luxury accommodation and exceptional service await you at Ballyvara House. All of the spacious rooms in our elegant 4**** country house have at least a queen sized bed, while our exclusive suites boast king sized sleigh beds. Every bath is either a jacuzzi or spa bath. Relax and unwind in Shane's Saloon, which serves wine and beer, or in the peaceful setting of our courtyard garden. AA ♦♦♦♦♦. Please enquire about Facilities for Persons with Mobility Impairment.

Member of Atlantis Holiday Group

*B&B from €50.00 to €120.00*
*Suites from €140.00 to €350.00*

*Rebecca Flanagan*
*Proprietor*

11

Closed 01 October - 30 April

# Doolin

## Cullinan's Seafood Restaurant & Guesthouse

GUESTHOUSE ★★★ MAP 5 E 9

Doolin,
Co. Clare

Tel: 065-707 4183 Fax: 065-707 4239
Email: cullinans@eircom.net
Web: www.cullinansdoolin.com

Unique setting overlooking the Aille River, centrally located in the heart of Doolin. Elegant bedrooms have spacious bathrooms with power showers, tea/coffee making facilities, DD phones & hairdryers. Complimentary WiFi throughout. Private car parking. Imaginative menus for breakfast & dinner are carefully chosen by the chef/owner, specializing in locally caught seafood. Reservations advisable. Highly recommended by Michelin, Fodors, Bridgestone, Georgina Campbell. AA & Le Guide du Routard. Accredited Best Restaurant Award 2007. Please enquire about Facilities for Persons with Mobility Impairment.

**B&B from €35.00 to €50.00**

*James & Carol Cullinan*
*Owners*

8

Closed 16 December - 15 February

## Hotel Doolin

HOTEL ★★★★ MAP 5 E 9

Doolin,
Co. Clare

Tel: 065-707 4111
Email: info@hoteldoolin.ie
Web: www.hoteldoolin.ie

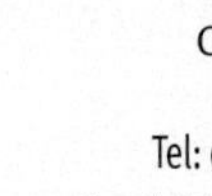

A warm Irish welcome awaits you at Hotel Doolin, located in the heart of Doolin, traditional Irish Music & Culture capital of Ireland. Against the backdrop of the Cliffs of Moher & on the fringes of the Burren National Park, Hotel Doolin village streetscape consists of 17 de luxe bedrooms, South Sound Restaurant, Fitzpatrick's Bar, Café Sonas, Pizza Café, banqueting suite, Atrium Bar, selection of retail outlets, outdoor terraces & tourist information point. Nearby attractions include Cliffs of Moher, Aran Islands, Doolin Cave, Lahinch & Doonbeg Golf Courses Please enquire about Facilities for Persons with Mobility Impairment.

*Bookable on www.irelandhotels.com*
*Special Offer: www.irelandhotels.com/offers*

**B&B from €50.00 to €85.00**

*John J. Burke*
*Director*

17

Closed 25 December

## O'Connors Farmhouse

GUESTHOUSE ★★★ MAP 5 E 9

Doolin,
Co. Clare

Tel: 065-707 4314 Fax: 065-707 4498
Email: joan@oconnorsdoolin.com
Web: www.oconnorsdoolin.com

Spacious modern guesthouse situated in the heart of Doolin, within 5 minutes stroll from pubs, shops and restaurants. Home-baking, breakfast menu and laundry facilities. We offer a high standard of accommodation in comfortable spacious bedrooms. All rooms are en suite with direct dial telephones, television, tea/coffee facilities and hairdryers. Recommended by travel writers. Tourism award winners. A warm Irish welcome awaits you. Group rates available on request. Please enquire about Facilities for Persons with Mobility Impairment.

**B&B from €35.00 to €45.00**

*Joan & Pat O'Connor*
*Owners*

10

Closed 01 November - 01 February



B&B Rates are per Person Sharing per Night incl. Breakfast. or Room Rates are per Room per Night - See also Page 8

## Tir Gan Ean House Hotel

HOTEL ★★★★ MAP 5 E 9

Doolin,
Co. Clare

Tel: 065-707 5726 Fax: 065-707 5734
Email: info@tirganean.ie
Web: www.tirganean.ie

Located in the centre of picturesque Doolin, this exclusive 4* boutique hotel features the best of luxurious accommodation and exceptional service. Relax with a cocktail on the Corcomroe Bar before dining in An tOiléain restaurant, offering contemporary cuisine from the finest local ingredients. With the Burren, Cliffs of Moher, Aran Islands, golfing & surfing all within easy reach, you couldn't choose a more ideal base to explore from. Please enquire about Facilities for Persons with Mobility Impairment.

Member of Atlantis Holiday Group

B&B from €50.00 to €120.00

*Martin Howley*
*Manager*

12

Open All Year

## Ardilaun Guesthouse

GUESTHOUSE ★★★ MAP 6 F 8

Galway Road,
Ennis,
Co. Clare

Tel: 065-682 2311 Fax: 065-684 3989
Email: purcells.ennis@eircom.net
Web: www.ardilaun.com

Ardilaun is a modern, architect designed 3*** guesthouse overlooking the River Fergus and Ballyallia Lake amenity area. Most rooms enjoy panoramic views of the river and all are superbly decorated with en suite, phone, TV, hairdryer, tea/coffee facilities. Our gym, sauna and fishing facilities also overlook the river and are available to guests only. Ardilaun is just 2 mins drive to the new Ennis swimming pool. Situated 20 mins drive from Shannon Airport on N18. Ideal touring base for Clare, Limerick and Galway. Received Certificate of Merit Award 2002.

*Bookable on www.irelandhotels.com*
*Special Offer: www.irelandhotels.com/offers*

B&B from €40.00 to €45.00

*Anne Purcell*
*Proprietress*

10

*Activities:*

Closed 23 - 28 December

## Ashford Court Boutique Hotel

HOTEL ★★★★ MAP 6 F 8

Old Mill Road,
Ennis,
Co. Clare

Tel: 065-689 4444 Fax: 065-689 4455
Email: sales@ashfordcourt.ie
Web: www.ashfordcourt.ie

The Ashford Court Hotel is a new boutique style hotel, conveniently located within walking distance of Ennis town centre. Each of the individually decorated rooms is en suite with power shower, satellite TV, DD phone, computer/internet access, ironing facilities and hairdryer. Kingsize beds & crisp white linens offer the ultimate in luxury, comfort & style. Juliano's Restaurant specialises in local seafood, Italian cuisine & certified Irish Angus Beef. Ideally situated within minutes of Shannon Airport, the Burren, Cliffs of Moher, Bunratty Castle, Ailwee Caves, Dunbeg & Lahinch Golf Courses. Meeting rooms. Parking.

*Bookable on www.irelandhotels.com*
*Special Offer: www.irelandhotels.com/offers*

B&B from €40.00 to €90.00

*Corinne Mannion*
*Proprietor*

27

Closed 24 - 28 December

## Ennis

### Banner Lodge

GUESTHOUSE ★★ MAP 6 F 8

Market Street,
Ennis,
Co. Clare
Tel: 065-682 4224 Fax: 065-682 1670
Email: bannerlodge_ennis@eircom.net
Web: www.bannerlodge.com

Located in the heart of Ennis Town within easy reach of shops and restaurants. 10 miles from Shannon International Airport and within 30 minutes drive of all county tourist attractions. Henry's Restaurant and Wine Bar downstairs. All bedrooms are en suite with TV, phone and tea/coffee facilities. Local attractions include the Aran Islands, The Burren, Cliffs of Moher and Bunratty Castle.

*B&B from €35.00 to €35.00*

*Noel Carr*

8

Closed 23 December - 08 January

B&B Rates are per Person Sharing per Night incl. Breakfast.
or Room Rates are per Room per Night - See also Page 8

## Magowna House Hotel

HOTEL ★★★ MAP 6 F 8

Inch,
Ennis,
Co. Clare

Tel: 065-683 9009 Fax: 065-683 9258

We are a beautifully located, country house hotel with extensive gardens and lovely views. Ideal for an active or purely relaxing break. Close to excellent golf courses, angling and walks. (Mid-Clare Way 1.5km). Shannon Airport, Cliffs of Moher, The Burren, Doolin, Bunratty Castle, Killimer Car Ferry to Kerry within easy reach. Close to new Ennis bypass. Function/Conference room (capacity 200). Enjoy hospitality, comfort, good food and a genuine welcome in the heart of County Clare. Please enquire about Facilities for Persons with Mobility Impairment.

B&B from €56.00 to €60.00

*Martin & Marianne Walsh*

10

Closed 24 - 27 December

## Old Ground Hotel

HOTEL ★★★ MAP 6 F 8

O'Connell Street,
Ennis,
Co. Clare

Tel: 065-682 8127 Fax: 065-682 8112

Email: reservations@oldgroundhotel.ie

Web: www.flynnhotels.com

Ivy-clad manor house dates to the 18th century. The hotel offers 83 de luxe rooms and luxurious new rooms with king beds and spacious suites. Our elegant formal dining room is renowned for excellent cuisine. Visit our recently opened Town Hall Café. The hotel is located in the heart of Ennis, 20 minutes drive from Shannon Airport, close to the Cliffs of Moher, The Burren, Bunratty Castle and many superb challenging golf courses, such as Doonbeg and Lahinch. GDS Access LE. Online reservations at www.flynnhotels.com

Member of Flynn Hotels

B&B from €62.50 to €115.00
Suites from €180.00 to €230.00

*Allen Flynn, Managing Dir*
*Mary Gleeson, Gen Manager*

83

Activities:

Closed 24 - 25 December

## Temple Gate Hotel

HOTEL ★★★ MAP 6 F 8

The Square,
Ennis,
Co. Clare

Tel: 065-682 3300 Fax: 065-682 3322

Email: info@templegatehotel.com

Web: www.templegatehotel.com

This charming town house hotel, family owned and managed is truly a haven in the heart of Ennis. Built on the site of a 19th century convent, it offers a unique combination of historical beauty and exceptional service. Preachers Pub features live music and an acclaimed bar menu. JM's Bistro - awarded the prestigious AA Rosette for 10 consecutive years. The Great Hall - Conference, Wedding & Banqueting suite, a unique venue. Near Shannon Intl. Airport, Bunratty, Cliffs of Moher and Lahinch & Doonbeg golf courses. Awarded Ireland's Best Service Excellence Award 2004.

***An IHF Quality Employer***

*Bookable on www.irelandhotels.com*
*Special Offer: www.irelandhotels.com/offers*

B&B from €75.00 to €110.00
Suites from €250.00 to €280.00

*Paul Madden*
*Managing Director*

70

Activities:

Closed 24 - 27 December

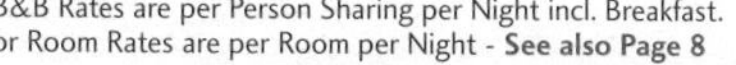

B&B Rates are per Person Sharing per Night incl. Breakfast.
or Room Rates are per Room per Night - **See also Page 8**

## Ennis / Ennistymon

### Westbrook House

GUESTHOUSE ★★★ MAP 6 F 8

Galway Road,
Ennis,
Co. Clare

Tel: 065-684 0173 Fax: 065-686 7777
Email: westbrook.ennis@eircom.net
Web: www.westbrookhouse.net

Westbrook House is a recently built luxury guesthouse in Ennis. All rooms are fitted to exceptionally high standards. Within walking distance of the centre of historic Ennis, with its friendly traditional pubs and fantastic shopping. Ideal base for golfing holidays, special discounts with local golf courses. A short drive to the majestic Cliffs of Moher, The Burren or Bunratty Castle and Folk Park. Only 15 minutes from Shannon Airport. Mobile: 087 798 5859. Member of Irish Hotels Federation. Please enquire about Facilities for Persons with Mobility Impairment.

*B&B from €40.00 to €45.00*

*Sheelagh & Domhnall Lynch*
*Proprietors*

10

Closed 23 - 26 December

### Falls Hotel & Spa

HOTEL ★★★ MAP 5 E 9

Ennistymon,
Co. Clare

Tel: 065-707 1004 Fax: 065-707 1367
Email: sales@fallshotel.ie
Web: www.fallshotel.ie

The Falls Hotel is conveniently located for touring The Burren and the Cliffs of Moher. For the golfer, the Championship Lahinch Golf Course is a mere 3 km away, with Doonbeg only a 20 mins drive. The hotel itself is surrounded by 50 acres of woodland and riverside walks. It has two restaurants, a large bar, Aqua Fitness Club, River Spa, 140 bedrooms and 9 duplex apartments. A full bar menu is available in Dylan Thomas Bar until 9pm daily.

***An IHF Quality Employer***

Member of Select Hotels of Ireland

*Bookable on www.irelandhotels.com*
*Special Offer: www.irelandhotels.com/offers*

*B&B from €65.00 to €95.00*
*Suites from €190.00 to €240.00*

*John & Michael McCarthy*
*Directors*

140

*Activities:*

Open All Year

### Grovemount House

GUESTHOUSE ★★★ MAP 5 E 9

Lahinch Road,
Ennistymon,
Co. Clare

Tel: 065-707 1431 Fax: 065-707 1823
Email: grovmnt@eircom.net
Web: www.grovemount-ennistymon.com

Grovemount House is a family-run guesthouse situated on the outskirts of Ennistymon Town. From here you can access with ease the renowned Cliffs of Moher and the spectacular and unique Burren. Just 5 minutes drive away is Lahinch championship golf links and Blue Flag Beach. Whatever is your pleasure: fishing, golfing, sightseeing, horse riding or the best traditional music, enjoy and then return to luxurious tranquillity in Grovemount House. Please enquire about Facilities for Persons with Mobility Impairment.

Member of Premier Guesthouses

*Bookable on www.irelandhotels.com*
*Special Offer: www.irelandhotels.com/offers*

*B&B from €35.00 to €40.00*

*Sheila Linnane*
*Owner*

7

*Activities:*

Closed 28 October - 30 April



B&B Rates are per Person Sharing per Night incl. Breakfast.
or Room Rates are per Room per Night - **See also Page 8**

## Halpin's Townhouse Hotel

HOTEL ★★★ MAP 5 D 7

Erin Street,
Kilkee,
Co. Clare

Tel: 065-905 6032 Fax: 065-905 6317

Email: halpinshotel@iol.ie

Web: www.halpinsprivatehotels.com

Highly acclaimed 3*** townhouse hotel. Combination of old world charm, fine food, vintage wines and modern comforts - overlooking old Victorian Kilkee, near Shannon Airport & Killimer car ferry. Ideal base for touring Cliffs of Moher, Bunratty, The Burren & Loop drive. Nearby major golf courses - Lahinch, Doonbeg & Ballybunion. Complimentary WiFi access. Accolades- AA, Times, Best Loved Hotels, Johansens. Sister property of Aberdeen Lodge and Merrion Hall both in Dublin 4.
USA toll free 1800 617 3178.
Global free phone +800 128 38155.
Direct Dial +353 65 905 6032.

Member of Épogue Boutique Hotels

*Bookable on www.irelandhotels.com*
*Special Offer: www.irelandhotels.com/offers*

*B&B from €49.00 to €69.00*

*Pat Halpin*
*Proprietor*

12

*Activities:*

**Closed 15 November - 15 March**

## Kilkee Bay Hotel

HOTEL ★★★ MAP 5 D 7

Kilrush Road,
Kilkee,
Co. Clare

Tel: 065-906 0060 Fax: 065-906 0062

Email: info@kilkeebayhotel.com

Web: www.kilkeebayhotel.com

The stylish and modern Kilkee Bay Hotel is located just a couple of minutes walk from one of Ireland's most beautiful beaches and picturesque towns. Enjoy luxurious treatments at the on site Sentosa Spa featuring Matis facials and Jessica nails. Indoor pool, sauna and jacuzzi. During July and August the hotel operates a Kids Club daily. Tennis court on site, close to Doonbeg, Lahinch and Ballybunion Golf Courses. Please enquire about Facilities for Persons with Mobility Impairment.

*B&B from €70.00 to €90.00*
*Suites from €160.00 to €240.00*

*George O'Gara*
*General Manager*

62

*Activities:*

**Closed 23 - 27 December**

## Strand Guest House

GUESTHOUSE ★★★ MAP 5 D 7

The Strand Line,
Kilkee,
Co. Clare

Tel: 065-905 6177 Fax: 065-905 6177

Email: thestrandkilkee@eircom.net

Web: www.clareguesthouse.com

Situated on the seafront in Kilkee, one of the most westerly seaside resorts in Europe. Kilkee is built around a 1.5km beach, considered one of the best and safest bathing places in the west with breathtaking coastal walks. The Strand makes an ideal touring base - visit The Burren, Cliffs of Moher, Ailwee Caves. For golf enthusiasts there is a local 18 hole course, Kilrush 13km, Doonbeg 13km, Lahinch 42km or Ballybunion 40km (via car ferry). Restaurant fully licenced, specialises in local seafood.

*Bookable on www.irelandhotels.com*
*Special Offer: www.irelandhotels.com/offers*

*B&B from €38.00 to €62.00*

*Johnny & Caroline Redmond*

6

**Open All Year**

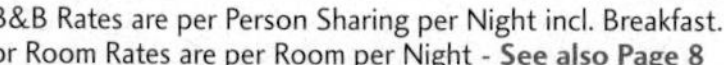

B&B Rates are per Person Sharing per Night incl. Breakfast.
or Room Rates are per Room per Night - **See also Page 8**

## Kilkee / Killaloe

### Thomond Guesthouse & Kilkee Thalassotherapy Centre

GUESTHOUSE ★★★ MAP 5 D 7

Grattan Street,
Kilkee,
Co. Clare

Tel: 065-905 6742 Fax: 065-905 6762
Email: info@kilkeethalasso.com
Web: www.kilkeethalasso.com

Thomond Guesthouse is a magnificent premises with 5 en suite rooms coupled with Kilkee Thalassotherapy Centre, offering natural seaweed baths, algae body wraps, beauty salon and other thalassotherapy treatments. Non-smoking. Children over 16 welcome. Ideal for those looking for a totally unique and relaxing break. Situated in beautiful Kilkee with golfing, scuba diving, deep sea angling, dolphin watching, swimming, pony trekking and spectacular cliff walks, nearby. Private car parking. Winner Best Day Spa 2004 - Irish Beauty Industry.

*B&B from €40.00 to €58.00*

*Eileen Mulcahy*
*Proprietor*

5

*Activities:*

Closed 20 - 29 December

### Lakeside Hotel & Leisure Centre

HOTEL ★★★ MAP 6 H 8

Killaloe,
Co. Clare

Tel: 061-376122 Fax: 061-376431
Email: info@lakeside-killaloe.com
Web: www.lakeside-killaloe.com

On the banks of the River Shannon, overlooking Lough Derg, the Lakeside is the ideal base for touring Counties Clare, Limerick and Tipperary. Enjoy our fabulous indoor leisure centre with its 40 metre water-slide, swimming pools, sauna and steam rooms, jacuzzi, gym and crèche rooms. Our 3*** hotel has 46 en suite bedrooms. Fully licensed restaurant and conference facilities available. Please enquire about Facilities for Persons with Mobility Impairment.

*B&B from €60.00 to €85.00*

*Christopher Byrnes*
*General Manager*

46

Closed 23 - 27 December

### Lantern House

GUESTHOUSE ★★★ MAP 6 H 8

Ogonnelloe,
Killaloe,
Co. Clare

Tel: 061-923034 Fax: 061-923139
Email: phil@lanternhouse.com
Web: www.lanternhouse.com

Ideally situated overlooking Lough Derg in a beautiful part of East Clare, 6 miles north of historic Killaloe and 45 minutes drive from Shannon Airport. Our en suite rooms are non-smoking, have semi-orthopaedic beds, direct dial phone, TV and radio. Residents' lounge, homely atmosphere and safe car parking. Enjoy the wonderful views from our fully licenced restaurant. Owner chef. Local activities include golf, watersports, fishing, pony trekking and walking.

*Elizabeth Coppen &*
*Philip Hogan*
*Owners*

6

Closed 01 November - 01 March

B&B Rates are per Person Sharing per Night incl. Breakfast. or Room Rates are per Room per Night - See also Page 8

## Atlantic Hotel

HOTEL ★★ MAP 5 E 9

Main Street,
Lahinch,
Co. Clare

Tel: 065-708 1049 Fax: 065-708 1029
Email: info@atlantichotel.ie
Web: www.atlantichotel.ie

The Atlantic Hotel is a family-run hotel where comfort and friendliness are our priority. The intimate dining room offers the very best in local seafood. All rooms are en suite and have direct dial phone, TV, hairdryer and tea/coffee making facilities. 51km from Shannon Airport, 5 minutes from the famous Lahinch championship golf courses, Cliffs of Moher and The Burren. Recently refurbished and upgraded, this charming little hotel has much to offer our special guests. A warm welcome awaits you.

*B&B from €55.00 to €70.00*

*Alan Logue*
*Managing Director*

15

*Activities:*

Open All Year

## Dough Mor Lodge

GUESTHOUSE ★★★ MAP 5 E 9

Station Road,
Lahinch,
Co. Clare

Tel: 065-708 2063 Fax: 065-707 1384
Email: dough@gofree.indigo.ie
Web: www.doughmorlodge.com

Purpose-built family-run guesthouse with residents' lounge and dining room. Private car parking and large garden. You can see Lahinch's famous golf links from the house. Tee times can be booked and arranged for guests. This is an ideal location for golfing, touring The Burren or visiting the Cliffs of Moher. The beach is within 5 minutes walk. Lahinch Sea World has a fine heated indoor swimming pool. The ideal place to unwind and enjoy your holiday.

Member of Premier Collection

*Bookable on www.irelandhotels.com*

*B&B from €40.00 to €65.00*

*Jim Foley*

6

*Activities:*

Closed 31 October - 31 March

## Greenbrier Inn Guesthouse

GUESTHOUSE ★★★ MAP 5 E 9

Lahinch,
Co. Clare

Tel: 065-708 1242 Fax: 065-708 1247
Email: gbrier@indigo.ie
Web: www.greenbrierinn.com

Luxurious 3*** guesthouse, overlooking Lahinch Golf Links and the Atlantic Ocean. Situated 300 yards from Lahinch Village with its excellent restaurants, pubs and shops. All rooms are en suite with antique style pine furnishings, pressurised showers, orthopaedic beds, DD phones, multi-channel TV, tea/coffee making facilities. An excellent base from which to visit the Cliffs of Moher, play the famous Lahinch Golf Links or the spectacular Greg Norman designed Doonbeg Golf Links 18 miles away. "Come and enjoy our home while away from your own".

Member of Premier Guesthouses of Ireland

*B&B from €35.00 to €85.00*

*Margaret & Victor Mulcahy*
*Proprietors*

14

*Activities:*

Closed 20 November - 07 March

B&B Rates are per Person Sharing per Night incl. Breakfast.
or Room Rates are per Room per Night - **See also Page 8**

## Lahinch

### Lahinch Golf & Leisure Hotel

HOTEL ★★★★ MAP 5 E 9


Lahinch,
Co. Clare

Tel: 065-708 1100 Fax: 065-708 1228
Email: info@lahinchgolfhotel.com
Web: www.lahinchgolfhotel.com

Situated on the former site of the Aberdeen Arms, this property has undergone an extensive renovation, which has transformed the hotel into a luxurious property in the heart of Lahinch. Relax and de-stress in our leisure centre or avail of our many treatments in the Lahinch Golf & Leisure Club. Enjoy an intimate dining experience in our Dunes Restaurant or relax in the cosy atmosphere of the Aberdeen Bar. Only 5 mins from Lahinch Golf Course, the hotel is an ideal base for the discerning golfer. The Blue Flag Beach at Lahinch is only a stroll away. The perfect base for touring The Burren and West Clare.

***An IHF Quality Employer***

*Bookable on www.irelandhotels.com*
*Special Offer: www.irelandhotels.com/offers*

*B&B from €70.00 to €105.00*
*Suites from €250.00 to €320.00*

*John O' Meara*
*General Manager*

144

*Activities:*

Open All Year

### Moy House

GUESTHOUSE ★★★★ MAP 5 E 9


Lahinch,
Co. Clare

Tel: 065-708 2800 Fax: 065-708 2500
Email: moyhouse@eircom.net
Web: www.moyhouse.com

Moy House prevails over the breathtaking seascape of Lahinch Bay, set on 15 acres of ground, adorned by mature woodland and a picturesque river. Major restoration has transformed this 18th century country house in keeping with present day expectations of superior standards, yet preserving its unique character style and period ambience. Dining at Moy House is a truly memorable experience in the new classical conservatory restaurant overlooking the Atlantic, with local ingredients that are prepared in a modern Irish style. Personal attention and outstanding service makes for an unforgettable experience.

Member of Ireland's Blue Book

*B&B from €115.00 to €135.00*
*Suites from €260.00 to €335.00*

*Brid O'Meara*
*General Manager*

9

Closed 01 January - 14 February

### Sancta Maria Hotel

HOTEL ★★ MAP 5 E 9


Lahinch,
Co. Clare

Tel: 065-708 1041 Fax: 065-708 1529
Email: sanctamaria01@eircom.net
Web: www.sancta-maria.ie

The McInerney Family have welcomed holiday makers to the Sancta Maria for over 50 years. Many of the attractive bedrooms overlook the famous Lahinch Golf Links and golden beach, which are within 100 metres of the hotel. Our restaurant specialises in fresh produce and special emphasis is placed on local seafoods and home-baking. The Sancta Maria is the ideal base for touring The Burren or visiting the Cliffs of Moher and Aran Islands. Please enquire about Facilities for Persons with Mobility Impairment.

*Bookable on www.irelandhotels.com*
*Special Offer: www.irelandhotels.com/offers*

*B&B from €44.00 to €55.00*

*Thomas McInerney*
*Proprietor*

24

*Activities:*

Closed 05 November - 01 March



B&B Rates are per Person Sharing per Night incl. Breakfast. or Room Rates are per Room per Night - **See also Page 8**

## Shamrock Inn Hotel

HOTEL ★★ MAP 5 E 9

Main Street,
Lahinch,
Co. Clare

Tel: 065-708 1700 Fax: 065-708 1029
Email: info@shamrockinn.ie
Web: www.shamrockinn.ie

Situated right in the heart of charming Lahinch. All tastefully decorated rooms have direct dial phone, TV, hairdryer and tea/coffee making facilities. Our restaurant is renowned for its warm and intimate atmosphere offering a choice of excellent cuisine, catering for all tastes. Delicious home-cooked bar food is served daily and by night the bar comes to life with the sound of music. Whatever your interest, golf, fishing or horse riding, we can arrange it for you.

*B&B from €55.00 to €70.00*

*Alan Logue*
*Managing Director*

10

Open All Year

## Vaughan Lodge and Seafood Restaurant

HOTEL ★★★★ MAP 5 E 9

Ennistymon Road,
Lahinch,
Co Clare

Tel: 065-708 1111 Fax: 065-708 1011
Email: info@vaughanlodge.ie
Web: www.vaughanlodge.ie

Michael & Maria Vaughan built this lovely lodge in 2005. The Vaughans have been taking care of guests in Lahinch for over 4 generations and it shows! Rooms are spacious with Power Showers, free broadband & WiFi. A drying room is provided for wet gear. The lodge has a highly acclaimed Seafood Restaurant open nightly except Mondays. The clubby lounge bar offers an extensive collection of fine malts & brandy. Vaughan Lodge is a real treat for those who crave individual attention & hearty Irish Hospitality. This is good old fashioned hotel - keeping for a modern era!

*Bookable on www.irelandhotels.com*
*Special Offer: www.irelandhotels.com/offers*

*B&B from €80.00 to €125.00*

*Maria & Michael Vaughan*
*Owners / Managers*

22

*Activities:*

Closed 01 November - 30 March



B&B Rates are per Person Sharing per Night incl. Breakfast.
or Room Rates are per Room per Night - See also Page 8

## Liscannor / Lisdoonvarna

### Cliffs of Moher Hotel

HOTEL ★★★★ MAP 5 E 9

Main Street,
Liscannor,
Co. Clare

Tel: 065-708 6770 Fax: 065-708 6771
Email: info@cliffsofmoherhotel.ie
Web: www.cliffsofmoherhotel.ie

The 4* Cliffs of Moher Hotel is situated in the tranquil and picturesque fishing village of Liscannor, 4km from the world famous Cliffs of Moher & Lahinch Golf Course. 23 luxurious en suite rooms combine with the splendid Puffin Restaurant & Submarine Bar to provide a luxurious & relaxed atmosphere. Our bar & restaurant provide exceptional service, quality food & drink from The Burren & west coast of Clare region. With the Aran Islands, picturesque Burren & the music Mecca that is Doolin on your doorstep, it's a superb place to base your exploring of Clare. Please enquire about Facilities for Persons with Mobility Impairment.

Member of Atlantis Holiday Group

B&B from €50.00 to €120.00
Suites from €150.00 to €250.00

*Michael Piwnik*
*Manager*

23

Open All Year

### Kincora House and Art Gallery

GUESTHOUSE ★★★ MAP 5 E 9

Lisdoonvarna,
Co. Clare

Tel: 065-707 4300 Fax: 065-707 4490
Email: kincorahotel@eircom.net
Web: www.kincorahotel.ie

Relaxing, romantic and dating from 1860, the property exudes charm, character and a lovely ambience. Comfortable en suite bedrooms with lovely views. Savour cooked-to-order breakfasts in our dining room, while enjoying the paintings of the owner/artist. 10 minutes from the Cliffs of Moher, Doolin and The Burren. 15 minutes Lahinch, 50 minutes Shannon Airport. Michelin recommended, Irish Inn of the Year, National Gardens Award.

Member of Signpost Premier Hotels

*Bookable on www.irelandhotels.com*
*Special Offer: www.irelandhotels.com/offers*

B&B from €35.00 to €65.00

*Doreen & Diarmuid Drennan*
*Proprietors*

14

Closed 01 October - 31 March

### Rathbaun Hotel

HOTEL ★★ MAP 5 E 9

Main Street,
Lisdoonvarna,
Co. Clare

Tel: 065-707 4009 Fax: 065-707 4009
Email: rathbaunhotel@eircom.net
Web: www.rathbaunhotel.com

Rathbaun Hotel is the most renowned hotel in Co. Clare for Irish Music - played nightly from June to September. Our hotel offers the best quality and value in accommodation and home-cooked food, with genuinely personal service. We offer maps and helpful information on The Burren, Aran Islands and Cliffs of Moher, etc. A welcoming and happy atmosphere is the hallmark of the Rathbaun Hotel. Shannon and Galway airports 60km. Céad Míle Fáilte.

Member of Countrywide Hotels - MinOtel Ireland

*Bookable on www.irelandhotels.com*
*Special Offer: www.irelandhotels.com/offers*

B&B from €35.00 to €60.00

*John Connolly*

12

Closed 10 October - 31 March



B&B Rates are per Person Sharing per Night incl. Breakfast.
or Room Rates are per Room per Night - See also Page 8

## Sheedy's Country House Hotel

HOTEL ★★★★ MAP 5 E 9

Lisdoonvarna,
Co. Clare

Tel: 065-707 4026 Fax: 065-707 4555

Email: info@sheedys.com

Web: www.sheedys.com

Set among herb and vegetable gardens, Sheedy's is described in the Campbell Guide as "One of the West of Ireland's Best Loved Small Hotels". Rooms are individually decorated with power showers, luxury bathrooms and music centres. The Sheedy house dates back to the mid 1700s, the oldest in the village. 5 minutes drive from Doolin. Cliffs of Moher and The Burren region are close by. WiFi available. John's cooking has been awarded 2 rosettes from AA & Best Breakfast in Munster 2004. Less than 1 hour from Shannon. Please enquire about Facilities for Persons with Mobility Impairment.

***An IHF Quality Employer***

Member of Manor House Hotels

*Bookable on www.irelandhotels.com*

*Special Offer: www.irelandhotels.com/offers*

*B&B from €68.50 to €95.00*

*Suites from €180.00 to €210.00*

*John & Martina Sheedy*

11

Closed 01 October - 15 March

## Armada Hotel

HOTEL ★★★ MAP 5 E 8

Spanish Point,
Milltown Malbay,
Co. Clare

Tel: 065-708 4110 Fax: 065-708 4632

Email: info@burkesarmadahotel.com

Web: www.burkesarmadahotel.com

Armada Hotel commands a superb ocean-front setting in the beautiful seaside resort of Spanish Point. All rooms are furnished to a very high standard with an additional 28 superior rooms & suites with spa facilities opening in Spring '08. The Cape Restaurant offers exceptional cusine under the attention of an award-winning culinary team, in contemporary modern surroundings with a private bar area. The hotel offers a private garden area overlooking Spanish Point Beach. Nearby attractions: Cliffs of Moher, Aran Islands, Doolin Cave, Lahinch & Doonbeg Golf Courses. Also extensive conference & banqueting facilities.

Member of Irish Country Hotels

*Bookable on www.irelandhotels.com*

*Special Offer: www.irelandhotels.com/offers*

*B&B from €55.00 to €90.00*

*Suites from €150.00 to €225.00*

*John J. Burke*
*Director*

61

Closed 25 December

B&B Rates are per Person Sharing per Night incl. Breakfast.
or Room Rates are per Room per Night - See also Page 8

# Milltown Malbay / Mountshannon / Newmarket-on-Fergus

## Bellbridge House Hotel

HOTEL ★★★ MAP 5 E 8

Spanish Point,
Milltown Malbay,
Co. Clare

Tel: 065-708 4038 Fax: 065-708 4830
Email: info@bellbridgehotelclare.com
Web: www.bellbridgehotelclare.com

A warm welcome & a relaxing atmosphere await you at this West Clare coastal hotel, not to mention our impeccable service and superb cuisine. Situated around the corner from Spanish Point's sandy beach and in close proximity to many of the counties scenic tourist attractions, word famous golf courses such as Lahinch & Doonbeg as well as surfing, horse riding & fishing, the hotel provides the ideal base for visiting Co. Clare. "Where Memories are Made & nothing is Overlooked but the Sea"

*Bookable on www.irelandhotels.com*
*Special Offer: www.irelandhotels.com/offers*

*B&B from €55.00 to €95.00*

*Derek Logue*
*Proprietor*

49

Activities:

Open All Year

## Mountshannon Hotel

HOTEL ★★ MAP 6 H 9

Mountshannon,
Co. Clare

Tel: 061-927162 Fax: 061-927272
Email: info@mountshannon-hotel.ie

The Mountshannon Hotel, situated in the rural and peaceful village of Mountshannon, offers you first class accommodation in friendly surroundings. All bedrooms are en suite with direct dial phone, TV, tea/coffee making facilities and hairdryer. Our continental style restaurant, which is known for excellent and reasonably priced cuisine, overlooks our garden and Lough Derg. Private car park. 4 mins walk from Mountshannon Harbour. Fishing, pony trekking and golf are available. Large function room catering for weddings & parties.

Member of Countrywide Hotels

*B&B from €40.00 to €50.00*

*Pauline & Michael Madden*
*Director / Owner*

16

Activities:

Closed 24 - 26 December

## Dromoland Castle

HOTEL ★★★★★ MAP 6 G 8

Newmarket-on-Fergus,
Co. Clare

Tel: 061-368144 Fax: 061-363355
Email: sales@dromoland.ie
Web: www.dromoland.ie

Located 13km from Shannon Airport. Stately halls, elegant public areas and beautifully furnished guest rooms are steeped in a timeless atmosphere that is unique to Dromoland. The international reputation for excellence is reflected in the award-winning cuisine in the castle's Earl of Thomond & Fig Tree Restaurant in the Dromoland Golf & Country Club. A completely renovated 18 hole championship golf course with our new golf academy which houses 10 automated driving bays, fishing, horse riding, clay shooting, gymnasium and the newly opened "Spa at Dromoland" which offers a full range of health and beauty treatments.

***An IHF Quality Employer***

Member of Preferred Hotels & Resorts WW

*Bookable on www.irelandhotels.com*

*Room Rate from €238.00 to €540.00*
*Suites from €499.00 to €1,365.00*

*Mark Nolan*
*General Manager*

98

Closed 24 - 27 December



B&B Rates are per Person Sharing per Night incl. Breakfast.
or Room Rates are per Room per Night - **See also Page 8**

## Hunters Lodge

GUESTHOUSE ★★★ MAP 6 G 8

The Square,
Newmarket-on-Fergus,
Co. Clare

Tel: 061-368577 Fax: 061-368057

Email: hunterslodge@eircom.net

Ideally situated for visitors arriving or departing from Shannon Airport (12km). We offer 6 comfortable en suite bedrooms with telephone and TV. Our olde worlde pub and restaurant specialise in good quality fresh food served in a relaxed atmosphere with a friendly and efficient service. Local tourist attractions include Bunratty Folk Park, castle banquets and many 18 hole golf courses. Ideal stopover for touring Co. Clare or commencing your trip to the West of Ireland.

*B&B from €45.00 to €55.00*

*Robert & Kathleen Healy*
*Proprietors*

6

Open All Year

## Oakwood Arms Hotel

HOTEL ★★★ MAP 6 G 7

Shannon,
Co. Clare

Tel: 061-361500 Fax: 061-361414

Email: reservations@oakwoodarms.com

Web: www.oakwoodarms.com

The Oakwood Arms enjoys an enviable location in the centre of Shannon just 3 kms from Shannon Airport, and a 20 minute drive from Ennis and Limerick. The hotel sets the standard on quality with its elegantly furnished guest rooms, state of the art gymnasium, sauna and steam room. Enjoy a relaxing drink or a light lunch in "Sophie's Lounge" or book a table in our "Palm Court" Restaurant. Please enquire about Facilities for Persons with Mobility Impairment.

*Bookable on www.irelandhotels.com*
*Special Offer: www.irelandhotels.com/offers*

*B&B from €65.00 to €75.00*
*Suites from €220.00 to €260.00*

*Victor O'Sullivan*
*Managing Director*

100

*Activities:*

Closed 24 - 26 December

## Park Inn Shannon Airport

HOTEL ★★★ MAP 6 G 7

Shannon Airport,
Shannon,
Co. Clare

Tel: 061-471122 Fax: 061-471526

Email: reservations.shannon-airport@rezidorparkinn.com

Web: www.shannon.parkinn.ie

Park Inn Shannon Airport is a hotel with exceptional style and comfort within walking distance of the terminal building at Shannon Airport. All 115 rooms are en suite with direct dial phone, TV, tea/coffee making facilities, hairdryer, trouser press and iron & ironing board. Leisure facilities include a gym and steam room. Within a short driving distance of Bunratty Castle, The Burren, Cliffs of Moher and the world famous Lahinch and Doonbeg Golf Links. Please enquire about Facilities for Persons with Mobility Impairment.

***An IHF Quality Employer***

Member of Rezidor SAS Hotels & Resorts

*Bookable on www.irelandhotels.com*
*Special Offer: www.irelandhotels.com/offers*

*Room Rate from €99.00 to €200.00*

*Louise O'Hara*
*General Manager*

115

*Activities:*

Closed 24 - 26 December

B&B Rates are per Person Sharing per Night incl. Breakfast.
or Room Rates are per Room per Night - **See also Page 8**

## Ardara / Ballybofey

### Nesbitt Arms Hotel

HOTEL ★★★ MAP 13 H 18

Main Street,
Ardara,
Co. Donegal

Tel: 074-954 1103 Fax: 074-954 1895
Email: info@nesbittarms.com
Web: www.nesbittarms.com

Family-run hotel. Built in 1838, refurbished 2004, in Heritage Town of Ardara, famed for tweeds, hand knits, unspoilt sandy beaches. Ideal base for touring Donegal. 49 modern en suite bedrooms, new function room, elevator. Excellent food. Choice of Weavens Bar / Bistro or Restaurant. Live music in bar. Locally, golf, fishing, horse riding, hill walking, cycling, boating. We have 3 bedrooms specially adapted for wheelchair users. Regional winners of Fáilte Ireland Welcome Awards 2005. Please enquire about Facilities for Persons with Mobility Impairment.

***An IHF Quality Employer***

*B&B from €50.00 to €65.00*

*Marie & Paul Gallagher*
*Proprietor / Manager* 49

Activities:

Closed 25 December

### Woodhill House

GUESTHOUSE ★★★ MAP 13 H 18

Ardara,
Co. Donegal

Tel: 074-954 1112 Fax: 074-954 1516
Email: yates@iol.ie
Web: www.woodhillhouse.com

An historic country house, the site dates back to the 17th century. Set in its own grounds, with an old Walled Garden overlooking the Donegal Highlands. There is a quality traditional French style restaurant, seafood a speciality, with fully licensed bar & occasional music. The area is famous for its Donegal tweeds & woollens, salmon & trout fishing, pony trekking, golf, boating, cycling, beaches, many archaeological sites, Sheskinmore Wildlife Reserve, Glenveagh National Park, Slieve League & some of the most unspoilt scenery in Europe. Additional garden rooms opening 2008. Special Packages available.

***An IHF Quality Employer***

*B&B from €48.00 to €75.00*

*Nancy & John Yates*
*Owners* 9

Closed 20 - 27 December

### Jackson's Hotel, Conference & Leisure Centre

HOTEL ★★★ MAP 13 J 19

Ballybofey,
Co. Donegal

Tel: 074-913 1021 Fax: 074-913 1096
Email: bjackson@iol.ie
Web: www.jacksons-hotel.ie

Located in lovely surroundings & set amongst its own gardens, Jackson's Hotel & Conference Centre is an award-winning, family-run property providing an array of amenities including 134 beautifully appointed guest rooms. Relax by the log fire and enjoy breathtaking views of the River Finn & Drumboe Woods, sample delicious dishes in the Ballybuffet Bistro or Garden Restaurant or unwind in the state-of-the-art Leisure Centre with its 22m swimming pool, jacuzzi, sauna, solarium & fully equipped gymnasium. Ideally located for touring all the sights of Donegal. 45 mins to Derry Airport.

***An IHF Quality Employer***

*Bookable on www.irelandhotels.com*
*Special Offer: www.irelandhotels.com/offers*

*B&B from €65.00 to €80.00*
*Suites from €100.00 to €400.00*

*Margaret & Barry Jackson*
*Proprietors* 134

Activities:

Open All Year



B&B Rates are per Person Sharing per Night incl. Breakfast. or Room Rates are per Room per Night - **See also Page 8**

## Kee's Hotel

HOTEL ★★★ MAP 13 J 19

Stranorlar,
Ballybofey,
Co. Donegal

Tel: 074-913 1018 Fax: 074-913 1917

Email: info@keeshotel.ie

Web: www.keeshotel.ie

Charming family-run hotel in village situation. A combination of excellent facilities, caring staff and management draws guests back time and again. One of the highlights of any stay is dinner in the elegant new restaurant. Delightful en suite rooms with all modern facilities. Leisure club with swimming pool, jacuzzi, sauna, steam room and gym. We also have a beauty salon.

Bookable on www.irelandhotels.com
Special Offer: www.irelandhotels.com/offers

B&B from €78.00 to €88.00

Richard, Jayne & Vicky Kee
Proprietors / Managers

53

Open All Year

## Villa Rose Hotel & V - Spa

HOTEL ★★★ MAP 13 J 19

Main Street,
Ballybofey,
Co. Donegal

Tel: 074-913 2266 Fax: 074-913 0666

Email: info@villarose.net

Web: www.villarose.net

A hidden gem, The Villa Rose Hotel has been extended & fully refurbished, to the new "Villa Rose & V-Spa". Deceptive on the outside, amazing on the inside, it offers the same quality & service with a few extra touches; the award-winning Spa & 58 executive bedrooms including 2 superior suites with circular beds & whirlpool baths. 10% off at local stores including McElhinney's. Ideal for golf, fishing and walking. Please enquire about Facilities for Persons with Mobility Impairment.

Bookable on www.irelandhotels.com
Special Offer: www.irelandhotels.com/offers

B&B from €76.00 to €99.00
Suites from €192.00 to €250.00

Thomas Gallen
Proprietor

58

Activities:

Closed 24 - 26 December

B&B Rates are per Person Sharing per Night incl. Breakfast.
or Room Rates are per Room per Night - **See also Page 8**

## Ballyliffin / Ballyshannon

### Ballyliffin Lodge & Spa

HOTEL ★★★★ MAP 14 K 21

Shore Road,
Ballyliffin,
Co. Donegal

Tel: 074-937 8200 Fax: 074-937 8985

Email: info@ballyliffinlodge.com

Web: www.ballyliffinlodge.com

The first thing to strike you about Ballyliffin Lodge is the panoramic views of the famous Ballyliffin Golf Club and Malin Head. Private and intimate and set in the heart of the village, the drama of its views is continued as you enter its beautifully designed interior, where traditional charm and luxury is woven into the very fabric of the exquisite décor. A stay in Ballyliffin Lodge & Spa whether for golf, wedding, walking or chilling out will calm your spirit, relax your body and rejuvenate your soul. Please enquire about Facilities for Persons with Mobility Impairment.

*B&B from €95.00 to €120.00*

*Tony McDermott*
*General Manager*

40

*Activities:*

Closed 25 December

### Dorrians Imperial Hotel

HOTEL ★★★ MAP 13 I 17

Main Street,
Ballyshannon,
Co. Donegal

Tel: 071-985 1147 Fax: 071-985 1001

Email: info@dorriansimperialhotel.com

Web: www.dorriansimperialhotel.com

Town centre family-run hotel (built 1781). All rooms are en suite with TV, telephone and tea/coffee facilities. Private car park. Open fire. The hotel was recently renovated, embracing old and new décor and has an elevator. Ideally suited for touring North West and North East Ireland and ideally located for golfing, fishing & beaches. Sligo 45km, Belfast 202km, Dublin 216km.

*Bookable on www.irelandhotels.com*

*B&B from €65.00 to €90.00*

*Ben & Mary Dorrian*
*Proprietors*

47

*Activities:*

Closed 22 December - 08 January

### Heron's Cove

GUESTHOUSE ★★★ MAP 13 I 17

Creevy, Rossnowlagh Road,
Ballyshannon,
Co. Donegal

Tel: 071-982 2070 Fax: 071-982 2075

Email: info@heronscove.ie

Web: www.heronscove.ie

Located close to the magnificent beach at Rossnowlagh and the little harbour at Creevy Pier in South Donegal, Heron's Cove is the ideal, intimate destination from which to explore the wonderful coastline and countryside of the northwest. The excellent family-run restaurant, with charming quiet accommodation, offers the best of Irish cuisine and hospitality. Many of Ireland's finest golf links courses are within driving distance. Excellent sea angling, surfing, hill walking and pony trekking are all available locally.

Member of Irish Country Hotels

*B&B from €60.00 to €75.00*

*Seoirse & Maeve O'Toole*
*Proprietors*

10

Closed 24 - 28 December



B&B Rates are per Person Sharing per Night incl. Breakfast.
or Room Rates are per Room per Night - **See also Page 8**

## Ostan Radharc Na Mara / Sea View Hotel

HOTEL ★★★ MAP 13 I 20

Bunbeg,
Co. Donegal

Tel: 074-953 1159 Fax: 074-953 2238
Email: info@seaviewhotel.ie
Web: www.visitgweedore.com

In an area where nature remains untouched, the air is rich and pure, ensuring a heavy appetite. In the Seaview Hotel, guests are treated to wonderful food. The à la carte menu always includes a seasonal selection of fresh, local seafood dishes, with salmon, trout, lobster and oysters a speciality.

***An IHF Quality Employer***

*B&B from €60.00 to €75.00*

*James Boyle*
*General Manager*

36

**Closed 23 - 28 December**

## Inishowen Gateway Hotel

HOTEL ★★★ MAP 14 K 20

Railway Road,
Buncrana, Inishowen,
Co. Donegal

Tel: 074-936 1144 Fax: 074-936 2278
Email: info@inishowengateway.com
Web: www.inishowengateway.com

Located on the shores of Lough Swilly on the Inishowen Peninsula, this hotel offers a picturesque & convenient location to explore the North West. 79 bedrooms with all the features of a modern 3*** hotel. Health club includes steam room, jacuzzi, sauna, & 20m pool. Seagrass Wellbeing Centre caters for all your beauty & pampering needs. The Peninsula Restaurant is renowned for its à la carte & dinner menus serving the finest local produce. Offering free golf on the adjacent 9 hole Buncrana and within 20 mins of three 18 hole link courses including Ballyliffin. Planet active soft adventure play centre.

*Bookable on www.irelandhotels.com*
*Special Offer: www.irelandhotels.com/offers*

*B&B from €60.00 to €70.00*

*Patrick Doherty*
*Proprietor*

79

Activities:

**Closed 24 - 26 December**

## Grand Central Hotel

HOTEL ★★★ MAP 13 I 17

Main Street,
Bundoran,
Co. Donegal

Tel: 071-984 2722 Fax: 071-984 2656
Email: info@grandcentralbundoran.com
Web: www.grandcentralbundoran.com

The Grand Central Hotel, located in the heart of Bundoran, has always been recognised as the best value for money 3*** family hotel in Bundoran. Along with our 62 en suite bedrooms which provide both comfort and luxury, we have sea views, a Féile Bia approved restaurant, Café GC, Ole Wine & Tapas venue, Bundo's Kids Club, free WiFi broadband access and music every weekend and nightly during July & August. Golfing, surfing, horse riding, angling, hill walking packages available. Please enquire about Facilities for Persons with Mobility Impairment.

*Bookable on www.irelandhotels.com*
*Special Offer: www.irelandhotels.com/offers*

*Room Rate from €79.00 to €139.00*

*Francois De Dietrich*
*Group General Manager*

62

**Open All Year**

B&B Rates are per Person Sharing per Night incl. Breakfast.
or Room Rates are per Room per Night - See also Page 8

## Bundoran / Culdaff / Donegal Town

### Great Northern Hotel

HOTEL ★★★★ MAP 13 I 17

Bundoran,
Co. Donegal

Tel: 071-984 1204 Fax: 071-984 1114
Email: reservations@greatnorthernhotel.com
Web: www.greatnorthernhotel.com

Great Northern Hotel, Conference & Leisure Centre Bundoran. The hotel is situated in the middle of an 18 hole championship golf course overlooking Donegal Bay. 4**** hotel with 96 bedrooms with top leisure facilities for all the family. This hotel has all en suite bedrooms, a restaurant, grill room, lounge, ballroom and syndicate rooms. Newly built leisure centre with swimming pool, gymnasium, sauna, steam room, childrens' area. Conference & banquet centre. Please enquire about Facilities for Persons with Mobility Impairment.

***An IHF Quality Employer***

Member of Brian McEniff Hotels

Bookable on www.irelandhotels.com
Special Offer: www.irelandhotels.com/offers

B&B from €70.00 to €115.00
Suites from €250.00 to €300.00

*Philip McGlynn*
*General Manager*

96

Activities:

Closed 17 - 27 December

### McGrorys of Culdaff

HOTEL ★★★ MAP 14 L 21

Culdaff,
Inishowen,
Co. Donegal

Tel: 074-937 9104 Fax: 074-937 9235
Email: reservations@mcgrorys.ie
Web: www.mcgrorys.ie

This contemporary and stylish premises located on scenic Inishowen Peninsula is an ideal base for touring the North and North West within easy distance of the City of Derry, Foyle Ferry and Ballyliffin. Our award-winning restaurant serves excellent seafood, steaks and house specialities. Famous Macs Backroom Bar features such acts as Altan, Tommy Emmanuel, Frankie Gavin, Ritchie Havens and more. Traditional sessions regularly in Front Bar. Please enquire about Facilities for Persons with Mobility Impairment.

B&B from €50.00 to €85.00

*John & Neil McGrory /*
*Anne Doherty*

17

Activities:

Closed 23 - 27 December

### Ard Na Breátha

GUESTHOUSE ★★★ MAP 13 I 18

Drumrooske Middle,
Donegal Town

Tel: 074-972 2288 Fax: 074-974 0720
Email: info@ardnabreatha.com
Web: www.ardnabreatha.com

Ard na Breatha Restaurant & Guesthouse, described by many as a hidden treasure, is located 1.5km from Donegal Town just off the road to lovely Lough Eske. You will be assured of a warm welcome in our cosy lounge, complete with open hearth, with views of the Bluestack Mountains. Our en suite bedrooms (all with bath) have tea/coffee facilities, TV, phone and hairdryer. Our fully licensed restaurant specialises in modern Irish cuisine with an emphasis on local & organic food where possible and an extensive wine list. AA ♦♦♦♦. Please enquire about Facilities for Persons with Mobility Impairment.

Bookable on www.irelandhotels.com
Special Offer: www.irelandhotels.com/offers

B&B from €40.00 to €55.00

*Theresa Morrow*
*Proprietor*

6

Closed 20 November - 14 February



B&B Rates are per Person Sharing per Night incl. Breakfast. or Room Rates are per Room per Night - See also Page 8

## Donegal Manor

GUESTHOUSE ★★★★ MAP 13 I 18

Letterkenny Road,
Donegal Town,
Co. Donegal

Tel: 074-972 5222 Fax: 074-972 5688

Email: info@donegalmanor.com

Web: www.donegalmanor.com

Enjoy the comforts of this newly built and Donegal Town's only 4 star guesthouse. Bright, spacious bedrooms decorated with style & elegance. All rooms are en suite with flat screen televisions etc. A delicious Irish breakfast and choice of continental starters served. Free on site parking, WiFi access, swimming vouchers when staying 3 or more nights. Conveniently situated 1 mile from centre of Donegal Town and close to Lough Eske. Highly rated on www.tripadvisor.

*Bookable on www.irelandhotels.com*

*Special Offer: www.irelandhotels.com/offers*

*B&B from €40.00 to €70.00*

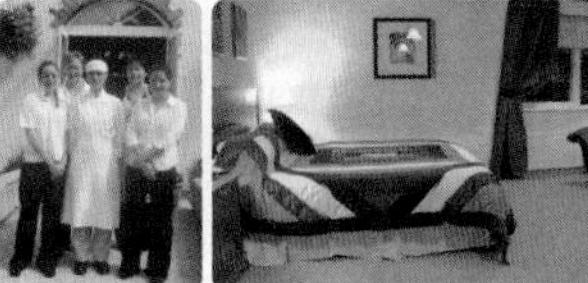

*Sian, Michelle & Staff*
*Hosts*

9

Closed 02 January - 01 March

## Harvey's Point Country Hotel

HOTEL ★★★★ MAP 13 I 18

Lough Eske,
Donegal Town,
Co. Donegal

Tel: 074-972 2208 Fax: 074-972 2352

Email: info@harveyspoint.com

Web: www.harveyspoint.com

Set in magical location amidst the natural beauty of the Bluestack Mountains and on the edge of the shimmering Lough Eske, Harvey's Point is an island of serenity and a truly unforgettable experience. Lavish accommodation with fine gourmet dining steeped in elegance and sophistication, 6km from Donegal Town. Michelin and Good Hotel Guide listed, AA and Fáilte Ireland 4****, 2 AA Rosettes, Optimus Award of Best practice 2005/6/7. Owned and managed by the Swiss Family Gysling since 1989. AA Hotel of the Year 2007.

***An IHF Quality Employer***

*Bookable on www.irelandhotels.com*

*Special Offer: www.irelandhotels.com/offers*

*B&B from €99.00 to €125.00*
*Suites from €290.00 to €580.00*

*Deirdre McGlone &*
*Marc Gysling*
*Proprietors*

60

Open All Year

## Mill Park Hotel, Conference Centre & Leisure Club

HOTEL ★★★ MAP 13 I 18

The Mullins,
Donegal Town,
Co. Donegal

Tel: 074-972 2880 Fax: 074-972 2640

Email: info@millparkhotel.com

Web: www.millparkhotel.com

The luxurious Mill Park Hotel is located only a few minutes stroll from Donegal Town. The interior design of the hotel is a fusion of traditional & contemporary styles with the main feature being the Granary Foyer at the heart of the hotel. Each of the 95 rooms and 5 suites reflect the luxury and comfort offered throughout the hotel. Enjoy a choice of 2 restaurants, superb leisure facilities & wellness centre. Please enquire about Facilities for Persons with Mobility Impairment.

Member of Irish Country Hotels

*Bookable on www.irelandhotels.com*

*Special Offer: www.irelandhotels.com/offers*

*B&B from €50.00 to €125.00*
*Suites from €170.00 to €320.00*

*Tony McDermott*

100

*Activities:*

Closed 23 - 27 December

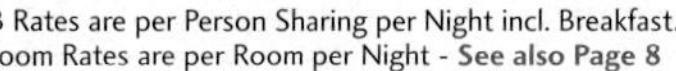

B&B Rates are per Person Sharing per Night incl. Breakfast.
or Room Rates are per Room per Night - See also Page 8

# Downings / Dunfanaghy

## Rosapenna Hotel and Golf Resort

HOTEL ★★★★ MAP 13 J 21

Downings,
Co. Donegal

Tel: 074-915 5301 Fax: 074-915 5128
Email: rosapenna@eircom.net
Web: www.rosapenna.ie

Situated in North West Donegal on the shore of Sheephaven Bay, the Rosapenna Hotel offers four star comfort and a quiet, relaxing atmosphere. Rosapenna has superb golfing facilities with two 18 hole links to choose from, the Old Tom Morris Course and the Sandy Hills Links, and a golf pavilion overlooking the courses.
Rosapenna...a place to remember...and return to.

***An IHF Quality Employer***

Bookable on www.irelandhotels.com
Special Offer: www.irelandhotels.com/offers

*B&B from €85.00 to €95.00*

*Hilary & Frank Casey*

53

Activities:

Closed 28 October - 14 March

## Arnolds Hotel

HOTEL ★★★ MAP 13 J 21

Dunfanaghy,
Co. Donegal

Tel: 074-913 6208 Fax: 074-913 6352
Email: enquiries@arnoldshotel.com
Web: www.arnoldshotel.com

Established in 1922 the hotel has been in the Arnold Family for three generations. Situated at the entrance to the village and overlooking Horn Head and Sheephaven Bay, we are an ideal base for touring North Donegal, Glenveagh National Park and Gardens close by. Enjoy one of the many activities organised by the hotel, horse riding from the hotel stables, golf on the local golf courses, fishing, walking, painting tuition, photography weekends and creative writing. Also bookable on www.irishcountryhotels.com Please enquire about Facilities for Persons with Mobility Impairment.

***An IHF Quality Employer***

Member of Irish Country Hotels

Bookable on www.irelandhotels.com
Special Offer: www.irelandhotels.com/offers

*B&B from €65.00 to €85.00*

*Arnold Family Proprietors*

30

Activities:

Closed 01 November - 29 March

## Shandon Hotel Spa and Wellness

HOTEL ★★★★ MAP 13 J 21

Marble Hill Strand,
Port-na-Blagh, Dunfanaghy,
Co. Donegal

Tel: 074-913 6137 Fax: 074-913 6430
Email: shandonhotel@eircom.net
Web: www.shandonhotel.com

Your room with picturesque sea views, friendly surroundings and turf fires. Be pampered in the luxurious spa.
Enjoy the indoor leisure centre, pitch & putt and tennis. Children have fun in the playhouse and grounds. Locally: famous golf links, water sport, horse riding, walking..... Discover the Heritage and culture of beautiful Sheephaven Bay, Donegal. Please enquire about Facilities for Persons with Mobility Impairment.

***An IHF Quality Employer***

Bookable on www.irelandhotels.com
Special Offer: www.irelandhotels.com/offers

*B&B from €85.00 to €140.00*
*Suites from €240.00 to €320.00*

*Dermot & Catherine McGlade*

50

Activities:

Closed 04 November - 15 March

B&B Rates are per Person Sharing per Night incl. Breakfast.
or Room Rates are per Room per Night - **See also Page 8**

## Ostan Na Rosann

HOTEL ★★★ MAP 13 | 19

Mill Road,
Dungloe,
Co. Donegal

Tel: 074-952 2444 Fax: 074-952 2400
Email: info@ostannarosann.com
Web: www.ostannarosann.com

The Ostan na Rosann is a family-run hotel in the heart of the Gaeltacht/Rosses, overlooking the spectacular Dungloe Bay. The hotel is warm, welcoming and is known for its friendly atmosphere. Our facilities include a leisure centre, childrens' play area, patio areas, restaurant, lounge bar and beautician. All our bedrooms are en suite, have tea & coffee making facilities, hairdryer, television, direct dial telephone. Please enquire about Facilities for Persons with Mobility Impairment.

***An IHF Quality Employer***

*Bookable on www.irelandhotels.com*
*Special Offer: www.irelandhotels.com/offers*

*B&B from €60.00 to €75.00*
*Suites from €160.00 to €190.00*

*Maurice McBride*
*Proprietor*

48

Open All Year

## Highlands Hotel

HOTEL ★★ MAP 13 | 19

Glenties,
Co. Donegal

Tel: 074-955 1111 Fax: 074-955 1564
Email: highlandhotel@eircom.net
Web: www.thehighlandshotel.com

The Highlands Hotel is situated in the pretty town of Glenties. The town has won awards both in the Tidy Towns and the European Entente Florale competition. The surrounding glens are a haven for the hill walkers and a series of marked walks meander through the countryside. Enjoy a meal in our restaurant and try our famous Donegal seafood chowder. Please enquire about Facilities for Persons with Mobility Impairment.

*B&B from €52.00 to €55.00*

*Johnny, Christine &*
*Sinead Boyle*

24

*Activities:*

Closed 24 - 28 December

## An Chúirt, Gweedore Court Hotel

HOTEL ★★★★ MAP 13 | 20

Gweedore,
Co. Donegal

Tel: 074-953 2900 Fax: 074-953 2929
Email: info@gweedorecourthotel.com
Web: www.gweedorecourthotel.com

Spectacularly set in the heart of the Donegal Gaeltacht, with magnificent views of Mount Errigal. An Chúirt Gweedore Court Hotel is family-run & proud to boast the highest of comfort & service in the area. Facilities: restaurant, health club with 20m pool, hair salon, beautician & spa treatments. Close to Glenveagh National Park, activties locally: mountain climbs, kyaking, horse-riding & angling. 10 mins from Donegal Airport, 45 mins from Letterkenny. Special offers always available on www.gweedorecourthotel.com
Please note we are also closed for Christmas.

*B&B from €70.00 to €120.00*

*Lewis Connon*
*General Manager*

66

*Activities:*

Closed December 31 - 16 January

# Killybegs / Laghey

## Bay View Hotel & Leisure Centre

HOTEL ★★★ MAP 13 H 18

Main Street,
Killybegs,
Co. Donegal

Tel: 074-973 1950 Fax: 074-973 1856
Email: info@bayviewhotel.ie
Web: www.bayviewhotel.ie

One of Donegal's finest hotels, overlooking the splendour of Donegal Bay. We offer 40 en suite bedrooms with satellite TV, hairdryer, trouser press, tea/coffee makers, DD phone. Theme bar and carvery, seafood restaurant. Fully equipped leisure centre, indoor swimming pool. Deep sea angling, fresh water fishing, golf, hill walking. Scenic boat trips. An ideal touring base. Wheelchair accessible rooms. Lift. Please enquire about Facilities for Persons with Mobility Impairment.

***An IHF Quality Employer***

*B&B from €55.00 to €80.00*

*Michael Heffernan*
*General Manager*

39

Closed 24-26 December

## Tara Hotel

HOTEL ★★★ MAP 13 H 18

Main Street,
Killybegs,
Co. Donegal

Tel: 074-974 1700 Fax: 074-974 1710
Email: info@tarahotel.ie
Web: www.tarahotel.ie

Opened in Sept 2004, luxury hotel built to 3 star standards in the centre of Killybegs, overlooking Killybegs Harbour. All of the 31 en suite bedrooms are beautifully appointed, with all modern facilities. Centrally located near all amenities and popular with many golfers, anglers and walkers. Our hotel is the perfect base for exploring South West Donegal and Slieve League (Europe's highest sea cliffs). Killybegs is fast becoming the gourmet capital of the North West and our panoramic Turntable Restaurant is no exception. We look forward to your visit. Special offers available online at www.tarahotel.ie

***Bookable on www.irelandhotels.com***
***Special Offer: www.irelandhotels.com/offers***

*B&B from €45.00 to €95.00*
*Suites from €140.00 to €270.00*

*Johnny, Paul &*
*Breege McGuinness*
*Owners*

31

Closed 25 - 26 December

## Coxtown Manor

GUESTHOUSE ★★★★ MAP 13 I 18

Laghey,
Donegal

Tel: 074-973 4575 Fax: 074-973 4576
Email: coxtownmanor@yahoo.ie
Web: www.coxtownmanor.com

Stay with us at Coxtown Manor, only 10 mins from Donegal Town. Our elegant country house (300 yrs old) offers 9 spacious rooms, delicious Belgian cuisine & the relaxed ambience of an Irish manor situated in the rolling hills of south Donegal. Within close reach of breathtaking beaches, cliffs, coastal scenery & challenging golf courses (4km). Relax in our drawing room with a turf fire or enjoy a Belgian beer in our wood panelled bar. English, French, Dutch & German spoken. Dublin 3 hrs, Galway 2 hrs, Belfast 2.5 hrs. Closed also 05 Jan to 10 Feb. Please enquire about Facilities for Persons with Mobility Impairment.

Member of Manor House Hotels

*B&B from €75.00 to €95.00*

*Eduard Dewael*

9

Closed 01 November - 12 December



B&B Rates are per Person Sharing per Night incl. Breakfast.
or Room Rates are per Room per Night - **See also Page 8**

## Moorland Guesthouse

GUESTHOUSE ★★★ MAP 13 I 18

Laghey, R.232,
Donegal Town,
Co. Donegal

Tel: 074-973 4319 Fax: 074-973 4319

Email: moorland@eircom.net

Web: www.moorland-guesthouse.com

Have a break from the hustle and bustle. A guesthouse with family character, situated in a wild, high moor/hill landscape. We offer good cuisine. Available on the premises: treatment with reflexology, body massage, cosmetics salon and sauna. Lounge with open fire and TV. Special relaxing weeks. Arrangements made for golf and fishing. Excellent 18-hole golf links not far away. Ideal place for relaxation. Very quiet and remote. German spoken.

*Bookable on www.irelandhotels.com*

*Special Offer: www.irelandhotels.com/offers*

*B&B from €35.00 to €42.00*

*Rosemarie & Walter Schaffner*
*Proprietors*

8

Open All Year

## Castle Grove Country House Hotel

HOTEL ★★★★ MAP 13 J 19

Ballymaleel,
Letterkenny,
Co. Donegal

Tel: 074-915 1118 Fax: 074-915 1384

Email: reservations@castlegrove.com

Web: www.castlegrove.com

Castle Grove is a 17th century country house set on its own rolling estate overlooking Lough Swilly. Its bedrooms are spacious and with all modern facilities. Downstairs in both drawing room and library you find a perfect blend of old and new. The dining room offers excellent cuisine, much of its produce from the Walled Garden. To the discerning guest Castle Grove has to be visited to be appreciated. While here you can fish, golf, or simply enjoy the locality. This house may be exclusively booked for family or business functions. Please enquire about Facilities for Persons with Mobility Impairment.

*Bookable on www.irelandhotels.com*

*Special Offer: www.irelandhotels.com/offers*

*B&B from €75.00 to €85.00*
*Suites from €250.00 to €350.00*

*Raymond & Mary T. Sweeney*
*Owners*

15

*Activities:*

Closed 22 - 29 December

## Downings Bay Hotel

HOTEL ★★★ MAP 13 J 19

Downings,
Letterkenny,
Co. Donegal

Tel: 074-915 5586 Fax: 074-915 4716

Email: info@downingsbayhotel.com

Web: www.downingsbayhotel.com

Situated on Sheephaven Bay & the picturesque Atlantic Drive. Newly built 3*** hotel. Spacious bedrooms, many of them interconnecting, are luxuriously finished. The Sheephaven Suite is available for 20-350 people. JC's Bar & The Haven dining rooms serve locally sourced fresh food daily. Secrets Beauty Salon is available for those who wish to pamper themselves. The newly built Magherabeg Leisure Centre is complimentary to hotel guests with 20m pool, kids pool, jacuzzi, sauna & gym. Local activities include golf, fishing, horse riding & water activities. Within driving distance of Glenveagh National Park. Golf specials available.

*Bookable on www.irelandhotels.com*

*B&B from €40.00 to €75.00*

*Eileen Rock*
*Manager*

40

*Activities:*

Closed 25 December

## Letterkenny

### Gleneany House

GUESTHOUSE ★★★ MAP 13 J 19

Port Road,
Letterkenny,
Co. Donegal
Tel: 074-912 6088 Fax: 074-912 6090
Email: gleneanyhouse@eircom.net
Web: www.gleneany.com

Gleneany House, located in the town centre, opposite the bus station in the heart of Letterkenny, offers both corporate and leisure clientèle an excellent level of personal and friendly service. Renowned for its consistency in excellent cuisine, food is served all day. Our 19 en suite bedrooms have satellite TV and direct dial telephone. Our lounge bar is the ideal place for a quiet relaxing drink. An ideal base for touring beautiful Donegal, private car parking available. A warm welcome awaits all at the Gleneany House. So when next in town, call and experience for yourself our hospitality.

B&B from €55.00 to €75.00

Paul Kelly

19

Closed 22 - 28 December

### Radisson SAS Hotel

HOTEL ★★★★ MAP 13 J 19

The Loop Road,
Letterkenny,
Co. Donegal
Tel: 074-919 4444 Fax: 074-919 4455
Email: info.letterkenny@radissonsas.com
Web: www.radissonsas.com

Welcome to the superb Radisson SAS Hotel Letterkenny, located just five minutes walk from the town centre with 114 bedrooms designed in a contemporary Irish style, featuring all the facilities one would expect from a four star standard de luxe hotel; such as cable and pay TV, fast internet connections with broadband, minibar, direct dial phones with voicemail, trouser press and 24hr room service. The hotel also boasts state of the art conference and banqueting facilities and full leisure centre including 17m pool. Please enquire about Facilities for Persons with Mobility Impairment.

Member of Radisson SAS Hotels & Resorts

Bookable on www.irelandhotels.com
Special Offer: www.irelandhotels.com/offers

B&B from €65.00 to €79.00

Ray Hingston
General Manager

114

Activities:

Open All Year

### Ramada Encore - Letterkenny

HOTEL ★★★ MAP 13 J 19

Lower Main Street,
Letterkenny,
Co. Donegal
Tel: 074-912 3100 Fax: 074-910 9862
Email: info@encoreletterkenny.com
Web: www.encoreletterkenny.com

The Ramada Encore Letterkenny offers 81 spacious en suite guest rooms designed with the guest in mind, all featuring direct dial telephone, remote control multi-channel TV with in-house movie channels, executive desk, PC modem connection with free broadband, hairdryer and complimentary tea and coffee making facilities. So whether you travel on business or for pleasure, for short or long stays, our accommodation will provide you the best at an affordable price. Ramada Encore Letterkenny...........Simply better. Please enquire about Facilities for Persons with Mobility Impairment.

Member of Ramada Worldwide

Bookable on www.irelandhotels.com
Special Offer: www.irelandhotels.com/offers

B&B from €59.00 to €99.00

Emma O'Carroll
General Manager

81

Closed 24 - 26 December



B&B Rates are per Person Sharing per Night incl. Breakfast.
or Room Rates are per Room per Night - See also Page 8

## Silver Tassie Hotel

HOTEL ★★★ MAP 13 J 19

Ramelton Road,
Letterkenny,
Co. Donegal

Tel: 074-912 5619 Fax: 074-912 4473

Email: info@silvertassiehotel.ie

Web: www.silvertassiehotel.com

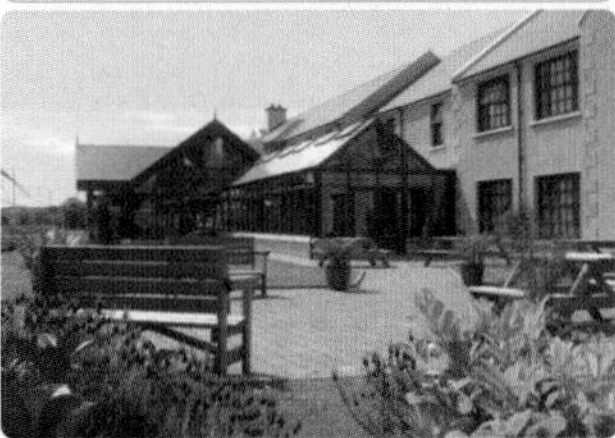

Nestled in the beautiful hills of Donegal overlooking Lough Swilly this charming family-run hotel combines old world charm with modern comfort & elegance. Luxurious en suite bedrooms (standard, superior or family) equipped with all modern facilities offer unrivalled comfort & luxury with an old country house feel. Renowned for excellent food & friendly service. Relax by the open fires or enjoy afternoon tea in the magnificent glass fronted foyer. Only 5 mins drive from the bustling town of Letterkenny. Ideal base for touring the stunning North West. Bookable online at www.theblaneygroup.com. Free WiFi.

Member of Select Hotels of Ireland

*Bookable on www.irelandhotels.com*
*Special Offer: www.irelandhotels.com/offers*

*B&B from €45.00 to €90.00*

*Rose & Ciaran Blaney*

36

*Activities:*

Closed 25 December

## Malin Hotel

HOTEL ★★ MAP 14 L 21

Malin Town,
Inishowen,
Co. Donegal

Tel: 074-937 0606 Fax: 074-937 0770

Email: info@malinhotel.ie

Web: www.malinhotel.ie

Situated at the tip of the Inishowen Peninsula, the Malin Hotel offers the very best in luxury boutique hotel accommodation. The beauty of the surrounding area is breathtaking, and the Malin Hotel is the perfect base to explore local attractions. The quality of the food preparation is evident in the award-winning Jack Yeats Restaurant, which is highly recommended in the Bridgestone and Georgina Campbell Guide. Please enquire about Facilities for Persons with Mobility Impairment.

*B&B from €65.00 to €90.00*

*John Keyes*
*Manager*

18

*Activities:*

Closed 25 December

## Milford Inn Hotel

HOTEL ★★★ MAP 13 J 20

Milford,
Co. Donegal

Tel: 074-915 3313 Fax: 074-915 3388

Email: info@milfordinnhotel.ie

Web: www.milfordinnhotel.com

Situated 10 miles from Letterkenny between the town of Milford and the Heritage Town of Ramelton, this luxurious family-run hotel is ideally located for the visitor to explore Donegal's rugged Atlantic Coast. Relax in comfort and style in a choice of standard or superior rooms all offering the highest standard. Renowned for its consistency in serving quality food with carvery lunches daily and food served all day. Close to championship golf courses, beaches, horse riding, clay pigeon shooting, Glenveigh National Park, hill walking. Check out www.theblaneygroup.com for special offers.

Member of Blaney Group

*Bookable on www.irelandhotels.com*
*Special Offer: www.irelandhotels.com/offers*

*B&B from €40.00 to €80.00*

*Mandy & Neil Blaney*

33

*Activities:*

Closed 25 - 27 December

B&B Rates are per Person Sharing per Night incl. Breakfast.
or Room Rates are per Room per Night - **See also Page 8**

## Moville / Portnoo / Rathmullan

### Carlton Redcastle Hotel & C Spa

HOTEL ★★★★ MAP 14 L 21

Redcastle,
Moville,
Co. Donegal

Tel: 074-938 5555 Fax: 074-938 5444

Email: info.redcastle@carlton.ie

Web: www.carlton.ie

Nestled along the banks of Lough Foyle, the Carlton Redcastle Hotel is perfect for a relaxing leisure break. Discover one of the most beautiful regions in the country, world-class golf courses, ancient monuments & Blue Flag beaches. 93 luxury rooms & suites all with spectacular views; fine dining Waters Edge Restaurant, Captains Bar, & spacious banqueting & conference Ocean Suite with panoramic views. The C Spa offers Thalasso spa & beauty treatments, complimentary use of the heated, multi-jet seawater Thalasso pool & gym. Room Reservations LoCall 1890 288 288.

Member of The Carlton Hotel Group

*Bookable on www.irelandhotels.com*

*Special Offer: www.irelandhotels.com/offers*

*B&B from €70.00 to €135.00*

*Suites from €240.00 to €570.00*

*John Varley*

*Group Operations Director*

93

Activities:

Open All Year

### Lake House Hotel

HOTEL ★★★ MAP 13 H 19

Narin,
Portnoo,
Co. Donegal

Tel: 074-954 5123 Fax: 074-954 5444

Email: lakehouse@iol.ie

Web: www.lakehousehotel.ie

A country house hotel overlooking Narin golf course, minutes away from the Blue Flag Beach at Narin. 14 en suite luxury bedrooms decorated with a feeling of elegance and spaciousness, with television, DD telephone, hairdryer and complimentary tea/coffee making facilities. Family rooms available. The hotel boasts dining experiences from fine dining in the award-winning restaurant to a grill/bar menu in the lounge. Conference and banqueting facilities also available. Please note the hotel is also closed 19 - 27 December. Please enquire about Facilities for Persons with Mobility Impairment.

*B&B from €60.00 to €65.00*

*Frank Barber*

*Managing Director*

14

Activities:

Closed 04 January - 08 February

### Fort Royal Hotel

HOTEL ★★★ MAP 14 K 20

Rathmullan,
Co. Donegal

Tel: 074-915 8100 Fax: 074-915 8103

Email: fortroyal@eircom.net

Web: www.fortroyalhotel.com

One of the most beautifully situated hotels in Ireland with 7 hectares of lovely grounds and gardens, beside Lough Swilly including a sandy beach, hard tennis court, par 3 golf course. Especially friendly welcome accounts for the large number of regular visitors from all parts of the world to this peaceful unspoilt part of Donegal. Irish Tourist Board and AA***. GDS Access Code: UI Toll Free 1-800-44-UTELL.

*Bookable on www.irelandhotels.com*

*Special Offer: www.irelandhotels.com/offers*

*B&B from €87.50 to €97.50*

*Tim & Tina Fletcher*

*Proprietor / Manager*

15

Activities:

Closed 01 November - 31 March



B&B Rates are per Person Sharing per Night incl. Breakfast.
or Room Rates are per Room per Night - **See also Page 8**

## Rathmullan House

HOTEL ★★★★ MAP 14 K 20

Lough Swilly,
Rathmullan,
Co. Donegal

Tel: 074-915 8188 Fax: 074-915 8200

Email: info@rathmullanhouse.com

Web: www.rathmullanhouse.com

A country house opening out to a long sandy beach at the bottom of the garden. Award-winning restaurant offering fresh fish and seafood along with seasonal fruit, salad crops and herbs from the walled garden. Supporters of the "Slow Food" movement and organic produce where possible. Bedrooms are decorated in different styles from garden view rooms to spacious family rooms. Leisure facilities, tennis courts and holistic therapy room on site.

***An IHF Quality Employer***

Member of Ireland's Blue Book

*Bookable on www.irelandhotels.com*

*Special Offer: www.irelandhotels.com/offers*

*B&B from €105.00 to €140.00*

Wheeler Family
Hosts

34

Closed 06 January - 13 February

## Waters Edge (The)

HOTEL MAP 14 K 20

Rathmullan,
Co. Donegal

Tel: 074-915 8182 Fax: 074-915 8314

Email: info@thewatersedge.ie

Web: www.theblaneygroup.com

Built to a 3*** specification. Set in an exclusive location, this boutique hotel boasts some of the most spectacular views that Donegal has to offer. All rooms offer breathtaking sea views equipped with all mod cons, TV, DVD, tea/coffee making facilities, hairdryer, robes, slippers. Food & wine is what we are famous for, come join us in our waterfront restaurant. Dine on the finest of fare as you enjoy panoramic views of Lough Swilly. The ideal location for golf, horse riding, surfing or hiking. Private weddings catered for. Member of Private Ireland. Please enquire about Facilities for Persons with Mobility Impairment.

Member of Blaney Group

*B&B from €45.00 to €90.00*

Mandy & Neil Blaney

10

*Activities:*

Closed 25 - 27 December

## Sandhouse Hotel

HOTEL ★★★★ MAP 13 I 17

Rossnowlagh,
Co. Donegal

Tel: 071-985 1777 Fax: 071-985 2100

Email: info@sandhouse.ie

Web: www.sandhouse.ie

A delightful seaside setting overlooking the Atlantic Ocean on Donegal Bay. This 4* luxury hotel, a transformed mid 19th century fishing lodge, is an oasis of comfort and relaxation on a 2 mile golden sandy beach. It combines elegant accommodation, open log fires, a marine spa and an award-winning restaurant. A splendid location to explore the spectacular Donegal landscapes. Nearby 3 championship golf links courses. Described as one of Ireland's west coast treasures. Dublin 3hrs, Shannon 4hrs. Please enquire about Facilities for Persons with Mobility Impairment.

***An IHF Quality Employer***

Member of Manor House Hotels

*Bookable on www.irelandhotels.com*

*Special Offer: www.irelandhotels.com/offers*

*B&B from €90.00 to €110.00*
*Suites from €200.00 to €350.00*

Paul Diver
Manager

55

*Activities:*

Closed 01 December - 01 February

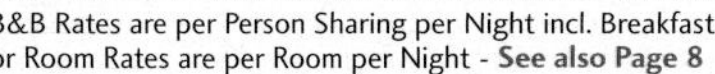

B&B Rates are per Person Sharing per Night incl. Breakfast.
or Room Rates are per Room per Night - **See also Page 8**

## Aran Islands

### Aran Islands Hotel

HOTEL ★★★ MAP 5 D 10

Cill Ronain,
Inis Mór, Aran Islands,
Co. Galway

Tel: 099-61104 Fax: 099-61225
Email: info@aranislandshotel.com
Web: www.aranislandshotel.com

Enjoy the serenity and beauty of The Aran Islands at Aran Islands Hotel. Inis Mór's only hotel, minutes away from the pier in Cill Rónáin. All bedrooms are spacious and beautifully appointed with a wide range of facilities. The luxurious balcony rooms with king-size beds boast breath taking views. Our stylish restaurant serves locally caught fish, showcasing the extraordinary quality of the area's seafood and organically grown vegetables. Aran Islands Hotel is the ideal base to explore the unique spirit and traditions of Aran. Please enquire about Facilities for Persons with Mobility Impairment.

*B&B from €55.00 to €139.00*

*PJ & Grace Flaherty*
*Fáilteoir*
20

Closed 20 December - 22 February

### Ard Einne Guesthouse

GUESTHOUSE ★★★ MAP 5 D 10

Inismor,
Aran Islands,
Co. Galway

Tel: 099-61126 Fax: 099-61388
Email: ardeinne@eircom.net
Web: www.ardeinne.com

Experience a unique quality of peace, serenity & unrivalled beauty at Ard Einne. The cosy atmosphere is perfect for a "getaway break". Spectacular sea views from all bedroom windows & overlooks own beach. Ard Einne provides high quality standard and comfortable accommodation. Renowned for excellent Irish cuisine. Perfect base for walkers, cyclists, artist and writers. Near cliffs, monastic monuments & historical sites. Beside airport, 2Km from pier. Please enquire about Facilities for Persons with Mobility Impairment.

Member of Premier Collection of Ireland

*B&B from €40.00 to €60.00*

*Clodagh Ni Ghoill*
*Manager*
14

Closed 06 December - 06 January

### Kilmurvey House

GUESTHOUSE ★★★ MAP 5 D 10

Kilronan,
Inismor, Aran Islands,
Co. Galway

Tel: 099-61218 Fax: 099-61397
Email: kilmurveyhouse@eircom.net
Web: www.kilmurveyhouse.com

Kilmurvey House is a 150 year old country house once the home of "The Ferocious O'Flahertys". We are situated at the foot of Dun Aonghus, just beside Dun Aonghus Visitor Centre. Just 3 minutes walk from a Blue Flag beach, we are an ideal location for cyclists, walkers and those who just wish to relax. Group rates available. Free access to Dun Aonghus National Monument available to our guests. Recommended by several travel guides including Bridge Stone and Georgina Campbell.

*B&B from €45.00 to €65.00*

*Treasa Joyce*
*Proprietor*
12

Activities:

Closed 30 October - 01 April



B&B Rates are per Person Sharing per Night incl. Breakfast.
or Room Rates are per Room per Night - See also Page 8

## Pier House Guesthouse

GUESTHOUSE ★★★ MAP 5 D 10

Lower Kilronan,
Aran Islands,
Co. Galway

Tel: 099-61417 Fax: 099-61122

Email: pierh@iol.ie

Web: www.pierhousearan.com

Pier House is perfectly located less than 100m from Kilronan Village, within walking distance of sandy beaches, pubs and historical remains. This modern house is finished to a very high standard and has many extra facilities, TV, tea/coffee facilities in bedrooms and a restaurant on the premises. The bedrooms are well appointed and have perfect sea and landscape views. If it is comfort and old fashioned warmth and hospitality you expect, then Pier House is the perfect location to enjoy it.

*B&B from €45.00 to €65.00*

*Maura Joyce*
*Proprietor*

12

**Closed 02 November - 16 March**

## Tigh Fitz

GUESTHOUSE ★★★ MAP 5 D 10

Killeany, Kilronan,
Inishmore, Aran Islands,
Co. Galway

Tel: 099-61213 Fax: 099-61386

Email: penny@tighfitz.com

Web: www.tighfitz.com

Tigh Fitz, a family-run guesthouse, bar and lounge is in Killeany, Inishmore. Offering luxurious accommodation in this unspoilt area of the Aran Isles. Tigh Fitz is unique in its situation, in its spaciousness and proximity to beaches and areas of archaeological and historical remains. In this area are the tall Cliffs of Aran and the magnificent pre-historic forts. Tigh Fitz is 1.6km from the island capital Kilronan and close to the Aer Arann airstrip.

*B&B from €40.00 to €60.00*

*Penny Fitzpatrick*
*Proprietor*

11

**Closed 01 - 28 December**

## Raheen Woods Hotel & Spa

HOTEL ★★★ MAP 6 G 10

Athenry,
Galway

Tel: 091-875888 Fax: 091-875444

Email: stay@raheenwoodshotel.ie

Web: www.raheenwoodshotel.ie

Raheen Woods Hotel & Tranquillity Leisure/Pool & Spa is "that special place", contemporary in style. Located in Athenry a designated walled Heritage Town. 50 bright well appointed spacious bedrooms & suites, all areas wheechair accessible by lift from basement carpark. Good food in McHales Bar or dine in The Clarin Bistro. The N6 is minutes away and Galway Airport just 15 minutes. We welcome guests with reduced mobility. Our friendly staff will be happy to assist you with your plans. Please enquire about Facilities for Persons with Mobility Impairment.

*Bookable on www.irelandhotels.com*
*Special Offer: www.irelandhotels.com/offers*

*B&B from €45.00 to €99.00*
*Suites from €180.00 to €225.00*

*Frank Corby*
*General Manager*

50

*Activities:*

**Closed 24 - 27 December**

# Ballinasloe / Ballynahinch / Barna

## Carlton Shearwater Hotel & C Spa

HOTEL MAP 6 I 11

Marina Point,
Ballinasloe,
Co. Galway

Tel: 0909-630400 Fax: 0909-630401

Email: info@carltonshearwaterhotel.com

Web: www.carltonshearwaterhotel.com

Built to a 4**** specification. Carlton Shearwater Hotel a new property adjoining the Marina in Ballinasloe, Co. Galway. It has 104 de luxe rooms including suites Marengo's Restaurant and Café with fine dining, a contemporary stylebar, a C Spa and leisure centre. A state of the art conference and banqueting centre with 9 meeting rooms and the Plaza Suite. This central location - the Gateway to the West is the perfect destination to tour Ireland. Please enquire about Facilities for Persons with Mobility Impairment.

Member of Carlton Hotel Group

*B&B from €75.00 to €140.00*
*Suites from €200.00 to €500.00*

*Dermot Birchall*
*General Manager*

104

*Activities:*

Closed 24 - 26 December

## Ballynahinch Castle Hotel

HOTEL ★★★★ MAP 5 D 11

Ballinafad,
Recess, Connemara,
Co. Galway

Tel: 095-31006 Fax: 095-31085

Email: bhinch@iol.ie

Web: www.ballynahinch-castle.com

Once home to the O'Flaherty Chieftains, pirate queen Grace O'Malley, Humanity Dick Martin & Maharajah Ranjitsinji, Ballynahinch is now a 4**** hotel. With casual country elegance, overlooking both river & mountains, offering an unpretentious service & an ideal centre from which to tour the West. Log fires & a friendly fisherman's pub complement a restaurant offering the best in fresh game, fish & produce. Voted in the Top 20 Hotels in the World by Fodor's, Ballynahinch is the jewel in Connemara's crown. RAC 2 Rosettes Dining Award and Food & Wine Magazine Hotel Restaurant of the Year.

***An IHF Quality Employer***

Member of Manor House Hotels

*Bookable on www.irelandhotels.com*
*Special Offer: www.irelandhotels.com/offers*

*B&B from €120.00 to €204.00*
*Suites from €385.00 to €460.00*

*Patrick O'Flaherty*
*General Manager*

40

*Activities:*

Closed Christmas Week & February

## Twelve (The)

HOTEL ★★★★ MAP 6 F 10

Barna Village,
Galway

Tel: 091-597000 Fax: 091-597003

Email: enquire@thetwelvehotel.ie

Web: www.thetwelvehotel.ie

A stone's throw from Galway City, on the fringe of Connemara, traditional and the new Ireland come together as one. The Twelve combines a modern and fun design with a uniquely refreshing and personal experience. Dine in West, a world class restaurant, pamper yourself with selected in-room treatments and enjoy a 'trad' session in the bar. As the sun sets on Galway Bay, step into your stylish suite and think..."I have arrived". Please enquire about Facilities for Persons with Mobility Impairment.

*Bookable on www.irelandhotels.com*
*Special Offer: www.irelandhotels.com/offers*

*B&B from €100.00 to €200.00*
*Suites from €200.00 to €600.00*

*Fergus O'Halloran*
*General Manager*

48

*Activities:*

Open All Year



B&B Rates are per Person Sharing per Night incl. Breakfast.
or Room Rates are per Room per Night - **See also Page 8**

## Lisdonagh House

GUESTHOUSE ★★★★ MAP 10 F 12

Caherlistrane,
Co. Galway

Tel: 093-31163 Fax: 093-31528
Email: cooke@lisdonagh.com
Web: www.lisdonagh.com

Lisdonagh House is located 20 mins from Galway City in a glorious tranquil setting. The house is early Georgian with commanding views over Lough Hackett. Over 100 acres of woodland on the estate where guests can meander on country walks. Fishing & horse riding can be arranged. Your hosts, John & Finola Cooke, have elegantly restored the house retaining the classical proportions. The oval entrance hall has murals depicting four virtues dating from 1790. The cooking is superb, innovatively using the best of local ingredients. A warm welcome is extended to guests at Lisdonagh House.

Member of Ireland's Blue Book

B&B from €90.00 to €140.00

*John & Finola Cooke*

9

Closed 01 Novemeber - 26 April

## Carna Bay Hotel

HOTEL ★★★ MAP 9 D 11

Carna,
Connemara,
Co. Galway

Tel: 095-32255 Fax: 095-32530
Email: carnabay@iol.ie
Web: www.carnabay.com

Carna Bay Hotel is located in the most magical scenery in Ireland. Connemara: unique landscape, flora and fauna, unspoilt beaches, mountain ranges. Beautiful Western Way walking routes. Our kitchen offers the finest fresh Irish produce. Locally: St. McDara's Island, Connemara National Park, Kylemore Abbey, Aran and Inisbofin Ferry 40 minutes drive. Please enquire about Facilities for Persons with Mobility Impairment.

Member of Irish Country Hotels

*Bookable on www.irelandhotels.com*
*Special Offer: www.irelandhotels.com/offers*

Room Rate from €45.00 to €130.00

*Michael & Sheamus Cloherty*
*Proprietors*

24

Closed 23 - 27 December

B&B Rates are per Person Sharing per Night incl. Breakfast.
or Room Rates are per Room per Night - **See also Page 8**

## Carraroe / Cashel / Cashel Bay

### Hotel Carraroe

HOTEL ★★ MAP 5 D 10

Carraroe,
Co. Galway

Tel: 091-595116 Fax: 091-595187

Email: hotelcarraroe@eircom.net

Web: www.hotelcarraroe.com

The Hotel Carraroe is a 25 bedroomed en suite family-run hotel situated in the heart of the Connemara Gaeltacht. The village of Carraroe itself is renowned for its traditional values and music. Daily boat trips to the Aran Islands are from nearby Rossaveal Harbour. Our local friendly staff will provide information on where to fish, play golf, horse ride or tour beautiful Connemara. Enjoy our new Irish Themed Bar.

*B&B from €100.00 to €100.00*

*Seosamh O Loideain*

25

Open All Year

### Cashel House Hotel

HOTEL ★★★★ MAP 5 D 11

Cashel,
Connemara,
Co. Galway

Tel: 095-31001 Fax: 095-31077

Email: res@cashel-house-hotel.com

Web: www.cashel-house-hotel.com

Elegance in a wilderness on the shores of the Atlantic. It is set amidst the most beautiful gardens in Ireland. Enjoy long walks, cycling and fishing. Later, relax in front of a peat fire in this elegant residence appointed with antique furniture and period paintings. Most guest rooms look onto the gardens and some onto the sea. Dine on bounty from the sea and garden - enjoy vintage wine. Please enquire about Facilities for Persons with Mobility Impairment.

Member of Ireland's Blue Book

*Bookable on www.irelandhotels.com*
*Special Offer: www.irelandhotels.com/offers*

*B&B from €95.00 to €174.00*
*Suites from €304.00 to €394.00*

*McEvilly Family*
*Proprietors*

32

*Activities:*

Closed 05 January - 05 February

### Zetland Country House Hotel

HOTEL ★★★★ MAP 5 D 11

Cashel Bay,
Connemara,
Co. Galway

Tel: 095-31111 Fax: 095-31117

Email: info@zetland.com

Web: www.zetland.com

Overlooking Cashel Bay this 19th century manor house is renowned for its peace and commanding views. The bedrooms and superb seafood restaurant overlook the gardens and Cashel Bay. Facilities include tennis court and billiard room and there are many activities, hill walking and golf in the surrounding area. Good Hotel Guide recommended, AA Courtesy of Care Award and Gilbeys Gold Medal Winner. 4**** Manor House Hotel.

Member of Manor House Hotels

*Bookable on www.irelandhotels.com*
*Special Offer: www.irelandhotels.com/offers*

*B&B from €114.00 to €125.00*
*Suites from €310.00 to €340.00*

*Ruaidhri Prendergast*
*Proprietor*

20

Open All Year

B&B Rates are per Person Sharing per Night incl. Breakfast.
or Room Rates are per Room per Night - **See also Page 8**

## Claregalway Hotel

HOTEL ★★★ MAP 6 11 G

Claregalway Village,
Co. Galway

Tel: 091-738300 Fax: 091-738311
Email: stay@claregalwayhotel.ie
Web: www.claregalwayhotel.ie

The Claregalway Hotel is a unique destination. The hotel is definitely different, with an innovative contemporary design; the hotel offers an indulgent experience in an interesting and energetic atmosphere. The Claregalway Hotel really looks forward to making their guests feel special. The hotel offers 48 cosy bedrooms, fantastic fun bars, luxurious leisure centre, contemporary restaurant and fabulous staff. Superbly located on the edge of Galway City on the junction of N17 and N18 routes. Please enquire about Facilities for Persons with Mobility Impairment.

Member of Irish Country Hotels

*Bookable on www.irelandhotels.com*
*Special Offer: www.irelandhotels.com/offers*

*B&B from €59.00 to €180.00*

*Paul & Nora Gill*
*Directors*

48

Closed 23 - 27 December

## Abbeyglen Castle Hotel

HOTEL ★★★★ MAP 9 C 12

Sky Road,
Clifden,
Co. Galway

Tel: 095-22832 Fax: 095-21797
Email: info@abbeyglen.ie
Web: www.abbeyglen.ie

Abbeyglen Castle Hotel was built in 1832 in the heart of Connemara by John D'Arcy of Clifden Castle. Romantically set in beautiful gardens with waterfalls & streams, a panoramic view of Clifden and the bay with a backdrop of the Twelve Bens. Abbeyglen provides a long list of indoor/outdoor facilities, international cuisine, unique qualities of peace, serenity & ambience. Complimentary afternoon tea a speciality. AA 2 rosettes for good food and service. Superior rooms available at a supplement see photo belown Reservations from USA 011 353 95 22832, from Europe 00 353 95 22832.

Member of Manor House Hotels

*Bookable on www.irelandhotels.com*
*Special Offer: www.irelandhotels.com/offers*

*B&B from €96.00 to €125.00*

*Brian / Paul Hughes*
*Manager / Proprietor*

45

Closed 06 January - 01 February

## Alcock and Brown Hotel

HOTEL ★★★ MAP 9 C 12

Clifden,
Connemara,
Co. Galway

Tel: 095-21206 Fax: 095-21842
Email: alcockandbrown@eircom.net
Web: www.alcockandbrown-hotel.com

Alcock and Brown Hotel is family owned and operated. Situated in the centre of Clifden Village, featuring Brownes Restaurant with AA Rosette for excellent food and service. Ideal base for touring Connemara. Pursuits to be enjoyed are pony trekking, golfing on Connemara championship links course. Sea angling, guided heritage walks and mountain climbing. Numerous sandy beaches nearby.

*Bookable on www.irelandhotels.com*
*Special Offer: www.irelandhotels.com/offers*

*B&B from €55.00 to €79.00*

*Deirdre Keogh*
*Manager*

19

*Activities:*

Closed 22 - 27 December

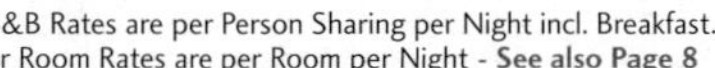

B&B Rates are per Person Sharing per Night incl. Breakfast.
or Room Rates are per Room per Night - **See also Page 8**

## Clifden

### Ardagh Hotel & Restaurant

HOTEL ★★★ MAP 9 C 12

Ballyconneely Road,
Clifden,
Co. Galway

Tel: 095-21384 Fax: 095-21314

Email: ardaghhotel@eircom.net

Web: www.ardaghhotel.com

A quiet family-run 3*** hotel, 2km from Clifden on Ardbear Bay, AA recommended. Bedrooms individually decorated with television, telephone and tea/coffee facilities. Award-winning restaurant, 2 AA rosettes. Specialises in lobsters, salmon, oysters and Connemara lamb with homegrown vegetables and a wide selection of wines. Local amenities: golf, fishing and beaches. Reservations by post, phone, fax, email and website. Superior suites with bay view available. WiFi available.

Member of Irish Country Hotels

*Bookable on www.irelandhotels.com*
*Special Offer: www.irelandhotels.com/offers*

*B&B from €75.00 to €110.00*
*Suites from €190.00 to €280.00*

*Stephane & Monique Bauvet*
*Proprietors / Manager / Chef*

17

Closed 29 October - 20 March

### Ben View House

GUESTHOUSE ★★ MAP 9 C 12

Bridge Street,
Clifden, Connemara,
Co. Galway

Tel: 095-21256 Fax: 095-21226

Email: benviewhouse@ireland.com

Web: www.benviewhouse.com

Dating from 1848, Ben View has been owned and managed by our family since 1926. See our history on website. Recommended by Frommer and Le Petit Fute Guides. RAC ♦♦♦ and AA ♦♦♦ approved. Enjoy all the modern comforts of this elegant guesthouse, surrounded by antiques and old world atmosphere. Ben view is withing walking distance of all amenities, harbour and seaside. Free on-street parking. Lock-up garage available for motorcycles and bicycles. Your hostess Eileen wishes everyone a safe and pleasant journey.

*B&B from €30.00 to €45.00*

*Eileen Morris*
*Proprietor*

9

*Activities:*

Closed 24 - 26 December

### Buttermilk Lodge

GUESTHOUSE ★★★ MAP 9 C 12

Westport Road,
Clifden,
Co. Galway

Tel: 095-21951 Fax: 095-21953

Email: buttermilklodge@eircom.net

Web: www.buttermilklodge.com

A warm friendly home from home, 400m from Clifden centre. Spacious bedrooms each with multi-channel TV, DD phone, personal toiletries, hairdryer, ironing facilities and private bath/shower room. Your warm welcome includes tea/coffee and home baking by the turf fire where there is always a cuppa available. Our breakfast options, tasteful décor, free WiFi, interesting cow collection, stunning mountain views, friendly Connemara Ponies and many extra touches ensure return visits. ITB 3***, AA 4 Red Diamonds. Children over 5 welcome.

*Bookable on www.irelandhotels.com*
*Special Offer: www.irelandhotels.com/offers*

*B&B from €35.00 to €50.00*

*Cathriona & Patrick O'Toole*
*Proprietors / Hosts*

11

Closed 02 January - 01 March



B&B Rates are per Person Sharing per Night incl. Breakfast.
or Room Rates are per Room per Night - **See also Page 8**

## Byrne Mal Dua House

GUESTHOUSE ★★★★ MAP 9 C 12

Galway Road,
Clifden, Connemara,
Co. Galway

Tel: 095-21171 Fax: 095-21739

Email: info@maldua.com

Web: www.maldua.com

Award-winning 4**** Byrne Mal Dua House offers luxury in a relaxed friendly atmosphere. Spacious rooms have all facilities for your comfort. Relax in our landscaped gardens. Perfect base to enjoy the beauty of Connemara. RAC Little Gem Award 2006, Les Routiers Award, RAC ♦♦♦♦♦ AA ♦♦♦♦♦, Karen Brown's Guide, Michele Erdvig. Internet access. Use of nearby leisure centre. Please enquire about Facilities for Persons with Mobility Impairment.

***An IHF Quality Employer***

Member of Premier Collection

*Bookable on www.irelandhotels.com*
*Special Offer: www.irelandhotels.com/offers*

*B&B from €45.00 to €85.00*

*The Byrne Family*

14

**Closed 22 - 26 December**

## Clifden Station House Hotel

HOTEL ★★★ MAP 9 C 12

Clifden,
Connemara,
Co. Galway

Tel: 095-21699 Fax: 095-21667

Email: info@clifdenstationhouse.com

Web: www.clifdenstationhouse.com

Anyone who loves shopping, wining and dining will feel instantly at home at the Clifden Station House. Here on your break, to get away from it all, you can do all those things you love to do but in a relaxed contemporary environment. In the courtyard surrounding the hotel is a wonderful selection of speciality shops, hair salon, body and skincare clinic, full leisure facilities, self catering apartments and museum. Please enquire about Facilities for Persons with Mobility Impairment.

***An IHF Quality Employer***

Member of Sweeney Hotels

*Bookable on www.irelandhotels.com*
*Special Offer: www.irelandhotels.com/offers*

*B&B from €60.00 to €139.00*
*Suites from €180.00 to €358.00*

*Wilson Bird*
*General Manager*

78

**Closed 24 - 25 December**

B&B Rates are per Person Sharing per Night incl. Breakfast.
or Room Rates are per Room per Night - **See also Page 8**

## Clifden

### Connemara Country Lodge

GUESTHOUSE ★★★ MAP 9 C 12

Westport Road,
Clifden,
Co. Galway

Tel: 095-22122 Fax: 095-21122

Email: connemara@unison.ie

Web: www.bedandbreakfastgalway.com

Delightful Georgian home with spacious bedrooms, 2 minutes walk from Clifden, on extensive grounds with large private car park. All bedrooms are en suite with TV, tea/coffee making facilities, telephones, safes and hairdryers. Why not join Mary for an evening of traditional Irish music and song in her large lounge - a truly unique experience - as Mary is a well known performer. Her home and ballad singing have been recorded for broadcasting on American TV. French and German spoken by Mary. Home-baking a speciality. Please enquire about Facilities for Persons with Mobility Impairment.

B&B from €25.00 to €50.00

*Mary Corbett*
*Proprietress*

10

Activities: ✓

T C ✽ U ♪ P ⊞ I

Closed 10 - 28 December

### Dun Ri Guesthouse

GUESTHOUSE ★★★ MAP 9 C 12

Hulk Street,
Clifden,
Co. Galway

Tel: 095-21625 Fax: 095-21635

Email: dunri@anu.ie

Web: www.connemara.net/dun-ri

Centrally located on a quiet street in the heart of picturesque Clifden. Dun Ri offers private parking with secure motorcycle parking. Our spacious rooms have private bathrooms (many with bath tubs), DD phone and TVs. The guest lounge is an ideal place to relax over a coffee/tea after a day of exploring Connemara. We are just 1 minute's walk from the town centre, its excellent restaurants, traditional pubs and a short pleasant drive to beaches, golf horse riding and many more attractions.

B&B from €30.00 to €45.00

*Michael & Aileen King*
*Proprietors*

13

T C U P

Closed 21 - 28 December

### Foyles Hotel

HOTEL ★★★ MAP 9 C 12

Clifden,
Connemara,
Co. Galway

Tel: 095-21801 Fax: 095-21458

Email: info@foyleshotel.com

Web: www.foyleshotel.com

One of Connemara's longest established hotels, trading since 1836 and owned by the Foyles for nearly a century. The hotel is situated in the centre of Clifden and is an ideal central point for exploring Connemara. The hotel's old world elegance and atmosphere have been gracefully retained through recent renovations, each room being individually decorated and furnished with charm and warmth. The Foyles and their staff offer you a warm welcome and will be happy to assist you in enjoying the area.

***An IHF Quality Employer***

Bookable on www.irelandhotels.com

B&B from €45.00 to €65.00

*Eddie Foyle*
*Proprietor*

25

T C ✽ U ♪ S

Closed 07 January - 02 March



B&B Rates are per Person Sharing per Night incl. Breakfast. or Room Rates are per Room per Night - See also Page 8

## Joyces Waterloo House

GUESTHOUSE ★★★ MAP 9 C 12

Galway Road,
Clifden, Connemara,
Co. Galway

Tel: 095-21688 Fax: 095-22044

Email: pkp@joyces-waterloo.com

Web: www.joyces-waterloo.com

Indulge yourself with our King or Queen sized beds, outdoor Hot Tub, power showers, spacious guest lounge with open fire, small library, private parking and bike hire, excellent dining, evening meals and our superb location. With the best of Connemara hospitality and yet the privacy and peacefulness of the old family-run hotels, we offer quality, value and comfort that has been our trademark for the past decade. We look forward to welcoming you to our home.

Member of Premier Collection

*Bookable on www.irelandhotels.com*

*Special Offer: www.irelandhotels.com/offers*

*B&B from €38.00 to €65.00*

*Patricia & P.K. Joyce*
*Hosts*

8

Closed 23 - 27 December

## Quay House (The)

GUESTHOUSE ★★★★ MAP 9 C 12

Beach Road,
Clifden,
Co. Galway

Tel: 095-21369 Fax: 095-21608

Email: thequay@iol.ie

Web: www.thequayhouse.com

The Quay House is Clifden's oldest building, c.1820. It now comprises 14 individually furnished rooms, some with balconies and working fireplaces, and has a wonderful collection of Georgian furniture and family portraits. It's just 7 minutes walk into town. Fishing, golf, pony-trekking, etc. are all nearby. Owned by Julia and Paddy Foyle whose family have been innkeepers in Connemara since 1917. Staying at the Quay House is a completely different experience. Outright winner of "Cesar" Award for Ireland 2003. Awarded Georgina Campbell's Guesthouse of the Year 2006.

Member of Hidden Ireland

*B&B from €70.00 to €85.00*

*Paddy & Julia Foyle*
*Owners*

14

Closed 05 November - 12 March

## Rock Glen Country House Hotel

HOTEL ★★★★ MAP 9 C 12

Clifden,
Connemara,
Co. Galway

Tel: 095-21035 Fax: 095-21737

Email: enquiry@rockglenhotel.com

Web: www.rockglenhotel.com

A delightful 4**** country house hotel. Spectacular views, tasteful décor & open fires. The restaurant is well known for its excellent cuisine. The quiet bedrooms offer all facilities for your comfort. A short drive to Connemara's 27 hole golf links, horse riding, trekking, fishing & hill walking. Clifden has many art galleries & shops where you can buy local handcrafts, tweeds, linens & gifts. Visit Kylemore Abbey, the Victorian Gardens & National Park. National AA Courtesy and Care Award winners 2000.

***An IHF Quality Employer***

Member of Manor House Hotels

*Bookable on www.irelandhotels.com*

*Special Offer: www.irelandhotels.com/offers*

*B&B from €75.00 to €105.00*

*Peadar Nevin*
*Host*

27

*Activities:* ✓

Closed 05 January - 05 March

# Clonbur (An Fháirche) / Craughwell / Furbo

## Fairhill House Hotel

HOTEL ★★★ MAP 9 E 12

Clonbur (An Fháirche),
Co. Galway

Tel: 094-954 6176 Fax: 094-954 6176
Email: fairhillhouse@eircom.net
Web: www.fairhillhouse.com

Established in 1830, Fairhill House Hotel is a beautifully refurbished hotel located in one of the most scenic parts of the west of Ireland. In the village of Clonbur, nestled between the magical lakes of Lough Mask and Lough Corrib, Fairhill House Hotel will give you an opportunity to explore the west from a luxurious, comfortable, friendly hotel. Fairhill House Hotel has been in the Lynch family for three generations. Very famous for its seafood menu, old world bar, open fires, traditional music entertainment, free fishing, hill walking and friendly atmosphere. You could meet anybody in Clonbur!

B&B from €55.00 to €85.00

Edward Lynch
Proprietor

20

Activities:

Closed 24 - 26 December

## St. Clerans Manor House

GUESTHOUSE ★★★★ MAP 6 G 10

Craughwell,
Co. Galway

Tel: 091-846555 Fax: 091-846600
Email: stclerans@iol.ie
Web: www.stclerans.com

St. Clerans is a truly magical 18th century manor house. The ambience here is wonderfully warm and relaxing and a very warm welcome awaits all who visit and experience the hospitality and home comfort that is "St. Clerans". Set in 45 acres of pure peace and tranquillity and described by its former owner, film director John Huston, as "one of the most beautiful houses in all of Ireland".

Member of Ireland's Blue Book 2007

Bookable on www.irelandhotels.com
Special Offer: www.irelandhotels.com/offers

B&B from €112.50 to €162.50
Suites from €375.00 to €450.00

Ken Bergin
General Manager

12

Activities:

Open All Year

## Connemara Coast Hotel

HOTEL ★★★★ MAP 6 F 10

Furbo,
Galway

Tel: 091-592108 Fax: 091-592065
Email: reservations@connemaracoast.ie
Web: www.sinnotthotels.com

With dedicated staff on hand to provide a warm welcome and great standards of service, this is the ideal place to stay when visiting the Galway/Connemara area. Spectacularly set on the shores of Galway Bay yet just ten minutes from the City Centre, facilities include restful lounges, restaurants, bars, extensive grounds, free car parking and an award-winning leisue centre.
Bookable on www.sinnotthotels.com

***An IHF Quality Employer***

Member of Sinnott Hotels Ireland

Bookable on www.irelandhotels.com

B&B from €70.00 to €170.00
Suites from €350.00 to €500.00

Karl Reinhardt
General Manager

112

Activities:

Open All Year



B&B Rates are per Person Sharing per Night incl. Breakfast.
or Room Rates are per Room per Night - See also Page 8

## Abbey House

GUESTHOUSE ★★ MAP 6 F 10

113 Upper Newcastle,
Galway

Tel: 091-524394 Fax: 091-528217
Email: abbeyhouse@eircom.net
Web: www.abbeyhousegalway.com

Family-run guesthouse located on the N59 leading to Connemara. Convenient to city centre. Rooms are en suite with cable TV and direct dial phones. Private car parking. Close to golf, fishing, tennis, swimming pool, horse riding, seaside and city centre. Excellent location for touring Connemara, Aran Islands and The Burren. A warm welcome awaits you from the Darby family.

*Bookable on www.irelandhotels.com*
*Special Offer: www.irelandhotels.com/offers*

*B&B from €30.00 to €55.00*

*John Darby*

10

Closed 01 - 28 December

## Adare Guest House

GUESTHOUSE ★★★ MAP 6 F 10

9 Father Griffin Place,
Galway

Tel: 091-582638 Fax: 091-586421
Email: adare@iol.ie
Web: www.adarebedandbreakfast.com

Adare Guesthouse is a family managed guesthouse, within 5 minutes of city centre (train/bus). Refurbished with old time pine furniture & floors, you can enjoy your multi-choice breakfast in our dining room overlooking our beautiful patio area. All bedrooms are en suite with direct dial phones, cable TV & hairdryers. Tea/coffee & ironing facilities are available. 2 new suites built to a high standard with baths, direct dial fax phone, trouser press/iron, tea/coffee, cable TV/radio. Please enquire about Facilities for Persons with Mobility Impairment.

Member of Galway Chamber of Commerce

*B&B from €45.00 to €60.00*

*Padraic & Grainne Conroy*
*Proprietors*

11

*Activities:*

Closed 21 - 27 December

## Anno Santo Hotel

HOTEL ★★ MAP 6 F 10

Threadneedle Road,
Salthill,
Galway

Tel: 091-523011 Fax: 091-522110
Email: info@annosantosalthill.com
Web: www.annosantosalthill.com

Small family-run hotel located in quiet residential area. Galway's major tennis/badminton and squash club lies opposite the hotel. The golf club is also close by (1km), while Galway City and beaches are within easy reach. We are also on a main bus route. All rooms are en suite, with TV, complimentary tea/coffee and direct dial telephone. Your hosts, the Vaughan family, provide high class service in comfortable bedrooms at budget prices.

*Bookable on www.irelandhotels.com*
*Special Offer: www.irelandhotels.com/offers*

*Room Rate from €50.00 to €160.00*

*Gerard & Joanna Vaughan*
*Proprietors*

14

*Activities:*

Closed 20 December - 20 January

## Galway City

### Ardawn House

GUESTHOUSE ★★★★ MAP 6 F 10

31 College Road,
Galway

Tel: 091-568833 Fax: 091-563454
Email: ardawn@iol.ie
Web: www.galway.net/pages/ardawn-house/

Ardawn House is a luxurious haven for the discerning visitor to Galway. Located within five minutes walking of city centre, train & bus. Antiques, fresh flowers, silver and china help to make our multi choice home-cooked breakfast famous. All bedrooms have en suite, direct dial phones, cable TV & hairdryers. Tea/coffee & ironing facilities are also available. Highly recommended in Guide du Routard, AA and many other guide books.

*Bookable on www.irelandhotels.com*
*Special Offer: www.irelandhotels.com/offers*

*B&B from €45.00 to €85.00*

*Mike & Breda Guilfoyle*
*Proprietors*

8

Closed 21 - 27 December

### Ardilaun Hotel, Conference Centre & Leisure Club

HOTEL ★★★★ MAP 6 F 10

Taylor's Hill,
Galway

Tel: 091-521433 Fax: 091-521546
Email: info@theardilaunhotel.ie
Web: www.theardilaunhotel.ie

The Ardilaun is a family owned hotel, newly refurbished to a 4**** standard, situated in its own five acres of landscaped grounds, minutes from city centre. 125 luxurious bedrooms to include garden rooms and unique suites. Comfortable spacious lounges, award-winning "Camilaun Restaurant" and superb leisure club with its 18m swimming pool, sauna, jacuzzi and gymnasium. Beauty salon on site. Conferencing facilities for up to 650 delegates. Complimentary car parking. Awarded Optimus "Best Practice". Please enquire about Facilities for Persons with Mobility Impairment.

***An IHF Quality Employer***
Member of Select Hotels of Ireland

*Bookable on www.irelandhotels.com*
*Special Offer: www.irelandhotels.com/offers*

*B&B from €75.00 to €300.00*
*Suites from €175.00 to €550.00*

*John Ryan*
*Managing Director*

125

*Activities:*

Closed 23 - 26 December

### Ashford Manor

GUESTHOUSE ★★★ MAP 6 F 10

No 7 College Road,
Galway City

Tel: 091-563941 Fax: 091-563941
Email: info@ashfordaccommodation.com
Web: www.ashfordaccommodation.com

City centre location. New wine bar and bistro serving food all day. Near train and bus station - 5 mins drive to Galway Airport, 1 hour and 15 mins to Shannon Airport, 1 hour to Knock Airport. All en suite rooms with TV, phone, tea and coffee making facilities. Car parking. Credit cards accepted. Featured in holiday programme "Bon Voyage". Tours organised for Connemara, Aran Islands, Burren and the Cliffs of Moher. Golfing trips arranged. Groups welcome. Fishing available. Full and half board rates packages available.

*B&B from €30.00 to €75.00*

*Corinne Mannion*
*Proprietor*

5

Closed 23 - 28 December



B&B Rates are per Person Sharing per Night incl. Breakfast.
or Room Rates are per Room per Night - See also Page 8

## Atlantic View Guesthouse

GUESTHOUSE ★★★ MAP 6 F 10

4 Ocean Wave,
Dr. Colohan Road,
Galway

Tel: 091-582109 Fax: 091-528566
Email: atlanticbandb@hotmail.com
Web: www.atlanticbandb.com

Atlantic View guesthouse is a luxurious haven overlooking Galway Bay with a large sun balcony. Some of our rooms have stunning views of the sea, with balconies. We are an ideal base to tour Connemara, Cliffs of Moher and The Burren. We are only a short walk to the city centre and are ideally located for shopping, theatres, art galleries, museums, pubs, restaurants and clubs. Free secure car parking. We are situated on the famous salthill promenade across the road from the beach. Mobile: 086 - 852 4579.

*B&B from €30.00 to €120.00*

*Jennifer Treacy*
*Proprietor*

5

Closed 23 - 28 December

## Best Western Flannery's Hotel

HOTEL ★★★ MAP 6 F 10

Dublin Road,
Galway City East,
Galway

Tel: 091-755111 Fax: 091-753078
Email: reservations@flanneryshotel.net
Web: www.flanneryshotel.net

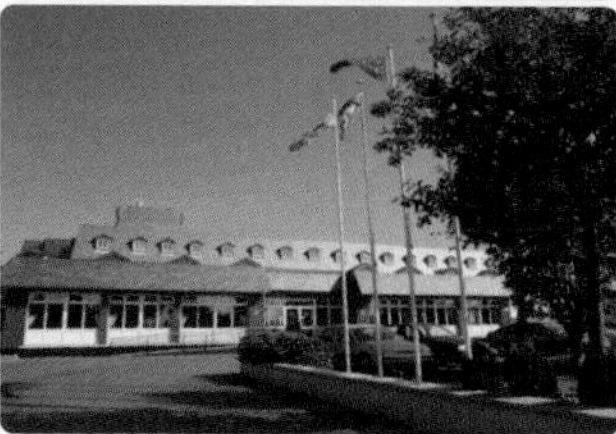

Flannerys Hotel is long established in Galway as a hotel offering comfort and style within relaxed surroundings. A welcome choice for the business traveller or leisure guest. We take pride in ensuring that a special emphasis is placed on guest comfort enhanced by a genuinely caring and efficient service. Recently refurbished, the hotel features 134 modern, comfortable bedrooms, restaurant and bar. Member of Best Western Hotels. Free extensive on-site car parking. Please enquire about Facilities for Persons with Mobility Impairment.

***An IHF Quality Employer***

Member of Best Western Hotels

*Bookable on www.irelandhotels.com*
*Special Offer: www.irelandhotels.com/offers*

*B&B from €40.00 to €150.00*

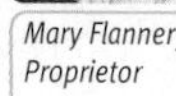

*Mary Flannery*
*Proprietor*

134

Activities:

Closed 21 - 28 December

B&B Rates are per Person Sharing per Night incl. Breakfast.
or Room Rates are per Room per Night - **See also Page 8**

## Galway City

### Corrib Haven Guest House

GUESTHOUSE ★★★ MAP 6 F 10

107 Upper Newcastle,
Galway

Tel: 091-524171 Fax: 091-582414
Email: corribhaven@eircom.net
Web: www.corribhaven.net

Corrib Haven's motto is quality hospitality for discerning people. Located in Galway City on the N59 leading to Connemara. All rooms en suite, power showers, posture sprung beds, cable TV, DD phones. Tea/coffee facility, breakfast menu, private parking. Convenient to city centre, restaurants, nightly entertainment. Ideal for touring Connemara, Aran Islands. Smooth professionalism with personal warmth to our visitors. Non-smoking. 20 mins drive from Galway Airport. Close to NUI Galway & hospital. Bus No.4 to city centre. Close to Westwood House Hotel & Glenlo Abbey Hotel. Wireless broadband throughout.

Member of Premier Guesthouses

*Bookable on www.irelandhotels.com*

*B&B from €35.00 to €70.00*

*Tom & Angela Hillary*
*Proprietors*

9

Closed 10 December - 10 January

### Courtyard By Marriott

HOTEL ★★★★ MAP 6 F 10

Headford Point,
Headford Road,
Galway City

Tel: 091-513200 Fax: 091-513201
Email: galway.reservations@courtyardgalway.com
Web: www.galwaycourtyard.com

Located at Headford Point within walking distance of Eyre Square & Shop St, the first Courtyard by Marriott in the West of Ireland is the ideal base to explore Galway City & its surrounds. Our 90 rooms are spacious & comfortable featuring high speed internet access, air-con, pay per view movies, built in mini fridge & safe. The Olive Tree Bistro features popular Irish cuisine with a contemporary & Mediterranean influence. Additional facilities: the Point Bar, Absolute Spa, a fitness suite, business centre & conference suites with secure underground car parking.

***An IHF Quality Employer***

Member of Marriott Hotel Group

*Bookable on www.irelandhotels.com*
*Special Offer: www.irelandhotels.com/offers*

*B&B from €95.00 to €400.00*

*Cian Landers*
*General Manager*

90

Open All Year

### Days Hotel Galway

HOTEL ★★★ MAP 6 F 10

Dublin Road,
Galway City East,
Galway

Tel: 1890-329329 Fax: 091-753187
Email: info@dayshotelgalway.com
Web: www.dayshotelgalway.com

Days Hotel has 363 spectacular guest rooms and suites. Situated just 2km from Galway City, the hotel has retained its renowned friendly service and welcoming atmosphere. Superb leisure centre with 20m pool, toddlers' pool, sauna, steam room, jacuzzi and gym. Kids Club operates at weekends and during school holidays. Reuben's Restaurant and Bar Solo open daily. Meeting rooms available for up to 120 delegates. Free parking. Hotel Direct Line: 091 381200.

***An IHF Quality Employer***

Member of Days Hotels Ireland

*Bookable on www.irelandhotels.com*
*Special Offer: www.irelandhotels.com/offers*

*B&B from €49.00 to €155.00*
*Suites from €128.00 to €380.00*

*Siobhán Burke*
*General Manager*

363

Activities:

Closed 22 - 26 December



B&B Rates are per Person Sharing per Night incl. Breakfast. or Room Rates are per Room per Night - **See also Page 8**

## Eyre Square Hotel

HOTEL ★★★ MAP 6 F 10

Forster Street,
Off Eyre Square,
Galway

Tel: 091-569633 Fax: 091-569641
Email: eyresquarehotel@eircom.net
Web: www.byrne-hotels-ireland.com

The Eyre Square Hotel is situated right in the heart of Galway adjacent to both bus and rail stations. The Eyre Square Hotel caters for both the tourist and business person offering a very high standard of accommodation. Rooms en suite with direct dial phone, satellite TV and tea/coffee making facilities. Enjoy excellent cuisine in our Red's Bistro or visit the lively Red Square Pub. A warm and friendly welcome awaits you at the Eyre Square Hotel.

Member of Byrne Hotel Group

*B&B from €55.00 to €150.00*

*Roger Carey*
*General Manager*

52

Closed 23 - 27 December

## G (The)

HOTEL ★★★★★ MAP 6 F 10

Wellpark,
Galway

Tel: 091-865200 Fax: 091-865203
Email: reservetheg@monogramhotels.ie
Web: www.monogramhotels.ie

Voted Best Hotel design in Travel & Leisure's 2007 Design Award, together with appearing in The Condé Nast hot list as one of the top hotels in the world to visit. The g hotel is situated overlooking Lough Atalia and Galway Bay. The exquisite creation of world renowned milliner Philip Treacy, the hotel has been created for both business and leisure traveller, where thoughtful service meets sophisticated style. award-winning ESPA at the g is set amidst a Zen rooftop garden. The restaurant Riva at the g offers breathtaking views over the bay as does "This must be the place" bar.

Member of Small Luxury Hotels of the World

*Bookable on www.irelandhotels.com*
*Special Offer: www.irelandhotels.com/offers*

*Room Rate from €200.00 to €310.00*
*Suites from €580.00 to €2,500.00*

*Irina Agostinelli*
*General Manager*

101

*Activities:*

Closed 23 - 27 December

## Galway Bay Hotel, Conference & Leisure Centre

HOTEL ★★★★ MAP 6 F 10

The Promenade,
Salthill,
Galway

Tel: 091-520520 Fax: 091-520530
Email: info@galwaybayhotel.com
Web: www.galwaybayhotel.com

Awarded best 4**** in Ireland, the hotel has all the advantages of a city centre location while being situated overlooking the famous Galway Bay and Ladies Beach which was awarded a Blue Flag this year. Facilities include Gymnasium, Pool, Steam Room, Sauna, Beauty Salon, Kids Club. The Lobster Pot Restaurant offers modern style cuisine with seafood specialities. Complimentary broadband access in all guest bedrooms and conference suites. Please enquire about Facilities for Persons with Mobility Impairment.

***An IHF Quality Employer***

*Bookable on www.irelandhotels.com*
*Special Offer: www.irelandhotels.com/offers*

*B&B from €95.00 to €165.00*
*Suites from €120.00 to €320.00*

*Dan Murphy*
*General Manager*

153

*Activities:*

Open All Year

B&B Rates are per Person Sharing per Night incl. Breakfast.
or Room Rates are per Room per Night - **See also Page 8**

## Galway City

### Glenlo Abbey Hotel

HOTEL ★★★★★ MAP 6 F 10

Bushypark,
Galway

Tel: 091-526666 Fax: 091-527800
Email: info@glenloabbey.ie
Web: www.glenlo.com

Glenlo Abbey Hotel - an 18th century country estate, is located on a 138 acre lakeside golf course just 4km from Galway City. A Fáilte Ireland rated 5***** hotel, Glenlo Abbey is one of the most entertaining properties in the West of Ireland. All 46 rooms are de luxe standard. There is a choice for dining including the Pullman Restaurant aboard the Orient Express. Golf, fishing, lake boating all on site with a spa being developed in the near future. Galway City 5 mins drive. Choice of suites available - enquire with reservations. Please enquire about Facilities for Persons with Mobility Impairment.

***An IHF Quality Employer***

Member of Ireland's Blue Book

*Bookable on www.irelandhotels.com*
*Special Offer: www.irelandhotels.com/offers*

*Room Rate from €250.00 to €400.00*
*Suites from €550.00 to €980.00*

*John & Peggy Bourke*
*Proprietors*

46

*Activities:*

Closed 24 - 27 December

### Harbour Hotel

HOTEL MAP 6 F 10

New Dock Road,
Galway

Tel: 091-569466 Fax: 091-569455
Email: stay@harbour.ie
Web: www.harbour.ie

Major refurbishment to 4 star specification taking place in Jan & Feb '08. Located in the city centre adjacent to the waterfront area. This contemporary style hotel offers 96 spacious rooms, a chic bar & restaurant along with "state of the art" meeting rooms to cater for up to 100 people. The Harbour also boasts Haven Health & Beauty, an exclusive leisure suite, which includes a gym, steam room, jacuzzi and treatment rooms. The Harbour prides itself on its outstanding levels of service and quality in refreshingly unique surroundings. Parking on-site. Glac do Scíth I gcroílár chathair na Gallimhe. Fáilte.

***An IHF Quality Employer***

*Bookable on www.irelandhotels.com*
*Special Offer: www.irelandhotels.com/offers*

*B&B from €99.00 to €350.00*

*Christopher Carson*
*General Manager*

96

*Activities:*

Closed 23 - 27 December

### Holiday Hotel (The)

HOTEL ★ MAP 6 F 10

181 Upper Salthill,
Galway

Tel: 091-523934 Fax: 091-522518
Email: theholidayhotel@hotmail.com

Holiday Hotel, Salthill Galway. Holiday Hotel is located in the heart of Salthill beside restaurants, Bars and shops. Salthill Golf Club and leisureland is 2 minutes away. We are a family-run hotel and can accommodate families and groups up to 25 people. Our hotel Bar "The Office" boast a warm and friendly atmosphere, ideally located in the prime of Salthill. Massage available in our therapy room for guests.

*B&B from €45.00 to €75.00*

*Zoe Ward*
*General Manager*

10

Closed 24 - 26 December



B&B Rates are per Person Sharing per Night incl. Breakfast. or Room Rates are per Room per Night - **See also Page 8**

## Hotel Meyrick

HOTEL ★★★★ MAP 6 F 10

Eyre Square,
Galway

Tel: 091-564041 Fax: 091-566704
Email: reshm@monogramhotels.ie
Web: www.hotelmeyrick.com

Originally built in 1845, this Victorian hotel's ground floor was extensively renovated in 2007. Best address in town, overlooking Eyre Square, the Hotel Meyrick, formerly the Great Southern Hotel, is a stylish combination of old world features and modern luxuries. Its 97 guest rooms offer a range of executive rooms, junior and senior suites. The award-winning Oyster Bar & Grill Restaurant has an extensive menu. The Square Spa & Health Club has a wide range of fitness equipment, outdoor Canadian hot tub and beauty treatments. Please enquire about Facilities for Persons with Mobility Impairment.

***An IHF Quality Employer***

Bookable on www.irelandhotels.com

Room Rate from €165.00 to €229.00
Suites from €325.00 to €650.00

*Cian O'Broin*
*General Manager*
97

Activities:

Closed 24 - 26 December

## House Hotel (The)

HOTEL ★★★★ MAP 6 F 10

Spanish Parade,
Galway

Tel: 091-538900 Fax: 091-568262
Email: info@thehousehotel.ie
Web: www.thehousehotel.ie

Welcome to the House, a luxurious boutique hotel located in the heart of Galway City. The House Hotel represents the ideal "Home away from home" with its cosy atmosphere, chic style, excellent facilities and personalised service. Features of the guestrooms include flat screen TVs, with internet access, laptop safe, tuck box and crisp white linen. The Parlour Bar and Grill specialises in modern international cuisine. Please enquire about Facilities for Persons with Mobility Impairment.

***An IHF Quality Employer***

Bookable on www.irelandhotels.com
Special Offer: www.irelandhotels.com/offers

Room Rate from €99.00 to €395.00
Suites from €220.00 to €650.00

*Elaine Hourigan*
*General Manager*
40

Open All Year

## Huntsman Inn

HOTEL ★★★ MAP 6 F 10

164 College Road,
Galway

Tel: 091-562849 Fax: 091-561985
Email: info@huntsmaninn.com
Web: www.huntsmaninn.com

Situated one kilometre from Eyre Square this stylish, comfortable boutique hotel offers excellent standards of accommodation and décor. All bedrooms are en suite with direct dial phone, internet access, flat screen TV, DVD player, safe and tea/coffee making facilities. Enjoy excellent food in our modern dining room or relax in our spacious lounge bars. Free car parking on site. Please enquire about Facilities for Persons with Mobility Impairment.

Bookable on www.irelandhotels.com

B&B from €50.00 to €80.00

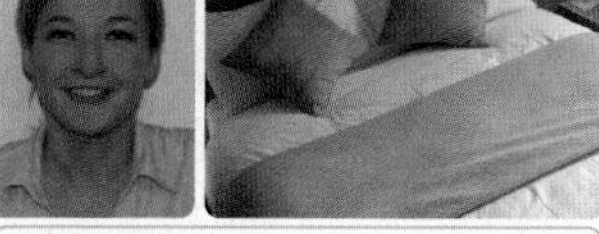

*Cathrina McManamon*
*Manager*
12

Closed 23 - 28 December

B&B Rates are per Person Sharing per Night incl. Breakfast.
or Room Rates are per Room per Night - **See also Page 8**

## Galway City

### Inishmore Guesthouse

GUESTHOUSE ★★★ MAP 6 F 10

109 Fr. Griffin Road,
Lower Salthill,
Galway

Tel: 091-582639 Fax: 091-589311
Email: inishmorehouse@eircom.net
Web: www.galwaybaygolfholidays.com

A charming family residence with secure carpark within 5 minutes walk of city and beach. All rooms contain direct dial phone, multi-channel TV and hairdryers. Tea/coffee and ironing facilities available. German spoken. An ideal base for touring the Aran Islands, Burren and Connemara. All day tours can be organised. Golf holidays, sea angling trips and coarse or game fishing arranged. Recommended by many leading travel guides. Specialise in Golf Package Holidays.

Bookable on www.irelandhotels.com
Special Offer: www.irelandhotels.com/offers

B&B from €35.00 to €65.00

*Marie & Peter*
*Proprietors*

8

*Activities:*

T C P S

Open All Year

### Jurys Inn Galway

HOTEL ★★★ MAP 6 F 10

Quay Street,
Galway

Tel: 091-566444 Fax: 091-568415
Email: jurysinngalway@jurysinns.com
Web: www.jurysinns.com

Jurys Inn is perfectly located in the heart of the city on Galways Quay Street with a host of bars and restaurants on its doorsteps. Overlooking the historic Spanish Arch and Galway Bay, Jurys Inn Galway is within short walking distance of the citys commercial and shopping districts. Please enquire about Facilities for Persons with Mobility Impairment.

***An IHF Quality Employer***

Member of Jurys Inns Group Ltd

Bookable on www.irelandhotels.com

Room Rate from €69.00 to €280.00

*Martha O'Grady*
*General Manager*

130

T C P I

Closed 24 - 26 December

### Marian Lodge Guesthouse

GUESTHOUSE ★★★ MAP 6 F 10

Knocknacarra Road,
Salthill Upper,
Galway

Tel: 091-521678 Fax: 091-528103
Email: celine@iol.ie
Web: www.marian-lodge.com

AA ♦♦♦♦ "A home from home". Family-run. Adjacent to promenade/beach in Salthill Upr. Private parking. Daily tours arranged Connemara/Burren/Aran Islands. City bus route. Home baking. Bedrooms en suite, cable TV, DD phone, clock radio, orthopaedic beds, hairdryers, tea/coffee facilities. Iron, trouser press available. Large family rooms. Children welcome. Convenient to nightly entertainment, Leisureland, Aquarium, tennis, windsurfing, fishing, horse-riding, Galway Bay, Ardilaun & Clybaun Hotels. Beside golf course, driving range, restaurant, pubs & shops. Internet access. Also contactable on 087 6184128.

Member of Premier Guesthouses of Ireland

B&B from €38.00 to €55.00

*Celine Molloy*

6

T C P S

Closed 19 - 29 December



B&B Rates are per Person Sharing per Night incl. Breakfast.
or Room Rates are per Room per Night - **See also Page 8**

## Menlo Park Hotel and Conference Centre

HOTEL ★★★★ MAP 6 F 10

Terryland,
Headford Road,
Galway

Tel: 091-761122 Fax: 091-761222

Email: reservations@menloparkhotel.com

Web: www.menloparkhotel.com

Located only half a mile from city centre. Traditional hospitality and great food. Completely refurbished 2007. Ten rooms with extra luxury décor and king beds. Bar food & carvery all day. Restaurant à la carte & table d'hote. Free parking, Conference Centre, WiFi throughout. Easy access. Weekend entertainment.

***An IHF Quality Employer***

Bookable on www.irelandhotels.com

B&B from €50.00 to €180.00

*David Keane*
*General Manager*

64

Closed 24 - 25 December

## Ocean Crest House

GUESTHOUSE ★★★ MAP 6 F 10

No 6 Ocean Wave,
Seapoint Promenade, Salthill,
Galway

Tel: 091-589028 Fax: 091-529399

Email: oceanbb@iol.ie

Web: www.oceanbb.com

We chose this site and built this guesthouse to provide what our guests love, a taste of subtropical elegance, overlooking Galway Bay and beaches with panoramic views of The Burren Mountains. We are walking distance from the bustling mediaeval city of Galway and across the road we have the Promenade. Our bedrooms are beautifully appointed with multi channel TV, en suite facilities, phone, trouser press, hairdryers, hospitality tray and armchairs. Please enquire about Facilities for Persons with Mobility Impairment.

B&B from €35.00 to €55.00

*Sharon McEvaddy*
*Manager*

9

Closed 25 December

## O'Connors Warwick Hotel

HOTEL ★★★ MAP 6 F 10

Salthill,
Galway

Tel: 091-522740 Fax: 091-521815

Email: info@thewarwick.com

Web: www.thewarwick.com

O'Connors Warwick Hotel is a modern family-run hotel in the heart of Salthill, across the road from the famous Salthill Prom. Our beautifully appointed rooms feature tea/coffee making facilities, safes, TV and free WiFi. A popular entertainment venue with live music and nightclub and Beo! Bar serving an excellent bar menu. The award-winning Butler Brasserie is open all day, serving a full à la carte menu.

B&B from €55.00 to €100.00

*Sandra Butler &*
*Dermot O'Connor*
*Proprietors*

32

Closed 22 - 30 December

## Galway City

### Oranmore Lodge Hotel, Conference & Leisure Centre

HOTEL ★★★★ MAP 6 G 10

Galway City

Tel: 091-794400 Fax: 091-790227
Email: info@oranmorelodge.ie
Web: www.oranmorelodgehotel.ie

This family owned manor house hotel is located Galway City East, 10 minutes city centre, adjacent to picturesque Oranmore which overlooks Galway Bay, 4km Galway Airport/Racecourse. Our rooms and suites are furnished to the highest standard. Ultra modern conference facilities and relaxing leisure centre. Your host and friendly staff look forward to welcoming you to sample our superb food and excellent service in the best traditions of Irish hospitality. Please enquire about Facilities for Persons with Mobility Impairment.

***An IHF Quality Employer***

*Bookable on www.irelandhotels.com*
*Special Offer: www.irelandhotels.com/offers*

*B&B from €45.00 to €150.00*
*Suites from €180.00 to €400.00*

*Brian J. O'Higgins*
*Managing Director*

68

*Activities:*

Closed 22 - 27 December

### Park House Hotel & Park Restaurant

HOTEL ★★★★ MAP 6 F 10

Forster Street,
Eyre Square,
Galway

Tel: 091-564924 Fax: 091-569219
Email: parkhousehotel@eircom.net
Web: www.parkhousehotel.ie

Superb and convenient location in the heart of Galway City centre, Park House Hotel is an oasis of luxury and hospitality. Air-conditioning and broadband access are standard in all bedrooms. Secure private car park on hotel grounds. Galway Chamber of Commerce Business of the Year Award 2005 for "Customer Care/Service". AA & RAC Rosettes for Fine Foods. Failte Ireland, AA, RAC 4**** hotel. Irish owned and managed.

*B&B from €49.50 to €250.00*
*Suites from €240.00 to €600.00*

*Eamon Doyle & Kitty Carr*
*Proprietors*

84

Closed 24 - 26 December

### Quality Hotel and Leisure Centre Galway

HOTEL ★★★ MAP 6 F 10

Oranmore,
Galway

Tel: 091-792244 Fax: 091-792246
Email: res.galway@qualityhotels.ie
Web: www.qualityhotelgalway.com

Excellently located on the N6, just 10 minutes drive from Galway city. 113 Spacious Bedrooms, Restaurant and Bar, Food served all day, Entertainment Programme. Conference Centre, Free Wireless Broadband. Superb Leisure Club with 20m Swimming Pool, Hi Tech Gym, Spa Pool, Steam Room, Sauna and Beauty Salon. Free Car Parking, Family Friendly Hotel, Kids Club. NEW Outdoor Playground. Beside the Hotel: Omniplex Cinema and City Limits Entertainment Centre including Bowling, Laser Quest etc. Easy access to Connemara, the Burren, Aran Islands and Salthill. Golf 4 Km.

***An IHF Quality Employer***

Member of Choice Hotels Ireland

*Bookable on www.irelandhotels.com*
*Special Offer: www.irelandhotels.com/offers*

*B&B from €49.00 to €124.00*

*Dermot Comerford*
*General Manager*

113

Closed 24 - 26 December



B&B Rates are per Person Sharing per Night incl. Breakfast. or Room Rates are per Room per Night - See also Page 8

## Racing Lodge (The)

HOTEL ★★★ MAP 6 F 10

Deoch Uisce,
Merlin Park,
Galway

Tel: 091-746666 Fax: 091-746667

Email: info@theracinglodge.com

Web: www.theracinglodge.com

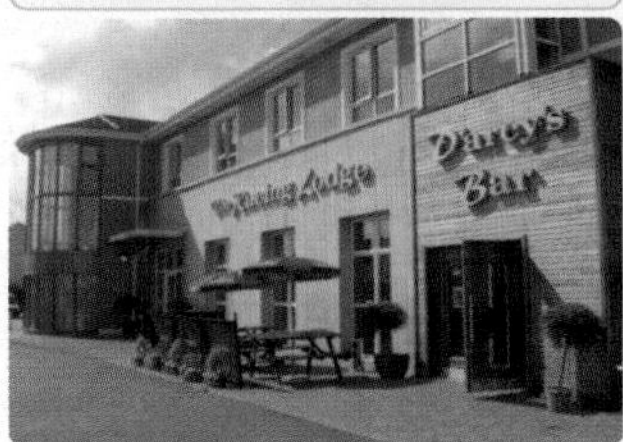


Welcome to The Racing Lodge. The lodge is situated just off the old Galway - Dublin Road and is just 5 minutes from Galway City. We are opposite the Galway Race Track and Galway Clinic. The Racing Lodge comprises 19 tastefully furnished en suite hotel guest rooms, D'Arcy's Bar, our Galway Races themed bar and Killanin Room, ideal for conferences, functions and private parties. With Galway 5 minutes away, you can pop in and sample the many delights that are on offer day and night. Please enquire about Facilities for Persons with Mobility Impairment.

*Bookable on www.irelandhotels.com*
*Special Offer: www.irelandhotels.com/offers*

*B&B from €39.50 to €150.00*

*Conor Mullin*
*General Manager*

19

*Activities:*

Closed 24 - 26 December

## Radisson SAS Hotel & Spa Galway

HOTEL ★★★★ MAP 6 F 10

Lough Atalia Road,
Galway

Tel: 091-538300 Fax: 091-538380

Email: sales.galway@radissonsas.com

Web: www.radissonhotelgalway.com

Located overlooking Lough Atalia, the Radisson SAS Hotel & Spa Galway is a few steps away from Eyre Square and the main bus and railway stations. Restaurant Marinas specialises in seafood and international cuisine. The Atrium Bar & Lounge and new Veranda Lounge serves a selection of light meals all day. Ireland's most exclusive Spa 'Spirit One Spa' offers many unique heat, steam & relaxation facilities. LEVEL 5, the panoramic club floor, guarantees privacy with secure members-only access in addition to individual terraces, club lounge, business centre & more spacious & luxurious rooms.

***An IHF Quality Employer***

Member of Radisson SAS Hotels & Resorts

*Bookable on www.irelandhotels.com*
*Special Offer: www.irelandhotels.com/offers*

*Room Rate from €160.00 to €550.00*
*Suites from €299.00 to €2,000.00*

*Tom Flanagan*
*General Manager*

261

*Activities:*

Open All Year

## Salthill Hotel

HOTEL ★★★ MAP 6 F 10

The Promenade,
Salthill,
Galway

Tel: 091-522711 Fax: 091-521855

Email: salthillhotel@eircom.net

Web: www.byrne-hotels-ireland.com

A Byrne Hotel, 50m from Salthill's sandy beach. All rooms en suite, direct dial phone, tea making facilities, hairdryer. Excellent cuisine and service. Live entertainment nightly with a choice of live bands or Trad on the Prom, which is a contemporary Irish show featuring an electrifying mix of music, song and dance. 100m from Leisureland and indoor swimming pool. Overlooking Galway Bay with a large car park. Less than 2 miles from the mediaeval City of Galway. Our new Spa & Leisure facility is opening Summer 2008.

Member of Byrne Hotel Group

*B&B from €75.00 to €105.00*
*Suites from €200.00 to €350.00*

*Pauline Griffin*
*General Manager*

68

*Activities:*

Closed 23 - 26 December

B&B Rates are per Person Sharing per Night incl. Breakfast.
or Room Rates are per Room per Night - **See also Page 8**

## Galway City

### Skeffington Arms Hotel

HOTEL ★★★ MAP 6 F 10

Eyre Square,
Galway

Tel: 091-563173 Fax: 091-561679
Email: reception@skeffington.ie
Web: www.skeffington.ie

Ideally located in an enviable position in Galway city, overlooking the new Eyre Square and within walking distance of rail and bus terminals. With 23 bedrooms, our guests are guaranteed a personal service from start to finish. All bedrooms are en suite, have multi channel tv, tea/coffee making facilities, direct dial phone and iron and ironing board. Serving fine food 7 days a week including breakfast, carvery lunch, sandwiches / juices and an à la carte menu in the evening, there is something to cater for everybody's taste. Please enquire about Facilities for Persons with Mobility Impairment.

*Bookable on www.irelandhotels.com*
*Special Offer: www.irelandhotels.com/offers*

*B&B from €50.00 to €150.00*

*Kerry Seward*
*Reservations Manager*

23

Closed 25 - 26 December

### Victoria Hotel

HOTEL ★★★ MAP 6 F 10

Victoria Place,
Eyre Square,
Galway

Tel: 091-567433 Fax: 091-565880
Email: victoriahotel@eircom.net
Web: www.byrne-hotels-ireland.com

The Victoria Hotel is centrally located just 100 yards off Eyre Square, within walking distance of all shops, theatres, pubs and cinemas. Each of the 57 spacious en suite rooms is beautifully appointed with direct dial phone, TV, tea/coffee making facilities and hairdryer. The hotel restaurant serving à la carte dinner, along with a lively bar serving lunches, will all add up to make your stay at the Victoria as enjoyable as possible. The Victoria is your enclave in the city, dedicated to pleasing you. Please enquire about Facilities for Persons with Mobility Impairment.

***An IHF Quality Employer***

Member of Byrne Hotel Group

*Bookable on www.irelandhotels.com*
*Special Offer: www.irelandhotels.com/offers*

*B&B from €45.00 to €150.00*

*Fabianne Rapinett*
*Group Sales & Marketing Manager*

57

*Activities:*

Closed 24 - 26 December

### Wards Hotel

HOTEL ★ MAP 6 F 10

Lower Salthill,
Galway

Tel: 091-581508 Fax: 091-520353
Email: wardshotel@eircom.net
Web: www.wardshotel.com

Wards comfortable family-run hotel is located 5 minutes from Galway's City centre and a short stroll from Salthill. All our rooms are en suite with hairdryer and multi channel TV. Secure car park. Renowned for its friendly service and convenient location - this provides an excellent base for business or pleasure.

*B&B from €45.00 to €65.00*

*Anthony Finnerty*
*Host*

10

Closed 23 - 28 December



B&B Rates are per Person Sharing per Night incl. Breakfast.
or Room Rates are per Room per Night - **See also Page 8**

## Waterfront Hotel

HOTEL ★★★ MAP 6 F 10

Salthill,
Galway

Tel: 091-588100 Fax: 091-588107
Email: info@waterfront.ie
Web: www.waterfront.ie

Our superbly located hotel sits on the shores of Galway Bay in the delightful suburb of Salthill, just 5 minutes from Galway's vibrant city centre. Each of our spacious 64 en suite rooms offers a dazzling, panoramic ocean view, and is amply furnished with a large lounge or kitchenette. Family rooms available and free, secure car parking. Reservations: Call Save 1850 588 488. www.waterfront.ie.

*B&B from €55.00 to €125.00*
*Suites from €140.00 to €280.00*

*Cathy Melia*
*General Manager*

64

Closed 21 - 28 December

## Western Hotel (The)

HOTEL ★★★ MAP 6 F 10

33 Prospect Hill,
Galway City Centre,
Galway

Tel: 091-562834 Fax: 091-565458
Email: info@thewestern.ie
Web: www.thewestern.ie

Located just off Eyre Square, The Western Hotel offers you the highest standard of accommodation at very affordable prices. Three impressive Georgian era buildings are incorporated to give an old style feel with modern facilities. Our large bar popular with Galwegians hosts traditional Irish music and dance throughout the week. Our delicious meals are prepared from fresh and local produce by our award-winning chef. Please enquire about Facilities for Persons with Mobility Impairment.

*Bookable on www.irelandhotels.com*
*Special Offer: www.irelandhotels.com/offers*

*B&B from €40.00 to €150.00*

*Joanna Majorek*
*Manager*

38

Closed 25 - 26 December

## Westwood (The)

HOTEL ★★★★ MAP 6 F 10

Dangan,
Upper Newcastle,
Galway City

Tel: 091-521442 Fax: 091-521400
Email: resmanager@westwoodhousehotel.com
Web: www.westwoodhousehotel.com

The Westwood stands amidst a rural landscape of greenery and combines a mellow taste of the countryside with the city's cutting edge. The hotel has recently completed a major refurbishment of all 58 guest bedrooms, hotel foyer, Meridian Restaurant, and banqueting suites. The hotel is air-conditioned throughout and offers complimentary internet access in all areas, and free private parking. Winner of CIE National Award of Excellence 2003/4. Locall 1850 366 000. Please enquire about Facilities for Persons with Mobility Impairment.

***An IHF Quality Employer***

*Bookable on www.irelandhotels.com*
*Special Offer: www.irelandhotels.com/offers*

*B&B from €99.00 to €199.00*
*Suites from €139.00 to €339.00*

*David Kelly*
*General Manager*

58

*Activities:*

Closed 24 - 26 December

## Galway City / Gort

### White House

GUESTHOUSE ★★★ MAP 6 F 10

2 Ocean Wave,
Seapoint Promenade, Salthill,
Galway

Tel: 091-529399 Fax: 091-529399
Email: whitehouseadsi@eircom.net
Web: www.oceanbb.com

New and beautiful purpose built guesthouse in Galway's finest location, overlooking Galway Bay and the Burren Mountains. Minutes walk to Galway's mediaeval city and Salthill's new hotel, the Galway Bay. Large bedrooms with armchairs and tables, iron and board, multi-channel TV, hospitality tray and hairdryer. Please enquire about Facilities for Persons with Mobility Impairment.

*B&B from €35.00 to €55.00*

*Sharon McEvaddy*
*Manager*

9

Closed 19-31 December

### Lady Gregory Hotel, Conference & Leisure Club

HOTEL ★★★ MAP 6 G 9

Ennis Road,
Gort,
Co. Galway

Tel: 091-632333 Fax: 091-632332
Email: sales@ladygregoryhotel.ie
Web: www.ladygregoryhotel.ie

Situated in the West of Ireland, near Coole Park, in the town of Gort, with its many local and historical attractions. A warm friendly welcome awaits you as you enter the architectural splendor of the Lady Gregory Hotel. 87 beautifully appointed rooms, Copper Beech Restaurant, lively Jack B. Yeats Bistro Bar and magnificent Gregory Suite for banqueting and conferencing, with broadband WiFi. Leisure Club incorporates an 18m swimming pool, children's pool, Technogym gymnasium, herb sauna, crystal steam, Jacuzzi, and a unique salt grotto with health showers - thus offering a hydro and thermal relaxing experience.

*B&B from €70.00 to €130.00*

*Leonard Murphy*
*General Manager*

87

*Activities:*

Closed 24 - 27 December

### Sullivan's Royal Hotel

HOTEL ★★ MAP 6 G 9

The Square,
Gort,
Co. Galway

Tel: 091-631257 Fax: 091-631916
Email: sullivansroyalhotel@eircom.net

Sullivan's Hotel is family-run hotel with 12 newly refurbished bedrooms, between Galway City (25 mins) and Shannon Airport (30 mins). Dining Pub of the Year winner 2000 - 2006 for service, quality and value. Additional phone number: 091-631401.

*B&B from €30.00 to €60.00*

*Johnny & Annie Sullivan*
*Proprietors*

12

Open All Year



B&B Rates are per Person Sharing per Night incl. Breakfast.
or Room Rates are per Room per Night - See also Page 8

## Anglers Rest Hotel

HOTEL ★★ MAP 10 F 12

Headford,
Co. Galway

Tel: 093-35528 Fax: 093-35749
Email: anglersresthotel@eircom.net

The Anglers Rest Hotel has been owned and managed by the Heneghan family since 1905. Just 3 miles from the eastern shore of Lough Corrib and 16 miles from Galway City. It is an ideal centre for the tourist or angler. With 16 bedrooms, dining room, 2 bars, open lounge, residents lounge and a function room with dining facilities. Meeting and conference facilities for over 100 people are also available on request. Please enquire about Facilities for Persons with Mobility Impairment.

B&B from €50.00 to €65.00

*Frank Heneghan*
*Manager*

16

*Activities:*

Closed 24 - 26 December

## Doonmore Hotel

HOTEL ★★ MAP 9 C 12

Inishbofin Island,
Co. Galway

Tel: 095-45804 Fax: 095-45804
Email: info@doonmorehotel.com
Web: www.doonmorehotel.com

Uniquely situated on a beautiful and historic island, commanding magnificent views of the surrounding sea and islands. Inishbofin, a haven for artists, fishermen, bird watchers, nature lovers or those who just wish to escape from the hectic pace of life. Fine sandy beaches. Sea trips and boat angling can be arranged. Facilities for divers. Excellent shore fishing. Doonmore Hotel is owned and managed by the Murray family, unpretentious but friendly and comfortable. Please enquire about Facilities for Persons with Mobility Impairment.

B&B from €48.00 to €65.00

*Aileen Murray*
*Manager*

19

*Activities:*

Closed 05 October - 01 April

## Inishbofin House Hotel

HOTEL ★★★ MAP 9 C 12

Inishbofin,
Connemara,
Co. Galway

Tel: 095-45809 Fax: 095-45803
Email: info@inishbofinhouse.com
Web: www.inishbofinhouse.com

Inishbofin lies 6 miles off the Galway coast and is one of Ireland's most thriving and beautiful islands. A 30 minute ferry journey from the north Connemara village of Cleggan. Inishbofin is a physical gem and a favourite haven among botanists, geologists and environmentalists due to its huge diversity of natural life. Inishbofin House is a new de luxe hotel with a marine spa which commands exquisite views of the beautiful harbour. Built on the site of the old Day's Hotel, this family owned hotel offers a warm welcome, friendly and efficient service and excellent food, particularly seafood!

B&B from €65.00 to €125.00

*Gerard Teahan*
*Manager*

34

*Activities:*

Closed 10 December - 01 March

## Kinvara / Kylemore / Leenane

### Merriman Inn & Restaurant

HOTEL ★★★ MAP 6 G 10

Main Street,
Kinvara,
Co. Galway

Tel: 091-638222 Fax: 091-637686

Email: merrimanhotel@eircom.net

Web: www.merrimanhotel.com

Old style country warmth permeates this charming, rustic 32 bedroom inn, situated in the picturesque village, Kinvara. On our doorstep are The Burren, Galway Bay and the Hills of Connemara, while across the harbour nestles Dunguaire Castle providing medieval banquets. Under the unique thatched roof of the hotel, named after the poet, Brian Merriman, sample the savoury delights of the "Quilty Room" Restaurant, or the quaintly named contemporary bar, "M'Asal Beag Dubh". Welcome. Please enquire about Facilities for Persons with Mobility Impairment.

Bookable on www.irelandhotels.com

Special Offer: www.irelandhotels.com/offers

B&B from €55.00 to €75.00

Terence Egan
Manager

32

Closed 07 January - 09 March

### Kylemore Pass Hotel

HOTEL ★★ MAP 9 D 12

Kylemore,
Connemara,
Co. Galway

Tel: 095-41141 Fax: 095-41377

Email: passinn@indigo.ie

Web: www.kylemore-pass-hotel-connemara.com

Beautifully situated, in the foot hills of the "Twelve Bens", overlooking some of Connemara's most spectacular scenery. There is something that will appeal to everyone in this "wild & wonderful" part of Ireland. Ideal for touring, walking, fishing etc, or "just a quiet relaxing break". Splendidly remote, with clean mountain air, and our own mountain spring water. The benign waters of Kylemore Lake lap peacefully below your bedroom window. Our restaurant has one of the most stunning views, also Sailors-Bar beer garden, both offer appetising home cooked meals.

Member of Countrywide Hotels

B&B from €42.00 to €63.00

Stuart & Rose Rima
Hosts

11

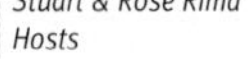

Closed 02 November - 16 March

### Leenane Hotel

HOTEL ★★★ MAP 9 D 12

Leenane,
Connemara,
Co. Galway

Tel: 095-42249 Fax: 095-42376

Email: info@leenanehotel.com

Web: www.leenanehotel.com

On the shores of Killary Harbour, Ireland's only Fjord, lies Ireland's oldest Coaching Inn. The Leenane Hotel, recently refurbished to the highest of standards, boasts the most spectacular views in Ireland. Being a family-run hotel, we understand the appreciation for traditional home-cooking. Fresh seafood from the harbour and vegetables and herbs from the hotel garden are brought in every day. The hotel's position makes it without doubt the best base for exploring Connemara, the most romantic and unspoiled region of Ireland.

Bookable on www.irelandhotels.com

Special Offer: www.irelandhotels.com/offers

B&B from €55.00 to €90.00

Conor Foyle
Manager

29

Closed 25 November - 14 March



B&B Rates are per Person Sharing per Night incl. Breakfast.
or Room Rates are per Room per Night - See also Page 8

## Portfinn

GUESTHOUSE ★★ MAP 9 D 12

Leenane,
Co. Galway

Tel: 095-42265 Fax: 095-42315
Email: orantaz@mac.com
Web: www.portfinn.com

Portfinn, run by the Daly family since 1977, is located overlooking the picturesque village of Leenane and Killary Harbor in Co. Galway. We offer 11 comfortable rooms all En suite with either a sea or mountain Views. Portfinn has a renowned seafood restaurant serving only locally caught and produced fish, meat and poultry. Activities such as Scuba diving, fishing, hiking, golf and much more is available at our door step. We look forward to hosting you in the future

*B&B from €40.00 to €50.00*

*Óran Daly*

11

*Activities:*

**Closed 01 November - 15 March**

## Rosleague Manor Hotel

HOTEL ★★★★ MAP 9 C 12

Letterfrack,
Connemara,
Co. Galway

Tel: 095-41101 Fax: 095-41168
Email: info@rosleague.com
Web: www.rosleague.com

Rosleague is a Regency manor now run as a first class country house hotel by Mark Foyle and Eddie Foyle. It lies 7 miles north west of Clifden on the coast overlooking a sheltered bay and surrounded by the Connemara Mountains, beside the National Park. It is renowned for its superb cuisine personally supervised by the owners with all the amenities expected by today's discerning guest.
Recommended by Good Hotel Guide, Bridgestone 100 Best, Karen Brown, Georgina Campbell, Alastair Sawday's and many more. Also a member of Ireland's Blue Book.

Member of I.C.H.R.A. (Blue Book)

*Bookable on www.irelandhotels.com*
*Special Offer: www.irelandhotels.com/offers*

*B&B from €75.00 to €110.00*
*Suites from €190.00 to €250.00*

*Eddie Foyle / Mark Foyle*
*Owner / Manager*

20

**Closed 15 November - 15 March**

## Meadow Court Hotel

HOTEL ★★★ MAP 6 H 10

Clostoken,
Loughrea,
Co. Galway

Tel: 091-841051 Fax: 091-842406
Email: meadowcourthotel@eircom.net
Web: www.meadowcourthotel.com

Newly extended and refurbished the Meadow Court Hotel's en suite rooms have full facilities, tea and coffee making facilities, multi channel TV, hairdryer and iron. Superb dining is on offer in our award-winning restaurant renowned for its outstanding cuisine. Enjoy after dinner drinks in our Derby Bar. Situated on the main Galway Dublin Road, 2 miles from Loughrea, 18 miles from Galway, convenient to all local 18-hole golf courses, angling, horse riding, water sports. Banqueting & conference facilities. Carpark. Please enquire about Facilities for Persons with Mobility Impairment.

*B&B from €45.00 to €90.00*
*Suites from €200.00 to €300.00*

*Tom & David Corbett*
*Directors*

21

*Activities:*

**Closed 24 - 26 December**

B&B Rates are per Person Sharing per Night incl. Breakfast.
or Room Rates are per Room per Night - **See also Page 8**

# Loughrea / Maam Cross / Oughterard

## O'Deas Hotel

HOTEL ★★★ MAP 6 H 10

Bride Street,
Loughrea,
Co. Galway

Tel: 091-841611 Fax: 091-842635

Email: odeashotel@eircom.net

Web: www.odeashotel.com

O'Deas Hotel is a family hotel, a Georgian town house hotel of character, with open fires and within walking distance of Loughrea's game fishing lake. It is an ideal touring base situated on the N6 (exactly halfway between Clonmacnoise, 35 miles to the east and the Cliffs of Moher, 35 miles to the west). The start of the Burren country is just 12 miles away. Galway City 20 miles.

Member of Countrywide Hotels - MinOtel Ireland

B&B from €55.00 to €65.00

*Mary O'Neill*
*Proprietor / Manager*

32

*Activities:*

Closed 24 - 26 December

## Peacockes Hotel & Complex

HOTEL MAP 5 E 11

Maam Cross,
Connemara,
Co. Galway

Tel: 091-552306 Fax: 091-552216

Email: info@peacockes.ie

Web: www.atlantisholidaygroup.ie

Built to a 3*** specification. Peacockes Hotel is an oasis of calm & luxury amidst the rugged beauty of Connemara. Ideal base for touring Connemara & for the great outdoor enthusiast with an abundance of excellent walks, hikes & cycle routes in the immediate vicinity. The hotel complex includes a luxury hotel with well appointed bedrooms, a lake view restaurant serving excellent food, coffee shop, banqueting room catering for all events large & small & a 20m viewing tower from where you can enjoy unspoilt Connemara as far as the eye can see. Gift & craft shop. A replica of "The Quiet Man" cottage also on site.

Member of Atlantis Holiday Group

B&B from €50.00 to €120.00
Suites from €150.00 to €300.00

*Caroline Fahy- Conneely*
*General Manager*

25

Closed 23 - 26 December

## Corrib Wave Guest House

GUESTHOUSE ★★★ MAP 5 E 11

Portacarron,
Oughterard, Connemara,
Co. Galway

Tel: 091-552147 Fax: 091-552147

Email: cwh@gofree.indigo.ie

Web: www.corribwave.com

Panoramic lakeside guesthouse - the home of Michael & Maria Healy. As our guests, you are assured of a warm welcome to a family home with every comfort and Irish hospitality, superb home-cooking, excellent wines, beautiful en suite bedrooms (all with double and single beds), TVs, hairdryers. Spectacular views, turf fire, peace and tranquility. Angling specialists, boats, engines, for hire. Lakeside walks. 18 hole golf 1km. Recommended by Le Guide Routard, Georgina Campbell best places to stay. For more info contact us direct. Please enquire about Facilities for Persons with Mobility Impairment.

B&B from €40.00 to €45.00

*Maria & Michael Healy*
*Proprietors*

10

*Activities:*

Closed 01 December - 15 January



B&B Rates are per Person Sharing per Night incl. Breakfast. or Room Rates are per Room per Night - **See also Page 8**

## Currarevagh House

GUESTHOUSE ★★★★ MAP 5 E 11

Oughterard,
Connemara,
Co. Galway

Tel: 091-552312 Fax: 091-552731
Email: mail@currarevagh.com
Web: www.currarevagh.com

A charming country mansion, built in 1842, romantically situated beside Lough Corrib in 180 acres of private woodlands. The relaxing atmosphere and classically simple menus receive much international praise. Own fishing, boats, tennis court, with golf & riding locally. Recommendations: Egon Ronay, Guide Michelin, Footprint Guide, Lonely Planet, Karen Brown's Irish Country Inns, Georgina Campbell's Best of the Best, Alistar Sawdays Guide, Good Hotel Guide & many other international hotel & food guides. They suggest that you stay at least 3 nights to absorb the atmosphere and gently explore Connemara.

Member of Ireland's Blue Book

Bookable on www.irelandhotels.com

B&B from €75.00 to €105.00

*Harry, June and Henry Hodgson*
*Proprietors*

15

Closed 20 October - 10 march

## Mountain View Guest House

GUESTHOUSE ★★★ MAP 5 E 11

Aughnanure,
Oughterard,
Co. Galway

Tel: 091-550306 Fax: 091-550133
Email: tricia.oconnor@eircom.net
Web: www.mountainviewgalway.com

Situated just off the N59, 24kms from Galway City and within 2-4 km of Oughterard, with the Connemara mountains in the distance and Lough Corrib nearby. Leisure activities include; golf at the renowned Oughterard Golf Club, established walks along scenic routes, boating or fishing on Lough Corrib. All bedrooms en suite, with TV, direct dial phones, tea/coffee making facilities and hairdryers. Please enquire about Facilities for Persons with Mobility Impairment.

Bookable on www.irelandhotels.com
Special Offer: www.irelandhotels.com/offers

B&B from €32.00 to €38.00

*Richard & Patricia O'Connor*
*Proprietors*

10

Closed 23 - 28 December

## Ross Lake House Hotel

HOTEL ★★★ MAP 5 E 11

Rosscahill,
Oughterard,
Co. Galway

Tel: 091-550109 Fax: 091-550184
Email: rosslake@iol.ie
Web: www.rosslakehotel.com

Ross Lake House is a wonderful Georgian house set in the magnificent wilderness of Connemara. Six acres of mature gardens surround the house creating an air of peace and tranquillity. Hosts Henry and Elaine Reid have beautifully restored this manor house to its former glory. A high quality Irish menu is prepared daily featuring a tempting variety of fresh produce from nearby Connemara hills, streams and lakes as well as fish straight from the Atlantic.

Member of Private Ireland

Bookable on www.irelandhotels.com
Special Offer: www.irelandhotels.com/offers

B&B from €75.00 to €100.00
Suites from €225.00 to €300.00

*Elaine & Henry Reid*
*Proprietors*

13

Closed 01 November - 14 March

B&B Rates are per Person Sharing per Night incl. Breakfast.
or Room Rates are per Room per Night - **See also Page 8**

## Portumna / Recess / Renvyle

### Shannon Oaks Hotel & Country Club

HOTEL ★★★ MAP 6 I 9

Portumna,
Co. Galway

Tel: 090-974 1777 Fax: 090-974 1357
Email: sales@shannonoaks.ie
Web: www.shannonoaks.ie

Shannon Oaks Hotel & Country Club lies adjacent to the 17th century Portumna Castle and estate, by the shores of Lough Derg. All our rooms have satellite television, DD phone and an en suite bathroom. A distinguished menu of classic and fusion Irish dishes are available each evening. Our White Flag award-winning leisure centre, with its indoor heated swimming pool, sauna, steam room and gymnasium provides the stress free atmosphere in which to relax and unwind. Please enquire about Facilities for Persons with Mobility Impairment.

***An IHF Quality Employer***

Member of Irish Country Hotels

*Bookable on www.irelandhotels.com*
*Special Offer: www.irelandhotels.com/offers*

*B&B from €95.00 to €115.00*

*Joe Groome*
*General Manager*

63

*Activities:*

Open All Year

### Lough Inagh Lodge

HOTEL ★★★★ MAP 5 D 11

Recess,
Connemara,
Co. Galway

Tel: 095-34706 Fax: 095-34708
Email: inagh@iol.ie
Web: www.loughinaghlodgehotel.ie

Lough Inagh Lodge was built in 1880. It offers all the comforts of an elegant modern hotel in an old world atmosphere, open log fires in the library and oak panelled bar symbolises the warmth of Inagh hospitality. The lodge is surrounded by famous beauty spots including the Twelve Bens Mountain Range and the Connemara National Park. Kylemore Abbey is also nearby. Ideal base for hill walking, cycling and fishing.

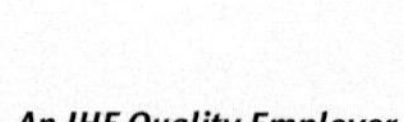

***An IHF Quality Employer***

Member of Manor House Hotels

*Bookable on www.irelandhotels.com*
*Special Offer: www.irelandhotels.com/offers*

*B&B from €193.00 to €284.00*

*Maire O'Connor*
*Proprietor*

13

*Activities:*

Closed 08 December - 06 March

### Maol Reidh Lodge

HOTEL ★★★ MAP 9 C 12

Tullycross,
Renvyle,
Co. Galway

Tel: 095-43844 Fax: 095-43784
Email: maolreidhhotel@eircom.net
Web: www.maolreidhhotel.com

Situated in the delightful village of Tullycross, Renvyle the Maol Reidh Lodge offers guests a high standard of luxury. We are close to Connemara National Park and Kylemore Abbey. For the active guest, we are nestled in the Twelve Bens and Maamturk Mountains, and only a few minutes drive from Scuba-Dive West and Oceans Alive sealife centre. A perfect place to enjoy the natural paradise of Connemara. Please enquire about Facilities for Persons with Mobility Impairment.

*Bookable on www.irelandhotels.com*
*Special Offer: www.irelandhotels.com/offers*

*B&B from €65.00 to €105.00*

*Jack & Monica Lydon*
*Proprietors*

12

Closed 30 October - 01 March



B&B Rates are per Person Sharing per Night incl. Breakfast.
or Room Rates are per Room per Night - **See also Page 8**

## Renvyle House Hotel

HOTEL ★★★ MAP 9 C 12

Renvyle,
Connemara,
Co. Galway

Tel: 095-43511 Fax: 095-43515
Email: info@renvyle.com
Web: www.renvyle.com

Historic coastal hotel set amid the magical beauty of sea, lake and mountains, the keynotes are warmth and comfort with award-winning fine fare. Turf fires and cosy lounges make you relax and feel at home. Golf, tennis, swimming pool (seasonal - outdoor, heated), snooker, boating, fishing are the facilities to name but a few. Wonderful walking and cycling routes throughout an area that hosts a vast National Park. Additional facilities include claypigeon shooting, canoeing, beauty treatment centre. Please enquire about Facilities for Persons with Mobility Impairment.

Member of Select Hotels of Ireland

*Bookable on www.irelandhotels.com*
*Special Offer: www.irelandhotels.com/offers*

*B&B from €30.00 to €125.00*
*Suites from €140.00 to €320.00*

*Zoe Fitzgerald*
*Sales & Marketing Manager*

70

Closed 08 January - 12 February

## Roundstone House Hotel

HOTEL ★★ MAP 9 C 11

Roundstone,
Connemara,
Co. Galway

Tel: 095-35864 Fax: 095-35944
Email: vaughanshotel@eircom.net
Web: www.irishcountryhotels.com

Roundstone House Hotel is a family hotel situated in the picturesque village of Roundstone. Roundstone is a fascinating place for a holiday offering a wide range of interests for the holidaymakers. Many outdoor activities are available locally including sea angling, watersports, hill walking, pony trekking and a championship 18 hole golf course nearby. Come to beautiful Roundstone for a holiday to remember. Please enquire about Facilities for Persons with Mobility Impairment.

Member of Irish Country Hotels

*Bookable on www.irelandhotels.com*

*B&B from €55.00 to €60.00*

*Maureen Vaughan*
*Proprietor*

13

Closed 31 October - 20 March

## An Crúiscín Lán Hotel

HOTEL ★★ MAP 5 E 10

Spiddal,
Co. Galway

Tel: 091-553148 Fax: 091-553712
Email: info@cruiscinlanhotel.com

An Crúiscín Lán Hotel is located in the heart of the Irish speaking Spiddal Village perfectly suited for touring the Gaeltacht, Connemara and the Islands. The hotel comprises a snug bar showing your favourite sports events, a lounge bar for meeting friends and making new ones and a dining conservatory with views of the Burren, Galway Bay and the Islands. We serve food all day long and are well known for quality.

*B&B from €50.00 to €75.00*

*David Concannon*

14

Closed 25 December

## Spiddal / Tuam

### Park Lodge Hotel

HOTEL ★★ MAP 5 E 10

Park,
Spiddal,
Co. Galway

Tel: 091-553159 Fax: 091-553494

Email: parklodgehotel@eircom.net

Web: www.parklodgehotel.com

The Park Lodge Hotel is owned and run by the Foyle Family. It is situated on the coast road from Galway to Connemara, 16km west of Galway City and just east of Spiddal Village. Most of the 23 bedrooms have a view of Galway Bay. There are also seven detached cottages on the grounds, each self-catering and fully equipped for 5 persons. Cottages open all year. Please enquire about Facilities for Persons with Mobility Impairment.

*B&B from €50.00 to €70.00*

*Jane Marie Foyle*
*Manager*

23

Activities:

Closed 01 October - 31 May

### Tigh Chualain

GUESTHOUSE ★★★ MAP 5 E 10

Kilroe East,
Spiddal,
Co. Galway

Tel: 091-553609 Fax: 091-553049

Email: tighchualain@eircom.net

Tigh Chualain is a charming, family-run 3*** guesthouse, 16km west of Galway City and 2km west of Spiddal Village, en route to the Aran Islands' Ferry. Overlooking Galway Bay, with a nearby Blue Flag beach, it is in the heart of the Connemara Gaeltacht. An obvious starting point for exploring the rugged beauty of Connemara with its manifold attractions. All bedrooms are en suite with direct dial telephone and colour TV.

*B&B from €30.00 to €40.00*

*Nora & Colm Folan*
*Proprietors*

9

Closed 31 October - 31 March

### Corralea Court

HOTEL ★★★ MAP 10 G 12

The Square,
Tuam,
Galway

Tel: 093-24188 Fax: 093-52794

Email: info@corraleacourthotel.com

Web: www.corralea_court_hotel.com

Located in the heart of Tuam, this newly built modern 3 star hotel is only a short drive from Galway & Knock making it the perfect meeting place for both business and pleasure. Krugers Bar - weekend entertainment, delicious carvery and bar food daily. Corrals restaurant serving the finest and freshest local produce. Mitre and O'Connor soite - Catering for all your banqueting needs. Please enquire about Facilities for Persons with Mobility Impairment.

*B&B from €80.00 to €160.00*

*Claire Coughlan*
*General Manager*

24

Closed 23 - 27 December



B&B Rates are per Person Sharing per Night incl. Breakfast. or Room Rates are per Room per Night - See also Page 8

## Commercial & Tourist Hotel

HOTEL ★★ MAP 11 J 15

Ballinamore,
Co. Leitrim

Tel: 071-964 4675 Fax: 071-964 4679
Email: commercialhotel@gmail.com
Web: www.hotelcommercial.com

Ideally situated in the centre of the greenest & most uncluttered part of Ireland in the heart of lovely Leitrim. Completely re-built to 3 star de luxe standard. Large comfortable rooms with queen size beds all en suite. Private car parking & elevator along with excellent cuisine & personal service. Local amenities include river cruising on the Shannon - Erne Waterway, scenic drives, hill walking & golfing. Fishing in the area is an absolute must. Special rates for golfers and commercial travellers. The Commericial Hotel is your ideal base for breathtaking tours or business. Dublin/Belfast 2 hrs, Shannon 3 hrs.

*Bookable on www.irelandhotels.com*
*Special Offer: www.irelandhotels.com/offers*

*B&B from €55.00 to €75.00*

*Karen Walsh*
*Director*

28

Closed 25 December

## Glenview Guesthouse

GUESTHOUSE ★★ MAP 11 J 15

Aughoo,
Ballinamore,
Co. Leitrim

Tel: 071-964 4157 Fax: 071-964 4814
Email: glenvhse@iol.ie
Web: www.glenview-house.com

Glenview House, 2 miles south of Ballinamore is a holiday haven, 500m from the Shannon-Erne Waterway. Exclusive fully licensed restaurant with extensive wine list. Enjoy Riverbus boat trips, country drives, horse riding, animal farm, golf and hill walking locally. Glenview has its own tennis court, games room, folk museum and play area for children. Self-catering houses within grounds, two of which are wheelchair friendly.

*B&B from €40.00 to €45.00*

*Teresa Kennedy*

6

Closed 23 - 28 December

## Aisleigh Guest House

GUESTHOUSE ★★★ MAP 10 I 14

Dublin Road,
Carrick-On-Shannon,
Co. Leitrim

Tel: 071-962 0313 Fax: 071-962 0675
Email: aisleigh@eircom.net
Web: www.aisleighguesthouse.com

A warm welcome awaits you at our family-run guesthouse situated 1km from the picturesque town of Carrick-on-Shannon, Ireland's best kept secret. Facilities include en suite bedrooms with TV, direct dial telephones. Internet access games room and sauna. Local genealogy a speciality. Private car parking. Ideal attractions Aura Leisure Centre, Docks Theatre & Gallery. Arigna Mining Museum, Strokestown House and Lough Key Forest Park, golfing, cruising, fishing (tackle & bait supplies) horse riding, walking, cycling, etc.

*Bookable on www.irelandhotels.com*
*Special Offer: www.irelandhotels.com/offers*

*B&B from €45.00 to €55.00*

*Sean & Charlotte Fearon*
*Owners*

10

Open All Year

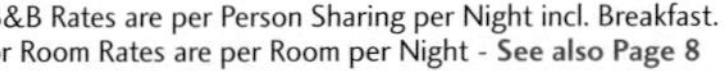

B&B Rates are per Person Sharing per Night incl. Breakfast.
or Room Rates are per Room per Night - **See also Page 8**

## Carrick-on-Shannon / Carrigallen

### Bush Hotel

HOTEL ★★★ MAP 10 I 14

Carrick-on-Shannon,
Co. Leitrim

Tel: 071-967 1000 Fax: 071-962 1180
Email: info@bushhotel.com
Web: www.bushhotel.com

An hotel of ambience, style and comfort, The Bush Hotel (one of Ireland's oldest) has just completed a major refurbishment and extension whilst still retaining its olde world charm and character. Centrally located in the town centre, the hotel has 50 modern bedrooms with all facilities, theme bars, coffee shop and restaurant. New state of the art business and banqueting centre. Attractions: Arigna Mining Museum, Strokestown House, King House, etc. Please enquire about Facilities for Persons with Mobility Impairment.

***An IHF Quality Employer***

*Bookable on www.irelandhotels.com*
*Special Offer: www.irelandhotels.com/offers*

*B&B from €59.50 to €84.50*
*Suites from €149.00 to €199.00*

*Joseph Dolan*
*Managing Director*

50

*Activities:*

Closed 24 - 27 December

### Ciúin House

GUESTHOUSE ★★★★ MAP 10 I 4

Hartley,
Carrick On Shannon,
Co. Leitrim

Tel: 071-967 1488 Fax: 071-967 1487
Email: info@ciuinhouse.com
Web: www.ciuinhouse.com

Ciúin House is a unique guest house experience - 4* luxury accommodation close to town centre. Our 15 deluxe bedrooms have orthopaedic beds, bath/power shower, tea/coffee making facilities & TV as standard. Superior rooms with queen size beds, jacuzzi bath, safe, etc. Relax in our stylish guest lounge with plasma screen TV, piped music & broadband access. Private gardens, seated patio area & secure car park. Our licensed restaurant serves breakfast, lunch & evening meals. Gourmet A la Carte dinner menu available & a selection of fine wines.

*B&B from €65.00 to €90.00*
*Suites from €160.00 to €180.00*

*Fiona & Barry Reynolds*

15

Closed 24 - 27 December

### Kilbrackan Arms Hotel

HOTEL ★★ MAP 11 K 14

Main Street,
Carrigallen,
Co. Leitrim

Tel: 049-433 9737 Fax: 049-433 9152
Email: info@kilbrackanarms.com
Web: www.kilbrackanarms.com

Carrigallen - a peaceful getaway. Convenient to all major towns. Set amongst rolling hills and lakes. An angler's paradise, close to many golf courses and walkways. Please enquire about Facilities for Persons with Mobility Impairment.

*B&B from €45.00 to €60.00*

*Donal Cadden*
*Host*

14

*Activities:*

Open All Year



B&B Rates are per Person Sharing per Night incl. Breakfast.
or Room Rates are per Room per Night - **See also Page 8**

## Ramada Hotel & Suites at Lough Allen

HOTEL ★★★★ MAP 10 I 15

Drumshambo,
Co. Leitrim

Tel: 071-964 0100 Fax: 071-964 0101
Email: info@loughallenhotel.com
Web: www.loughallenhotel.com

Close to the picturesque town of Drumshanbo, located on the shores of Lough Allen. Many rooms with balconies, decking area with stunning view of the lake. The best base for touring the surrounding countryside. Yeat's Country, Verdant County Fermanagh, rocky coastline of Co. Mayo, the many lakes of County Leitrim. In a word IDYLLIC! Please enquire about Facilities for Persons with Mobility Impairment.

Member of Ramada Worldwide

Bookable on www.irelandhotels.com
Special Offer: www.irelandhotels.com/offers

Room Rate from €85.00 to €160.00
Suites from €165.00 to €200.00

Erik Speekenbrink
Resort General Manager

72

Activities:

Open All Year

## Glebe House

GUESTHOUSE ★★★ MAP 11 J 14

Ballinamore Road,
Mohill,
Co. Leitrim

Tel: 071-963 1086 Fax: 071-963 1886
Email: glebehse@gmail.com
Web: www.glebehouse.com

At the end of a sweeping driveway this lovely Georgian former Rectory dating to 1823, is set on 50 acres of mature trees and farmland and has been carefully restored by the Maloney family. Enjoy the tranquility of this unspoilt part of Ireland. Ideal touring base. Assistance given with genealogy. Internet/computer for visitor use. Discount on bookings if more than one night.

Bookable on www.irelandhotels.com
Special Offer: www.irelandhotels.com/offers

B&B from €45.00 to €50.00

Laura Maloney
Manager

8

Closed 31 October - 31 December

## Lough Rynn Castle

HOTEL ★★★★ MAP 11 J 14

Mohill,
Co. Leitrim

Tel: 071-963 2700 Fax: 071-963 2710
Email: enquires@loughrynn.ie
Web: www.loughrynn.ie

Lough Rynn castle is the original 19th century home of the Clements family. The development comprises a luxury 40 bedroomed hotel with restored Victorian walled gardens. A world class spa and leisure facility, and a championship golf course designed by Nick Faldo will be completed by 2008. The entire facility is situated on 300 acres of an Ireland that is idyllic, rich in history and charmed with natural beauty. Please enquire about Facilities for Persons with Mobility Impairment.

Member of The Hanly Castle Hotel Group

Room Rate from €99.00 to €255.00
Suites from €295.00 to €595.00

Ciaran Reidy
General Manager

40

Activities:

Open All Year

## Rooskey / Adare

### Flynns Shannon Key West Hotel

HOTEL ★★★ MAP 11 J 13

The Waters Edge,
Rooskey,
Co. Leitrim

Tel: 071-963 8800 Fax: 071-963 8811
Email: info@shannonkeywest.com
Web: www.shannonkeywest.com

Situated on N4 Dublin Sligo route. Rooskey is an elegant marina village nestling between Carrick-On-Shannon & Longford Town. Dromod Train Station 2km from hotel. Friendly 40 bedroom hotel, with quirky architectural details offers beautiful views over the River Shannon from bedrooms, terraces & roof gardens. Tasty seasonal food served all day, with a choice of fine dining in the Kilglass Restaurant and à la carte in the bar. Facilities: gym, steam room & outdoor tennis or basketball. In-house beauty salon & golf courses nearby. Rooskey is a stress free comfort zone. Online booking www.shannonkeywest.com.

*Bookable on www.irelandhotels.com*
*Special Offer: www.irelandhotels.com/offers*

*B&B from €62.50 to €80.00*

*Niall Flynn*
*Proprietor*

40

Activities:

Open All Year

### Adare Manor Hotel & Golf Resort

HOTEL ★★★★★ MAP 6 G 7

Adare,
Co. Limerick

Tel: 061-396566 Fax: 061-396124
Email: reservations@adaremanor.com
Web: www.adaremanor.com

Located 20 miles from Shannon Airport. Adare Manor Hotel & Golf Resort provides a historical backdrop for a romantic getaway, a golfing break or group event. Elegant, rooms boast complimentary internet access. Our internationally acclaimed head chef prepares haute cuisine laced with Irish charm, as home of the Irish Open, play a course that challenges some of the finest golfers in the world. Other pursuits include indoor heated pool, fitness room, spa, fishing & laser shooting.

***An IHF Quality Employer***

Member of Leading Small Hotels of the World

*Bookable on www.irelandhotels.com*

*Room Rate from €306.50 to €789.00*
*Suites from €1,362.00 to €1,362.00*

*Anita Higgins*
*General Manager*

62

Activities:

Closed 24 - 26 December

### Carriage House (The)

HOTEL ★★★★ MAP 6 G 7

The Adare Manor Hotel & Golf Resort,
Adare,
Co. Limerick

Tel: 061-396566 Fax: 061-396124
Email: reservations@adaremanor.com
Web: www.adaremanor.com/accomodation_club_house

The Carriage House at Adare Manor Hotel & Golf Resort now provides superior guest accommodation for the Golfer & non golfer alike. Dine in the Carriage house Restaurant overlooking the putting green or share a post golf drink in the Carriage House Bar with friends. Home of the Irish Open, a round of golf on this superb Robert Trent Jones Sr. designed course is a must. Pursuits include access to indoor swimming pool & fitness room located in the manor plus spa, fishing & laser shooting.

*Room Rate from €227.00 to €295.00*

*Anita Higgins*
*General Manager*

10

Activities:

Closed 24 - 26 December

B&B Rates are per Person Sharing per Night incl. Breakfast. or Room Rates are per Room per Night - See also Page 8

## Dunraven Arms Hotel

HOTEL ★★★★ MAP 6 G 7

Adare,
Co. Limerick

Tel: 061-605 900 Fax: 061-396 541
Email: reservations@dunravenhotel.com
Web: www.dunravenhotel.com

Established in 1792 a 4**** old world hotel surrounded by ornate thatched cottages, in Ireland's prettiest village. Each bedroom, including 24 suites, is beautifully appointed with antique furniture, dressing room and bathroom en suite. Award-winning restaurant, AA Three Red Rosettes. Leisure centre comprised of a 17m pool, steam room, gymnasium and massage and beauty therapy rooms. Equestrian and golf holidays a speciality. 30 minutes from Shannon Airport. Hotel of the Year 2004 - Georgina Campbell Jameson Guide. Complimentary WiFi access throughout the hotel. Please enquire about Facilities for Persons with Mobility Impairment.

***An IHF Quality Employer***

Member of Small Luxury Hotels of the World

Bookable on www.irelandhotels.com
Special Offer: www.irelandhotels.com/offers

Room Rate from €135.00 to €200.00
Suites from €260.00 to €335.00

*Louis Murphy*
*Proprietor*

86

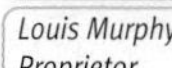

Activities:

Open All Year

## Fitzgeralds Woodlands House Hotel, Health and Leisure Spa

HOTEL ★★★ MAP 6 G 7

Knockanes,
Adare,
Co. Limerick

Tel: 061-605100 Fax: 061-396073
Email: reservations@woodlands-hotel.ie
Web: www.woodlands-hotel.ie

A sleep to remember with a 10cm mattress topper. Elegant dining in Brennans or Timmy Mac's Bistro which boasts great food in a homely environment with local memorabilia. Our leisure club comprises a 20m pool, kids' pool, a 1500sq ft gym, sauna, steam room & jacuzzi. Revas Spa includes a thermal suite, rasul chamber, outdoor rock pool, foot spa, couples rooms and a hair salon. A Destination to Remember. Please enquire about Facilities for Persons with Mobility Impairment.

***An IHF Quality Employer***

Member of Irish Country Hotels

Bookable on www.irelandhotels.com
Special Offer: www.irelandhotels.com/offers

B&B from €70.00 to €100.00
Suites from €225.00 to €300.00

*Mary & David Fitzgerald*
*Hosts*

94

Activities:

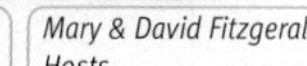

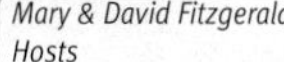

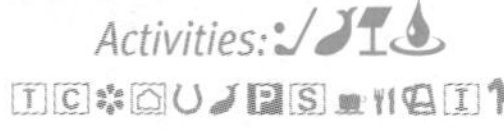

Closed 24 - 25 December

## Castle Oaks House Hotel & Country Club

HOTEL ★★★ MAP 6 H 7

Castleconnell,
Co. Limerick

Tel: 061-377666 Fax: 061-377717
Email: info@castleoaks.ie
Web: www.castleoaks.ie

Experience our casual country elegance. Located on N7 just 7 minutes from Limerick City, just off the new Limerick by-pass. The Castle Oaks House Hotel and Leisure Club is situated on 26 acres of mature gardens. The hotel boasts 20 lavishly appointed bedrooms and 22 (2 bedroomed) suites with individual private lounges, 19 4**** self-catering homes and new day spa. Extensive conference and banqueting facilities. Award-winning Acorn Restaurant. Fishing on site. Golf, equestrian facilities nearby. Shannon Airport 40 minutes.

Member of Great Fishing Houses of Ireland

Bookable on www.irelandhotels.com
Special Offer: www.irelandhotels.com/offers

B&B from €55.00 to €120.00
Suites from €195.00 to €300.00

*Gobnait O'Connell*
*Managing Director*

62

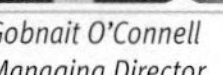

Closed 23 - 26 December

## Kilmallock / Limerick City

### Deebert House Hotel

HOTEL MAP 6 H 6

Deebert,
Kilmallock,
Co. Limerick

Tel: 063-31200 Fax: 063-31212
Email: info@deeberthousehotel.com
Web: www.deeberthousehotel.com

Built to a 3*** specification. Nestled at the foothills of the Ballyhoura mountains in the historic town of Kilmallock, the charm of Deebert House Hotel awaits you. Originally a flour mill dating back to 1807, the new building has many unique and individual features which have been maintained in the current design. The hotel offers 20 elegant bedrooms Restaurant and bar, meeting room and banqueting facilities for 100 delegates. Experience the true taste of Ballyhoura country where walking and mountain biking holidays are our specialty.

B&B from €50.00 to €75.00

*Margaret Atalla*
*Manager*

20

Activities:

Closed 24 - 28 December

### AbsoluteHotel.com

HOTEL MAP 6 H 7

Sir Harry's Mall,
Limerick

Tel: 061-463600 Fax: 061-463601
Email: info@absolutehotel.com
Web: www.absolutehotel.com

Built to a 4**** specification. AbsoluteHotel.com is located in the heart of Limerick city centre. Features of our guestrooms include rain-dance shower, plasma screen TVs with internet access, air-conditioning, hairdryer, WiFi internet access and sound proof windows. Our exceptional dining options include ,The Riverbank Restaurant & Bar and Refuel Café, which flow onto our terrace overlooking the river. Our breathtaking Spa has 6 treatment rooms, a thermal suite and the hotel also features a fitness gym. Please enquire about Facilities for Persons with Mobility Impairment.

B&B from €57.50 to €137.50

*Brenda Murphy*
*Group Sales & Marketing Manager*

99

Open All Year

### Best Western Pery's Hotel

HOTEL ★★★ MAP 6 H 7

Glentworth Street,
Limerick

Tel: 061-413822 Fax: 061-413073
Email: info@perys.ie
Web: www.perys.ie

An historic city centre boutique hotel in the heart of Georgian Limerick. Recently achieved the Ireland's Best Award for Service Excellence. Prides itself in creating exceptional service surrounded by a friendly and welcoming ambience. For evening dining choose from the elegant Tait's Restaurant or more informail Tait's Bar. Bus and Rail Station, shopping, theathres, museums, restaurants, nightlife all within minutes. Gym, Sauna and private car park. Shannon Airport 20 minutes drive. Please enquire about Facilities for Persons with Mobility Impairment.

Member of Best Western

*Bookable on www.irelandhotels.com*
*Special Offer: www.irelandhotels.com/offers*

B&B from €50.00 to €95.00

*Marie Tynan*
*Hotel Manager*

62

Closed 25 - 26 December



B&B Rates are per Person Sharing per Night incl. Breakfast. or Room Rates are per Room per Night - **See also Page 8**

## Castletroy Park Hotel

HOTEL ★★★★ MAP 6 H 7

Dublin Road,
Limerick

Tel: 061-335566 Fax: 061-331117
Email: sales@castletroy-park.ie
Web: www.castletroy-park.ie

The Hotel offers splendid luxury accommodation, and spacious guestrooms. The hotel is just 3 miles from Limerick City. If you are looking for a relaxing weekend away, you will find what you are looking for at Limerick's finest hotel. Avail of the extensive Aqua & Fitness Club and Beauty at Blue Door Salon. The Internationally acclaimed University Sports Arena and Concert Hall is adjacent to the hotel.

***An IHF Quality Employer***

*Bookable on www.irelandhotels.com*
*Special Offer: www.irelandhotels.com/offers*

*B&B from €85.00 to €140.00*
*Suites from €350.00 to €450.00*

*Fiona O'Shea*
*General Manager*

107

*Activities:*

Open All Year

## Clarion Hotel Limerick

HOTEL ★★★★ MAP 6 H 7

Steamboat Quay,
Limerick

Tel: 061-444100 Fax: 061-444101
Email: info@clarionhotellimerick.com
Web: www.clarionlimerick.com

Clarion Hotel Limerick, Ireland's tallest hotel, boasts a riverside location with magnificent views of the River Shannon. All rooms & suites are finished to an excellent standard. The Sinergie Restaurant offers the ultimate dining experience from its waterfront location, while Kudos Bar specialises in Malaysian food. Health & Leisure club: swimming pool, gym, sauna, steam room & jacuzzi. Within 10 mins of hotel: 20 dining options, Hunt Museum, King Johns Castle, Bunratty Castle & Folk Park, Limerick Racecourse & a wide variety of golf courses. 20 mins from Shannon International Airport.

***An IHF Quality Employer***
Member of Choice Hotels Ireland

*Bookable on www.irelandhotels.com*
*Special Offer: www.irelandhotels.com/offers*

*B&B from €65.00 to €145.00*
*Suites from €180.00 to €295.00*

*Sean Lally*
*Managing Partner*

158

*Activities:*

Closed 24 - 26 December

## Clarion Hotel Suites Limerick

HOTEL ★★★★ MAP 6 H 7

Ennis Road,
Limerick,

Tel: 061-582900 Fax: 061-582901
Email: info@clarionsuiteslimerick.com
Web: www.clarionsuiteslimerick.com

Limerick's only all suites hotel, located walking distance from Limerick City Centre. 61, one and two bedroom hotel suites with separate dining room equipped with kettle, toaster, fridge and microwave. Kudos Restaurant & Bar. Gymnasium onsite. Use of leisure facilities at The Clarion Steamboat Quay, 10mins away. Complimentary car parking. Within 10 minutes are: 20 other dining options, Bunratty Castle & Folk Park, Limerick racecourse & a variety of golf courses. 15 minutes from Shannon International Airport. Please enquire about Facilities for Persons with Mobility Impairment.

***An IHF Quality Employer***
Member of Choice Hotels Ireland

*Bookable on www.irelandhotels.com*
*Special Offer: www.irelandhotels.com/offers*

*Room Rate from €89.00 to €360.00*

*Sean Lally*
*Managing Partner*

61

Open All Year

B&B Rates are per Person Sharing per Night incl. Breakfast.
or Room Rates are per Room per Night - **See also Page 8**

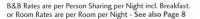

## Limerick City

### Clifton House Guest House

GUESTHOUSE ★★★ MAP 6 H 7

Ennis Road,
Limerick

Tel: 061-451166 Fax: 061-451224
Email: cliftonhouse@eircom.net

Set in 1 acre of landscaped gardens. All sixteen rooms are en suite, with multi-channel TV, trouser press, hairdryers and direct dial telephone. Complimentary tea/coffee is available in our spacious TV lounge. We are situated on the main Limerick / Shannon Road. Within 15 minutes walk of city centre. 22 space car park. AA listed. Friendly welcome awaits you.

Member of Premier Guesthouses

Bookable on www.irelandhotels.com

B&B from €45.00 to €45.00

*Michael & Mary Powell*
*Proprietors*

16

Closed 20 December - 05 January

### Greenhills Hotel Conference/Leisure

HOTEL ★★★ MAP 6 H 7

Ennis Road,
Limerick

Tel: 061-453033 Fax: 061-453307
Email: info@greenhillsgroup.com
Web: www.greenhillsgroup.com

The newly refurbished Greenhills Hotel, set in 3.5 acres of tended gardens offers a superb base to explore the attractions of the South West. 5 minutes from Limerick City and 15 minutes from Shannon Airport. Enjoy "Bryan's" Bar and "Hughs on the Greene" Restaurant. Relax in our award-winning Leisure Centre, which includes an 18m pool. State of the art conference and banqueting facilities catering for up to 400. Lots of local attractions and amenities. Newly added is Rachael's Beauty Rooms, offering a range of various pamper treatments. Please enquire about Facilities for Persons with Mobility Impairment.

***An IHF Quality Employer***

Bookable on www.irelandhotels.com
Special Offer: www.irelandhotels.com/offers

Room Rate from €75.00 to €129.00

*Daphne Greene*
*General Manager*

58

Closed 24 - 26 December

B&B Rates are per Person Sharing per Night incl. Breakfast.
or Room Rates are per Room per Night - See also Page 8

## Hilton Limerick

HOTEL ★★★★ MAP 6 H 7

Ennis Road,
Limerick

Tel: 061-421800 Fax: 061-421866
Email: reservations.limerick@hilton.com
Web: www.hilton.com/limerick

The 4 star Hilton Hotel Limerick is situated on the banks of the river Shannon & only 2 minute walk to the centre of Limericks shopping district. The hotel is in the perfect location for business, conferences or weddings & is only 15 mins drive from Shannon Airport. The hotel can accommodate 420 conference delegates or 400 guests for private dining. Wireless is available on ground floor public areas free of charge. All bedrooms as standard laptop safe, Mini bar PPV, television, with some offering views of the river. Please enquire about Facilities for Persons with Mobility Impairment.

*An IHF Quality Employer*

Member of Hilton International

*Room Rate from €85.00 to €240.00*
*Suites from €175.00 to €330.00*

*Eoin Little*
*General Manager*

184

*Activities:*

Closed 24-27 December

## Jurys Inn Limerick

HOTEL ★★★ MAP 6 H 7

Lower Mallow Street,
Limerick

Tel: 061-207000 Fax: 061-400966
Email: jurysinnlimerick@jurysinns.com
Web: www.jurysinns.com

Set in the heart of the city along the banks of the Shannon and just a two minute stroll from the shopping and cultural centre of Limerick. This very welcoming Inn provides an excellent base from which to explore many scenic delights in Limerick City, Co. Limerick and Co. Clare. Please enquire about Facilities for Persons with Mobility Impairment.

*An IHF Quality Employer*

Member of Jurys Inns Group Ltd

*Bookable on www.irelandhotels.com*
*Special Offer: www.irelandhotels.com/offers*

*Room Rate from €59.00 to €99.00*

*Aileen Phelan*
*General Manager*

151

Closed 23 - 27 December

## Kilmurry Lodge Hotel

HOTEL ★★★ MAP 6 H 7

Castletroy,
Limerick

Tel: 061-331133 Fax: 061-330011
Email: info@kilmurrylodge.com
Web: www.kilmurrylodge.com

This newly refurbished hotel set among four acres of landscaped gardens is perfectly located adjacent to the University of Limerick on the Dublin road (N7), whilst still only minutes from the thriving city centre. The business and conference services (for up to 300 people) exceed the highest of expectations and the hotel's "Olde World" character and charm is complemented by the latest in technology including free broadband access in all guest bedrooms. Please enquire about Facilities for Persons with Mobility Impairment.

*An IHF Quality Employer*

*Bookable on www.irelandhotels.com*
*Special Offer: www.irelandhotels.com/offers*

*B&B from €49.00 to €90.00*
*Suites from €120.00 to €200.00*

*Siobhan Hoare*
*Proprietor*

100

*Activities:*

Closed 24 - 27 December

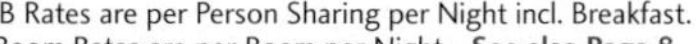

B&B Rates are per Person Sharing per Night incl. Breakfast.
or Room Rates are per Room per Night - **See also Page 8**

## Limerick City

### Limerick Marriott Hotel

HOTEL MAP 6 H 7

Henry Street,
Limerick

Tel: 061-448700 Fax: 061-448701
Email: info@limerickmarriott.ie
Web: www.limerickmarriott.com

Built to a 5***** specification. The first Marriott in Munster is on Henry Street in the heart of Limerick city close to the main shopping and business districts. Within short walking distance of this impressive eight story hotel are popular tourist attractions such as the 13th century King John's Castle, the Hunt Museum, the Treaty Stone, the 11th century St. Mary's Cathedral and the many and varied attractions of the Riverside City. Please enquire about Facilities for Persons with Mobility Impairment.

*B&B from €85.00 to €150.00*

*Donnacha Hurley*
*General Manager*

94

*Activities:*

Closed 24 - 26 December

### Old Quarter Lodge

GUESTHOUSE ★★★ MAP 6 H 7

Denmark Street,
Limerick

Tel: 061-315320 Fax: 061-316995
Email: lodge@oldquarter.ie
Web: www.oldquarter.ie

Old Quarter Lodge, formerly known as Cruises House. Newly refurbished, luxurious en suite rooms, situated in the heart of Limerick City centre, convenient to our finest shops & tourist attractions. All rooms en suite with DD telephone, hairdryer, tea/coffee making facilities, satellite TV. Additional facilities include room service, selection of suites, conference rooms, guest lounge, wireless internet access, fax/photocopying & bureau de change. Old Quarter Bar & Café also located within the building. A warm & friendly welcome awaits you. AA ♦♦♦ recognition.

*Bookable on www.irelandhotels.com*
*Special Offer: www.irelandhotels.com/offers*

*B&B from €40.00 to €50.00*
*Suites from €99.00 to €129.00*

*Carole Kelly*
*Lodge Manager*

26

Closed 24 December - 02 January

B&B Rates are per Person Sharing per Night incl. Breakfast.
or Room Rates are per Room per Night - See also Page 8

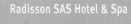

## Quality Hotel & Leisure Centre Limerick

HOTEL ★★★ MAP 6 H 7

John Carew Link Road,
Roxboro,
Limerick

Tel: 061-436100 Fax: 061-436110

Email: info.limerick@qualityhotels.ie

Web: www.qualityhotellimerick.com

Opened August 2006. This brand new hotel is situated just off the newly opened Southern Ring Motorway and just 5 minutes drive to Limerick city centre. The Quality Hotel and Leisure Centre is the perfect location whatever the reason for your visit to Limerick. Our 143 superior guestrooms, 26 two bedroomed suites and 4 one bedroomed suites with superb Club Vitae Leisure Centre and wide range of guest facilities make this the perfect base for family holidays short breaks or business needs in this vibrant city. Please enquire about Facilities for Persons with Mobility Impairment.

Member of Choice Hotels Ireland

*Bookable on www.irelandhotels.com*
*Special Offer: www.irelandhotels.com/offers*

*Room Rate from €79.00 to €199.00*
*Suites from €129.00 to €398.00*

*Tara Lyng*
*Sales & Marketing Manager*

199

*Activities:*

Closed 23 - 26 December

## Radisson SAS Hotel & Spa

HOTEL ★★★★ MAP 6 H 7

Ennis Road,
Limerick

Tel: 061-456200 Fax: 061-327418

Email: sales.limerick@radissonsas.com

Web: www.limerick.radissonsas.com

Located on the N18, 5 minutes drive from Limerick City, 15 minutes from Shannon Airport. Set in landscaped gardens, the hotel boasts 154 spacious bedrooms. Dine in our award-winning restaurant or relax in one of our two bars. Complimentary WiFi in all areas. Ladies level and business class room available. Renaissance spa, offering Elemis products, includes 9 treatment rooms, thermal suite, hot tub, relaxation suite and wet treatment rooms.

***An IHF Quality Employer***

Member of Rezidor SAS Hotels & Resorts

*Bookable on www.irelandhotels.com*
*Special Offer: www.irelandhotels.com/offers*

*B&B from €50.00 to €75.00*
*Suites from €250.00 to €380.00*

*Stephen Hanley*
*General Manager*

154

*Activities:*

Open All Year

## Railway Hotel

HOTEL ★★ MAP 6 H 7

Parnell Street,
Limerick

Tel: 061-413653 Fax: 061-419762

Email: sales@railwayhotel.ie

Web: www.railwayhotel.ie

Family-run hotel, owned and managed by the McEnery/Collins Family, this hotel offers Irish hospitality at its best. Personal attention is a way of life, along with an attractive lounge/bar, comfortable en suite accommodation and good home cooked food, one can't ask for more. Ideally situated, opposite rail/bus station, convenient to city centre, it is the perfect stop for the tourist and business person alike. All major credit cards accepted.

*B&B from €35.00 to €52.00*

*Pat & Michele McEnery*
*Owners / Managers*

25

5

Closed 24 - 26 December

## Limerick City / Newcastle West

### Sarsfield Bridge Hotel

HOTEL ★★★ MAP 6 H 7

Sarsfield Bridge,
Limerick City

Tel: 061-317179 Fax: 061-317182
Email: info@tsbh.ie
Web: www.sarsfieldbridgehotel.com

The Sarsfield Bridge Hotel located in the heart of Limerick City beside the River Shannon. Ease of access for sightseeing, shopping, sports events or business makes our hotel the perfect city centre location. All 55 en suite bedrooms are bright, comfortable and relaxing. On the ground floor, our very attractive Pier One Bar & Restaurant overlooking the Shannon offers excellent cuisine. 20 minutes from Shannon Airport. GDS Access Code UI. Please enquire about Facilities for Persons with Mobility Impairment.

Member of UTELL

*Bookable on www.irelandhotels.com*
*Special Offer: www.irelandhotels.com/offers*

*B&B from €55.00 to €70.00*

*Daragh O'Neill*
*Proprietor*

55

Open All Year

### Woodfield House Hotel

HOTEL ★★★ MAP 6 H 7

Ennis Road,
Limerick

Tel: 061-453022 Fax: 061-326755
Email: woodfieldhotel@eircom.net
Web: www.woodfieldhousehotel.com

Enjoy a warm & friendly welcome at our family-run hotel. Situated a short stroll from Limerick City Centre on the upmarket Ennis Rd, close to Thomand Park & adjacent to the Gaelic Grounds. All rooms en suite, free parking. Excellent dining facilities. Range of conference suites available. Public areas and ground floor rooms WiFi enabled. Ideal for visiting all major attractions.

***An IHF Quality Employer***

Member of MinOtel Ireland Hotel Group

*Bookable on www.irelandhotels.com*
*Special Offer: www.irelandhotels.com/offers*

*B&B from €49.00 to €69.00*

*Dermot & Suzanne Fehily*
*Proprietors*

26

Closed 24 - 26 December

### Courtenay Lodge Hotel

HOTEL ★★★ MAP 2 F 6

Newcastle West,
Co. Limerick

Tel: 069-62244 Fax: 069-77184
Email: res@courtenaylodge.iol.ie
Web: www.courtenaylodgehotel.com

A warm welcome awaits you at the Courtenay Lodge Hotel situated on the main Limerick to Killarney Road and only 15 minutes from the picturesque village of Adare. The newly-built, tastefully decorated, en suite rooms complete with TV, direct dial phone, power showers, trouser press, tea/coffee facilities, etc. ensure a level of comfort second to none. The ideal base for touring the Shannon and South West regions and the perfect location for golfers to enjoy some of the most renowned courses.

***An IHF Quality Employer***

*Bookable on www.irelandhotels.com*
*Special Offer: www.irelandhotels.com/offers*

*B&B from €50.00 to €75.00*
*Suites from €150.00 to €170.00*

*Declan O'Grady*
*General Manager*

39

*Activities:*

Closed 24 - 25 December



B&B Rates are per Person Sharing per Night incl. Breakfast. or Room Rates are per Room per Night - **See also Page 8**

## Rathkeale House Hotel

HOTEL ★★★ MAP 6 G 6

Rathkeale,
Co. Limerick

Tel: 069-63333 Fax: 069-63300
Email: info@rathkealehousehotel.ie
Web: www.rathkealehousehotel.ie

Rathkeale House Hotel, located just off the N21 Limerick to Killarney route and 4 miles west of Ireland's prettiest village, Adare. 26 superior en suite rooms, O'Deas Bistro open each evening 6-9.30pm. Chestnut Tree Bar where carvery lunch is available each day. Conference & banqueting facilities for 300 guests. Golf packages a speciality. Local courses, Adare, Adare Manor, Newcastle West (Ardagh), Charleville. Spacious gardens for your relaxation. A warm welcome awaits you. Please enquire about Facilities for Persons with Mobility Impairment.

***An IHF Quality Employer***

*Bookable on www.irelandhotels.com*
*Special Offer: www.irelandhotels.com/offers*

*B&B from €50.00 to €80.00*

*Gerry O'Connor*
*General Manager*

26

*Activities:*

*Closed 25 December*

## Achill Cliff House Hotel

HOTEL ★★★ MAP 9 C 14

Keel,
Achill Island,
Co. Mayo

Tel: 098-43400 Fax: 098-43007
Email: info@achillcliff.com
Web: www.achillcliff.com

New family-run smoke free hotel in a superb location. Keel Beach, ideal for walking is only 2 minutes away. The hotel commanding magnificent views offers excellent home-made food, comfortable accommodation and good value. Fine wines and an extensive breakfast menu are available. All facilities are nearby, fishing, horse riding, golf, walking, painting, photography. The Deserted Village and House of Prayer. There is no nightclub. Check out our website for last minute special offers. RAC Dining Award 2005. Michelin Recommended 2007.

***An IHF Quality Employer***

*Bookable on www.irelandhotels.com*
*Special Offer: www.irelandhotels.com/offers*

*B&B from €40.00 to €80.00*

*Teresa McNamara*
*Proprietor*

10

*Closed 23 -27 December*

## Grays Guest House

GUESTHOUSE ★★★ MAP 9 C 14

Dugort,
Achill Island,
Co. Mayo

Tel: 098-43244

Vi McDowell welcomes you to Grays where you are assured of a restful holiday, with good food, comfort and personal attention. Turf fires and electric blankets. Late dinner is served at 7pm. There are three lounges, colour TV, table tennis room and croquet lawn and swings in an enclosed garden. Art gallery for use of artists staying in guesthouse.

Member of Turasoireacht Acla

*B&B from €50.00 to €55.00*

*Vi McDowell*
*Owner / Manager*

15

*Closed 23 - 30 December*

B&B Rates are per Person Sharing per Night incl. Breakfast.
or Room Rates are per Room per Night - **See also Page 8**

# Achill Island / Ballina

## Ostán Oileán Acla

HOTEL ★★★ MAP 9 C 14

Achill Sound,
Co. Mayo

Tel: 098-45138 Fax: 098-45198
Email: reservations@achillislandhotel.com
Web: www.achillislandhotel.com

Enjoy the panoramic views of Achill Island from our new luxury hotel situated at the gateway to Achill Island. In our elegant Seafood Restaurant choose from a wide range of local produce. Relax and enjoy a drink in our friendly traditional bar. Convenient to 5 Blue Flag beaches, the highest cliffs in Europe, golf courses, pitch and putt course, outdoor activities. A warm friendly welcome awaits you at Ostán Oileán Acla.

*Michael & Una McLoughlin*
*Proprietors*

26

Activities:

Open All Year

## Belleek Castle

HOTEL ★ MAP 10 F 15

Belleek,
Ballina,
Co. Mayo

Tel: 096-22400 Fax: 096-71750
Email: belleekcastlehotel@eircom.net
Web: www.belleekcastle.com

Historic, romantic, set in 1000 acres of woodland on banks of River Moy - wine/dine till midnight - Gourmet organic food enthusiasts welcomed - 'Perchance to Dream' in a four poster. For your added pleasure: tour of 16th century castle armoury, giant fossil exhibits, Spanish Armada Bar, dramatic artefacts and timbers salvaged from Galleons wrecked off the Irish West Coast 1588. Sporting: international surfing, golf, fishing, tennis, riding, ten stables in castle. Please enquire about Facilities for Persons with Mobility Impairment.

*B&B from €75.00 to €130.00*

*Jacqueline Doran*
*Host*

15

Closed 09 January - 25 March

## Downhill House Hotel & Eagles Leisure Club

HOTEL ★★★ MAP 10 F 15

Ballina,
Co. Mayo

Tel: 096-21033 Fax: 096-21338
Email: info@downhillhotel.ie
Web: www.downhillhotel.ie

A privately owned country house hotel, a short walk from shops, bars & restaurants of Ballina Town, offering a perfect blend of olde world charm and new world comfort. This stylish hotel is set in mature tranquil gardens, offering excellent cuisine with superb facilities. Eagles Leisure Club, holder of White Flag incorporates 2 swimming pools, steam room, sauna, jaccuzi & floodlit tennis courts. Conference centre, piano bar (national & international entertainment). 18 hole golf courses nearby. River, lake & deep sea fishing. Freephone 1800-215095 (Ireland only). Please enquire about Facilities for Persons with Mobility Impairment.

Member of D'Arcy Marketing

*Bookable on www.irelandhotels.com*
*Special Offer: www.irelandhotels.com/offers*

*B&B from €88.50 to €107.50*
*Suites from €350.00 to €350.00*

*Rachael Moylett*

60

Activities:

Closed 22 - 27 December



B&B Rates are per Person Sharing per Night incl. Breakfast.
or Room Rates are per Room per Night - **See also Page 8**

## Downhill Inn

HOTEL ★★★ MAP 10 F 15

Sligo Road,
Ballina,
Co. Mayo

Tel: 096-73444 Fax: 096-73411
Email: info@downhillinn.ie
Web: www.downhillinn.com

A family-run 3*** hotel, located 1 mile outside Ballina Town on the main Sligo Road (N59). Contemporary in its design with 45 well-appointed triple rooms. All rooms are en suite with multi-channel TV, hairdryer, tea/coffee facilities and DD phone. The region offers superb fishing on the River Moy, Lough Conn and Killala Bay. An excellent selection of golf courses: Enniscrone, Ballina, Carne, to mention but a few. Special green fees available with our golf packages - see our website. 2 B&B and 1 dinner with 3 golf from €180pps. Enjoy a drink at the bar or a meal in our Terrace Restaurant. Rest assured!

***An IHF Quality Employer***

Member of Holiday Ireland Hotels

*Bookable on www.irelandhotels.com*
*Special Offer: www.irelandhotels.com/offers*

*B&B from €45.00 to €75.00*

*John Raftery / Nicola Moylett*
*Proprietors*

45

Closed 21 - 27 December

## Mount Falcon Country House Hotel

HOTEL ★★★★ MAP 10 F 15

Foxford Road,
Ballina,
Co. Mayo

Tel: 096-74472 Fax: 096-74473
Email: info@mountfalcon.com
Web: www.mountfalcon.com

Mount Falcon Country House Hotel is a de luxe 32 bedroomed 4**** family-run destination located on the west bank of the River Moy between Foxford and Ballina in County Mayo. The hotel facilities include: The first class Kitchen Restaurant, the welcoming "Boathole Bar", 30 self catering luxury suites, 2 miles of private fishing on the River Moy, a leisure centre with a 17m swimming pool, treatment rooms and state of the art conference facilities. Golf and fishing packages available. Please enquire about Facilities for Persons with Mobility Impairment.

Member of Manor House Hotels

*B&B from €90.00 to €110.00*
*Suites from €400.00 to €500.00*

*Alan Maloney*
*Proprietor*

32

*Activities:*

Closed 24 - 26 December

## Ramada Ballina

HOTEL MAP 10 F 15

Old Dublin Road,
Ballina,
Co. Mayo

Tel: 096-23600 Fax: 096-23623
Email: stay@ramadaballina.ie
Web: www.ramadaballina.ie

Built to a 4**** specification. With 87 en suite bedrooms. The Ramada Ballina is minutes from the bustling town centre with all its shops, entertainment, bars and restaurants. Full leisure facilities and spa incl. 20 m pool & gym. Conference facilities from 2 to 550 delegates in 3 state of the art business suites. Ideal hotel for business, leisure and activity breaks with access to fishing, golf, walking, shopping or entertainment. Ramada Ballina, leave the rest to us. Please enquire about Facilities for Persons with Mobility Impairment.

Member of Ramada Group

*B&B from €80.00 to €110.00*
*Suites from €240.00 to €360.00*

*Richard Swarbrick*
*General Manager*

87

Closed 25 - 27 December

# Ballinrobe / Ballycastle / Belmullet

## JJ Gannon's Hotel

HOTEL ★★★ MAP 9 F 12

Main Street,
Ballinrobe (Lake District),
Co. Mayo

Tel: 094-954 1008 Fax: 094-952 0018
Email: info@jjgannons.com
Web: www.jjgannons.com

Situated in the heart of the lake district and built in 1838, Niki & Jay Gannon restored the building (3rd generation) in 2004. At Gannon's, guests enjoy much more than the luxurious accommodation with large bedrooms, boasting stunning balcony views and super-king size beds. A special little place in a special little town. JJ Gannon's is a delicious secret. Great food, warmth and atmosphere hiding in Ireland's own national playground.

Member of Private Ireland

*B&B from €60.00 to €150.00*
*Suites from €150.00 to €220.00*

*Niki & Jay Gannon*
*Proprietors*

11

Closed 25 December

## Stella Maris Country House Hotel

HOTEL ★★★★ MAP 9 E 16

Ballycastle,
Co. Mayo

Tel: 096-43322 Fax: 096-43965
Email: Info@StellaMarisIreland.com
Web: www.StellaMarisIreland.com

Stella Maris Country House Hotel is one of Bridgestone Guide's Top 100 Restaurants in Ireland, the 2006 Georgina Campbell Guide's 'Hideaway of the Year' and Irish Golf Tour Operators Association 'Small Hotel of the Year'. Stella Maris sits majestically on Bunatrahir Bay featuring mesmerizing views of the Atlantic Ocean. It is strategically located between the world-class golf links of Enniscrone and Carne, and is recommended by most travel guides. Please enquire about Facilities for Persons with Mobility Impairment.

Member of Ireland's Blue Book

*Bookable on www.irelandhotels.com*

*B&B from €100.00 to €125.00*

*Frances Kelly / Terence McSweeney*
*Proprietors*

12

Closed 01 October - 24 April

## Sea Rod Inn

GUESTHOUSE ★★ MAP 9 C 16

Doohoma,
Belmullet, Ballina,
Co. Mayo

Tel: 097-86767 Fax: 097-86809
Email: info@thesearodinn.ie
Web: www.thesearodinn.ie

Located on the southern shore of Doohoma Peninsula, The Sea Rod Inn is a fully licensed premises with a beautifully decorated bar and lounge, and nine magnificent bedrooms all of which are en suite with TV and central heating. Tea/coffee making facilities are all available in a separate sitting room, exclusive to guests, where you can enjoy panoramic views of Achill Island and the Atlantic Ocean. Our in-house entertainment during the summer months ensures that parents with young families can have a carefree holiday with no childcare worries.

Member of North & West Coast Links Ireland

*B&B from €30.00 to €40.00*

*Michael & Bernadette Barrett*

9

*Activities:*

Open All Year



B&B Rates are per Person Sharing per Night incl. Breakfast.
or Room Rates are per Room per Night - See also Page 8

## Western Strands Hotel

HOTEL ★ MAP 9 C 16

Main Street,
Belmullet,
Co. Mayo

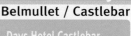

Tel: 097-81096 Fax: 097-81096
Email: reception@westernstrandshotel.com

A small, family-run hotel situated in the centre of Belmullet Town. Easy access to safe, sandy beaches, some with Blue Flag awards. Local amenities include deep sea angling and fresh water fishing, 5 minutes drive to Carne Golf Links, rated No. 5 golf links course in Ireland. Close to U.I.S.C.E, a water sports centre with sailing and surfing, near Aughleim Heritage Centre (archaeology, local history and folklore centre). There are 10 en suite bedrooms with TV and telephone. Also closed Good Friday.

B&B from €35.00 to €35.00

*Emer O'Toole*
*Manager*

10

*Activities:*

Closed 24 - 25 December

## Days Hotel Castlebar

HOTEL ★★★ MAP 9 E 14

Westport Road,
Castlebar,
Co. Mayo

Tel: 1890-329 329 Fax: 094-928 6201
Email: res@dayshotelcastlebar.com
Web: www.dayshotelcastlebar.com

Located in Castlebar Town centre, Days Hotel is a spectacular development, newly opened in November 2006. Located adjacent to the TF Royal Concert & Theatre venue, the hotel offers the ultimate in cool, clean design, with chic décor throughout. 90 stylish bedrooms, all with flat screen TV, ironing station, safe, hairdryer and free broadband. Light, spacious suites with small kitchen and living area. Restaurant and café bar open throughout the day. Host of conference and function rooms with capacity for 150. Car parking available in the adjacent multi storey car park. Hotel direct: 094-928 6200.

Member of Days Hotels Ireland

*Bookable on www.irelandhotels.com*
*Special Offer: www.irelandhotels.com/offers*

Room Rate from €79.00 to €189.00
Suites from €99.00 to €229.00

*Pat & Mary Jennings*
*Owners*

90

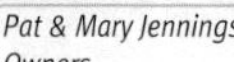

Closed 24 - 26 December

## Castlebar

### Kennys Guest House

GUESTHOUSE ★★★ MAP 9 E 14

Lucan Street,
Castlebar,
Co. Mayo
Tel: 094-902 3091
Email: kennys@castlebar.ie
Web: www.kennysguesthouse.com

Castlebar's only 3 star family-run guesthouse offers luxury and comfort. Decorated and furnished to a very high standard. All rooms are en suite with TV, DD telephone, Wi-Fi and hairdryer. Relax in the residents lounge with complimentary tea/coffee or avail of the numerous facilities nearby e.g. organised walks, fishing, bowling, swimming, golf, fine restaurants and entertainment. Location: town centre. Private car park. Mobile: 087 984 0759. Please enquire about Facilities for Persons with Mobility Impairment.

Bookable on www.irelandhotels.com

B&B from €40.00 to €50.00

*Susanna & Raymond Kenny*

8

Open All Year

### TF Royal Hotel & Theatre

HOTEL ★★★ MAP 9 E 14

Old Westport Road,
Castlebar,
Co. Mayo
Tel: 094-902 3111 Fax: 094-902 3111
Email: info@tfroyalhotel.com
Web: www.tfroyalhotel.com

The TF Royal Hotel & Theatre is a luxury boutique 3*** family hotel adjacent to Castlebar Town centre. Renovation & refurbishment has provided luxurious bedrooms decorated to an excellent standard with air con, security safe, ISDN lines, TV, VCR, trouser press, hairdryer. Executive/master suites & connecting family rooms. Modern conference & theatre facility. Café Bar & Bistro. Tamarind Seed Restaurant. Dedicated business centre. Adjacent to Institute of Technology, Mayo General Hospital, Harlequin Shopping Centre and main shopping. Please enquire about Facilities for Persons with Mobility Impairment.

Member of Countrywide Hotels

Bookable on www.irelandhotels.com

B&B from €65.00 to €85.00

*Pat & Mary Jennings*
*Proprietors*

28

Activities:

Closed 24 - 26 December

B&B Rates are per Person Sharing per Night incl. Breakfast.
or Room Rates are per Room per Night - See also Page 8

## Riverside Guesthouse & Restaurant

GUESTHOUSE ★★ MAP 10 G 14

Church Street,
Charlestown,
Co. Mayo

Tel: 094-925 4200 Fax: 094-925 4207
Email: riversiderestaurant@eircom.net
Web: www.riversiderest.com

Situated on the intersection of N17 & N5 primary routes. 10 minutes to Knock Ireland West International Airport, 20 minutes to Knock Shrine. Ideal base for touring Mayo, Sligo, Roscommon and Galway. A charming family-run guesthouse with all rooms en suite and with TV. Modern Irish food served and prepared in our Olde World restaurant by award-winning chef/owner Anthony Kelly and his wife Anne. Special restaurant licence to serve all alcohol to diners. A warm Irish welcome awaits you.

Member of Countrywide Hotels

*B&B from €39.00 to €43.00*

*Anthony & Anne Kelly*
*Proprietors*

8

2

Closed 24 - 27 December

## McWilliam Park Hotel (The)

HOTEL ★★★★ MAP 10 F 13

Knock Road,
Claremorris,
Co. Mayo

Tel: 094-937 3333 Fax: 094-937 3631
Email: info@mcwilliamparkhotel.ie
Web: www.mcwilliamparkhotel.ie

This Best Western premier 4**** hotel is superbly located in the heart of the West, halfway between Galway & Sligo on the N17, Ireland West Airport Knock 19 minutes drive, Knock Shrine 10 minutes, situated on direct rails & bus routes. A 30 minute drive from the rugged Atlantic coastline surrounded by plains, rivers, lakes & golf courses with a backdrop of Croagh Patrick & the Partry mountains. This luxurious four star hotel is equipped with state of the art leisure centre & health & beauty studios to make The McWilliam Park a unique location for retreat, business or pleasure. "A haven of tranquillity".

Member of Best Western

*Bookable on www.irelandhotels.com*
*Special Offer: www.irelandhotels.com/offers*

*B&B from €85.00 to €130.00*
*Suites from €210.00 to €300.00*

*Fergal Ryan*
*General Manager*

103

Activities:

Open All Year

## Ashford Castle

HOTEL ★★★★★ MAP 9 E 12

Cong,
Co. Mayo

Tel: 094-954 6003 Fax: 094-954 6260
Email: ashford@ashford.ie
Web: www.ashford.ie

13th Century Castle located 40 minutes from Galway City. Once the estate of Lord Ardilaun and the Guinness Family. Ashford Castle opened as a luxury hotel in 1939. 83 guest rooms are of the highest standards with incredible lake or river views. We offer 9 hole golf and tennis complimentary to residents. Our activities include archery, clay pigeon, fishing, horseback riding, cruising on the lake and falconry. Our Health Centre comprises: sauna, jacuzzi, steam room, gym area and treatment rooms. Various suites and staterooms available. Email enquiries to reservations@ashford.ie.

***An IHF Quality Employer***

Member of The Leading Small Hotels of the World

*Bookable on www.irelandhotels.com*

*Room Rate from €244.00 to €590.00*
*Suites from €522.00 to €1,187.00*

*Niall Rochford*
*General Manager*

83

Activities:

Open All Year

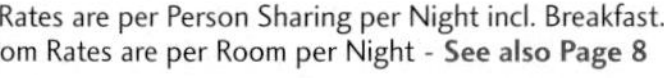
B&B Rates are per Person Sharing per Night incl. Breakfast.
or Room Rates are per Room per Night - **See also Page 8**

## Cong / Kiltimagh

### Lydons Lodge Hotel

HOTEL ★★ MAP 9 E 12

Cong,
Co. Mayo

Tel: 094-954 6053 Fax: 094-954 6523
Email: lydonslodge@eircom.net

Lydons Lodge combines the most modern amenities with old world charm. Located in Cong, village of 'Quiet Man' film fame it offers salmon, pike and famous Lough Corrib wild brown trout fishing. Boats, engines and boatmen can be arranged. Choice of 3 local golf clubs, horse riding and tennis. Minutes' walk from Ashford Castle and gardens. Hill walks and mountain climbing with spectacular lake views, an archaeological and geological paradise. Traditional music and bar food.

B&B from €35.00 to €60.00

*Frank & Carmel Lydon*
*Owners*

11

Closed 01 December - 01 February

### Michaeleen's Manor

GUESTHOUSE ★★★ MAP 9 E 12

Lisloughrey,
Quay Road,
Cong, Co. Mayo

Tel: 094-954 6089 Fax: 094-954 6448
Email: info@quietman-cong.com
Web: www.quietman-cong.com

Guesthouse themed on Quiet Man Film in the heart of Quiet Man Country. Promising a unique experience for all Quiet Man enthusiasts with TV, DVD, hot tub, sauna, tennis court. Located only 1/2 mile from Lough Corrib which is a fisherman's paradise. Historical sites, monuments, forest walks, hill climbing. One of the most central guesthouses for touring Connemara, Galway, Westport, Achill Island, The Aran Islands. Also mini-golf and falconry. Cong once seen is never forgotten. Please enquire about Facilities for Persons with Mobility Impairment.

B&B from €35.00 to €65.00

*Margaret Collins*
*Owner / Manager*

11

Open All Year

### Cill Aodain Hotel

HOTEL ★★★ MAP 10 F 14

Main Street,
Kiltimagh,
Co. Mayo

Tel: 094-938 1761 Fax: 094-938 1838
Email: info@cillaodain.ie
Web: www.cillaodainhotel.com

The newly refurbished 3*** Cill Aodain Court Hotel has a number of excellent facilities for your pleasure. Our renowned bistro serves continental & country cuisine sourced locally. Our Court Bar has open fires and a welcoming atmosphere. Our spacious en suite bedrooms have all the modern facilities you should expect. We are situated only 20 kms from Ireland West Airport Knock, making us an ideal base in which to explore the local amenities (including the Knock Marian Shrine) in Co. Mayo. Our friendly staff are waiting to make your stay a home from home experience.

Member of Irish Country Hotels

B&B from €55.00 to €80.00

*Mary Halligan*
*Director*

17

Closed 24 - 26 December



B&B Rates are per Person Sharing per Night incl. Breakfast. or Room Rates are per Room per Night - **See also Page 8**

## Park Hotel Kiltimagh

HOTEL ★★★ MAP 10 F 14

Swinford Road,
Kiltimagh,
Mayo

Tel: 094-937 4922 Fax: 094-937 4924
Email: info@parkhotelmayo.com
Web: www.parkhotelmayo.com

Our newly built Park Hotel Kiltimagh is located in east Mayo 15 minutes from Ireland West Airport Knock, situated adjacent to the local wildlife park and a few minutes walk from the town centre. The hotel is an ideal base for touring the west. Enjoy our individually decorated de luxe or executive rooms, full fitness centre and state of the art wellness centre. Relax in our comfortable lobby or dine in our café bar or à la carte restaurant. Member of Signature Park Hotels. Please enquire about Facilities for Persons with Mobility Impairment.

Member of Irish Country Hotels

*B&B from €50.00 to €90.00*
*Suites from €85.00 to €135.00*

*Noel Lafferty*
*Manager*

46

*Activities:*

Closed 24 - 27 December

## Belmont Hotel

HOTEL ★★★ MAP 10 G 13

Knock,
Co. Mayo

Tel: 094-938 8122 Fax: 094-938 8532
Email: reception@belmonthotel.ie
Web: www.belmonthotel.ie

A haven of hospitality nestled at the rear entrance to Knock Shrine off N17. The hotel radiates old country warmth from the moment you arrive. RAC 3***, Failte Ireland 3*** and AA 3*** status. Daily carvery and sumptuous bar food menu complement our award-winning Bialann Restaurant. Our specially developed Natural Health Therapy packages are very professional and attractive. Tastefully furnished bedrooms with facilities. Please enquire about Facilities for Persons with Mobility Impairment.

*Bookable on www.irelandhotels.com*
*Special Offer: www.irelandhotels.com/offers*

*B&B from €55.00 to €80.00*
*Suites from €130.00 to €160.00*

*Evelyn Fleming*
*Manager*

62

*Activities:*

Closed 24-26 December

## Knock House Hotel

HOTEL ★★★ MAP 10 G 13

Ballyhaunis Road,
Knock,
Co. Mayo

Tel: 094-938 8088 Fax: 094-938 8044
Email: info@knockhousehotel.ie
Web: www.knockhousehotel.ie

Located in over 100 acres of parkland and nestling behind the Basilica, this 8 year old hotel is a gem! With 68 comfortable bedrooms, of which 6 are designed for wheelchair users, every need is catered for. The superb Four Seasons Restaurant - open all day - and the glazed reception and lounge areas, surrounded by local limestone, overlook countryside. This well run, tranquil hotel will be hard to leave. Please enquire about Facilities for Persons with Mobility Impairment.

***An IHF Quality Employer***

*Bookable on www.irelandhotels.com*

*B&B from €58.00 to €80.00*

*Brian Crowley*
*General Manager*

68

*Activities:*

Open All Year

B&B Rates are per Person Sharing per Night incl. Breakfast.
or Room Rates are per Room per Night - **See also Page 8**

# Mulranny / Newport / Pontoon

## Park Inn Mulranny

HOTEL ★★★★ MAP 9 D 14

Mulranny,
Westport,
Co. Mayo

Tel: 098-36000 Fax: 098-36899

Email: info@parkinnmulranny.ie

Web: www.parkinnmulranny.ie

A stunning hotel on a unique site, overlooking Clew Bay on 42 acres of woodland. All rooms have spectacular sea or woodland views. Its original character and charm has been retained, with the elegant Nephin Restaurant, lively Waterfront Bar and relaxing lounge. Extensive conference facilities are available. Complimentary use of leisure facilities for all our guests. Excellent midweek breaks available. For further details on this unique hotel, call 098-36000. Reservations 1850 33 6000. Please enquire about Facilities for Persons with Mobility Impairment.

Member of Rezidor SAS

*Bookable on www.irelandhotels.com*
*Special Offer: www.irelandhotels.com/offers*

*B&B from €75.00 to €120.00*

*Stephen O'Connor*
*General Manager*

41

*Activities:*

Closed 24 - 26 December

## Hotel Newport

HOTEL ★★★ MAP 9 E 14

Main Street,
Newport,
Co. Mayo

Tel: 098-41155 Fax: 098-42548

Email: info@hotelnewportmayo.com

Web: www.hotelnewportmayo.com

Hotel Newport is located in the picturesque town of Newport, Co. Mayo. It's central location means guests are within easy reach of all regional towns and golf courses in Mayo. Our hotel has 30 bedrooms all of which are completed to the highest possible standards. Our Inish Kee Restaurant boasts a choice of menus, while the Seven Arches Bar is the place to relax and enjoy the craic. Newport is located approx. 15 mins drive from Castlebar and Westport is only 20 mins from Mulranny. The area is known for its scenic walks and great golf courses.

*B&B from €50.00 to €75.00*
*Suites from €150.00 to €180.00*

30

Closed 25 December

## Healys Restaurant & Country House

HOTEL ★★ MAP 9 F 14

Pontoon,
Foxford,
Co. Mayo

Tel: 094-925 6443 Fax: 094-925 6572

Email: info@healyspontoon.com

Web: www.healyspontoon.com

Boutique Country House located on the shores of Loughs Conn & Cullin set in the heart of Mayo's best golf & fishing region. Dining room & restaurant serving award-winning food & a selection of 80 wines. Hotel bar open to all. Accreditations; AA rosette for cuisine, Georgina Campbell Guide, Trout & Salmon magazine, Dining Pub of the Year - 6 consecutive years, Féile Bia, Great Fishing Houses of Ireland, Hooked on the Moy, Ireland West & many more. Golf & fishing can be arranged. 5 mins to R. Moy, world renowned for salmon fishing. 30 mins from Enniscrone Golf links & Westport GC. Horse riding/scenic walks close by.

Member of Great Fishing Houses of Ireland

*B&B from €45.00 to €65.00*

*John Dever & Josette Maurer*
*Proprietors*

14

*Activities:*

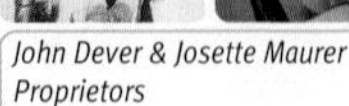

Closed 25 - 26 December



B&B Rates are per Person Sharing per Night incl. Breakfast. or Room Rates are per Room per Night - See also Page 8

## Pontoon / Swinford / Westport

### Pontoon Bridge Hotel

HOTEL ★★★ MAP 10 F 14

Pontoon,
Foxford,
Co. Mayo

Tel: 094-925 6120 Fax: 094-925 6688
Email: relax@pontoonbridge.com
Web: www.pontoonbridge.com

Family managed hotel on the shores of Lough Conn & Cullin in the centre of Mayo. Famous trout & salmon fishing - Rr. Moy, golf, horse riding, scenery, central for touring. Twin Lakes Restaurant boasts the best food in Mayo. Geary's Waterfront Bar & Bistro with seasonal live music. Two panoramic restaurants on water's edge. Tennis court, sandy beaches, archery school locally, conference facilities. Families welcome. School of fly fishing, landscape painting & cookery. Friendly welcome. Hot tub, sauna, treatment rooms & small gym. Wonderful lake-view suites. Member of Select Hotels. See you soon in Pontoon!

Member of Great Fishing Houses of Ireland

*Bookable on www.irelandhotels.com*
*Special Offer: www.irelandhotels.com/offers*

*B&B from €75.00 to €160.00*
*Suites from €250.00 to €300.00*

*Breeta Geary*
*General Manager*

58

*Activities:*

Closed 24 - 26 December

### Kelly's Gateway Hotel

HOTEL ★★★ MAP 10 G 14

Main Street,
Swinford,
Co. Mayo

Tel: 094-925 2156 Fax: 094-925 1328
Email: info@gatewayswinford.com
Web: www.gatewayswinford.com

Situated in the bustling town of Swinford, Kelly's Gateway Hotel is a stylish and modern hotel, perfect for a relaxing break. In the heart of Mayo, it is the ideal gateway to the West. Only 15 mins from Ireland West Airport Knock. Swinford is renowned for its fishing waters, as it is located beside the famous River Moy and the Callow Lakes. It is also within travelling distance of many of Ireland's leading golf courses. Please enquire about Facilities for Persons with Mobility Impairment.

*B&B from €45.00 to €75.00*

*Cathal Kelly*
*Proprietor*

22

*Activities:*

Closed 25 - 26 Decmeber

### Ardmore Country House Hotel and Restaurant

HOTEL ★★★★ MAP 9 E 13

The Quay,
Westport,
Co. Mayo

Tel: 098-25994 Fax: 098-27795
Email: ardmorehotel@eircom.net
Web: www.ardmorecountryhouse.com

Ardmore House is a small exclusive 4**** boutique hotel offering individual style, superb cuisine and the highest level of personal service. Idyllically situated overlooking Clew Bay with breathtaking sunsets in the shadow of Croagh Patrick. A perfect home from home. All 13 bedrooms are non-smoking.

*B&B from €85.00 to €120.00*

*Noreen & Pat Hoban*

13

Closed 20 December - 14 Februrary

B&B Rates are per Person Sharing per Night incl. Breakfast.
or Room Rates are per Room per Night - See also Page 8

## Westport

### Augusta Lodge

GUESTHOUSE ★★★ MAP 9 E 13

Golf Links Road,
Westport,
Co. Mayo

Tel: 098-28900 Fax: 098-28995

Email: info@augustalodge.ie

Web: www.augustalodge.ie

Augusta Lodge is a purpose built 3*** guesthouse situated in Westport. A warm and friendly welcome awaits you in this family-run guesthouse and Liz and Dave will ensure that your stay is a memorable one. A golfer's haven with tee times and green fees arranged at Westport and adjacent courses. All-weather synthetic putting green on-site for guests' use. Listed in all leading guides.

*Bookable on www.irelandhotels.com*
*Special Offer: www.irelandhotels.com/offers*

*B&B from €35.00 to €50.00*

*Liz O'Regan*

10

Closed 23 - 27 December

### Boffin Lodge

GUESTHOUSE ★★★ MAP 9 E 13

The Quay,
Westport,
Co. Mayo

Tel: 098-26092 Fax: 098-28690

Email: pa@achh.iol.ie

Web: www.boffinlodge.com

Boffin Lodge was purpose built in 1999. It is located very close to the fashionable quay area of Westport where many of the town's best hotels, restaurants and pubs are located. Boffin Lodge has many special features such as a four poster room, a bedroom with a steam room and another with a jet stream bath. Our breakfast menu is extensive and can be seen on www.boffinlodge.com. We look forward to meeting you.

*Bookable on www.irelandhotels.com*
*Special Offer: www.irelandhotels.com/offers*

*B&B from €40.00 to €55.00*

*Patrick Aylward*
*Proprietor*

10

Closed 22-27 December

### Carlton Atlantic Coast Hotel

HOTEL ★★★★ MAP 9 E 13

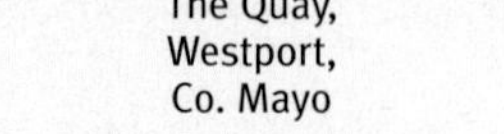

The Quay,
Westport,
Co. Mayo

Tel: 098-29000 Fax: 098-29111

Email: info@atlanticcoasthotel.com

Web: www.atlanticcoasthotel.com

Established as one of Westport's finest & most popular hotels, on the waterfront at Westport Quay overlooking Clew Bay. Superb contemporary cuisine in our unique top floor award-winning Blue Wave Restaurant. The Aqua Club features pool, gym, sauna, steam room and Float & Light Therapy treatment. The new C Spa with 9 treatments rooms offers an extensive range of therapies & treatments. Championship golf, angling, scenic walks, island trips & Blue Flag beaches nearby. Mark of Best Practice '07 - '08. Please enquire about Facilities for Persons with Mobility Impairment.

***An IHF Quality Employer***

Member of Carlton Hotel Group

*Bookable on www.irelandhotels.com*
*Special Offer: www.irelandhotels.com/offers*

*B&B from €70.00 to €135.00*
*Suites from €180.00 to €310.00*

*Lynda Foley*
*General Manager*

85

*Activities:*

Closed 20 - 27 December



B&B Rates are per Person Sharing per Night incl. Breakfast. or Room Rates are per Room per Night - See also Page 8

## Castlecourt Hotel Conference and Leisure Centre

HOTEL ★★★ MAP 9 E 13

Castlebar Street,
Westport,
Co. Mayo

Tel: 098-55088 Fax: 098-28622
Email: info@castlecourthotel.ie
Web: www.castlecourthotel.ie

This stunning family hotel is now one of the largest leisure hotels in the West of Ireland. It offers guests indoor heated swimming pool, spa jacuzzi, sauna, steam room, children's pool, hairdressing salon, beautician and health suites for aromatherapy and massage. Additional choice of restaurants and bars in adjoining Westport Plaza Hotel. Spa opening Spring 2008. A short stay with us and you will soon see why we are so famously known for our warm and welcoming atmosphere!! Please enquire about Facilities for Persons with Mobility Impairment.

***An IHF Quality Employer***

Bookable on www.irelandhotels.com
Special Offer: www.irelandhotels.com/offers

B&B from €45.00 to €119.00
Suites from €130.00 to €340.00

*Anne Corcoran / Joseph Corcoran*
*Managers*

148

*Activities:*

Closed 24 - 26 December

## Clew Bay Hotel

HOTEL ★★★ MAP 9 E 13

James Street,
Westport,
Co. Mayo

Tel: 098-28088 Fax: 098-25783
Email: info@clewbayhotel.com
Web: www.clewbayhotel.com

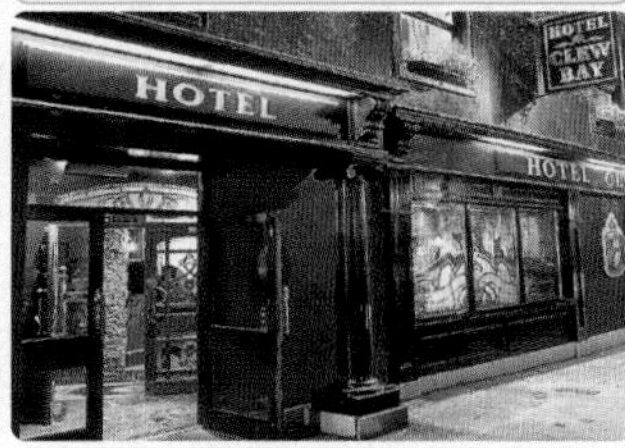


Our newly refurbished hotel is located in the heart of Westport Town. This family-run hotel offers a warm welcome to all our guests. Renowned for good food whether you choose to dine in our bistro or Riverside Restaurant. Our popular new bar features music regularly. Guests can enjoy free access to Westport Leisure Park. The hotel is ideally located for exploring the stunning sites of the West. Please enquire about Facilities for Persons with Mobility Impairment.

***An IHF Quality Employer***
Member of Irish Country Hotels

Bookable on www.irelandhotels.com
Special Offer: www.irelandhotels.com/offers

B&B from €50.00 to €120.00

*Maria Ruddy & Darren Madden*
*Proprietors*

40

*Activities:*

Closed 22 - 28 December

B&B Rates are per Person Sharing per Night incl. Breakfast.
or Room Rates are per Room per Night - **See also Page 8**

## Westport

### Hotel Westport leisure - spa - conference

HOTEL ★★★ MAP 9 E 13

Newport Road,
Westport,
Co. Mayo

Tel: 098-25122 Fax: 098-26739
Email: reservations@hotelwestport.ie
Web: www.hotelwestport.ie

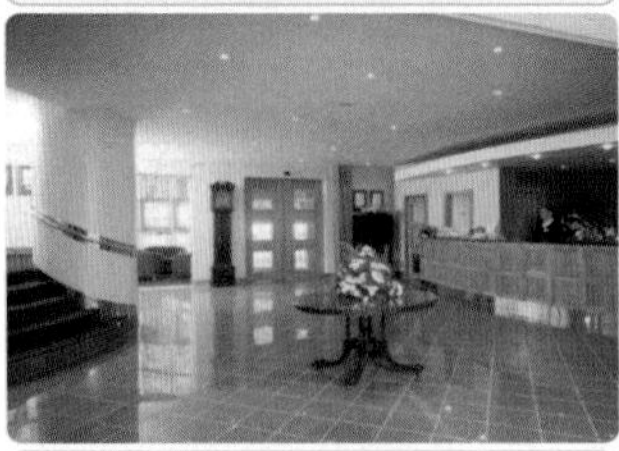

Set in private woodlands and just a short river walk into Westport, this Award-Winning Hotel is a place to truly pamper yourself! Facilities include: Westport's Premier Ocean Spirit Spa & Leisure, Islands Restaurant, Maple Bar, Patio Gardens, outdoor children's play area and much more. A variety of Theme and Leisure holidays are available: Bridge, Bowling, Golf and Murder Mystery! Family holidays with children's 'Panda Club', seasonal. "One of Ireland's best loved hotels!" Locall Reservations (RoI) 1850 53 63 73 (NI/UK) 0870 876 54 32. Please enquire about Facilities for Persons with Mobility Impairment.

***An IHF Quality Employer***

Bookable on www.irelandhotels.com
Special Offer: www.irelandhotels.com/offers

B&B from €55.00 to €140.00
Suites from €175.00 to €345.00

*Gerry Walshe*
*General Manager*

129

Activities:

Open All Year

### Knockranny House Hotel & Spa

HOTEL ★★★★ MAP 9 E 13

Westport,
Co. Mayo

Tel: 098-28600 Fax: 098-28611
Email: info@khh.ie
Web: www.khh.ie

Spectacular views of Croagh Patrick and Clew Bay combine with open log fires, antique furniture and classical music to create a warm and relaxed atmosphere at one of Ireland's premier luxury properties. The recently opened new rooms and suites are beautifully designed and offer facilities and space above and beyond that of many five star hotel rooms in Ireland. Among its wide range of facilities, the spectacular Spa Salveo features a wonderful vitality pool, expansive thermal spa suites and twelve spacious treatment rooms. Please enquire about Facilities for Persons with Mobility Impairment.

***An IHF Quality Employer***

Member of Manor House Hotels

Bookable on www.irelandhotels.com
Special Offer: www.irelandhotels.com/offers

B&B from €70.00 to €145.00
Suites from €170.00 to €350.00

*Geraldine & Adrian Noonan*
*Proprietors*

97

Activities:

Closed 24 - 26 December

### Knockranny Lodge

GUESTHOUSE ★★★★ MAP 9 E 13

Knockranny,
Westport,
Co. Mayo

Tel: 098-28595 Fax: 098-28805
Email: info@knockrannylodge.ie
Web: www.knockrannylodge.ie

Perched on an elevated position overlooking the town of Westport, Croagh Patrick and the island-studded waters of Clew Bay, Knockranny Lodge is Mayo's only 4 star guesthouse. All rooms are designed to a luxury hotel standard with pressure jet shower, TV, trouser press and hairdryer. De luxe rooms available. We are the only guesthouse or bed and breakfast in the area to offer free use of Westport's award-winning leisure centre, the C-Club Leisure Centre located in the Castlecourt Hotel. Discounted rates for dinner in two sister hotels. Please enquire about Facilities for Persons with Mobility Impairment.

Bookable on www.irelandhotels.com
Special Offer: www.irelandhotels.com/offers

B&B from €40.00 to €65.00

*Mary McDermott*

16

Closed 01 December - 30 January

B&B Rates are per Person Sharing per Night incl. Breakfast.
or Room Rates are per Room per Night - **See also Page 8**

## Westport Inn Hotel

HOTEL ★★ MAP 9 E 13

Town Centre,
Mill Street, Westport,
Co. Mayo

Tel: 098-29200 Fax: 098-29250
Email: info@westportinn.ie
Web: www.westportinn.ie

The Westport Inn Hotel is a boutique hotel ideally situated in the heart of Westport where the visitor can immerse themselves in all of the amenities that the town has to offer. The hotel boasts beautifully appointed bedrooms, a charming lounge, quality restaurant and a lively bar. The Westport Inn Hotel prides itself on high customer service standards, quality accommodation, fine food and entertainment. Relax, unwind and enjoy a warm and friendly atmosphere at this charming hotel. Please enquire about Facilities for Persons with Mobility Impairment.

*Bookable on www.irelandhotels.com*
*Special Offer: www.irelandhotels.com/offers*

*B&B from €39.00 to €105.00*
*Suites from €130.00 to €280.00*

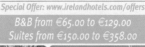

*Stephen Barry*
*General Manager*

34

Closed 24 - 26 December

## Westport Plaza Hotel

HOTEL ★★★★ MAP 9 E 13

Castlebar Street,
Westport,
Co. Mayo

Tel: 098-51166 Fax: 098-51133
Email: info@westportplazahotel.ie
Web: www.westportplazahotel.ie

Step into the Westport Plaza Hotel and the world outside will seem far away. A fusion of contemporary chic and classic elegance awaits as you relax and unwind in ultimate luxury. Will it be an Indian head massage, sophisticated dining at the Restaurant Merlot or a peaceful night in one of luxurious suites. Just across the courtyard, in our resort leisure centre, you'll find a range of facilities to help you unwind including a health suite for aromatherapy and massage and a hair dressing salon. Our Resort Spa is due to open in Spring 2008. Please enquire about Facilities for Persons with Mobility Impairment.

*Bookable on www.irelandhotels.com*
*Special Offer: www.irelandhotels.com/offers*

*B&B from €65.00 to €129.00*
*Suites from €150.00 to €358.00*

*Anne Corcoran, Joseph Corcoran*

88

*Activities:*

Closed 24 - 26 December

## Westport Woods Hotel & Spa

HOTEL ★★★ MAP 9 E 13

Quay Road,
Westport,
Co. Mayo

Tel: 098-25811 Fax: 098-26212
Email: info@westportwoodshotel.com
Web: www.westportwoodshotel.com

The hotel is conveniently located between the charming town of Westport and the quay, nestled in mature woodlands. We have a delightful lakeview restaurant, leisure centre, spa, bench café bar and a horse riding centre. Your holiday can be as eventful as you wish, with our get!together! co-ordinators who organise a diverse range of activities. Enjoy unforgettable family holidays with our go!kids! club. Please enquire about Facilities for Persons with Mobility Impairment.

***An IHF Quality Employer***
Member of Brian McEniff Hotels

*Bookable on www.irelandhotels.com*
*Special Offer: www.irelandhotels.com/offers*

*B&B from €65.00 to €110.00*
*Suites from €170.00 to €270.00*

*Michael Lennon & Joanne McEniff*
*Management Team*

111

*Activities:*

Open All Year

B&B Rates are per Person Sharing per Night incl. Breakfast.
or Room Rates are per Room per Night - **See also Page 8**

# Westport / Ballaghaderreen / Ballinlough

## Wyatt Hotel

HOTEL ★★★ MAP 9 E 13

The Octagon,
Westport,
Co. Mayo

Tel: 098-25027 Fax: 098-26316

Email: info@wyattehotel.com

Web: www.wyatthotel.com

The award-winning Wyatt Hotel is a stunning boutique style hotel, commanding one of the finest locations in the heart of Westport. The Wyatt is renowned for its friendly efficient service, superb cuisine and relaxing ambience. Croagh Patrick, Westport Leisure Park, Blue Flag beaches, golf, islands, scenic drives, lively bars and restaurants, whether for business or leisure, The Wyatt Hotel is your perfect Westport base. FREEPHONE 1800 205270.

Member of Select Hotels of Ireland

*Bookable on www.irelandhotels.com*

*Special Offer: www.irelandhotels.com/offers*

*B&B from €59.00 to €120.00*
*Suites from €179.00 to €300.00*

*Chris McGauley*
*General Manager*

52

*Activities:*

Closed 24 - 26 December

## Abbeyfield Hotel Conference and Leisure Centre

HOTEL MAP 10 H 14

Sligo Road,
Ballaghaderreen,
Co. Roscommon

Tel: 094-986 2736 Fax: 094-986 2738

Email: info@abbeyfieldhotel.ie

Web: www.abbeyfieldhotel.ie

UNDER CONSTRUCTION - OPENING APRIL 2008

Built to a 4**** specification. Luxurious 70 bedroom hotel located on mature grounds once the setting of the bishops palace, the hotel is situated in the cathedral town of Ballaghaderreen, historically know as the gateway to the west. The hotel boasts a selection of superior executive & family suites, conference rooms, leisure & spa facilities including swimming pool, fitness club, spa bath & treatment rooms. Ideally located 15 minutes drive from Ireland West Airport Knock. Golf, angling & horse racing nearby. Please enquire about Facilities for Persons with Mobility Impairment.

*B&B from €65.00 to €160.00*

*Martin Carty*
*Managing Director*

70

Open All Year

## Whitehouse Hotel

HOTEL ★★★ MAP 10 H 13

Ballinlough,
Co. Roscommon

Tel: 094-964 0112 Fax: 094-964 0993

Email: thewhitehousehotel@eircom.net

Web: www.white-house-hotel.com

Located on the Roscommon Mayo border stands the luxurious Whitehouse Hotel. Enjoy our lunchtime carvery in the bar whilst our Blue Room Restaurant offers the finest in contemporary and traditional cuisine. Frequent live music and traditional sessions throughout the year add to the ambience of this unique hotel. The hotel is just a short drive from Lough O'Flynn and within 6 miles of Ballyhaunis and Castlerea Golf Clubs.

*Bookable on www.irelandhotels.com*

*B&B from €49.50 to €60.00*
*Suites from €135.00 to €165.00*

*Olivia Mc Dermott*
*General Manager*

19

*Activities:*

Closed 25 December



B&B Rates are per Person Sharing per Night incl. Breakfast. or Room Rates are per Room per Night - **See also Page 8**

## Royal Hotel

HOTEL ★★ MAP 10 I 14

Bridge Street,
Boyle,
Co. Roscommon

Tel: 071-966 2016 Fax: 071-966 4949

Email: royalhotelboyle@hotmail.com

Est. 1782, The Royal is one of Irelands historic purpose built continuously run family Hotels. 16 refurbished en suites and dining room. Situated literally on the Boyle River, in the Heritage Town of Boyle. The 12th century Abbey, Lough Key, castles and islands, make this a dream location for fishermen to fish from the balcony of their bedrooms. Excellent home cooked food served all day, carvery lunch 7 days, car park. Please enquire about Facilities for Persons with Mobility Impairment.

B&B from €45.00 to €65.00

*Shirley Regan*
*Proprietor*

16

Activities:

Closed 25 - 27 December

## Abbey Hotel, Conference and Leisure Centre

HOTEL ★★★★ MAP 10 I 12

Galway Road,
Roscommon Town

Tel: 090-666 6200 Fax: 090-662 6021

Email: info@abbeyhotel.ie

Web: www.abbeyhotel.ie

Charming 18th century Manor House Hotel set in picturesque private grounds. The 'Abbey' is the perfect choice for business or pleasure. Our facilities include 50 spacious bedrooms including our Manor Suites. Visit our award-winning leisure club with 20m pool, gymnasium and therapy room. Our conference suites will cater for groups of 2 - 200 people. Relax and dine in our restaurant where casual elegance meets a timeless relaxed atmosphere. Please enquire about Facilities for Persons with Mobility Impairment.

Member of Irish Country Hotels

*Bookable on www.irelandhotels.com*
*Special Offer: www.irelandhotels.com/offers*

B&B from €55.00 to €140.00

*Tom Grealy*
*Operations Manager*

50

Activities:

Closed 24 - 26 December

## Gleesons Townhouse & Restaurant

GUESTHOUSE ★★★ MAP 10 I 12

Market Square,
Roscommon Town,
Co. Roscommon

Tel: 090-662 6954 Fax: 090-662 7425

Email: info@gleesonstownhouse.com

Web: www.gleesonstownhouse.com

Gleesons is ideally located inn the centre of Roscommon, overlooking the town's historic square. If you are seeking comfort, value for money & superb home-cooking & baking, this is the place. Eamonn & Mary Gleeson have lovingly restored their listed 19th century townhouse to a very high standard. The combination of superbly appointed rooms, suites, café, fully licensed restaurant, private car park, meeting rooms, complimentary broadband access mixed in with the Gleeson's charming hospitality creates a relaxed buzz. Member of AA, Good Food Ireland, Premier Guesthouses of Ireland.

***An IHF Quality Employer***

Member of Good Food Ireland

*Bookable on www.irelandhotels.com*
*Special Offer: www.irelandhotels.com/offers*

B&B from €60.00 to €80.00
Suites from €160.00 to €195.00

*Mary & Eamonn Gleeson*
*Proprietors*

19

Activities:

Closed 25 - 26 December

B&B Rates are per Person Sharing per Night incl. Breakfast.
or Room Rates are per Room per Night - **See also Page 8**

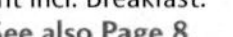

## Roscommon Town / Ballintogher / Ballygawley

### O'Gara's Royal Hotel

HOTEL ★★ MAP 10 I 12

Castle Street,
Roscommon Town

Tel: 090-662 6317 Fax: 090-662 6225
Email: royalhotelros@eircom.net
Web: www.ogarasroyalhotel.com

O'Gara's Royal Hotel family-run, situated on the Dublin to Castlebar/Westport route. 19 bedrooms en suite, radio, direct dial phone, TV, video, hairdryer, ironing and tea/coffee facilities. Comfortable modern dining room with good food and friendly service. Coffee dock/carvery. Spacious lounge bar with pleasant surroundings. Private car park. A warm welcome awaits you. 3 new conference rooms are available, catering for up to 500 people, fully equipped with the latest facilities. Golfing holidays a speciality with a number of top golf courses locally. Please enquire about Facilities for Persons with Mobility Impairment.

*Bookable on www.irelandhotels.com*
*Special Offer: www.irelandhotels.com/offers*

*B&B from €45.00 to €65.00*

*Aileen & Larry O'Gara*
*Proprietors*

19

*Activities:*

Closed 25 December & Good Friday

### Kingsfort Country House

GUESTHOUSE MAP 10 H 15

Ballintogher,
Co. Sligo

Tel: 071-911 5111 Fax: 071-911 5979
Email: info@kingsfortcountryhouse.com
Web: www.kingsfortcountryhouse.com

Built to a 4**** specification. Located in the quaint and scenic village of Ballintogher, Kingsfort Country House is a peaceful and relaxing haven 15 minutes from the town of Sligo. This recently refurbished 18th century house is your ideal base for visiting the North West of Ireland. All of our rooms are to the highest standards and all requirements are catered for. Close to 5 golf courses, fishing spots and lovely walks. Please enquire about Facilities for Persons with Mobility Impairment.

Member of Private Ireland

*Bookable on www.irelandhotels.com*
*Special Offer: www.irelandhotels.com/offers*

*B&B from €50.00 to €110.00*

*Bernard Eucher-Lahon*
*Proprietor*

8

*Activities:*

Closed 04 November - 13 March

### Castle Dargan Golf Hotel Wellness

HOTEL ★★★★ MAP 10 H 15

Ballygawley,
Co. Sligo

Tel: 071-911 8080 Fax: 071-911 8090
Email: info@castledargan.com
Web: www.castledargan.com

Combining timeless opulence with a rich and romantic heritage to offer an unrivalled resort experience. The Edwardian House and crumbling Castle ruins stand testament to the wonderful sense of history that still lives in what is now a modern contemporary retreat for the discerning traveller. Presenting exquisite cuisine, accommodation and ambience. The Darren Clarke designed Golf Course is incredible with Icon the destination Medi Spa; luxury abounds at Castle Dargan. Please enquire about Facilities for Persons with Mobility Impairment.

*Bookable on www.irelandhotels.com*
*Special Offer: www.irelandhotels.com/offers*

*B&B from €80.00 to €150.00*
*Suites from €230.00 to €400.00*

*Noel Conlon*
*General Manager*

22

*Activities:*

Closed 24 - 26 December

B&B Rates are per Person Sharing per Night incl. Breakfast. or Room Rates are per Room per Night - See also Page 8

## Castlebaldwin / Collooney / Curry

### Cromleach Lodge Country House

HOTEL ★★★★ MAP 10 H 15

Castlebaldwin,
Via Boyle,
Co. Sligo

Tel: 071-916 5155 Fax: 071-916 5455
Email: info@cromleach.com
Web: www.cromleach.com

"Hideaway of the Year 2004" - Cromleach Lodge is set in the quiet hills above Lough Arrow. All rooms & suites are exceptionally spacious and well appointed. For a quiet weekend or an exclusive destination wedding the atmosphere is warm and relaxed. Cromleach Lodge's piece de resistance is its restaurant, where dishes created by Moira, "Irish Chef of the Year 2000" and her team are a gastronomic delight. The perfect haven in which to explore the natural beauty of the North West. Cromleach Spa just opened in 2007. Please enquire about Facilities for Persons with Mobility Impairment.

Member of Ireland's Blue Book

B&B from €75.00 to €199.00
Suites from €199.00 to €700.00

*Moira & Christy Tighe*
*Proprietors*

24

Closed 23 - 28 December

### Markree Castle

HOTEL ★★★ MAP 10 H 15

Collooney,
Co. Sligo

Tel: 071-916 7800 Fax: 071-916 7840
Email: markree@iol.ie
Web: www.markreecastle.ie

A spectacular castle set in lovely gardens and large estate, in the same ownership for over 350 years. Markree Castle offers a relaxing, friendly and quiet place to stay. Wonderful wood and plaster work complements the friendly service and the restaurant enjoys a reputation of excellence throughout Ireland. Please enquire about Facilities for Persons with Mobility Impairment.

**An IHF Quality Employer**

Member of Best Loved Hotels

B&B from €87.50 to €97.50
Suites from €230.00 to €240.00

*Adrian O'Connor*
*General Manager*

30

Closed 24 - 27 December

### Yeats County Inn Hotel

HOTEL ★★ MAP 10 G 14

Curry,
Co. Sligo

Tel: 094-925 5050 Fax: 094-925 5053
Email: mail@yeatscountyinn.com
Web: www.yeatscountyinn.com

A warm welcome awaits you at this family-run hotel, a comfortable and relaxing venue, situated on the N17 between Charlestown and Tubbercurry. All our spacious bedrooms are en suite with tea and coffee making facilities, hairdryer and direct dial telephone. We provide free car parking facilities, and we are ideally based for fishing, golfing and touring the west of Ireland. Situated just 8 miles from Knock Airport and 25 miles from Sligo Airport, with access to major bus routes just outside our door. Relax and unwind at The Yeats County Inn.

B&B from €45.00 to €50.00

*Sven Anders*
*Manager*

10

Closed 25 December

B&B Rates are per Person Sharing per Night incl. Breakfast.
or Room Rates are per Room per Night - **See also Page 8**

## Mullaghmore / Rosses Point

### Beach Hotel and Leisure Club

HOTEL ★★ MAP 13 H 17

The Harbour,
Mullaghmore,
Co. Sligo

Tel: 071-916 6103 Fax: 071-916 6448
Email: beachhot@iol.ie
Web: www.beachhotelmullaghmore.com

Overlooking the beach in the picturesque fishing village of marvellous Mullaghmore. Leisure club with 15m swimming pool, jacuzzi, steam room, sauna, gym, sunbed, excellent restaurant and trendy bars all on site. Golf, fishing, horse riding, scuba diving, watersports and boat trips locally. Murder Mystery weekends. Family friendly. Romantic location.

***An IHF Quality Employer***

*Bookable on www.irelandhotels.com*
*Special Offer: www.irelandhotels.com/offers*

*B&B from €45.00 to €65.00*

*Paddy Donnelly*
*Manager*

28

Activities:

Open All Year

### Pier Head Hotel, Spa and Leisure Centre

HOTEL ★★★ MAP 13 H 17

Mullaghmore,
Co. Sligo

Tel: 071-916 6171 Fax: 071-916 6473
Email: pierheadreception@eircom.net
Web: www.pierheadhotel.ie

With its unique setting in the picturesque seaside village of Mullaghmore, the Pier Head Hotel has two bars and a very popular restaurant. All 40 rooms are ensuite, many with balconies or access to the roof garden with stunning views of Mullaghmore Harbour and Donegal Bay. Nearby activities include surfing, sailing, horse riding, hiking and fishing to name a few. The hotel offers luxurious accommodation and excellent facilities such as swimming pool, hot tub and seaweed baths making it the ideal venue for your stay in the North West. Please enquire about Facilities for Persons with Mobility Impairment.

*B&B from €50.00 to €80.00*

*John McHugh*

40

Activities:

Closed 20 - 27 December

### Yeats Country Hotel, Spa & Leisure Club

HOTEL ★★★ MAP 10 H 16

Rosses Point,
Co. Sligo

Tel: 071-917 7211 Fax: 071-917 7203
Email: info@yeatscountryhotel.com
Web: www.yeatscountryhotel.com

A family-run, 3* hotel. All rooms en suite, cable TV, DD phone, tea/coffee facilities, hairdryer. Within walking distance of sandy beaches and Sligo's 18 hole championship golf courses. Our wonderful Eros Spa is located in the hotel offering seaweed baths, hydro baths, Yon-ka Paris body products & much more. Amenities: leisure club with 18m swimming pool, sauna, jacuzzi, steam room & hi-tech gym. Also available tennis, basketball. Supervised crèche & indoor play areas during the months of July & August & Bank Holiday Weekends. Local activities: golf, yachting, fishing, scenic drives. Also closed 20 - 27 Dec.

Member of McEniff Hotels

*Bookable on www.irelandhotels.com*
*Special Offer: www.irelandhotels.com/offers*

*B&B from €65.00 to €105.00*

*Fiona McEniff*
*Managing Director*

98

Activities:

Closed 10 - 25 January



B&B Rates are per Person Sharing per Night incl. Breakfast. or Room Rates are per Room per Night - See also Page 8

## Clarion Hotel Sligo

HOTEL ★★★★ MAP 10 H 16

Clarion Road,
Sligo

Tel: 071-911 9000 Fax: 071-911 9001
Email: info@clarionhotelsligo.com
Web: www.clarionhotelsligo.com

White Egyptian linen, fluffy white towels, cable TV and free broadband are all standard in each of the 312 bedrooms and suites. Our conference centre offers small suites perfect for private dining or board meetings, the ballroom for conferences or weddings. Our Sinergie Restaurant serves beautifully presented modern European flavours. Kudos Bar offers Asian food freshly prepared from wok stations. Sanovitae offers pool, treatment rooms, sauna, gym, aerobics room and childrens' club.

Member of Clarion Group

*Bookable on www.irelandhotels.com*
*Special Offer: www.irelandhotels.com/offers*

*Room Rate from €99.00 to €290.00*
*Suites from €124.00 to €224.00*

*Jason Sleator*
*Sales & Marketing Manager*

312

Open All Year

## Glasshouse Hotel (The)

HOTEL ★★★★ MAP 10 H 16

Swan Point,
Sligo

Tel: 071-919 4300 Fax: 071-919 4301
Email: info@theglasshouse.ie
Web: www.theglasshouse.ie

Towering dramatically over the banks of the Garavogue river, The Glasshouse is the first design hotel of its kind in Ireland - in the centre of one of Ireland's emerging vibrant and scenic cities and within metres of Sligo's main O'Connell Street. With stylish rooms and designer junior suites, many with stunning views of the river and Hyde Bridge, the Glasshouse has set a completely new standard of luxury accommodation, at an affordable price. Please enquire about Facilities for Persons with Mobility Impairment.

Member of The Gleneagle Group

*B&B from €60.00 to €130.00*
*Suites from €250.00 to €300.00*

*Roisin Buckley*
*General Manager*

116

*Activities:*

Open All Year

## Radisson SAS Hotel & Spa, Sligo

HOTEL ★★★★ MAP 10 H 16

Ballincar,
Rosses Point,
Sligo

Tel: 071-914 0008 Fax: 071-914 0005
Email: info.sligo@radissonsas.com
Web: www.sligo.radissonsas.com

Located in beautiful Rosses Point with stunning views of Sligo Bay. 132 luxurious bedrooms. Classiebawn Restaurant serving local and international cuisine and Benwiskin Bar with an extensive bar menu. Magnificent leisure facilities include 18m swimming pool, steam room, sauna, jacuzzi and outdoor Canadian hot tub. Solas Spa and Wellness centre boasts a relaxation suite, 7 modern treatment rooms, a luxurious thermal suite, a Balneotherapy bath and a dry floatation tank. Within easy reach of some of Ireland's best golf courses. Please enquire about Facilities for Persons with Mobility Impairment.

***An IHF Quality Employer***

Member of Rezidor SAS

*Bookable on www.irelandhotels.com*
*Special Offer: www.irelandhotels.com/offers*

*B&B from €75.00 to €225.00*

*Fergus O'Donovan*
*General Manager*

132

Open All Year

## Sligo Town

### Sligo City Hotel

HOTEL ★★★ MAP 10 H 16

Quay Street,
Sligo

Tel: 071-914 4000 Fax: 071-914 6888
Email: info@sligocityhotel.com
Web: www.sligocityhotel.com

The Sligo City Hotel is located in the heart of Sligo Town, with immediate access to Sligo's new shopping centre and a host of lively bars on its doorstep. All 60 bedrooms are en suite with cable TV and direct dial phone, fast internet connections with broadband and tea/coffee making facilities. The Sligo City Hotel offers a warm welcome to all our guests and prides itself on delivering service excellence. Specialising in room only rates, commercial traveller rates and golfing holidays. Room only rate. Please enquire about Facilities for Persons with Mobility Impairment.

*Bookable on www.irelandhotels.com*
*Special Offer: www.irelandhotels.com/offers*

*Room Rate from €79.00 to €180.00*
*Suites from €99.00 to €250.00*

*M.Mulholland & B. Mullen*

60

*Activities:*

**Closed 24 - 29 December**

### Sligo Park Hotel & Leisure Club

HOTEL ★★★★ MAP 10 H 16

Pearse Road,
Sligo

Tel: 071-919 0400 Fax: 071-916 9556
Email: sligo@leehotels.com
Web: www.leehotels.com

Situated one mile south of Sligo on the old Dublin Road, just a short walk or suburban bus ride into town. The Sligo Park Hotel is set in lush landscaped gardens. A 3 star hotel with 137 new bedrooms, and one of the finest health and leisure clubs in the country. In the heart of Yeats Country, surrounded by the most scenic countryside ranging from the majestic Benbulben to the gentle waters of Lough Gill. For that special break, the Sligo Park offers everything for your enjoyment. Please enquire about Facilities for Persons with Mobility Impairment.

***An IHF Quality Employer***

Member of Lee Hotels

*Bookable on www.irelandhotels.com*
*Special Offer: www.irelandhotels.com/offers*

*B&B from €49.00 to €135.00*

*Gerard Moore*
*General Manager*

137

*Activities:*

**Open All Year**

### Sligo Southern Hotel & Leisure Centre

HOTEL ★★★ MAP 10 H 16

Strandhill Road,
Sligo Town

Tel: 071-916 2101 Fax: 071-916 0328
Email: reservations@sligosouthernhotel.com
Web: www.sligosouthernhotel.com

The Sligo Southern Hotel is situated in the heart of Sligo Town, adjacent to the railway and bus stations. The Sligo Southern Hotel blends old world intimacy with every modern convenience. All 99 rooms are en suite, cable TV, phone, hairdryers, tea/coffee making facilities. Indoor swimming pool, gym, jacuzzi, sauna and steam room. Entertainment most nights in high season. Reservations Tel: 071 916 2101. www.sligosouthernhotel.com.

***An IHF Quality Employer***

Member of Brian McEniff Hotels

*Bookable on www.irelandhotels.com*
*Special Offer: www.irelandhotels.com/offers*

*Room Rate from €89.00 to €150.00*
*Suites from €220.00 to €300.00*

*Kevin McGlynn*
*General Manager*

99

*Activities:*

**Closed 23 - 27 December**



B&B Rates are per Person Sharing per Night incl. Breakfast.
or Room Rates are per Room per Night - See also Page 8

## Cawley's

GUESTHOUSE ★★ MAP 10 G 15

Emmet Street,
Tubbercurry,
Co. Sligo
Tel: 071-918 5025 Fax: 071-918 5963
Email: cawleysguesthouse@eircom.net

Cawley's is a large 3 storey family-run guesthouse with full bar license. We offer high standards in accommodation with tastefully decorated rooms. Our home cooking and personal service make this premises your home for the duration of your stay. Private parking, landscaped gardens, easily accessed by air, rail and bus. Local amenities include fishing, 9 hole golf course and horse riding. Seaside resorts close by. Major credit cards accepted. For further information please contact a member of the Cawley family on 071-918 5025. Please enquire about Facilities for Persons with Mobility Impairment.

*B&B from €35.00 to €39.00*

*Teresa Cawley / Pierre Krebs*

13
3

Closed 23 - 27 December

## Murphy's Hotel

HOTEL ★★★ MAP 10 G 15

Teeling Street,
Tubbercurry,
Co. Sligo
Tel: 071-918 5598 Fax: 071-918 5034
Email: info@murphyshotel.ie
Web: www.murphyshotel.ie

Murphy's Hotel provides the perfect combination of traditional Irish Hospitality and modern comforts and facilities. Completely refurbished in 2006, it combines elegance and style in designed with friendly atmosphere you expect in a family-run hotel. Relax in comfort in one of our 17 spacious rooms - all with en suite bathrooms, wireless broadband access & satellite TV. During your stay, enjoy excellent food from our team of international chefs. Please enquire about Facilities for Persons with Mobility Impairment.

*B&B from €45.00 to €60.00*

*Mr Paul Murphy*
*General Manager*

17

Closed 23 December - 03 January

B&B Rates are per Person Sharing per Night incl. Breakfast.
or Room Rates are per Room per Night - See also Page 8

**For Detailed Maps of this Region See Pages 477-492**

**Each Hotel or Guesthouse has a Map Reference to these detailed maps under their photograph.**

**See page 477 for map with access points and driving distances**

Welcome to Ireland South. Seven counties, like seven jewels adorning Ireland's golden southern shores.

Welcome to a land of unparalleled scenic beauty, a land of picturesque valleys and ancient roadways, vibrant streets and spectacular coastline. A land where the lilt of a fiddler's tune entwined with peat smoke and conversation in a city bar, is as eloquent an expression of its beauty as are the run of its waters, the vaunt of its peaks, or the glint of a leaping salmon in the fading evening light. Ireland South is special for so many reasons – the drama of its diverse yet spectacular landscapes, the naturally sculpted beauty of its award-winning beaches, the mystical charms of its ancient past, the quality and variety of its world-class visitor attractions, the unique personalities of its many famous cities, towns and villages and perhaps, most of all, the open warmth and creative spirit of its extraordinary people. All of this is waiting for you here, to explore, to discover, to fall in love with.

**Carlow**, framed by the River Barrow to the west and the River Slaney to the east, Carlow is a county defined by its rivers. The Barrow Navigation is hugely popular with tourists for pleasure boating, angling and walking, one of the best ways to get to know this beautiful river. Carlow is steeped in history and amoung its top visitor attractions are Altamont Gardens, Huntingdon Castle, Saint Lazerian's Cathedral, Duckett's Grove and Ballykeenan Pet Farm & Aviary.

**Cork**, perhaps no other corner of Ireland contains so much to see, do and experience as County Cork. Cork City is a thriving metropolis with a distinctively continental air. The east of the county is ripe with fertile farmlands, verdant river valleys and picturesque towns and villages while the west boasts a long, magnificent coastline, which stretches 200 miles from Youghal to Ardgroom on the Beara Peninsula.

This beautiful county is also brimming with must see visitor attractions, like the world famous island garden of Ilnacullin, Bantry House and Gardens, Blarney Castle, the Old Middleton Distillery, the Michael Collins Centre at Clonakilty and Fota Arboretum and Gardens.

**Kerry**, perhaps the most popular tourist destination in Ireland, Kerry is also considered by many to be the most beautiful. From the spectacular Ring of Kerry, to the extraordinary 25,000 acre Killarney National Park – home to Muckross House, to beauty spots like the Gap of Dunloe and Torc Waterfall, Kerry is replete in awe inspiring natural beauty. The county is rich in archaeological treasures too, none more famous or inspiring as the 6th century Skelligs UNESCO World Heritage Site, situated 12km off the southwest coast of Ireland. Among the many world class visitor attractions that have been developed in recent years, are The Geraldine Centre and the Kerry County Museum in Tralee, Derrynane House, Ardfert Cathedral, The Barracks Heritage Centre, Cahersiveen, the Skellig Experience and the Great Blasket Island Interpretative Centre.

**Kilkenny**, whether you're fishing for trout on the Nore, sinking a putt at Mount Juliet, or driving through pretty towns and villages like Thomastown and Inistioge, you'll be struck by the peaceful beauty of Kilkenny. The county has a wealth of fascinating visitor attractions, from the wonders of Dunmore Cave and Jerpoint Abbey, to the magnificently restored Kilkenny Castle or the many faceted Castlecomer Demesne. The ancient medieval city of Kilkenny itself is today a thriving, modern capital that has protected its precious heritage whilst evolving as one of Ireland's most vibrant and enjoyable cities in which to stay.

**Tipperary**, there's probably no livelier a collection of market towns in all Ireland than Carrick-on-Suir, Clonmel, Cahir, Tipperary and Cashel. Nor a more distinctive set of landmarks than Cahir Castle on its island in the middle of the River Suir and the great Rock of Cashel, rising like a sentinel above the Golden Vale and the Glen of Aherlow. Tipperary also has some fascinating visitor attractions, like Mitchelstown Cave, one of Europe's most spectacular, and the captivating

BrúBorú Cultural Centre, commemorating Brian Boru, the Last of the High Kings, with a 'cultural village' dedicated to the study and celebration of native Irish music, song, dance and theatre.

**Waterford**, famous the world over for the beauty and craftsmanship of its master glass cutters at the Waterford Crystal Visitor Centre, Waterford offers visitors a choice between a cosmopolitan vibrant city, charming seaside resorts with miles of sandy beaches and countryside getaway locations set against the backdrop of the Comeragh Mountains. From the charm of rural towns and villages like Dungarvan, Lismore, Cappoquin and BallyMcCarbry to the resort villages of Ardmore, Dunmore and Tramore there is something to appeal to all tastes. There is also an excellent choice of world-class visitor attractions to enjoy including The Waterford Museum of Treasures which is complemented by the Jack Burtchaell Walking Tour both of which tell the story of Waterford - Ireland's oldest city. For families, the newly restored Waterford to Kilmeaden narrow gauge railway is a fabulous way to take in the sweep of the Suir Valley and to go back 450 million years you can take a tour of the spectacular Copper Coast UNESCO Geopark.

**Wexford**, located in the sunny South East of Ireland is fast becoming the spa capital of Ireland. With new developments such as the Monart destination spa and Seafield and Kelly's resort spas, Wexford is the ideal location for a restful and rejuvenating break. But long before the arrival of 'spas', Wexford was famous for its rich history, the story of which is told through the numerous visitor attractions in the county. The most fascinating include the remarkable Irish National Heritage Park at Wexford – which will take you on a tour of how the Irish lived, worshiped and died from the stone age to the 12 Century; the Dunbrody Heritage Ship in New Ross - a replica of a 19th century famine ship that transported the Irish to the new world; the medieval Hook Lighthouse – where monks kept the fire alight as far back as the 5th Century; add to these the Irish Agricultural Museum at Johnstown Castle, the National 1798 Rebellion Centre in Enniscorthy, Ireland's premier wildfowl sanctuary, the Wexford Wildfowl Reserve and the JFK Arboretum and you get the finest array of quality visitor attractions in the country.

**Heritage**

With a rich cultural tapestry of towering castles, magnificent stately homes, ancient Celtic monuments, early Christian ecclesiastical sites, fascinating museums and intriguing city architecture, Ireland South boasts a wealth of world-class cultural and heritage visitor centres.

In every corner of these seven counties you'll find a thread of ancient times so alive it seems still woven to the present day; captivating history brought to life through enthralling tales, working museums, and state-of-the-art interpretative centres.

Discover the medieval splendour of the Rock of Cashel, boost your powers of eloquence by kissing the famous Blarney Stone at Blarney Castle, or take an easy wander round the magnificent Kilkenny Castle and Gardens overlooking the picturesque River Nore. There's also the fully restored elegance of Ross Castle in Kerry, and the fascinating war-entangled history of Charles Fort at Kinsale to explore.

**GUINNESS CALENDAR OF EVENTS**

**May**
Carlsberg Kilkenny Rhythm, Kilkenny City

**June**
Smithwick's Cat Laughs Festival, Kilkenny City

**July/August**
Killarney Summer Fest, Killarney, Co. Kerry
Trafest Music Festival, Tramore, Co. Waterford
Waterford Spraoi Festival, Waterford City
Guinness Puck Fair, Killorglin, Co. Kerry
Guinness Dunmore East, Bluegrass Festival, Dunmore East, Co. Waterford

**September**
Listowel Racing Festival, Listowel, Co. Kerry

**October/November**
Guinness Jazz Festival, Cork City
Wexford Festival Opera, Wexford Town

## Carlow Town

### Barrowville Town House

GUESTHOUSE ★★★ MAP 7 M 8

Kilkenny Road,
Carlow Town,
Co. Carlow

Tel: 059-914 3324 Fax: 059-914 1953
Email: barrowvilletownhouse@eircom.net
Web: www.barrowvillehouse.com

A period listed residence in own grounds, 3 minutes walk to town centre. Well appointed rooms with all facilities and Internet access. Antique furnishing. Traditional or buffet breakfast served in conservatory overlooking the gardens. Ideal location for Golf at Carlow, Mt Wolseley, touring the South East, Glendalough, Kilkenny, Waterford and visiting various gardens. Orthopaedic beds, crisp linen. Multi Night Discount.

*B&B from €50.00 to €70.00*

*Anna & Dermot Smyth*
*Proprietors*

7

Closed 24 - 28 December

### Dolmen Hotel and River Court Lodges

HOTEL ★★★ MAP 7 M 8

Kilkenny Road,
Carlow Town,
Co. Carlow

Tel: 059-914 2002 Fax: 059-914 2375
Email: reservations@dolmenhotel.ie
Web: www.dolmenhotel.ie

Nestled along the scenic banks of the River Barrow and set in 20 acres of landscaped beauty is the Dolmen Hotel, 1.5km from Carlow. Fishing, golf, shooting and horse riding are just some of the sporting facilities surrounding the hotel. With 93 beautifully appointed rooms (81 rooms & 12 lodges) including 3 luxury suites with en suite, TV, direct dial phone, trouser press and hairdryer. Our 1 bedroomed lodges are ideal for the sporting enthusiast. One of the largest conference and banqueting facilities in the South East. Please enquire about Facilities for Persons with Mobility Impairment.

*B&B from €35.00 to €90.00*
*Suites from €160.00 to €300.00*

*Colin Duggan*
*General Manager*

93

*Activities:*

Closed 25 - 27 December

### Ramada Hotel & Suites at Killerig Golf Resort

HOTEL ★★★ MAP 7 M 8

Killerig,
Co. Carlow

Tel: 059-916 3050 Fax: 059-916 3051
Email: info@ramadakillerig.com
Web: www.ramadakillerig.com

The chic and stylish Ramada Hotel & Suites at Killerig Golf Resort, situated on the Kildare / Carlow border is innovative in design, gushing with natural light and offering panoramic views of the course and countryside. Providing unsurpassed hospitality for all, the property offers modern spacious guest rooms, all with private balconies overlooking the course, 48 holiday lodges, conference rooms, a fully equipped spa and leisure centre, three bars and Sir Henry's Restaurant. Please enquire about Facilities for Persons with Mobility Impairment.

Member of Ramada Worldwide

***Bookable on www.irelandhotels.com***
***Special Offer: www.irelandhotels.com/offers***

*B&B from €39.50 to €110.00*

*Alan Scully*
*Resort Manager*

80

*Activities:*

Closed 24 - 25 December



B&B Rates are per Person Sharing per Night incl. Breakfast.
or Room Rates are per Room per Night - See also Page 8

## Seven Oaks Hotel

HOTEL ★★★ MAP 7 M 8

Athy Road,
Carlow Town,
Co. Carlow

Tel: 059-913 1308 Fax: 059-913 2155
Email: info@sevenoakshotel.com
Web: www.sevenoakshotel.com

Ideally located just 3 mins walk to Carlow Town centre and bus/train station. We specialise in the best of Irish foods in our Oaks Bar carvery and intimate T.D. Molloy's Restaurant. Individually designed rooms, combining a selection of executive suites. Rooms are accessible by lift. Fully equipped conference facilities, with professional and friendly staff make the Seven Oaks Hotel an ideal venue for all such occasions whether large or small. Work out in our fully equipped Greenbank Health and Leisure Club with 20m swimming pool, gym, sauna and steam room.

***An IHF Quality Employer***

Member of Irish Country Hotels

*Bookable on www.irelandhotels.com*
*Special Offer: www.irelandhotels.com/offers*

**B&B from €75.00 to €100.00**

*Michael Murphy*
*Managing Director*

89

*Activities:*

**Closed 25 - 27 December**

## Talbot Hotel Carlow

HOTEL ★★★★ MAP 7 M 8

Portlaoise Road,
Carlow Town,
Co. Carlow

Tel: 059-915 3000 Fax: 059-915 3001
Email: sales@talbothotelcarlow.ie
Web: www.talbotcarlow.ie

The Talbot Carlow is a luxurious 4 star hotel situated off the N80 from Dublin and 2km walk into Carlow town centre. Facilities include 84 guestrooms, Liberty Tree 4th floor restaurant, Corries Bar and Bistro with live music every Friday & Saturday night, conference and banqueting facilities, fully equipped Leisure Centre and beauty salon, complimentary car parking and the hotel is located beside "The Dome" (Kids Entertainment Centre). The Talbot Group are renowned for impeccable service, mouth watering cuisine, great locations and the Talbot Carlow is no exception. Please enquire about Facilities for Persons with Mobility Impairment.

***An IHF Quality Employer***

Member of Talbot Hotel Group

*Bookable on www.irelandhotels.com*
*Special Offer: www.irelandhotels.com/offers*

**B&B from €55.00 to €120.00**

*Larry Bowe*
*General Manager*

84

*Activities:*

**Closed 23 - 27 December**

## Leighlinbridge / Tullow / Allihies

### Lord Bagenal Inn

HOTEL ★★★★ MAP 7 M 8

Main Street,
Leighlinbridge,
Co. Carlow

Tel: 059-977 4000 Fax: 059-972 2629
Email: info@lordbagenal.com
Web: www.lordbagenal.com

Situated in the picturesque Heritage Village of Leighlinbridge along the River Barrow, with private marina and gardens, we are the perfect location to explore the South East. Our new en suite bedrooms are luxuriously furnished to the highest standards. Award-winning Lord Bagenal Restaurant is renowned for fine food & excellent wines. Locals and visitors frequent our bar and carvery daily. New classical, fine dining Waterfront Restaurant with decked area overlooking river. Weddings, conferences, banquets catered for. Children welcome. Please enquire about Facilities for Persons with Mobility Impairment.

**B&B from €65.00 to €95.00**
**Suites from €170.00 to €300.00**

*James & Mary Kehoe*

39

Activities:

**Closed 25 - 26 December**

### Mount Wolseley Hotel Spa & Country Club

HOTEL ★★★★ MAP 8 N 8

Tullow,
Co. Carlow

Tel: 059-918 0100 Fax: 059-915 2123
Email: info@mountwolseley.ie
Web: www.mountwolseley.ie

This charming and exclusive resort is an eclectic blend of contemporary design and lavish country house details. Featuring 143 bedrooms and conference facilities for up to 750 delegates. The hotel overlooks the 18th hole of the magnificent, Christy O'Connor designed, championship golf course. Other leisure facilities include a spa with 14 treatment rooms and a health club with 20 meter deck pool, sauna, steam bath, gym and aerobics studio. Please enquire about Facilities for Persons with Mobility Impairment.

***An IHF Quality Employer***

***Bookable on www.irelandhotels.com***
*Special Offer: www.irelandhotels.com/offers*

**B&B from €70.00 to €200.00**
**Suites from €220.00 to €340.00**

*Odhran Lawlor*
*General Manager*

143

Activities:

**Closed 25 - 27 December**

### Sea View Guest House

GUESTHOUSE ★★★ MAP 1 C 2

Cluin Village,
Allihies, Beara,
Co. Cork

Tel: 027-73004 Fax: 027-73211
Email: seaviewg@iol.ie
Web: www.allihiesseaview.com

Sea View Guesthouse is a family-run concern in the remote and unspoilt Beara Peninsula. All bedrooms are en suite with TV and telephone. Situated in the village of Allihies, it is within walking distance of a beach, playground and tennis court. The nearby hills afford excellent opportunities for walking, offering breathtaking views. Traditional Irish music and a friendly welcome can be found in the village pubs.

**B&B from €40.00 to €45.00**

*John & Mary O'Sullivan*
*Proprietors*

10

**Closed 31 October - 01 March**



B&B Rates are per Person Sharing per Night incl. Breakfast.
or Room Rates are per Room per Night - See also Page 8

## Oriel House Hotel, Leisure Club & Spa

HOTEL ★★★★ MAP 2 H 3

Ballincollig,
Co. Cork

Tel: 021-420 8400 Fax: 021-487 5880
Email: info@orielhousehotel.ie
Web: www.orielhousehotel.ie

The Oriel House Hotel Leisure Club & Spa is located on the west side of Cork city. Close proximity to Cork Airport, train station and gateway to Co. Kerry. The Oriel House is a listed building dating back to 1805, sits comfortably alongside the contemporary new building. Our facilities include 78 guest rooms, extensive conference and banqueting facilities, fully equipped business centre, bright and airy leisure Club and The Oriel Spa. The Oriel House Hotel is luxury and relaxation, pure and simple. Please enquire about Facilities for Persons with Mobility Impairment.

Member of Cork Luxury Hotel Group

*Bookable on www.irelandhotels.com*
*Special Offer: www.irelandhotels.com/offers*

*B&B from €100.00 to €200.00*
*Suites from €250.00 to €320.00*

*Breda Keane Shortt*
*General Manager*

78

Activities:

Closed 24 - 27 December

## Bayview Hotel

HOTEL ★★★★ MAP 3 J 3

Ballycotton,
Co. Cork

Tel: 021-464 6746 Fax: 021-464 6075
Email: res@thebayviewhotel.com
Web: www.thebayviewhotel.com

Nestled in the unspoilt fishing village of Ballycotton, the Bayview Hotel directly overlooks miles of spectacular coastline. Embrace the invigorating sea air while relaxing in the original gardens. The Capricho Restaurant provides dishes with a balance of flavour, texture and presentation. Our chefs emphasise fish dishes caught literally on the doorstep. From the cold, crystal depths of the Atlantic Ocean to your plate in a matter of hours. A short distance away are Fota Wildlife Park, Heritage Centres, Trabolgan Holiday Village & an abundance of arts & crafts.

Member of Manor House Hotels

*Bookable on www.irelandhotels.com*
*Special Offer: www.irelandhotels.com/offers*

*B&B from €85.00 to €111.00*

*Stephen Belton*
*General Manager*

35

Closed 30 October - 10 April

## Seaview House Hotel

HOTEL ★★★★ MAP 2 E 2

Ballylickey,
Bantry,
Co. Cork

Tel: 027-50073 Fax: 027-51555
Email: info@seaviewhousehotel.com
Web: www.seaviewhousehotel.com

Delightful country house hotel & restaurant, set back in extensive grounds on main Bantry/Glengarriff Road. All bedrooms en suite, D.D. telephone & colour TV. Ideal for touring West Cork & Kerry. 2 golf courses nearby. Recommended Egon Ronay, Good Hotel Guide etc. For the restaurant, AA Rosettes & Failte Ireland Awards of Excellence. Seafood a speciality. Member of Manor House Hotels. A wing of new superior rooms and a conservatory to the dining room was added in Winter 2000. Special midweek & weekend rates, subject to availability. Bookable on www.manorhousehotels.com

Member of Manor House Hotels

*Bookable on www.irelandhotels.com*
*Special Offer: www.irelandhotels.com/offers*

*B&B from €85.00 to €95.00*
*Suites from €175.00 to €200.00*

*Kathleen O'Sullivan*
*Proprietor*

25

Closed 15 November - 15 March

B&B Rates are per Person Sharing per Night incl. Breakfast.
or Room Rates are per Room per Night - See also Page 8

## Ballyvourney / Baltimore

### Abbey Hotel

HOTEL ★★ MAP 2 F 3

Ballyvourney,
Co. Cork

Tel: 026-45324 Fax: 026-45830
Email: abbeyhotel@eircom.net
Web: www.theabbeyhotel.net

Family-run hotel nestles in the valley of the Sullane River among the Cork and Kerry Mountains on the N22. It combines a friendly atmosphere and excellent catering. An ideal base for touring Kerry and Cork. A wide range of activities is available to you at the hotel including fishing, mountaineering, nature walks and golfing. 39 bedrooms with private facilities, direct dial phone & colour TV. Within 20 minutes drive are two 18 hole golf courses and trout fishing on the Sullane River. Fully licensed function room for weddings, dinner dances and parties. Please enquire about Facilities for Persons with Mobility Impairment.

**B&B from €45.00 to €60.00**

*Cornelius Creedon*
*Proprietor*

39

Activities:

**Closed 30 October - 01 March**

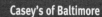

### Baltimore Harbour Hotel & Leisure Centre

HOTEL ★★★ MAP 2 E 1

Baltimore,
Co. Cork

Tel: 028-20361 Fax: 028-20466
Email: info@baltimoreharbourhotel.ie
Web: www.baltimoreharbourhotel.ie

The hotel is situated overlooking the Harbour & Islands in the charming coastal village of Baltimore. It is the ideal haven from which to explore the beauty and wonders of West Cork and the sea and to enjoy the many varied activities available locally, including sailing, golfing, angling, diving, horse riding, walking, cycling and, of course, the Islands. We are especially suited for families and offer childrens' entertainment during peak season. Enjoy our superb indoor leisure centre.

*Bookable on www.irelandhotels.com*
*Special Offer: www.irelandhotels.com/offers*

**B&B from €60.00 to €90.00**
**Suites from €220.00 to €290.00**

*William Buckley*
*General Manager*

64

**Closed 20 December - 01 January**

### Casey's of Baltimore

HOTEL ★★★ MAP 2 E 1

Baltimore,
Co. Cork

Tel: 028-20197 Fax: 028-20509
Email: info@caseysofbaltimore.com
Web: www.caseysofbaltimore.com

A warm welcome awaits you at Casey's of Baltimore. Situated at the entrance to Baltimore with its lovely views overlooking the bay, this superb family-run hotel is the perfect place to spend some time. All rooms feature en suite bathrooms, satellite TV, tea/coffee facility, direct dial phone, hairdryer and trouser press. The traditional pub and restaurant feature natural stone and wood décor, a spectacular view, extensive menu - seafood is our speciality. Activities can be arranged.

***An IHF Quality Employer***
Member of Irish Country Hotels

*Bookable on www.irelandhotels.com*
*Special Offer: www.irelandhotels.com/offers*

**B&B from €77.00 to €91.00**

*Ann & Michael Casey*
*Owners*

14

**Closed 20 - 27 December**



B&B Rates are per Person Sharing per Night incl. Breakfast.
or Room Rates are per Room per Night - **See also Page 8**

## Waterfront (The)

GUESTHOUSE ★★★ MAP 2 E 1

Baltimore,
Co. Cork

Tel: 028-20600 Fax: 028-20495

Email: res@waterfronthotel.ie

Web: www.waterfronthotel.ie

Superbly appointed premises that recently added 5 generous en suite bedrooms, reception area, bar & restaurant on to 8 existing spacious rooms. Satellite TV, tea/coffee facilities, and access to a comfortable residents' lounge. A family-run premises located on the square with stunning views of Baltimore Bay & The Islands. Convenient to its associated family pizza & grill, La Jolie Brise, and the famous Chez Youen Seafood Restaurant. Please enquire about Facilities for Persons with Mobility Impairment.

*Bookable on www.irelandhotels.com*

*Special Offer: www.irelandhotels.com/offers*

**B&B from €40.00 to €60.00**

*Youen Jacob*
*Owner-Manager*

13

**Open All Year**

## Munster Arms Hotel

HOTEL ★★ MAP 2 G 2

Oliver Plunkett Street,
Bandon,
Co. Cork

Tel: 023-41562 Fax: 023-41562

Email: info@munsterarmshotel.com

Web: www.munsterarmshotel.com

Set at the gateway to West Cork, 30 high quality en suite bedrooms with tea/coffee facilities, direct dial telephone, remote control TV radio and hairdryer. Set in beautiful scenic West Cork accessible by the N71 route from Cork City. Renowned for its homely atmosphere and superb quality. Ideal touring base and easily accessible from Kinsale, Cork City, Blarney, Killarney and West Cork. Relax and be pampered! Guests of the Munster Arms Hotel may use the leisure facilities at the local Bandon Leisure Centre for a nominal fee payable direct to the leisure centre.

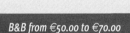

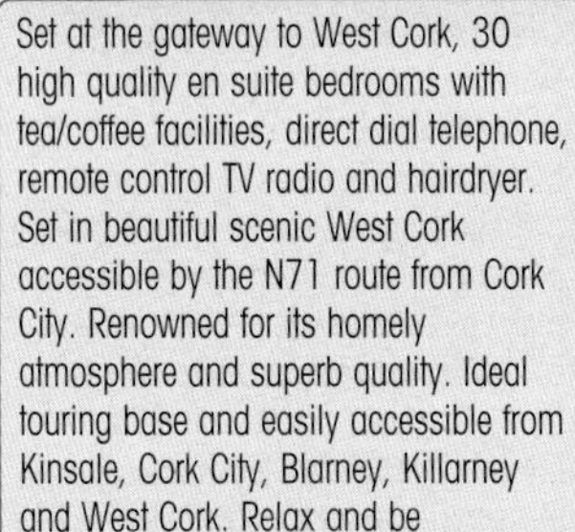

**B&B from €50.00 to €70.00**

*Don O'Sullivan*

30

**Closed 25 - 26 December**



B&B Rates are per Person Sharing per Night incl. Breakfast.
or Room Rates are per Room per Night - **See also Page 8**

## Bantry

### Bantry Bay Hotel

**HOTEL ★★ MAP 2 E 2**

Wolfe Tone Square,
Bantry,
Co. Cork

Tel: 027-50062 Fax: 027-50261
Email: info@bantrybayhotel.ie
Web: www.bantrybayhotel.ie

The Bantry Bay has been operated by the O'Callaghan family since 1946 in the centre of historic Bantry. Extensively renovated from 1995 to present, we offer a choice of family, tourist and commercial accommodation. All rooms offer every expected amenity. They are complemented by our award-winning maritime themed bar and restaurant. Perfect touring base for South West. Guests are assured of a hearty O'Callaghan welcome. Please enquire about Facilities for Persons with Mobility Impairment.

**B&B from €55.00 to €71.50**

*Vivian & Pauline O'Callaghan*
*Manager / Proprietor*

14

**Closed 24 - 27 December**

### Maritime Hotel (The)

**HOTEL ★★★★ MAP 2 E 2**

The Quay,
Bantry,
Co. Cork

Tel: 027-54700 Fax: 027-54701
Email: info@themaritime.ie
Web: www.themaritime.ie

Overlooking Bantry bay, the new Maritime Hotel offers modern and contemporary 4**** standards in beautiful Bantry. Our one and two bedroomed suites are ideal for families, offering flexibility along the way with many of the comforts of home. The Club Maritime Leisure Centre, Ocean Resturant and Maritime Bar make the hotel a perfect venue for work or pleasure - and an ideal base for exploring the wonders of West Cork. Please enquire about Facilities for Persons with Mobility Impairment.

Member of Gleneagle Group

***Bookable on www.irelandhotels.com***
***Special Offer: www.irelandhotels.com/offers***

**B&B from €55.00 to €130.00**
**Suites from €150.00 to €280.00**

*George Hook*
*General Manager*

117

**Closed 24 - 26 December**

### Westlodge Hotel

**HOTEL ★★★ MAP 2 E 2**

Bantry,
Co. Cork

Tel: 027-50360 Fax: 027-50438
Email: reservations@westlodgehotel.ie
Web: www.westlodgehotel.ie

3*** hotel situated in the scenic surroundings of Bantry Bay. Super health & leisure centre including indoor heated swimming pool, childrens' pool, toddlers' pool, sauna, steam room, jacuzzi, gym, aerobics, squash. Outdoor amenities include tennis, pitch & putt, woodland walks. The Westlodge specialises in family holidays with organised activities during Jul & Aug. A warm & friendly welcome awaits you at the Westlodge. Self-catering cottages available. Mighty Duck's Club opens during Jul & Aug. Guaranteed Tee Times at Bantry Bay Golf Club. Themed breaks now available: wellness & golf. Optimus Mark of Best Practice.

***An IHF Quality Employer***

Member of Holiday Ireland Hotels

***Bookable on www.irelandhotels.com***
***Special Offer: www.irelandhotels.com/offers***

**B&B from €70.00 to €80.00**
**Suites from €199.00 to €249.00**

*Eileen M O'Shea FIHI*
*General Manager*

90

Activities:

**Closed 22 - 28 December**



B&B Rates are per Person Sharing per Night incl. Breakfast. or Room Rates are per Room per Night - See also Page 8

## Ashlee Lodge

GUESTHOUSE ★★★★ MAP 2 H 3

Tower,
Blarney,
Co. Cork

Tel: 021-438 5346 Fax: 021-438 5726

Email: info@ashleelodge.com

Web: www.ashleelodge.com

This charming 4**** boutique style property is a rare find striking the perfect balance between traditional comfort and a contemporary atmosphere. A member of the Best Loved Hotels of the World, it holds AA Red Five Diamonds and RAC ♦♦♦♦♦ awards. 10 luxurious bedrooms and suites with all that one expects of a private hotel. Air-conditioning, king sized beds, widescreen TV/CD units and sittingroom areas. Relax in our sauna and Canadian hot tub. RAC Little Gem Award 2005 and National Accommodation Services Award Winner 2004 and 2005. AA 'Country House of the Year 2006'.

Member of Best Loved Hotels of the World

*Bookable on www.irelandhotels.com*

*Special Offer: www.irelandhotels.com/offers*

**B&B from €55.00 to €120.00**
**Suites from €180.00 to €300.00**

*John O'Leary*
*Proprietor*

10

*Activities:*

**Open All Year**

## Blarney Castle Hotel

HOTEL ★★★ MAP 2 H 3

Blarney,
Co. Cork

Tel: 021-438 5116 Fax: 021-438 5542

Email: info@blarneycastlehotel.com

Web: www.blarneycastlehotel.com

Established in 1837, still run by the Forrest family. Picturesque inn on a peaceful village green, 5 miles from Cork City. Tastefully appointed spacious bedrooms. Unspoilt traditional bar. Restaurant specialising in finest local produce. Killarney, Kenmare, Kinsale, Cobh, West Cork, Waterford and numerous golf courses all an easy drive. Immediately to the left the magnificent grounds of Blarney Castle guarding that famous stone, to the right, Blarney Woollen Mills. Private car park for hotel guests. Quality entertainment nightly in village.

*Bookable on www.irelandhotels.com*

*Special Offer: www.irelandhotels.com/offers*

**B&B from €55.00 to €75.00**

*Ian Forrest / Una Forrest*
*Manager / Reservations*

13

*Activities:*

**Closed 24 - 25 December**

## Blarney Golf Resort

HOTEL ★★★★ MAP 2 H 3

Tower,
Blarney,
Co. Cork

Tel: 021-438 4477 Fax: 021-451 6453

Email: reservations@blarneygolfresort.com

Web: www.blarneygolfresort.com

Blarney Golf Resort is set amongst 164 acres fo the beautiful wooded Shournagh Valley. Complimenting the hotel is the superb John Daly golf course, the only one outside the U.S. Spacious function space is perfect for any event, large or small. Our health club and spa provides peace and relaxation, while The Inniscarra Restaurant serves gourment cuisine. Please enquire about Facilities for Persons with Mobility Impairment.

*Bookable on www.irelandhotels.com*

*Special Offer: www.irelandhotels.com/offers*

**Room Rate from €60.00 to €125.00**
**Suites from €150.00 to €250.00**

*Peter Borrowdale*
*General Manager*

62

*Activities:*

**Closed 24 - 26 December**

B&B Rates are per Person Sharing per Night incl. Breakfast.
or Room Rates are per Room per Night - See also Page 8

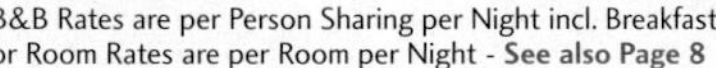

## Blarney / Carrigaline

### Blarney Woollen Mills Hotel

HOTEL ★★★ MAP 2 H 3


Blarney,
Co. Cork

Tel: 021-438 5011 Fax: 021-438 5350
Email: info@blarneywoollenmillshotel.com
Web: www.blarneywoollenmillshotel.com

Blarney Woollen Mills 3*** Hotel with 48 beautifully appointed superior rooms including 3 executive suites. Many of the rooms have spectacular views of the famous Blarney Castle. All rooms have been tastefully decorated in the traditional style. All day dining in our Millroom Restaurant and evening dining in Christys Grill Bar. The hotel boasts one of the finest fitness centres in the area. Located within the old Mill buildings in the famous Blarney Woollen Mills complex where you can enjoy a relaxing drink and experience some Irish hospitality in Christy's Pub. Please enquire about Facilities for Persons with Mobility Impairment.

Member of The Blarney Group

*Bookable on www.irelandhotels.com*
*Special Offer: www.irelandhotels.com/offers*

**B&B from €65.00 to €80.00**
**Suites from €180.00 to €260.00**

*Dominic Heaney*
*General Manager*

48

Closed 20 - 26 December

### Muskerry Arms

GUESTHOUSE ★★★ MAP 2 H 3


Blarney,
Co. Cork

Tel: 021-438 5200 Fax: 021-438 1013
Email: info@muskerryarms.com
Web: www.muskerryarms.com

With all the attributes of a small hotel, the Muskerry Arms is ideally located for your stay in Blarney. Stylish, spacious guest rooms and family suites offer power showers and tea/coffee making facilities. Live music is a regular feature in the popular Muskerry Bar and two delicious menus are available in the bar and main restaurant. All within walking distance of Blarney Castle and Woollen Mills. Please enquire about Facilities for Persons with Mobility Impairment.

*Bookable on www.irelandhotels.com*
*Special Offer: www.irelandhotels.com/offers*

**B&B from €49.00 to €59.00**
**Suites from €140.00 to €160.00**

*Nell O' Connor*

11

Closed 24 - 25 December

### Carrigaline Court Hotel & Leisure Centre

HOTEL ★★★★ MAP 3 H 3


Carrigaline,
Co. Cork

Tel: 021-485 2100 Fax: 021-437 1103
Email: reception@carrigcourt.com
Web: www.carrigcourt.com

AA 4**** hotel, located just minutes from city centre, airport and ferry terminal. 91 spacious bedrooms with broadband internet access, satellite TV, tea/coffee facilities, in-room safe, trouser press and all modern comforts as standard. Superb contemporary restaurant with unique design features. Atmospheric and spacious bar. Exquisite leisure centre including 20m pool, sauna, jacuzzi, steam room and gym. Golf arranged at Cork's best courses. Sailing, angling, horse riding and a host of other activities all available in this beautiful area. Please enquire about Facilities for Persons with Mobility Impairment.

***An IHF Quality Employer***

*Bookable on www.irelandhotels.com*
*Special Offer: www.irelandhotels.com/offers*

**B&B from €70.00 to €110.00**
**Suites from €200.00 to €300.00**

*David Harney*
*General Manager*

91

Activities:

Closed 25 December



B&B Rates are per Person Sharing per Night incl. Breakfast.
or Room Rates are per Room per Night - See also Page 8

## Fernhill Carrigaline Hotel, Golf & Health Club

HOTEL ★★ MAP 3 H 3

Fernhill,
Carrigaline,
Co. Cork

Tel: 021-437 2226 Fax: 021-437 1011
Email: info@fernhillgolfhotel.com
Web: www.fernhillgolfhotel.com

Set on the perimeters of an 80 acre golf course, overlooking the Owenabue Valley. Experience somewhere where you can enjoy golf, dining, tennis and a health and leisure club. Located 10 minutes from the city centre, 10 from the airport and 5 from Cork ferry. Offering 38 spacious guest rooms and 10 holiday houses, designed with your comfort in mind. Fernhill operates with the services of a hotel but with the intimacy and friendliness you would find at a great country house.

Member of Central Reservations

***Bookable on www.irelandhotels.com***
***Special Offer: www.irelandhotels.com/offers***

***B&B from €55.00 to €85.00***

*Alan Bowes*
*General Manager*

38

*Activities:*

**Closed 23 - 26 December**

## Glenwood House

GUESTHOUSE ★★★★ MAP 3 H 3

Ballinrea Road,
Carrigaline,
Co. Cork

Tel: 021-437 3878 Fax: 021-437 3878
Email: info@glenwoodguesthouse.com
Web: www.glenwoodguesthouse.com

Glenwood House is a purpose built, self contained guesthouse, designed with all guest requirements in mind. The rooms are large and spacious, offering similar facilities to those of quality hotels, firm orthopaedic beds, heated towel rails, complimentary beverages, trouser press, satellite TV, power shower, WiFi broadband communication and many more. Located close to Ringaskiddy Ferry Port (5mins), Cork City (7mins), Kinsale (15mins), Crosshaven (5mins), Airport (10mins). We offer secure car parking, and have facilities to look after disabled guests. All accommodation is of hotel quality.

Member of Premier Guesthouses

***Bookable on www.irelandhotels.com***

***B&B from €49.00 to €59.00***

*Adrian Sheedy*
*Proprietor*

15

**Closed 07 December - 06 January**

## Capella Castlemartyr

HOTEL MAP 3 I 3

Castlemartyr,
Co. Cork

Tel: 021-464 4050 Fax: 021-464 4051
Email: reservations.castlemartyr@capellahotels.com
Web: www.capellacastlemartyr.com

Built to a 5***** specification. 20 minutes east of Cork City, 220 acres are home to a 109 bedroomed Capella Hotel with the centerpiece a 17th century Manor House. Featuring Knights Bar, Belltower Restaurant, the Garden Room and Terrace, 24,400 sqft spa with café, 3 boardrooms, private dining room and presidential suite. An 18 hole inland links golf course, designed by Mr. Ron Kirby, with clubhouse, 10 mews style houses and 42 lodges are within the estate. Please enquire about Facilities for Persons with Mobility Impairment.

Member of Capella Hotels

***Room Rate from €360.00 to €750.00***
***Suites from €1,450.00 to €3,250.00***

*Peter Bowling*
*General Manager*

109

*Activities:*

**Open All Year**





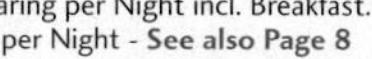

## Castletownshend / Clonakilty

### Castle (The)

GUESTHOUSE ★ MAP 2 F 1

Castletownshend,
Near Skibbereen,
Co. Cork

Tel: 028-36100 Fax: 028-36166

Email: castle_townshend@hotmail.com

Web: www.castle-townshend.com

18th century Townshend family home overlooking Castlehaven Harbour. Set in its own grounds at water's edge with access to small beach and woods. Most bedrooms en suite on second floor with excellent sea views. Panelled hall/sitting room with TV and open fire. Breakfast in elegant dining room. Mary Ann's Restaurant close by. Ideal for touring Cork and Kerry. Also self-catering apartments and cottages. Guided tours of The Castle in May, June & September & October by arrangement.
Website www.castle-townshend.com

*B&B from €50.00 to €85.00*

*Anne & Malcolm Cochrane Townshend*

7

**Closed 15 December - 15 January**

### Dunmore House Hotel

HOTEL ★★★ MAP 2 G 2

Muckross,
Clonakilty,
Co. Cork

Tel: 023-33352 Fax: 023-34686

Email: enq@dunmorehousehotel.ie

Web: www.dunmorehousehotel.ie

Situated on the South West coast of Ireland, Dunmore House Hotel is family owned. Rooms are beautifully decorated, with spectacular views of the Atlantic Ocean. Sample a true taste of West Cork with our home-cooked local produce and seafood. Private foreshore available for sea angling. Green fees at the on-site golf club are free to residents. Horse riding available by arrangement. Interesting collection of local and modern Irish art. Please enquire about Facilities for Persons with Mobility Impairment.

***An IHF Quality Employer***

*B&B from €85.00 to €105.00*

*Derry & Mary O'Donovan*
*Proprietors*

29

Activities:

**Closed 13 January - 06 March**

### Emmet Hotel

HOTEL ★★ MAP 2 G 2

Emmet Square,
Clonakilty,
Co. Cork

Tel: 023-33394 Fax: 023-35058

Email: emmethotel@eircom.net

Web: www.emmethotel.com

Family-run Hotel in a quiet Georgian Square in the bustling Town of Clonakilty. All rooms are furnished to a high standard with very comfortable beds & duvets, all en suite with TV, DD telephone, tea/coffee making facilities & Wireless Internet Access. Delicious food, using fresh seasonal & organic (where possible), at very reasonable prices served in The Bistro & the bar from noon to 10pm. The heated courtyard can be reserved for private barbeques & there are function & meeting rooms available. The hotel also has a heated smoking area & contemporary night club. Beautiful beaches, sea fishing & golfing are a short drive away.

*B&B from €50.00 to €80.00*

*The O'Keeffe Family*
*Proprietors*

20

Activities:

**Closed 24 - 26 December**



B&B Rates are per Person Sharing per Night incl. Breakfast.
or Room Rates are per Room per Night - **See also Page 8**

## Fernhill House Hotel

HOTEL ★★ MAP 2 G 2

Clonakilty,
Co. Cork

Tel: 023-33258 Fax: 023-34003
Email: info@fernhillhousehotel.com
Web: www.fernhillhousehotel.com

Fernhill House is a family-run old Georgian style hotel located on picturesque grounds 0.8km from Clonakilty. All bedrooms are en suite with tea/coffee making facilities, phone, TV and hairdryer. Conference and function facilities available. Our hotel offers an intimate homely atmosphere, excellent food and a comfortable bar. Holiday with us and enjoy scenic West Cork from centrally situated Fernhill House Hotel. Please enquire about Facilities for Persons with Mobility Impairment.

***An IHF Quality Employer***

***B&B from €60.00 to €70.00***

*Michael & Teresa O'Neill*
*Proprietors*

16

Activities:

**Closed 23 December - 01 January**

## Inchydoney Island Lodge & Spa

HOTEL ★★★★ MAP 2 G 2

Clonakilty,
West Cork

Tel: 023-33143 Fax: 023-35229
Email: reservations@inchydoneyisland.com
Web: www.inchydoneyisland.com

Situated on the idyllic island of Inchydoney, adjacent to a stunning EU Blue Flag beach, this luxurious hotel offers de luxe rooms, a fully equipped thalassotherapy (seawater) spa, award-winning restaurant, Dunes Pub and function and meeting facilities. Within a short distance guests can enjoy sailing, golf, riding and deep sea fishing, whale watching and surfing. The style of cooking in the Gulfstream Restaurant reflects the wide availability of fresh seafood and organically grown vegetables. Please enquire about Facilities for Persons with Mobility Impairment.

***An IHF Quality Employer***

***Bookable on www.irelandhotels.com***
***Special Offer: www.irelandhotels.com/offers***

***B&B from €180.00 to €200.00***

*The Team at Inchydoney*
*Island Lodge & Spa*

67

Activities:

**Closed 24 - 27 December**

## O'Donovan's Hotel

HOTEL ★★ MAP 2 G 2

Pearse Street,
Clonakilty,
West Cork

Tel: 023-33250 Fax: 023-33250
Email: info@odonovanshotel.com
Web: www.odonovanshotel.com

Charles Stewart Parnell, Marconi and Gen. Michael Collins found time to stop here. This fifth generation, family-run hotel is located in the heart of Clonakilty Town. Abounding in history, the old world charm has been retained whilst still providing the guest with facilities such as bath/shower en suite, TV etc. Our restaurant provides snacks and full meals and is open to non-residents. Ideal for conferences, private functions, meetings etc., with lock up car park.

***An IHF Quality Employer***

***B&B from €60.00 to €60.00***

*O'Donovan Family*
*Proprietors*

21

**Closed 25 - 28 December**

## Clonakilty / Cobh

### Quality Hotel & Leisure Centre Clonakilty

HOTEL ★★★ MAP 2 G 2

Clonakilty,
Co. Cork

Tel: 023-36400 Fax: 023-35404
Email: info.clonakilty@qualityhotels.ie
Web: www.qualityhotelclonakilty.com

Clonakilty is a thriving and busy attractive town with a wealth of musical, artistic and family activities. Our unique hotel, 10 minutes from Clonakilty town centre, offers you the following superb facilities, 96 en suite guest rooms including 17 executive family rooms, 20 two bedroomed suites, 5 holiday homes, Lannigans Restaurant, Oscars Bar, an award-winning Health & Fitness Club, 3 Screen Cinema, Crèche, Playroom & Playground and 2 Treatment & Therapy Suites.

***An IHF Quality Employer***

Member of Quality Hotels

***Bookable on www.irelandhotels.com***
***Special Offer: www.irelandhotels.com/offers***

***B&B from €39.00 to €109.00***
***Suites from €79.00 to €199.00***

*David Henry*
*General Manager*

96

Activities:

Closed 22 - 26 December

### Commodore Hotel

HOTEL ★★ MAP 3 I 3

Cobh,
Co. Cork

Tel: 021-481 1277 Fax: 021-481 1672
Email: commodorehotel@eircom.net
Web: www.commodorehotel.ie

The Commodore Hotel, owned and managed by the O'Shea family for 38 years - overlooks Cork Harbour. 25 minutes from city centre. Facilities: indoor swimming pool, sauna - entertainment and roof garden. Locally (subject to availability at clubs) free golf and pitch & putt. Ideal location for visiting Fota Wildlife Park, Fota Golf Course, Blarney etc, The Jameson and Queenstown Heritage Centres. All 42 rooms have full facilities, (21 overlook Cork Harbour - supplement applies). Ringaskiddy Ferryport 15 minutes via river car ferry.

***An IHF Quality Employer***

***Bookable on www.irelandhotels.com***
***Special Offer: www.irelandhotels.com/offers***

***B&B from €47.00 to €80.00***

*Patrick O'Shea*
*General Manager*

42

Activities:

Closed 24 - 25 December

### WatersEdge Hotel

HOTEL ★★★ MAP 3 I 3

(Next To Cobh Heritage Centre),
Cobh,
Co. Cork

Tel: 021-481 5566 Fax: 021-481 2011
Email: info@watersedgehotel.ie
Web: www.watersedgehotel.ie

Situated on the waterfront overlooking Cork Harbour. All rooms en suite with satellite TV, tea making facilities, direct dial phone, modem, hairdryer, trouser press. Our restaurant, Jacobs Ladder, is renowned for its seafood, steaks, ambience and friendly staff. Local activities and sightseeing include Cobh Heritage Centre (next door), Cathedral, Titanic Trail, Fota Wildlife Park, Fota House & Gardens, golf, sailing, angling, tennis, horse riding. Ideal touring base for Cork City, Kinsale & Blarney. Please enquire about Facilities for Persons with Mobility Impairment.

Member of Cork Luxury Hotels

***Bookable on www.irelandhotels.com***
***Special Offer: www.irelandhotels.com/offers***

***B&B from €55.00 to €100.00***
***Suites from €180.00 to €250.00***

*Dudley Fitzell*
*Group General Manager*

19

Activities:

Closed 24 - 26 December



B&B Rates are per Person Sharing per Night incl. Breakfast.
or Room Rates are per Room per Night - See also Page 8

## Cork International Airport Hotel

HOTEL ★★★★ MAP 2 H 3

Cork Airport,
Co. Cork

Tel: 021-454 9800 Fax: 021-454 9999
Email: info@corkairporthotel.com
Web: www.corkinternationalairporthotel.com

Opposite Cork Airport with a walkway to the door, located in Cork Airport Business Park and 15 mins to the city, this new 150 bedroomed four star hotel's striking aviation-themed interior and avant-garde design help to set the hotel apart. Spacious guest rooms with views over Cork City. Uniquely designed public spaces, Strata Restaurant, The Ó Bar, on-site bakery supplying fresh bread and pastries all day, sandwich bar, Café Tucano, florist, hairdresser, large conference & banqueting space. Free parking and WiFi. Spa open 2007/2008. Book online www.corkinternationalairporthotel.com

Member of Mercer Accommodation Group

*Bookable on www.irelandhotels.com*
*Special Offer: www.irelandhotels.com/offers*

***B&B from €55.00 to €200.00***

*Gabriele Molari*
*General Manager*

150

Open All Year

## Radisson SAS Hotel, Cork Airport

HOTEL ★★★★ MAP 2 H 3

Cork Airport,
Co. Cork

Tel: 021-494 7500 Fax: 021-494 7501
Email: reservations.airport.cork@radissonsas.com
Web: www.radissonsas.com

The Radisson Hotel Cork Airport is a stylish contemporary hotel conveniently located within walking distance of the terminal at Cork Airport. With a wide range of meeting rooms, a business centre and a leisure centre with gymnasium, steam room and jacuzzi, it is the perfect base for business meetings or for first or last night stays. Bookable worldwide through Rezidor Hotel Reservations or In House Reservations: 021-494 7500. Please enquire about Facilities for Persons with Mobility Impairment.

***An IHF Quality Employer***

*Bookable on www.irelandhotels.com*
*Special Offer: www.irelandhotels.com/offers*

***Room Rate from €89.00 to €270.00***

*Rose O'Donovan*
*General Manager*

81

*Activities:*

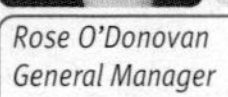

Closed 24 - 27 December

B&B Rates are per Person Sharing per Night incl. Breakfast.
or Room Rates are per Room per Night - See also Page 8

## Cork City

### Achill House

GUESTHOUSE ★★★ MAP 2 H 3


Western Road,
Cork City

Tel: 021-427 9447
Email: info@achillhouse.com
Web: www.achillhouse.com

Stay in luxury, comfort and style at Achill House. This elegant period house is ideally located in the heart of Cork City and opposite UCC. All rooms have de luxe en suite bathrooms with optional jacuzzi. An extensive breakfast menu caters for all tastes, from hearty Irish breakfasts to lighter options. Achill House is convenient to ferry, airport and bus termini, the perfect base for exploring Cork and Kerry. A warm and relaxed atmosphere awaits you, whether on business or pleasure.

*Bookable on www.irelandhotels.com*
*Special Offer: www.irelandhotels.com/offers*

**B&B from €45.00 to €65.00**

*Helena McSweeney*
*Manager*

6

**Open All Year**

### Ambassador Hotel

HOTEL ★★★★ MAP 2 H 3


Military Hill,
St. Lukes,
Cork

Tel: 021-453 9000 Fax: 021-455 1997
Email: info@ambassadorhotel.ie
Web: www.ambassadorhotel.ie

Located on a hilltop, the Ambassador Hotel commands spectacular views over Cork City and Harbour. 70 spacious bedrooms luxuriously decorated to the highest standards. A gourmet award-winning "Season's Restaurant", Cocktail Bar, Embassy Bar, Conference Centre and Banqueting facilities, all combine to ensure a memorable stay. Health Centre (gym, jacuzzi, sauna, steam room) allows guests to unwind at leisure. An excellent base to explore Cork City and county. Free wireless access in all bedrooms.

***An IHF Quality Employer***

Member of Best Western Hotels

*Bookable on www.irelandhotels.com*
*Special Offer: www.irelandhotels.com/offers*

**B&B from €62.50 to €92.50**
**Suites from €175.00 to €250.00**

*John McCarthy*
*General Manager*

70

*Activities:*

**Closed 24 - 27 December**

### Ashley Hotel

HOTEL ★★ MAP 2 H 3


Coburg Street,
Cork City

Tel: 021-450 1518 Fax: 021-450 1178
Email: info@ashleyhotel.com
Web: www.ashleyhotel.com

Superbly located in the city centre with a lock up car park, north of the River Lee near the bus and railway station. This family-run hotel offers you a comfortable stay with all bedrooms offering bathroom en suite, satellite television, wireless Broadband access, complimentary tea/coffee making facilities and direct dial telephone. For a relaxing drink, why not try the Hotel Bar.

*Bookable on www.irelandhotels.com*
*Special Offer: www.irelandhotels.com/offers*

**B&B from €55.00 to €100.00**

*Anita Coughlan*

27

**Closed 22 December - 07 January**



B&B Rates are per Person Sharing per Night incl. Breakfast.
or Room Rates are per Room per Night - See also Page 8

## Blarney Stone

GUESTHOUSE ★★★ MAP 2 H 3

Western Road,
Cork City

Tel: 021-427 0083 Fax: 021-427 0471

Email: bsgh@eircom.net

Web: www.blarneystoneguesthouse.ie

This newly refurbished Victorian residence has character and charm and offers you luxurious accommodation in the heart of the city. Situated opposite University College Cork and within close proximity of a selection of restaurants, bars and entertainment places. Also ideally located for ferry, airport, train and bus. Rooms are tastefully decorated to the highest standard with de luxe en suite optional jacuzzi, TV, DD phone, tea/coffee making facilities. A warm and friendly atmosphere awaits you.

**B&B from €40.00 to €75.00**

*Angela Hartnett*
*Proprietor*

8

T C P S I

**Open All Year**

## Brookfield Hotel

HOTEL ★★★ MAP 2 H 3

Brookfield Holiday Village,
College Road,
Cork

Tel: 021-480 4700 Fax: 021-480 4793

Email: brookfieldhotel@eircom.net

Web: www.brookfieldcork.ie

Brookfield Hotel, College Road is just 1 mile from Cork City centre. Set on 10 acres of rolling parkland, it is truly a rural setting. *24 bright, modern bedrooms. *Family rooms. *Interconnecting rooms. *Enjoy our leisure and fitness centre which incorporates 25m indoor pool. Kiddies pool, water slide, saunas, steam room, spa jacuzzi, outdoor hot tub, massage, gym, sunbeds, outdoor tennis courts. Please enquire about Facilities for Persons with Mobility Impairment.

**B&B from €60.00 to €110.00**

*Jean Cassidy*
*Reservations*

24

T C P I

**Closed 21 December - 03 January**

B&B Rates are per Person Sharing per Night incl. Breakfast.
or Room Rates are per Room per Night - See also Page 8

## Cork City

### Clarion Hotel

HOTEL ★★★★ MAP 2 H 3


Lapps Quay,
Cork City

Tel: 021-422 4900 Fax: 021-422 4901
Email: info@clarionhotelcorkcity.com
Web: www.clarionhotelcorkcity.com

Overlooking Cork's River Lee, the Clarion Hotel is situated in the heart of Cork City. Our contemporary bedrooms and suites are furnished to the highest standards. Enjoy a range of eating experiences from Sinergie Restaurant with an Irish/European menu and Kudos Bar serving Asian cuisine. The Atrium Lounge offers light snacks throughout the day. The hotel is completed by SanoVitae Health Club and Spa offering full leisure facilities. The Clarion Hotel is located 15 minutes from Cork Airport. Please enquire about Facilities for Persons with Mobility Impairment.

***Bookable on www.irelandhotels.com***
***Special Offer: www.irelandhotels.com/offers***

***Room Rate from €120.00 to €320.00***
***Suites from €185.00 to €350.00***

*Charlie Sheil*
*General Manager*

191

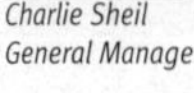

*Activities:*

**Closed 24 - 26 December**

### Commons Inn

HOTEL ★★★ MAP 3 H 3


New Mallow Road,
Cork

Tel: 021-421 0300 Fax: 021-421 0333
Email: info@commonsinn.com
Web: www.commonsinn.com

Close to Cork City, on the main Cork to Blarney road, this family-run hotel contains the popular Commons Bar, Baileys Restaurant and the Roebuck Room function centre. All rooms contain two queen sized beds and are priced per room. Enjoy carvery lunch in the bar or dinner in one of Cork's best restaurants. Whether you're in Cork on business or for pleasure, we are at your service. Please enquire about Facilities for Persons with Mobility Impairment.

***Room Rate from €65.00 to €90.00***

*Ashley Colson*
*Accommodation Manager*

40

*Activities:*

**Closed 24 - 31 December**

### Crawford Guesthouse

GUESTHOUSE ★★★ MAP 3 H 3


Western Road,
Cork

Tel: 021-427 9000 Fax: 021-427 9927
Email: info@crawfordhouse.ie
Web: www.crawfordhouse.ie

One of Cork's finest guesthouses offering bed & breakfast in a contemporary setting. All the bedrooms provide comfort and luxury with oak-wood furniture and orthopaedic 6ft beds. De luxe en suites include jacuzzi baths and power showers. Fax/modem points in all rooms. Located directly across from University College Cork. 10 minutes walk to city centre. Private car park. AA ♦♦♦♦ & RAC ♦♦♦♦ and Sparkling Diamond Award. Recommended by Lonely Planet Guide, Time Out Guide, Bradt City Guide and Gourmet Magazine.

***Bookable on www.irelandhotels.com***

***B&B from €50.00 to €65.00***

*Cecilia O'Leary*
*Manager*

12

**Closed 22 December - 15 January**



B&B Rates are per Person Sharing per Night incl. Breakfast.
or Room Rates are per Room per Night - **See also Page 8**

## East Village Hotel

HOTEL ★★ MAP 3 H 3

Douglas,
Cork

Tel: 021-436 7000 Fax: 021-436 7001
Email: info@eastvillage.ie
Web: www.eastvillage.ie

East Village is a welcome addition to the Cork area with a large and vibrant sports bar, award-winning restaurant and just 10 bedrooms. This contemporary hotel provides easy access to all amenities close to Cork City centre, Cork Airport & the Jack Lynch Tunnel. This hotel offers the oft-forgotten personal touch. All rooms are en suite and have private balcony, TV etc. and are decorated in a modern fashion. Please enquire about Facilities for Persons with Mobility Impairment.

**Room Rate from €89.00 to €119.00**

*Derry O'Regan*
*Proprietor*

10

**Open All Year**

## Fitzgeralds Vienna Woods Hotel Cork

HOTEL ★★★ MAP 3 H 3

Glanmire,
Cork

Tel: 021-455 6800 Fax: 021-482 1120
Email: info@viennawoodshotel.com
Web: www.viennawoodshotel.com

A country house hotel, set in 20 acres of woodlands, overlooking Cork Harbour. Excellent location, only 7 minutes from Cork city centre, and close to Fota Wildlife Park and Cork International Airport. An ideal base for touring the Cork region. Superb dining facilities serving à la carte, table d'hôte and snack menus. Excellent wedding and conference facilities with generous private car parking. Fitzgeralds Woodlands House Hotel and Spa is a sister hotel located in Adare, Co. Limerick. Please enquire about Facilities for Persons with Mobility Impairment.

***An IHF Quality Employer***
Member of Irish Country Hotels

*Bookable on www.irelandhotels.com*
*Special Offer: www.irelandhotels.com/offers*

**B&B from €70.00 to €250.00**
**Suites from €140.00 to €400.00**

*David Fitzgerald, Michael Magner*
*Proprietors*

50

*Activities:*

**Closed 24 - 26 December**

Step back in time to see what 19th & early 20th Century life was like in Cork - inside & outside prison walls! Amazingly lifelike figures, furnished cells, sound effects and fascinating exhibitions.

**OPEN 7 DAYS**
Throughout the year.
At same location the
RADIO MUSEUM

Sunday's Well, Cork City
Tel: 021-430 50 22
Email: corkgaol@indigo.ie
www.corkcitygaol.com

B&B Rates are per Person Sharing per Night incl. Breakfast.
or Room Rates are per Room per Night - See also Page 8

## Cork City

### Garnish House

GUESTHOUSE ★★★ MAP 3 H 3

Western Road,
Cork

Tel: 021-427 5111 Fax: 021-427 3872
Email: garnish@iol.ie
Web: www.garnish.ie

RAC 4♦♦♦♦ and AA 4♦♦♦♦. Offers a homely atmosphere and personal attention normally reserved for old friends. Individually styled rooms, some with Jacuzzi baths, are tranquil and charming and our traditional welcome is more than mere words with tea, pastries and an award-winning gourmet breakfast as featured on national TV. 24/7 reception, central to the city and opposite Cork University. Awards: Sparkling Diamond, Bridgestone Chosen Place to Stay. 4**** studios/suites available. Free internet (wireless) access.

***Bookable on www.irelandhotels.com***

**B&B from €45.00 to €100.00**
**Suites from €130.00 to €200.00**

*Johanna Lucey*
*Manageress*

14

**Open All Year**

### Gresham Metropole

HOTEL ★★★ MAP 3 H 3

MacCurtain Street,
Cork

Tel: 021-464 3789 Fax: 021-450 6450
Email: info@gresham-metropolehotel.com
Web: www.gresham-hotels.com

The Gresham Metropole is an architectural landmark in the centre of Cork City. Behind our historical façade you'll find 113 beautifully refurbished rooms. Facilities include the Riverview Restaurant and the Met Bar. In Cork, everything is close by. Whether it's shopping, eating or drinking, you'll find it all within minutes of the hotel. Secure complimentary parking for guests. AA approved.

***An IHF Quality Employer***

Member of Gresham Hotel Group

***Bookable on www.irelandhotels.com***
***Special Offer: www.irelandhotels.com/offers***

**Room Rate from €90.00 to €260.00**

*Thys Vogels*
*General Manager*

113

Activities:

**Open All Year**

### Hayfield Manor Hotel

HOTEL ★★★★★ MAP 2 H 3

Perrott Avenue,
College Road,
Cork

Tel: 021-484 5900 Fax: 021-431 6839
Email: enquiries@hayfieldmanor.ie
Web: www.hayfieldmanor.ie

Hayfield Manor is a unique Irish experience with our staff dedicated to providing you with individual & memorable service. Our spacious rooms have been individually designed in classical style with elegant marble bathrooms. As a resident, you have exclusive access to The Beautique Spa. We offer two award-winning & distinctive restaurants, The Manor Bar & our renowned Afternoon Tea. Awarded IGTOA Hotel of the Year 2005, Georgina Campbell's Ireland Hotel of the Year 2006 & AA Irish Hotel of the Year 2003 /2004. Hotel & Catering Review Gold Medal Awards 5* Hotel of the Year 2007.

***An IHF Quality Employer***

Member of Small Luxury Hotels of the World

***Bookable on www.irelandhotels.com***
***Special Offer: www.irelandhotels.com/offers***

**Room Rate from €200.00 to €380.00**
**Suites from €400.00 to €1,030.00**

*Joe Scally*
*Proprietor*

88

Activities:

**Open All Year**



B&B Rates are per Person Sharing per Night incl. Breakfast.
or Room Rates are per Room per Night - **See also Page 8**

## Hotel Isaacs

HOTEL ★★★ MAP 3 H 3

48 MacCurtain Street,
Cork

Tel: 021-450 0011 Fax: 021-450 6355
Email: cork@isaacs.ie
Web: www.isaacs.ie

Unique Victorian Hotel tucked away underneath an archway in Cork's city centre. Minutes from bus and train stations. Beautifully furnished standard and air-conditioned superior rooms plus serviced holiday apartments. Facilities include television, phone, hospitality tray, hairdryer, ironing facilities and personal safe. Wi-Fi and broadband available throughout the hotel. Greenes Restaurant, overlooking the floodlit waterfall offers modern creative cuisine. Dine al fresco all year in the heated courtyard garden. Limited free parking close to the hotel.

*Bookable on www.irelandhotels.com*
*Special Offer: www.irelandhotels.com/offers*

*Room Rate from €89.00 to €119.00*

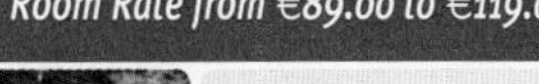

*Paula Lynch*
*General Manager*

47

Activities:

**Closed 24 - 27 December**

## Imperial Hotel with Escape Salon and Spa

HOTEL ★★★★ MAP 3 H 3

South Mall,
Cork

Tel: 021-427 4040 Fax: 021-427 5375
Email: reservations@imperialhotelcork.ie
Web: www.flynnhotels.com

Nestled amongst the charm and magic of Cork City is one of Cork's most exclusive properties. The recent refurbishment has touched on every aspect of the hotel to create 130 beautifully appointed guest rooms, including 42 new contemporary designed superior rooms, a fantastic penthouse suite boasting stunning views of Cork's cityscape and Ireland's first Aveda Lifestyle Salon and Spa. We want your time at the Imperial Hotel with Escape Salon and Spa to be a memorable treat, a haven from a busy world. Please enquire about Facilities for Persons with Mobility Impairment.

Member of Flynn Hotels

*Bookable on www.irelandhotels.com*
*Special Offer: www.irelandhotels.com/offers*

*Room Rate from €99.00 to €150.00*
*Suites from €139.00 to €190.00*

*Joe Kennedy*
*General Manager*

130

Activities:

**Closed 24 - 27 December**

## Jurys Cork Hotel

HOTEL ★★★★ MAP 2 H 3

Western Road,
Cork

Tel: 021-425 2700 Fax: 021-427 4477
Email: cork@jurysdoyle.com
Web: www.jurysdoyle.com

Jurys Cork Hotel returns to the city steeped in luxury throughout - the elegant interior deftly exploiting its spectacular riverside backdrop. Designed to delight the eye and capitalise on its commanding location on the banks of the River Lee. The hotel bridges the gap between home & work by providing spacious, luxurious bedrooms with up to date entertainment systems, an excellent restaurant & bar serving fresh healthy food, meeting rooms with state-of-the-art technology and leisure centre.

***An IHF Quality Employer***

Member of Jurys Doyle Hotel Group

*Bookable on www.irelandhotels.com*
*Special Offer: www.irelandhotels.com/offers*

*Room Rate from €149.00 to €249.00*

*Fergal Somers*
*General Manager*

182

**Open All Year**

B&B Rates are per Person Sharing per Night incl. Breakfast.
or Room Rates are per Room per Night - **See also Page 8**

## Cork City

### Jurys Inn Cork

HOTEL ★★★ MAP 2 H 3

Anderson's Quay,
Cork

Tel: 021-494 3000 Fax: 021-427 6144
Email: jurysinncork@jurysinns.com
Web: www.jurysinns.com

Jurys Inn Cork enjoys a superb location right in the heart of Cork City, overlooking the River Lee. Vibrant business and shopping districts and a host of restaurants, bars, museums and galleries are literally within a few minutes' walk. An excellent base to explore the city or the very stunning Co. Cork countryside. Please enquire about Facilities for Persons with Mobility Impairment.

***An IHF Quality Employer***

Member of Jurys Inns Group Ltd

***Bookable on www.irelandhotels.com***
*Special Offer: www.irelandhotels.com/offers*

**Room Rate from €85.00 to €169.00**

*Julieann Brennan*
*General Manager*

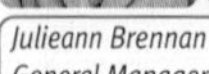

133

**Closed 24 - 26 December**

### Killarney Guest House

GUESTHOUSE ★★★ MAP 2 H 3

Western Road,
(Opp. UCC),
Cork City

Tel: 021-427 0290 Fax: 021-427 1010
Email: killarneyhouse@iol.ie
Web: www.killarneyguesthouse.com

This charming, distinctive, delightful and different guesthouse is renowned for its unique blend of comfort, style and hospitality. Its sumptuous breakfast menu includes a buffet table laden with fresh produce and home baking. All rooms are en suite with optional jacuzzi bath. A close walk to the city centre and opposite the University College Cork. Large car park for your security. AA ♦♦♦♦ acclaimed and RAC ♦♦♦♦. Also available, superb self catering apartments.

***Bookable on www.irelandhotels.com***

**B&B from €45.50 to €75.00**

*Margaret O'Leary*
*Manageress*

19

**Closed 24 - 27 December**

### Kingsley Hotel & Residences

HOTEL ★★★★★ MAP 2 H 3

Victoria Cross,
Cork

Tel: 021-480 0500 Fax: 021-480 0527
Email: resv@kingsleyhotel.com
Web: www.kingsleyhotel.com

Nestled on the River Lee, located only minutes from Cork's Airport. An elegant atmosphere and tranquil surroundings. The hotel features Ireland's only Ayurvedic Spa, Yauvana Spa, 200 seater conference & events area, 18 two bed residences (for long stay guests), health & fitness club, spectacular Riverside Restaurants and walkways. Please enquire about Facilities for Persons with Mobility Impairment.

***An IHF Quality Employer***

***Bookable on www.irelandhotels.com***
*Special Offer: www.irelandhotels.com/offers*

**B&B from €80.00 to €160.00**
**Suites from €375.00 to €1,500.00**

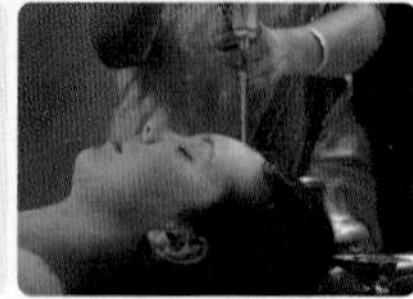

*Michelle Maloney*
*General Manager*

131

*Activities:*

**Open All Year**

B&B Rates are per Person Sharing per Night incl. Breakfast.
or Room Rates are per Room per Night - See also Page 8

## Lancaster Lodge

GUESTHOUSE ★★★★ MAP 2 H 3

Western Road,
Cork

Tel: 021-425 1125 Fax: 021-425 1126
Email: info@lancasterlodge.com
Web: www.lancasterlodge.com

Newly refurbished 4**** Boutique Accommodation located in the heart of Cork City centre between the University and the Courthouse. All rooms have wide screen LCD TV, king sized beds with crisp white duvets, digital safe and armchair with footstools. Jacuzzi Suites. Meeting room facilities. Free private car park. Complimentary morning newspapers. Free Wi-Fi in all rooms. Please enquire about Facilities for Persons with Mobility Impairment.

***Bookable on www.irelandhotels.com***
***Special Offer: www.irelandhotels.com/offers***

*B&B from €65.00 to €85.00*
*Suites from €160.00 to €200.00*

*Susan Leahy*
*General Manager*

48

Activities:

**Closed 23 - 27 December**

## Lotamore House

GUESTHOUSE ★★★★ MAP 3 H 3

Lower Glanmire Road,
Tivoli,
Cork

Tel: 021-482 2344 Fax: 021-482 2219
Email: lotamore@iol.ie
Web: www.lotamorehouse.com

An elegant Georgian residence of outstanding character, Lotamore House is the perfect place to escape from it all to the graciousness of times past. Pleasantly secluded, yet only 5 minutes drive from city centre, welcoming fires, lavish décor and antique furnishings combine to offer the perfect balance of luxury and charm. The stylish elegance in each guest room is individual. Lotamore House offers an uncompromising level of service. Ideally situated, near airport, ferry terminals and golf courses, making it the perfect base when visiting the scenic South West. Please enquire about Facilities for Persons with Mobility Impairment.

***Bookable on www.irelandhotels.com***
***Special Offer: www.irelandhotels.com/offers***

*B&B from €65.00 to €75.00*
*Suites from €150.00 to €170.00*

*Geraldine McElhinney*
*Proprietor / Manager*

18

**Closed 22 December - 05 January**

## Maryborough Hotel & Spa

HOTEL ★★★★ MAP 3 H 3

Maryborough Hill,
Douglas,
Cork

Tel: 021-436 5555 Fax: 021-436 5662
Email: info@maryborough.ie
Web: www.maryborough.com

One of Cork's leading hotels, The Maryborough is a unique experience. This 4**** de luxe hotel offers sophistication and luxury in an intimate atmosphere; an exclusive product with premier service, where customer service is the main focus and is the perfect destination for business and pleasure. 93 executive rooms and suites, Zings Restaurant & Café Bar, 11 conference rooms, Maryborough Club and ESPA Spa. Impeccable Hospitality, elegant and individual, you will enjoy the service excellence that Maryborough Hotel & Spa has to offer. Please enquire about Facilities for Persons with Mobility Impairment.

***An IHF Quality Employer***

***Bookable on www.irelandhotels.com***
***Special Offer: www.irelandhotels.com/offers***

*B&B from €89.00 to €250.00*
*Suites from €300.00 to €500.00*

*Justin McCarthy*
*General Manager*

93

Activities:

**Closed 24 - 26 December**

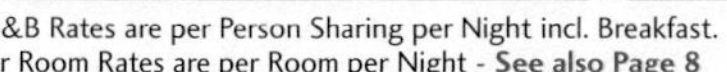

B&B Rates are per Person Sharing per Night incl. Breakfast.
or Room Rates are per Room per Night - **See also Page 8**

## Cork City

### Montenotte Hotel

HOTEL ★★★★ MAP 2 H 3

Montenotte,
Cork

Tel: 021-453 0050 Fax: 021-453 0060
Email: reservations@themontenottehotel.com
Web: www.themontenottehotel.com

Nestled along the leafy streets of Cork's most exclusive suburb, The Montenotte commands a spectacular position overlooking the wonderful city of Cork. Just minutes from the bustling city centre, this stylish hotel offers modern guest rooms and apartments, superb bar and dining options and all the comforts expected from today's discerning business and leisure travellers, including gym, 18m pool, sauna and steam room. Further information and online bookings at www.themontenottehotel.com

Member of Select Hotels

*Bookable on www.irelandhotels.com*
*Special Offer: www.irelandhotels.com/offers*

**B&B from €89.00 to €139.00**
**Suites from €190.00 to €300.00**

*John Gately*
*MD/Proprietor*

107

**Open All Year**

### Quality Hotel & Leisure Centre, Cork

HOTEL ★★★ MAP 2 H 3

John Redmond Street,
Cork

Tel: 021-452 9200 Fax: 021-452 9222
Email: info@qualityhotels.ie
Web: www.qualityhotelcork.com

A great location for city breaks or an ideal base to explore Cork County. Spacious guest rooms, relaxing surroundings, imaginative menus available at Lannigans Restaurant and Bell's Bar - a perfect place for a relaxing drink, serving bar food daily from 10.30am until 9pm. Entertainment Wednesday through to Sunday. Club Vitae boasts a superb 20m pool, gym, jacuzzi, steam room, sauna and treatment room. Complimentary but limited car parking. WiFi broadband. Wheelchair accessible. Please enquire about Facilities for Persons with Mobility Impairment.

***An IHF Quality Employer***

Member of Quality Hotels

*Bookable on www.irelandhotels.com*
*Special Offer: www.irelandhotels.com/offers*

**Room Rate from €79.00 to €199.00**

*Aidan Moynihan*
*General Manager*

101

Activities:

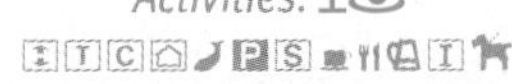

**Closed 24 - 27 December**

### Radisson SAS Hotel & Spa, Cork

HOTEL ★★★★ MAP 2 H 3

Ditchley House,
Little Island,
Cork

Tel: 021-429 7000 Fax: 021-429 7101
Email: info.cork@radissonsas.com
Web: www.cork.radissonsas.com

Nestled on 9 acres of landscaped gardens, in close proximity to the city centre and Cork International Airport, the hotel is a fusion of old world charm and new world sophistication, offering 129 luxurious guest rooms and suites. The extravagant Retreat Spa & Fitness Centre includes nine treatment rooms and a hydrotherapy treatment pool. Boasting extensive meeting and events facilities. Dining options include the intimate "Island Grillroom" and the "Banks Bar" for lighter meals and cocktails. Please enquire about Facilities for Persons with Mobility Impairment.

*Bookable on www.irelandhotels.com*

**B&B from €60.00 to €120.00**

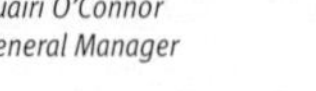

*Ruairi O'Connor*
*General Manager*

129

Activities:

**Open All Year**



B&B Rates are per Person Sharing per Night incl. Breakfast.
or Room Rates are per Room per Night - See also Page 8

## Rochestown Park Hotel

HOTEL ★★★★ MAP 3 H 3

Rochestown Road,
Douglas,
Cork City

Tel: 021-489 0800 Fax: 021-489 2178

Email: info@rochestownpark.com

Web: www.rochestownpark.com

The 4* Rochestown Park Hotel enjoys a superb location just 5 minutes from Cork City and Cork International Airport. Built among 11 acres of mature gardens, the property allows its guests to unwind & relax in luxury. Facilities include an award-winning leisure centre & spa, 163 large bedrooms, 2 dining options & the largest conference & banqueting facilities in Cork. Complimentary parking & WiFi access makes this hotel the perfect choice for corporate and leisure guests. Please enquire about Facilities for Persons with Mobility Impairment.

***An IHF Quality Employer***

Member of Mary Brown Associates

***Bookable on www.irelandhotels.com***
*Special Offer: www.irelandhotels.com/offers*

*B&B from €45.00 to €200.00*
*Suites from €300.00 to €500.00*

*Shay Livingstone*
*General Manager*

163

*Activities:*

**Closed 24 - 26 December**

## Silver Springs Moran Hotel

HOTEL ★★★★ MAP `

Tivoli,
Cork

Tel: 021-450 7533 Fax: 021-450 7641

Email: silverspringsinfo@moranhotels.com

Web: www.silverspringshotel.ie

This 4**** hotel has been completely re-designed and re-furbished. The hotel is located only minutes from Cork City. 109 bedrooms including 5 de luxe suites all with cable TV, trouser press and tea/coffee facitlities. Centrally located only 5 minutes from the city centre and 7 miles from Cork Intenational Airport. Excellent base for touring Cork's many visitor attractions. Full leisure facilities available include 25m pool. Free parking. A Moran Hotel. Please enquire about Facilities for Persons with Mobility Impairment.

***An IHF Quality Employer***

Member of Moran Hotel Group

***Bookable on www.irelandhotels.com***
*Special Offer: www.irelandhotels.com/offers*

*B&B from €60.00 to €150.00*
*Suites from €210.00 to €350.00*

*Tom Moran*
*Managing Director*

109

*Activities:*

**Closed 24 - 27 December**

## Victoria Hotel

HOTEL ★★ MAP 3 H 3

Patrick Street,
Cook Street,
Cork

Tel: 021-427 8788 Fax: 021-427 8790

Email: info@thevictoriahotel.com

Web: www.thevictoriahotel.com

The Victoria Hotel is situated in Cork City centre. All rooms have bath & shower, direct dial phone, TV and hairdryer. Family suites available. Built in 1810, it was frequented by European Royalty and was home to some of our own great political leaders, including Charles Stewart Parnell, who made his major speeches from its upper balcony. James Joyce recounts his stay in Portrait of an Artist. Conference room available. Children under 6 free when sharing parents' room. WiFi broadband area available and in selected bedrooms.

Member of Countrywide Hotels

*B&B from €40.00 to €90.00*

*King Family*
*Managers*

29

**Closed 24 - 26 December**

## Crosshaven / Fota Island / Glengarriff

### Whispering Pines Hotel

HOTEL ★★ MAP 3 I 3

Crosshaven,
Co. Cork

Tel: 021-483 1843 Fax: 021-483 1679
Email: reservations@whisperingpineshotel.com
Web: www.whisperingpineshotel.com

Whispering Pines, personally run by the Twomey Family, is a charming hotel sheltered by surrounding woodland and overlooking the Owenabue River. In this idyllic setting one can enjoy good company, quality home-cooked food and a host of amenities to ensure your stay is a restful and memorable experience. All rooms with direct dial phone, tea/coffee facilities and TV. Our 3 angling boats fish daily from April-October. Ideal base for touring Cork/Kerry Region. Cork Airport 12km and Cork City 19km. AA approved.

**B&B from €45.00 to €75.00**

*Norma Twomey*
*Proprietor*

15

Activities:

**Closed 01 December - 28 Feburary**

### Sheraton Fota Island Hotel & Spa (The)

HOTEL MAP 3 I 3

Fota Island,
Co. Cork

Tel: 021-467 3000 Fax: 021-467 3456
Email: reservations.fota@sheraton.com
Web: sheraton.com/cork

Built to a 5***** specification. Discover Cork's newest luxury destination, situated 20 minutes from Cork International Airport, the Sheraton offers an 18 hole championship course, the world class Fota Island Spa complete with 18 treatment rooms, hydrotherapy and thermal suites and an indoor swimming pool. Three individual eating experiences await: dine at the Gourmet Cove Restaurant, or enjoy all day dining with distinction at The Fota Restaurant or perhaps a light snack or afternoon tea in The Amber Lounge. Please enquire about Facilities for Persons with Mobility Impairment.

Member of Starwood

*Bookable on www.irelandhotels.com*
*Special Offer: www.irelandhotels.com/offers*

**Room Rate from €179.00 to €330.00**
**Suites from €214.00 to €700.00**

*John O'Flynn*
*General Manager*

131

Activities:

**Closed 25 - 27 December**

### Casey's Hotel

HOTEL ★★ MAP 1 D 2

The Village,
Glengarriff,
Co. Cork

Tel: 027-63010 Fax: 027-63072
Email: info@caseyshotelglengarriff.ie
Web: www.caseyshotelglengarriff.ie

Casey's Hotel is owner managed by the Deasy family. Offering a personal, friendly service with old fashioned courtesy. All our rooms are en suite with telephone, TV and tea/coffee. Private off road car parking and gardens. The perfect base for day trips to Killarney, Sheep's Head and Gougane Barra. Come and discover the unspoilt beauty of the Beara Peninsula. Fine food assured in our bar and à la carte restaurant.

**B&B from €48.00 to €57.00**

*Donal & Eileen Deasy*
*Proprietors*

19

Activities:

**Closed 01 November - 15 March**



B&B Rates are per Person Sharing per Night incl. Breakfast.
or Room Rates are per Room per Night - See also Page 8

## Glengarriff Eccles Hotel

HOTEL ★★★ MAP 2 D 2

Glengarriff,
Co. Cork

Tel: 027-63003 Fax: 027-63319
Email: info@eccleshotel.com
Web: www.eccleshotel.com

Located opposite Garnish Island, in beautiful Bantry Bay. The Glengarriff Eccles Hotel is one of the oldest established hotels in Ireland (1745). Now fully restored, this family-run hotel boasts 66 en suite bedrooms, many with panoramic views, restaurant and bar. Ideally situated to explore the beauty of the Beara Peninsula. Golf (3 courses within 20 km), fishing, hill walking and sailing are all nearby. 17km from Bantry. Please enquire about Facilities for Persons with Mobility Impairment.

***An IHF Quality Employer***

*Bookable on www.irelandhotels.com*
*Special Offer: www.irelandhotels.com/offers*

**B&B from €55.00 to €120.00**
**Suites from €200.00 to €400.00**

*Thos O'Brien*
*General Manager*

66

Activities:

**Closed 23 - 28 December**

## Glengarriff Park Hotel

HOTEL MAP 1 D 2

Glengarriff,
Co. Cork

Tel: 027-63000 Fax: 027-63526
Email: info@glengarriffpark.com
Web: www.glengarriffpark.com

Built to a 3*** specification. A new luxury hotel perfectly located in the very heart of Glengarriff Village at the entrance to the Blue Pool Park and Garnish Island. The hotel boasts 28 luxurious bedrooms and suites, traditional Irish bar and exquisite dining facilities. Walk, cycle, climb, swim or sail through the 60 acres of parks, gardens and bays on our doorstep. Please enquire about Facilities for Persons with Mobility Impairment.

*Bookable on www.irelandhotels.com*
*Special Offer: www.irelandhotels.com/offers*

**B&B from €40.00 to €99.00**
**Suites from €130.00 to €260.00**

*Paul Cullinan*
*General Manager*

28

Activities:

**Open All Year**

## Gougane Barra Hotel

HOTEL ★★★ MAP 2 E 3

Gougane Barra,
Ballingeary,
Co. Cork

Tel: 026-47069 Fax: 026-47226
Email: gouganebarrahotel@eircom.net
Web: www.gouganebarrahotel.com

Our family-run hotel hotel is nestled in one of the most scenic & romantic glens in the south west of Ireland, at the source of the River Lee, overlooking Gougane Barra Lake and St. Finbarr's sixth century hermitage. A favourite place for visitors, this small imtimate hotel is renowned for its fine food, comfort, relaxed atmosphere, warm welcome and splendid views of the lake, the glen and hills beyond.

Member of Irish Country Hotels

*Bookable on www.irelandhotels.com*
*Special Offer: www.irelandhotels.com/offers*

**B&B from €65.00 to €75.00**

*Katy & Neil Lucey*

26

**Closed 20 October - 05 April**

B&B Rates are per Person Sharing per Night incl. Breakfast.
or Room Rates are per Room per Night - **See also Page 8**

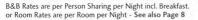

# Innishannon / Kinsale

## Innishannon House Hotel

HOTEL ★★★ MAP 2 G 2

Innishannon,
Co. Cork

Tel: 021-477 5121 Fax: 021-477 5609
Email: info@innishannon-hotel.ie
Web: www.innishannon-hotel.ie

The most romantic hotel in Ireland built in 1720 in the Petit Château style on the banks of the River Bandon, close to Kinsale. All rooms are en suite with TV, DD phone, radio, etc. Award-winning restaurant (AA**, RAC, Egon Ronay) serving fresh fish. Superb wine cellar, stunning views, free salmon and trout fishing from the grounds. Horse riding and golf nearby. GDS code: UI Toll Free 1-800-44 UTELL.

**B&B from €70.00 to €85.00**

David Roche
General Manager

12

**Closed 24 - 26 December**

## Actons Hotel

HOTEL ★★★ MAP 2 H 2

Pier Road,
Kinsale,
Co. Cork

Tel: 021-477 9900 Fax: 021-477 2231
Email: res@actonshotelkinsale.com
Web: www.actonshotelkinsale.com

Superior 3 star hotel located in landscaped gardens overlooking Kinsale's beautiful harbour. Renowned for its welcoming and friendly atmosphere, Actons also features an award-winning restaurant (Kinsale Good Food Circle Member), bar/bistro, and health & fitness club with new lobby, lounges and gardens. Conference and banqueting facilities available. Located in the historic town of Kinsale with restaurants, pubs, cafés, art and craft shops. Activities nearby: golfing, fishing, sailing, walking, historical sites.

***An IHF Quality Employer***

Member of Select Hotels of Ireland

*Bookable on www.irelandhotels.com*
*Special Offer: www.irelandhotels.com/offers*

**Room Rate from €89.00 to €179.00**

Jack Walsh
General Manager

73

1

Activities:

**Closed 06 January - 08 February**

## Blue Haven Kinsale (The)

HOTEL ★★★ MAP 2 H 3

3 Pearse Street,
Kinsale,
Co. Cork

Tel: 021-477 2209 Fax: 021-477 4268
Email: info@bluehavenkinsale.com
Web: www.bluehavenkinsale.com

A luxury boutique style hotel situated in the heart of Kinsale. Each room is individually furnished with exquisite furniture, the ultimate in luxury pocket sprung beds, plasma TVs and finer touches to make each room unique. The new Blue Haven Bar is now open. Luxuriously refurbished to the highest standards, it has launched an exciting new menu serving 7 days a week from 12 noon. First class cocktail menu also available, all professionally prepared from premium ingredients. Please enquire about Facilities for Persons with Mobility Impairment.

***An IHF Quality Employer***

*Bookable on www.irelandhotels.com*
*Special Offer: www.irelandhotels.com/offers*

**B&B from €85.00 to €125.00**

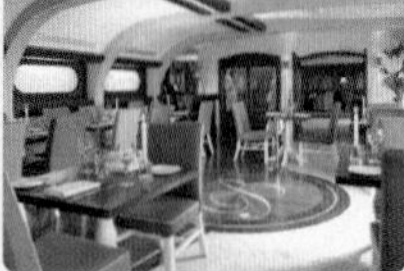

Declan Delaney / Loretto Kiernan
Managers

17

Activities:

**Open All Year**



B&B Rates are per Person Sharing per Night incl. Breakfast.
or Room Rates are per Room per Night - See also Page 8

## Captains Quarters

GUESTHOUSE ★★★ MAP 2 H 2

5 Dennis Quay,
Kinsale,
Co. Cork
Tel: 021-477 4549 Fax: 021-477 4944
Email: captquarters@eircom.net
Web: www.captains-kinsale.com

This Georgian period townhouse is situated close to the yacht club marina and within easy walking distance of restaurants and town centre amenities. It offers quality accommodation in a maritime ambience. The tranquil lounge on the 1st floor overlooks the harbour. The WHEELCHAIR ACCESSIBLE GROUND FLOOR ROOMS (1 twin / 1 single, sharing accessible shower / toilet) are also very convenient for the elderly. TV, direct dial phone, tea/coffee making facilities, hairdryer in all rooms. Please enquire about Facilities for Persons with Mobility Impairment.

*B&B from €35.00 to €50.00*

*Justina Jachimovic & Aiste Ungulaityte*
*Managers*

4
2

**Closed 01 - 28 February**

## Carlton Kinsale Hotel & C Spa

HOTEL ★★★★ MAP 2 H 2

Rathmore Road,
Kinsale,
Co. Cork
Tel: 021-470 6000 Fax: 021-470 6001
Email: info@carltonkinsalehotel.com
Web: www.carlton.ie

Situated on 90 acres of mature wooded parkland, the new Carlton Kinsale Hotel & C Spa is committed to providing the highest of standards. 90 luxury bedrooms and garden suites, most with views overlooking Oysterhaven Bay. Our restaurant offers superb cuisine with fine menus & spectacular views. Captain's Bar serves food all day. Conference & banqueting facilities are magnificent. Guests can enjoy our luxury leisure club & indulge in the C Spa. 5 minutes from Kinsale Town & 20 minutes from Cork City. Complimentary parking for all our guests. Room Reservations LoCall 1890 288 288.

Member of the Carlton Hotel Group

*Bookable on www.irelandhotels.com*
*Special Offer: www.irelandhotels.com/offers*

*B&B from €85.00 to €145.00*
*Suites from €450.00 to €650.00*

*Jerry Healy*
*General Manager*

90

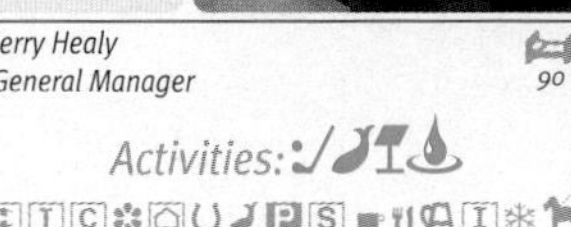


**Closed 24 - 26 December**

## Kinsale

### Friar's Lodge

GUESTHOUSE ★★★★ MAP 2 H 2

Friar's Street,
Kinsale,
Co. Cork

Tel: 021-477 7384 Fax: 021-477 4363

Email: mtierney@indigo.ie

Web: www.friars-lodge.com

Welcome! Friar's Lodge is situated in the heart of beautiful, award-winning, historical Kinsale. An ideal base for exploring the wonders of West Cork. All the rooms are luxurious, offering our guest every facility. A short stroll to the world famous restaurants and lively bars. Golfers welcomed, tee times can be arranged and we have a golf club drying room. Secure off street car park. RAC ♦♦♦♦♦, AA ♦♦♦♦♦. Please enquire about Facilities for Persons with Mobility Impairment.

*Bookable on www.irelandhotels.com*

*B&B from €45.00 to €75.00*

*Maureen Tierney*
*Owner*

18

**Closed 22 - 27 December**

### Harbour Lodge

GUESTHOUSE ★★★★ MAP 2 H 2

Scilly,
Kinsale,
Co. Cork

Tel: 021-477 2376 Fax: 021-477 2675

Email: relax@harbourlodge.com

Web: www.harbourlodge.com

Harbour Lodge is a hidden gem of luxury on Kinsale's waterfront. Our stunning location on the water's edge looks out over magnificent Kinsale Harbour and marina. Guests can watch the world sail by as they gaze out over the balconies, enjoying home-made chocolates and complimentary champagne. Our conservatory is the perfect setting for enjoying our fine dining experience overlooking the water. Local activities: golfing, sailing, deep sea fishing.

*Bookable on www.irelandhotels.com*
*Special Offer: www.irelandhotels.com/offers*

*B&B from €82.50 to €120.00*
*Suites from €220.00 to €330.00*

*Peter Tiernan*
*Manager*

9

*Activities:*

**Closed 20 December - 03 January**

### Jim Edwards

GUESTHOUSE ★★ MAP 2 H 2

Market Quay,
Kinsale,
Co. Cork

Tel: 021-477 2541 Fax: 021-477 3228

Email: info@jimedwardskinsale.com

Web: www.jimedwardskinsale.com

Family-run since 1971, Jim Edwards has a tradition of a warm, friendly welcome. All rooms are en suite and tastefully decorated with TV, telephone, tea/coffee making facilities. The guesthouse boasts an excellent seafood restaurant (fully licensed) which is a member of Kinsale Good Food Circle. The bar with its nautical theme throughout serves bar food all day. Being situated in the heart of the town means easy access to all the lively bars and entertainment. Local amenities include golf, deep sea angling, sailing, horse riding.

*B&B from €35.00 to €50.00*

*Jim Edwards*

7

**Open All Year**



B&B Rates are per Person Sharing per Night incl. Breakfast.
or Room Rates are per Room per Night - **See also Page 8**

## Kilcaw House

GUESTHOUSE ★★★ MAP 2 H 2

Kinsale,
Situated On R600,
Co. Cork

Tel: 021-477 4155 Fax: 021-477 4755

Email: info@kilcawhouse.com

Web: www.kilcawhouse.com

A family-run guesthouse, just 1km from Kinsale Town centre, with safe off the road parking and beautifully landscaped gardens. The guesthouse is built with a traditional flair yet is modern and luxurious. The bedrooms are spacious, furnished in antique pine and are en suite with TV, phone and tea/coffee making facilities. Just a 20 minute drive from Cork Airport and ferry. An ideal base for touring Blarney, Cobh, West Cork and Old Head of Kinsale. We welcome you to experience the warmth and hospitality of our home.

*B&B from €30.00 to €50.00*

*Henry & Christina Mitchell*
*Owners*

7

**Open All Year**

## Long Quay House

GUESTHOUSE ★★★ MAP 2 H 2

Long Quay,
Kinsale,
Co. Cork

Tel: 021-477 4563 Fax: 021-477 4563

Email: longquayhouse@eircom.net

Web: www.longquayhousekinsale.com

Long Quay House is a Georgian residence which typifies its era with rooms of splendid dimensions, furnished to afford the greatest possible guest comfort. Bedrooms are en suite (majority with bath), TV, direct dial phone, tea-making facilities and hairdryer. Located centrally overlooking inner harbour, yacht marina and within walking distance of all Kinsale's gourmet restaurants and many tourist attractions. Sea angling trips by local skippers arranged.

*B&B from €30.00 to €70.00*

*Jim & Peter Deasy*
*Hosts*

8

*Activities:*

**Closed 15 November - 27 December**

## Old Bank House

GUESTHOUSE ★★★★ MAP 2 H 2

11 Pearse Street,
Next To Post Office, Kinsale,
Co. Cork

Tel: 021-477 4075 Fax: 021-477 4296

Email: info@oldbankhousekinsale.com

Web: www.oldbankhousekinsale.com

The Old Bank House in the heart of Kinsale has been individually & tastefully designed & decorated to the highest standard with luxury pocket sprung beds & flat screen televisions in all rooms, with the finest gourmet breakfast. Most rooms enjoy views of the harbour town of Kinsale. All offer comfort & luxury with full en suites, every facility expected in an establishment of this quality. Complimentary broadband available to our guests. Golf friendly, tee times arranged. Voted one of the 'Top 100 Places to Stay in Ireland' every year since 1990. Winner of Les Routiers Irish Guesthouse of the Year 2005.

*B&B from €60.00 to €125.00*
*Suites from €200.00 to €270.00*

*Marguerite Cullen*
*Manageress*

17

*Activities:*

**Closed 22 - 29 December**

B&B Rates are per Person Sharing per Night incl. Breakfast.
or Room Rates are per Room per Night - **See also Page 8**

## Kinsale

### Tierney's Guest House

GUESTHOUSE ★★ MAP 2 H 2

Main Street,
Kinsale,
Co. Cork

Tel: 021-477 2205

Email: info@tierneys-kinsale.com

Web: www.tierneys-kinsale.com

Tierney's Guesthouse is a well established guesthouse situated in the heart of award-winning Kinsale. We offer TV, hairdryer, tea/coffee in each room, all of which are en suite and have been newly refurbished to a high standard. Browse in our craft outlet and enjoy our Courtyard Conservatory Café. A warm welcome is guaranteed and we will be only too happy to direct you to the many activities available and places to visit in Kinsale.

***Bookable on www.irelandhotels.com***
***Special Offer: www.irelandhotels.com/offers***

***B&B from €33.00 to €40.00***

*Fiona O'Mahony*
*Owner*

*10*

**Closed 23 - 26 December**

### Trident Hotel

HOTEL ★★★★ MAP 2 H 2

World's End,
Kinsale,
Co. Cork

Tel: 021-477 9300 Fax: 021-477 4173

Email: info@tridenthotel.com

Web: www.tridenthotel.com

The Trident has a spectacular setting on the water's edge in Kinsale. Now a 4**** hotel, it has 75 bedrooms and luxury suites. There are magnificent views from almost every vantage point in the hotel, particularly from the Schooner Lounge and the redesigned 'Pier One' Restaurant, where local seafood is a speciality. The cosy Wharf Tavern serves excellent bar food and has a lovely sheltered terrace overlooking the hotel's marina. Please enquire about Facilities for Persons with Mobility Impairment.

***An IHF Quality Employer***

***Bookable on www.irelandhotels.com***
***Special Offer: www.irelandhotels.com/offers***

***B&B from €70.00 to €125.00***
***Suites from €200.00 to €600.00***

*Hal McElroy*
*Managing Director*

*75*

*Activities:*

**Closed 24 - 26 December**

### White House

GUESTHOUSE ★★★ MAP 2 H 2

Pearse St. & The Glen,
Kinsale,
Co. Cork

Tel: 021-477 2125 Fax: 021-477 2045

Email: whitehse@indigo.ie

Web: www.whitehouse-kinsale.ie

The White House epitomises Kinsale hospitality with 3*** accommodation, Le Restaurant d'Antibes and a thoroughly modern bar and bistro where all the old values of guest satisfaction, comfort and value for money prevail. We have welcomed both visitors and locals since the 1850s and from its earliest days it has enjoyed a reputation for fine food, drinks of good cheer and indulgent service. Today we pride ourselves on enhancing that tradition. A member of Kinsale's Good Food Circle, West Cork Fuschia branding and Féile Bia Charter.

***An IHF Quality Employer***
Member of Premier Guesthouses

***Bookable on www.irelandhotels.com***
***Special Offer: www.irelandhotels.com/offers***

***B&B from €50.00 to €80.00***

*Rose & Michael Frawley*
*Proprietors*

*10*

*Activities:*

**Closed 24 - 25 December**



B&B Rates are per Person Sharing per Night incl. Breakfast. or Room Rates are per Room per Night - See also Page 8

## Castle Hotel & Leisure Centre

HOTEL ★★★★ MAP 2 F 3

Main Street,
Macroom,
Co. Cork

Tel: 026-41074 Fax: 026-41505
Email: castlehotel@eircom.net
Web: www.castlehotel.ie

Nestled between Blarney and Killarney, Macroom is the ideal base to explore the scenic South West. Our luxurious 4**** facilities feature executive and contemporary bedrooms and superior suites, "B's" award-winning restaurant (AA Rosette '92 - '07), Dan Buckley's Bar (Black & White Munster Hotel Bar of the Year), continental style café and "The Ardilaun" conference and banqueting suite. Relax in our extensive health and leisure club or treat yourself in our holistic therapy suite. Reduced green fees on Macroom's 18 hole golf course.

***An IHF Quality Employer***

Member of Irish Country Hotels

***Bookable on www.irelandhotels.com***

***Special Offer: www.irelandhotels.com/offers***

*B&B from €75.00 to €95.00*

*Don & Gerard Buckley*
*Proprietors*

56

Closed 24 - 28 December

## Coolcower House

GUESTHOUSE ★★ MAP 2 F 3

Coolcower,
Macroom,
Co. Cork

Tel: 026-41695 Fax: 026-42119
Email: coolcowerhouse@eircom.net

Coolcower House is a large country residence on picturesque grounds. The house is ideally located within easy driving distance of all the tourist attractions in the Cork-Kerry region including Killarney, Kenmare, Kinsale, Blarney, Bantry, Cobh and Midleton. Located on the edge of the River Lee for coarse fishing and boating. Our bedrooms offer TVs, tea/coffee making facilities, DD telephones and hairdryers. Fully licensed bar and home cooked meals available. Outdoor tennis court for residents use. We look forward to welcoming you to Coolcower House.

*B&B from €38.00 to €48.00*

*Evelyn Casey*
*Proprietor*

12

Activities:

Closed 07 December - 07 March

## Riverside Park Hotel (The)

HOTEL MAP 2 F 3

Killarney Road,
Macroom,
Co. Cork

Tel: 026-20090 Fax: 026-20093
Email: info@riversideparkhotel.ie
Web: www.riversideparkhotel.ie

Built to a 4**** specification. Nestled on the banks of the River Sullane, we are on the main Cork to Killarney road on the outskirts of Macroom. With Macroom's old town charm, a golf club adjacent to the hotel, game and coarse angling nearby and a holistic room on site we are ideally situated for those looking for the perfect break. We boast 33 luxurious rooms, some with magnificent river views. Please enquire about Facilities for Persons with Mobility Impairment.

Member of The Mulcahy Hotel Group

*B&B from €70.00 to €85.00*
*Suites from €90.00 to €120.00*

*Susan O'Driscoll*
*General Manager*

33

Activities:

Closed 25 - 26 December

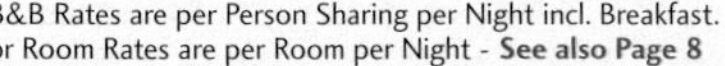

B&B Rates are per Person Sharing per Night incl. Breakfast.
or Room Rates are per Room per Night - **See also Page 8**

## Mallow

### Hibernian Hotel and Leisure Centre

HOTEL ★★★ MAP 2 G 4

Main Street,
Mallow,
Co. Cork

Tel: 022-58200 Fax: 022-22632
Email: info@hibernianhotelmallow.com
Web: www.hibernianhotelmallow.com

The Hibernian Hotel and Leisure Centre is located in the centre of Mallow, at the heart of the Munster region within easy access of Cork, Limerick, Blarney and Killarney. The hotel boasts full leisure facilities including swimming pool, steam room, sauna, jacuzzi and gym. Conference rooms with WiFi, lively pub with evening entertainment and all day Coffee Dock. Spacious en suite rooms feature courtesy tray, iron, satellite TV, phone and hairdryer. The hotel has been fully refurbished since August '07. Please enquire about Facilities for Persons with Mobility Impairment.

*Bookable on www.irelandhotels.com*
*Special Offer: www.irelandhotels.com/offers*

*B&B from €65.00 to €80.00*

*Shane McShortall*
*General Manager*

54

*Activities:*

**Closed 24 - 25 December**

### Longueville House Hotel

HOTEL ★★★★ MAP 2 G 4

Mallow,
Co. Cork

Tel: 022-47156 Fax: 022-47459
Email: info@longuevillehouse.ie
Web: www.longuevillehouse.ie

Set in a 500 acre wooded estate in the heart of the Blackwater Valley, Longueville House is a 1720 listed Georgian mansion owned and run by the O'Callaghan family. With organic gardens, vineyard and orchards, Longueville is a gourmande's paradise! Ideal venue for smaller weddings (60 - 120) and prestigious business meetings. Activities include fly fishing on site, clay shoots, live shoot (Nov - Jan) and country walks. Well stocked library and wine cellar.

***An IHF Quality Employer***

Member of Ireland's Blue Book

*B&B from €100.00 to €130.00*
*Suites from €275.00 to €360.00*

*William & Aisling O'Callaghan*

20

*Activities:*

**Closed 08 January - 16 March**

### Springfort Hall Hotel

HOTEL ★★★ MAP 2 G 4

Mallow,
Co. Cork

Tel: 022-21278 Fax: 022-21557
Email: stay@springfort-hall.com
Web: www.springfort-hall.com

Springfort Hall 18th century Georgian manor house, owned by the Walsh Family. Highly recommended restaurant, fully licensed bar, bedrooms en suite with colour TV and direct outside dial. 6km from Mallow off the Limerick Road, N20. Ideal for touring the South West, Blarney, Killarney, Ring of Kerry. Local amenities, 18-hole golf course, horse riding, angling on River Blackwater. Gulliver Central Reservations. Please enquire about Facilities for Persons with Mobility Impairment.

***An IHF Quality Employer***

*Bookable on www.irelandhotels.com*
*Special Offer: www.irelandhotels.com/offers*

*B&B from €75.00 to €95.00*

*Walsh Family*
*Proprietors*

49

*Activities:*

**Closed 24 - 27 December**



B&B Rates are per Person Sharing per Night incl. Breakfast. or Room Rates are per Room per Night - See also Page 8

## Midleton Park Hotel

HOTEL ★★★ MAP 313

Old Cork Road,
Midleton,
Co. Cork

Tel: 021-463 5100 Fax: 021-463 5101
Email: resv@midletonpark.com
Web: www.midletonpark.com

The 3 star Midleton Park Hotel is ideal for business or pleasure. Located 20 minutes drive east of Cork City in the bustling town of Midleton. The hotel boasts luxurious guest rooms and award-winning leisure facilities. Our wellness centre specialises in alternative therapies and treatments designed to revitalise body and mind. Local attractions include Old Midleton Distillery, Fota Wildlife Park and Queenstown Story. Please enquire about Facilities for Persons with Mobility Impairment.

***An IHF Quality Employer***

*Bookable on www.irelandhotels.com*
*Special Offer: www.irelandhotels.com/offers*

***B&B from €70.00 to €75.00***
***Suites from €225.00 to €250.00***

*John Villiers-Tuthill*
*General Manager*

79

*Activities:*

**Closed 24 - 26 December**

B&B Rates are per Person Sharing per Night incl. Breakfast.
or Room Rates are per Room per Night - **See also Page 8**

## Mitchelstown / Rosscarbery / Schull

### Fir Grove Hotel

HOTEL ★★ MAP 3 I 5

Cahir Hill,
Mitchelstown,
Co. Cork

Tel: 025-24111 Fax: 025-84541
Email: info@firgrovehotel.com
Web: www.firgrovehotel.com

The Fir Grove Hotel is a modern newly renovated hotel, set in its own grounds in the shadow of the Galtee Mountains. Situated on the N8, main Cork/Dublin route, we are the ideal base for touring Munster. Our Mulberry Restaurant and Gradoge Bar serve good local food at affordable prices. All bedrooms are en suite with multi channel TV. Local facilities include golf, fishing, hill walks, pony-trekking and Mitchelstown Caves. Please enquire about Facilities for Persons with Mobility Impairment.

**B&B from €55.00 to €65.00**

*Brenda & Pat Tangney*
*Proprietors*

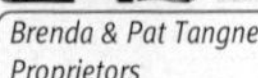

14

**Closed 24 - 26 December**

### Celtic Ross Hotel Conference & Leisure Centre

HOTEL ★★★ MAP 2 F 1

Rosscarbery,
West Cork

Tel: 023-48722 Fax: 023-48723
Email: info@celticrosshotel.com
Web: www.celticrosshotel.com

West Cork is an area of outstanding beauty; the Celtic Ross Hotel nestled in Rosscarbery Bay, is at the heart of this charming and historical region - the ideal base for touring West Cork and the islands. Superior 3 star hotel with 66 well appointed rooms, many with sea views. Druids Restaurant offers table d'hôte and à la carte menu, our Kingfisher Bar and lounge offers high quality meals all day. Conference and banqueting facilities for up to 250 people. Leisure centre: 15m heated pool, bubble pool, baby pool, steam room, sauna and gym. Beauty and massage therapies in our Holistic Suite!

***An IHF Quality Employer***

Member of Select Hotels

***Bookable on www.irelandhotels.com***
***Special Offer: www.irelandhotels.com/offers***

**B&B from €50.00 to €110.00**

*Steven Ward*
*Operations Manager*

66

*Activities:*

**Closed 07 January - 14 February**

### Corthna-Lodge Guesthouse

GUESTHOUSE ★★★ MAP 1 D 1

Airhill,
Schull,
Co. Cork

Tel: 028-28517 Fax: 028-28032
Email: info@corthna-lodge.net
Web: www.corthna-lodge.net

Charming high standard guesthouse in a quiet setting, within walking distance of the lovely village of Schull. Ideally positioned for touring in West Cork, golfing in Bantry or walking on the beautiful Barleycove Beach, boat trips to Cape Clear, etc. In our large garden an outdoor hot tub and sauna house are the ideal places to relax. All bedrooms are en suite. Free use of our gym and BBQ area. Our guests have a separate lounge with wireless internet access.

**B&B from €42.50 to €47.50**

*Andrea & Martin Mueller*
*Owners*

7

**Closed 07 October - 25 April**



B&B Rates are per Person Sharing per Night incl. Breakfast.
or Room Rates are per Room per Night - **See also Page 8**

## Harbour View Hotel

HOTEL MAP 1 D 1

East End,
Schull,
Co. Cork

Tel: 028-28101 Fax: 028-27557
Email: harbourviewhotel@gmail.com
Web: www.harbourhotelviewschull.com

Built to a 3*** specification. This newly opened hotel overlooks Schull Harbour. The 30 bedrooms are finished to the highest standard and offer many breathtaking views of the harbour. The leisure centre includes 16 metre pool, steam room, sauna, hydrotherapy pool, gym and two treatment rooms. Lunch served daily from 12.30 - 3pm. Comprehensive bar menu from 12.30 - 9.30pm, Restaurant from 6.00pm - 9.30pm offering à la carte and table d'hôte menus. All functions catered for up to 200 people. Please enquire about Facilities for Persons with Mobility Impairment.

B&B from €60.00 to €80.00

Shane Nallan
General Manager

30

Closed 25 - 27 December

## Ballymaloe House

GUESTHOUSE ★★★★ MAP 3 I 3

Shanagarry,
Midleton,
Co. Cork

Tel: 021-465 2531 Fax: 021-465 2021
Email: res@ballymaloe.ie
Web: www.ballymaloe.ie

A large country house on a 400 acre farm near the coast, owned and run by the Allen family. Home and locally grown produce is served in the award-winning restaurant. Small golf course, tennis court, outdoor pool, woodlands, gardens and pleasant walks are on the premises, also a craft and kitchen shop. The Ballymaloe Cookery School is nearby. Sea and river fishing can be arranged. Approx. 6 miles south of the N25 highway. Turn off outside Midleton or at Castlemartyr. Two miles beyond Cloyne on the Ballycotton Road. See map No. 3 at rear of guide.

***An IHF Quality Employer***
Member of Ireland's Blue Book

B&B from €110.00 to €160.00

Myrtle Allen
Proprietor

33

Closed Christmas & 07 - 23 January

B&B Rates are per Person Sharing per Night incl. Breakfast.
or Room Rates are per Room per Night - See also Page 8

## Shanagarry / Skibbereen / Youghal

### Garryvoe Hotel

HOTEL ★★★ MAP 3 J 3

Ballycotton Bay,
Shanagarry,
Co. Cork

Tel: 021-464 6718 Fax: 021-464 6824

Email: res@garryvoehotel.com

Web: www.garryvoehotel.com

The coastal location of Garryvoe Hotel directly overlooking 5 km of one of Ireland's finest beaches, is an ideal holiday destination. The hotel provides the holidaymakers with a warm and friendly feeling which will be long remembered. This beautiful area of Cork has an abundance of sporting and leisure pursuits. Combined with the above and only 30 minutes drive from Cork City, Garryvoe Hotel's new bedrooms enhance the spectacular views from the hotel. Please enquire about Facilities for Persons with Mobility Impairment.

Member of Irish Country Hotels

*Bookable on www.irelandhotels.com*
*Special Offer: www.irelandhotels.com/offers*

*B&B from €85.00 to €95.00*

*Stephen Belton*
*General Manager*

55

**Closed 24 - 26 December**

### West Cork Hotel

HOTEL ★★★ MAP 2 E 1

Ilen Street,
Skibbereen,
Co. Cork

Tel: 028-21277 Fax: 028-22333

Email: info@westcorkhotel.com

Web: www.westcorkhotel.com

The West Cork Hotel offers one of the warmest welcomes you will find in Ireland, and combines old-fashioned courtesy with the comfort of tastefully decorated and well-equipped accommodation. Guests can enjoy the friendly bar atmosphere or dine in the elegant restaurant. However long your stay, the West Cork Hotel is the perfect base from which to discover and explore the glorious surroundings and activities available in West Cork.

*Bookable on www.irelandhotels.com*

*B&B from €55.00 to €75.00*

*Sharon Cleary*
*General Manager*

30

*Activities:*

**Closed 23 - 28 December**

### Aherne's Townhouse & Seafood Restaurant

GUESTHOUSE ★★★★ MAP 3 J 3

163 North Main Street,
Youghal,
Co. Cork

Tel: 024-92424 Fax: 024-93633

Email: ahernes@eircom.net

Web: www.ahernes.com

Open turf fires and the warmest of welcomes await you in this family-run guesthouse in the historic walled port of Youghal. Our rooms exude comfort and luxury, stylishly furnished with antiques and paintings. Our restaurant and bar food menus specialise in the freshest of locally landed seafood. Youghal is on the N25, 35 minutes from Cork Airport and is a golfer's paradise. There are 18 golf courses within 1 hour's drive. Find us in Ireland's Blue Book and other leading guides. Please enquire about Facilities for Persons with Mobility Impairment.

Member of Ireland's Blue Book

*Bookable on www.irelandhotels.com*
*Special Offer: www.irelandhotels.com/offers*

*B&B from €85.00 to €105.00*
*Suites from €220.00 to €240.00*

*The Fitzgibbon Family*

12

**Closed 23 - 29 December**



B&B Rates are per Person Sharing per Night incl. Breakfast.
or Room Rates are per Room per Night - **See also Page 8**

## Quality Hotel and Leisure Centre Youghal

HOTEL ★★★ MAP 3 J 3

Redbarn,
Youghal,
Co. Cork

Tel: 024-93050 Fax: 024-20699
Email: info.youghal@qualityhotels.ie
Web: www.qualityhotelyoughal.com

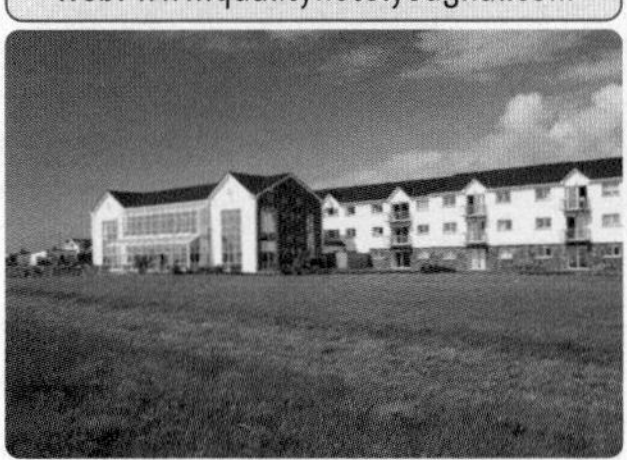

Commanding the perfect location on Redbarn Beach, with breathtaking views of the Atlantic Ocean, this superb hotel has something for everyone. Facilities include Club Vitae, our Health & Fitness Club incorporating 4 treatment and therapy suites, 2 outdoor sports pitches, Childrens' Crèche, Playground, Movie Room, Games Room, along with Lannigans Restaurant and the Coast Bar which are both ocean facing. Our accommodation offering includes both standard and family guest rooms, 2 bedroom apartments and 3 bedroom holiday homes.

Member of Quality Hotels

*Bookable on www.irelandhotels.com*
*Special Offer: www.irelandhotels.com/offers*

*B&B from €39.00 to €109.00*
*Suites from €79.00 to €199.00*

*Allen McEnery*
*General Manager*

25

*Activities:*

**Closed 22 - 26 December**

## Walter Raleigh Hotel

HOTEL ★★★ MAP 3 J 3

O'Brien Place,
Youghal,
Co. Cork

Tel: 024-92011 Fax: 024-93560
Email: walterraleighhotel@eircom.net
Web: www.walterraleighhotel.com

Breathtaking sea views, a warm welcome and an ideal location for tourists and golfers alike await you at the Walter Raleigh Hotel. Combining luxury with a taste of country living, a sea-front location beside a beautiful green park, spectacular sea views, close to golf and Youghal's pristine Blue Flag beach, coastline and countryside. We guarantee you a comfortable and pleasant stay at the Walter Raleigh Hotel. Golf packages a speciality. Please enquire about Facilities for Persons with Mobility Impairment.

*Bookable on www.irelandhotels.com*
*Special Offer: www.irelandhotels.com/offers*

*B&B from €44.50 to €80.00*
*Suites from €120.00 to €170.00*

*Aiden Fleming*
*General Manager*

41

*Activities:*

**Closed 24 - 25 December**



B&B Rates are per Person Sharing per Night incl. Breakfast.
or Room Rates are per Room per Night - **See also Page 8**

## Ballybunion / Ballyferriter / Caherdaniel

### Eagle Lodge

GUESTHOUSE ★ MAP 5 D 6

Ballybunion,
Co. Kerry

Tel: 068-27224

Owner managed, delightful guesthouse situated in town centre. All bedrooms with bathrooms and central heating throughout. A beautiful lounge and private car park for guests. Local amenities include two championship golf courses, sea fishing, tennis, pitch and putt, swimming and boating. Extra value reduced green fees at Ballybunion Golf Club. Cliff walks and surfing also available.

***B&B from €35.00 to €70.00***

*Mildred Gleasure* — 8

**Open All Year**

### Óstán Cheann Sibéal

HOTEL ★★★ MAP 1 B 5

Ballyferriter,
Dingle,
Co. Kerry

Tel: 066-915 6433 Fax: 066-915 6577
Email: info@ceannsibealhotel.com
Web: www.ceannsibealhotel.com

Hotel Óstán Cheann Sibéal is a high quality hotel situated in the village of Ballyferriter in the heart of the West Kerry Gaeltacht. It is 8 miles west of Dingle and half way on the Slea Head Drive. The hotel comprises 26 spacious and tastefully designed bedrooms all en suite and some with spectacular views of the local scenery. It also includes a stylish restaurant and trendy bar with live music on certain weekends in the summertime. We offer the ideal stop off point for lunch, dinner, drinks and overnight stays. Please enquire about Facilities for Persons with Mobility Impairment.

***B&B from €45.00 to €80.00***

*Diarmuid Curran*
*Manager* — 26

**Closed 01 November - 09 April**

### Derrynane Hotel

HOTEL ★★★ MAP 1 C 2

Caherdaniel,
Ring Of Kerry,
Co. Kerry

Tel: 066-947 5136 Fax: 066-947 5160
Email: info@derrynane.com
Web: www.derrynane.com

Amidst the most spectacular scenery in Ireland, halfway round the famous Ring of Kerry (on the N70) lies the Derrynane Hotel. 70 en suite bedrooms. Facilities: 15m outdoor heated pool, steam room, sauna, gym, luxurious seaweed bath, childrens' games room, tennis court & gardens. Surrounded by beautiful beaches, hills, lovely walks & Derrynane House & National Park. Deep sea angling, lake fishing, golf, horse riding, sea sports, boat trips to Skelligs Rock all within short distance. Hotel's own walking guide with maps to the area. Luxury self catering available on site. Special rates at Skelling Bay Golf Course.

***An IHF Quality Employer***

***Bookable on www.irelandhotels.com***

***B&B from €75.00 to €95.00***

*Mary O'Connor*
*Manager / Director* — 70

Activities:

**Closed 02 October - 12 April**



B&B Rates are per Person Sharing per Night incl. Breakfast.
or Room Rates are per Room per Night - **See also Page 8**

## Ring of Kerry Hotel

HOTEL ★★★ MAP 1 B 3

Valentia Road,
Cahersiveen,
Co. Kerry

Tel: 066-947 2543 Fax: 066-947 2893

Email: ringhotel@eircom.net

Web: www.ringofkerryhotel.ie

This is a small family-run hotel located on the coast, close to Blue Flag beaches. Bar, restaurant and comfortable rooms, some with a jacuzzi. We offer regular live music and information on local heritage. Enjoy the friendly atmosphere, excellent cuisine and discover beautiful South Kerry. Bíodh sos, suaimhneas agus spóirt agat. Fáilte roimh gach éinne. Please enquire about Facilities for Persons with Mobility Impairment.

*Bookable on www.irelandhotels.com*

*Special Offer: www.irelandhotels.com/offers*

*B&B from €40.00 to €90.00*

*Suites from €130.00 to €280.00*

*Marian O'Sullivan*
*Manager*

23

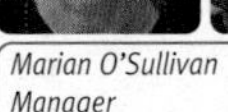

Activities:

**Open All Year**

## Watermarque Boutique Hotel

HOTEL MAP 1 B 3

The Quays,
Cahersiveen,
Co. Kerry

Tel: 066-947 2222 Fax: 066-948 1230

Email: info@watermarquehotel.ie

Web: www.watermarquehotel.ie

Built to a 4**** specification. Savour the beauty of the Ring of Kerry from the luxury of the new Watermarque Boutique Hotel Cahersiveen. Located on the Ring of Kerry in a place of incredible natural beauty, we offer gorgeous rooms, luxurious Health & Wellness Centre & Therapy Spa, conference facilities and a beautiful setting for your wedding. Our restaurant features the finest modern Irish cuisine while the Ivy Bar is the ideal venue to relax after a day touring. Please enquire about Facilities for Persons with Mobility Impairment.

*B&B from €72.00 to €100.00*

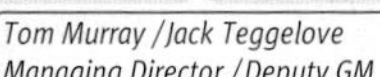

*Tom Murray / Jack Teggelove*
*Managing Director / Deputy GM*

53

Activities:

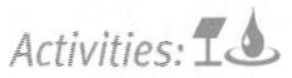

**Open All Year**



B&B Rates are per Person Sharing per Night incl. Breakfast.
or Room Rates are per Room per Night - See also Page 8

# Caragh Lake / Castlegregory

## Ard-Na-Sidhe

HOTEL ★★★★ MAP 1 D 4

Caragh Lake,
Killorglin,
Co. Kerry

Tel: 066-976 9105 Fax: 066-976 9282

Email: hotelsales@liebherr.com

Web: www.killarneyhotels.ie

18 bedroomed 4**** de luxe Victorian mansion delightfully located in its own park on Caragh Lake. Tastefully furnished with antiques and open fireplaces. Luxurious lounges and restaurant. Free boating, fishing and facilities of sister hotels - Hotel Europe and Hotel Dunloe Castle - available to guests. 10 major golf courses nearby. Special green fees. Central Reservations Tel: 064-71350 Fax: 064-37900. Please enquire about Facilities for Persons with Mobility Impairment.

Member of Killarney Hotels Ltd

*Bookable on www.irelandhotels.com*
*Special Offer: www.irelandhotels.com/offers*

**B&B from €85.00 to €150.00**

*Nuala Naughton*

18

Activities:

**Closed 15 October - 01 May**

## Carrig Country House

GUESTHOUSE ★★★★ MAP 1 D 4

Caragh Lake,
Killorglin,
Co. Kerry

Tel: 066-976 9100 Fax: 066-976 9166

Email: info@carrighouse.com

Web: www.carrighouse.com

Charming Victorian Manor on acres of woodlands & gardens (935 plant species) running down to the lake shore. Furnished in period style with antique furniture. Central to 12 superb golf courses, fishing, shooting, hill walking or just lazing by the fireside with a good book. Award-winning restaurant (open to non residents). Ideal for touring the Ring of Kerry, Dingle & Killarney. Recommended by Bridgestone Guide, 100 Best Places to Stay in Ireland 2006, Georgina Campbell's Jameson Guide, The Good Hotel Guide, an AA "Country House of the Year" & Best Loved Hotels, The Michelin Guide.

Member of Private Ireland

*Bookable on www.irelandhotels.com*
*Special Offer: www.irelandhotels.com/offers*

**B&B from €80.00 to €130.00**

*Frank & Mary Slattery*
*Hosts / Proprietors*

17

Activities:

**Closed 01 December - 01 March**

## Crutch's Hillville House Hotel

HOTEL ★★ MAP 1 C 5

Conor Pass Road, Castlegregory,
Dingle Peninsula,
Co. Kerry

Tel: 066-713 8118 Fax: 066-713 8159

Email: macshome@iol.ie

Web: www.dinglehotel.com

Step back in time at this delightful country house hotel overlooking Brandon Bay on the scenic Dingle Peninsula. Bedrooms are tastefully decorated, some offering sea views, 4 poster beds, all with spacious bathrooms. We offer a friendly country house atmosphere with a cosy bar & open fires. The restaurant offers traditional home cooking using local fresh produce & has an established reputation for fine foods & wine. 4km west of Stadbally Village on the Conor Pass Road. Local activities: golf, walks, sea & river fishing, surf & dive schools, pony trekking, bird watching & island tours.

Member of Irish Country Hotels

*Bookable on www.irelandhotels.com*
*Special Offer: www.irelandhotels.com/offers*

**B&B from €45.00 to €85.00**

*Ron & Sandra*
*Proprietors*

19

**Open All Year**



B&B Rates are per Person Sharing per Night incl. Breakfast. or Room Rates are per Room per Night - See also Page 8

## Castlegregory / Cloghane / Dingle (An Daingean)

### Harbour House & Leisure Centre

GUESTHOUSE ★★★ MAP 1 C 5

Scraggane Pier,
Castlegregory,
Co. Kerry

Tel: 066-713 9292 Fax: 066-713 9557

Email: stay@iol.ie

Web: www.maharees.ie

The family-run Harbour House is superbly located on the tip of the Maharees Peninsula and has its own indoor heated swimming pool, sauna and gym. Its Islands Restaurant has panoramic views of the breathtaking scenery of the Maharees Islands and offers an excellent range of locally caught seafood, prime steak, meat and vegetarian dishes. If you want tranquillity, serenity, charm and true Irish hospitality, this is the place for you. Local amenities include golf, walking, scuba diving, windsurfing, surfing, fishing, horse riding, cycling etc.

*Bookable on www.irelandhotels.com*

*Special Offer: www.irelandhotels.com/offers*

*B&B from €35.00 to €50.00*

*Pat & Ronnie Fitzgibbon*

8

*Activities:*

**Closed 23 - 30 December**

### O'Connor's Guesthouse

GUESTHOUSE ★★ MAP 1 B 5

Cloghane,
Dingle Peninsula,
Co. Kerry

Tel: 066-713 8113 Fax: 066-713 8270

Email: oconnorsguesthouse@eircom.net

Web: www.cloghane.com

A long established, spacious country home with spectacular views of sea and mountains, overlooking Brandon Bay and within easy reach of Dingle on the Dingle Way. Private car park, guest lounge, open fire, home cooked meals, pub and a warm welcome are just some of the things awaiting our guests. Ideal area for walking, fishing, cycling, pony trekking, swimming, birdwatching or just relaxing.

*B&B from €40.00 to €60.00*

*Micheal & Elizabeth O'Dowd*
*Owners*

9

**Closed 01 November - 28 February**

### Alpine House

GUESTHOUSE ★★★ MAP 1 B 4

Mail Road,
Dingle,
Co. Kerry

Tel: 066-915 1250 Fax: 066-915 1966

Email: alpinedingle@eircom.net

Web: www.alpineguesthouse.com

Superb guesthouse run by the O'Shea Family. AA ♦♦♦♦ and RAC ♦♦♦♦ highly acclaimed. Elegant en suite bedrooms with TV, direct dial phone, hairdryers, central heating and tea/coffee facilities. Spacious dining room with choice of breakfast. Delightful guest lounge. 2 minutes walk to town centre, restaurants, harbour and bus stop. Local amenities include Slea Head Drive and Blasket Islands. Also pony trekking, angling and boat trips to Fungi the dolphin. Non-smoking premises.

*B&B from €35.00 to €60.00*

*Paul O'Shea*
*Proprietor*

10

**Open All Year**

B&B Rates are per Person Sharing per Night incl. Breakfast.
or Room Rates are per Room per Night - See also Page 8

## Dingle (An Daingean)

### An Bothar Guesthouse, Restaurant & Bar

GUESTHOUSE ★★★ MAP 1 B 5

Cuas, Ballydavid,
Dingle Peninsula, Tralee,
Co. Kerry

Tel: 066-915 5342

Email: botharpub@eircom.net

Web: www.botharpub.com

An Bóthar Guesthouse, Restaurant and Bar is a family-run guesthouse and pub situated at the foot of Mount Brandon just 6 miles from Dingle. Where the Dingle Way Walk passes the door at the start of the next day's stage. An ideal base for a walking holiday close to beaches, fishing & golf. In the heart of the Gaeltacht, Gaelic is the first language of the house. À la carte menu and bar menu available during season, March - September. Meals arranged by request out of season. Home-baking & local produce on menu. Additional Tel No's: 066-915 5519 & 087 236 5608

**B&B from €40.00 to €60.00**

*Maurice & Aileen Walsh*
*Owners*

7

**Closed 24 - 25 December**

### An Portán

GUESTHOUSE ★★ MAP 1 B 4

Dunquin,
Co. Kerry

Tel: 066-915 6212

Email: donn@eircom.net

Web: www.anportan.com

Located in Dún Chaoin, the most westerly village in Ireland, opposite Blasket Islands. 15 - 20 minute drive from An Daingean / Dingle. Ferry to the Blasket Islands, 1km, 18 hole golf links 4 km, horse riding 4.5 km, shore angling. Award-winning restaurant fully licensed, small conference room, 14 bedrooms each with separate entrance in secluded setting. Private car park. Please enquire about Facilities for Persons with Mobility Impairment.

**B&B from €40.00 to €45.00**

*Rónán O'Donnchadha*

14

**Closed 01 October - 01 April**

### Bambury's Guest House

GUESTHOUSE ★★★ MAP 1 B 4

Mail Road,
Dingle,
Co. Kerry

Tel: 066-915 1244 Fax: 066-915 1786

Email: info@bamburysguesthouse.com

Web: www.bamburysguesthouse.com

AA Selected ♦♦♦♦, new house, excellent location, 2 minutes walk to town centre. Offering peaceful accommodation in spacious, double, twin or triple rooms all en suite with direct dial telephone and satellite TV. Attractive guest lounge to relax in. Private car parking, choice of breakfast in spacious dining room. Local attractions, Dingle Peninsula, horse riding, angling and golf on local 18 hole golf links. Reduced green fees can be arranged. Listed in all leading guides. Please enquire about Facilities for Persons with Mobility Impairment.

**B&B from €35.00 to €65.00**

*Bernie Bambury*
*Proprietor*

12

**Open All Year**



B&B Rates are per Person Sharing per Night incl. Breakfast.
or Room Rates are per Room per Night - **See also Page 8**

## Barr na Sraide Inn

**GUESTHOUSE ★★★ MAP 1 B 4**

Upper Main Street,
Dingle,
Co. Kerry

Tel: 066-915 1331 Fax: 066-915 1446

Email: barrnasraide@eircom.net

Web: www.barrnasraide.com

Family-run guesthouse and bar. Located in the town centre. The Barr na Sraide Inn has been recently refurbished to a very high standard. An extensive menu awaits our guests for breakfast. End each day with a relaxing drink in our comfortable bar amongst the locals. Private enclosed car park. Ideal base for your stay in the South West. Golf, fishing, sailing, cycling, horse riding and trips to Fungi the dolphin available nearby. Please enquire about Facilities for Persons with Mobility Impairment.

*Bookable on www.irelandhotels.com*

*Special Offer: www.irelandhotels.com/offers*

*B&B from €40.00 to €70.00*

*Patricia Geaney*

26

**Closed 18 - 26 December**

## Boland's Guesthouse

**GUESTHOUSE ★★ MAP 1 B 4**

Upper Main Street,
Dingle,
Co. Kerry

Tel: 066-915 1426

Email: bolanddingle@eircom.net

Web: www.ireland.com

Boland's Guesthouse is situated at the top of Main Street overlooking Dingle Bay. Minutes walk to restaurants, pubs, entertainment, fishing, golfing, horse riding, hill walking and trips to Fungi the dolphin. Our guest rooms are bright and spacious with modern amenities, some with views of Dingle Bay. Full breakfast is served in our conservatory dining room. You can relax in our guest lounge overlooking Dingle Bay. Can also be contacted at 085 714 2297. Please enquire about Facilities for Persons with Mobility Impairment.

*Bookable on www.irelandhotels.com*

*Special Offer: www.irelandhotels.com/offers*

*B&B from €35.00 to €60.00*

*Breda Boland*
*Owner*

8

**Closed 1 - 30 December**

## Castlewood House

**GUESTHOUSE ★★★★ MAP 1 B 4**

The Wood,
Dingle,
Co. Kerry

Tel: 066-915 2788

Email: castlewoodhouse@eircom.net

Web: www.castlewooddingle.com

At Castlewood House a warm welcome awaits you. Luxurious 4**** guesthouse located on the shores of Dingle Bay offering de luxe rooms and junior suites. All rooms are spacious and individually styled to a very high standard. Facilities include en suite bathrooms with whirlpool bath, power showers, TV, DD phone, internet access and hospitality tray. Elevator access. Speciality breakfast served in our dining room with its collection of art, or relaxing in our antique filled drawing room. AA ♦♦♦♦♦. Non smoking premises. Please enquire about Facilities for Persons with Mobility Impairment.

*Bookable on www.irelandhotels.com*

*Special Offer: www.irelandhotels.com/offers*

*B&B from €45.00 to €85.00*
*Suites from €120.00 to €200.00*

*Helen Woods Heaton &*
*Brian Heaton*

12

**Closed 10 January -03 February**

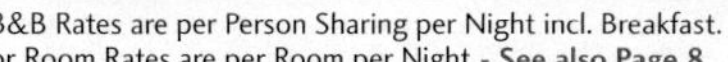

B&B Rates are per Person Sharing per Night incl. Breakfast.
or Room Rates are per Room per Night - See also Page 8

## Dingle (An Daingean)

### Coastline Guesthouse

GUESTHOUSE ★★★ MAP 1 B 4


The Wood,
Dingle,
Co. Kerry

Tel: 066-915 2494 Fax: 066-915 2493

Email: coastlinedingle@eircom.net

Web: www.coastlinedingle.com

Beautiful seafront guesthouse on the water's edge of Dingle Harbour. All rooms are en suite with direct dial phone, TV, hairdryer, tea/coffee facilities and most have panoramic views of the harbour. Ground floor rooms available. Enjoy our excellent breakfast. Relax in our guest lounge or garden and watch the local fishing fleet return with their catch. Private car parking. 5 minute walk to town centre. Ideal base to enjoy all Dingle has to offer - excellent restaurants and pubs. Please enquire about Facilities for Persons with Mobility Impairment.

**B&B from €35.00 to €55.00**

*Vivienne O'Shea*
*Proprietor*

7

**Closed 30 November - 01 March**

### Dingle Bay Hotel

HOTEL ★★★ MAP 1 B 4


Strand Street,
Dingle,
Co. Kerry

Tel: 066-915 1231 Fax: 066-915 2740

Email: info@dinglebayhotel.com

Web: www.dinglebayhotel.com

Dingle's newest Hotel, located by the pier and marina in Dingle Town. The hotel has been designed to the highest standards throughout. Unwind and relax in the very stylish Paudie's Bar and sample the renowned food - seafood is a specialty. The hotel offers regular live entertainment. Guest receive reduced green fees at Dingle Golf Links and discounts at the Harmony Health Club and Dingle World of Leisure. Please enquire about Facilities for Persons with Mobility Impairment.

**B&B from €50.00 to €110.00**

*Kathleen Sheehy*
*General Manager*

25

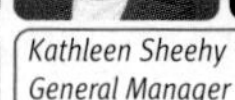

**Closed 16 - 26 December**

### Dingle Benners Hotel

HOTEL ★★★ MAP 1 B 4


Main Street,
Dingle,
Co. Kerry

Tel: 066-915 1638 Fax: 066-915 1412

Email: info@dinglebenners.com

Web: www.dinglebenners.com

Located in the heart of Dingle Town, the hotel is favoured for its old world charm and style. Luxuriously appointed bedrooms provide an intimate cosy atmosphere complemented by authentic Irish antique furnishings. Mrs. Benner's Bar & Lounges will captivate you on arrival, have a warm friendly welcome and will fill you with a sense of yesteryear. Special weekend and midweek packages available. Please enquire about Facilities for Persons with Mobility Impairment.

***An IHF Quality Employer***

Member of Manor House Hotels

***Bookable on www.irelandhotels.com***
***Special Offer: www.irelandhotels.com/offers***

**B&B from €60.00 to €105.00**

*Muireann Nic Giolla Ruaidh*
*General Manager*

52

Activities:

**Closed 21 - 27 December**



B&B Rates are per Person Sharing per Night incl. Breakfast. or Room Rates are per Room per Night - See also Page 8

## Dingle Skellig Hotel & Peninsula Spa

HOTEL ★★★★ MAP 1 B 4

Dingle,
Co. Kerry

Tel: 066-915 0200 Fax: 066-915 1501
Email: reservations@dingleskellig.com
Web: www.dingleskellig.com

Renowned hotel situated on the beautiful harbour of Dingle Bay. Luxurious leisure club & pool. Fungi Kid's Club & Crèche on weekends & holidays (crèche daily Apr - Oct). Awarded Georgina Campbell's Family Friendly Hotel of the Year 2007. Excellent cuisine in our Coastguard Restaurant. Established conference & banqueting centre with stunning views for up to 250 people. The Peninsula Spa features Yon-Ka face & body treatments, hydrotherapy, signature wraps etc. Relaxation suite & outdoor hot tub overlooking bay. Yon-Ka's Destination Spa of the Year 2004.

*Bookable on www.irelandhotels.com*
*Special Offer: www.irelandhotels.com/offers*

**B&B from €78.00 to €127.00**

*Graham Fitzgerald*
*General Manager*

113

Activities:

**Closed 21 - 27 December**

## Doyles Seafood Bar & Town House

GUESTHOUSE ★★★★ MAP 1 B 4

John Street,
Dingle,
Co. Kerry

Tel: 066-915 1174 Fax: 066-915 1816
Email: cdoyles@iol.ie
Web: www.doylesofdingle.com

The Town House has some of the most delightful rooms in Dingle. All 8 en suite spacious rooms have recently been refurbished in a most comfortable style. Satellite TV, phone, trouser press/iron, tea/coffee facilities. The world renowned restaurant has an old range & sugán chairs. Natural stone & wood combination gives Doyles a cosy country atmosphere. The menu consists only of fresh food and is chosen on a daily basis from the fish landed on Dingle boats. AA♦♦♦♦, RAC♦♦♦♦, Les Routiers "Restaurant of the Year" 2002. Bushmills Fish Restaurant of the Year 2005/6. Open from 27 Dec to 06 Jan.

Member of Blue Book

**B&B from €55.00 to €80.00**

*John Cluskey*
*Host*

8

**Closed 15 November - 14 February**

## Gorman's Clifftop House and Restaurant

GUESTHOUSE ★★★★ MAP 1 B 5

Glaise Bheag, Ballydavid,
Dingle Peninsula, Tralee,
Co. Kerry

Tel: 066-915 5162 Fax: 066-915 5003
Email: info@gormans-clifftophouse.com
Web: www.gormans-clifftophouse.com

A welcoming cliff-top refuge on the western edge of the Dingle Peninsula. All rooms pay homage to the landscape, offering breathtaking views. Our emphasis is on comfort, mini suites boasting king sized beds and jacuzzi baths. Downstairs guests can gather around the fire to read or chat, dine in our fully licensed restaurant. AA ♦♦♦♦♦ Premier Select. Les Routiers "Hidden Gem Ireland" 2001 & "Hotel of the Year" 2001. Georgina Campbell 'Guesthouse of the Year' 2002 (Jameson Guide). Good Food Ireland. Guesthouse and Restaurant of the Year 2006.

**B&B from €60.00 to €95.00**

*Vincent & Sile O'Gormain*
*Proprietors*

9

**Closed 24 - 26 December**

B&B Rates are per Person Sharing per Night incl. Breakfast.
or Room Rates are per Room per Night - **See also Page 8**

## Dingle (An Daingean)

### Greenmount House

GUESTHOUSE ★★★★ MAP 1 B 4

Upper John Street,
Dingle,
Co. Kerry

Tel: 066-915 1414 Fax: 066-915 1974
Email: info@greenmount-house.com
Web: www.greenmount-house.com

Greenmount House is the proud recipient of several awards for its accommodations & breakfasts. A charming 4**** country house yet centrally located. Spacious lounges to relax in and take advantage of its magnificent scenic location overlooking Dingle Town and harbour. All bedrooms have private bathroom, TV/ radio, direct dial phone & WiFi. Breakfast is served in a conservatory. This year all rooms have been upgraded & a hot tub has been installed in the garden. Wine Bar also new to premises. Recognised by all leading guides. Please enquire about Facilities for Persons with Mobility Impairment.

**B&B from €45.00 to €85.00**

*John & Mary Curran*
*Owners*

14

**Closed 10 - 27 December**

### Heaton's Guesthouse

GUESTHOUSE ★★★★ MAP 1 B 4

The Wood,
Dingle,
Co. Kerry

Tel: 066-915 2288 Fax: 066-915 2324
Email: heatons@iol.ie
Web: www.heatonsdingle.com

Superb 4**** family-run guesthouse situated on the shore of Dingle Bay with spectacular views, 5 minutes walk from the town. All rooms are en suite (pressure shower and bath), with TV, DD phone and tea/coffee welcome tray. Breakfast is our speciality. Luxury junior suites and de luxe rooms recently opened (rates available on request). Local amenities include golf, sailing, fishing, surfing, cycling, walking, horse riding and the renowned gourmet restaurants. Awarded Guesthouse of the Year for Ireland 2002 - Les Routiers. Please enquire about Facilities for Persons with Mobility Impairment.

Member of Lucinda O'Sullivan

*Bookable on www.irelandhotels.com*
*Special Offer: www.irelandhotels.com/offers*

**B&B from €47.00 to €69.00**
**Suites from €140.00 to €190.00**

*Nuala & Cameron Heaton*
*Proprietors*

16

**Closed 1 - 27 December**

### Hillgrove (The)

GUESTHOUSE ★ MAP 1 B 4

Spa Road,
Dingle,
Co. Kerry

Tel: 066-915 1131 Fax: 066-915 1272
Email: hillgrovedingle@eircom.net
Web: www.hillgroveinn.com

The Hillgrove is family owned and managed. Located 5 minutes walk from Dingle's main street. Our rooms are all en suite, with DD phone, TV and tea/coffee making facilities. Our private lounge is the ideal place to relax with full bar facilities available. The Hillgrove offers a perfect combination of professional service with cheerful and helpful staff. We will ensure that your stay is the highlight of your visit to our beautiful town. Please enquire about Facilities for Persons with Mobility Impairment.

*Bookable on www.irelandhotels.com*
*Special Offer: www.irelandhotels.com/offers*

**B&B from €40.00 to €70.00**

*Kieran Ashe*

12

*Activities:*

**Closed (Sun-Thur) 01 October - 01 March**



B&B Rates are per Person Sharing per Night incl. Breakfast. or Room Rates are per Room per Night - See also Page 8

## Milltown House

GUESTHOUSE ★★★★ MAP 1 B 4

Dingle,
Co. Kerry

Tel: 066-915 1372 Fax: 066-915 1095
Email: info@milltownhousedingle.com
Web: www.milltownhousedingle.com

Award-winning family-run Milltown House is ideally located overlooking Dingle Bay and town from our private gardens. All rooms which retain the character of the 130 year old house are en suite, have tea/coffee making facilities, direct dial phone, TV, trouser press, hairdryer and safety deposit box. The house was home to Robert Mitchum during the making of David Lean's epic movie "Ryan's Daughter". Assistance in planning your day. One of the most scenic and tranquil locations in the town area, less than 15 minutes walk or 2 minutes drive! Secure booking on www.milltownhouse.com

*Bookable on www.irelandhotels.com*

*B&B from €65.00 to €80.00*

*Tara Kerry*

10

**Closed 28 October - 03 May**

## Old Pier, Restaurant and Guesthouse

GUESTHOUSE ★★★ MAP 1 B 4

An Fheothanach,
Ballydavid, Dingle,
Co. Kerry

Tel: 066-915 5242
Email: info@oldpier.com
Web: www.oldpier.com

Situated in the heart of the West Kerry Gaeltacht on the Dingle Peninsula overlooking beautiful Smerwick Harbour and the Atlantic Ocean. This family-run establishment offers 3*** accommodation with beautiful sea and mountain vistas. The Old Pier Restaurant offers a broad range of locally caught seafood, prime steak and meat dishes. Adjacent activities include 18 hole golf course, deep sea angling, mountain walking and archaeology sites. A warm welcome awaits you. Please enquire about Facilities for Persons with Mobility Impairment.

*B&B from €30.00 to €50.00*

*Padraig & Jacqui O'Connor*

6

**Open All Year**



B&B Rates are per Person Sharing per Night incl. Breakfast.
or Room Rates are per Room per Night - See also Page 8

## Dingle (An Daingean) / Inch Beach

### Pax House

GUESTHOUSE ★★★★ MAP 1 B 4

Upper John Street,
Dingle,
Co. Kerry

Tel: 066-915 1518 Fax: 066-915 0865
Email: paxhouse@iol.ie
Web: www.pax-house.com

Voted one of the top ten places to stay in Ireland. Pax House has undeniably one of the most spectacular views in peninsula - overlooking Dingle Bay, Ring of Kerry, Blasket Island and the entrance to the harbour. Sit back on the balcony and enjoy the activity in the bay and a sighting of Fungi the Dolphin, gulls diving and little fishing boats heading back with the daily catch. Please enquire about Facilities for Persons with Mobility Impairment.

Member of Premier Guesthouses

**B&B from €50.00 to €65.00**
**Suites from €140.00 to €170.00**

*John O'Farrell*

12

Closed 01 December - 01 March

### Smerwick Harbour Hotel

HOTEL ★★★ MAP 1 B 5

Ballyferriter,
Dingle,
Co. Kerry

Tel: 066-915 6470 Fax: 066-915 6473
Email: info@smerwickhotel.ie
Web: www.smerwickhotel.ie

Smerwick Harbour Hotel & Seafood Restaurant, with its old world bar, is located a short distance from Dingle Town. Our local 18 hole golf course is 4km away, with reduced green fees for guests. All rooms en suite (family rooms also). Spacious lounge. Enjoy excellent cuisine in our seafood restaurant, specialising in local seafood & char grilled steaks. Quality bar food also available. Old world ambience, as featured on our website. The best sandy beaches in Ireland nearby. Suitable for Disabled. Groups & weddings catered for. Please enquire about Facilities for Persons with Mobility Impairment.

***An IHF Quality Employer***

Member of Atlantis Holiday Group

**B&B from €50.00 to €120.00**
**Suites from €110.00 to €220.00**

*Fionnbar Walsh*
*Manager*

33

*Activities:*

Closed 01 November - 01 April

### Inch Beach Guest House

GUESTHOUSE ★★★ MAP 1 C 5

Inch Beach,
Inch,
Co. Kerry

Tel: 066-915 8118 Fax: 066-915 8388
Email: inch@iol.ie
Web: www.inchbeachguesthouse.com

Overlooking the beautiful Blue Flag beach of Inch Strand this purpose built, family-run Inch Beach Guest House where a traditional warm Kerry welcome awaits. This magnificent location famed for Ryan's Daughter is the perfect base for touring the splendours of County Kerry. All rooms are en suite with power showers, television, DD telephone, tea and coffee making facilities, king and queen size beds, we also have an antique suite. An ideal location at the end of the day. New bar/restaurant located within walking distance. Please enquire about Facilities for Persons with Mobility Impairment.

***Bookable on www.irelandhotels.com***
*Special Offer: www.irelandhotels.com/offers*

**B&B from €35.00 to €65.00**

*Hussain Family*
*Proprietors*

9

Open All Year



B&B Rates are per Person Sharing per Night incl. Breakfast.
or Room Rates are per Room per Night - **See also Page 8**

## Coachmans Townhouse

HOTEL ★★ MAP 1 D 3

8 Henry Street,
Kenmare,
Co. Kerry

Tel: 064-41311 Fax: 064-89193

Email: info@thecoachmans.com

Web: www.thecoachmans.com

Newly re-built luxury hotel, the Coachmans offers state of the art accommodation in Kenmare Town centre. Rooms & suites have AC, king sized beds, sofas, jacuzzi bath & power showers, plasma TVs, ESPN, underfloor heating. We also offer a small local bar, an informal restaurant, a good chef, an intimate live music venue & "Ireland's finest" pub courtyard. The Jones family have run the Coachmans for generations & offer a wealth of info. Check out our website for images & special offers. Good service & hospitality. Please enquire about Facilities for Persons with Mobility Impairment.

**B&B from €55.00 to €75.00**
**Suites from €250.00 to €300.00**

*Siobhan Jones*
*Proprietor*

10

**Closed 24 - 26 December**

## Foleys Shamrock Guesthouse

GUESTHOUSE ★★★ MAP 1 D 3

Henry Street,
Kenmare,
Co. Kerry

Tel: 064-42162 Fax: 064-41799

Email: foleyest@iol.ie

Web: www.foleyskenmare.com

Award-winning townhouse offering quality hospitality in the centre of Kenmare. Our traditional Irish gastro pub, with Irish music and open fires, serves local seafood, beef and lamb. All rooms are en suite with colour TV and tea/coffee facilities. For information and our best room rate guarantee, visit us online at www.foleyskenmare.com

**B&B from €39.00 to €59.00**

*Marion Foley*
*Owner / Manager*

10

**Open All Year**

## Lansdowne Arms Hotel

HOTEL ★★★ MAP 1 D 3

Main Street,
Kenmare,
Co. Kerry

Tel: 064-41368 Fax: 064-41114

Email: info@lansdownearms.com

Web: www.lansdownearms.com

Built in the 1790s and situated at the top of Kenmare Town. The Lansdowne Arms Hotel, now owned by the Quill family, has undergone extensive refurbishment throughout. Enjoy a relaxed atmosphere in front of the open fires and the hospitality from the warm and friendly staff. All of the 26 rooms and bathrooms have been redecorated and finished to a very high standard with king sized beds, safes, hairdryers, tea/coffee facility, telephone, TV and ironing presses. Private parking. Enjoy a pint in The Bold Thady Quills Traditional Irish Pub & Restaurant, or a relaxing afternoon tea in The Poets Bar.

Member of AA Hotels

***Bookable on www.irelandhotels.com***
***Special Offer: www.irelandhotels.com/offers***

**B&B from €45.00 to €85.00**

*The Quill Family*
*Proprietors*

26

Activities:

**Closed 24 - 25 December**

## Kenmare

### Lodge (The)

GUESTHOUSE ★★★★ MAP 1 D 3

Killowen Road,
Kenmare,
Co. Kerry

Tel: 064-41512 Fax: 064-42724
Email: thelodgekenmare@eircom.net
Web: www.thelodgekenmare.com

Purpose built luxury guesthouse situated opposite Kenmare's 18 hole golf course. Within 3 minutes walk of some of the finest restaurants & pubs in Ireland. All rooms are elegantly furnished with king beds and en suite bathrooms. All rooms are extremely well appointed with DD telephone, TV, safes, controllable central heating, iron, tea/coffee facilities. The Lodge is renowned for its vast home cooked breakfast and freshly baked breads. 4 of the rooms are at ground level, 1 of which is especially equipped for wheelchair use. Please enquire about Facilities for Persons with Mobility Impairment.

**B&B from €45.00 to €60.00**

*Anne Duncan*
*General Manager*

10

**Closed November - March**

### O'Donnabhain's

GUESTHOUSE ★★★ MAP 1 D 3

Henry Street,
Kenmare,
Co. Kerry

Tel: 064-42106 Fax: 064-42321
Email: info@odonnabhain-kenmare.com
Web: www.odonnabhain-kenmare.com

Conveniently located in the centre of Kenmare Town, providing affordable accommodation with lashings of charm. Spacious en suite rooms (direct dial phone, TV-6 channels). Some with king size beds, finished with the comfort of the guests in mind. Rooms are located away from the bar, so as to ensure no sleepless nights - quietness in the centre of town. Ideal base to discover the south's attractions. Private car park.

***Bookable on www.irelandhotels.com***
*Special Offer: www.irelandhotels.com/offers*

**B&B from €36.00 to €56.00**

*Jeremiah Foley*
*Owner*

10

**Open All Year**

### Park Hotel Kenmare

HOTEL ★★★★★ MAP 1 D 3

Kenmare,
Co. Kerry

Tel: 064-41200 Fax: 064-41402
Email: info@parkkenmare.com
Web: www.parkkenmare.com

Since 1897 travellers have enjoyed the gracious elegance of the Park Hotel Kenmare. In a heavenly location overlooking Kenmare Bay the hotel is renowned for its attentive service and international standards. In the de luxe Destination Spa SAMAS guests can indulge in the ethos of a true spa to rejuvenate the body, mind & spirit. A host of classes & activities encompass the wonderful location of this special corner of Ireland. 18 hole golf course, tennis, 12 acres of gardens & 40 acre National Park adjoin the grounds. Enjoy Ireland in one of its most magnificent locations. Please enquire about Facilities for Persons with Mobility Impairment.

***An IHF Quality Employer***
Member of Ireland's Blue Book

***Bookable on www.irelandhotels.com***
*Special Offer: www.irelandhotels.com/offers*

**B&B from €182.00 to €249.00**
**Suites from €696.00 to €846.00**

*Francis Brennan*
*Proprietor*

46

Activities:

**Closed 26 November - 23 December**



B&B Rates are per Person Sharing per Night incl. Breakfast. or Room Rates are per Room per Night - See also Page 8

## Sea Shore Farm

**GUESTHOUSE ★★★ MAP 1 D 3**

Tubrid,
Kenmare,
Co. Kerry

Tel: 064-41270 Fax: 064-41270
Email: seashore@eircom.net
Web: www.seashorekenmare.com

Our setting on the bay is uniquely peaceful and private yet only 1 mile from town. Our farm extends to the shore affording unspoilt field walks in natural habitat with plentiful bird/wildlife. Large en suite rooms with panoramic seascapes, king beds, phone, tea facilities, etc. AA ♦♦♦♦ Selected, Recommended Guide du Routard, Los Angeles Times & Fodors Guide. Sign posted 300m from Kenmare by Esso Station - junction N71/N70 Killarney/Ring of Kerry Sneem Road. Please enquire about Facilities for Persons with Mobility Impairment.

Member of Friendly Homes of Ireland

*B&B from €50.00 to €65.00*

*Mary Patricia O'Sullivan*
*Proprietor*

6

Closed 01 November - 10 March

## Sheen Falls Lodge

**HOTEL ★★★★★ MAP 1 D 3**

Kenmare,
Co. Kerry

Tel: 064-41600 Fax: 064-41386
Email: info@sheenfallslodge.ie
Web: www.sheenfallslodge.ie

Uniquely set on the shores of Kenmare Bay & Sheen River, only 2km from the Heritage Town of Kenmare, on a 300 acre woodland estate. Our restaurant La Cascade, offers a distinctive fine dining experience overlooking the Sheen Waterfalls. We also offer casual dining in Oscar's Bar & Bistro situated on the riverside. Choose from an extensive array of estate activities from salmon fishing to clay pigeon shooting, or unwind with a visit to the Health Club. Dedicated staff uphold the most outstanding service to make your stay as unforgettable & unique as Ireland itself.

***An IHF Quality Employer***

Member of Relais et Châteaux

***Bookable on www.irelandhotels.com***
***Special Offer: www.irelandhotels.com/offers***

*Room Rate from €310.00 to €455.00*
*Suites from €465.00 to €1,870.00*

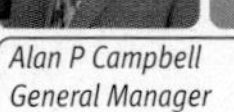

*Alan P Campbell*
*General Manager*

66

*Activities:*

Closed 03 January - 01 February

B&B Rates are per Person Sharing per Night incl. Breakfast.
or Room Rates are per Room per Night - **See also Page 8**

## Virginia's Guesthouse

GUESTHOUSE ★★★ MAP 1 D 3

36 Henry Street,
Kenmare,
Co. Kerry
Tel: 064-41021
Email: virginias@eircom.net
Web: www.virginias-kenmare.com

Welcome to Virginia's 3*** (AA ♦♦♦♦) family-run guesthouse in the heart of Kenmare. Guest rooms are bright, spacious & beautifully appointed with power showers, 40 channel digital TV and extremely comfortable beds. Excellent varied breakfast menu featuring home-baked breads and organic local produce. Virginia's is recommended by "The Good Hotel Guide", "The Rough Guide", Georgina Campbell, Lucinda O'Sullivan and Alistair Sawday. Mulcahy's Award - Winning Restaurant on ground floor of house.

***B&B from €40.00 to €60.00***

*Noreen & Neil Harrington*

8

**Closed 23 - 25 December**

## 19th Green (The)

GUESTHOUSE ★★★ MAP 2 E 4

Lackabane,
Fossa, Killarney,
Co. Kerry
Tel: 064-32868 Fax: 064-32637
Email: 19thgreen@eircom.net
Web: www.19thgreen-bb.com

Family-run guesthouse 3km from Killarney Town. Ring of Kerry Road; adjacent to Killarney's 3 x 18 hole championship courses. Ideal for golfers playing Killarney, Beaufort, Dooks, Waterville, Tralee or Ballybunion. All tee times arranged. Tours arranged: Gap of Dunloe, Ring of Kerry and Dingle Peninsula. All rooms en suite with direct dial phone and TV, tea/coffee facilities in guest rooms.

***Bookable on www.irelandhotels.com***
*Special Offer: www.irelandhotels.com/offers*

***B&B from €35.00 to €60.00***

*John & Freda Sheehan*
*Proprietors*

13

**Closed 01 November - 01 February**

## Abbey Lodge

GUESTHOUSE ★★★★ MAP 2 E 4

Muckross Road,
Killarney,
Co. Kerry
Tel: 064-34193 Fax: 064-35877
Email: abbeylodgekly@eircom.net
Web: www.abbey-lodge.com

Built to a 4**** specification. A genuine Irish welcome awaits you at Abbey Lodge. Our guesthouse is family-run and boasts 15 luxurious en suite rooms with TV, direct dial phone, power showers and central heating. We are conveniently located on the Muckross Road (N71) a mere three minute walk to the town centre. The house is tastefully decorated throughout and features many interesting antiques and art. With 30 years in the business - anywhere else is a compromise. Please enquire about Facilities for Persons with Mobility Impairment.

Member of Premier Guesthouses

***Bookable on www.irelandhotels.com***
*Special Offer: www.irelandhotels.com/offers*

***B&B from €45.00 to €85.00***

*Muireann King*
*Host*

15

**Closed 20 - 28 December**



B&B Rates are per Person Sharing per Night incl. Breakfast.
or Room Rates are per Room per Night - See also Page 8

## Aghadoe Heights Hotel & Spa

HOTEL ★★★★★ MAP 2 E 4

Lakes of Killarney,
Killarney,
Co. Kerry

Tel: 064-31766 Fax: 064-31345

Email: info@aghadoeheights.com

Web: www.aghadoeheights.com

Located in Ireland's most spectacular natural setting Aghadoe Heights Hotel & Spa is the premier destination Spa resort in Ireland. Consistently recognised for its service, guest rooms, suites & penthouse Aghadoe is one of only 4 hotels in Ireland to have achieved five Red Stars from the Automobile Association. We invite you to visit with us and be inspired by the breathtaking views, spellbound by the myth and legend, soothed by our Spa and enchanted by our people. Www.thespakillarney.com

***An IHF Quality Employer***

Member of Virtuoso

***Bookable on www.irelandhotels.com***
***Special Offer: www.irelandhotels.com/offers***

**B&B from €210.00 to €450.00**
**Suites from €350.00 to €2,500.00**

*Marie Chawke*
*General Manager*

74

*Activities:*

**Closed 31 December - 14 February**

## Arbutus Hotel

HOTEL ★★★★ MAP 2 E 4

College Street,
Killarney,
Co. Kerry

Tel: 064-31037 Fax: 064-34033

Email: stay@arbutuskillarney.com

Web: www.arbutuskillarney.com

The Arbutus Hotel and the Buckley family - at the heart of Killarney hospitality since 1926. Generations of visitors have enjoyed their personal introduction to the many attractions of the area whilst enjoying the warmth of a townhouse hotel where loving attention to detail is evident in home-cooked food, the original Buckley's Bar and the marvellous Celtic Deco design throughout. A truly special hotel. Please enquire about Facilities for Persons with Mobility Impairment.

***Bookable on www.irelandhotels.com***
***Special Offer: www.irelandhotels.com/offers***

**B&B from €65.00 to €110.00**

*Sean Buckley*
*Proprietor*

34

*Activities:*

**Closed 15 December - 05 January**

## Ashville House

GUESTHOUSE ★★★ MAP 2 E 4

Rock Road,
Killarney,
Co. Kerry

Tel: 064-36405 Fax: 064-36778

Email: info@ashvillekillarney.com

Web: www.ashvillekillarney.com

Ashville is a spacious family-run guesthouse, 2 mins walk from town centre, on main Tralee Road (N22). Private car park. Comfortably furnished en suite rooms include DD telephone, multi channel TV, hairdryer. Sample our varied breakfast menu. Convenient to Killarney National Park, pony trekking, golf & fishing. Ideal touring base for Ring of Kerry, Dingle & Beara. Declan & Elma assure you of a warm welcome at Ashville. Awarded AA ♦♦♦♦, RAC ♦♦♦♦ & Sparkling Diamond Award & Hospitality Award. Ground floor rooms available. Complimentary WiFi access.

***An IHF Quality Employer***

Member of Premier Guesthouses

***Bookable on www.irelandhotels.com***

**B&B from €35.00 to €60.00**

*Declan & Elma Walsh*
*Proprietors*

12

**Closed 01 November - 01 March**

B&B Rates are per Person Sharing per Night incl. Breakfast.
or Room Rates are per Room per Night - See also Page 8

# Killarney

## Best Western Eviston House Hotel

HOTEL ★★★ MAP 2 E 4

New Street,
Killarney,
Co. Kerry

Tel: 064-31640 Fax: 064-33685
Email: evishtl@eircom.net
Web: www.evistonhouse.com

Our hotel is family-run, ensuring guests a genuine Irish welcome. Located in the town centre, yet only minutes from the National Park. Choose from excellent value standard rooms to new superior rooms with broadband and contemporary decor. For an extra special stay try one of our luxurious deluxe rooms with whirlpool bath and king bed. Enjoy excellent cuisine and the best of lively traditional Irish music in our "Danny Mann" pub. Health conscious guests will appreciate our fitness suite, sauna, hot tub and solarium. A warm welcome is just the beginning!

***An IHF Quality Employer***

Member of Best Western Hotels

***Bookable on www.irelandhotels.com***
***Special Offer: www.irelandhotels.com/offers***

**B&B from €39.00 to €89.00**
**Suites from €120.00 to €200.00**

*Edward Eviston*
*Proprietor*

103

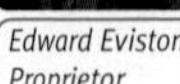

Activities:

**Open All Year**

## Best Western International

HOTEL ★★★ MAP 2 E 4

Killarney,
Co. Kerry

Tel: 064-31816 Fax: 064-31837
Email: inter@iol.ie
Web: www.killarneyinternational.com

Nestled in the heart of beautiful Killarney, blending the charm & intimacy of times past with contemporary elegance. Recently refurbished, boasting 90 luxurious guestrooms furnished to an exceptional standard. Executive room available complete with Italian furniture & flatscreen TVs and an en suite jacuzzi to soothe those aching muscles. Relax in our fitness suite or play world famous courses on our 3D golf simulator. Facilities include Hannigan's award-winning traditional bar & restaurant, live music nightly, golfers drying room & snooker room. Killarney National Park opposite the hotel.

***An IHF Quality Employer***

Member of Best Western Hotels

***Bookable on www.irelandhotels.com***
***Special Offer: www.irelandhotels.com/offers***

**Room Rate from €140.00 to €280.00**
**Suites from €260.00 to €400.00**

*Terence Mulcahy*
*General Manager*

90

**Closed 23 - 26 December**

## Brehon (The)

HOTEL ★★★★ MAP 2 E 4

Muckross Road,
Killarney,
Co. Kerry

Tel: 064-30700 Fax: 064-30701
Email: info@thebrehon.com
Web: www.thebrehon.com

The Brehon & Angsana Spa, a member of The Gleneagle Group, is a luxurious hotel of unique grace and elegance set amid Killarney's alluring landscape. Each guestroom and suite reflects a contemporary blend of beauty, style and space. Angsana Spa at the Brehon provides a sanctuary for the inner self. The experienced Thai therapists offer a range of holistic spa treatments and massages to refresh and revitalise the spirit, mind and physical being. Please enquire about Facilities for Persons with Mobility Impairment.

***An IHF Quality Employer***

Member of Luxury Lifestyle Hotels & Resorts

***Bookable on www.irelandhotels.com***
***Special Offer: www.irelandhotels.com/offers***

**Room Rate from €180.00 to €320.00**
**Suites from €286.00 to €1,500.00**

*Seán O'Driscoll*
*General Manager*

125

Activities:

**Open all Year**



B&B Rates are per Person Sharing per Night incl. Breakfast.
or Room Rates are per Room per Night - See also Page 8

## Brook Lodge Hotel

HOTEL ★★★★ MAP 2 E 4

High Street,
Killarney,
Co. Kerry

Tel: 064-31800 Fax: 064-35001

Email: brooklodgekillarney@eircom.net

Web: www.brooklodgekillarney.com

De luxe family-run 4* hotel in Killarney Town centre off the street with private parking and landscaped gardens. Large bedrooms & junior suites include tea/coffee facilities, hairdryer, iron and ironing board, TV, elevator, wheelchair friendly. Free internet access available. Our hotel has justifiably earned an outstanding reputation for its friendly personal service and relaxed atmosphere, excellent cuisine in Brooks Restaurant or a nightcap in the residents' bar. Please enquire about Facilities for Persons with Mobility Impairment.

*Bookable on www.irelandhotels.com*
*Special Offer: www.irelandhotels.com/offers*

**B&B from €55.00 to €85.00**
**Suites from €180.00 to €240.00**

*Joan Counihan*
*Owner*

24

**Closed 01 November - 04 April**

## Cahernane House Hotel

HOTEL ★★★★ MAP 2 E 4

Muckross Road,
Killarney,
Co. Kerry

Tel: 064-31895 Fax: 064-34340

Email: reservations@cahernane.com

Web: www.cahernane.com

Formerly the residence of the Herbert family, Earls of Pembroke, Cahernane House dates back to the 17th century. Cahernane House Hotel is situated on its own parklands on the edge of Killarney's National Park, an area of outstanding natural beauty with its untamed landscape of mountains, lakes and woodland walks and is only 10 minutes walk from Killarney Town. All of the 38 bedrooms are beautifully appointed, many with antique furniture, jacuzzis and private balconies. No pets allowed. Conference & Spa facility opening Spring 2007. Please enquire about Facilities for Persons with Mobility Impairment.

Member of Manor House Hotels

*Bookable on www.irelandhotels.com*
*Special Offer: www.irelandhotels.com/offers*

**B&B from €90.00 to €150.00**
**Suites from €320.00 to €390.00**

*Jimmy Browne*
*Proprietor*

38

**Closed 23 December - 05 January**

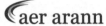

B&B Rates are per Person Sharing per Night incl. Breakfast.
or Room Rates are per Room per Night - See also Page 8

# Killarney

## Castlelodge Guesthouse

GUESTHOUSE ★★ MAP 2 E 4

Muckross Road,
Killarney,
Co. Kerry

Tel: 064-31545 Fax: 064-32325
Email: castlelodge@eircom.net

Conveniently located, just two minutes walk from Killarney Town centre. Open all year round excluding Christmas, our guesthouse offers very friendly staff, a homely atmosphere and easy access to all the major attractions and magnificent scenery in Killarney. Good restaurants and live music will be recommended, come and see the sights, hear the music and taste the atmosphere. Please enquire about Facilities for Persons with Mobility Impairment.

**B&B from €45.00 to €60.00**

*Aoife O'Shea & Michelle Corcoran*
*Hosts*

25

**Closed 24 - 26 December**

## Castlerosse Hotel and Golf Resort

HOTEL ★★★ MAP 2 E 4

Lower Lake,
Killarney,
Co. Kerry

Tel: 064-31144 Fax: 064-31031
Email: res@castlerosse.ie
Web: www.castlerossehotel.com

The Castlerosse Hotel & Golf Resort is located on the lakeside 2kms from Killarney town with panoramic views of the lakes and mountains. It is flanked on one side by the National Park and on the other by Killarney Golf & Fishing Club. There is a choice of double twin and family rooms, some with lake and mountain view. Leisure facilities: Onsite 9 hole golf course, health and leisure club with 20m pool, gym, jacuzzi, sauna and spa treatment rooms.

***An IHF Quality Employer***

***Bookable on www.irelandhotels.com***
*Special Offer: www.irelandhotels.com/offers*

**B&B from €45.00 to €90.00**

*Danny Bowe*
*General Manager*

120

Activities:

**Closed 04 November - 14 March**

## Crystal Springs

GUESTHOUSE ★★★ MAP 2 E 4

Ballycasheen (Off N22),
Killarney,
Co. Kerry

Tel: 064-33272 Fax: 064-35518
Email: crystalsprings@eircom.net
Web: http://www.crystalspringsbb.com/

Located on the banks of the peaceful River Flesk offering fishing on location. Just off N22/Cork Road, only a short walk to town centre, where many traditional pubs and fine restaurants can be found. Close to lakes, National Park, Ring of Kerry and I.N.E.C. Spacious en suite rooms, AA ♦♦♦♦ award. TV, tea/coffee facilities, hairdryers, DD phones, trouser press and refrigerators. Extensive menus including vegetarian and home specialities. Ample safe parking. Please enquire about Facilities for Persons with Mobility Impairment.

***Bookable on www.irelandhotels.com***
*Special Offer: www.irelandhotels.com/offers*

**B&B from €39.00 to €65.00**

*Eileen & Tim Brosnan*

8

**Closed 20 - 29 December**



B&B Rates are per Person Sharing per Night incl. Breakfast.
or Room Rates are per Room per Night - See also Page 8

## Darby O'Gill's Country House Hotel

HOTEL ★★★ MAP 2 E 4

Lissivigeen,
Mallow Road, Killarney,
Co. Kerry
Tel: 064-34168 Fax: 064-36794
Email: darbyogill@eircom.net
Web: www.darbyogillskillarney.com

Darby O'Gill's is a spacious, family-run hotel located 5 mins drive from Killarney. All 43 bedrooms are en suite and fully equipped. Private car park onsite. Newly installed elevator. Darby O'Gill's also boasts the refurbished "Rathcullen Lounge & Sport Bar" serving superb bar food all day. Entertainment every weekend and nightly during peak season. Excellent cuisine served daily in Cluricaune's Restaurant. Personal attention is guaranteed. Families most welcome. Please enquire about Facilities for Persons with Mobility Impairment.

***An IHF Quality Employer***

Member of Countrywide Hotels - MinOtel Ireland

*Bookable on www.irelandhotels.com*
*Special Offer: www.irelandhotels.com/offers*

*B&B from €40.00 to €85.00*

*Pat & Joan Gill & Family*

43

**Closed 24 - 26 December**

## Dromhall Hotel

HOTEL ★★★★ MAP 2 E 4

Muckross Road,
Killarney,
Co. Kerry
Tel: 064-39300 Fax: 064-39301
Email: info@dromhall.com
Web: www.dromhall.com

Killarney's famous mountain scenes provide a magnificent backdrop for the Dromhall Hotel. Located 5 minutes walk from town, the hotel offers the comfort and service one associates with a first class hotel while retaining the friendliness and welcome of a family-run hotel. From the moment you enter the elegant marbled lobby the scene is set for a special experience. Banquet and conference facilities for up to 300. Award-winning Kaynes Bistro. Club Santé leisure facilities are available to all guests. For sheer indulgence pay a visit to our Zen Day Spa.

***An IHF Quality Employer***

*Bookable on www.irelandhotels.com*
*Special Offer: www.irelandhotels.com/offers*

*B&B from €55.00 to €115.00*

*Bernadette Randles*
*Managing Director*

70

*Activities:*

**Closed 23 - 27 December**

B&B Rates are per Person Sharing per Night incl. Breakfast.
or Room Rates are per Room per Night - **See also Page 8**

## Killarney

### Earls Court House

HOTEL ★★★★ MAP 2 E 4

Woodlawn Junction, Muckross Road, Killarney, Co. Kerry

Tel: 064-34009 Fax: 064-34366

Email: info@killarney-earlscourt.ie

Web: www.killarney-earlscourt.ie

Luxury 4 star residence, family-run, offering peace & relaxation in a quiet suburb, only 7 mins walk to town centre. Winner of the "Romantic Elegance Award for Ireland" 2006 & "Ireland's Best Breakfast Award". Experience the elegance & charm of a country house, open fires, tea & home baking. Enjoy spacious rooms graced with antiques, king beds, full bathrooms, four poster suites some with jacuzzi. Wheelchair friendly, tea facilities, elevator & private parking, internet access. Tours & golf arranged. Light snack menu until 8pm. Wine licence. Please enquire about Facilities for Persons with Mobility Impairment.

*Bookable on www.irelandhotels.com*

*Special Offer: www.irelandhotels.com/offers*

**B&B from €60.00 to €75.00**
**Suites from €140.00 to €200.00**

*Emer & Ray Moynihan*
*Owners*

30

**Closed 15 November - 15 February**

### Failte Hotel

HOTEL ★★ MAP 2 E 4

College Street, Killarney, Co. Kerry

Tel: 064-33404 Fax: 064-36599

Email: failtehotel@eircom.net

The Failte Hotel, furnished to a very high standard, is owned and managed by the O'Callaghan family. It is internationally known for its high standard of cuisine. Paudie supervises the award-winning bar. It is situated in the town centre, adjacent to railway station, new factory outlet, shopping complex. Also close by are many local cabarets and night clubs. Local amenities include golfing, fishing, walking.

**B&B from €45.00 to €75.00**

*Dermot & Eileen O'Callaghan*
*Proprietors*

14

*Activities:*

**Closed 23 - 27 December**

### Fairview Guesthouse

GUESTHOUSE ★★★★ MAP 2 E 4

Michael Collins Place, College Street, Killarney, Co. Kerry

Tel: 064-34164 Fax: 064-71777

Email: info@fairviewkillarney.com

Web: www.fairviewkillarney.com

Superbly located in the heart of Killarney Town, yet out of noise's way, Fairview is a luxurious boutique style guesthouse that is unique in quality, location, service & elegance. Parking, spacious rooms with optional jacuzzi suites, all modern amenities including lift & wheelchair facilities, category 3 VAS. A base from which to tour, golf or socialise. Privately owned & managed. Awards: AA and RAC ♦♦♦♦♦, Sparkling Diamond & Warm Welcome Award, Killarney Best New Development & Guesthouse Awards & the prestigious Little Gem Awards. New Fifth Season Restaurant & additional executive deluxe rooms & penthouse now open.

*Bookable on www.irelandhotels.com*

**B&B from €45.00 to €85.00**
**Suites from €150.00 to €300.00**

*The Fifth Season*

*James & Shelley O' Neill*
*Proprietors*

29

*Activities:*

**Closed 24 - 25 December**



B&B Rates are per Person Sharing per Night incl. Breakfast. or Room Rates are per Room per Night - **See also Page 8**

## Foley's Townhouse & Restaurant

GUESTHOUSE ★★★★ MAP 2 E 4

23 High Street,
Killarney,
Co. Kerry

Tel: 064-31217 Fax: 064-34683
Email: info@foleystownhouse.com
Web: www.foleystownhouse.com

Originally a 19th Century Coaching Inn, this old house has hosted generations of travellers. Newly refurbished, this is a 4**** family-run town centre guesthouse. Luxury bedrooms are individually designed for comfort with every modern amenity, including lift, wheelchair access and 2 de luxe suites. Downstairs is our award-winning seafood & steak restaurant. Chef / owner Carol provides meals from fresh local produce. Choose from approx 300 wines. Personal supervision. Private parking. Awarded AA ♦♦♦♦♦, RAC Highly Acclaimed. Please enquire about Facilities for Persons with Mobility Impairment.

Member of Premier Guesthouses

*Bookable on www.irelandhotels.com*
*Special Offer: www.irelandhotels.com/offers*

*B&B from €65.00 to €85.00*
*Suites from €280.00 to €300.00*

*Carol Hartnett*
*Proprietor*

28

*Activities:*

**Closed 01 December - 27 December**

## Friars Glen

GUESTHOUSE ★★★★ MAP 2 E 4

Mangerton Road,
Muckross, Killarney,
Co. Kerry

Tel: 064-37500 Fax: 064-37388
Email: friarsglen@eircom.net
Web: www.friarsglen.ie

"Magnificent, extremely beautiful, delightful, absolutely wonderful, stunning, peaceful and tranquil, fantastic, charming, delicious, relaxing, gracious, comfortable, We'll be back!" Some of the words used by guests to describe Friars Glen in the guest book. Set in its own 28 acres within the world renowned Killarney National Park, Friars Glen is a 4**** country house that offers the highest standards of accommodation and service. The ideal base for exploring Killarney National Park and Ireland's Southwest. Please enquire about Facilities for Persons with Mobility Impairment.

*Bookable on www.irelandhotels.com*
*Special Offer: www.irelandhotels.com/offers*

*B&B from €50.00 to €70.00*

*Mary Fuller*
*Proprietor*

10

**Closed 30 November - 01 March**

## Killarney

### Fuchsia House

GUESTHOUSE ★★★★ MAP 2 E 4

Muckross Road,
Killarney,
Co. Kerry

Tel: 064-33743 Fax: 064-36588
Email: fuchsiahouse@eircom.net
Web: www.fuchsiahouse.com

We invite you to enjoy the affordable luxury of Fuchsia House which is set well back from Muckross Road in mature leafy gardens. Only 7 minutes walk from Killarney Town centre. Purpose built to combine the amenities of a modern 4**** guesthouse with the elegance of an earlier age. We offer spacious rooms with orthopaedic beds, dressed in crisp cotton and linen, DD phone, private bath with power shower. Separate guest kitchen with tea/coffee making facilities. Spacious lounges & conservatory. Complimentary WiFi access throughout. Irish & vegetarian menus. Recognized by all leading guidebooks.

*B&B from €45.00 to €70.00*

*Neil & Marie Burke*
*Proprietors/Managers*

10

*Activities:*

T C ✲ U P S I

**Closed 01 November - 14 March**

### Gleann Fia Country House

GUESTHOUSE ★★★ MAP 2 E 4

Old Deerpark,
Killarney,
Co. Kerry

Tel: 064-35035 Fax: 064-35000
Email: info@gleannfia.com
Web: www.gleannfia.com

Gleann Fia Country House, open year round, is located 2km from Killarney Town. Situated on acres of gardens, river & woodland walks. Our location is perfect for touring scenic sights of Kerry, playing golf on world renowned championship parklands & links courses, fishing & hill walking. All bedrooms are tastefully decorated, some furnished with antiques & all rooms have pleasant views of the surrounding countryside. Breakfast is hot & cold buffet with fresh juices, breads, yogurts, cheese platters. Safe & secure parking. A professional & friendly home style service.

Member of Premier Collection

**Bookable on www.irelandhotels.com**
*Special Offer: www.irelandhotels.com/offers*

*B&B from €30.00 to €75.00*

*Bridget & Conor O'Connell*
*Proprietors / Managers*

19

*Activities:*

T C ✲ U P S I

**Open All Year**

### Glena Guesthouse

GUESTHOUSE ★★★ MAP 2 E 4

Muckross Road,
Killarney,
Co. Kerry

Tel: 064-32705 Fax: 064-35611
Email: glena@iol.ie
Web: www.glenahouse.com

Glena House - Killarney's award-winning 3 star guesthouse, AA ♦♦♦♦, RAC ♦♦♦♦, Sparkling Diamond Award 2003/2004, Failte Ireland approved. It's the simple things that make it a great place to stay - great location 5 minutes from town centre, evening meals available during season, orthopaedic beds to rest in, a shower/bath en suite to invigorate, tea/coffee when you want, homebaking & preserves, healthy options breakfast, a bowl of ice, dispense bar service & a host and staff eager to make your stay happy & memorable. Parking on site. Access to internet. Please enquire about Facilities for Persons with Mobility Impairment.

Member of Ireland B&B

**Bookable on www.irelandhotels.com**
*Special Offer: www.irelandhotels.com/offers*

*B&B from €38.00 to €50.00*

*Kayan Culloty Rice*
*Manager*

20

T C ✲ P S

**Open All Year**



B&B Rates are per Person Sharing per Night incl. Breakfast.
or Room Rates are per Room per Night - **See also Page 8**

## Gleneagle Hotel

HOTEL ★★★ MAP 2 E 4

Killarney,
Co. Kerry

Tel: 064-36000 Fax: 064-32646
Email: info@gleneaglehotel.com
Web: www.gleneaglehotel.com

Ireland's leading leisure and conference/convention hotel, adjacent to Killarney's National Park with beautifully furnished rooms. Ireland's National Events Centre is ideally suited for conventions, conferences, exhibitions, sporting events, concerts and theatrical productions. Our award-winning chefs will delight you in both our restaurants. We have a great line-up of entertainment all year round. Relax and unwind using our indoor/outdoor leisure facilities.

***An IHF Quality Employer***

Member of Gleneagle Group

***Bookable on www.irelandhotels.com***
***Special Offer: www.irelandhotels.com/offers***

*B&B from €50.00 to €120.00*
*Suites from €150.00 to €380.00*

*John Dolan*
*General Manager*

246

*Activities:*

**Open All Year**

## Heights Hotel - Killarney (The)

HOTEL ★★★ MAP 2 E 4

Cork Road,
Killarney,
Co. Kerry

Tel: 064-31158 Fax: 064-35198
Email: info@killarneyheights.ie
Web: www.killarneyheights.ie

Situated 1km from Killarney Town centre, this beautiful 70 bedroomed hotel overlooks the breathtaking Torc and Mangerton Mountains. Privately owned and family-run, the hotel offers unparalleled standards of service, luxury accommodation, fine dining and entertainment. The Heights Hotel Killarney is the perfect venue to begin your holiday or tour of our beautiful scenic countryside. Two conference rooms available, facilities include broadband and audio visual equipment. Please enquire about Facilities for Persons with Mobility Impairment.

***Bookable on www.irelandhotels.com***
***Special Offer: www.irelandhotels.com/offers***

*B&B from €45.00 to €90.00*

*Tom O'Mahony*
*General Manager*

70

*Activities:*

**Closed 24 - 26 December**



B&B Rates are per Person Sharing per Night incl. Breakfast.
or Room Rates are per Room per Night - **See also Page 8**

## Killarney

### Holiday Inn Killarney

HOTEL ★★★ MAP 2 E 4

Muckross Road,
Killarney,
Co. Kerry

Tel: 064-33000 Fax: 064-33001

Email: reservations@holidayinnkillarney.com

Web: www.holidayinnkillarney.com

Holiday Inn Killarney enjoys a quiet but central location close to Killarney Town centre. Its 100 spacious en suite guest rooms including 24 family suites, are tastefully decorated to the highest standards. Our fully equipped leisure centre is the perfect place to relax and unwind. Our Library Point Restaurant serves the finest of local cuisine while Saddlers Pub serves food daily and has a live entertainment programme. A haven for all seasons!

***An IHF Quality Employer***

***B&B from €55.00 to €130.00***
***Suites from €140.00 to €290.00***

*Misja Herfurt*
*General Manager*

100

**Closed 24 - 25 December**

### Hotel Dunloe Castle

HOTEL ★★★★★ MAP 2 E 4

Killarney,
Co. Kerry

Tel: 064-44111 Fax: 064-44583

Email: hotelsales@liebherr.com

Web: www.killarneyhotels.ie

5 star resort hotel overlooking the famous Gap of Dunloe. 98 spacious rooms including suites, all with balconys overlooking Gap of Dunloe or surrounding parkland. Historical park & botanic gardens with ruins of castle. Elegant décor with many valuable antiques. Luxurious lounges, cocktail bar, gourmet restaurant. Extensive leisure facilities: pool, sauna, gym, riding, putting green, tennis, jogging track. 10 ch'ship courses nearby. Sister hotels: Ard-na-Sidhe & Hotel Europe. Central Res: Tel: 064-71350, Fax: 064-37900. Please enquire about Facilities for Persons with Mobility Impairment.

Member of Killarney Hotels Ltd

***Bookable on www.irelandhotels.com***
***Special Offer: www.irelandhotels.com/offers***

***B&B from €105.00 to €145.00***
***Suites from €600.00 to €600.00***

*Hilary O'Mara*
*Manager*

98

*Activities:*

**Closed 31 October - 01 April**

### Hotel Europe

HOTEL ★★★★★ MAP 2 E 4

Killarney,
Co. Kerry

Tel: 064-71300 Fax: 064-37900

Email: hotelsales@liebherr.com

Web: www.killarneyhotels.ie

UNDER REFURBISHMENT - RE-OPENING MARCH 2008

5 star resort hotel, internationally known for its location on the Lakes of Killarney. 190 bedrooms and suites, all refurbished with balconies. Extensive renovation has seen the introduction of the Espa at the Europe which incorporates health, wellbeing, beauty and fitness. New conference facilities offer the perfect balance between an inspiring work environment and a relaxing oasis. On site activities include tennis, pony trekking, walking, children's outdoor playground. Boating and fishing available for a charge at the lake shore. Please enquire about Facilities for Persons with Mobility Impairment.

Member of Killarney Hotels Ltd

***Bookable on www.irelandhotels.com***
***Special Offer: www.irelandhotels.com/offers***

***B&B from €105.00 to €175.00***
***Suites from €400.00 to €1,750.00***

*Michael W. Brennan*

190

*Activities:*

**Closed 15 December - 12 February**



B&B Rates are per Person Sharing per Night incl. Breakfast.
or Room Rates are per Room per Night - See also Page 8

## Husseys Townhouse & Bar

GUESTHOUSE ★★★ MAP 2 E 4

43 High Street,
Killarney,
Co. Kerry

Tel: 064-37454 Fax: 064-33144

Email: geraldine@husseystownhouse.com

Web: www.husseystownhouse.com

Centrally located, within walking distance of Killarney National Park, the principal shopping areas and the best restaurants in town. This family owned house offers peaceful accommodation in tastefully decorated rooms, equipped to a high standard. Enjoy a choice of breakfast in our delightful dining room, relax in our comfortable guest lounge or cosy friendly bar. For walkers, cyclists, golfers or touring Kerry, this is the discerning traveller's perfect choice. Private parking. Please enquire about Facilities for Persons with Mobility Impairment.

**B&B from €35.00 to €50.00**

*Geraldine O'Leary*
*Owner*

5

**Closed 01 November - 14 March**

## Inveraray Farm Guesthouse

GUESTHOUSE ★★ MAP 2 E 4

Beaufort,
Killarney,
Co. Kerry

Tel: 064-44224 Fax: 064-44775

Email: inver@indigo.ie

Web: www.inver-aray.com

A luxury farm guesthouse in a quiet sylvan setting. Views of Killarney Lakes, Mountains and Gap of Dunloe. 9km west of Killarney, 1km off N72, left over Laune Bridge at shop. Free private trout and salmon fishing on River Laune. A walkers' paradise, angling, walking and golfer groups catered for. Tours arranged. Tea room, playroom, playground and pony for children. Singing pubs, horse riding locally. Home-baking, seafood and dinner a speciality with good, wholesome home cooking. Recommended Le Guide du Routard 2007 and Michelin 2007. Internet Access.

*Bookable on www.irelandhotels.com*

*Special Offer: www.irelandhotels.com/offers*

**B&B from €34.00 to €40.00**

*Eileen & Noel Spillane*
*Proprietors*

9

Activities:

**Closed 15 November - 20 February**

## Kathleens Country House

GUESTHOUSE ★★★★ MAP 2 E 4

Madams Height, Tralee Road,
Killarney,
Co. Kerry

Tel: 064-32810 Fax: 064-32340

Email: info@kathleens.net

Web: www.kathleens.net

Attentiveness, friendliness, traditional hospitality make Kathleens special. Awarded 'Small Hotel of the Year' for Ireland, AA ♦♦♦♦♦. A tranquil oasis on 3 acres of mature gardens with private car park only one mile to Killarney Town. Sumptuous breakfasts using fresh local produce. Spacious bedrooms, full bathrooms, orthopaedic beds, tea/coffee facilities, hairdryer, telephone & internet access. WiFi/Computer for guests use in library. Customised itineraries and golfing tee times arranged. Ideal golfing/touring base. Singles welcome. Non smoking. Easy to get to! Hard to leave!

***An IHF Quality Employer***

*Bookable on www.irelandhotels.com*

*Special Offer: www.irelandhotels.com/offers*

**B&B from €50.00 to €75.00**

*Kathleen O'Regan Sheppard*
*Proprietor*

17

Activities:

**Closed 21 October - 19 March**

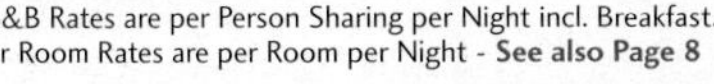

B&B Rates are per Person Sharing per Night incl. Breakfast.
or Room Rates are per Room per Night - **See also Page 8**

## Killarney

### Killarney Avenue Hotel

HOTEL ★★★★ MAP 2 E 4

Town Centre,
Killarney,
Co. Kerry

Tel: 064-32522 Fax: 064-33707

Email: kavenue@odonoghue-ring-hotels.com

Web: www.odonoghue-ring-hotels.com

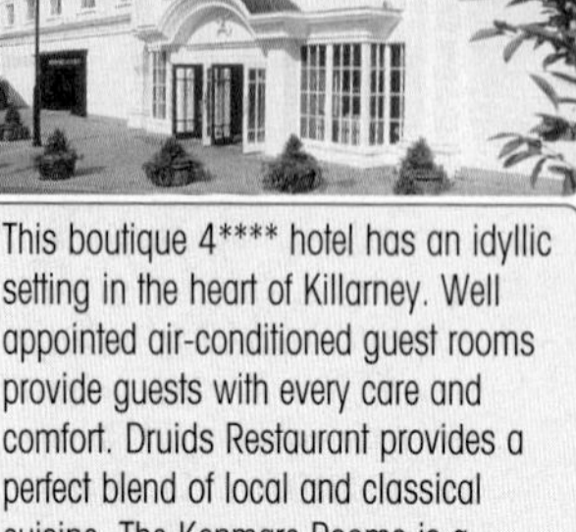

This boutique 4**** hotel has an idyllic setting in the heart of Killarney. Well appointed air-conditioned guest rooms provide guests with every care and comfort. Druids Restaurant provides a perfect blend of local and classical cuisine. The Kenmare Rooms is a distinctly different hotel bar. Guests are welcome to use the leisure facilities of our sister hotel (Killarney Towers Hotel), 100m away. Underground garage parking available. Close to shopping, vistor attractions and Kerry's premier golf courses.

*Bookable on www.irelandhotels.com*

*Special Offer: www.irelandhotels.com/offers*

**B&B from €60.00 to €115.00**

*Denis McCarthy*
*General Manager*

66

**Closed 24 December - 02 January**

### Killarney Lodge

GUESTHOUSE ★★★★ MAP 2 E 4

Countess Road,
Killarney,
Co. Kerry

Tel: 064-36499 Fax: 064-31070

Email: klylodge@iol.ie

Web: www.killarneylodge.net

Welcome to Killarney Lodge, a purpose built four star guesthouse set in private walled-in gardens, yet only 2 minutes walk from Killarney Town centre. The Lodge provides private parking, spacious en suite air-conditioned bedrooms with all modern amenities. Guests can avail of internet access at the Lodge. Enjoy an extensive breakfast menu, relax in comfortable lounges with open fires where traditional home baking is served. The Lodge has justifiably earned an outstanding reputation for quality of service, relaxed atmosphere and friendliness.

**B&B from €50.00 to €72.00**

*Catherine Treacy*
*Owner*

16

*Activities:*

**Closed 01 November - 01 February**

### Killarney Oaks

HOTEL ★★★ MAP 2 E 4

Muckross Road,
Killarney,
Co. Kerry

Tel: 064-37600 Fax: 064-37619

Email: info@killarneyoaks.com

Web: www.killarneyoaks.com

The hotel has 70 newly refurbished deluxe and superior bedrooms, all en suite, offering every modern comfort and amenity. Enjoy traditional Irish music, great bar food and a drink in the Acorn Bar. Guests can have a choice to dine in our two evening restaurants, The Oaks and Hayden's Eurotoque Restaurant, both offering guests a broad selection of superb local and international dishes . Launched in November 2006, our new conference and banqueting centre which can hold up to 350 guests, suitable for conference meetings, functions and weddings.

*Bookable on www.irelandhotels.com*

*Special Offer: www.irelandhotels.com/offers*

**B&B from €50.00 to €120.00**
**Suites from €140.00 to €280.00**

*Eamon Courtney*
*Proprietor*

70

**Closed 24 - 26 December**



B&B Rates are per Person Sharing per Night incl. Breakfast.
or Room Rates are per Room per Night - See also Page 8

## Killarney Park Hotel

HOTEL ★★★★★ MAP 2 E 4

Town Centre,
Killarney,
Co. Kerry

Tel: 064-35555 Fax: 064-35266
Email: info@killarneyparkhotel.ie
Web: www.killarneyparkhotel.ie

Superbly located in the heart of Killarney Town on its own grounds, this family owned hotel is renowned as a place of elegance laced with warmth and hospitality. The hotel offers 68 beautifully appointed guest rooms and suites complemented by a luxurious full service spa. Other hotel features include a 20m swimming pool, outdoor hot-tub, jacuzzi, library, drawing room, billiards room, games room, golf locker and drying room. Conference facilities for up to 150 delegates. A warm welcome awaits you. Please enquire about Facilities for Persons with Mobility Impairment.

***An IHF Quality Employer***

Member of Leading Small Hotels of the World

*Bookable on www.irelandhotels.com*
*Special Offer: www.irelandhotels.com/offers*

*B&B from €137.50 to €200.00*
*Suites from €385.00 to €580.00*

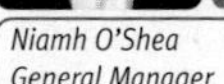

*Niamh O'Shea*
*General Manager*

68

*Activities:*

**Closed 24 - 27 December**

## Killarney Plaza Hotel & Spa

HOTEL ★★★★ MAP 2 E 4

Town Centre,
Killarney,
Co. Kerry

Tel: 064-21111 Fax: 064-21190
Email: info@killarneyplaza.com
Web: www.killarneyplaza.com

The Killarney Plaza successfully blends gracious hospitality, quality service and amenities in such a way that guests using the hotel for business or pleasure feel at ease. This elegant hotel enjoys a wonderful location in Killarney. The leisure area and Molton Brown Spa allow guests to unwind and relax in luxurious surroundings. All bedrooms and suites are luxuriously furnished and air-conditioned. The Killarney Plaza is a "must see, must stay" rendezvous.

*Bookable on www.irelandhotels.com*
*Special Offer: www.irelandhotels.com/offers*

*B&B from €90.00 to €250.00*
*Suites from €400.00 to €500.00*

*Michael O'Donoghue*
*Managing Director*

198

*Activities:*

**Closed 16 December - 01 February**



B&B Rates are per Person Sharing per Night incl. Breakfast.
or Room Rates are per Room per Night - **See also Page 8**

## Killarney

### Killarney Royal

HOTEL ★★★★ MAP 2 E 4

College Street,
Killarney,
Co. Kerry

Tel: 064-31853 Fax: 064-34001
Email: info@killarneyroyal.ie
Web: www.killarneyroyal.ie

Privately owned by the Scally family & located in the heart of Killarney, the Killarney Royal is the perfect base for walking, golfing, & touring the South West of Ireland. Air-conditioned throughout, this 4 star standard boutique property boasts 24 de luxe rooms and also has 5 junior suites tastefully designed by the proprietor Mrs. Scally, who modestly uses a country classical design at the Killarney Royal Hotel. "Overall, outstanding service with a positive attitude. I would recommend it to anyone looking for a small hotel with charm & loads of hospitality" - Peter Zummo.

**Bookable on www.irelandhotels.com**
*Special Offer: www.irelandhotels.com/offers*

**B&B from €75.00 to €160.00**
**Suites from €95.00 to €160.00**

*Noreen Cronin &*
*Gillian O'Dea*
*Operations Managers*

29

Activities:

**Closed 23 - 27 December**

### Killeen House Hotel

HOTEL ★★★ MAP 2 E 4

Aghadoe,
Lakes Of Killarney,
Co. Kerry

Tel: 064-31711 Fax: 064-31811
Email: charming@indigo.ie
Web: www.killeenhousehotel.com

The Killeen House is truly a charming little hotel. With only 23 rooms, 8 of them de luxe, it is the ideal base for touring 'God's own country', the magical Kingdom of Kerry. With our DIY Golf Pub and Rozzers elegant dining room you are assured of a memorable experience. Go on, do the smart thing and call us now! We look forward to extending the 'hostility of the house' to you! Please enquire about Facilities for Persons with Mobility Impairment.

***An IHF Quality Employer***

**Bookable on www.irelandhotels.com**
*Special Offer: www.irelandhotels.com/offers*

**B&B from €70.00 to €120.00**

*Geraldine & Michael Rosney*
*Owners*

23

**Closed 01 January - 10 April**

### Kingfisher Lodge Guesthouse

GUESTHOUSE ★★★ MAP 2 E 4

Lewis Road,
Killarney,
Co. Kerry

Tel: 064-37131 Fax: 064-39871
Email: kingfisherguesthouse@eircom.net
Web: www.kingfisherkillarney.com

Kingfisher Lodge is an award-winning family-run Fáilte Ireland approved and AA ♦♦♦♦ registered guesthouse. Quietly located yet just 4 minutes walk from town centre pubs, restaurants, entertainment and shopping. Beautifully decorated spacious bedrooms with TV, phone, hairdryer, tea/coffee, internet access available. Guest lounge with satellite TV, books, magazines. Varied breakfast menu. Private parking, large gardens. Tackle, drying rooms. Tours, golfing, walking, angling arranged with Donal, a qualified guide. Non-smoking house.

Member of Insight Web Marketing

**Bookable on www.irelandhotels.com**
*Special Offer: www.irelandhotels.com/offers*

**B&B from €35.00 to €55.00**

*Ann & Donal Carroll*
*Proprietors*

10

Activities:

**Closed 10 December - 10 February**



B&B Rates are per Person Sharing per Night incl. Breakfast. or Room Rates are per Room per Night - **See also Page 8**

## Lake Hotel

HOTEL ★★★★ MAP 2 E 4

On Lake Shore,
Muckross Road, Killarney,
Co. Kerry

Tel: 064-31035 Fax: 064-31902

Email: info@lakehotel.com

Web: www.lakehotel.com

The most beautiful location in Ireland, set on Killarney's lakeshore. Open log fires, double height ceilings, relaxed & friendly atmosphere. Woodland view rooms; superior lakeside rooms with jacuzzi & balcony; deluxe lakeside rooms with jacuzzi, balcony & refrigerator; four poster deluxe lakeside rooms with jacuzzi, balcony, fireplace & refrigerator; master deluxe rooms with jacuzzi & balcony. Spa Sensations with hot tub on the lakeside, sauna, steam room, gym & treatment rooms. Library, free WiFi, tennis court & 3 state of the art meeting rooms. Safety deposit boxes. Customer & Care Award from AA for 2007.

***An IHF Quality Employer***

***Bookable on www.irelandhotels.com***

***Special Offer: www.irelandhotels.com/offers***

**B&B from €50.00 to €160.00**
**Suites from €120.00 to €320.00**

*Niall Huggard*
*General Manager*

120

*Activities:*

**Closed 08 December - 15 January**

## Lime Court

GUESTHOUSE ★★★ MAP 2 E 4

Muckross Road,
Killarney,
Co. Kerry

Tel: 064-34547 Fax: 064-35611

Email: limecrt@iol.ie

Web: www.hoztel.com

Lime Court has the perfect location for those wishing to completely unwind. Just 5 minutes walk from Killarney Town centre, easy on street parking, on the main Ring of Kerry route and Muckross Road. Located beside 4 excellent pubs offering traditional Irish music and good food. Lime Court is also ideally located to take advantage of the INEC, which is 5 minutes walk away. If you would care to walk for another 5 minutes, you are in the heart of Killarney National Park, with the ripples from the world famous Lakes of Killarney breaking at your feet. Lime Court offers a truly serene environment. Access to internet.

Member of Ireland B&B

**B&B from €38.00 to €50.00**

*Kayan Culloty Rice*
*Manager*

16

**Open All Year**

## Loch Lein Country House

HOTEL ★★★★ MAP 2 E 4

Golf Course Road,
Fossa, Killarney,
Co. Kerry

Tel: 064-31260 Fax: 064-36151

Email: stay@lochlein.com

Web: www.lochlein.com

A secluded Country House with magnificent uninterrupted views over Killarney's famous Lower Lake and the MacGillicuddy Reeks. The hotel's emphasis is on friendly personal service and high standards of food and accommodation. Spacious non-smoking bedrooms have many thoughtful touches to enhance a comfortable and relaxing stay. Ideally located on the Ring of Kerry/Dingle roads, near the Gap of Dunloe. Nearby four golf courses, fishing and horse riding. May we welcome you. Please enquire about Facilities for Persons with Mobility Impairment.

***Bookable on www.irelandhotels.com***

***Special Offer: www.irelandhotels.com/offers***

**B&B from €50.00 to €85.00**

*Paul & Annette Corridan*
*Hosts*

25

**Closed 01 November - 31 March**

B&B Rates are per Person Sharing per Night incl. Breakfast.
or Room Rates are per Room per Night - See also Page 8

## Killarney

### Malton (The)

HOTEL ★★★★ MAP 2 E 4

Town Centre,
Killarney,
Co. Kerry

Tel: 064-38000 Fax: 064-31642
Email: res@themalton.com
Web: www.themalton.com

The Malton, formerly the Great Southern Hotel Killarney, is a stunning Victorian hotel and much-loved Irish landmark. Since opening our doors in 1854, this historic hotel has been a cherished destination, welcoming visitors from all over the world. Tucked away on six acres of landscaped gardens, fountains and pathways for rambling, The Malton is unique in combining wide-open space with the convenience of town.

***An IHF Quality Employer***

*Bookable on www.irelandhotels.com*
*Special Offer: www.irelandhotels.com/offers*

**B&B from €95.00 to €153.00**
**Suites from €350.00 to €550.00**

*Conor Hennigan*
*General Manager*

172

*Activities:*

**Open All Year**

### McSweeney Arms Hotel

HOTEL ★★★ MAP 2 E 4

College Street,
Killarney,
Co. Kerry

Tel: 064-31211 Fax: 064-34553
Email: mcsweeneyarms@eircom.net
Web: www.mcsweeneyarms.com

McSweeney Arms Hotel is a superior 3 star hotel, situated in Killarney Town centre, an ideal base for golfing, touring and shopping. It boasts 26 beautifully appointed bedrooms with private bathroom, TV and direct dial phone. Tony's Sandtrap Bar & Restaurant, where we boast our own lobster tank, specialises in fresh seafood and traditional Irish cuisine. Both the bar and the restaurant host a relaxed, friendly atmosphere.

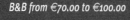

**B&B from €70.00 to €100.00**

*Tony McSweeney*
*Proprietor*

26

*Activities:*

**Closed 02 January - 14 February**

### Muckross Park Hotel & Cloisters Spa

HOTEL ★★★★★ MAP 2 E 4

Lakes Of Killarney,
Killarney,
Co. Kerry

Tel: 064-23400 Fax: 064-31965
Email: info@muckrosspark.com
Web: www.muckrosspark.com

Excellence surrounded by beauty - elegant, luxurious guest rooms and suites, award-winning bars & restaurants, superb business facilities and our world class Cloisters Spa ensure an enjoyable stay. Combine this with our unique location in Killarney National Park, surrounded by magnificent mountains, lakes and 7 championship golf courses and you will discover that The Muckross Park Hotel & Cloisters Spa is truly a unique hotel experience. Please enquire about Facilities for Persons with Mobility Impairment.

Member of Preffered Hotel

*Bookable on www.irelandhotels.com*
*Special Offer: www.irelandhotels.com/offers*

**Room Rate from €190.00 to €300.00**
**Suites from €250.00 to €1,200.00**

*Jackie Lavin*
*Proprietor*

68

*Activities:*

**Closed 24 - 25 Dec & 07 - 24 Jan**



B&B Rates are per Person Sharing per Night incl. Breakfast.
or Room Rates are per Room per Night - See also Page 8

## Murphys of Killarney

GUESTHOUSE ★★★ MAP 2 E 4

College Street,
Killarney,
Co. Kerry

Tel: 064-31294 Fax: 064-31294
Email: info@murphysofkillarney.com
Web: www.murphysofkillarney.com

Murphy's of Killarney: a town centre family-run guesthouse with all rooms newly refurbished, adjacent to bus and rail stations. Incorporating Lord Kenmare's renowned restaurant, Murphy's Traditional Irish Bar, where you can enjoy live Irish music and the more contemporary Squires Bar. Sean, Maire & the staff will make sure that your visit to "Murphy's" is enjoyable and memorable. Amenities include: golf, fishing, horse riding, scenic walks and shopping. Local tours arranged. "Murphy's - a sense of Tradition".

**B&B from €45.00 to €65.00**

*Sean Murphy*
*Proprietor*

20

**Closed 17 - 26 December**

## Old Weir Lodge

GUESTHOUSE ★★★★ MAP 2 E 4

Muckross Road,
Killarney,
Co. Kerry

Tel: 064-35593 Fax: 064-35583
Email: oldweirlodge@eircom.net
Web: www.oldweirlodge.com

A magnificent, luxurious, family-run 4* (AA ♦♦♦♦♦) guesthouse 5 minutes walk from town, on main road, towards National Park. Set in 3/4 acre landscaped gardens. 30 large bedrooms, some with king sized beds, bath, power showers, orthopaedic beds, telephone, multi-channel TV, tea/coffee facilities, ice and hairdryers. 2 lounges, fresh flowers, private parking, home baking, traditional, vegetarian, coeliac breakfasts. Friendly staff, ground floor bedrooms and elevator, drying room. Local advice offered, all tours arranged. Non-smoking guesthouse. Please enquire about Facilities for Persons with Mobility Impairment.

*Bookable on www.irelandhotels.com*
*Special Offer: www.irelandhotels.com/offers*

**B&B from €50.00 to €70.00**

*Maureen & Dermot O'Donoghue*
*Proprietors*

30

*Activities:*

**Closed 23 - 26 December**

## Quality Resort Killarney

HOTEL ★★★ MAP 2 E 4

Cork Road,
Killarney,
Co. Kerry

Tel: 064-26200 Fax: 064-32438
Email: reservations@qualityhotelkillarney.com
Web: www.qualitykillarney.com

The Quality Resort Killarney: Quality accommodation to suit everyone, luxury guest rooms, holiday homes, family apartments and suites in Ireland's favourite holiday destination. A real guest welcome in a fun, friendly atmosphere. A wealth of dining facilities and entertainment. A holiday the whole family can agree on. Please enquire about Facilities for Persons with Mobility Impairment.

***An IHF Quality Employer***

Member of Quality Hotels

*Bookable on www.irelandhotels.com*
*Special Offer: www.irelandhotels.com/offers*

**Room Rate from €69.00 to €209.00**
**Suites from €89.00 to €239.00**

*Patrick Dillon*
*General Manager*

288

**Closed 14 - 27 December**

B&B Rates are per Person Sharing per Night incl. Breakfast.
or Room Rates are per Room per Night - **See also Page 8**

## Killarney

### Randles Court Clarion Hotel

HOTEL ★★★★ MAP 2 E 4

Muckross Road,
Killarney,
Co. Kerry

Tel: 064-35333 Fax: 064-35206
Email: info@randlescourt.com
Web: www.randlescourt.com

This AA/RAC 4**** hotel is one of Killarney's gems. Family owned and run, this de luxe hotel offers all the elegance and charm of a country house. Dating back to 1906, the hotel has been tastefully restored with beautiful furniture and open fires. Checker's Restaurant is truly a unique dining experience. Club Santé leisure facilities are available to all guests. For sheer indulgence, pay a visit to Zen Day Spa. The fully automated conference suite is ideal for all events and WiFi is available throughout the hotel. The perfect setting for a special wedding day and available for Civil Ceremonies.

***An IHF Quality Employer***

Member of Clarion Hotel Group

***Bookable on www.irelandhotels.com***

***B&B from €75.00 to €200.00***

*Tom Randles*
*General Manager*

68

*Activities:*

**Closed 23 - 27 December**

### Rivermere

GUESTHOUSE ★★★★ MAP 2 E 4

Muckross Road,
Killarney,
Co. Kerry

Tel: 064-37933 Fax: 064-37944
Email: info@killarney-rivermere.com
Web: www.killarney-rivermere.com

Rivermere is a custom built, family-run 4**** guesthouse within walking distance of lakes and National Park and only 7 minutes walk from town centre. All rooms are spacious with TV, radio, direct dial phone, orthopaedic beds, bath, power showers, hairdryer. A luxurious half suite is available also. Rivermere is in a delightful setting and combines luxury with charm, elegance and serenity, walkers' and golfers' paradise. Drying room available. Private parking. Choose from our delicious breakfast menu. A warm welcome awaits you.

***B&B from €45.00 to €65.00***

*Kayan Culloty Rice / Don Culloty*

8

*Activities:*

**Open All Year**

### Ross (The)

HOTEL ★★★★ MAP 2 E 4

Town Centre,
Killarney,
Co. Kerry

Tel: 064-31855 Fax: 064-27633
Email: info@theross.ie
Web: www.theross.ie

The Ross is an exciting new addition to Killarney town and perfectly situated adjacent to our sister property the Killarney Park Hotel. A seamless fusion of luxury and cool, The Ross provides the services and amenities of a luxury hotel within a stylish environment. This 29 bedroomed hotel is also home to our unique Cellar One Restaurant and the lively Lane Café Bar. Just steps from Killarney National Park, local bars, restaurants and great shopping, The Ross is simply the best address in town. Please enquire about Facilities for Persons with Mobility Impairment.

***Bookable on www.irelandhotels.com***
***Special Offer: www.irelandhotels.com/offers***

***B&B from €85.00 to €122.50***
***Suites from €220.00 to €275.00***

*Padraig & Janet Treacy*
*Proprietors*

29

*Activities:*

**Closed 24 - 27 December**



B&B Rates are per Person Sharing per Night incl. Breakfast. or Room Rates are per Room per Night - See also Page 8

## Scotts Hotel

HOTEL ★★★ MAP 2 E 4

Killarney,
Co. Kerry

Tel: 064-31060 Fax: 064-36656
Email: info@scottshotelkillarney.com
Web: www.scottshotelkillarney.com

The newly rebuilt Scotts Hotel is located in the heart of Killarney Town centre. Set amidst Killarney's cosmopolitan quarter, Scotts Hotel is the ideal choice for sightseeing, shopping and dining. Facilities include an excellent choice of en suite bedrooms, one and two-bedroom suites, a selection of bars and a stylish restaurant. Scotts Bar & Courtyard features nightly live entertainment during the summer months and weekends throughout the rest of the year. Please enquire about Facilities for Persons with Mobility Impairment.

Member of The Gleneagle Group

*Bookable on www.irelandhotels.com*
*Special Offer: www.irelandhotels.com/offers*

**B&B from €65.00 to €105.00**
**Suites from €250.00 to €400.00**

*Maurice Eoin O'Donoghue*
*Managing Director*

120

*Activities:* ✓

**Closed 23 - 26 December**

## Valley Suites (The)

HOTEL ★★★★ MAP 2 E 4

Fossa,
Killarney,
Co. Kerry

Tel: 064-23600 Fax: 064-23601
Email: info@thevalleysuites.ie
Web: www.valleysuites.ie

The Valley Suites is located at the gateway to the Ring of Kerry, making It the ideal location to explore the Kingdom of Kerry. Facilities include a selection of comfortable en suite bedrooms with panoramic views as well as one and two bedroom suites, a spacious bar and stylish restaurant. Please enquire about Facilities for Persons with Mobility Impairment.

Member of Gleneagle Group

*Bookable on www.irelandhotels.com*
*Special Offer: www.irelandhotels.com/offers*

**Room Rate from €89.00 to €179.00**
**Suites from €89.00 to €279.00**

*Pat Galvin*
*General Manager*

63

*Activities:* ✓

**Closed 01 November - 01 February**

## Victoria House Hotel

HOTEL ★★★ MAP 2 E 4

Muckross Road,
Killarney,
Co. Kerry

Tel: 064-35430 Fax: 064-35439
Email: info@victoriahousehotel.com
Web: www.victoriahousehotel.com

Traditional family-run hospitality, overlooking Killarney National Park, our cosy and charming Boutique Hotel offers an exceptional warm welcome and personal service. Our Restaurant and Ivy Room Bar provides excellent choice of local produce with frequent live traditional entertainment. Newly refurbished elegant bedrooms now offer upgrades of Deluxe and Superior rooms. Pampering within, and cycling, walking and National Park on our doorstep. Let us make your Killarney experience the most unique- your way! Member of www.irishfamilyrun.com and Best Loved Hotels.

Member of Best Loved Hotels

*Bookable on www.irelandhotels.com*
*Special Offer: www.irelandhotels.com/offers*

**B&B from €60.00 to €100.00**
**Suites from €180.00 to €300.00**

*John Courtney*
*Proprietor*

35

**Closed 15 December - 01 February**

B&B Rates are per Person Sharing per Night incl. Breakfast.
or Room Rates are per Room per Night - **See also Page 8**

## Killarney / Killorglin

### Woodlawn House

GUESTHOUSE ★★★ MAP 2 E 4

Woodlawn Road,
Killarney,
Co. Kerry
Tel: 064-37844 Fax: 064-36116
Email: woodlawn@ie-post.com
Web: www.woodlawn-house.com

Old style charm and hospitality. Family-run. Relaxed atmosphere. All modern conveniences. Ideally located 5 minutes walk from town centre. Near leisure centre, lakes and golf courses. Tours arranged. Private parking. Decorated with natural pine wood. Orthopaedic beds dressed in white cotton and linen. Irish and vegetarian menus. Our wholesome breakfasts include freshly squeezed orange juice, homemade preserves and bread. Early bird breakfast also available. A warm welcome assured.

Member of Kerry - Insight

**B&B from €45.00 to €65.00**

*The Wrenn Family*

10

**Closed 23 - 30 December**

### Bianconi

GUESTHOUSE ★★★ MAP 1 D 4

Killorglin,
Ring Of Kerry,
Co. Kerry
Tel: 066-976 1146 Fax: 066-976 1950
Email: bianconi@iol.ie
Web: www.bianconi.ie

Family-run inn on The Ring of Kerry. Gateway to Dingle Peninsula, Killarney 18km. On the road to Glencar - famous for its scenery, lakes, hill walking and mountain climbing. Famous for its table. High standard of food in bar. Table d'hôte and à la carte available. 50 minutes to Waterville, Tralee & Ballybunion golf courses. 15 minutes to Dooks & Beaufort courses. 5 minutes to Killorglin course. 15 mins to Killarney course. Private access to Caragh Lake. Own boat. Mentioned by many guides.

**B&B from €55.00 to €65.00**

*Ray Sheehy*
*Owner*

14

*Activities:*

**Closed 23 - 28 December**

### Grove Lodge Riverside Guesthouse

GUESTHOUSE ★★★ MAP 1 D 4

Killarney Road,
Killorglin,
Co. Kerry
Tel: 066-976 1157 Fax: 066-976 2330
Email: info@grovelodge.com
Web: www.grovelodge.com

Peace and tranquillity. Relax in luxury riverside accommodation, with spacious de luxe bedrooms and stroll through our mature gardens and riverside walks. Delia prepares an extensive gourmet breakfast menu, home baking from local fresh produce. We are a short walk to Killorglin Town centre which has many fine restaurants and lively Irish pubs. We are centrally located to all of Kerry's tourist anemities and attractions. We are highly acclaimed where the majority of our business is repeated and referrals from satisfied customers. Please enquire about Facilities for Persons with Mobility Impairment.

Member of Premier Guesthouses

**B&B from €45.00 to €65.00**

*Fergus & Delia Foley*
*Owners & Managers*

10

*Activities:*

**Closed 01 December - 31 January**



B&B Rates are per Person Sharing per Night incl. Breakfast. or Room Rates are per Room per Night - See also Page 8

## Westfield House

GUESTHOUSE ★★★ MAP 1 D 4

Killorglin,
Co. Kerry

Tel: 066-976 1909 Fax: 066-976 1996
Email: westhse@iol.ie
Web: www.westfieldhse.com

Westfield House is a family-run guesthouse. All rooms are bright and spacious en suite, orthopaedic beds, direct dial telephone, TV, tea/coffee maker. Extra large family room available. We are situated on the Ring of Kerry in a quiet peaceful location only 5 minutes walk from town with panoramic views of McGillycuddy Reeks. There are five 18 hole golf courses within 20 minutes drive. Recognised stop for many weary cyclists. Ideal location for the hill walker and climber.

***Bookable on www.irelandhotels.com***

*B&B from €40.00 to €42.50*

*Marie & Leonard Clifford*
*Proprietors*

10

**Closed 01 November - 01 March**

## Moorings (The)

GUESTHOUSE ★★★ MAP 1 B 3

Portmagee,
Co. Kerry

Tel: 066-947 7108 Fax: 066-947 7220
Email: moorings@iol.ie
Web: www.moorings.ie

The award-winning Moorings overlooks Portmagee harbour and provides tasteful and spacious accommodation and a renowned dining experience. Winner of "Licensing World Tourist Bar of the Year" 2007, The Bridge Bar adjoining, hosts Irish set dancing and live music throughout the year. Our delightful new gift shop, Cois Cuain offers a selection of quality gifts, many with a nautical theme in keeping with the harbour-side location. Visit our updated website for details of our exciting new Skelligs Package. Please enquire about Facilities for Persons with Mobility Impairment.

***An IHF Quality Employer***

*B&B from €45.00 to €70.00*
*Suites from €120.00 to €140.00*

*Patricia & Gerard Kennedy*
*Proprietors*

16

**Closed 19 December - 09 January**

## Parknasilla Hotel

HOTEL ★★★★ MAP 1 C 3

Sneem,
Co. Kerry

Tel: 064-45122 Fax: 064-45323
Email: info@parknasillahotel.ie
Web: www.parknasillahotel.ie

UNDER REFURBISHMENT - RE-OPENING JUNE 2008

One of Ireland's finest resort hotels, 500 acres of on-site facilities; walks, tennis, golf, archery, swimming & clay pigeon shooting. Exceptional standards of service within plush surroundings and a warm Irish welcome. Standard rooms, superior rooms & suites with views over Kerry countryside. Dine in style at the Pygmalion Restaurant and Doolittle Bar. Balmy subtropical vegetation, mountainous backdrop and tranquil waters - it is the perfect place to relax. New spa with large open windows overlooking the sea & mountains. Call 01 474 4120. Please enquire about Facilities for Persons with Mobility Impairment.

***An IHF Quality Employer***

***Bookable on www.irelandhotels.com***
***Special Offer: www.irelandhotels.com/offers***

*B&B from €200.00 to €1,000.00*
*Suites from €1,000.00 to €2,000.00*

*Klaus H. Voss*
*General Manager*

95

**Closed January - June 08**

B&B Rates are per Person Sharing per Night incl. Breakfast.
or Room Rates are per Room per Night - See also Page 8

## Sneem / Tahilla / Tarbert

### Sneem Hotel

HOTEL ★★★★ MAP 1 C 3

Goldens Cove,
Sneem,
Co. Kerry

Tel: 064-75100 Fax: 064-75782

Email: information@sneemhotel.com

Web: www.sneemhotel.com

Family-run the Sneem Hotel, the Ring of Kerry's latest addition is stylish and contemporary in design, a hidden gem set on 22 acres of mature gardens, surrounded with stunning views of Sneem Estuary and the McGillycuddy Reeks. Purpose built this four star standard property is conveniently located 150 yards from the picturesque village of Sneem. It boasts 69 luxurious bedrooms with ultra modern facilities, dining room, bar, banquet and conference facilities for up to 300. Please enquire about Facilities for Persons with Mobility Impairment.

*Bookable on www.irelandhotels.com*
*Special Offer: www.irelandhotels.com/offers*

**B&B from €65.00 to €95.00**
**Suites from €190.00 to €250.00**

*Louis Moriarty*
*Proprietor*

69

*Activities:*

**Open All Year**

### Tahilla Cove Country House

GUESTHOUSE ★★★ MAP 1 D 3

Tahilla,
Near Sneem,
Co. Kerry

Tel: 064-45204 Fax: 064-45104

Email: tahillacove@eircom.net

Web: www.tahillacove.com

Travel writers have described this family-run, fully licensed seashore guesthouse as the most idyllic spot in Ireland - the haunt of Irish/British dignitaries. Located on The Ring of Kerry seashore. 14 acre estate boasts mature gardens and private pier. Ideal place for a relaxing holiday/touring centre. Each room has en suite facilities, phone, TV, radio, hairdryer, iron and tea/coffee facilities. Log fires, superb views, home cooking. Take Sneem Road from Kenmare (N70).

**B&B from €60.00 to €75.00**

*James / Deirdre /Chas Waterhouse*
*Owners*

9

**Closed 15 October - 20 April**

### Kirby's Lanterns Hotel

HOTEL ★★★ MAP 5 E 7

Glin / Tarbert Coast Road,
Tarbert,
Co. Kerry

Tel: 068-36210 Fax: 068-36553

Email: reservations@thelanternshotel.ie

Web: www.thelanternshotel.ie

Kirby's Lanterns Hotel overlooking the majestic Shannon Estuary is an ideal tourist base for Kerry, Limerick & Clare. Central to world famous golf courses at Ballybunion, Tralee, Killarney, Adare, Doonbeg and Lahinch. Enjoy a day Angling, Horse riding or walking. Relax on golden beaches. Visit Kirby's Lanterns Hotel where a warm Kirby welcome awaits you. Superb accommodation, great food & friendly service. Food served from 6.30 to 10 pm daily. Music sessions every weekend. Special mid-week and weekend breaks available year round. Please enquire about Facilities for Persons with Mobility Impairment.

*Bookable on www.irelandhotels.com*
*Special Offer: www.irelandhotels.com/offers*

**B&B from €50.00 to €100.00**

*Marie Kirby Meade*
*Manager*

22

**Closed 24 - 26 December**



B&B Rates are per Person Sharing per Night incl. Breakfast. or Room Rates are per Room per Night - See also Page 8

## Abbey Gate Hotel

HOTEL ★★★ MAP 1 D 5

Maine Street,
Tralee,
Co. Kerry

Tel: 066-712 9888 Fax: 066-712 9821

Email: info@abbeygate-hotel.com

Web: www.abbeygate-hotel.com

Welcome to the Abbey Gate Hotel, located in the heart of Tralee. Providing a warm, intimate atmosphere & the utmost in personal attentions. All 100 guest bedrooms are tastefully designed & equipped with satellite TV, direct dial telephone, hairdryer & tea/coffee facilities. The old market place pub is Tralee's liveliest venue with bar food served all day, casual dining in the bistro marché. Please enquire about Facilities for Persons with Mobility Impairment.

***An IHF Quality Employer***

***Bookable on www.irelandhotels.com***

***Special Offer: www.irelandhotels.com/offers***

*B&B from €75.00 to €110.00*

*Suites from €210.00 to €250.00*

*Laura Moore*
*Proprietor*

100

*Activities:*

**Closed 24 - 26 December**

## Ballygarry House Hotel & Spa

HOTEL ★★★★ MAP 1 D 5

Killarney Road,
Tralee,
Co. Kerry

Tel: 066-712 3322 Fax: 066-712 7630

Email: info@ballygarryhouse.com

Web: www.ballygarryhouse.com

Set amidst six acres of mature landscaped gardens at the foot of the Kerry Mountains offering guests an inspiring mixture of mountain, lake woodland and sea. Ballygarry House offers you the complete country house experience where the warmest of welcomes awaits you. Luxurious guest rooms and suites, library, drawing room, Brooks Restaurant and our latest addition 'Nádúr Spa' combine to create an atmosphere of unhurried tranquility. 1.5km from Tralee and 6km from Kerry Airport - perfect for golfing or touring the South West.

***An IHF Quality Employer***

Member of Johansens

***Bookable on www.irelandhotels.com***

***Special Offer: www.irelandhotels.com/offers***

*B&B from €75.00 to €95.00*

*Suites from €180.00 to €250.00*

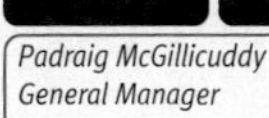

*Padraig McGillicuddy*
*General Manager*

64

*Activities:*

**Closed 23 - 27 December**

## Ballyroe Heights Hotel

HOTEL ★★★ MAP 1 D 5

Ballyroe,
Tralee,
Co. Kerry

Tel: 066-712 6796 Fax: 066-712 5066

Email: info@ballyroe.com

Web: www.ballyroe.com

De luxe hotel set in woodland and sloping gardens. Our new bedrooms, which include 5 executive balcony rooms, have flat screen TV, remote lighting, tea/coffee facilities, designer table top wash hand basins and heated mirrors. Conferences for 20-400 delegates. Drop down screens, data projectors, wireless broadband as standard. Free car parking. Memorable weddings where personal attention is guaranteed - special midweek discounts. Please enquire about Facilities for Persons with Mobility Impairment.

***Bookable on www.irelandhotels.com***

***Special Offer: www.irelandhotels.com/offers***

*B&B from €75.00 to €100.00*

*Suites from €85.00 to €120.00*

*Mark Sullivan*
*General Manager*

69

*Activities:*

**Open All Year**

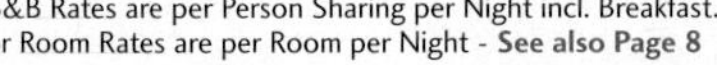

B&B Rates are per Person Sharing per Night incl. Breakfast.
or Room Rates are per Room per Night - **See also Page 8**

## Tralee

### Ballyseede Castle Hotel

HOTEL ★★★★ MAP 1 D 5

Ballyseede,
Tralee,
Co. Kerry

Tel: 066-712 5799 Fax: 066-712 5287
Email: info@ballyseedecastle.com
Web: www.ballyseedecastle.com

Ballyseede Castle is steeped in history. Be a king or queen for the night in our elegant bedrooms. Drink wine or chat with the locals in our cosy cocktail bar and enjoy the best of traditional and continental food in our elegant restaurant. Located on 30 acres of pasture and gardens off the main Tralee Killarney road (N21). We are ideally located for touring both the Ring of Kerry or the Dingle Peninsula and within reach of several championship golf courses.

Member of Manor House Hotels

*Bookable on www.irelandhotels.com*
*Special Offer: www.irelandhotels.com/offers*

*B&B from €75.00 to €110.00*
*Suites from €220.00 to €250.00*

*Marnie Corscadden*
*General Manager*
20

Closed 06 January - 10 March

### Benners Hotel

HOTEL ★★★ MAP 1 D 5

Upper Castle Street,
Tralee,
Co. Kerry

Tel: 066-712 1877 Fax: 066-712 2273
Email: info@bennershoteltralee.com
Web: www.bennershoteltralee.com

Benners Hotel is a historic Hotel ideally situated in the heart of Tralee, close to all visitor attractions, abundant shopping & minutes from bus & rail stations. A perfect base to tour Irelands most spectacular county. Following extensive refurbishment the hotel has re-opened as a modern stylish property featuring the Deacon Bar, Tralee's most fashionable night spot & The Cooperage, a contemporary & innovative Restaurant. 45 elegant & spacious rooms with all facilities. Private & secure resident parking. Please enquire about Facilities for Persons with Mobility Impairment.

*B&B from €55.00 to €80.00*

*Declan Ryan & Joe Magann*
*Proprietors*
45

Closed 24 - 26 December

### Brandon Hotel Conference and Leisure Centre

HOTEL ★★★ MAP 1 D 5

Princes Street,
Tralee,
Co. Kerry

Tel: 066-712 3333 Fax: 066-712 5019
Email: sales@brandonhotel.ie
Web: www.brandonhotel.ie

Renowned, privately owned premises ideally located in the heart of Tralee Town, close to shopping and visitor attractions. The hotel offers a range of accommodation - standard rooms, de luxe rooms and suites, with a choice of bars and restaurants. It is also equipped with full leisure centre incorporating swimming pool, sauna, steam room, jacuzzi, gymnasium and beauty treatment rooms, as well as extensive conference and banqueting facilities. Private parking available. Tralee is accessible by mainline rail and air with Kerry Airport just 10 miles away. Please enquire about Facilities for Persons with Mobility Impairment.

*Bookable on www.irelandhotels.com*
*Special Offer: www.irelandhotels.com/offers*

*B&B from €55.00 to €120.00*
*Suites from €299.00 to €350.00*

*Liam Power*
*Manager*
183

Activities:

Closed 23 - 29 December



B&B Rates are per Person Sharing per Night incl. Breakfast. or Room Rates are per Room per Night - See also Page 8

## Brook Manor Lodge

GUESTHOUSE ★★★★ MAP 1 D 5

Fenit Road,
Tralee,
Co. Kerry

Tel: 066-712 0406 Fax: 066-712 7552
Email: brookmanor@eircom.net
Web: www.brookmanorlodge.com

Luxury 4 star Guesthouse situated on the outskirts of Tralee Town. The Slieve Mish Mountains form an ever changing backdrop - A most wonderful scene to wake up to! Spacious bedrooms with en suite facilities. Complimentary tea/coffee, TV, DVD. WiFi. Guest lounge offers a tranquil space to read or browse the internet. Extensive Breakfast menu to be enjoyed in our bright conservatory. Ideal base for Golf or Touring Holidays.

**B&B from €50.00 to €75.00**
**Suites from €130.00 to €160.00**

*Sandra & Jerome Lordan*
*Owners*

8

**Open All Year**

## Fels Point Hotel

HOTEL MAP 1 D 5

Fels Point,
Tralee,
Co. Kerry

Tel: 066-711 9986 Fax: 066-711 9987
Email: info@felspointhotel.ie
Web: www.felspointhotel.ie

Built to a 4**** specification. Opened in June 2007, this new stylish Hotel has been designed to four star standard 166 air-conditioned guest rooms with internet access, health & leisure suite, Clarets Bar and Morels restaurant. Extensive conference and banqueting facilities. Parking provided on-site. Ideally located 5 minutes walk from Tralee Town centre and close to numerous golf courses and visitor attractions, Fels Point Hotel offer new standards in hospitality combining modern comfort with an excellent location. Please enquire about Facilities for Persons with Mobility Impairment.

***Bookable on www.irelandhotels.com***
*Special Offer: www.irelandhotels.com/offers*

**Room Rate from €55.00 to €80.00**

*Peter McDermott*
*General Manager*

166

*Activities:*

**Closed 24 - 27 December**

## Glenduff House

GUESTHOUSE ★★★ MAP 1 D 5

Kielduff,
Tralee,
Co. Kerry

Tel: 066-713 7105 Fax: 066-713 7099
Email: glenduffhouse@eircom.net
Web: www.glenduff-house.com

Enter the old world charm of the 19th century in our family-run period house set on 6 acres with mature gardens. Refurbished to give the comforts of the modern day, yet keeping its original character with antiques & paintings. Personal attention assured. Relax & enjoy a drink in our friendly bar. Also self catering cottages in the courtyard. Ideally situated for golf and sports amenities. From Tralee take route to racecourse off N21 at Joe Keohane Roundabout. Continue for 4.5 miles and turn right at large sign on right.

***An IHF Quality Employer***
Member of Premier Guesthouses

**B&B from €39.00 to €52.00**

*Joe & Elizabeth Goodfellow*
*Owners*

7

**Closed 18 December - 06 January**

B&B Rates are per Person Sharing per Night incl. Breakfast.
or Room Rates are per Room per Night - **See also Page 8**

## Tralee

### Grand Hotel

HOTEL ★★★ MAP 1 D 5

Denny Street,
Tralee,
Co. Kerry

Tel: 066-712 1499 Fax: 066-712 2877
Email: info@grandhoteltralee.com
Web: www.grandhoteltralee.com

The Grand Hotel is a 3*** hotel situated in Tralee Town centre. Established in 1928, its open fires, ornate ceilings and mahogany furnishings offer guests old world charm in comfortable surroundings. All our rooms are equipped with direct dial telephone, computer point, satellite TV and tea/coffee welcoming trays. Residents can avail of reduced rates to the fabulous Aqua Dome Waterworld complex. Family rooms are available at discounted rates. Limited parking available.

***An IHF Quality Employer***

***Bookable on www.irelandhotels.com***
***Special Offer: www.irelandhotels.com/offers***

***B&B from €55.00 to €85.00***

*Dick Boyle*
*General Manager*

44

Activities:

Closed 24 - 27 December

### Manor West Hotel, Spa & Leisure Club

HOTEL ★★★★ MAP 1 D 5

Manorwest,
Tralee,
Co. Kerry

Tel: 066-719 4500 Fax: 066-719 4545
Email: info@manorwesthotel.ie
Web: www.manorwesthotel.ie

Tralee's luxury destination with 75 bedrooms, the AA 4**** Manor West Hotel is designed with the discerning guest in mind. Situated on the site of Kerry's largest shopping destination, Manor West Retail Park, the hotel's location in the heart of Kerry makes it the ideal base for exploring the jewels of the kingdom. The hotel provides all the facilities you would associate with a deluxe hotel and the Harmony Leisure Club & Wellness Suites are a must for all guests. Situated on the main Limerick/Killarney road, the Manor West Hotel is less than 20 mins from Kerry International Airport.

Member of Select Hotels of Ireland

***Bookable on www.irelandhotels.com***
***Special Offer: www.irelandhotels.com/offers***

***B&B from €60.00 to €149.00***
***Suites from €210.00 to €468.00***

*Jim Feeney*
*General Manager*

75

Activities:

Closed 25 - 26 December

### Meadowlands Hotel

HOTEL ★★★★ MAP 1 D 5

Oakpark,
Tralee,
Co. Kerry

Tel: 066-718 0444 Fax: 066-718 0964
Email: info@meadowlands-hotel.com
Web: www.meadowlands-hotel.com

A charming and intimate hotel, set in a tranquil corner of Tralee, on its own beautiful landscaped gardens. This luxurious hotel comprises 57 superbly appointed rooms, including suites. Our award-winning restaurant specialises in the freshest of locally caught seafood and shellfish cuisine. State of the art conference centre. Ideal base for golfing enthusiasts and touring the Dingle Peninsula, The Ring of Kerry. Experience an experience!

***An IHF Quality Employer***

***Bookable on www.irelandhotels.com***
***Special Offer: www.irelandhotels.com/offers***

***B&B from €80.00 to €120.00***
***Suites from €250.00 to €300.00***

*Padraig & Peigi O' Mathuna*
*Owners*

57

Activities:

Closed 24 - 26 December



B&B Rates are per Person Sharing per Night incl. Breakfast. or Room Rates are per Room per Night - See also Page 8

## Tralee Townhouse

GUESTHOUSE ★★★ MAP 1 D 5

High Street,
Tralee,
Co. Kerry

Tel: 066-718 1111 Fax: 066-718 1112

Email: traleetownhouse@eircom.net

Web: www.traleetownhouse.com

Centrally located beside all of Tralee's visitor attractions; - Siamsa Tire, Aqua Dome, Geraldine Experience, Kerry County Museum, Blennerville Windmill, Steam Train and the new Tralee Marina. Local amenities include - for the golf enthusiast, the world renowned Tralee & Ballybunion Golf Courses are only a few miles away. 2 excellent 9 hole courses are within 1 mile of the town centre. Fishing, horse riding, hill walking, sports centre with indoor pool, etc. 3*** AA. Please enquire about Facilities for Persons with Mobility Impairment.

Member of Holiday Tralee

*Bookable on www.irelandhotels.com*

*Special Offer: www.irelandhotels.com/offers*

*B&B from €35.00 to €45.00*

*Eleanor Collins*
*Manager*

19

**Closed 24 - 28 December**

## Brookhaven Country House

GUESTHOUSE ★★★★ MAP 1 B 3

New Line Road,
Waterville,
Co. Kerry

Tel: 066-947 4431 Fax: 066-947 4724

Email: brookhaven@esatclear.ie

Web: www.brookhavenhouse.com

Welcome to Brookhaven, a 4 star family-run, luxury guesthouse, on the Ring of Kerry. All our spacious en suite rooms have king beds, multi-channel TV, free internet access and tea and coffee making facilities. Rooms view the Atlantic Ocean and the Waterville golf course. Skelllig Bay golf course 2mins drive. 10% discount offered. Centrally located to all amenities, golf, fishing lake and sea, beaches, surfing, horse riding, bird watching historic skellig islands, walking, Kerry way route, cycling and gourmet restaurants. Recommended by all leading guide books.

Member of Premier Collection Marketing Group

*Bookable on www.irelandhotels.com*

*Special Offer: www.irelandhotels.com/offers*

*B&B from €45.00 to €65.00*
*Suites from €110.00 to €130.00*

*Mary Clifford*
*Proprietor*

6

Activities:

**Closed 15 November - 01 March**

## Butler Arms Hotel

HOTEL ★★★★ MAP 1 B 3

Waterville,
Co. Kerry

Tel: 066-947 4144 Fax: 066-947 4520

Email: reservations@butlerarms.com

Web: www.butlerarms.com

This charming hotel, on the scenic Ring of Kerry, has been run by 4 generations of the Huggard family. Tastefully furnished bedrooms, many with magnificent seaviews, cosy lounges, award-winning restaurant specializing in local seafood and the Fishermens Bar with its cosmopolitan ambience. Only 1 mile from Waterville's Championship Golf Links. Renowned salmon and seatrout fishing, sandy beaches, horse riding, hill walking. Please enquire about Facilities for Persons with Mobility Impairment.

***An IHF Quality Employer***

Member of Manor House Hotels

*Bookable on www.irelandhotels.com*

*Special Offer: www.irelandhotels.com/offers*

*B&B from €75.00 to €155.00*
*Suites from €225.00 to €325.00*

*Paula & Louise Huggard*
*Proprietors*

40

Activities:

**Closed 20 December - 15 March**

B&B Rates are per Person Sharing per Night incl. Breakfast.
or Room Rates are per Room per Night - See also Page 8

## Waterville / Graiguenamanagh

### Lakelands Farm Guesthouse

GUESTHOUSE ★★★ MAP 1 B 3

Lake Road,
Waterville,
Co. Kerry

Tel: 066-947 4303 Fax: 066-947 4678

Email: lakelands@eircom.net

Web: www.lakelandshouse.com

Refurbished in 2007, Lakelands is set in a unique location overlooking Lough Currane. Spacious en suite rooms with panoramic views over the lake and mountains, some boosted with balcony or jacuzzi. TV lounge and library. Proprietor professional guide with own boats and motors for hire. Trips to Church Island. Very close to Skellig Bay & Waterville Golf Course. Activities nearby, horse riding, surfing, beaches, Kerry Way. Trips to Skellig Island. 2km from village.

***Bookable on www.irelandhotels.com***

***Special Offer: www.irelandhotels.com/offers***

*B&B from €40.00 to €50.00*

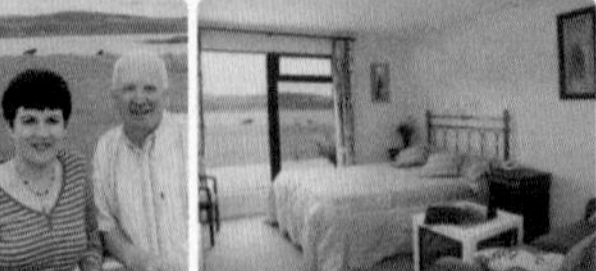

*Anne & Frank Donnelly*
*Proprietors*

12

Activities:

**Closed 20 - 27 December**

### Smugglers Inn

GUESTHOUSE ★★★ MAP 1 B 3

Cliff Road,
Waterville,
Co. Kerry

Tel: 066-947 4330 Fax: 066-947 4422

Email: thesmugglersinn@eircom.net

Web: www.the-smugglers-inn.com

The Smugglers Inn, family-run, was an 180 year old farmhouse restored by the Hunt Family in 1980. Since then it has become renowned world-wide for its warm welcome and super restaurant. Situated in a quiet location on a 2km sandy beach, adjacent to Waterville Golf Links, a haven for golfing, fishing, surfing, scuba diving, walking. Comfortable guest bedrooms many with sea views. Panoramic views from our conservatory restaurant. Chef/proprietor Henry Hunt. Fully licenced bar serving bar food. It has been said "if our fish was any fresher it would have to be cooked underwater". Helicopter Landing.

***Bookable on www.irelandhotels.com***

***Special Offer: www.irelandhotels.com/offers***

*B&B from €50.00 to €75.00*

*Henry Hunt*
*Proprietors*

14

Activities:

**Closed 07 Novemeber - 15 March**

### Waterside

GUESTHOUSE ★★★ MAP 7 M 7

The Quay,
Graiguenamanagh,
Co. Kilkenny

Tel: 059-972 4246 Fax: 059-972 4733

Email: info@watersideguesthouse.com

Web: www.watersideguesthouse.com

A beautifully restored 19th century cornstore with feature wooden beams and imposing granite exterior. Riverside location, all rooms have a view of the River Barrow. Excellent base for boating, fishing, hill walking. 16km from Mount Juliet for golf. Nearby 13th century Duiske Abbey. 27km from historical Kilkenny. Superb restaurant features continental cuisine and international flavour wine list. Relaxed and friendly approach. Perfect for small groups. Graiguenamanagh hosts annual 'Town of Books' Festival.

*B&B from €39.00 to €55.00*

*Brian & Brigid Roberts*

10

Activities:

**Closed 01 - 31 January**



B&B Rates are per Person Sharing per Night incl. Breakfast.
or Room Rates are per Room per Night - **See also Page 8**

## Berkeley House

GUESTHOUSE ★★★ MAP 7 L 7

5 Lower Patrick Street,
Kilkenny

Tel: 056-776 4848 Fax: 056-776 4829

Email: berkeleyhouse@eircom.net

Web: www.berkeleyhousekilkenny.com

A warm and genuine welcome awaits you here at this charming owner operated period residence, uniquely situated in the very heart of mediaeval Kilkenny City. Berkeley House boasts ample private car parking, 10 spacious & tastefully decorated rooms, all en suite with multi channel TV, direct dial phone & tea/coffee facilities. We pride ourselves on a dedicated and professional team and ensure that every effort will be made to make your stay with us a most enjoyable one. Please enquire about Facilities for Persons with Mobility Impairment.

**B&B from €35.00 to €75.00**

*Trish Kiely*
*Manager*

10

T C P

**Closed 23 - 28 December**

## Brog Maker Hotel

HOTEL ★ MAP 7 L 7

Castlecomer Road,
Kilkenny

Tel: 056-775 2900 Fax: 056-777 1455

Email: thebrogmaker@gmail.com

Web: www.thebrogmaker.com

The Bróg Maker was established in 1994. Notwithstanding this, the design and atmosphere of both its lounge and bar is "Old Worlde" as if from a time gone by - the perfect place to relax, enjoy a pint and savour excellent food. Our achievements are: one Black & White Best Newcomer award, two Black & White Kilkenny County Winner awards and Dining Pub of the Year award 2003 presented by Dining Pub Guide. Our facilities include 13 en suite bedrooms. Lunches and bar food are served all day.

**B&B from €40.00 to €55.00**

*Bobby & Breda Quinn*
*Proprietors*

13

T C P

**Open All Year**

## Kilkenny City

### Butler House

GUESTHOUSE ★★★ MAP 7 L 7

Patrick Street,
Kilkenny

Tel: 056-776 5707 Fax: 056-776 5626
Email: res@butler.ie
Web: www.butler.ie

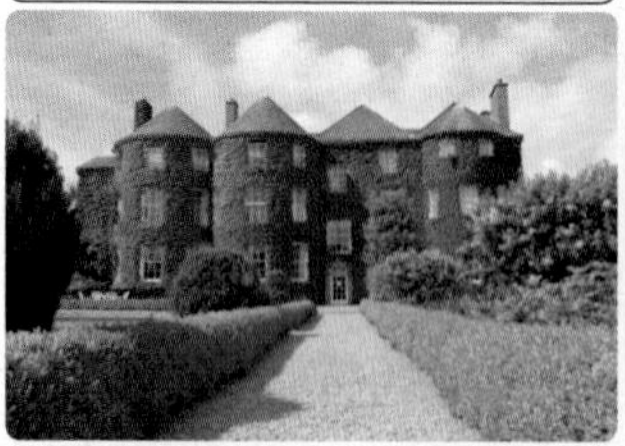

This magnificent Dower House of Kilkenny Castle, Situated in the centre of Kilkenny City has recently undergone a refurbishment. Sweeping staircases magnificent plastered ceilings and marble fireplaces are all features of this 16th century house. The house is a combination of contemporary furnishing and period elegance. The larger superior rooms and suite have graceful bow windows with lovely views of the Georgian garden and Kilkenny Castle. Private parking. Chairlift available.

*B&B from €60.00 to €100.00*
*Suites from €180.00 to €250.00*

*Gabrielle Hickey*
*Manager*

13

Activities:

**Closed 23 - 29 December**

### Club House Hotel

HOTEL ★★ MAP 7 L 7

Patrick Street,
Kilkenny

Tel: 056-772 1994 Fax: 056-777 1920
Email: clubhse@iol.ie
Web: www.clubhousehotel.com

Situated uniquely in a cultural & artistic centre and against the background of Kilkenny's mediaeval city, the magnificent 18th century Club House Hotel maintains a 200 year old tradition of effortless comfort, hospitality and efficiency. En suite rooms are decorated in both modern & period style with complimentary beverages, TV, hairdryer & phone. Food is locally sourced, cooked and presented to highest standards. Victors Bar has old world charm & luxury. Live music Saturday nights, traditional Irish song & dance Wednesday nights July & August.

***An IHF Quality Employer***

Member of Countrywide Hotels - MinOtel Ireland

***Bookable on www.irelandhotels.com***
***Special Offer: www.irelandhotels.com/offers***

*B&B from €45.00 to €125.00*

*James P. Brennan*
*Managing Director*

28

**Closed 24 - 30 December**

### Days Hotel Kilkenny

HOTEL ★★★ MAP 7 L 7

Springhill,
Smithsland South,
Kilkenny

Tel: 1890-329329 Fax: 056-778 3101
Email: info@dayshotelkilkenny.com
Web: www.dayshotelkilkenny.com

Days Hotel is situated just 2km from the wonderful medieval city centre of Kilkenny, and less than five minutes drive from the city centre. The hotel comprises of 80 superb bedrooms with TV/DVD player, ironing station, tea/coffee making facilities, hairdryer, safe and free broadband. Rueben's restaurant and bar open throughout the day. Meeting rooms can accommodate from 2 to 60 delegates, with excellent audio visual equipment on site. Complimentary wireless in the lobby and bar. Car parking is offered free of charge. Hotel direct line 056 778 3100. Please enquire about Facilities for Persons with Mobility Impairment.

***An IHF Quality Employer***

Member of Days Hotels Ireland

***Bookable on www.irelandhotels.com***
***Special Offer: www.irelandhotels.com/offers***

*Room Rate from €79.00 to €249.00*

*Clement Gleeson*
*General Manager*

80

Activities:

**Closed 21 - 26 December**



B&B Rates are per Person Sharing per Night incl. Breakfast. or Room Rates are per Room per Night - See also Page 8

## Fanad House

GUESTHOUSE ★★★ MAP 7 L 7

Castle Road,
Kilkenny

Tel: 056-776 4126 Fax: 056-775 6001
Email: fanadhouse@hotmail.com
Web: www.fanadhouse.com

Overlooking Kilkenny Castle Park, Fanad House is a five minute walk from the city centre. The newly built guesthouse offers all en suite rooms with complimentary beverages, multi-channel TV, hairdryer and direct dial phone. Extensive breakfast menu available. Private and secure parking provided. An ideal base for exploring the mediaeval city. We are adjacent to Kilkenny Tennis Club. Owner operated is your guarantee for an enjoyable stay. Please enquire about Facilities for Persons with Mobility Impairment.

Member of Premier Guesthouses

*B&B from €45.00 to €110.00*

*Pat Wallace*
*Proprietor*

8

**Open All Year**

## Glendine Inn

GUESTHOUSE ★★ MAP 7 L 7

Castlecomer Road,
Kilkenny

Tel: 056-772 1069 Fax: 056-777 0714
Email: info@glendineinn.com
Web: www.glendineinn.com

The Glendine Inn has been a licensed tavern for over 200 years. It consists of 7 bedrooms (all en suite), a residents' lounge, residents' dining room, and public lounge and bars serving snack or bar lunches. We are ideally located for golf (course 200m away), the railway station and the historic city of Kilkenny are only 1.5km away. We assure you of a friendly welcome. Under new ownership of the Phelan family. Please enquire about Facilities for Persons with Mobility Impairment.

***Bookable on www.irelandhotels.com***
***Special Offer: www.irelandhotels.com/offers***

*B&B from €30.00 to €80.00*

*The Phelan Family*
*Proprietors*

7

*Activities:*

**Closed 24 - 26 December**

## Kilkenny City

### Hotel Kilkenny

HOTEL ★★★★ MAP 7 L 7

College Road,
Kilkenny

Tel: 056-776 2000 Fax: 056-776 5984
Email: experience@hotelkilkenny.ie
Web: www.hotelkilkenny.ie

The new 4 star Hotel Kilkenny is now open. The city's best located hotel, accessible from all major routes, yet only minutes from Kilkenny's heart, the new hotel offers 138 spacious bedrooms, stylish new lobby, bar & restaurant and exceptional leisure facilities with Olympic specification gym and 20m pool. Hairdressers, onsite beauty spa and children's play programme are also available. There is also an abundance of complimentary parking. Please enquire about Facilities for Persons with Mobility Impairment.

***An IHF Quality Employer***

Member of Griffin Hotel Group

*Bookable on www.irelandhotels.com*
*Special Offer: www.irelandhotels.com/offers*

*B&B from €71.00 to €130.00*
*Suites from €192.00 to €310.00*

*Richard Butler*
*General Manager*

138

*Activities:*

**Open All Year**

### Kilford Arms Hotel

HOTEL ★★★ MAP 7 L 7

John Street,
Kilkenny

Tel: 056-776 1018 Fax: 056-776 1128
Email: info@kilfordarms.ie
Web: www.kilfordarmshotel.com

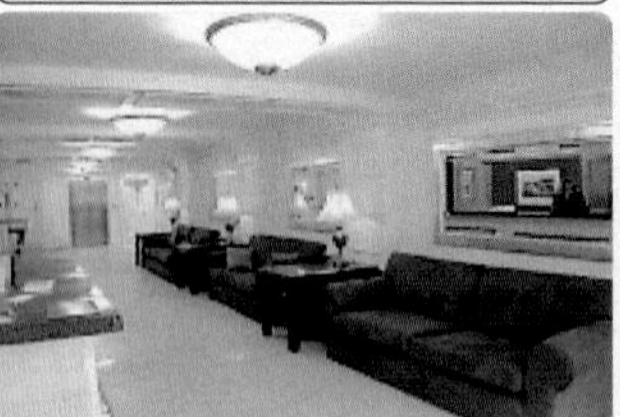

Enviably located, just minutes walk from city centre and railway station, the Kilford Arms Hotel offers a personal service and great range of facilities. The White Oak Restaurant serves fresh local produce in comfortable surroundings. PV's traditional bar has entertainment nightly, with food served daily. O'Faolain's Bar is Kilkenny's most vibrant bar, with 3 levels of stunning architecture, DJs and late bar nightly. Welcome to the Kilford Arms Hotel. Please enquire about Facilities for Persons with Mobility Impairment.

*Bookable on www.irelandhotels.com*
*Special Offer: www.irelandhotels.com/offers*

*B&B from €45.00 to €120.00*

*Pius Phelan*
*Owner*

60

**Open All Year**

### Kilkenny Hibernian Hotel

HOTEL ★★★★ MAP 7 L 7

1 Ormonde Street,
Kilkenny City

Tel: 056-777 1888 Fax: 056-777 1877
Email: info@kilkennyhibernianhotel.com
Web: www.kilkennyhibernianhotel.com

Experience old warm charm in Kilkenny's finest boutique hotel. Located in the city centre, this gracious old Victorian bank has been transformed into a unique hotel offering 46 luxury bedrooms. Guests can relax in the Black and White award-winning Hibernian Bar or sample the livelier atmosphere of Morrissons Bar. For exceptional food, Jacobs Cottage Restaurant is a must. Experience Kilkenny with us - you will find it difficult to leave!

***An IHF Quality Employer***

*Bookable on www.irelandhotels.com*
*Special Offer: www.irelandhotels.com/offers*

*B&B from €65.00 to €85.00*
*Suites from €160.00 to €230.00*

*John McNena*
*General Manager*

46

*Activities:*

**Closed 24 - 26 December**

 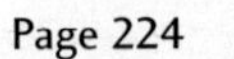 

B&B Rates are per Person Sharing per Night incl. Breakfast.
or Room Rates are per Room per Night - See also Page 8

## Kilkenny House Hotel

HOTEL ★★★ MAP 7 L 7

Freshford Road,
Talbot's Inch,
Kilkenny

Tel: 056-777 0711 Fax: 056-777 0698
Email: kilkennyhouse@eircom.net
Web: www.kilkennyhousehotel.ie

Enter the warmth and traditional style of Kilkenny House Hotel, ideally located between St Lukes and Aut Even Hospitals on the R693. Built to 3*** perfection with spacious and tastefully decorated bedrooms. Dore's Public Bar serves bar food daily from 12.30pm to 8.00pm and offers you a personal service while serving the best of local produce. The Talbots Inch Suite caters for meetings and events. Situated enviably on 2 acres with 100 car parking spaces. Owner operated guarantees Kilkenny's best value accommodation, food and beverage.

*Bookable on www.irelandhotels.com*
*Special Offer: www.irelandhotels.com/offers*

**Room Rate from €50.00 to €150.00**

*Ted Dore*
*Proprietor*
30

Activities:

**Closed 24 - 28 December**

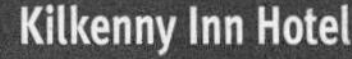

## Kilkenny Inn Hotel

HOTEL ★★★ MAP 7 L 7

15/16 Vicar Street,
Kilkenny

Tel: 056-777 2828 Fax: 056-776 1902
Email: info@kilkennyinn.com
Web: www.kilkennyinn.com

We offer exceptional value in a great location in the city. We are Fáilte Ireland and AA 3*** approved . Close to all tourist attractions, bars, restaurants and night life. 30 en suite bedrooms with flatscreen TV, free broadband access and tea/coffee facilities. The hotel has 2 bars, grill room and meeting room. We cater for private parties, large and small groups and family occasions etc. Free parking available. Please enquire about Facilities for Persons with Mobility Impairment.

*Bookable on www.irelandhotels.com*
*Special Offer: www.irelandhotels.com/offers*

**Room Rate from €60.00 to €160.00**

*John & Noeleen Breen*
*Proprietors*
30

Activities:

**Closed 24 - 26 December**

## Kilkenny Ormonde Hotel

HOTEL ★★★★ MAP 7 L 7

Ormonde Street,
Kilkenny

Tel: 056-772 3900 Fax: 056-772 3977
Email: info@kilkennyormonde.com
Web: www.kilkennyormonde.com

The 4**** de luxe Kilkenny Ormonde Hotel is the most extensive hotel in the city. Ideally situated just off the High Street with Kilkenny Castle on its doorstep. Complete with 118 of the largest bedrooms in Kilkenny, fully equipped leisure centre with 21 metre swimming pool and 2 award-winning restaurants. A complimentary activity packed Childrens Club is open throughout mid-term breaks and summer season. Also offering complimentary parking. The Kilkenny Ormonde is the perfect choice for both corporate & leisure guests. Please enquire about Facilities for Persons with Mobility Impairment.

***An IHF Quality Employer***

*Bookable on www.irelandhotels.com*
*Special Offer: www.irelandhotels.com/offers*

**B&B from €64.00 to €130.00**
**Suites from €228.00 to €360.00**

*Tom Walsh*
*General Manager*
118

Activities:

**Closed 24 - 27 December**

B&B Rates are per Person Sharing per Night incl. Breakfast.
or Room Rates are per Room per Night - See also Page 8

## Kilkenny City

### Kilkenny River Court

HOTEL ★★★★ MAP 7 L 7

The Bridge,
John Street,
Kilkenny

Tel: 056-772 3388 Fax: 056-772 3389
Email: info@rivercourthotel.com
Web: www.rivercourthotel.com

Award-winning RAC/AA 4**** hotel, leisure club and conference centre. City centre location, stunning views of Kilkenny Castle and the River Nore. Ideal as a conference venue or simply sheer relaxation. Leisure facilities include swimming pool, sauna, geyser pool, jacuzzi, fully equipped gymnasium and treatment rooms. Limited free car-parking. Within easy access of Dublin, Waterford and Cork. Please enquire about Facilities for Persons with Mobility Impairment.

***An IHF Quality Employer***

Member of Spectra Group Hotels

*Bookable on www.irelandhotels.com*
*Special Offer: www.irelandhotels.com/offers*

*B&B from €55.00 to €140.00*
*Suites from €320.00 to €400.00*

*Colin Ahern*
*General Manager*
*90*

*Activities:*

**Closed 24 - 26 December**

### Lacken House

GUESTHOUSE ★★★ MAP 7 L 7

Dublin Road,
Kilkenny

Tel: 056-776 1085 Fax: 056-776 2435
Email: info@lackenhouse.ie
Web: www.lackenhouse.ie

Stay at Lacken House & enjoy high quality accommodation & a friendly welcome. Family-run guest house, situated in Kilkenny City where you can enjoy exploring the medieval city. Superior & standard rooms available, all en suite with colour TV & tea/coffee facilities. Private car parking available for all residents. Full breakfast included. Winners of national Féile Bia award 2005, Best Tourism Provider Kilkenny 2005, AA rosette Award 2005.

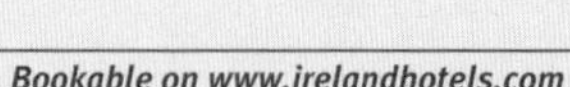

*Bookable on www.irelandhotels.com*
*Special Offer: www.irelandhotels.com/offers*

*B&B from €65.00 to €99.00*
*Suites from €150.00 to €190.00*

*Clodagh O'Gorman*
*Manager*
*10*

**Closed 24 - 27 December**

### Langton House Hotel

HOTEL ★★★ MAP 7 L 7

67-69 John Street,
Kilkenny

Tel: 056-776 5133 Fax: 056-776 3693
Email: reservations@langtons.ie
Web: www.langtons.ie

The Langton Group, incorporating Langtons Hotel; Bar & Restaurant; The Marble City Bar, are all located in the heart of Kilkenny City. Langtons Hotel, complete with thirty bedrooms, incorporating executive, penthouse and art-deco suites. Having won "National Pub of the Year" a record 4 times, the Langton Bar, Garden Restaurant, (member of the Kilkenny Good Food Circle) and "Club Langton" disco complete the picture that is Langtons. Please enquire about Facilities for Persons with Mobility Impairment.

*B&B from €45.00 to €100.00*
*Suites from €200.00 to €240.00*

*Eamon Langton*
*Proprietor*
*30*

*Activities:*

**Closed 25-26 December**



B&B Rates are per Person Sharing per Night incl. Breakfast. or Room Rates are per Room per Night - See also Page 8

## Laragh Guest House

GUESTHOUSE ★★★★ MAP 7 L 7

Smithsland North,
Waterford Road,
Kilkenny City

Tel: 056-776 4674 Fax: 056-770 3605

Email: info@laraghhouse.com

Web: www.laraghhouse.com

Laragh House is a new modern guesthouse offering luxurious, individually styled en suite rooms with TV, DD phones, tea/coffee facilities, hairdryer, power shower and/or whirlpool bath. Guests can expect a warm welcome, comfortable accommodation and an appetising breakfast. We are easily located 1km from the city centre's shops, restaurants and historic sights, on main road to Waterford near bypass roundabout. There is off street parking for guests. Broadband Available.

**B&B from €40.00 to €50.00**

Helen Cooney
Manager

8

**Closed 24 - 25 December**

## Laurels

GUESTHOUSE ★★★ MAP 7 L 7

College Road,
Kilkenny

Tel: 056-776 1501 Fax: 056-777 1334

Email: laurels@eircom.net

Web: www.thelaurelskilkenny.com

Purpose built townhouse 6-10 minutes walk from city centre and castle. Private car parking. All rooms en suite (some with whirlpool baths & super king sized beds). TV, Hairdryer, Tea/Coffee in all rooms. Some of the comments in Visitors Book: "Absolutely Wonderful", "Best B&B we had in Ireland", "First class & recommendable", "What more could one ask for, and a whirlpool bath too", "Wonderful". Opposite Hotel Kilkenny beside the famous Sceilp Pub.

Member of Premier Guesthouses

*Bookable on www.irelandhotels.com*
*Special Offer: www.irelandhotels.com/offers*

**B&B from €35.00 to €65.00**

Brian & Betty McHenry

9

**Open All Year**

## Lyrath Estate Hotel, Spa & Convention Centre

HOTEL ★★★★★ MAP 7 L 7

Dublin Road,
Kilkenny

Tel: 056-776 0088 Fax: 056-776 0089

Email: info@lyrath.com

Web: www.lyrath.com

Lyrath is delighted to welcome its guests to a place of contemporary elegance and sophistication, where we guarantee a memorable and unique hospitality experience. Situated on 170 acres, Lyrath's 17th century house plays an integral part in the overall development. At the Oasis Spa, we offer you a unique and exclusive opportunity to unwind and take time out just for you. A courtesy service is available to take you to the city centre just 5 mins away. Please enquire about Facilities for Persons with Mobility Impairment.

Member of Spectra Group Hotels

*Bookable on www.irelandhotels.com*
*Special Offer: www.irelandhotels.com/offers*

**B&B from €70.00 to €180.00**
**Suites from €440.00 to €660.00**

Patrick Joyce
General Manager

137

Activities:

**Closed 19 - 26 December**

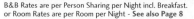

## Kilkenny City

### Newpark Hotel

HOTEL ★★★★ MAP 7 L 7

Castlecomer Road,
Kilkenny

Tel: 056-776 0500 Fax: 056-776 0555
Email: info@newparkhotel.com
Web: www.newparkhotel.com

Newpark Hotel 4**** & AA 4****. Tranquil parkland setting close to city centre, "The Creative Heart of Ireland". 129 superior rooms & suites. Full conference and banqueting facilities, additional facilities include: health spa & leisure complex, 17m pool, extensive air conditioned gym and aerobics studio. Choice of dining facilities: Scott Dove Bar, offering carvery lunch & evening menu, and fine dining in Gullivers Restaurant. Live entertainment at weekends. Fully equipped business & conference centre, ideal for seminars, sales conference & training courses. Please enquire about Facilities for Persons with Mobility Impairment.

***An IHF Quality Employer***

Member of Best Western Hotels

***Bookable on www.irelandhotels.com***
***Special Offer: www.irelandhotels.com/offers***

***B&B from €65.00 to €95.00***
***Suites from €135.00 to €150.00***

*David O'Sullivan*
*Managing Director*

129

Activities:

**Open All Year**

### Pembroke Hotel

HOTEL MAP 7 L 7

Patrick Street,
Kilkenny

Tel: 056-778 3500 Fax: 056-778 3535
Email: info@pembrokehotel.ie
Web: www.pembrokekilkenny.com

Built to a 4**** specification. The Pembroke, sophisticated elegance, a true gem in the heart of the Marble City. Indulge yourself in the stylish comfort, linger by the fire and soak up the atmosphere which abounds in this chic residence. Please enquire about Facilities for Persons with Mobility Impairment.

***B&B from €99.00 to €160.00***

*Tom Walsh*
*General Manager*

75

**Closed 24 - 27 December**

### Rosquil House

GUESTHOUSE ★★★★ MAP 7 L 7

Castlecomer Road,
Kilkenny

Tel: 056-772 1419 Fax: 056-775 0398
Email: info@rosquilhouse.com
Web: www.rosquilhouse.com

Located a short walk from the centre of the medieval Kilkenny City, Rosquil House offers the ambience of a hotel with the best traditions of Irish hospitality. With seven luxury en suite bedrooms with all the facilities, a guest lounge to enjoy a glass of wine and breakfast a culinary treat, all adds up to an experience not to be missed. Extensive private parking. Please enquire about Facilities for Persons with Mobility Impairment.

***B&B from €45.00 to €60.00***

*Jenny Nolan*
*Manager*

7

**Closed 23 - 27 December**



B&B Rates are per Person Sharing per Night incl. Breakfast.
or Room Rates are per Room per Night - See also Page 8

## San Antonio

GUESTHOUSE ★★ MAP 7 L 7

Castlecomer Road,
Kilkenny

Tel: 056-777 1834 Fax: 056-775 6393
Email: sanantonio@eircom.net
Web: www.kilkennycitybandb.com

San Antonio is a family-run guesthouse. Just a 10 minute walk to Kilkenny City centre. All our rooms are en suite with tea/coffee making facilities, multi channel TV, hairdryers and telephones. Private car parking available for all residents. Ideally located to explore the Mediaeval City and South East area. You are assured a warm and friendly welcome.

**B&B from €40.00 to €50.00**

*Luke & Marie Roche*
*Owners*

8

**Closed 15 December - 01 February**

## Springhill Court Hotel, Conference, Leisure & Spa Hotel

HOTEL ★★★ MAP 7 L 7

Waterford Road,
Kilkenny

Tel: 056-772 1122 Fax: 056-776 1600
Email: reservations@springhillcourt.com
Web: www.springhillcourt.com

Located only minutes from the bustling centre of "the Marble City". We boast one of Kilkenny's most modern leisure clubs. Our facilities include a 19m deck level pool, sauna, jacuzzi, steam room and fully equipped gymnasium. Unwind in "AquaSpa" offering 7 treatment rooms including floatation therapy. This compliments our superb restaurant, friendly bar, conference centre and 85 well appointed bedrooms. Member of Brennan Hotel Group. Sister Hotels: The Arklow Bay Conference & Leisure Hotel, Co. Wicklow, Bettystown Court Hotel Co. Meath & Clonmel Park Hotel, Co. Tipperary. Please enquire about Facilities for Persons with Mobility Impairment.

***An IHF Quality Employer***

Member of Brennan Hotel Group

***Bookable on www.irelandhotels.com***
***Special Offer: www.irelandhotels.com/offers***

**B&B from €45.00 to €100.00**

*Seamus O'Carroll*
*General Manager*

85

Activities:

**Open All Year**

## Zuni Restaurant & Townhouse

HOTEL ★★★ MAP 7 L 7

26 Patrick Street,
Kilkenny

Tel: 056-772 3999 Fax: 056-775 6400
Email: info@zuni.ie
Web: www.zuni.ie

A city centre boutique hotel, Zuni has earned its reputation as one the best places to stay and eat in Ireland. An award winning restaurant with fine cooking by eurotoque chef Maria Raftery and thirteen newly refurbished bedrooms, this property is ideally located in the heart of Kilkenny city with private parking and within walking distance of Kilkenny Castle, excellent shopping, restaurants and the many tourist attractions of Kilkenny.

***Bookable on www.irelandhotels.com***
***Special Offer: www.irelandhotels.com/offers***

**B&B from €50.00 to €85.00**
**Suites from €150.00 to €250.00**

*Paul Byrne*
*Proprietor*

13

**Closed 23 - 27 December**

B&B Rates are per Person Sharing per Night incl. Breakfast.
or Room Rates are per Room per Night - **See also Page 8**

## Knocktopher / Mullinavat / Thomastown

### Carrolls Hotel

HOTEL ★★ MAP 7 L 6

Knocktopher,
Co. Kilkenny

Tel: 056-776 8082 Fax: 056-776 8290
Email: info@carrollshotel.com
Web: www.carrollshotel.com

Situated on the N10 between Kilkenny and Waterford. Enjoy the excellent service, warmth and luxury of our family-run hotel. All rooms are en suite with TV and direct dial phone. Our Sionnach Sioc Restaurant has an excellent reputation for good food. The hotel provides live music 2 nights a week. Golfing, karting, fishing, horse riding and shooting are available nearby.

*B&B from €45.00 to €90.00*

*Padraig Carroll*
*General Manager*

10

**Closed 24 - 26 December**

### Rising Sun

GUESTHOUSE ★★★ MAP 4 L 6

Mullinavat,
Via Waterford,
Co. Kilkenny

Tel: 051-898173 Fax: 051-898435
Email: info@therisingsun.ie
Web: www.therisingsun.ie

A family-run guesthouse, 14km from Waterford City on the main Waterford-Dublin road. It has 10 luxurious bedrooms all en suite with D/D telephone, TV and tea/coffee making facilities. The Rising Sun Guesthouse is an ideal base for sports enthusiasts, surrounded by some beautiful golf courses within 15-30 minutes drive. The old world charm of stone and timberwork sets the tone of comfort and relaxation in the bar and lounge. Traditional home cooked lunches and bar food served daily. The Restaurant offers full à la carte menu and wine list.

*B&B from €50.00 to €65.00*

*Kathrena O'Connor*
*General Manager*

10

Activities:

**Closed 23 - 29 December**

### Mount Juliet Conrad

HOTEL ★★★★ MAP 7 L 6

Thomastown,
Co. Kilkenny

Tel: 056-777 3000 Fax: 056-777 3019
Email: mountjulietinfo@conradhotels.com
Web: www.conradhotels.com

At 1500 acres, Mount Juliet is one of the oldest surviving walled estates in the world. Guests can choose from accommodation in the carefully refurbished 18th century manor house overlooking the meandering waters of the River Nore, or in the Club Rooms at the estate's old stable yards, restored just over a decade ago. For longer stays, The Rose Garden Lodges offer privacy, flexibility & comfort. On site activities include horse riding, fishing, clay shooting & archery, golf on the 18 hole Nicklaus course or the 18 hole putting course and a luxurious spa & leisure centre.

***An IHF Quality Employer***

Member of Conrad Group of Hotels

***Bookable on www.irelandhotels.com***
***Special Offer: www.irelandhotels.com/offers***

*B&B from €74.50 to €225.00*
*Suites from €310.00 to €499.00*

*William Kirby*
*General Manager*

57

Activities:

**Open All Year**



B&B Rates are per Person Sharing per Night incl. Breakfast. or Room Rates are per Room per Night - **See also Page 8**

## Cahir House Hotel

HOTEL ★★★ MAP 3 J 6

The Square,
Cahir,
Co. Tipperary

Tel: 052-43000 Fax: 052-42728

Email: info@cahirhousehotel.ie

Web: www.cahirhousehotel.ie

Now under new management Cahir House Hotel is dedicated to providing excellent service and facilities. Ideal location for touring. Situated in the historic village of Cahir and situated within walking distance of Cahir Castle and 'The Swiss Cottage', and also close to Mitchelstown Caves and the famous rock of Cashel. Located within ten miles of 8 top class Golf Courses, golf breaks are a speciality. Bar food is available all day, with an á la carte menu served in our beautiful Pantry Restaurant. Member of Féile Bia promotion of Irish food. We serve the finest locally produced food. New Spa & Leisure facilities open.

***An IHF Quality Employer***

***Bookable on www.irelandhotels.com***

***Special Offer: www.irelandhotels.com/offers***

*B&B from €45.00 to €100.00*

*Brendan Kehoe*
*General Manager*

42

*Activities:*

**Closed 25 - 26 December**

## Kilcoran Lodge Hotel, Lodges & Leisure Centre

HOTEL ★★★ MAP 3 J 6

Cahir,
Co. Tipperary

Tel: 052-41288 Fax: 052-41994

Email: info@kilcoranlodgehotel.com

Web: www.kilcoranlodgehotel.com

Kilcoran, a former hunting lodge, is set in 20 acres of manicured gardens overlooking beautiful countryside. An ideal holiday base located equal distance from Cork, Kilkenny, Limerick and Waterford. The hotel has the charm of bygone days yet all the modern facilities of a good 3*** hotel. Guests have free access to our leisure centre with indoor pool. There are also 17 luxury holiday lodges, self catering for up to 6 persons, ideal for golf, walking and fishing breaks. Special bed and breakfast rates available for lodges and mews.

*Room Rate from €110.00 to €130.00*
*Suites from €180.00 to €200.00*

*Pierce Connell*
*General Manager*

22

*Activities:*

**Closed 08 January - 01 February**



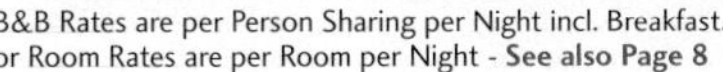

B&B Rates are per Person Sharing per Night incl. Breakfast.
or Room Rates are per Room per Night - See also Page 8

## Carrick-on-Suir / Cashel

### Carraig Hotel

HOTEL ★★★ MAP 3 K 5


Main Street,
Carrick-on-Suir,
Co. Tipperary

Tel: 051-641455 Fax: 051-641604

Email: info@carraighotel.com

Web: www.carraighotel.com


Located in the town centre of Carrick in the heart of the Suir Valley, close to Waterford, Kilkenny and the coast. Welcoming bar and restaurant with a great reputation for food. Excellent salmon & trout fishing on the Suir, golf on the local course with commanding views over the Suir Valley, or simply browse some great local shops, Farmer's market and Design centre. Visit The Ormonde Castle or simply enjoy Irish Hospitality at it's best. Live music at weekends.

***An IHF Quality Employer***

*Bookable on www.irelandhotels.com*

*Special Offer: www.irelandhotels.com/offers*

**B&B from €55.00 to €80.00**

*Bobby Carrigan*
*General Manager*

24

**Closed 24 - 26 Dec & 20 - 21 Mar**

### Aulber House

GUESTHOUSE ★★★ MAP 3 J 6


Deerpark,
Golden Road, Cashel,
Co. Tipperary

Tel: 062-63713 Fax: 062-63715

Email: info@aulberhouse.com

Web: www.aulberhouse.com

Aulber House - newly built luxury guesthouse. Idealy located on the outskirts of the historic town of Cashel. Home away from home. Perfect base for touring the South. Beautiful views of the Rock of Cashel and Hoare Abbey from some rooms and lobby. All rooms are spacious with en suite, power showers, direct dial phones, TV, hairdryers and broadband. Non-smoking guesthouse. Golf and angling facilities available locally. AA ♦♦♦♦. WiFi internet access available. Please enquire about Facilities for Persons with Mobility Impairment.

Member of Premier Guesthouses

**B&B from €50.00 to €80.00**

*Bernice & Sean Alley*

12

**Closed 02 December - 01 January**

### Baileys of Cashel

HOTEL ★★★★ MAP 3 J 6


Main Street,
Cashel,
Co. Tipperary

Tel: 062-61937 Fax: 062-63957

Email: info@baileys-ireland.com

Web: www.baileys-ireland.com


Baileys is a beautifully restored listed Georgian house ideally situated in the town centre with private off-street parking. The fully licensed Cellar Bar serves food all day in a cosy environment, while at No. 42 superb bistro style food is served each evening. Elegant rooms provide DD phone, broadband internet & interactive TV with on-demand movies. Leisure facilities: 20m swimming pool, fully equipped gym, sauna, steam room & jacuzzi. Baileys offers old-world charm in a modern world. AA ♦♦♦♦, Bridgestone recommended, member of Lucinda O'Sullivan & Great Places to Stay.

*Bookable on www.irelandhotels.com*

*Special Offer: www.irelandhotels.com/offers*

**B&B from €95.00 to €95.00**
**Suites from €225.00 to €275.00**

*Phil Delaney*
*Manager*

20

**Closed 24 - 28 December**

B&B Rates are per Person Sharing per Night incl. Breakfast. or Room Rates are per Room per Night - See also Page 8

## Cashel Palace Hotel

HOTEL ★★★★ MAP 3 J 6

Main Street,
Cashel,
Co. Tipperary
Tel: 062-62707 Fax: 062-61521
Email: reception@cashel-palace.ie
Web: www.cashel-palace.ie

Built in 1730 as an Archbishop's Palace, the Cashel Palace is complemented by tranquil walled gardens and a private walk to the famous Rock of Cashel. Our 23 bedrooms are all en suite with TV, phone & trouser press. Our Bishop's Buttery Restaurant is open for lunch & dinner, while the Guinness Bar is open for light snacks daily. The hotel has recently been completely restored & guests can now enjoy the finest furnishings, fabrics, art & antiques in the most elegant surroundings. AA 4**** hotel. AA Rosette Award for Culinary Excellence 2007/2008.

Member of Ireland's Blue Book

*Bookable on www.irelandhotels.com*
*Special Offer: www.irelandhotels.com/offers*

**B&B from €130.00 to €180.00**
**Suites from €345.00 to €480.00**

*Susan & Patrick Murphy*
*Proprietors*

23

Activities:

**Closed 24 - 26 December**

## Dundrum House Hotel

HOTEL ★★★ MAP 3 I 7

Dundrum,
Cashel,
Co. Tipperary
Tel: 062-71116 Fax: 062-71366
Email: dundrumh@iol.ie
Web: www.dundrumhousehotel.com

One of Ireland's best inland resort hotels, Dundrum House Hotel is surrounded by the manicured fairways of its own 18-hole c'ship course designed by Ryder Cup hero Philip Walton. The Country Club features the Venue Clubhouse Bar/Restaurant, 'White-Flag' award-winning Health & Leisure Centre with 20m indoor pool, gym, jacuzzi, sauna & steam room. Beauty treatments/massage by appointment. 84 rooms including two junior suites, six apartments & eighteen superior rooms and 16 luxury self catering apartments. Please enquire about Facilities for Persons with Mobility Impairment.

Member of Manor House Hotels

*Bookable on www.irelandhotels.com*
*Special Offer: www.irelandhotels.com/offers*

**B&B from €55.00 to €120.00**

*Austin & Mary Crowe*
*Proprietors*

84

Activities:

**Closed 24 - 26 December**

## Legends Townhouse & Restaurant

GUESTHOUSE ★★★ MAP 3 J 6

The Kiln,
Cashel,
Co. Tipperary
Tel: 062-61292
Email: info@legendsguesthouse.com
Web: www.legendsguesthouse.com

Legends is your home from home, a place to relax and unwind after your day's travelling. You can enjoy your breakfast, lunch or dinner in our comfortable surroundings with spectacular views of the Rock of Cashel. Recommended consistently by leading guides such as AA Hotel Guide, Michelin, Karen Brown, Bridgestone 100 Best and Rick Steves. An ideal base to explore Kilkenny, Waterford and Limerick or simply sit back and be inspired by the historical monument that is the Rock of Cashel. Unmissable!

*Bookable on www.irelandhotels.com*

**B&B from €45.00 to €70.00**

*Grazielle & John Quinlan*

7

**Closed 07 - 30 November**

B&B Rates are per Person Sharing per Night incl. Breakfast.
or Room Rates are per Room per Night - **See also Page 8**

## Clonmel

### Brighton House

GUESTHOUSE ★★ MAP 3 K 5

1 Brighton Place,
Clonmel,
Co. Tipperary

Tel: 052-23665 Fax: 052-80209
Email: brighton@iol.ie
Web: www.tipp.ie/brightonhouse.htm

Family-run 3 storey Georgian guesthouse, with a hotel ambience and antique furnishings. Clonmel Town centre - the largest inland town in Ireland bridging Rosslare Harbour (132km) with Killarney (160km) and the South West. Host to Fleadh Cheoil na hEireann 2003/04. Visit the Rock of Cashel, Mitchelstown Caves, Cahir Castle etc. Golf, fishing and pony trekking arranged locally. All rooms have direct dial phones, TV, radio, hairdryer and tea/coffee making facilities. Situated opposite Dunnes Stores Oakville Shopping Centre.

*B&B from €45.00 to €65.00*

*Bernie & Pat Morris*
*Proprietors*

6

**Closed 24 - 29 December**

### Clonmel Park Conference Leisure & Spa Hotel

HOTEL ★★★★ MAP 3 K 5

Cahir Road Roundabout,
Clonmel,
Co. Tipperary

Tel: 052-88700 Fax: 052-88766
Email: info@clonmelparkhotel.com
Web: www.clonmelparkhotel.com

Tipperary's newest hotel offers 99 modern guestrooms and all you would expect of a modern 4 star standard hotel. Enjoy dinner in Howards followed by drinks in the lively Wheat Bar. Why not book at treat at Eco Spa! Conference & Banqueting facilities for up to 500 people. A leisure centre and ample free parking completes a wonderful stay. Please enquire about Facilities for Persons with Mobility Impairment.

***An IHF Quality Employer***

Member of Brennan Hotels

*Bookable on www.irelandhotels.com*
*Special Offer: www.irelandhotels.com/offers*

*B&B from €65.00 to €110.00*
*Suites from €180.00 to €310.00*

*Michael Boyle*
*General Manager*

99

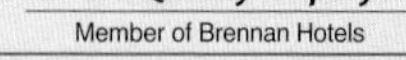

**Open All Year**

### Fennessy's Hotel

HOTEL ★★ MAP 3 K 5

Gladstone Street,
Clonmel,
Co. Tipperary

Tel: 052-23680 Fax: 052-23783
Email: info@fennessyshotel.com
Web: www.fennessyshotel.com

This beautiful Georgian building is recently restored and refurbished. Right in the centre of Clonmel, it is easily located opposite the town's main church. All bedrooms are en suite and have security safes, DD phone, multi channel TV, hairdryer, tea/coffee facilities, some with jacuzzis. Family-run hotel. Elegant ambience throughout. Main shopping area, swimming pool, leisure centre, riverside walks are a stone's throw from our front door. Golf, hill walking, fishing, pony trekking. After your visit, you will wish to return.

*Bookable on www.irelandhotels.com*
*Special Offer: www.irelandhotels.com/offers*

*B&B from €35.00 to €80.00*

*Richard & Esther Fennessy*
*Proprietors*

10

**Open All Year**



B&B Rates are per Person Sharing per Night incl. Breakfast.
or Room Rates are per Room per Night - See also Page 8

## Hotel Minella & Leisure Club

HOTEL ★★★★ MAP 3 K 5

Clonmel,
Co. Tipperary

Tel: 052-22388 Fax: 052-24381
Email: frontdesk@hotelminella.ie
Web: www.hotelminella.ie

Situated on the banks of the River Suir, the Minella has been owned and managed by the Nallen family who are noted for their warm and attentive hospitality. A €5 million development has recently been completed, and the contemporary style penthouse floor boasts a selection of superior king bedrooms, two boardrooms and four superbly appointed suites with balconies overlooking the river, two with indoor hot tubs. Club Minella boasts a 20m pool, jacuzzi, steam room, gymnasium, treatment rooms and hot tub overlooknig the River Suir. Minella is an ideal location for touring, golfing, mountain climbing and hill walking.

Member of Irish Country Hotels

***Bookable on www.irelandhotels.com***
***Special Offer: www.irelandhotels.com/offers***

*B&B from €80.00 to €180.00*
*Suites from €250.00 to €500.00*

*John Nallen*
*Managing Director*

*90*

*Activities:*

**Closed 23 - 29 December**

## Mulcahys

HOTEL ★★ MAP 3 K 5

47 Gladstone Street,
Clonmel,
Co. Tipperary

Tel: 052-25054 Fax: 052-24544
Email: info@mulcahys.ie
Web: www.mulcahys.ie

Mulcahys is run by the Higgins family and is located in the centre of town. Our bedrooms are tastefully designed, all en suite with tea/coffee making facilities, multi channel TV and hairdryer. The carvery opens for lunch from 12pm and our "East Lane" menu is served from 6pm. "Dance the night away" at our award-winning nightclub "Dannos". Some of Ireland's best golf courses are within easy reach of Clonmel and the River Suir has been described as an "angler's paradise".

*B&B from €40.00 to €80.00*

*Sharon Higgins*
*Manager*

*10*

**Closed 24 - 28 December**

## Aherlow House Hotel and Lodges

HOTEL ★★★ MAP 3 I 6

Glen of Aherlow,
Co. Tipperary

Tel: 062-56153 Fax: 062-56212
Email: reservations@aherlowhouse.ie
Web: www.aherlowhouse.ie

Aherlow House Hotel and 4**** de luxe lodges. The hotel & lodges are set in the middle of a coniferous forest just 4 miles from Tipperary Town. Originally a hunting lodge now converted into an exquisitely furnished hotel. Aherlow House welcomes you to its peaceful atmosphere, enhanced by a fine reputation for hospitality, excellent cuisine and unique wines. Aherlow House overlooks the Glen of Aherlow and has beautiful views of the Galtee Mountains. Activities can be arranged. Please enquire about Facilities for Persons with Mobility Impairment.

Member of Premier Guesthouse

***Bookable on www.irelandhotels.com***
***Special Offer: www.irelandhotels.com/offers***

*B&B from €79.50 to €89.50*
*Suites from €250.00 to €250.00*

*Ferghal & Helen Purcell*
*Owners*

*29*

**Open All Year**

B&B Rates are per Person Sharing per Night incl. Breakfast.
or Room Rates are per Room per Night - **See also Page 8**

## Glen of Aherlow / Horse and Jockey / Killenaule

### Glen Hotel

HOTEL ★★ MAP 3 I 6

Glen of Aherlow,
Co. Tipperary

Tel: 062-56146 Fax: 062-56152
Email: info@theglenhotel.ie
Web: www.theglenhotel.ie

The Glen Hotel set in the shadows of the majestic Galtee Mountains, amidst the splendour of the Aherlow Valley is just 5 miles from Tipperary Town. To relax, dream, reminisce or plan - this is the ideal haven. Our bedrooms are all en suite. This family owned and operated hotel has built up a fine reputation for excellent cuisine and offers friendly and efficient service. Hill walking, horse riding, fishing and golf. Musical entertainment weekly.

**B&B from €60.00 to €75.00**

*Cormac & Joseph Rose*
*Proprietors*

18

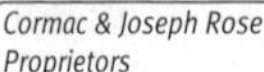

**Open All Year**

### Horse and Jockey Hotel

HOTEL ★★★★ MAP 7 J 7

Horse and Jockey,
(Near Cashel),
Co. Tipperary

Tel: 0504-44192 Fax: 0504-44747
Email: info@horseandjockeyhotel.com
Web: www.horseandjockeyhotel.com

Suitably located on one of the major crossroads in Ireland on the N8 approximately 1 1/4 hours from all main cities. Our facilities include award-winning restaurant, traditional Irish Bar, 67 luxurious bedrooms featuring plasma TV and WiFi. Superior conference centre comprising of 10 meeting rooms and a tiered auditorium for up to 200 delegates. Leisure complex includes 21m pool, steam room, sauna, jacuzzi, hydro-therapy area and gymnasium. The Spa is a haven of relaxation incorporating 7 treatment rooms using the Elemis Spa products.

**B&B from €75.00 to €90.00**
**Suites from €180.00 to €210.00**

*Tom Egan*
*Proprietor*

67

*Activities:*

**Closed 25 - 26 December**

### Ardagh House

GUESTHOUSE ★ MAP 3 K 7

Killenaule,
Co. Tipperary

Tel: 052-56224 Fax: 052-56224
Email: ahouse@iol.ie
Web: www.ardaghhouse.ie

Fully licensed family guesthouse, piano lounge bar, residents' lounge, rooms en suite, home-cooking. Set in the shadow of romantic Slievenamon, in the area of the Derrynaflan Chalice, the famous Coolmore Stud, in the heart of the Golden Vale. Near Holycross Abbey, Cashel and Kilkenny. Central for hunting, fishing, shooting, golf, horse riding and less strenuous walks through the hills of Killenaule. Finally, just one hour from the sea.

**B&B from €35.00 to €40.00**

*Mary & Michael McCormack*
*Managers*

6

**Closed 24 - 27 December**



B&B Rates are per Person Sharing per Night incl. Breakfast.
or Room Rates are per Room per Night - See also Page 8

## Abbey Court Hotel, Lodges & Trinity Leisure Spa

HOTEL ★★★ MAP 6 I 8

Dublin Road,
Nenagh,
Co. Tipperary

Tel: 067-41111 Fax: 067-41022

Email: info@abbeycourt.ie

Web: www.abbeycourt.ie

A Friendly and Warm Welcome awaits you at The Abbey Court Hotel. Situated in the historic town of Nenagh, an ideal gateway to Lough Derg, just off the Dublin to Limerick Road (N7). Set in its own magnificent landscaped gardens, the hotel presents 82 tastefully decorated superior Bedrooms, exclusive Conference & Banqueting facilities, Cloisters Restaurant, Abbots Bar, coupled with a 20m Indoor Pool, Techno Gym, Rugrats Kiddies Club, Crèche, Hair Salon, Spa and Beauty Centre. Also, stunning 3, 5 or 8 Bedroomed Lodges, all uniquely designed.

***An IHF Quality Employer***

***Bookable on www.irelandhotels.com***

***Special Offer: www.irelandhotels.com/offers***

*B&B from €70.00 to €95.00*
*Suites from €250.00 to €270.00*

*Matthias Muller MIHI*
*General Manager*

82

Activities:

Closed 25 - 26 December

## Racket Hall Country House Golf & Conference Hotel

HOTEL ★★★ MAP 7 J 9

Dublin Road,
Roscrea,
Co. Tipperary

Tel: 0505-21748 Fax: 0505-23701

Email: reservations@rackethall.ie

Web: www.rackethall.ie

Located on the main N7 just outside the Heritage Town of Roscrea and set in the heart of the monastic Midlands beneath the Slieve Bloom Mountains, this charming family-run olde world residence boasts 40 new luxurious guest rooms. The ideal location for the avid golfer, hill walker, fishing enthusiast or history buff. An extremely convenient stopping off point from Dublin to Limerick, Shannon, Clare or Kerry. Award-winning Lily Bridges Steakhouse Bar and Willow Tree Restaurant. Fully wheelchair accessible. Special Golf/Fishing packages available all year.
www.valuegolfireland.com

*B&B from €69.00 to €129.00*
*Suites from €269.00 to €299.00*

*Michael Costello*
*Proprietor*

40

Activities:

Open All Year

## Templemore Arms Hotel

HOTEL ★★ MAP 7 J 8

Main Street,
Templemore,
Co. Tipperary

Tel: 0504-31423 Fax: 0504-31343

Email: info@templemorearms.com

Web: www.templemorearms.com

The Templemore Arms Hotel is located in the shadow of one of Ireland's most prominent landmarks, The Devil's Bit, in the centre of the town of Templemore. Recently rebuilt to match the demands of the most discerning guests, it boasts lounge bars, carvery, restaurant, banqueting suite and conference room, providing first class service. Visit the Templemore Arms Hotel and experience an enjoyable getaway.

*B&B from €50.00 to €80.00*
*Suites from €145.00 to €145.00*

*Dan Ward*

14

Activities:

Closed 25 December

## Thurles / Tipperary Town

### Anner Hotel & Leisure Centre

HOTEL ★★★ MAP 7 J 7


Dublin Road,
Thurles,
Co. Tipperary

Tel: 0504-21799 Fax: 0504-22111

Email: info@annerhotel.ie

Web: www.annerhotel.ie

The Anner Hotel located on the outskirts of Thurles, 5 minutes walk from the town centre with beautiful landscaped gardens. We offer our guests a warm welcome, excellent food and a friendly service in comfortable surroundings. Superb leisure facilities boasts 18m pool, kiddies pool, jacuzzi, sauna and gym. Close to Holy Cross Abbey and The Rock of Cashel. Ideal base for touring, golf, walking, leisure breaks, conference and banqueting.

**B&B from €75.00 to €100.00**

*Gerard Laffan*
*General Manager*

96

Activities:

**Closed 25 - 26 December**

### Ach Na Sheen Guesthouse

GUESTHOUSE ★★ MAP 3 I 6


Clonmel Road,
Tipperary Town,
Co. Tipperary

Tel: 062-51298 Fax: 062-80467

Email: gernoonan@eircom.net

Web: www.achnasheen.net

Family-run guesthouse, 5 minutes walk from the town centre with a spacious sun lounge and diningroom overlooking gardens and the beautiful Galtee Mountains. Our 8 rooms are all en suite, equipped with TV and tea/coffee making facilities. Ach-na-Sheen is adjacent to the picturesque Glen of Aherlow where fishing and hill walking can be arranged. Golf can be enjoyed at any number of nearby championship courses. G & S Noonan offer you the utmost in Irish hospitality.

**B&B from €40.00 to €55.00**

*Sylvia & Ger Noonan*
*Proprietors*

8

Activities:

**Closed 11 December - 14 January**

### Ballyglass Country House

HOTEL ★★ MAP 3 I 6


Glen Of Aherlow Road,
Ballyglass,
Tipperary Town

Tel: 062-52104 Fax: 062-52229

Email: info@ballyglasshouse.com

Web: www.ballyglasshouse.com

Ballyglass Country House is an 18th century country residence set in its own grounds on the outskirts of Tipperary and just 2km from the beautiful Glen of Aherlow. Here at this family-run hotel you can enjoy the best of local produce in our "Colonel's Restaurant" and relax in front of a real coal fire in our "Forge Bar". Ballyglass Country House is perfectly situated for touring Munster. Golfing, fishing, hill walking and horse riding are all available locally.

**B&B from €50.00 to €60.00**

*Joan & Bill Byrne*
*Proprietors*

10

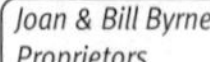

**Closed 24 - 26 December**



B&B Rates are per Person Sharing per Night incl. Breakfast.
or Room Rates are per Room per Night - **See also Page 8**

## Ballykisteen Hotel & Golf Resort

HOTEL ★★★★ MAP 6 I 6

Limerick Junction,
Near Tipperary Town,
Co. Tipperary

Tel: 062-33333 Fax: 062-31555
Email: info@ballykisteenhotel.com
Web: www.ballykisteenhotel.com

Ballykisteen Hotel & Golf Resort is a relaxing country location set in the lea of the Galtee Mountains close to Limerick Junction railway station and Shannon Airport. The hotel offers a Des Smyth designed championship golf course, beauty suite, leisure facilities and children's playroom. Situated amidst 170 acres of the former Ballykisteen Stud, there is an overwhelming sense of space, the perfect haven of peace and tranquility. Please enquire about Facilities for Persons with Mobility Impairment.

***Bookable on www.irelandhotels.com***
***Special Offer: www.irelandhotels.com/offers***

**Room Rate from €95.00 to €149.00**
**Suites from €179.00 to €190.00**

*George Graham*
*General Manager*
85

Activities:

**Closed 25 - 26 December**

## Cliff House Hotel

HOTEL MAP 3 K 3

Dysert Street,
Ardmore,
Co. Waterford

Tel: +44 (0) 207 259 3621
Email: uksales@steinhotels.com
Web: www.cliffhouse.steinhotels.com

UNDER CONSTRUCTION - OPENING DECEMBER 2007

Built to a 5***** specification. The Cliff House in Ardmore on the Irish Riviera is one of Ireland's standout properties. Its décor is contemporary Irish with 39 rooms all with stunning views over Ardmore Bay. The hotel also features a restaurant, a spa, an indoor pool, a sauna, a steam room, a fully equipped gym & 3 meeting rooms which can also be used for banqueting. Please enquire about Facilities for Persons with Mobility Impairment.

Member of Stein Hotels & Resorts

**Room Rate from €350.00 to €450.00**
**Suites from €650.00 to €1,250.00**

*Michael Conrad-Pickles*
*General Manager*
39

Activities:

**Open All Year**

## Newtown Farm Guesthouse

GUESTHOUSE ★★★ MAP 3 K 3

Grange,
Ardmore, Via Youghal,
Co. Waterford

Tel: 024-94143 Fax: 024-94054
Email: newtownfarm@eircom.net
Web: www.newtownfarm.com

This is a charming guesthouse set in its own lands. Located near the coastal resort of Ardmore. Our guest rooms offer a haven of relaxation and are tastefully furnished with a country house feel, a fully equipped sauna and a hard tennis court are extras we offer our guests. Breakfast is served overlooking the garden with a view of the Atlantic Ocean. The breakfast includes local ingredients. Situated on N25 halfway between Waterford and Cork. Rosslare 2 hours drive.

Member of Premier Guesthouses

***Bookable on www.irelandhotels.com***

**B&B from €40.00 to €45.00**

*Teresa O'Connor*
*Proprietor*
7

**Closed 01 November - 01 April**

B&B Rates are per Person Sharing per Night incl. Breakfast.
or Room Rates are per Room per Night - **See also Page 8**

## Ardmore / Ballymacarbry / Cappoquin

### Round Tower Hotel

**Hotel ★★ Map 3 K 3**

College Road,
Ardmore,
Co. Waterford

Tel: 024-94494 Fax: 024-94254

Email: rth@eircom.net

Situated within walking distance of Ardmore's award-winning beach, the Round Tower Hotel offers 12 well appointed en suite bedrooms. Fresh local produce features prominently on both the bar and restaurant menus. The ancient monastic settlement of St. Declan & the Round Tower are situated behind the hotel. Ardmore also boasts some world famous cliff walks and breathtaking scenery. 21kms from Dungarvan and a 2 hour drive from the port of Rosslare on the Primary N25 route. Please enquire about Facilities for Persons with Mobility Impairment.

Member of Irish Countrywide Hotels

*Bookable on www.irelandhotels.com*

*Special Offer: www.irelandhotels.com/offers*

**B&B from €55.00 to €65.00**

*Patricia Quirke & Aidan Quirke M.I.H.C.I.*
*Proprietors*

12

**Closed 23 - 28 December**

### Hanoras Cottage

**Guesthouse ★★★★ Map 3 K 5**

Nire Valley,
Ballymacarbry,
Co. Waterford

Tel: 052-36134 Fax: 052-36540

Email: hanorascottage@eircom.net

Web: www.hanorascottage.com

A haven of peace and tranquillity in the Comeragh Mountains, Hanoras has everything for discerning guests. Relax in the sheer bliss of an adult only house with the soothing sounds of the Nire River running by. Spacious rooms with jacuzzi tubs. Superior rooms for that special occasion! Enjoy excellent cuisine from our Ballymaloe School chefs who cater for all diets. AA ♦♦♦♦♦. Recommended in Bridgestone Guide 100 Best Places in Ireland. Georgina Campbell's Best of the Best National award winners. Guesthouse Of The Year and Breakfast Of The Year. "The Wall Family Welcomes You".

**B&B from €85.00 to €125.00**

*The Wall Family*
*Proprietors*

10

**Closed 20 - 28 December**

### Richmond House

**Guesthouse ★★★★ Map 3 J 4**

Cappoquin,
Co. Waterford

Tel: 058-54278 Fax: 058-54988

Email: info@richmondhouse.net

Web: www.richmondhouse.net

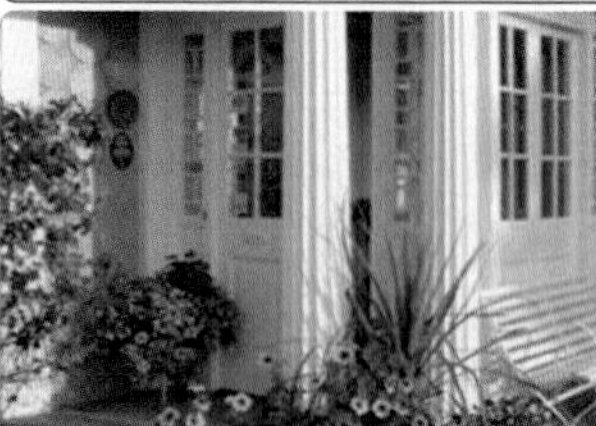

Delightful 18th century Georgian country house and fully licenced award-winning restaurant set in private grounds. Relax in total peace and tranquillity in front of log fires. Each room is a perfect blend of Georgian splendour combined with all modern comforts for the discerning guest. AA ♦♦♦♦♦. Recommended in the Bridgestone Guides; 100 Best Places to Stay, 100 Best Restaurants in Ireland and all leading guides. Ideal location for a short break. Georgina Campbell's Féile Bia Award 2006.

**B&B from €80.00 to €130.00**

*Paul & Claire Deevy*
*Proprietors*

9

**Closed 23 December - 10 January**



B&B Rates are per Person Sharing per Night incl. Breakfast. or Room Rates are per Room per Night - **See also Page 8**

## Three Rivers Guest House

GUESTHOUSE ★★★ MAP 4 M 5

Cheekpoint,
Co. Waterford

Tel: 051-382520 Fax: 051-382542

Email: mail@threerivers.ie

Web: www.threerivers.ie

3*** award-winning guesthouse, a haven of peace and tranquillity with magnificent views of Waterford Estuary. Situated on the outskirts of the historic village Cheekpoint, with its award-winning pubs and seafood restaurants. Sample the delights of breakfast in our estuary view dining room or relax over coffee in our spacious lounge. Ideal base for touring sunny South East. Close to Waterford, Dunmore East, Tramore and 2km from Faithlegg Golf Course. All rooms en suite.

*B&B from €45.00 to €60.00*

*Brian & Theresa Joyce* — 14

**Closed 20 - 28 December**

## Barnawee Bridge Guesthouse

GUESTHOUSE ★★★ MAP 3 K 4

Kilminion,
Dungarvan,
Co. Waterford

Tel: 058-42074

Email: michelle@barnawee.com

Web: www.barnawee.com

Our established guesthouse with fabulous sea and mountain views near all local amenities including three 18 hole golf courses, indoor swimming, sea angling, tennis, fishing and bird watching. Also various countryside walks. Food and drinks available locally, also a kitchennette for tea/coffee and snacks available for all our customers. All rooms are very spacious with en suite and color TV, making for a very enjoyable stay. Mobile number: 087 262 0269.

*B&B from €38.00 to €45.00*
*Suites from €80.00 to €100.00*

*Michelle Dwane / Gary Treen*
*Proprietors* — 6

**Open All Year**

## Clonea Strand Hotel, Golf & Leisure

HOTEL ★★★ MAP 3 K 4

Clonea,
Dungarvan,
Co. Waterford

Tel: 058-45555 Fax: 058-42880

Email: info@clonea.com

Web: www.clonea.com

Clonea Strand Hotel overlooking Clonea Beach. Family-run by John and Ann McGrath. All rooms en suite with tea/coffee making facilities, hairdryer and colour TV. Indoor leisure centre with heated pool, jacuzzi, sauna, Turkish bath, gymnasium and ten pin bowling alley. Situated close by is our 18 hole golf course bordering on the Atlantic Ocean with a scenic background of Dungarvan Bay and Comeragh Mountains. Our Bay Restaurant specialises in locally caught seafood. 1 thousand sq foot children's soft play facility. www.playloft.net. GPS Co ordinates: N52 303 W 007 37 386.

*B&B from €34.75 to €95.00*

*Mark Knowles*
*Resort Director* — 58

**Open All Year**

## Dungarvan / Dunmore East

### Park Hotel, Leisure Centre & Holiday Homes

HOTEL ★★★ MAP 3 K 4

Dungarvan,
Co. Waterford

Tel: 058-42899 Fax: 058-42969
Email: reservations@parkhoteldungarvan.com
Web: www.flynnhotels.com

Overlooking the Colligan River Estuary, nestled beneath the Comeragh Mountains and minutes from beautiful beaches and Championship Golf Courses, The Park Hotel provides the ideal setting for leisure or business. The hotel's 87 spacious rooms and suites are elegantly furnished with flair and imagination. The hotel also boasts its own state of the art Aqua & Fitness centre with 20m swimming pool, sauna, steam room and gym. There are also 15 luxurious self catering holiday homes on the grounds of the hotel. Please enquire about Facilities for Persons with Mobility Impairment.

Member of Flynn Hotels

*Bookable on www.irelandhotels.com*
*Special Offer: www.irelandhotels.com/offers*

*B&B from €70.00 to €85.00*
*Suites from €120.00 to €160.00*

*Pierce Flynn*
*Manager*
87

Activities:

Closed 24 - 25 December

### Seaview

GUESTHOUSE ★★★ MAP 3 K 4

Windgap,
N25 / Youghal Road, Dungarvan,
Co. Waterford

Tel: 058-41583 Fax: 058-41679
Email: faheyn@gofree.indigo.ie
Web: www.seaviewdungarvan.com

Want your vacation to never stop being a vacation? Enjoy breakfast overlooking the sea? Play one of Dungarvan's three 18 hole golf courses or take a bus tour of the area and let someone else do the driving. How about dinner, entertained by traditional Irish musicians, at the nearby Marine Bar? Make every ounce of your vacation count. Try Seaview on N25, 5km west of Dungarvan. Fax and e-mail facilities available. Continental and full Irish breakfast served. Laundry service available. Please enquire about Facilities for Persons with Mobility Impairment.

Member of Premier Guesthouses

*Bookable on www.irelandhotels.com*
*Special Offer: www.irelandhotels.com/offers*

*Room Rate from €60.00 to €80.00*

*Martin & Nora Fahey*
*Owners*
8

Closed 1 December - 31 January

### Beach Guest House

GUESTHOUSE ★★★★ MAP 4 M 5

1 Lower Village,
Dunmore East,
Co. Waterford

Tel: 051-383316 Fax: 051-383319
Email: beachouse@eircom.net
Web: www.dunmorebeachguesthouse.com

Newly built in a superb location overlooking Dunmore East Strand. The Beach Guesthouse provides luxury accommodation, stunning sea views and private parking. A central base from which to explore charming hidden coves, superb cliff walks and neat rows of pretty thatched cottages in this picturesque village 10 miles from Waterford, in the centre of Dunmore East with excellent restaurants and sporting amenities nearby including 4 championship golf courses within 10 miles. AA/RAC ♦♦♦♦. Disabled access room available. Please enquire about Facilities for Persons with Mobility Impairment.

Member of Premier Guesthouses

*Bookable on www.irelandhotels.com*
*Special Offer: www.irelandhotels.com/offers*

*B&B from €40.00 to €50.00*
*Suites from €90.00 to €100.00*

*Breda Battles*
*Host*
7

Closed 01 November - 28 February



B&B Rates are per Person Sharing per Night incl. Breakfast.
or Room Rates are per Room per Night - See also Page 8

## Ocean Hotel

HOTEL ★★ MAP 4 M 5

Dunmore East,
Co. Waterford

Tel: 051-383136 Fax: 051-383576
Email: info@theoceanhotel.com
Web: www.theoceanhotel.com

The Ocean Hotel 15 minutes drive from Waterford City, is situated in one of Ireland's most picturesque villages. The jewel of the sunny South East. We offer you the personal attention and service only a family-run hotel can provide. Our extensive à la carte menu is available in both dining room and bar with a strong emphasis on seafood dishes. Our menu is reasonably priced. Golf packages arranged. Our new Alfred D Snow Bar is air-conditioned with décor depicting a nautical theme. Entertainment in the bar most nights during the summer and Saturday nights all year around.

**B&B from €50.00 to €80.00**

*Colm Gallagher*
*Proprietor*

12

Activities:

**Closed 25 December**

# Top Two Visitor Attractions
## Lismore, Co. Waterford.

### Lismore Castle Gardens & Art Gallery

Prince John first built a castle in Lismore in 1185,and a round tower, dating from the 13th century still stands today. Within the defensive walls of the castle, the gardens at Lismore provide spectacular views, and the herbaceous border gives an impressive show of colour throughout summer. There is also a fine selection of specimen magnolias, camellias, and rhododendrons, and a remarkable yew walk where Edmund Spenser is said to have written the 'Faerie Queen'. While wandering the gardens, visitors are invited to enjoy several pieces of contemporary sculpture, and the West-Wing of the Castle has been developed as a gallery for contemporary art, providing a vibrant programme to be enjoyed by the local community and tourists alike. Visitors to the gardens are welcome to visit the gallery free of charge. Lismore Castle is the Irish home of the Duke of Devonshire and his family and, when not in residence, the castle may be rented, fully staffed, to guests.

*Tel: 058 54424 Fax: 058 54896*
*E-mail: lismoreestates@eircom.net*
*Website: www.lismorecastle.com*
*www.lismorecastlearts.ie*
*Open daily 1.45p.m. to 4.45p.m. from 7th. April to 30th. September. (11 a.m. opening during high season).*
*Admission charges:*
*€7 (adults) €3.50 (children)*

### Lismore Heritage Centre

Situated in the centre of the town, is a must for those who wish to experience the rich history of the town and its surroundings. Your host Brother Declan (alias Niall Toibin) will take you on a fascinating journey through time in "The Lismore Experience" – an exciting audio-visual presentation which tells the story of the town since St. Carthages arrival in 636AD. Also exhibition galleries on Monastic, Norman and Medieval Lismore and a science exhibition room on the life and works of Robert Boyle, 'the Father of Modern Chemistry' who was born at Lismore Castle. Guided tours of this monastic town leave the Heritage Centre at appointed times each day.

*Open 9.30am – 5.30pm*
*Monday – Friday (year round)*
*10am – 5.30pm Saturday*
*(April – September)*
*12noon – 5.30pm Sunday*
*(April – September)*

*Admission charges €4.50 (adults)*
*Special rates for families and OAP's*
*Tel: 058 54975 Fax: 058 53009*
*e-mail: lismoreheritage@eircom.net*

B&B Rates are per Person Sharing per Night incl. Breakfast.
or Room Rates are per Room per Night - **See also Page 8**

## Faithlegg / Lismore / Tramore

### Faithlegg House Hotel and Golf Club

HOTEL ★★★★ MAP 4 M 5

Faithlegg,
Co. Waterford

Tel: 051-382000 Fax: 051-382010
Email: reservations@fhh.ie
Web: www.faithlegg.com

A Tower Group Hotel - Faithlegg House Hotel is located on the already renowned 18-hole championship golf course, overlooking the estuary of the River Suir. This elegantly restored country house hotel incorporates 82 bedrooms, including 14 master rooms in the original house; a unique fitness, health and beauty club featuring a 17m pool; plus comprehensive meeting, conference and event management facilities. AA 4**** approved. Special offers available on www.towerhotelgroup.com. Please enquire about Facilities for Persons with Mobility Impairment.

***An IHF Quality Employer***

Member of Tower Hotel Group

***Bookable on www.irelandhotels.com***
*Special Offer: www.irelandhotels.com/offers*

**B&B from €95.00 to €170.00**
**Suites from €250.00 to €300.00**

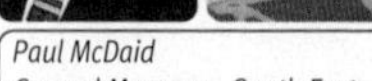

*Paul McDaid*
*General Manager - South East*
82

Activities:

**Closed 02 January- 09 February**

### Lismore House Hotel

HOTEL MAP 3 J 4

Main Street,
Lismore,
Co. Waterford

Tel: 058-72966 Fax: 058-53068
Email: info@lismorehousehotel.com
Web: www.lismorehousehotel.com

Built to a 4**** specification. Built in 1797 and located in the heart of Lismore, the hotel has been completely restored and refurbished to retain the glory of it's Georgian old world style and charm and reflect the heritage of Lismore Castle and surrounds. The team look forward to welcoming you in the true Traditional Irish style and to offering you the best in personal service. Lismore Castle, gardens, heritage centre and so much more, from our doorstep. Please enquire about Facilities for Persons with Mobility Impairment.

***Bookable on www.irelandhotels.com***
*Special Offer: www.irelandhotels.com/offers*

**B&B from €70.00 to €142.00**

*Mervyn Boyle*
*General Manager*
29

Activities:

**Open All Year**

### Beach Haven House

GUESTHOUSE ★★★ MAP 4 L 5

Tivoli Terrace,
Tramore,
Co. Waterford

Tel: 051-390208 Fax: 051-330971
Email: beachhavenhouse@eircom.net
Web: www.beachhavenhouse.com

This luxurious home in the heart of Tramore has a warm and friendly atmosphere. Finished to the highest standards and with your comfort in mind. We are located just a few minutes walk to the beach, town centre, Splashworld and the racecourse. Tramore has great restaurants and pubs and lots to do for the whole family. All rooms are en suite with TV, phone and coffee and tea making facilities. Extensive breakfast menu, family suites, comfy guest lounge, private parking. AA ♦♦♦♦ accredited.

Member of Irish Guests

***Bookable on www.irelandhotels.com***
*Special Offer: www.irelandhotels.com/offers*

**B&B from €40.00 to €50.00**

*Avery & Niamh Coryell*
*Owners*
8

**Open All Year**



B&B Rates are per Person Sharing per Night incl. Breakfast.
or Room Rates are per Room per Night - **See also Page 8**

## Grand Hotel

HOTEL ★★★ MAP 4 L 5

Tramore,
Co. Waterford

Tel: 051-381414 Fax: 051-386428

Email: reservations@grand-hotel.ie

Web: www.grand-hotel.ie

The Grand Hotel is owned and managed by the Treacy family & combines its traditional surroundings with friendly staff to create its unique atmosphere. 82 en suite bedrooms with tea/coffee making facilities, hairdryers, multi-channel TV and DD phone. The award-winning Doneraile Restaurant has a panoramic view of Tramore Strand & extensive menus with something for everyone. Visit Duffy's Bar with exciting bar menus & live entertainment at weekends and every night in July & August. For details on special offers please visit www.grand-hotel.ie. Please enquire about Facilities for Persons with Mobility Impairment.

***An IHF Quality Employer***

***Bookable on www.irelandhotels.com***

***Special Offer: www.irelandhotels.com/offers***

***B&B from €58.00 to €73.00***

*Tom & Anna Treacy*
*Proprietors*

82

**Closed 01 December - 31 January**

## Majestic Hotel

HOTEL ★★★ MAP 4 L 5

Tramore,
Co. Waterford

Tel: 051-381761 Fax: 051-381766

Email: info@majestic-hotel.ie

Web: www.majestic-hotel.ie

A warm welcome awaits you at the award-winning Majestic Hotel, overlooking Tramore Bay and its famous 5km of sandy beach. Only 10km from Waterford City. All 59 bedrooms are en suite with TV, phone, hairdryer and tea/coffee facilities. Full internet access. Complimentary leisure facilities available to guests at Splashworld Health and Fitness Club near hotel. Golf packages are our speciality on South East sunshine circuit. Tee-times arranged.

***An IHF Quality Employer***

***Bookable on www.irelandhotels.com***

***Special Offer: www.irelandhotels.com/offers***

***B&B from €60.00 to €80.00***

*Annette Devine*
*Managing Director*

59

*Activities:* ✓

**Closed 24 - 26 December**

## O'Shea's Hotel...by the sea

HOTEL ★★★ MAP 4 L 5

Strand Street,
Tramore,
Co. Waterford

Tel: 051-381246 Fax: 051-390144

Email: info@osheas-hotel.com

Web: www.osheas-hotel.com

Noreen & Joe O'Shea are the proud owners of this intimate family-run hotel that opened its doors to guests in 1968 (celebrating 40 years) & has maintained an outstanding reputation for customer care, good food & genuine hospitality. Located by the sea in downtown Tramore, minutes from "Splashworld" (discount for guests). Bedrooms are located in the main hotel or the annex. We specialise in the best of Irish foods, in the Copper Room Restaurant & O'Shea's Bar where all the old values of good food, customer satisfaction, comfort & value for money prevails. Secure car-parking. Golfing packages a speciality.

***An IHF Quality Employer***

***Bookable on www.irelandhotels.com***

***Special Offer: www.irelandhotels.com/offers***

***B&B from €45.00 to €85.00***

*Joe & Noreen O'Shea*
*Proprietors*

30

*Activities:* ✓

**Closed 24 - 27 December**

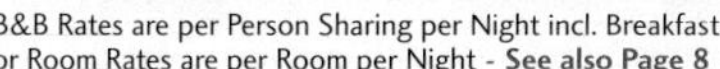

B&B Rates are per Person Sharing per Night incl. Breakfast.
or Room Rates are per Room per Night - See also Page 8

## Tramore / Waterford City

### Sands Hotel (The)

HOTEL ★★★ MAP 4 L 5

Turkey Road,
Tramore,
Co. Waterford

Tel: 051-381355 Fax: 051-393869

Email: enquiries@sands-hotel-tramore.com

Web: www.sands-hotel-tramore.com

Overlooking Tramore Beach and next door to Splashworld Health and Fitness Centre (discounts for guests), The Sands Hotel features 20 bedrooms, all en suite, with stylish, modern and tasteful decor, including TV, phone, tea and coffee facilities, iron and board. The Sands Hotel is integral to a visit to Tramore, boasting an extensive award-winning bar food menu, choice of 2 bars offering live music and exclusive night club called Redz and Oakroom Restaurant.

**B&B from €55.00 to €70.00**
**Suites from €170.00 to €170.00**

*Paul Mitchell*
*General Manager*

20

**Closed 24 - 26 December**

### Arlington Lodge Town House & Restaurant

HOTEL ★★★★ MAP 4 L 5

John's Hill,
Waterford City

Tel: 051-878584 Fax: 051-878127

Email: info@arlingtonlodge.com

Web: www.arlingtonlodge.com

Maurice Keller's Arlington Lodge Hotel is a gracious 18th century Georgian house, formerly the Bishop's Palace for over 200 years. Converted to a luxury town house & restaurant in 2000, it is situated in its own private grounds yet only 8 minutes walk from the city centre. The emphasis is on hospitality, good food and wine. Breakfast is a delight and should never be missed. Maurice's attention to detail and easy informality make Arlington Lodge the perfect venue for any occasion. Boardroom/meeting room facilities, complimentary broadband in all bedrooms.

Member of Good Food Ireland

*Bookable on www.irelandhotels.com*

**B&B from €85.00 to €145.00**

*Maurice Keller*
*Manager / Proprietor*

20

**Closed 24 - 27 December**

### Athenaeum House Hotel

HOTEL ★★★★ MAP 4 L 5

Christendom,
Ferrybank,
Waterford

Tel: 051-833999 Fax: 051-833977

Email: info@athenaeumhousehotel.com

Web: www.athenaeumhousehotel.com

Athenaeum House Hotel is a 4**** boutique hotel set amidst 6 acres of parkland on the banks of the River Suir overlooking Waterford City. Offering a lifestyles elegance, with modern chic décor. Providing the ultimate in comfort and luxury for discerning travellers. Featuring Zaks Restaurant, state of the art meeting rooms, all bedrooms, including de luxe rooms & suites, are individually designed with TV, mini-hi-fi, mini-bar, voicemail and broadband.

***An IHF Quality Employer***

Member of Manor House Hotels

*Bookable on www.irelandhotels.com*
*Special Offer: www.irelandhotels.com/offers*

**B&B from €50.00 to €90.00**
**Suites from €150.00 to €250.00**

*Mailo & Stan Power*
*Joint Proprietors*

29

Activities:

**Closed 24 - 27 December**



B&B Rates are per Person Sharing per Night incl. Breakfast. or Room Rates are per Room per Night - **See also Page 8**

## Belfry Hotel

HOTEL ★★★ MAP 4 L 5

Conduit Lane,
Waterford

Tel: 051-844800 Fax: 051-844814
Email: info@belfryhotel.ie
Web: www.belfryhotel.ie

The Belfry is a family-run hotel that has a special ambience, combining traditional charm with superb modern amenities. Bedrooms are spacious and luxurious. Riada's Restaurant offers a well chosen and varied à la carte menu for dinner, while an extensive bar menu is available daily in the popular and stylish Chapter House Bar. City centre location, close to bus and rail station. Superb range of golf courses nearby. Golf packages available. Please enquire about Facilities for Persons with Mobility Impairment.

Member of Good Food Ireland

*Bookable on www.irelandhotels.com*
*Special Offer: www.irelandhotels.com/offers*

*B&B from €45.00 to €95.00*
*Suites from €130.00 to €240.00*

*Sharon Mansfield*
*General Manager*

61

**Closed 24 - 30 December**

## Waterford City

### Coach House

GUESTHOUSE ★★★ MAP 4 L 5

Butlerstown Castle,
Butlerstown, Cork Road,
Waterford

Tel: 051-384656 Fax: 051-384751
Email: coachhse@iol.ie
Web: www.butlerstowncastle.com

Built during the late 1700's, remodelled by Sir Samuel Ferguson in 1874 and restored in 1992 - retaining many original features - the Coach House offers the best of traditional country home en suite accommodation in a tranquil and unique historical setting (walled cottage garden, 13th century castle ruins on grounds). Situated in countryside, 5 mins from Waterford city which has excellent pubs and restaurants. Michelin recommended.

***Bookable on www.irelandhotels.com***
***Special Offer: www.irelandhotels.com/offers***

**B&B from €55.00 to €55.00**

*Des O'Keeffe*
*Proprietor*

7

**Closed 01 November - 01 April**

### Days Hotel Waterford

HOTEL ★★★ MAP 4 L 5

No 1 The Quay,
Waterford

Tel: 1890-329 329 Fax: 051-877229
Email: res@dayshotelwaterford.com
Web: www.dayshotelwaterford.com

The newly rebranded 130 bedroom hotel has undergone a €5 million refurbishment, transformed to one of Waterford's finest hotels. Overlooking the River Suir, 3 minutes from both bus and train stations and centrally located in Waterford City. Timbertoes Bar offers the perfect pint, an excellent bar menu with live entertainment on most nights. Corporate, golf, family, golden years and many other seasonal packages available. Hotel direct line 051 877 222. Please enquire about Facilities for Persons with Mobility Impairment.

Member of Days Hotels Ireland

***Bookable on www.irelandhotels.com***
***Special Offer: www.irelandhotels.com/offers***

**B&B from €49.00 to €110.00**

*Barry Twomey*
*General Manager*

130

Activities:

**Closed 24 - 27 December**

### Diamond Hill Country House

GUESTHOUSE ★★★ MAP 4 L 5

Slieverue,
Waterford

Tel: 051-832855 Fax: 051-832254
Email: info@stayatdiamondhill.com
Web: www.stayatdiamondhill.com

Situated 2.5km from Waterford City off the Rosslare Waterford Road N25. Convenient to ferries. A long established guesthouse of considerable charm and friendliness, set in its own national award-winning gardens. The house has been extensively refurbished incorporating family heirlooms and antiques resulting in a countryside oasis, a haven of luxury and tranquillity, yet only minutes from the bustling city of Waterford. Recommended by Frommers, Foders, Michelin, AA ♦♦♦♦. Member of Premier Guesthouses. Please enquire about Facilities for Persons with Mobility Impairment.

Member of Premier Guesthouses

***Bookable on www.irelandhotels.com***

**B&B from €35.00 to €45.00**

*Bernard Smith-Lehane*
*Proprietor*

17

**Closed 20 - 26 December**



B&B Rates are per Person Sharing per Night incl. Breakfast. or Room Rates are per Room per Night - See also Page 8

## Dooley's Hotel

HOTEL ★★★ MAP 4 L 5

The Quay,
Waterford

Tel: 051-873531 Fax: 051-870262
Email: hotel@dooleys-hotel.ie
Web: www.dooleys-hotel.ie

The waters of the River Suir swirl past the door of this renowned hotel, which is situated on The Quay in Waterford. Dooley's is an ideal choice for a centrally located hotel, close to all amenities, cultural and business centres. This family owned and managed hotel caters for the corporate/leisure traveller. The hotel has a purpose-built conference centre with full facilities. Enjoy the style and comfort of The New Ship Restaurant and Dry Dock Bar. Dooley's Hotel serving the customer for three generations. 24 hour online booking www.dooleys-hotel.ie. Please enquire about Facilities for Persons with Mobility Impairment.

***An IHF Quality Employer***

Member of Holiday Ireland Hotels

*Bookable on www.irelandhotels.com*
*Special Offer: www.irelandhotels.com/offers*

*B&B from €50.00 to €99.00*

*Margaret & Tina Darrer*
*Directors*

113

*Activities:*

**Closed 25 - 28 December**

## Granville Hotel

HOTEL ★★★ MAP 4 L 5

Meagher Quay,
Waterford

Tel: 051-305555 Fax: 051-305566
Email: stay@granville-hotel.ie
Web: www.granville-hotel.ie

One of Waterford's most prestigious city centre hotels, RAC**** overlooking the River Suir. This family-run hotel is one of Ireland's oldest with significant historical connections. Justly proud of the Granville's heritage, owners Liam and Ann Cusack today vigourously pursue the Granville's long tradition of hospitality, friendliness and comfort. It has been elegantly refurbished, retaining its old world Georgian character. Award-winning Bianconi Restaurant, Thomas Francis Meagher Bar. Bookable now on www.granville-hotel.ie Please enquire about Facilities for Persons with Mobility Impairment.

***An IHF Quality Employer***

Member of Best Western Hotels

*Bookable on www.irelandhotels.com*
*Special Offer: www.irelandhotels.com/offers*

*B&B from €50.00 to €100.00*

*Ann & Liam Cusack*
*Managers / Proprietors*

98

*Activities:*

**Closed 24 - 27 December**

## Ramada Viking Hotel

HOTEL ★★★ MAP 4 L 5

Cork Road,
Waterford

Tel: 051-336933 Fax: 051-336969
Email: info@vikinghotel.ie
Web: www.vikinghotel.ie

Ideally located on the main Cork to Rosslare Road (N25) with extensive free car parking our hotel is the ideal gateway to all that the 'Sunny South East' has to offer. FREE high speed broadband and 11 FREE Sky movie channels are provided in each of our 100 spacious and comfortable bedrooms. Valhalla Restaurant and Asgard Bar both offer a superb variety of food. Please enquire about Facilities for Persons with Mobility Impairment.

*Bookable on www.irelandhotels.com*
*Special Offer: www.irelandhotels.com/offers*

*Room Rate from €79.00 to €159.00*

*Geoff Kinsella*
*General Manager*

100

*Activities:*

**Closed 24 - 26 December**

B&B Rates are per Person Sharing per Night incl. Breakfast.
or Room Rates are per Room per Night - **See also Page 8**

## Waterford City

### Rhu Glenn Country Club Hotel

HOTEL ★★★ MAP 4 L 5


Luffany,
Slieverue,
Waterford

Tel: 051-832242 Fax: 051-832242

Email: info@rhuglennhotel.com

Web: www.rhuglennhotel.com

Built within its own grounds with parking for cars, coaches, etc., the hotel is family-run. Situated on the N25 Rosslare to Waterford Road, convenient to ferries, it offers a superb location whether your pleasure be golfing, fishing, or simply exploring the South East. All rooms are en suite with direct dial phone and multi-channel TV. Our Luffany Restaurant is renowned for its service of fine food. Relax and enjoy our Sliabh Mór lounge bars and the Country Club for ballroom dancing with live entertainment provided by Ireland's top artistes. Please enquire about Facilities for Persons with Mobility Impairment.

***Bookable on www.irelandhotels.com***
***Special Offer: www.irelandhotels.com/offers***

**B&B from €40.00 to €70.00**

*Liam Mooney*
*Proprietor*

30

Activities:

**Closed 24 - 25 December**

### Rice Guesthouse & Batterberry's Bar

GUESTHOUSE ★ MAP 4 L 5


35 & 36 Barrack Street,
Waterford

Tel: 051-371606 Fax: 051-357013

Email: info@riceguesthouse.com

Web: www.riceguesthouse.com

Waterford's premier city centre guesthouse, located 2 minutes from Waterford's City Square Shopping Centre and Waterford Crystal Gallery. Offering our customers hotel accommodation at guesthouse prices. Purpose built in 1997, all rooms en suite with cable TV, direct dial phones & tea/coffee facilities. Full bar and residents' bar, Batterberry's Bar offers ceol and craic with live music 5 nights a week, bar food and the finest Irish hospitality. Tee times arranged for golfers. Midweek and weekend break specials available.

Member of Premier Guesthouses

***Bookable on www.irelandhotels.com***
***Special Offer: www.irelandhotels.com/offers***

**B&B from €40.00 to €55.00**

*John & Jimmy Fitzgerald*

20

Activities:

**Closed 23 - 27 December**

### St. Albans Guesthouse

GUESTHOUSE ★★ MAP 4 L 5


Cork Road,
Waterford

Tel: 051-358171 Fax: 051-358171

Email: stalbansbandb@yahoo.com

Web: www.stalbanswaterford.com

St. Albans is a well established family-run guesthouse. Ideally located minutes walk from Waterford City centre and Waterford Crystal. Our very spacious superbly appointed rooms are all en suite with multi-channel TV, tea/coffee facilities and hairdryer. Secure parking at rear of premises. 4 championship golf courses in vicinity. Horse riding 3km. Tennis courts, swimming pool 2 minutes. Several local beaches and breathtaking scenery. Bus and train station a short distance.
Freephone: UK: 0800 912 3910.
Please enquire about Facilities for Persons with Mobility Impairment.

**B&B from €40.00 to €55.00**

*Helen & Tom Mullally*
*Proprietors*

8

**Closed 18 - 28 December**



B&B Rates are per Person Sharing per Night incl. Breakfast.
or Room Rates are per Room per Night - **See also Page 8**

## Tower Hotel & Leisure Centre

HOTEL ★★★ MAP 4 L 5

The Mall,
Waterford

Tel: 051-862300 Fax: 051-870129
Email: reservations@thw.ie
Web: www.towerhotelwaterford.com

A Tower Group Hotel, with its riverside location in the heart of Waterford City & 139 guest rooms offering every modern amenity, the Tower Hotel is the flagship hotel of the Tower Hotel Group. The Tower Hotel is the ideal base to discover this wonderful city & county, with two restaurants - traditional carvery and award-winning bistro, Adelphi Riverside Bar, leisure centre with 20m pool, extensive conference facilities & private guest car park. Free internet access in each guest bedroom. Special online offers available on www.towerhotelgroup.com. Please enquire about Facilities for Persons with Mobility Impairment.

***An IHF Quality Employer***

Member of Tower Hotel Group

*Bookable on www.irelandhotels.com*
*Special Offer: www.irelandhotels.com/offers*

*B&B from €70.00 to €159.00*

*Alicia Maguire*
*General Manager*

139

*Activities:*

**Closed 24 - 28 December**

## Waterford Castle Hotel & Golf Club

HOTEL ★★★★ MAP 4 L 5

The Island,
Ballinakill,
Waterford

Tel: 051-878203 Fax: 051-879316
Email: info@waterfordcastle.com
Web: www.waterfordcastle.com

Waterford Castle Hotel & Golf Club is uniquely situated on a 310 acre island overlooking the estuary of the River Suir, 3 miles from Waterford City. Access to the island is by a chain linked car ferry. Furnished with antiques and open fireplaces. The 15th century castle combines gracious living of an elegant past with every modern comfort, service and convenience. Own 18 hole championship golf course. Excellent dining experience. Lodges 'Castle Gardens' available to rent 2008.

Member of Best Loved Hotels

*Bookable on www.irelandhotels.com*
*Special Offer: www.irelandhotels.com/offers*

*Room Rate from €195.00 to €380.00*
*Suites from €375.00 to €640.00*

*Gillian Butler*
*General Manager*

19

*Activities:*

**Closed 01 - 31 January**

## Waterford Marina Hotel

HOTEL ★★★ MAP 4 L 5

Canada Street,
Waterford

Tel: 051-856600 Fax: 051-856605
Email: info@waterfordmarinahotel.com
Web: www.waterfordmarinahotel.com

The Waterford Marina Hotel is ideally located in the heart of Waterford City, nestled on the banks of the River Suir, 5 minutes walk from the city centre. 81 superbly appointed en suite guest rooms, all offering the essentials for an enjoyable stay. Relax by the River Suir in our Waterfront Bar and Restaurant. Other facilities include a range of conference suites, our riverside terrace and complimentary on-site parking. Free WiFi installed in all bedrooms, bar, lobby and conference suites.

***An IHF Quality Employer***

*Bookable on www.irelandhotels.com*
*Special Offer: www.irelandhotels.com/offers*

*B&B from €39.00 to €120.00*

*Karen Dollery*
*General Manager*

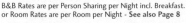

81

*Activities:*

**Closed 19 - 26 December**

## Waterford City / Barntown / Bunclody

### Woodlands Hotel

HOTEL ★★★ MAP 4 L 5

Dunmore Road,
Waterford

Tel: 051-304574 Fax: 051-304575
Email: info@woodlandshotel.ie
Web: www.woodlandshotel.ie

This contemporary hotel offers 47 stylish bedrooms, modern leisure centre (pool, sauna, jacuzzi, steam room, gym), lively bar with regular entertainment, stylish Arbutus Restaurant and air-conditioned conference and banqueting facilities. Our new addition is Caroline's Hair & Beauty Salon offering a wide variety of hair and beauty treatments. Just 3 miles from Waterford's City centre and a short drive from local golf courses and sandy beaches. Please enquire about Facilities for Persons with Mobility Impairment.

Member of Select Hotels of Ireland

***Bookable on www.irelandhotels.com***
***Special Offer: www.irelandhotels.com/offers***

**Room Rate from €109.00 to €189.00**

*Billy Brenner*
*General Manager*

47

Activities:

**Closed 25 - 26 December**

### Stanville Lodge Hotel

HOTEL ★★★ MAP 4 N 6

Barntown,
Co. Wexford

Tel: 053-913 4300 Fax: 053-913 4989
Email: info@stanville.ie
Web: www.stanville.ie

This beautiful family-run hotel, which opened in 2003, just minutes from Wexford town is the ideal getaway, located in the foothills of Fort Mountain, the Stanville Lodge Hotel offers a warm, friendly & relaxed atmosphere. Top quality food and friendly service is assured in O'Nuaills Restaurant, with food served all day in O'Nuaills Bar & Lounge. Please enquire about Facilities for Persons with Mobility Impairment.

***Bookable on www.irelandhotels.com***
***Special Offer: www.irelandhotels.com/offers***

**B&B from €50.00 to €100.00**

*John Likely*
*General Manager*

32

Activities:

**Closed 25 - 27 December**

### Carlton Millrace Hotel & C Spa

HOTEL ★★★★ MAP 8 N 7

Riversedge,
Bunclody,
Co. Wexford

Tel: 053-937 5100 Fax: 053-937 5124
Email: reservations.millrace@carlton.com
Web: www.carltonmillracehotel.com

Located on the edge of the beautiful 800 acre Hall-Dare estate & the River Slaney. This 4**** hotel has 60 well appointed bedrooms including family suites. Lady Lucy's fine dining rooftop restaurant overlooks the picturesque town of Bunclody. The C Spa is a real treasure with 10 treatment suites and dedicated relaxation room with heated loungers. Bunclody is situated on the N80 between Carlow and Enniscorthy, 80 mins drive from Dublin, 45 mins from Rosslare. Conference facilities for up to 350 delegates. Room Reservations
LoCall 1890 288 288.

Member of The Carlton Hotel Group

***Bookable on www.irelandhotels.com***
***Special Offer: www.irelandhotels.com/offers***

**B&B from €70.00 to €135.00**
**Suites from €180.00 to €310.00**

*James O'Brien*
*General Manager*

60

Activities:

**Open All Year**



B&B Rates are per Person Sharing per Night incl. Breakfast.
or Room Rates are per Room per Night - **See also Page 8**

## Courtown Hotel

HOTEL ★★ MAP 8 O 7

Courtown Harbour,
Gorey,
Co. Wexford

Tel: 053-942 5210 Fax: 053-942 5304

Email: info@courtownhotel.com

Web: www.courtownhotel.com

The family-run Courtown Hotel & Leisure Centre is renowned for its friendly atmosphere and excellent cuisine. This is an AA 3*** hotel and features our new bistro V for excellent food in stylish surroundings and a selection of lounge bars. Our Pear Tree beer garden offers food from 1pm to 8pm daily. All rooms are en suite with TV and direct dial telephone. Residents enjoy complimentary use of our leisure facilities which include an indoor heated swimming pool, sauna, jacuzzi & steam room. Entertainment nightly in July & August and at weekends all year round.

**B&B from €40.00 to €85.00**

*Paul & Sandra Kinch*
*Manager/Proprietor*

22

**Closed 01 November - 01 March**

## Harbour House Guesthouse

GUESTHOUSE ★★ MAP 8 O 7

Courtown Harbour,
Courtown, Gorey,
Co. Wexford

Tel: 053-942 5117 Fax: 053-942 5117

Email: stay@harbourhouseguesthouse.com

Web: www.harbourhouseguesthouse.com

Harbour House just off the main Rosslare/Dublin N11 route and only 6km from Gorey is ideally located in the renowned seaside resort of Courtown Harbour. Harbour House is the ideal base for both business and holiday travellers and is central to all amenities and only three minutes from Courtown's sandy beaches. All rooms are en suite. Private car park. Come and enjoy Courtown's new 25m swimming pool. 2 kiddies pools and a 65m water slide all set within 63 acres of woodland with beautiful river walks.

***An IHF Quality Employer***

**B&B from €42.50 to €50.00**

*Donal & Margaret O'Gorman*
*Proprietors*

13

**Closed 31 October - 10 April**



B&B Rates are per Person Sharing per Night incl. Breakfast.
or Room Rates are per Room per Night - **See also Page 8**

## Curracloe / Enniscorthy

### Hotel Curracloe

HOTEL ★★ MAP 4 O 6

Curracloe,
Co. Wexford

Tel: 053-913 7308 Fax: 053-913 7587
Email: hotelcurracloe@eircom.net
Web: www.hotelcurracloe.com

Hotel Curracloe is ideally situated, only five miles from Wexford Town, minutes from Blue/Green Flag beaches and central to golfing, angling, bird-watching, hill walking and horse riding amenities. Our 29 rooms are en suite with modern facilities and our award-winning Blake Restaurant and Tavern Pub serve the best of home produce. The Brent Banqueting Room will cater for every special occasion. Our friendly staff will ensure that Hotel Curracloe is the perfect base for your leisure time in the sunny South East. Please enquire about Facilities for Persons with Mobility Impairment.

**B&B from €40.00 to €65.00**

*John & Margaret Hanrahan*
*Owners*

29

**Open All Year**

### Lemongrove House

GUESTHOUSE ★★★ MAP 4 N 6

Blackstoops,
Enniscorthy,
Co. Wexford

Tel: 053-923 6115 Fax: 053-923 6115
Email: lemongrovehouse@iolfree.ie
Web: www.euroka.com/lemongrove

Elegant country house 1km north of Enniscorthy just off roundabout on Dublin/Rosslare Road (N11). Lemongrove House is set in mature gardens with private parking. All rooms en suite with direct dial phone, TV, hairdryer and tea/coffee making facilities. Recommended by Guide du Routard, AA and other leading guides. Within walking distance of a choice of restaurants, pubs and new pool and leisure centre. Locally we have beaches, golf, horse riding, walking and quad track. Please enquire about Facilities for Persons with Mobility Impairment.

**B&B from €35.00 to €40.00**

*Colm & Ann McGibney*
*Owners*

9

**Closed 20 - 29 December**

### Pines Country House Hotel

HOTEL ★★ MAP 4 N 6

Camolin,
Enniscorthy,
Co. Wexford

Tel: 053-938 3600 Fax: 053-938 3588
Email: thepines@eircom.net
Web: www.pinescountryhousehotel.com

Family-run hotel with award-winning resturant, European and real Indian food. Top class accommodation, state of the art gym, sauna, steam room, plunge pool, pony trekking, hill walking, birdwatching. Nearby Courtown and Curracloe beaches, historic Ferns, heritage park, quad trekking, fishing, music and on-site bouncy castle/slide, horse riding, trampolines and sunshine. Music on Saturdays. Please enquire about Facilities for Persons with Mobility Impairment.

***Bookable on www.irelandhotels.com***
***Special Offer: www.irelandhotels.com/offers***

**B&B from €40.00 to €75.00**

*Frank Murhill*
*Director Manager*

11

*Activities:* ✓

**Open All Year**



B&B Rates are per Person Sharing per Night incl. Breakfast.
or Room Rates are per Room per Night - **See also Page 8**

### Riverside Park Hotel and Leisure Club

HOTEL ★★★ MAP 4 N 6

The Promenade,
Enniscorthy,
Co. Wexford

Tel: 053-923 7800 Fax: 053-923 7900
Email: info@riversideparkhotel.com
Web: www.riversideparkhotel.com

Nestling along the scenic banks of the River Slaney, the Riverside Park Hotel and Leisure Club is an ideal base for touring the treasures of the sunny South East. With a choice of two superb restaurants, The Moorings and The Alamo, Tex-Mex at its best. A luxurious bar with spectacular views. Relax and unwind in our 15m indoor swimming pool, sauna, steam room, jacuzzi and gym. Please enquire about Facilities for Persons with Mobility Impairment.

*Bookable on www.irelandhotels.com*
*Special Offer: www.irelandhotels.com/offers*

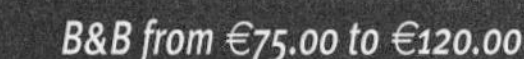

**B&B from €75.00 to €120.00**

*Jim Maher*
*General Manager*

60

Activities:

**Closed 24 - 26 December**

### Treacy's Hotel

HOTEL ★★★ MAP 4 N 6

Templeshannon,
Enniscorthy,
Co. Wexford

Tel: 053-923 7798 Fax: 053-923 7733
Email: info@treacyshotel.com
Web: www.treacyshotel.com

Situated in the heart of beautiful Enniscorthy, Treacy's Hotel is the ideal location for both excitement and relaxation. Boasting two restaurants, European and Thai, and the Temple Bar serving gourmet bar food daily. Live entertainment nightly and Benedicts superpub provides entertainment at weekends. A range of activities can be organised in the hotel for you. Golf, Quad Biking and Murder Mystery weekends throughout the year. Only 15 minutes from Blue Flag beaches. Treacys Hotel undergoing major refurbishment Jan/Feb 2008.

*Bookable on www.irelandhotels.com*
*Special Offer: www.irelandhotels.com/offers*

**B&B from €55.00 to €95.00**

*Anton Treacy*

48

**Closed 24 - 26 December**

### Horse and Hound Hotel

HOTEL ★★ MAP 4 N 5

Ballinaboola,
Foulksmills,
Co. Wexford

Tel: 051-428323 Fax: 051-428471
Email: info@horseandhoundinn.ie
Web: www.horseandhoundinn.ie

The Horse and Hound Hotel is a family-run hotel in picturesque Ballinaboola, a small village on the N25 from Rosslare. Accommodation is provided in 27 tastefully decorated guest rooms. Catering for all needs - from private parties and weddings to conferences. A haven for weary tourists or busy delegate. Food served all day in our renowned restaurant. You are sure of a friendly welcome from the Murphy family and their professional staff.

**B&B from €55.00 to €70.00**

*Christy & Brendan Murphy*

27

**Closed 25 December**

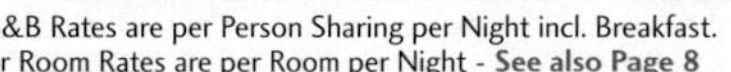

B&B Rates are per Person Sharing per Night incl. Breakfast.
or Room Rates are per Room per Night - **See also Page 8**

## Gorey

### Amber Springs Hotel and Health Spa

HOTEL ★★★★ MAP 807

Wexford Road,
Gorey,
Co. Wexford

Tel: 053-948 4000 Fax: 053-948 4494
Email: info@amberspringshotel.ie
Web: www.amberspringshotel.ie

A Redmond Hotel Group member & sister hotel to Ashdown Park Hotel, the newest 4**** luxury hotel in Gorey, Amber Springs Hotel & Health Spa is centrally located only walking distance from both the train station & town centre. Offering 69 luxurious spacious guest rooms with 11 executive suites, Kelbys Bistro, Brookes Bar, state of the art conference and banqueting facilities, fully equiped leisure centre & Cocoon Health & Beauty Spa. Complimentary car parking. Abundance of historical, cultural & sporting activities nearby. Please enquire about Facilities for Persons with Mobility Impairment.

*Bookable on www.irelandhotels.com*
*Special Offer: www.irelandhotels.com/offers*

**B&B from €85.00 to €115.00**
**Suites from €220.00 to €280.00**

*Sandra Wogan*
*General Manager*

80

*Activities:*

**Closed 23 - 26 December**

### Ashdown Park Hotel Conference & Leisure Centre

HOTEL ★★★★ MAP 807

Coach Road,
Gorey,
Co. Wexford

Tel: 053-948 0500 Fax: 053-948 0777
Email: info@ashdownparkhotel.com
Web: www.ashdownparkhotel.com

Part of the Redmond Hotel Group and sister of the Amber Springs. The Ashdown Park has 79 beautifully appointed guest rooms and suites, each tastefully designed. Enjoy the food on offer all day or just relax with regular live entertainment. Facilities include conference & banqueting facilities, the award-winning Rowan Tree Restaurant, Ivy & Coach Bars, Leisure Club & Beauty Studio and complimentary car park. All public areas are wheelchair friendly. The Ashdown Park Hotel has been awarded RAC **** AA **** ITB****.

***An IHF Quality Employer***

*Bookable on www.irelandhotels.com*
*Special Offer: www.irelandhotels.com/offers*

**B&B from €90.00 to €135.00**

*Liam Moran*
*General Manager*

79

*Activities:*

**Closed 24 - 26 December**

### Marlfield House Hotel

HOTEL ★★★★ MAP 807

Gorey,
Co. Wexford

Tel: 053-942 1124 Fax: 053-942 1572
Email: info@marlfieldhouse.ie
Web: www.marlfieldhouse.com

This fine Regency period house is set in 36 acres of grounds and filled with antiques. The Bowe family opened its doors to guests in 1978 and has maintained an outstanding reputation for food, comfort and service ever since. The 20 bedrooms are filled with antiques, paintings and flowers and all have marble bathrooms. There are six sumptuous state rooms overlooking the lake. Member of Relais & Chateaux, AA Red Star and RAC Gold Ribbon. Highly acclaimed conservatory restaurant. Please enquire about Facilities for Persons with Mobility Impairment.

***An IHF Quality Employer***
Member of Relais et Chateaux

*Bookable on www.irelandhotels.com*
*Special Offer: www.irelandhotels.com/offers*

**B&B from €115.00 to €275.00**

*Mary Bowe*
*Proprietor*

20

**Closed 17 December - 26 January**



B&B Rates are per Person Sharing per Night incl. Breakfast. or Room Rates are per Room per Night - See also Page 8

## Seafield Hotel

HOTEL MAP 8 O 7

Ballymoney,
Gorey,
Co. Wexford

Tel: 053-942 4000 Fax: 053-942 4050
Email: reservations@seafieldhotel.com
Web: www.seafieldhotel.com

Built to a 4**** specification. The stunning Seafield Hotel & Oceo Spa is set on 160 acres of lush parkland grounds just an hour south of county Dublin on the sands of the Ballymoney shore. Designed by Italian architect Francesco Bria in a clean contemporary style, natural daylight floods through & awe inspiring sea views have been maximized. This four star venue has something for everyone with its fabulous hotel, exquisite Spa & championship 18 hole golf course as designed by Peter McEvoy. Please enquire about Facilities for Persons with Mobility Impairment.

***Bookable on www.irelandhotels.com***
*Special Offer: www.irelandhotels.com/offers*

***B&B from €85.00 to €120.00***

*Rita Barcoe*
*Operations Director*

265

*Activities:*

**Open All Year**

## Hotel Saltees

HOTEL ★★ MAP 4 N 5

Kilmore Quay,
Co. Wexford

Tel: 053-912 9601 Fax: 053-912 9602
Email: info@hotelsaltees.ie
Web: www.hotelsaltees.ie

Hotel Saltees is situated in the picturesque fishing village of Kilmore Quay. Renowned for its thatched cottages and maritime flavour, it is located just 22km from Wexford Town and 19km from the international port of Rosslare. Offering excellent accommodation, with all rooms en suite, TV, telephone and all well designed to cater for families. Le Saffron Restaurant is renowned for its relaxed atmosphere where diners can afford good food at their own leisurely pace. Eurotoque chef Dominique Dayot specialises in modern and French cuisine. Please enquire about Facilities for Persons with Mobility Impairment.

***B&B from €60.00 to €80.00***

*Dominique Dayot*
*Executive Chef*

10

*Activities:*

**Closed 25 December**

## Sean Og's Hotel & Holiday Cottages

HOTEL MAP 8 O 7

Kilmuckridge,
Gorey,
Co. Wexford

Tel: 053-913 0982 Fax: 053-913 0163
Email: info@seanogs.ie
Web: www.seanogs.ie

Built to a 3*** specification. Sean Og's Hotel & Holiday Cottages are the ideal venue for Summer, Autumn or indeed Winter vacations or breaks with stunning beaches, fishing and walking on the doorstep. At Sean Og's Hotel there are 20 luxurious en suite bedrooms including 10 large family bedrooms opened in June 2007. For golfers we are the ideal location with more than seven outstanding courses within 40 minute drive, while some are only minutes away. Please enquire about Facilities for Persons with Mobility Impairment.

***B&B from €50.00 to €70.00***

*Graham Bell*
*Manager*

20

**Closed 24 - 25 December**

B&B Rates are per Person Sharing per Night incl. Breakfast.
or Room Rates are per Room per Night - **See also Page 8**

## New Ross / Newbawn / Rosslare

### Brandon House Hotel, Health Club & Spa

HOTEL ★★★ MAP 4 M 6

New Ross,
Co. Wexford

Tel: 051-421703 Fax: 051-421567
Email: reception@brandonhousehotel.ie
Web: www.brandonhousehotel.ie

A de luxe country manor house set in landscaped grounds with panoramic views overlooking the River Barrow. Dine in the Gallery Restaurant or relax in the Library Bar. All rooms are elegantly furnished. Luxurious health & leisure club with 20m pool, sauna, steam room, jacuzzi, fully equipped gym, kiddies pool & hydrotherapy grotto. An ideal base for touring the sunny South East. Conference and banqueting for up to 400 people. Solas Croí Eco Spa open from September 2007. This unique structure will provide Tri - Dosha ayurvedic natural therapies & 5 star Kerstin Florian Products.

***An IHF Quality Employer***

*Bookable on www.irelandhotels.com*
*Special Offer: www.irelandhotels.com/offers*

**Room Rate from €79.00 to €189.00**
**Suites from €99.00 to €209.00**

*Garth MacKenzie*
*General Manager*

79

*Activities:*

**Closed 24 - 27 December**

### Cedar Lodge Hotel & Restaurant

HOTEL ★★★★ MAP 4 N 6

Carrigbyrne,
Newbawn, (Near New Ross),
Co. Wexford

Tel: 051-428386 Fax: 051-428222
Email: cedarlodge@eircom.net
Web: www.prideofeirehotels.com

Charming boutique country hotel located in a picturesque setting, 30 minutes drive from Rosslare Port on the N25 New Ross Road. All bedrooms en suite with direct dial phone and TV. The restaurant, which concentrates on freshly prepared produce, is noted for its good food. Recommended by Michelin, Good Hotel Guide, AA. Forest walks nearby. Golf, horse riding, JF Kennedy Park, county museum, heritage park and sandy beaches within easy driving distance. Please enquire about Facilities for Persons with Mobility Impairment.

*Bookable on www.irelandhotels.com*
*Special Offer: www.irelandhotels.com/offers*

**B&B from €75.00 to €100.00**

*Tom Martin*
*Proprietor*

28

**Closed 20 December - 01 February**

### Churchtown House

GUESTHOUSE ★★★★ MAP 4 O 5

Tagoat,
Rosslare,
Co. Wexford

Tel: 053-913 2555 Fax: 053-913 2577
Email: info@churchtownhouse.com
Web: www.churchtownhouse.com

This delightful award-winning Queen Anne Country House, set in its own 8 acres; offers a peaceful escape from the bustling world. 1/2 mile from the N25, Rosslare Harbour, Wexford, Cork, Dublin Road, 2 miles from the renowned seaside resort of Rosslare Strand. Superior and ground floor rooms available. A non-smoking house. Country house style dinner offered at 7.30pm - 8pm commences with complimentary sherry, Tuesday to Saturday inclusive. Good wines. Please book by noon. AA 5 Red Diamonds. Welcome to our "Special Home".

Member of Manor House Hotels

*Bookable on www.irelandhotels.com*
*Special Offer: www.irelandhotels.com/offers*

**B&B from €55.00 to €75.00**

*Austin & Patricia Cody*
*Owners*

12

**Closed 30 November - 01 March**



B&B Rates are per Person Sharing per Night incl. Breakfast.
or Room Rates are per Room per Night - **See also Page 8**

## Crosbie Cedars Hotel

HOTEL ★★★ MAP 405

Rosslare,
Co. Wexford

Tel: 053-913 2124 Fax: 053-913 2243
Email: info@crosbiecedarshotel.com
Web: www.crosbiecedarshotel.com

In Rosslare resort, only 3 minutes from the beach, and 5 minutes from Rosslare Golf Course, Crosbie Cedars Hotel provides a warm welcome with traditional hospitality. All rooms en suite with TV, radio, direct dial telephone, hairdryer and tea/coffee facilities. Restaurant menus of excellent quality and variety. Extensive bar menu. Entertainment weekends and nightly July & August. Available nearby tennis, watersports, childrens' playground, crazy golf. 15 minutes to ferry. Please enquire about Facilities for Persons with Mobility Impairment.

*Bookable on www.irelandhotels.com*

**B&B from €50.00 to €75.00**

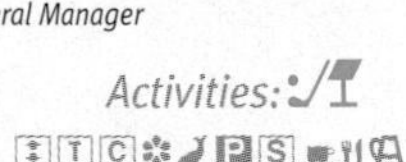

*Anthony Spencer*
*General Manager*

34

*Activities:*

**Closed 03 January - 14 February**

## Danby Lodge Hotel

HOTEL ★★★ MAP 405

Rosslare Road,
Killinick, Rosslare,
Co. Wexford

Tel: 053-915 8191 Fax: 053-915 8191
Email: info@danbylodge.ie
Web: www.danbylodge.com

Under new management, a friendly & warm welcome awaits you at Danby Lodge Hotel. Former home of Francis Danby, renowned international artist, built around 1730 and situated in the sunny South East. Located 5 minutes from Rosslare Euro Port & Wexford's most beautiful sandy beaches and only 10 minutes from Wexford Town. Our restaurant is well know and has earned itself a reputation for its excellence in food & service. We offer a wide range of conference & banqueting facilities & can accommodate up to 350 delegates. A perfect setting for a special wedding day.

**B&B from €40.00 to €70.00**

*Gavin McGuire*
*General Manager*

29

*Activities:*

**Closed 22 - 30 December**

## Kelly's Resort Hotel & Spa

HOTEL ★★★★ MAP 405

Rosslare,
Co. Wexford

Tel: 053-913 2114 Fax: 053-913 2222
Email: info@kellys.ie
Web: www.kellys.ie

Since 1895 the Kelly Family has personally overseen this truly fine beach side resort hotel. Locally produced food, specially selected wines and nightly entertainment are very much part of the tradition as well as tennis, snooker, bowls, croquet and a choice of local championship golf courses. Pamper yourself and relax in our luxurious 14,000 square foot 'SeaSpa', incorporating thermal spa, 12 treatment rooms, seaweed bath and serail Mud Chamber. Focus on health and well-being in our Aqua Club and gym or come for our special activity midweek breaks in Spring and Autumn.

***An IHF Quality Employer***

*Bookable on www.irelandhotels.com*
*Special Offer: www.irelandhotels.com/offers*

**B&B from €99.00 to €132.00**
**Suites from €352.00 to €462.00**

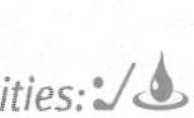

*William J Kelly*
*Manager / Director*

118

*Activities:*

**Closed 09 December - 15 February**

B&B Rates are per Person Sharing per Night incl. Breakfast.
or Room Rates are per Room per Night - **See also Page 8**

## Rosslare Harbour

### Best Western Hotel Rosslare

HOTEL ★★★ MAP 4 0 5

Rosslare Harbour,
Co. Wexford

Tel: 053-913 3110 Fax: 053-913 3386
Email: reservations@hotelrosslare.ie
Web: www.hotelrosslare.ie

Situated on the cliff-top overlooking Rosslare Harbour, Best Western Hotel Rosslare boasts stunning views of the bay and Irish Sea. 25 en suite bedrooms, many with sea views and private balconies located 2 minutes from Rosslare Europort, ideal for ferry travel. The historic town of Wexford with its quaint streets, boutiques and arts & crafts outlets is only 15 minutes away. Best Western Hotel Rosslare offers the perfect location for business, leisure and family breaks all year round.

*Bookable on www.irelandhotels.com*
*Special Offer: www.irelandhotels.com/offers*

**B&B from €60.00 to €75.00**

*John Walsh*
*General Manager*

25

**Closed 24 - 25 December**

### Ferryport House

GUESTHOUSE ★★★ MAP 4 0 5

Rosslare Harbour,
Co. Wexford

Tel: 053-913 3933 Fax: 053-916 1707
Email: info@ferryporthouse.com
Web: www.ferryporthouse.com

400m from Rosslare Euro Port & train station.16 beautifully appointed en suite bedrooms. Fantastic new restaurant opened which boasts fresh fish dishes from Kilmore Quay and fuses authentic cooking from the Far East. Fusion Restaurant is a unique dining experience. Local amenities include Blue Flag Beach, local golf courses, horse riding and fishing. Please enquire about Facilities for Persons with Mobility Impairment.

**B&B from €30.00 to €50.00**

*Billy & Patricia Roche*
*Proprietors*

16

**Closed 24 - 27 December**

### Harbour View Hotel

HOTEL ★★★ MAP 4 0 5

Rosslare Harbour,
Co. Wexford

Tel: 053-916 1450 Fax: 053-916 1455
Email: info@harbourviewhotel.ie
Web: www.harbourviewhotel.ie

Overlooking Rosslare Euro Port, this charming hotel is situated ideally on the N25 within walking distance of the ferry terminal, train and bus stations. It boasts 24 beautifully appointed guest rooms, all en suite with TV, coffee/tea making facilities, hairdryer, telephone and safe. You can enjoy the finest Asian and European cuisine in the exquisite surroundings of the newly refurbished Seasons Chinese Restaurant or the warm atmosphere of the Mail Boat Bar. Local amenities include golf, angling, horse riding and sandy beaches. Please enquire about Facilities for Persons with Mobility Impairment.

*Bookable on www.irelandhotels.com*
*Special Offer: www.irelandhotels.com/offers*

**B&B from €45.00 to €75.00**

*James & Grace Chan*

24

**Open All Year**



B&B Rates are per Person Sharing per Night incl. Breakfast.
or Room Rates are per Room per Night - See also Page 8

## St. Helens Hotel (formerly Great Southern Hotel)

HOTEL ★★★ MAP 4 O 5

Rosslare Harbour,
Co. Wexford

Tel: 053-913 3233 Fax: 053-913 3543
Email: res@sthelenshotel.ie
Web: www.sthelenshotel.ie

In Rosslare, a favourite resort, St. Helens Hotel provides a warm welcome with traditional hospitality. The hotel is beautifully situated on a cliff-top overlooking Rosslare Harbour. All rooms are en suite with TV, radio, hairdryer and tea/coffee facilities. Enjoy the leisure centre with indoor swimming pool, jacuzzi, steam room, the comfortable lounges and excellent food of the Mariner's Restaurant.

***An IHF Quality Employer***

**Room Rate from €79.00 to €160.00**

*Eoin O'Sullivan*
*General Manager*

100

*Activities:*

**Closed 30 November - 15 February**

## Faythe Guest House

GUESTHOUSE ★★★ MAP 4 O 6

The Faythe,
Swan View,
Wexford

Tel: 053-912 2249 Fax: 053-912 1680
Email: faythhse@iol.ie
Web: www.faytheguesthouse.com

Family-run guesthouse in a quiet part of the town centre, is built on the grounds of a former castle of which one wall remains today. All rooms refurbished recently to the highest standard. Some of our rooms overlook Wexford Harbour. All rooms have bathroom en suite, colour TV, DVD player, direct dial phone, clock radios and tea/coffee facilities. Rosslare Ferry Port is only 15 minutes drive (early breakfast on request). We also have a large private car park. We are a non smoking house. Please enquire about Facilities for Persons with Mobility Impairment.

Member of Premier Guesthouses

*Bookable on www.irelandhotels.com*
*Special Offer: www.irelandhotels.com/offers*

**B&B from €30.00 to €50.00**

*Damian & Siobhan Lynch*
*Proprietors*

10

**Closed 25 - 27 December**

## Ferrycarrig Hotel

HOTEL ★★★★ MAP 4 N 6

Ferrycarrig,
Wexford

Tel: 053-912 0999 Fax: 053-912 0982
Email: info@ferrycarrighotel.com
Web: www.ferrycarrighotel.ie

Renowned Ferrycarrig Hotel has one of the most spectacular locations of any hotel in Ireland, with every room providing memorable views of the River Slaney Estuary. Offers contemporary luxurious, spacious bedrooms, award-winning service, excellent waterfront dining, award-winning waterfront bar, 5***** health and fitness club with 20m pool, on site Beauty and Wellness Lodge and hair salon. Abundance of historic, cultural and sporting amenities, including golf are nearby. Excellent conference facilities for 4 - 400 delegates. Please enquire about Facilities for Persons with Mobility Impairment.

***An IHF Quality Employer***

*Bookable on www.irelandhotels.com*
*Special Offer: www.irelandhotels.com/offers*

**B&B from €80.00 to €500.00**

*Jeanette O'Keeffe*
*General Manager*

102

*Activities:*

**Open All Year**

B&B Rates are per Person Sharing per Night incl. Breakfast.
or Room Rates are per Room per Night - **See also Page 8**

## Wexford Town

### Newbay Country House

GUESTHOUSE ★★★ MAP 406

Newbay,
Wexford

Tel: 053-914 2779 Fax: 053-914 6318
Email: newbay@newbayhouse.com
Web: www.newbaycountryhouse.com

Newbay Country House is a beautiful Georgian guesthouse in an idyllic countryside setting, yet only 5 minutes from the historic town of Wexford. Most bedrooms boast traditional 4 poster beds as well as views of the well manicured gardens. We are fully licensed and serve a la carte and bar food 7 days a week. AA rosette restaurant with piano music at weekends. Newbay Casino Club open daily. Also closed 31 December - 01 January. Please enquire about Facilities for Persons with Mobility Impairment.

**B&B from €65.00 to €85.00**
**Suites from €130.00 to €170.00**

Alex Scallan
General Manager

11

**Closed 25 December**

### Quality Hotel & Leisure Club Wexford

HOTEL ★★★ MAP 406

Ballindinas,
Barntown,
Wexford

Tel: 053-917 2000 Fax: 053-917 2001
Email: info.wexford@qualityhotels.ie
Web: www.qualitywexford.com

Superb 3*** modern hotel with 107 generously sized rooms including family, interconnecting and balcony rooms. Great restaurant and lively bar with entertainment at the weekends and during summer. Free WiFi in all public areas and excellently equipped leisure club and spa available. Supervised crèche and outdoor playground, new 18 hole crazy golf course onsite. 4 meeting rooms, perfect for all your conference needs.

***An IHF Quality Employer***
Member of Quality Hotels

***Bookable on www.irelandhotels.com***
***Special Offer: www.irelandhotels.com/offers***

**B&B from €49.00 to €109.00**

Rory Fitzpatrick
General Manager

107

Activities:

**Closed 24 - 26 December**

### Riverbank House Hotel

HOTEL ★★★ MAP 406

The Bridge,
Wexford

Tel: 053-912 3611 Fax: 053-912 3342
Email: info@riverbankhousehotel.com
Web: www.riverbankhousehotel.com

The Riverbank House Hotel commands magnificent views of the old Viking town, the River Slaney and the miles of golden beach surrounding Wexford. The hotel boasts an excellent à la carte menu, delicious bar food together with an exciting wine list. Benefiting from its own private car park, the hotel offers easy access to five of the best golf courses in the South East, sea angling sites and shooting - ensuring that whatever your stay, business or leisure, it will be most enjoyable. Conference facilities available. Please enquire about Facilities for Persons with Mobility Impairment.

***Bookable on www.irelandhotels.com***
***Special Offer: www.irelandhotels.com/offers***

**B&B from €45.00 to €110.00**

Colm Campbell
General Manager

23

**Closed 25 December**

B&B Rates are per Person Sharing per Night incl. Breakfast.
or Room Rates are per Room per Night - See also Page 8

## St. George Guest House

GUESTHOUSE ★★ MAP 406

Georges Street,
Wexford

Tel: 053-914 3474 Fax: 053-912 4814
Email: info@stgeorgeguesthouse.com
Web: www.stgeorgeguesthouse.com

Under new management. We are 3 minutes' walk from town centre and bus station. All our bedrooms are en suite and have thermostatically controlled heating. Wireless internet access available. Private lock up car parking free of charge. Our varied breakfast menu proves popular with customers. Credit card facilities available. Michael's staff will be available to help make your stay most enjoyable. Please enquire about Facilities for Persons with Mobility Impairment.

*B&B from €35.00 to €45.00*

*Michael Power*

9

Closed 24 December - 02 January

## Talbot Hotel Conference and Leisure Centre

HOTEL ★★★★ MAP 406

On The Quay,
Wexford Town

Tel: 053-912 2566 Fax: 053-912 3377
Email: sales@talbothotel.ie
Web: www.talbothotel.ie

Overlooking the quay in the heart of Wexford town, the Talbot dates back to 1905 and offers all that is best in traditional style and hospitality. Luxuriously appointed guest rooms, Ballast Bank Bar & Grill with live music weekly. Award-winning Oyster Lane Restaurant, Conference & Banqueting Centre, Quay Leisure Centre, Essence Nail and Beauty Therapy. Complimentary car parking. Enjoy hospitality at its best, upgrade to the Talbot Hotel, a locally owned and managed hotel. Please enquire about Facilities for Persons with Mobility Impairment.

***An IHF Quality Employer***

Member of Talbot Hotel Group

***Bookable on www.irelandhotels.com***
***Special Offer: www.irelandhotels.com/offers***

*B&B from €55.00 to €95.00*

*Declan Moriarty*
*General Manager*

101

7

*Activities:*

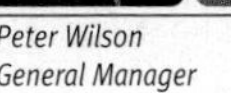

Closed 23 - 26 December

## Whites of Wexford

HOTEL ★★★★ MAP 406

Abbey Street,
Wexford

Tel: 053-912 2311 Fax: 053-914 5000
Email: info@whitesofwexford.ie
Web: www.whitesofwexford.ie

Whites of Wexford offers guests a truly world class hotel experience with 157 bedrooms & luxury suites. Centrally located in Wexford Town, it is the ideal base for touring the sunny South East. Our facilities include our Tranquillity Spa, leisure club & Cryotherapy Clinic. We cater for all palates including business lunch, afternoon tea or a romantic meal for two in our Terrace Restaurant, Library Bar or La Speranza Café Bar. The hotel also includes an outdoor courtyard to dine al fresco, extensive conference facilities, panoramic views & underground car parking.

***An IHF Quality Employer***

Member of Select Hotels of Ireland

***Bookable on www.irelandhotels.com***
***Special Offer: www.irelandhotels.com/offers***

*B&B from €65.00 to €105.00*
*Suites from €250.00 to €298.00*

*Peter Wilson*
*General Manager*

157

*Activities:*

Closed 24 - 26 December

## Wexford Town

### Whitford House Hotel Health & Leisure Club

HOTEL ★★★ MAP 4 N 5

New Line Road,
Wexford

Tel: 053-914 3444 Fax: 053-914 6399
Email: info@whitford.ie
Web: www.whitford.ie

One of Ireland's leading family-run hotels situated 2km from Wexford Town. Renowned for hospitality and luxury accommodation. Experience our multi award-winning Seasons Restaurant or alternatively, enjoy the Forthside Bar/Bistro which has earned the prestigious Dining Pub of the Year award or choose al fresco dining. Music 6 nights peak season. Our superb award-winning state of the art leisure club is simply awe inspiring. Kiddies outdoor play area & video room in season. Enjoy the ultimate relaxation in our beauty treatment rooms. Whitford, where hospitality is a tradition.

*Bookable on www.irelandhotels.com*
*Special Offer: www.irelandhotels.com/offers*

**B&B from €55.00 to €109.00**

*The Whitty Family*

36

TC❀⌂U♪PS ▪ 🍴 ▫ I

**Closed 24 - 26 December**

B&B Rates are per Person Sharing per Night incl. Breakfast. or Room Rates are per Room per Night - See also Page 8

# DUBLIN & IRELAND EAST

**For Detailed Maps of this Region See Pages 477-492**

**Each Hotel or Guesthouse has a Map Reference to these detailed maps under their photograph.**

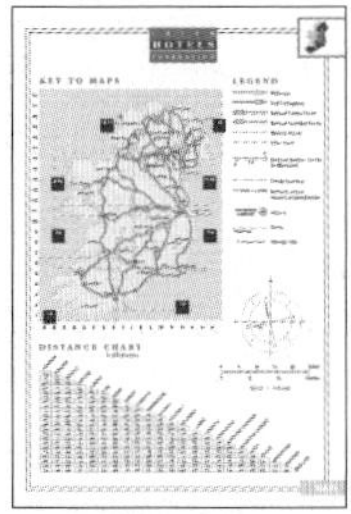

**See page 477 for map with access points and driving distances**

# DUBLIN & IRELAND EAST

Feast your senses on bewitching scenery, fantastic city life, sensational sporting events and compelling historical sights.

The republic's capital city **Dublin** lies at the heart of a region that enchants the visitor with a selection of lakes, rivers and stretches of coastline. Dublin is usually the first port of call for visitors and this energetic, youthful city pulsates with a compelling mix of history, culture, hip bars and pubs, elegant architecture, great shopping and some of the country's most sophisticated restaurants. Cosmopolitan and diverse, Dublin is now one of Europe's top urban hotspots.

Ireland's capital is steeped in history and youthful energy. Dublin is a city where the charming and cosmopolitan converge in delightful diversity. Medieval, Georgian and modern architecture provide a backdrop to this friendly bustling port. Attractions are many, from castles, museums and art galleries to the lively spirit of Temple Bar. As one of the oldest cities in Europe, Dublin provides you with a multitude of cultural riches from the ancient to the ultra-modern and from history, architecture and literature to the performing arts. Dublin has lively pedestrian shopping streets at the heart of the city, alive with buskers and street performers, and there are a number of huge shopping centres in the outskirts offering excellent choice all under one roof, or go further a field to the surrounding towns and villages where you'll find boutiques and craft shops. Rich culture, gourmet cuisine, lively pubs, fabulous shopping, music for all, and plenty of sport are just some of the experiences Dublin has to offer. There has never been a better time to visit Dublin! Visit the official online tourist office for Dublin www.visitdublin.com. The Dublin pass offers the visitor the best in attraction, sightseeing, shopping, service and restaurant offers, all in one complete package. The purchase price of the pass covers entrance to over thirty of Dublin's top attraction and gives access to over twenty five special offers, added value and preferential rates at selected venues, theatres, retail outlets, restaurants, transport and tours. For more information see **www.dublinpass.ie**

Ireland East & Dublin will shower you with friendship and unforgettable memories and your adventures begin now…

Beyond Dublin, the east of Ireland tells a different story with the counties of Cavan, Kildare, Laois, Longford, Louth, Offaly, Meath, Monaghan, Westmeath and Wicklow offering a contrasting slice of life. This region is famed for its rich natural charms, ancient sites of Newgrange and Clonmacnoise, top golfing and world-renowned horseracing. The county of Kildare, in particular, is home to some of the world's finest thoroughbreds and of course the 2006 Ryder Cup.

But what really defines the east is the unspoilt countryside. With glistening lakes, tranquil rivers, authentic rural life, scenic pastureland, rolling hills and forest parks, this area is a haven for outdoors enthusiasts with cycling, watersports, walking, angling, golfing, horseriding and cruising in plentiful supply.

Cruising, fishing, golfing and equestrian enthusiasts should look no further than **Laois** and **Offaly**. The heritage town of Tullamore has put Offaly firmly on the map as a short break location and from here the ancient monastic site of Clonmacnoise, and of course the famous Tullamore Dew Heritage Centre, can be visited. For those who enjoy country walks and visiting gardens, Laois provides both. Tranquillity reigns along the banks of the Grand Canal at Vicarstown or the walking routes of the Slieve Blooms. Splendid gardens surround the Gandon House at Emo or the Lutyens Gardens at Heywood.

**Kildare**, host of the prestigious international Ryder Cup, is also home of the Irish horse. The county boasts three of the country's premier race courses as well as the Irish National Stud, Japanese and St. Fiachra's Gardens. Other attractions include Castletown House, Leixlip Castle, Ballindoolin Gardens and Mondello International Motor Race Course. While neighbouring **Wicklow**, known as the Garden of Ireland, contains outstanding scenery of mountains, valleys, lakes and coastlines. Renowned for its walking trails, The Wicklow Way is one of the most famous. The ancient monastic site of Glendalough, Powerscourt Gardens, Mount Usher Gardens, Wicklow Gaol and Parnell's Avondale House are some of the many attractions well worth a visit.

The royal county of **Meath** has some of the most spectacular attractions in the country including the passage Graves at Newgrange, the historic Trim Castle and the famous Hills of Tara and Slane. The vibrant towns of Navan, Trim and Kells provide the ideal base for touring. **Louth** also has a rich medieval past. The town of Dundalk has connections with the mythical hero Cuchulainn. It is a vibrant shopping town and has a newly refurbished Town Hall & Basement Gallery, an award-winning County Museum and the magnificent St. Patrick's Cathedral that dates back to 1837. Drogheda, on the River Boyne, has many fascinating buildings including St. Laurence's Gate, Milmount Motte and Martello Tower. The relics of St. Oliver Plunkett, martyred in 1681, are preserved in St. Peter's Church. The heritage town of Carlingford displays its past in King John's Castle and the interpretive centre.

**Cavan** is known as the Lake County. Discover the mystery and magic of the Lake County – a county with an ancient and colourful heritage. Come for a weekend, a week or longer and discover that Cavan is a fun place to visit. Buzzing with friendly people, lively towns and villages, spectacular scenery, a vibrant arts and theatre scene, walks, cycle routes, museums, heritage centres, sparkling lakes, fishing, cruising and activities, Cavan is a popular destination. Ireland's longest river – the mighty River Shannon rises in Dowra, Co. Cavan and forms part of the Shannon Erne Waterway. Why not hire a cruiser and meander your way through the longest navigable waterway in Europe. There is no better place to start than Cavan...

**Monaghan** has a landscape you can reach out and touch. It resounds with the poetry of Patrick Kavanagh. The renowned poet is celebrated in the Patrick Kavanagh Rural and Literary Resource Centre in Inniskeen – a must for anyone interested in the poet's life and work. Monaghan has long been known as an angler's paradise and with this attraction and so many more it is well worth a visit. There are several walking routes in the Sliabh Beagh area. These include the Sliabh Beagh Way, a 46km long distance walk, way marked from St. Patrick's Chair & Well in Co. Tyrone, entering Co. Monaghan at Lough More, going over Bragan Mountain, winding its way through Tully Forest and aptly ending at Donagh. There are also 36 loop walks, throughout the Sliabh Beagh region, all of which are way marked and vary in length from 4km – 15km. these routes take the walker through a variety of landscapes.

Counties **Longford** and **Westmeath** with their rivers, lakes and canal ensure many watersports are enjoyed here as well as top class angling with all species of coarse fish and brown trout. An area noted for its history and varied heritage, visitor attractions include the Heritage Centre in Ardagh, Corlea Trackway near Kenagh, the Bog Oak Sculptures in Newtowncashel, the magnificent Belvedere House and Gardens outside Mullingar, Athlone Castle and Locke's Distillery situated in the town of Kilbeggan which also hosts horse racing during the summer months. Literary associations include Maria Edgeworth, Padraic Colum, Oliver Goldsmith, James Joyce and Jonathan Swift.

## GUINNESS CALENDAR OF EVENTS

**April/May**
Bray Jazz Festival, Bray, Co. Wicklow
Nissan Irish Open, Co. Kildare

**June**
Budweiser Irish Derby, The Curragh Racecourse, Co. Kildare

**July**
Carlsberg Arklow Seabreeze, Arklow, Co. Wicklow
The Smurfit European Open, K Club, Co. Kildare

**August**
Birr Vintage Week, Birr, Co. Offaly
Tullamore Phoenix Festival, Tullamore, Co. Offaly
Wicklow Regatta, Wicklow Town

**September**
Guinness All Ireland Hurling Championship Final, Croke Park, Dublin
Baileys Champion Stakes, Leopardstown Racecourse, Dublin

## Arvagh / Bailieborough / Ballyconnell

### Breffni Arms Hotel

HOTEL ★★ MAP 11 K 14

Arvagh,
Co. Cavan

Tel: 049-433 5127 Fax: 049-433 5799
Email: breffniarms@hotmail.com
Web: www.breffniarms.com

The Breffni Arms is a 12 bedroomed en suite family-run licensed hotel and leisure centre. Ideally situated for a choice of golf courses, fishing, horse riding and pitch & putt, etc. Facilities include 15m indoor swimming pool, sauna, steam room, jacuzzi and fitness room. All our rooms have TV, phone, computer point and tea/coffee making facilities. Please enquire about Facilities for Persons with Mobility Impairment.

**B&B from €70.00 to €80.00**

Philomena & Eamonn Gray

12

**Open All Year**

### Bailie Hotel

HOTEL ★★ MAP 11 M 14

Main Street,
Bailieborough,
Co. Cavan

Tel: 042-966 5334 Fax: 042-966 6506
Email: hotelbailie@eircom.net
Web: www.bailiehotel.com

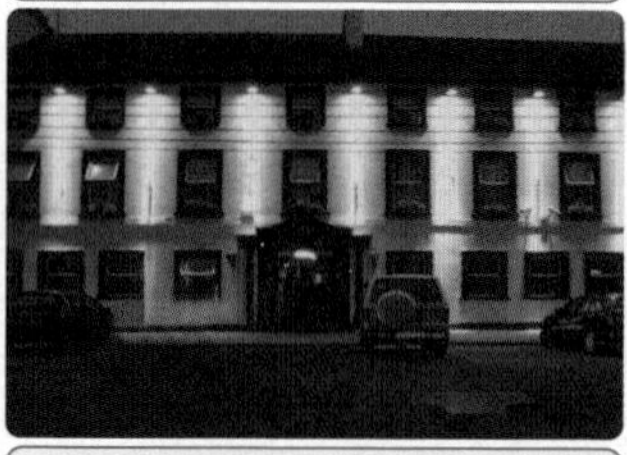

This newly refurbished family-run hotel is the perfect location for holiday, business or relaxation. Our 18 beautifully appointed en suite bedrooms are fitted out to the highest standard with TV, direct dial phone and tea/coffee facilities. Excellent reputation for good food with carvery lunches served daily, also à la carte and bar food. Our bar and lounge enjoy live music every weekend. Coarse fishing, golf course and mountain climbing close by. Swimming pool and leisure centre in town. Please enquire about Facilities for Persons with Mobility Impairment.

**B&B from €56.00 to €65.00**

Geraldine McEnaney
Proprietor

18

**Closed 24 - 26 December**

### Keepers Arms

GUESTHOUSE ★★ MAP 11 K 15

Bridge Street,
Bawnboy, Ballyconnell,
Co. Cavan

Tel: 049-952 3318 Fax: 049-952 3008
Email: keepers@iol.ie
Web: www.keepersarms.com

Situated in West Cavan the village of Bawnboy boasts The Keepers Arms. It offers top of the range quality approved accommodation and fully licenced bar. Ideally based for fishing, golfing and walking holidays. All our eleven en suite rooms have been decorated and equipped with your comfort in mind. (TV'S, Tea/Coffee, DD Phone). So if you require a king, single, double, twin, or family room we are able to satisfy your needs. Our aim is to make your stay a comfortable one. Please enquire about Facilities for Persons with Mobility Impairment.

*Bookable on www.irelandhotels.com*

**B&B from €55.00 to €65.00**

Sheila McKiernan

11

**Closed 24 - 26 December**



B&B Rates are per Person Sharing per Night incl. Breakfast. or Room Rates are per Room per Night - See also Page 8

## Cavan Town / Ballyconnell

### Slieve Russell Hotel Golf & Country Club

HOTEL ★★★★ MAP 11 K 15

Ballyconnell,
Co. Cavan

Tel: 049-952 6444 Fax: 049-952 6046
Email: slieve-russell@quinn-hotels.com
Web: www.quinnhotels.com

The Slieve Russell Hotel Golf & Country Club with Ciúin Spa & Wellness Centre, is a luxury 4 star resort with 222 stylish rooms set amidst 300 acres of landscaped gardens, including 50 acres of lakes. Our state of the art conference centre enables us to cater for conferences with up to 1200 delegates. For the golfer, our 18 hole Championship Golf Course ensures a challenging game. Our 9 hole par 3 course & driving range are also available. Located just 90 miles from Dublin & Belfast, the Slieve Russell Hotel offers a haven of comfort & relaxation.

***An IHF Quality Employer***

Member of Quinn Hotels

*Bookable on www.irelandhotels.com*
*Special Offer: www.irelandhotels.com/offers*

*B&B from €85.00 to €309.00*

*Tony Walker*
*General Manager*

222

*Activities:*

**Open All Year**

### Cavan Crystal Hotel

HOTEL ★★★★ MAP 11 L 14

Dublin Road,
Cavan Town,
Co. Cavan

Tel: 049-436 0600 Fax: 049-436 0699
Email: info@cavancrystalhotel.com
Web: www.cavancrystalhotel.com

Cavan Crystal Hotel is a contemporary 4**** hotel. 85 superbly appointed bedrooms, 9 conference and banqueting suites, 2 bars, award-winning Opus One Restaurant, award-winning Zest Health & Fitness Club including an 18 metre deck level pool, sauna, jacuzzi, steam room and fully equipped gymnasium. Why not relax in our IBPA Salon of the Year 2005, Utopia Health & Beauty Clinic or hair salon and do a spot of shopping in our own Cavan Crystal showroom. Located on the N3, a few minutes drive from town centre, 1.5 hours Dublin / Belfast.

*Bookable on www.irelandhotels.com*
*Special Offer: www.irelandhotels.com/offers*

*B&B from €85.00 to €115.00*
*Suites from €220.00 to €350.00*

*Siobhan Smyth*
*General Manager*

85

*Activities:*

**Closed 24 - 26 December**

### Farnham Arms Hotel

HOTEL ★★ MAP 11 L 14

Main Street,,
Cavan Town,
Co. Cavan

Tel: 049-433 2577 Fax: 049-436 2606
Email: info@farnhamarmshotel.com
Web: www.farnhamarmshotel.com

Centrally located in the heart of Cavan Town, The Farnham Arms Hotel has it all at its doorstep. Horse riding, Cinema, Cavan Sports and Swimming Centre, Fishing, Golfing and Shopping to name a few. Enjoy fine food in our Lough-Tree Restaurant and Fine Drink in our award-winning Percy French Bar. All rooms are en suite with DD telephone, tea/coffee facilitites and television. We're the ideal location for any Conference (Large/Small) or Private Function. Private Car Park, Special Rates and Packages available. Please enquire about Facilities for Persons with Mobility Impairment.

*B&B from €49.50 to €75.00*

*Oliver & Ann Sheils*
*Proprietors*

32

**Closed 25 December**



B&B Rates are per Person Sharing per Night incl. Breakfast.
or Room Rates are per Room per Night - **See also Page 8**

## Hotel Kilmore

HOTEL ★★★ MAP 11 L 14

Dublin Road,
Cavan Town,
Co. Cavan

Tel: 049-433 2288 Fax: 049-433 2458
Email: info@hotelkilmore.ie
Web: www.hotelkilmore.ie

On the doorsteps of Ireland's lakelands, the charming Hotel Kilmore offers guests a perfect blend of old world charm and contemporary design. Relax and enjoy the benefits of the afternoon sun in our Victorian sunroom bar, dine in sumptuous elegance in our Annalee Restaurant or enjoy a pint and a friendly chat in our Killykeen Lounge. A vibrant venue for any conference or private function. Please enquire about Facilities for Persons with Mobility Impairment.

***An IHF Quality Employer***

*Bookable on www.irelandhotels.com*
*Special Offer: www.irelandhotels.com/offers*

*B&B from €78.00 to €95.00*
*Suites from €175.00 to €220.00*

*Paul Henry*
*General Manager*

38

*Activities:*

**Closed 24 - 26 December**

## Radisson SAS Farnham Estate Hotel

HOTEL ★★★★ MAP 11 L 14

Farnham Estate,
Cavan,
Co. Cavan

Tel: 049-437 7700 Fax: 049-437 7701
Email: info.farnham@radissonsas.com
Web: www.farnhamestate.com

Located on a magnificent 1,300 acre country estate, 4km from Cavan Town, the beautiful 400 year old Farnham Estate opened in July 2006. The Estate incorporates a luxury 158 bedroom Radisson SAS Hotel and the world class Farnham Estate Health Spa. Designed to focus on wellbeing, health and luxury, Farnham offers guests a complete 'Retreat to Nature'. There are 7km of walking trails and fishing to be enjoyed. Our golf course opens in mid 2008. Please enquire about Facilities for Persons with Mobility Impairment.

***An IHF Quality Employer***

Member of Radisson SAS

*Bookable on www.irelandhotels.com*
*Special Offer: www.irelandhotels.com/offers*

*B&B from €65.00 to €102.50*
*Suites from €280.00 to €355.00*

*Sheila Gray*
*General Manager*

158

*Activities:*

**Open All Year**

## Errigal Country House Hotel

HOTEL ★★★ MAP 11 L 15

Cavan Road,
Cootehill,
Co. Cavan

Tel: 049-555 6901 Fax: 049-555 6902
Email: info@errigalhotel.com
Web: www.errigalhotel.com

The Errigal Hotel is a contemporary high quality hotel located just outside Cootehill Town centre, deep in the heart of Cavan's Lake District. The hotel's luxurious bedrooms have been designed with the busy traveller and the relaxing holiday resident in mind, and have been furnished to a very high standard. Our award-winning Reynards Restaurant offers a superb choice of menus. The hotel's gothic themed Brewery Bar provides a perfect retreat to relax with live entertainment on weekends. This small luxury hotel is the perfect destination for conferencing, golfing, business and leisure.

Member of Irish Country Hotels

*Bookable on www.irelandhotels.com*
*Special Offer: www.irelandhotels.com/offers*

*B&B from €60.00 to €90.00*

*Pat & Bernie Kelly*
*Proprietors*

22

**Open All Year**

B&B Rates are per Person Sharing per Night incl. Breakfast.
or Room Rates are per Room per Night - See also Page 8

## Kingscourt / Mountnugent / Virginia

### Cabra Castle Hotel

HOTEL ★★★★ MAP 11 M 14

Kingscourt,
Co. Cavan

Tel: 042-966 7030 Fax: 042-966 7039

Email: sales@cabracastle.com

Web: www.cabracastle.com

Follow in the footsteps of Oliver Cromwell and James II, and treat yourself to a stay in a castle. Cabra Castle stands on 88 acres of gardens and parkland, with its own nine hole golf course. The bar and restaurant offer views over countryside, famous for its lakes and fishing, as well as Dun a Ri Forest Park. An ideal venue for that holiday, specialising in golfing and equestrian holidays. Member of: Manor House Hotels Tel: 01-295 8900. www.manorhousehotels.com. Sister hotel of Ballyseede Castle Hotel, Tralee, Co. Kerry. Please enquire about Facilities for Persons with Mobility Impairment.

Member of Manor House Hotels

*Bookable on www.irelandhotels.com*

*Special Offer: www.irelandhotels.com/offers*

*B&B from €75.00 to €121.00*
*Suites from €185.00 to €277.00*

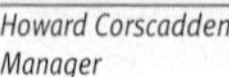

*Howard Corscadden*
*Manager*

86

Closed 23 - 26 December

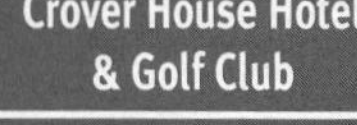

### Crover House Hotel & Golf Club

HOTEL ★★★ MAP 11 L 13

Lough Sheelin,
Mountnugent,
Co. Cavan

Tel: 049-854 0206 Fax: 049-854 0356

Email: crover@iol.ie

Web: www.croverhousehotel.ie

Crover House Hotel & Golf Club is a luxurious destination situated on the shores of Lough Sheelin. The hotel has 37 en suite bedrooms. The hotel has several dining options to offer. Enjoy our superb bar or snack menu in our intimate Sailor's Bar or the more contemporary Lakeview Bar. Fine dining is also available in our elegant Sheelin Room. Enjoy a round of golf on our executive 9 hole golf course or maybe stroll around our beautiful scenic gardens. Please enquire about Facilities for Persons with Mobility Impairment.

*B&B from €80.00 to €95.00*

*Aaron Mansworth*
*General Manager*

37

Activities:

Closed 25 - 27 December

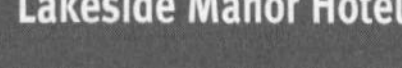

### Lakeside Manor Hotel

HOTEL ★★★ MAP 11 L 13

Dublin Road,
Virginia,
Co. Cavan

Tel: 049-854 8200 Fax: 049-854 8279

Email: info@lakesidemanor.ie

Web: www.lakesidemanor.ie

This luxurious hotel located on the shores of scenic Lough Ramor offers something to suit everyone's taste. Relaxing in the Manor Bar with its breathtaking view of the lake and surrounding countryside. An excellent central location for golfing and all other leisure activities. For the fisherman, boat hire is available at your request and boat trips can also be arranged. This friendly hotel with its helpful and courteous staff is an ideal venue for a relaxing weekend or just to escape the hustle and bustle of the city. Please enquire about Facilities for Persons with Mobility Impairment.

*B&B from €60.00 to €80.00*
*Suites from €140.00 to €180.00*

*Meabh & Jim Brady*
*Proprietors*

30

Activities:

Closed 24 - 26 December



B&B Rates are per Person Sharing per Night incl. Breakfast. or Room Rates are per Room per Night - See also Page 8

## Park Manor House Hotel & Estate

HOTEL ★★★ MAP 11 L 13

Virginia,
Co. Cavan

Tel: 049-854 6100 Fax: 049-854 7203
Email: reservations@parkhotelvirginia.com
Web: www.parkhotelvirginia.com

The Park Manor House Hotel is a beautifully restored 18th century country estate, situated on Lough Ramor. The 100 acre estate features golf course, orchards, herb gardens, rose gardens, picnic areas, walking trails. The perfect place for weddings, conferences, business meetings and more. Dine in our rosette award-winning Marquis Restaurant. The beautifully restored Arch Bar hosts an array of events from weddings & conferences to traditional music nights. Special rates for golf societies. Please enquire about Facilities for Persons with Mobility Impairment.

*Bookable on www.irelandhotels.com*
*Special Offer: www.irelandhotels.com/offers*

*B&B from €59.00 to €89.00*
*Suites from €75.00 to €90.00*

*Joey Dempsey*
*Managing Director*

29

*Activities:*

Closed 24 - 26 December

## Bracken Court Hotel

HOTEL ★★★ MAP 12 O 12

Bridge Street,
Balbriggan,
Co. Dublin

Tel: 01-841 3333 Fax: 01-841 5118
Email: info@brackencourt.ie
Web: www.brackencourt.ie

The Bracken Court Hotel is conveniently located in the seaside town of Balbriggan, 30 minutes north of Dublin City and 15 minutes from Dublin Airport making it an ideal location for access to the city, airport and as a gateway to the north. The 85 bedroomed hotel provides luxurious surroundings where comfort and a wide range of facilities combine to satisfy the needs of both business and leisure guest. Ireland's Best Service Excellence Award 2002 & 2003. Please enquire about Facilities for Persons with Mobility Impairment.

Member of The Moriarty Group

*Bookable on www.irelandhotels.com*
*Special Offer: www.irelandhotels.com/offers*

*B&B from €75.00 to €100.00*
*Suites from €260.00 to €500.00*

*Luke Moriarty*
*Owner*

85

*Activities:*

Open All Year

## Airportview Hotel & Spa

HOTEL ★★★ MAP 8 O 11

Cold Winters,
Blakes Cross,
Co. Dublin

Tel: 01-843 8756 Fax: 01-807 1949
Email: gerrybutterly@hotmail.com
Web: www.airportviewhotel.ie

Airport View Hotel & Spa newly built 2007. Luxurious hotel 8 mins from Dublin Airport built on a 7 acre site, incorporates a state of the art spa, four poster bedroom with jacuzzi baths, dvd, TV, tea/coffee, fax, computer outlet facilities & large rooms, TV lounge, large car park, conference rooms. Award-winning Winter's Restaurant with its excellent reputation for superb cuisine (fish & fillets speciality dishes). Conveniently located on R129, 50yds off old main Dublin/Belfast Road, now called R132. It has all the features of a 4* luxury Hotel. New health Spa & spa pool, sauna, steam etc now open. See you there!!

*B&B from €65.00 to €85.00*
*Suites from €150.00 to €200.00*

*Gerard Butterly / Annemarie Beggs*
*Proprietor*

20

*Activities:*

Closed 24 - 25 December

B&B Rates are per Person Sharing per Night incl. Breakfast.
or Room Rates are per Room per Night - See also Page 8

# Donabate / Dublin Airport

## Waterside House Hotel (The)

HOTEL ★★★ MAP 12 O 12

On the Beach,
Donabate,
Co. Dublin

Tel: 01-843 6153 Fax: 01-843 6111

Email: reservations@watersidehousehotel.ie

Web: www.watersidehousehotel.ie

Overlooking Lambay Island, Irelands Eye & Howth Head, this 3* property boasts 35 en suite recently refurbished bedrooms. It's ideal for golfers with 24 golf courses in the surrounding area & Corballis Golf Links on its doorstep. 20 mins from city centre & just 10 mins from Dublin Airport & Swords. Award-winning Signal Restaurant is open for breakfast, lunch & dinner daily. The Tower Bar & Bistro serves food from 7am-8.30pm. Telephone for special offers. Awarded two years in a row "Best Customer Service" Swords Fingal Chamber of Commerce. Please enquire about Facilities for Persons with Mobility Impairment.

*Bookable on www.irelandhotels.com*

*B&B from €60.00 to €120.00*
*Suites from €150.00 to €320.00*

*Chris & Thelma Slattery*
*Proprietors*

35

*Activities:*

**Open All Year**

## Airport Manor

GUESTHOUSE ★★★★ MAP 12 O 12

Naul Road,
Knocksedan, Swords,
Co. Dublin

Tel: 01-840 1818 Fax: 01-870 0010

Email: info@airportmanor.com

Web: www.airportmanor.com

Airport Manor combines the warmth of an Irish welcome with the luxury of private and convenient accommodation. The perfect location to enjoy the peace and tranquillity of the countryside, yet only 5 minutes from Dublin Airport, 20 minutes from city centre and easily accessible from all major routes. Whether you are arriving or departing from Dublin Airport, Airport Manor is the ideal overnight accommodation. Please enquire about Facilities for Persons with Mobility Impairment.

*Bookable on www.irelandhotels.com*

*B&B from €50.00 to €85.00*

*Michelle Lynch*
*Manager*

17

**Closed 24 December - 02 January**

## Bewley's Hotel Dublin Airport

HOTEL ★★★ MAP 12 O 12

Baskin Lane,
Swords,
Co. Dublin

Tel: 01-871 1000 Fax: 01-871 1001

Email: dublinairport@bewleyshotels.com

Web: www.bewleyshotels.com

Welcome to a comfortable new hotel, ideally located near the airport just off the M1 / M50 interchange. Offering 466 contemporary soundproofed rooms and built with the latest technology, all rooms offer complimentary high-speed internet access. Our brasserie and lounge offer a wide range of dining options throughout the day, and meetings are well catered for, with 16 highly specified executive boardrooms. Real-time online reservations and availability at www.BewleysHotel.com. Please enquire about Facilities for Persons with Mobility Impairment.

Member of BewleysHotels.com

*Room Rate from €89.00 to €99.00*

*The Team at*
*Bewley's Hotel Dublin Airport*

466

**Closed 24 - 26 December**



B&B Rates are per Person Sharing per Night incl. Breakfast.
or Room Rates are per Room per Night - See also Page 8

## Carlton Dublin Airport Hotel

HOTEL ★★★★ MAP 12 O 11

Old Airport Road,
Cloghran,
Co. Dublin

Tel: 01-866 7500 Fax: 01-862 3114

Email: info@carltondublinairport.com

Web: www.carlton.ie

Conveniently located adjacent to Dublin Airport. Elegantly designed & built to the highest international 4* standards the Carlton offers every facility for both our business & leisure customers. 100 luxury suites & bedrooms & incorporating a fully equipped conference centre boasting 19 meeting rooms. Clouds Rooftop Restaurant & Kitty Hawks Bistro, each with their own extensive menus using high quality produce in sumptuous surroundings. Stay, park & ride offers are available & include our complimentary shuttle service to & from the airport. Room reservations Lo Call 1890 288 288.

***An IHF Quality Employer***

Member of The Carlton Hotel Group

*Bookable on www.irelandhotels.com*
*Special Offer: www.irelandhotels.com/offers*

*Room Rate from €99.00 to €300.00*
*Suites from €149.00 to €330.00*

*Declan Meagher*
*General Manager*

100

*Activities:*

**Closed 24 - 27 December**

## Clarion Hotel Dublin Airport

HOTEL ★★★★ MAP 12 O 11

Dublin Airport,
Co. Dublin

Tel: 01-808 0500 Fax: 01-844 6002

Email: reservations@clarionhoteldublinairport.com

Web: www.clarionhoteldublinairport.com

Modern 4**** hotel, located at Dublin Airport, a 3 minute journey from the main terminal by 24 hour courtesy coach. All rooms are air-conditioned, offer tea/making faclilities, trouser press, multi-purpose fridge and blackout curtains. A choice of dining experiences are offered at Café Savour and Kudos Bar & Restaurant. Within walking distance, residents can enjoy complimentary use of ALSAA swimming pool, sauna and gym. Elevator available for luggage only. Please enquire about Facilities for Persons with Mobility Impairment.

Member of Choice International Hotels

*Bookable on www.irelandhotels.com*
*Special Offer: www.irelandhotels.com/offers*

*Room Rate from €94.00 to €300.00*

*Andrew O'Neill*
*General Manager*

248

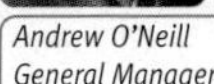

**Closed 24 - 26 December**

B&B Rates are per Person Sharing per Night incl. Breakfast.
or Room Rates are per Room per Night - See also Page 8

## Dublin Airport

### Crowne Plaza Dublin Northwood

HOTEL ★★★★ MAP 8 O 11

Northwood Park,
Santry Demesne,
Santry, Dublin 9

Tel: 01-862 8888 Fax: 01-862 8800

Email: info@crowneplazadublin.ie

Web: www.cpdublin-airport.com

Crowne Plaza is a luxurious 4**** hotel with extensive conference facilities catering for 1000 delegates, 25 meeting rooms, 2 restaurants, bar and coffee lounge. Located in a mature parkland setting only 15 minutes from the City Centre and 5 minutes from Dublin Airport, close to M1/M50 motorways. Courtesy coach to/from Dublin Airport and large car park. AA Business Hotel Of The Year. Please enquire about Facilities for Persons with Mobility Impairment.

***An IHF Quality Employer***

Member of Intercontintal Hotel Group

*Bookable on www.irelandhotels.com*
*Special Offer: www.irelandhotels.com/offers*

**Room Rate from €110.00 to €320.00**
**Suites from €250.00 to €550.00**

*Mary Buckley*
*General Manager*

204

*Activities:*

**Closed 24 - 25 December**

### Days Hotel Dublin Airport

HOTEL ★★★ MAP 8 O 11

Santry Cross,
Ballymun Road,
Dublin 11

Tel: 1890-329 329 Fax: 01-866 9501

Email: info@dayshoteldublinairport.com

Web: www.dayshoteldublinairport.com

Days Hotel Dublin Airport is part of a groundbreaking €2.5 billion development at Ireland's newest and most radically transformed regeneration area, just off the M50 at Ballymun. The hotel comprises 88 superb bedrooms, with TV/DVD player, ironing station, tea/coffee making facilities, safe and free broadband. Excellent meeting and conference facilities on site for up to 80 delegates. Free WiFi in lobby & bar. Rueben's Café Bar open all day. Complimentary transfers to/from Dublin Airport, while Dublin City centre is just 4 miles away, and is easily accessible by public transport. Hotel direct tel line (01) 866 9500.

***An IHF Quality Employer***

Member of Days Hotels Ireland

*Bookable on www.irelandhotels.com*
*Special Offer: www.irelandhotels.com/offers*

**Room Rate from €89.00 to €229.00**
**Suites from €89.00 to €259.00**

*Mark Williams*
*General Manager*

88

*Activities:*

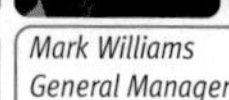

**Open All Year**

### Express by Holiday Inn

HOTEL ★★★ MAP 12 O 12

Northwood Park,
Santry Demesne,
Near Dublin Airport, Dublin 9

Tel: 01-862 8866 Fax: 01-862 8800

Email: info@hiexpressdublin-airport.ie

Web: www.hiexpressdublin-airport.ie

The 3*** standard hotel is set in a mature and tranquil parkland, 5 minutes from Dublin Airport and 15 minutes from the city centre. 114 contemporary bedrooms, with broadband internet access. Continental buffet breakfast is included in the room rate. Restaurant, Bar and Conference facilities at the adjacent Crowne Plaza Hotel. Airport courtesy coach and on site multi-story car park. Please enquire about Facilities for Persons with Mobility Impairment.

Member of Intercontinental Hotel Group

*Bookable on www.irelandhotels.com*
*Special Offer: www.irelandhotels.com/offers*

**Room Rate from €89.00 to €190.00**

*Stephan Cox*
*Hotel Manager*

114

**Closed 23 - 25 December**



B&B Rates are per Person Sharing per Night incl. Breakfast.
or Room Rates are per Room per Night - See also Page 8

## Glenmore House

GUESTHOUSE ★★★ MAP 12 O 12

Airport Road,
Nevinstown, Swords,
Co. Dublin

Tel: 01-840 3610 Fax: 01-840 4148

Email: glenmoreh@eircom.net

Web: www.glenmorehouse.com

Located beside Dublin Airport and just 20 mins to Dublin city centre, Glenmore House is the perfect choice for vistors travelling into or out of Dublin Airport or visiting Dublin City. Glemore House is a spacious family-run guesthouse with large gardens and private car park. All rooms have bathroom, TV, DD telephone and tea/coffee facilities. On main bus routes to airport and city centre and pick up service available by arrangement. Great location and accommodation at a very reasonable cost.

*Room Rate from €59.00 to €109.00*

*Rebecca Gibney*
*Proprietor*

30

**Closed 24 - 25 December**

## Hilton Dublin Airport

HOTEL ★★★★ MAP 12 O 12

Northern Cross,
Malahide Road,
Dublin 17

Tel: 01-866 1800 Fax: 01-866 1866

Email: dublin.airport@hilton.com

Web: www.hilton.com

Your experience of Ireland's famously warm hospitality starts at the Hilton Dublin Airport. Purpose built with sleek design, the hotel is situated close to Dublin, the airport and Ireland's picturesque east coast. Its location, combined with second to none business facilities and an exceptionally welcoming environment, offers the very best in comfort convenience for the business or leisure traveller. Please enquire about Facilities for Persons with Mobility Impairment.

***An IHF Quality Employer***

Member of Hilton Hotels Corporation

***Bookable on www.irelandhotels.com***

*Room Rate from €95.00 to €240.00*
*Suites from €175.00 to €320.00*

*Peter Mikkelsen*
*Hotel Manager*

166

*Activities:*

**Open All Year**

## Radisson SAS Hotel, Dublin Airport

HOTEL ★★★★ MAP 12 O 11

Dublin Airport,
Co. Dublin

Tel: 01-844 6000 Fax: 01-844 6001

Email: reservations.airport.dublin@radisson.sas.com

Web: www.airport.dublin.radissonsas.com

Situated within the airport complex, just two minutes from the main terminal, the Radisson SAS Hotel provides a tranquil haven for the busy traveller. The guest rooms have every convenience & allow guests unwind in stylish surroundings. The hotel has a wide range of conference rooms. Bookable through our in-house reservations on 01-844 6000. Please enquire about Facilities for Persons with Mobility Impairment.

***An IHF Quality Employer***

Member of Radisson

***Bookable on www.irelandhotels.com***
*Special Offer: www.irelandhotels.com/offers*

*Room Rate from €109.00 to €399.00*

*Fergal O'Connell*
*General Manager*

229

*Activities:*

**Open All Year**

B&B Rates are per Person Sharing per Night incl. Breakfast.
or Room Rates are per Room per Night - **See also Page 8**

## Dublin Airport / Dublin City

### Tulip Inn Dublin Airport

HOTEL ★★★ MAP 12 O 11

Airside Retail Park,
Swords,
Co. Dublin

Tel: 01-895 7777 Fax: 01-895 7700
Email: info@tulipinndublinairport.ie
Web: www.tulipinndublinairport.ie

Stylish, comfortable, friendly and informal hotel with excellent standards of accommodation and décor. Catering for those travellers looking for a pleasant meal, relaxing drink in the bar followed by a good night's sleep all at a great price. Fully air-conditioned hotel located just 1.5km from Dublin Airport for which there is a courtesy shuttle. Being close to the motorway network makes travel around the area very easy. Please enquire about Facilities for Persons with Mobility Impairment.

Member of Golden Tulip

*Bookable on www.irelandhotels.com*
*Special Offer: www.irelandhotels.com/offers*

*Room Rate from €79.00 to €155.00*

*Helen Devlin*
*General Manager*

155

**Open All Year**

### Abberley Court Hotel

HOTEL ★★★ MAP 8 O 11

High Street,
Tallaght Town Centre,
Dublin 24

Tel: 01-459 6000 Fax: 01-462 1000
Email: info@abberley.ie
Web: www.abberley.ie

This hotel is situated in the town centre of Tallaght, only 5 minutes from the M50 motorway and 8 miles from Dublin City Centre. Easily accessible from Dublin Airport, Dublin City Centre, Dublin & Dun Laoghaire's Ferry Ports. It is within minutes walking distance of hundreds of shops, superstores, cinemas, restaurants, pubs & nightclubs. Facilities include 40 bedrooms, choice of two bars, Chinese Restaurant & complimentary secure multi storey car parking. All bedrooms are equipped with plasma TV screens, DVD players, mini refrigerator, ironing station, complimentary WiFi. 4 minute walk from LUAS Red Line to city centre.

***An IHF Quality Employer***

*Bookable on www.irelandhotels.com*
*Special Offer: www.irelandhotels.com/offers*

*Room Rate from €35.00 to €164.00*

*Mairead Slye & Karen Garry*

40

**Closed 24 - 02 January**

### Abbey Hotel

HOTEL ★★ MAP 8 O 11

52 Middle Abbey Street,
Dublin 1

Tel: 01-872 8188 Fax: 01-872 8585
Email: reservations@abbey-hotel.ie
Web: www.abbey-hotel.ie

Small, intimate hotel in the heart of Dublin city centre. It is close to all main shopping areas and night life. The stylish rooms are decorated to a high standard. The hotel offers a full à la carte menu daily to 9pm. Only minutes walk from O'Connell Street and Temple Bar. Facilities include TV, telephone, car park, bar, restaurant, entertainment and lift. 21 rooms all en suite. Please enquire about Facilities for Persons with Mobility Impairment.

*Bookable on www.irelandhotels.com*

*B&B from €25.00 to €125.00*

*Agneiszka Hilt*
*Front Office Manager*

21

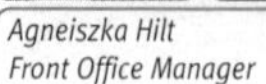

**Closed 24 - 26 December**



B&B Rates are per Person Sharing per Night incl. Breakfast.
or Room Rates are per Room per Night - **See also Page 8**

## Aberdeen Lodge

GUESTHOUSE ★★★★ MAP 8 O 11

53 Park Avenue,
Off Ailesbury Road, Ballsbridge,
Dublin 4

Tel: 01-283 8155 Fax: 01-283 7877

Email: aberdeen@iol.ie

Web: www.halpinsprivatehotels.com

The perfect balance of luxury, privacy and location, Aberdeen Lodge is one of Dublin's gems. The classic and de luxe bedrooms are spacious and elegant, several with four poster beds, spa baths, complimentary WiFi broadband, landscaped gardens and car park. Close to city centre, airport and car ferry terminals by DART or bus. Accolades: AA ♦♦♦♦♦, JDB Hotels, Times, Alaistair Sawdays, Bridgestone 100 Best Places to Stay Ireland 2007, The Good Hotel Guide, Best Loved Hotels.
USA toll free 1800 617 3178.
Global free phone +800 1283 8155.

Member of Private Ireland

*Bookable on www.irelandhotels.com*
*Special Offer: www.irelandhotels.com/offers*

**B&B from €69.00 to €99.00**
**Suites from €220.00 to €300.00**

*Pat Halpin*
*Proprietor*

20

*Activities:*

**Open All Year**

## Abrae Court

GUESTHOUSE ★★★ MAP 8 O 11

9 Zion Road,
Rathgar,
Dublin 6

Tel: 01-492 2242 Fax: 01-492 3944

Email: abrae@eircom.net

Web: www.abraecourt.ie

Built in 1864, family-run, 3*** Victorian guesthouse is located in the prestigious residential area of Rathgar, just ten minutes from the heart of Dublin City. Guest rooms are furnished with en suite bathroom, colour TV, direct dial phone and coffee/tea making facilities. Laundry service and a lock up car park are available. Bus routes, a good selection of restaurants, pubs, tourist attractions and various sports. We are "Kosher Friendly".

*Bookable on www.irelandhotels.com*
*Special Offer: www.irelandhotels.com/offers*

**B&B from €50.00 to €60.00**

*Alina Ignat*
*Manageress*

18

**Open All Year**

## Adams Trinity Hotel

HOTEL ★★★ MAP 8 O 11

28 Dame Street,
Dublin 2

Tel: 01-670 7100 Fax: 01-670 7101

Email: reservations@adamstrinityhotel.com

Web: www.adamstrinityhoteldublin.com

What better location in Dublin than the Adams Trinity Hotel? Located mid-way between Dublin Castle, Grafton Street and Trinity College; it faces the vibrant Temple Bar area. Traditional style bedrooms are finished to an exceptionally luxurious standard. The hotel features the Mercantile Bar and Restaurant, O'Brien's Traditional Bar and café style Brokers Bar. The Adams Trinity Hotel offers all guests that same personal attention and warmth, it has that little something special. Special rates apply from Sunday - Thursday. Please enquire about Facilities for Persons with Mobility Impairment.

*Bookable on www.irelandhotels.com*
*Special Offer: www.irelandhotels.com/offers*

**B&B from €49.50 to €102.00**

*Fran Ryder / Peter Hanahoe*
*Proprietors*

28

**Closed 24 - 27 December**

## Dublin City

### An Glen Guesthouse

GUESTHOUSE ★★ MAP 8 O 11

84 Lower Gardiner Street,
Dublin 1

Tel: 01-855 1374 Fax: 01-855 2506
Email: theglen@eircom.net
Web: www.glenguesthouse.com

The Glen is a beautifully restored and maintained guesthouse. Located in the heart of Dublin City, adjacent to shops, theatres, cinemas, galleries, museums and Dublin's famous night spots. Close to bus and train stations en route to airport. Rooms en suite, TV, direct dial phones, tea and coffee facilities in all rooms.

*Bookable on www.irelandhotels.com*
*Special Offer: www.irelandhotels.com/offers*

*B&B from €35.00 to €65.00*

*Martin Tynan & Rossi Borisova*
*Joint Managers*
15

T C S

**Closed 23 - 27 December**

### Anchor Guest House

GUESTHOUSE ★★★ MAP 8 O 11

49 Lower Gardiner Street,
Dublin 1

Tel: 01-878 6913 Fax: 01-878 6877
Email: info@anchorguesthouse.com
Web: www.anchorguesthouse.com

Our location is city central. Use the 747 Airport shuttle bus to the central bus station to reach us. Car spaces are available, but need to be reserved. We suggest that a car is not required during your stay with us. We serve a substantial "Full Irish Breakfast" (or a lighter menu selection) each morning, to properly set energy levels, prior to any exploration of Dublin City.

*B&B from €40.00 to €85.00*

*Joan & Gerry Coyne*
*Proprietors*
22

T C P S I

**Open All Year**

### Ardagh House

GUESTHOUSE ★★★ MAP 8 O 11

No.1 Highfield Road,
Rathgar,
Dublin 6

Tel: 01-497 7068 Fax: 01-497 3991
Email: enquiries@ardagh-house.ie
Web: www.ardagh-house.ie

Having been recently totally refurbished, Ardagh House is conveniently situated in a premier residential area. This imposing turn of the century premises contains many of the gracious and spacious features of a fine detached residence of that era and yet incorporating modern creature comforts. Within easy distance of the city centre, RDS, etc. This fine property stands on approximately 1/2 acre with ample off street car parking and good gardens.

*Bookable on www.irelandhotels.com*

*B&B from €45.00 to €75.00*

*Willie & Mary Doyle*
*Proprietors*
19

T C P I

**Closed 23 December - 03 Januray**



B&B Rates are per Person Sharing per Night incl. Breakfast. or Room Rates are per Room per Night - See also Page 8

## Ardmore Hotel

HOTEL ★★★ MAP 8 O 11

Tolka Valley,
Dublin 11

Tel: 01-864 8300 Fax: 01-864 8311
Email: reservations@ardmore-hotel.com
Web: www.ardmore-hotel.com

The Ardmore Hotel is a new, purpose built hotel situated 10 minutes from both Dublin Airport and Dublin City centre. This contemporary styled hotel offers 96 superbly appointed rooms which include iron and ironing board, tea and coffee facilities, flat screen cable television, DD telephone and high speed internet access. We also provide excellent conference facilities including state of the art audiovisual equipment. Secure private parking is also available. A spacious bar and international restaurant along with the launch of the executive floor in 2007 make this the perfect hotel for both business and pleasure.

Member of Cara Hotels

*Bookable on www.irelandhotels.com*
*Special Offer: www.irelandhotels.com/offers*

*Room Rate from €79.00 to €199.00*

*Sheila Baird*
*General Manager*

96

Activities:

Closed 23 - 27 December

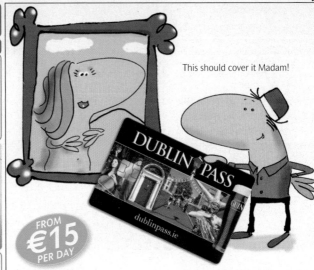



B&B Rates are per Person Sharing per Night incl. Breakfast.
or Room Rates are per Room per Night - **See also Page 8**

## Dublin City

### Ariel House

GUESTHOUSE ★★★★ MAP 8 O 11

50 - 54 Lansdowne Road,
Ballsbridge,
Dublin 4

Tel: 01-668 5512 Fax: 01-668 5845
Email: reservations@ariel-house.net
Web: www.ariel-house.net

Newly refurbished, Victorian mansion, built in 1850, remains true to its antique roots while incorporating the best of the modern townhouse hotel. Situated on Lansdowne Road, Ballsbridge, close to the Dart and bus routes. Its 37 stylish bedrooms boast a unique mix of period furniture with modern comforts. Breakfast is served in our light filled and airy garden room and afternoon tea is available in our elegant drawing room. Your stylish residence in Ballsbridge.

***An IHF Quality Employer***

*Bookable on www.irelandhotels.com*
*Special Offer: www.irelandhotels.com/offers*

**B&B from €49.50 to €95.00**
**Suites from €60.00 to €120.00**

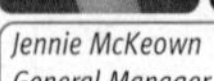

*Jennie McKeown*
*General Manager*

37

**Closed 23 - 28 December**

### Arlington Hotel

HOTEL ★★★ MAP 8 O 11

23/25 Bachelors Walk,
O'Connell Bridge,
Dublin 1

Tel: 01-804 9100 Fax: 01-804 9152
Email: info@arlington.ie
Web: www.arlington.ie

The most central hotel in Dublin, overlooking the River Liffey at O'Connell Bridge. Dublin's top attractions and shopping districts on your doorstep. 131 en suite bedrooms, limited free underground parking, meeting room. Magnificent medieval Knightsbridge Bar with live Irish music and dancing 7 nights a week all year round (free admission). Carvery lunch and à la carte bar menu available, candle-lit Knights Bistro. Perfect base for business or pleasure. Please enquire about Facilities for Persons with Mobility Impairment.

***An IHF Quality Employer***

*Bookable on www.irelandhotels.com*
*Special Offer: www.irelandhotels.com/offers*

**B&B from €55.00 to €130.00**

*Ken McEntee*
*General Manager*

131

**Closed 24 - 26 December**

### Ashling Hotel

HOTEL ★★★ MAP 8 O 11

Parkgate Street,
Dublin 8

Tel: 01-677 2324 Fax: 01-679 3783
Email: info@ashlinghotel.ie
Web: www.ashlinghotel.ie

A spacious hotel in a superb location, the Ashling provides excellent access to Dublin City centre and the rest of Ireland. Modern en suite bedrooms, conference/meeting rooms, free car/coach parking. 20 minutes walk to city centre/Temple Bar, or by bus, taxi or Dublin's new tram system, the LUAS. Adjacent to intercity rail station Heuston, Guinness Brewery, Phoenix Park and more. Easy access to the M50 motorway and all major routes. Direct "Airlink" bus from Dublin Airport to Heuston Station. Please enquire about Facilities for Persons with Mobility Impairment.

***An IHF Quality Employer***
Member of Best Western Hotels

*Bookable on www.irelandhotels.com*
*Special Offer: www.irelandhotels.com/offers*

**B&B from €55.00 to €150.00**

*Alan Moody*
*General Manager*

150

*Activities:*

**Closed 24 - 26 December**



B&B Rates are per Person Sharing per Night incl. Breakfast. or Room Rates are per Room per Night - **See also Page 8**

## Aston Hotel

HOTEL ★★★ MAP 8 O 11

7/9 Aston Quay,
Dublin 2

Tel: 01-677 9300 Fax: 01-677 9007
Email: stay@aston-hotel.com
Web: www.aston-hotel.com

A warm welcome awaits you at the Aston Hotel, located in Temple Bar and overlooking the River Liffey. Friendly staff and pleasant surroundings will make your stay a memorable one. All our 27 rooms are en suite and offer every guest comfort including direct dial phone, colour TV, hairdryer and tea/coffee making facilities. A leisurely stroll from the Aston brings you to all Dublin's top attractions and amenities and makes it an ideal base for exploring the capital. Please enquire about Facilities for Persons with Mobility Impairment.

*Bookable on www.irelandhotels.com*
*Special Offer: www.irelandhotels.com/offers*

**Room Rate from €70.00 to €300.00**

*Ann Walsh*
*Manager*

27

**Closed 24 - 26 December**

## Ballsbridge Court

HOTEL MAP 8 O 11

Lansdowne Road,
Ballsbridge,
Dublin 4

Email: rooms@d4hotels.com
Web: www.d4hotels.com

Book on d4hotels.com. Located on the same site as the Inn and Towers, the Court offers full ground floor services with style and panache. 188 superb bedrooms in a club style atmosphere in leafy Ballsbridge. The Bar is reminiscent of the classic 30s with Jazz music and white jacketed bartenders serving Martinis with Olives. A Bistro overlooking the gardens with food so good you will lick your fingers. If you are looking for great accommodation in a great location and services tailored to a city visit you have found home. If you stay once with us you will be back. Perfect for a host of reasons.

***An IHF Quality Employer***
Member of d4hotels.com

*Bookable on www.irelandhotels.com*

**Room Rate from €135.00 to €235.00**

*Patrick Hanley*
*General Manager*

188

**Open All Year**



B&B Rates are per Person Sharing per Night incl. Breakfast.
or Room Rates are per Room per Night - See also Page 8

## Dublin City

### Ballsbridge Inn & Towers

HOTEL MAP 8 O 11

Pembroke Road,
Ballsbridge,
Dublin 4

Email: rooms@d4hotels.com
Web: www.d4hotels.com

Book on d4hotels.com. The Ballsbridge Inn is ideal for that special break or short business trip, with well equipped bedrooms. In an unusual twist on a traditional hotel we offer a fine Food Hall with well known, respected outlets serving all you need. Gastro Bar brings a party atmosphere. RDS & DART 5 mins walk. The Ballsbridge Towers is a de luxe hotel within a hotel, in the same building as the Ballsbridge Inn, offering a private ground floor lounge & luxurious, spacious rooms with sitting area. Ideal for business or a romantic escape. Watch a Hollywood Classic in our 22 seater cinema.

***An IHF Quality Employer***

Member of d4hotels.com

***Bookable on www.irelandhotels.com***

***Room Rate from €105.00 to €195.00***

*Andrew Phelan*
*General Manager*
404

**Open All Year**

### Ballymun Plaza Hotel

HOTEL ★★★ MAP 8 O 11

Ballymun,
Dublin 11

Tel: 01-842 2000 Fax: 01-842 3000
Email: reservations@ballymunplaza.ie
Web: www.ballymunplaza.ie

This modern hotel opened its doors in August 2006, located 5 minutes from Dublin Airport and 15 minutes from the city centre. Offering 125 4**** standard unique guest rooms and suites, with exceptional facilities for both leisure and business guests including high speed internet. Coffee lounge, bar and restaurant and 24 hour room service available. Please enquire about Facilities for Persons with Mobility Impairment.

***Bookable on www.irelandhotels.com***
***Special Offer: www.irelandhotels.com/offers***

***Room Rate from €89.00 to €285.00***

*Kolvi Rutz*
*General Manager*
125

*Activities:*

**Closed 24 - 27 December**

### Best Western Academy Plaza Hotel

HOTEL ★★★ MAP 8 O 11

Findlater Place,
Off O'Connell Street,
Dublin 1

Tel: 01-817 4141 Fax: 01-878 0600
Email: stay@academyplazahotel.ie
Web: www.academyplazahotel.ie

The new Academy Plaza Hotel has an enviable location in the heart of Dublin. A short stroll to international shopping & attractions such as Temple Bar, Trinity College & Croke Park. The city's main transport services incl. Bus, Rail & LUAS are only minutes away. 285 de luxe bedrooms & suites provide the ultimate in luxury, LCD TV's, air-con & complimentary WiFi. Enjoy lunch or a drink in Sir Harry's Bar & Brasserie, breakfast in Oscars Restaurant or dine in "Abacus" our exclusive Asian restaurant. Conference facilities for up to 100 delegates, gym, business centre & games room available. Car parking opposite.

Member of Best Western Hotels

***Bookable on www.irelandhotels.com***
***Special Offer: www.irelandhotels.com/offers***

***B&B from €59.50 to €112.50***
***Suites from €169.00 to €325.00***

*Peter Collins*
*Manager*
285

*Activities:*

**Closed 23 - 29 December**



B&B Rates are per Person Sharing per Night incl. Breakfast.
or Room Rates are per Room per Night - See also Page 8

## Bewley's Hotel Ballsbridge

HOTEL ★★★ MAP 8 O 11

Merrion Road,
Ballsbridge,
Dublin 4

Tel: 01-668 1111 Fax: 01-668 1999

Email: ballsbridge@bewleyshotels.com

Web: www.bewleyshotels.com

Bewley's Hotel Ballsbridge is situated next to the RDS and minutes away from the attractions of the city centre. Accommodating you in style with 304 de luxe bedrooms and 9 well-equipped meeting rooms. Award-winning O'Connell's Restaurant offers a wide range of wonderful dining options. Bewley's Hotel provides a setting that is contemporary, relaxed and informal, at a fixed room rate - Every Room Every Night. The hotel is serviced by Aircoach. Real time on line reservations and availability at www.BewleysHotels.com. Please enquire about Facilities for Persons with Mobility Impairment.

***An IHF Quality Employer***

*Room Rate from €109.00 to €119.00*

*Carol Burke*
*General Manager*

*304*

**Closed 24 - 26 December**

B&B Rates are per Person Sharing per Night incl. Breakfast.
or Room Rates are per Room per Night - **See also Page 8**

## Dublin City

### Bewley's Hotel Leopardstown

HOTEL ★★★ MAP 8 O 11

Central Park,
Leopardstown Road,
Leopardstown, Dublin 18

Tel: 01-293 5000 Fax: 01-293 5099

Email: Leop@bewleyshotels.com

Web: www.bewleyshotels.com

A contemporary, relaxed and informal hotel, located just off the M50 and N11 and close to several corporate and business parks. Leopardstown racecourse and the LUAS tram station are a short walk away, while Aircoach links the hotel with the airport. Our Brasserie and Lounge allow a choice of flexible dining options throughout the day. Free high speed internet is provided in all rooms. Real-time online reservations and availability at www.bewleyshotels.com Please enquire about Facilities for Persons with Mobility Impairment.

Member of BewleysHotels.com

**Room Rate from €89.00 to €99.00**

*Joleen Donoghue*
*General Manager*

352

Closed 24 - 25 December

### Bewley's Hotel Newlands Cross

HOTEL ★★★ MAP 8 O 11

Newlands Cross,
Naas Road (N7),
Dublin 22

Tel: 01-464 0140 Fax: 01-464 0900

Email: res@bewleyshotels.com

Web: www.bewleyshotels.com

A unique blend of quality, value and flexibility for independent discerning guests. Located just off the N7, minutes from the M50, Dublin Airport and the city centre. Our large spacious family size rooms are fully equipped with all modern amenities. The Brasserie offers you a range of dining options, from traditional Irish breakfast to full table service à la carte. Real time on line reservations and availability at www.bewleyshotels.com Please enquire about Facilities for Persons with Mobility Impairment.

***An IHF Quality Employer***

Member of BewleysHotels.com

**Room Rate from €89.00 to €99.00**

*The Team at Bewley's Hotel*

299

Closed 24 - 26 December

### Blooms Hotel

HOTEL ★★★ MAP 8 O 11

6 Anglesea Street,
Temple Bar,
Dublin 2

Tel: 01-671 5622 Fax: 01-671 5997

Email: info@blooms.ie

Web: www.blooms.ie

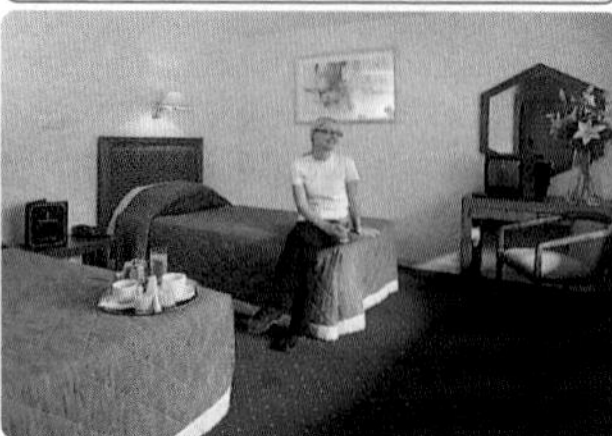

Blooms Hotel is situated at the centre of Dublin's cultural and artistic heart - Temple Bar. The hotel itself is only a few minutes stroll from Grafton Street's shopping and most of the city's best sights. And for those who want to set the town alight, Blooms is on the doorstep of Dublin's most famous nightlife - not least of which is its own nightclub, Club M. Blooms Hotel is a perfect choice for everyone looking to experience Temple Bar and Dublin's city centre.

*Bookable on www.irelandhotels.com*

**B&B from €50.00 to €125.00**

*Barry O'Sullivan*
*General Manager*

86

Closed 24 - 26 December



B&B Rates are per Person Sharing per Night incl. Breakfast.
or Room Rates are per Room per Night - See also Page 8

## Brooks Hotel

HOTEL ★★★★ MAP 8 O 11

Drury Street,
Dublin 2

Tel: 01-670 4000 Fax: 01-670 4455
Email: reservations@brookshotel.ie
Web: www.sinnotthotels.com

Brooks is a 4**** designer / boutique hotel located in the fashionable heart of Dublin, just two minutes stroll from Grafton St, Temple Bar and Trinity College. Air-conditioned throughout, the staff are well trained and deliver high standards of customer care. Superb accommodation with internet access includes Francesca's Restaurant, Jasmine Bar, private lounge, fitness suite with sauna and state of the art screening room. Ideal for discerning travelers, Drury St car park is also directly opposite the hotel. Bookable on www.sinnotthotels.com.

***An IHF Quality Employer***

Member of Sinnott Hotel Group

*Bookable on www.irelandhotels.com*
*Special Offer: www.irelandhotels.com/offers*

*Room Rate from €160.00 to €375.00*
*Suites from €375.00 to €650.00*

*Mark O'Sullivan*
*General Manager*

98

*Activities:*

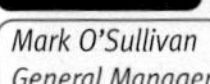

**Open All Year**

## Brownes Dublin

GUESTHOUSE ★★★★ MAP 12 O 11

22 St. Stephens Green,
Dublin 2

Tel: 01-638 3939 Fax: 01-638 3900
Email: info@brownesdublin.com
Web: www.steinhotels.com/brownes

Situated in a stylishly restored 18th Century Georgian Townhouse. Brownes is considered one of Dublin's finest luxury boutique properties in the centre of the city. Each of the 11 rooms and suites has been individually designed, all are en suite and well equipped with today's mod cons. Brownes also features meeting facilities as well as pleasant and cosy public areas, with one of Dublin's most celebrated restaurants.

Member of Stein Hotels and Resorts

*Room Rate from €205.00 to €265.00*
*Suites from €525.00 to €525.00*

*John Clarke*
*General Manager*

11

*Activities:*

**Open All Year**

## Burlington (The)

HOTEL ★★★★ MAP 8 O 11

Upper Leeson Street,
Dublin 4

Tel: 01-660 5222 Fax: 01-660 8496
Email: info@burlingtonhotel.com
Web: www.burlingtonhotel.com

UNDER REFURBISHMENT JAN - RE-OPENING SUMMER 08

The Burlington is a Dublin institution, always at the heart of the action and central to the whole whirl of Dublin life. Its lively bars and restaurants and friendly open charm conspire to create an atmosphere that is hard to forget. Dublin City's largest conference hotel, it is centrally located - just a 5 minute stroll to the city centre. Please enquire about Facilities for Persons with Mobility Impairment.

***An IHF Quality Employer***

Member of Jurys Doyle Hotel Group

*Bookable on www.irelandhotels.com*
*Special Offer: www.irelandhotels.com/offers*

*Room Rate from €130.00 to €450.00*

500

**Open All Year**

## Dublin City

### Buswells Hotel

HOTEL ★★★ MAP 8 O 11

23/27 Molesworth Street,
Dublin 2

Tel: 01-614 6500 Fax: 01-676 2090
Email: buswells@quinn-hotels.com
Web: www.quinnhotels.com

Ideally located in the centre of Dublin City, we are minutes walk from St. Stephen's Green, Trinity College and the fashionable Grafton Street. Refurbished throughout in 2005, our 67 classic bedrooms allow you to relax and unwind after a long day in the busy city centre. WiFi access available in all bedrooms and public areas. Secure overnight car parking available in Dawson car park to all our guests from 5.30pm to 9.30am. Please enquire about Facilities for Persons with Mobility Impairment.

***An IHF Quality Employer***

Member of Quinn Hotels

*Bookable on www.irelandhotels.com*
*Special Offer: www.irelandhotels.com/offers*

*B&B from €70.00 to €144.00*
*Suites from €95.00 to €169.00*

*Paul Gallagher*
*General Manager*

67

Activities:

**Closed 24 - 26 December**

### Butlers Town House

GUESTHOUSE ★★★★ MAP 8 O 11

44 Lansdowne Road,
Ballsbridge,
Dublin 4

Tel: 01-667 4022 Fax: 01-667 3960
Email: info@butlers-hotel.com
Web: www.butlers-hotel.com

An oasis of country tranquillity in the heart of Dublin, Butlers Town House is an experience as opposed to a visit. Opened in March 1997, fully restored to reflect its former glory, but with all modern comforts from air-conditioning to modem points. Butlers Town House is renowned for its elegance and premier guest service. Private secure car park available. 5 Diamond RAC rated.

Member of Manor House Hotels

*Bookable on www.irelandhotels.com*

*B&B from €80.00 to €85.00*

*Suzanne Cole*
*General Manager*

20

**Closed 21 December - 13 January**

### Camden Court Hotel

HOTEL ★★★ MAP 8 O 11

Camden Street,
Dublin 2

Tel: 01-475 9666 Fax: 01-475 9677
Email: sales@camdencourthotel.com
Web: www.camdencourthotel.com

The Camden Court Hotel is situated in the heart of Dublin within a 5 minute walk of Grafton Street, adjacent to the LUAS line on Harcourt Street. The hotel comprises 246 well-appointed bedrooms all en suite with hairdryer, direct dial phone, flat screen TV, trouser press, Wi-Fi internet access and tea/coffee making facilities. We also provide excellent conference facilities, restaurant and modern bar. Our state of the art leisure centre consists of a 16m swimming pool, sauna, steam room, jacuzzi and a fully equipped gym. Complimentary secure carparking on site. Please enquire about Facilities for Persons with Mobility Impairment.

***An IHF Quality Employer***

Member of Cara Hotels

*Bookable on www.irelandhotels.com*
*Special Offer: www.irelandhotels.com/offers*

*Room Rate from €105.00 to €165.00*

*Stephen Hanna*
*General Manager*

246

Activities:

**Closed 23 - 28 December**

B&B Rates are per Person Sharing per Night incl. Breakfast.
or Room Rates are per Room per Night - See also Page 8

## Cassidys Hotel

HOTEL ★★★ MAP 8 O 11

Cavendish Row,
Upper O'Connell St.,
Dublin 1

Tel: 01-878 0555 Fax: 01-878 0687
Email: stay@cassidyshotel.com
Web: www.cassidyshotel.com

"A little gem in the heart of Dublin" Cassidy's is a comfortable 113 bed-roomed boutique styled hotel located in 3 converted Georgian buildings opposite the famous Gate Theatre. Trinity College, shopping and the vibrant Temple Bar quarter are all a short walk away. Groomes Bar & Bistro adds a relaxing air and offers quality, character & comfort. On-site Fitness Suite free to guest. Complementary WiFi.

***An IHF Quality Employer***

*Bookable on www.irelandhotels.com*
*Special Offer: www.irelandhotels.com/offers*

*B&B from €60.00 to €130.00*

*Martin Cassidy*
*General Manager*

113

Activities:

**Closed 23 - 26 December**

## Castle Hotel

HOTEL ★★★ MAP 8 O 11

2-4 Gardiner Row,
Dublin 1

Tel: 01-874 6949 Fax: 01-872 7674
Email: info@castle-hotel.ie
Web: www.castle-hotel.ie

Elegant Georgian hotel close to Dublin's main shopping district, renowned for its friendly service. One of Dublin's oldest hotels. Authentically restored, the décor and furnishings offer modern comfort combined with olde world features: crystal chandeliers, antique mirrors, marble fireplaces and period staircases. The individually decorated rooms offer private bathroom, TV, direct dial phone, hairdryers and beverage making facilities. The hotel has an intimate residents' bar and private parking. Please enquire about Facilities for Persons with Mobility Impairment.

Member of Castle Hotel Group

*Bookable on www.irelandhotels.com*
*Special Offer: www.irelandhotels.com/offers*

*B&B from €54.00 to €105.00*

*Yvonne Evans*
*Manageress*

38

**Closed 24 - 27 December**

B&B Rates are per Person Sharing per Night incl. Breakfast.
or Room Rates are per Room per Night - **See also Page 8**

## Dublin City

### Castleknock Hotel and Country Club

HOTEL ★★★★ MAP 8 O 11

Porterstown Road,
Castleknock,
Dublin 15

Tel: 01-640 6300 Fax: 01-640 6303

Email: reservations@chcc.ie

Web: www.towerhotelgroup.com

Built to an exceptionally high 4* standard, this modern & stylish hotel is located just outside Castleknock Village with stunning views of an 18 hole golf course & surrounding countryside. Ideal for business & leisure guests. 9km from Dublin City, 13km from Dublin Airport & within easy access of the M50 motorway. Extensive conference facilities, magnificent leisure, health & beauty facilities, 2 bars & 2 restaurants which includes the stunning Park Restaurant which overlooks the surrounding golf course. Ample parking. Special offers available online - www.towerhotelgroup.com

***An IHF Quality Employer***

Member of Tower Hotel Group

*Bookable on www.irelandhotels.com*
*Special Offer: www.irelandhotels.com/offers*

*B&B from €77.50 to €165.00*
*Suites from €250.00 to €350.00*

*John Caffrey*
*General Manager*

144

*Activities:*

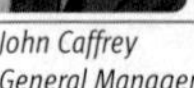

**Closed 23 - 25 December**

### Celtic Lodge Guesthouse

GUESTHOUSE ★ MAP 8 O 11

81/82 Talbot Street,
Dublin 1

Tel: 01-878 8732 Fax: 01-878 8698

Email: celticguesthouse@eircom.net

Web: www.celticaccommodation.net

This gracious Victorian residence is in the heart of the city centre adjacent to the bus and train stations and 15 minutes from the airport. A stroll from our door is the vibrant Temple Bar district with its numerous pubs, restaurants and clubs. Trinity College, Christchurch Cathedral, Dublin Castle and a number of theatres are within a stone's throw. All rooms en suite and finished to a very high standard with cable TV & tea/coffee making facilities. Next door a traditional bar with Irish music seven nights a week, free. Bar Food Available 2007. Bookable online at www.celticlodge.ie

*Bookable on www.irelandhotels.com*
*Special Offer: www.irelandhotels.com/offers*

*B&B from €35.00 to €65.00*

*Caroline Kearns*
*Reservations Manager*

29

**Closed 22 - 27 December**

### Charleville Lodge

GUESTHOUSE ★★★ MAP 8 O 11

268-272 North Circular Road,
Phibsborough,
Dublin 7

Tel: 01-838 6633 Fax: 01-838 5854

Email: info@charlevillelodge.ie

Web: www.charlevillelodge.ie

Charleville Lodge, (former home of Lord Charleville), is a Victorian property located 15 minutes walk from the city centre, Trinity College, Temple Bar and en route to Dublin Airport and car ferry. Modernised to offer all the facilities normally associated with a larger hotel, while retaining the family-run atmosphere. There is a free car park, tea/coffee facility and broadband internet access. Group evening meals available upon request. 2 Nights B&B & 1 green fee in Island Golf Links from €150.00 to €200.00 per person sharing. Please enquire about Facilities for Persons with Mobility Impairment.

***An IHF Quality Employer***

Member of Premier Collection

*Bookable on www.irelandhotels.com*
*Special Offer: www.irelandhotels.com/offers*

*B&B from €35.00 to €150.00*

*Paul Stenson*
*Director*

30

*Activities:*

**Closed 20 - 26 December**



B&B Rates are per Person Sharing per Night incl. Breakfast. or Room Rates are per Room per Night - See also Page 8

## Clarence (The)

HOTEL ★★★★★ MAP 8 0 11

6-8 Wellington Quay,
Dublin 2

Tel: 01-407 0800 Fax: 01-407 0820
Email: reservations@theclarence.ie
Web: www.theclarence.ie

Built to a 5***** specification. Located on the River Liffey, in the heart of the city, The Clarence was built in 1852 and was transformed into a boutique hotel in 1996. Owned by Bono and The Edge of the rock group U2, The Clarence has 49 individually designed bedrooms and suites. A massage and treatment room, fitness room and valet parking are all available. The renowned Tea Room Restaurant and Octagon Bar, famous for its cocktails, are located here. Please enquire about Facilities for Persons with Mobility Impairment.

*Bookable on www.irelandhotels.com*
*Special Offer: www.irelandhotels.com/offers*

*Room Rate from €189.00 to €420.00*
*Suites from €439.00 to €2,700.00*

*Oliver Sevestre*
*General Manager*

49

*Activities:*

**Closed 24 - 26 December**

## Clarion Hotel Dublin IFSC

HOTEL ★★★★ MAP 8 0 11

Excise Walk,
International Financial Services Centre,
Dublin 1

Tel: 01-433 8800 Fax: 01-433 8801
Email: info@clarionhotelifsc.com
Web: www.clariondublincity.com

Set along the banks of the River Liffey, the 4 Star Clarion IFSC boasts 180 fully refurbished en suite bedrooms, each offering state of the art technology, and providing every comfort for the discerning business & leisure guest. Following a €13m refurbishment, the hotel property features an extensive range of meeting facilities. For those wishing to enjoy a leisure break, relaxing spa treatments will be available from October 2007. On-site amenities include a leisure centre, complete with indoor pool & beauty treatments. Kudos restaurant offers a diverse & exotic menu including oriental & European dishes.

***An IHF Quality Employer***
Member of Choice Hotels Ireland

*Bookable on www.irelandhotels.com*
*Special Offer: www.irelandhotels.com/offers*

*Room Rate from €165.00 to €325.00*

*Dermot De Loughry*
*General Manager*

180

*Activities:*

**Open all year**

## Clarion Hotel Dublin Liffey Valley

HOTEL ★★★★ MAP 8 0 11

Liffey Valley,
Dublin 22

Tel: 01-625 8000 Fax: 01-625 8001
Email: info@clarionhotelliffeyvalley.com
Web: www.clarionhotelliffeyvalley.com

This stylish new hotel is conveniently located on the N4 beside the Liffey Valley Shopping Centre (85 shops), close to the M50, and just 6 miles from the city centre. Spacious and comfortable guest bedrooms with Sinergie Restaurant (Irish cuisine with Mediterranean influences), Kudos Bar with Asian Wok Station, 24 hour room service and SanoVitae Health & Fitness Club, make this a hotel you will want to re-visit. Conference facilities for up to 400 people, ample car parking. Please enquire about Facilities for Persons with Mobility Impairment.

***An IHF Quality Employer***
Member of Clarion Hotels

*Bookable on www.irelandhotels.com*
*Special Offer: www.irelandhotels.com/offers*

*Room Rate from €95.00 to €270.00*
*Suites from €125.00 to €470.00*

*Eamon Daly*
*General Manager*

292

*Activities:*

**Closed 24 - 29 December**

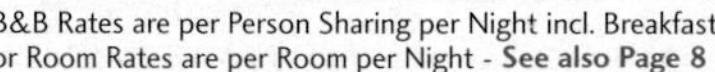

B&B Rates are per Person Sharing per Night incl. Breakfast.
or Room Rates are per Room per Night - **See also Page 8**

## Dublin City

### Clifden Guesthouse

GUESTHOUSE ★★★ MAP 8 O 11

32 Gardiner Place,
(off middle Gardiner Street),
Dublin 1

Tel: 01-874 6364 Fax: 01-874 6122
Email: info@clifdenhouse.com
Web: www.clifdenhouse.com

A refurbished city centre Georgian home. Our private car park provides security for guests' cars, even after check-out. All rooms are non-smoking and have shower, WC, WHB, TV, direct dial phone and tea-making facilities. We cater for single, twin, double, triple and family occupancies. Convenient to airport, ferryports, Bus Aras (bus station) and DART. We are only 5 minutes walk from O'Connell Street. AA approved.

Member of Premier Collection

*Bookable on www.irelandhotels.com*
*Special Offer: www.irelandhotels.com/offers*

*B&B from €25.00 to €130.00*

*Jack & Mary Lalor*

15

Closed 20 - 27 December

### Clontarf Castle Hotel

HOTEL ★★★★ MAP 8 O 11

Castle Avenue,
Clontarf,
Dublin 3

Tel: 01-833 2321 Fax: 01-833 0418
Email: info@clontarfcastle.ie
Web: www.clontarfcastle.ie

Clontarf Castle Hotel is part of a privately owned Irish hotel collection. Dating back to 1172 we offer the perfect blend of contemporary and traditional. From the strikingly historical exterior, to the warm Irish welcome waiting inside, the emphasis throughout is on luxury and glamour. 111 distinctively designed bedrooms and suites. 8 meeting rooms facilitating up to 600 delegates. Banqueting facilities for up to 450 guests. 2 bars; the chic Indigo Lounge & the time honoured Knights Bar... Unique restaurant, Farenheit Grill specialising in steak & fish. Please enquire about Facilities for Persons with Mobility Impairment.

***An IHF Quality Employer***

*Bookable on www.irelandhotels.com*
*Special Offer: www.irelandhotels.com/offers*

*B&B from €75.00 to €200.00*
*Suites from €400.00 to €600.00*

*Dermot Hennessy*
*General Manager*

111

Activities:

Closed 24 - 25 December

### Comfort Inn Citywest

HOTEL MAP 8 O 11

Kingswood Villiage,
Naas Road,
Dublin 22

Tel: 01-461 9900 Fax: 01-461 9911
Email: info.citywest@comfortinns.ie
Web: www.comfortinns.ie

Built to a 3*** specification. The new Comfort Inn Citywest is situated in the heart of the Citywest Business Park, convenient to city centre, minutes drive from Dublin Airport. Easy access into the city centre via the LUAS Light Rail Service. Our spacious 129 en suite rooms are tastefully decorated to the highest standard with DD phone, multi-channel TV, hairdryer and tea/coffee facilities. Disabled rooms available. Complimentary broadband internet available in all guest rooms. Please enquire about Facilities for Persons with Mobility Impairment.

Member of Choice Hotels Ireland

*Room Rate from €89.00 to €249.00*

*Mario Cossani*
*General Manager*

129

Closed 23 - 27 December



B&B Rates are per Person Sharing per Night incl. Breakfast.
or Room Rates are per Room per Night - See also Page 8

## Comfort Inn Granby Row

HOTEL ★★★ MAP 8 O 11

Parnell Square,
Dublin 1

Tel: 01-871 6800 Fax: 01-871 6810
Email: info@comfortinns.ie
Web: www.comfortinns.ie

Built to a 3*** specification. The new Comfort Inn Granby Row is a purpose built contemporary inn, which is superbly located on the grounds of the former Dublin Wax Museum. The Comfort Inn Granby Row is in the heart of Dublin city, a short walk from O'Connell Street Dublin's main thoroughfare, and the entertainment area as well as the airport and main bus and rail stations. Up to the minute technology, including free broadband in all 126 bedrooms as standard. Air-conditioning in each bedroom and public area. Please enquire about Facilities for Persons with Mobility Impairment.

Member of Choice Hotels Ireland

**Bookable on www.irelandhotels.com**

**Room Rate from €89.00 to €249.00**
**Suites from €109.00 to €299.00**

Mr Philip Uzice
General Manager

126

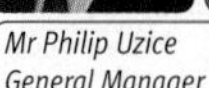

**Closed 23 - 26 December**

## Comfort Inn Parnell Square

HOTEL ★★ MAP 8 O 11

Great Denmark Street,
Off Parnell Square,
Dublin 1

Tel: 01-873 7700 Fax: 01-873 7776
Email: reservations@comfortinnparnell.com
Web: www.comfortparnellsquare.com

One minute off O'Connell Street in the heart of Georgian Dublin, The Comfort Inn Parnell Square offers the ideal base for the leisure or business traveller. Lose yourself in a world of literary and artistic genius in the many theatres and museums within walking distance of the hotel. We take great delight in offering you spacious rooms with free internet access, bath & power shower and satellite TV. Please enquire about Facilities for Persons with Mobility Impairment.

**An IHF Quality Employer**

Member of Choice Hotels

**Bookable on www.irelandhotels.com**
**Special Offer: www.irelandhotels.com/offers**

**Room Rate from €89.00 to €249.00**

Denise Batt
General Manager

92

**Closed 23 - 27 December**

## Comfort Inn Smithfield

HOTEL ★★★ MAP 8 O 11

Smithfield Village,
Dublin 7

Tel: 01-485 0900 Fax: 01-485 0910
Email: res.smithfield@comfortinns.ie
Web: www.comfortinns.ie

The Comfort Inn Smithfield is a newly built contemporary inn, located on the Smithfield Plaza. The Comfort Inn is within a short walk of the main shopping, entertainment, sightseeing and business districts of the city. On its doorstep is one of the main LUAS light rail stations giving easy access to the airport and main bus and rail stations. Bedroom facilities include power showers, satellite TV plus free broadband. Free WiFi and broadband available in meeting rooms. Secure car parking is provided by Parkrite, overnight rate starting from €10. Please enquire about Facilities for Persons with Mobility Impairment.

Member of Choice Hotels Ireland

**Bookable on www.irelandhotels.com**
**Special Offer: www.irelandhotels.com/offers**

**Room Rate from €89.00 to €249.00**
**Suites from €109.00 to €299.00**

Mark Long
General Manager

92

**Closed 23 - 27 December**

## Dublin City

### Conrad Dublin

HOTEL ★★★★★ MAP 8 O 11

Earlsfort Terrace,
Dublin 2

Tel: 01-602 8900 Fax: 01-676 5424
Email: dublininfo@conradhotels.com
Web: www.conraddublin.com

Conrad Dublin completed its refurbishment in 2005. Located in the heart of Dublin's city centre, only a few minutes walk from Grafton Street, the hotel has 192 de luxe guest rooms including 16 suites. Each room comes complete with CD player, ergonomic work stations, broadband internet, multi-channel television, air-conditioning, turndown service, bathrobes, slippers and hairdryer. The hotel offers a choice of two bars, a restaurant, 24 hour room service, a state of the art fitness centre, fully equipped business centre and extensive conference and meeting facilities.

***An IHF Quality Employer***

Member of Hilton Hotels Corporation

*Bookable on www.irelandhotels.com*
*Special Offer: www.irelandhotels.com/offers*

*Room Rate from €185.00 to €380.00*
*Suites from €250.00 to €1,500.00*

*Laurens Zieren*
*General Manager*

192

Activities:

Open All Year

### Days Hotel Park West

HOTEL ★★★ MAP 8 O 11

Park West Business Campus,
Nangor Road,
Dublin 12

Tel: 1890-329329 Fax: 01-642 9101
Email: info@dayshotelparkwest.com
Web: www.dayshotelparkwest.com

Situated just off the M50 at the Naas Road exit, Days Hotel is located within the award-winning Park West Business Campus, close to all the major road networks, and just six miles from Dublin City centre. With 146 impressive guest rooms, all with free broadband, TV/DVD player, ironing station, hairdryer, tea/coffee making facilities and safe, the hotel offers dedicated conference and meeting facilities for up to 100 delegates. Rueben's Café Bar open throughout the day, with an appetizing menu of snacks and hot dishes. Car parking is available free of charge for residents. Hotel direct Tel line: 01 642 9100.

***An IHF Quality Employer***

Member of Days Hotels Ireland

*Bookable on www.irelandhotels.com*
*Special Offer: www.irelandhotels.com/offers*

*Room Rate from €79.00 to €299.00*

*Andrea Wallace*
*General Manager*

146

Closed 23 - 29 December

### Days Inn Rathmines

HOTEL ★★★ MAP 8 O 11

Lower Rathmines Road,
Dublin 6

Tel: 1890-329329 Fax: 01-406 6200
Email: reservations@dayshotelrathmines.com
Web: www.dayshotelrathmines.com

Situated just fifteen minutes walk from the city centre, in the bustling area of Rathmines. Days Hotel comprises 66 rooms, including a selection of luxurious suites with living room and small fitted kitchen. All rooms offer iron & ironing board, trouser press, tea/coffee station and safe. The spectacular Tram Co. Bar, Restaurant and Club, offers complimentary admission to residents. Secure underground car parking available free of charge. The ultimate shopping experience, Dundrum Town Centre is located ten minutes drive away. Hotel direct Tel line: (01) 406 6100.

***An IHF Quality Employer***

Member of Days Hotels Ireland

*Bookable on www.irelandhotels.com*
*Special Offer: www.irelandhotels.com/offers*

*Room Rate from €79.00 to €249.00*

*Jane Dunleavy*
*General Manager*

66

Open All Year



B&B Rates are per Person Sharing per Night incl. Breakfast. or Room Rates are per Room per Night - See also Page 8

## Days Inn Talbot Street

GUESTHOUSE ★★★ MAP 8 O 11

95-98 Talbot Street,
Dublin 1

Tel: 1890-329329 Fax: 01-874 9672
Email: info@daysinntalbot.com
Web: www.daysinntalbot.com

Newly refurbished in 2007, Days Inn Talbot Street boasts the perfect location, just 2 minutes walk from O'Connell Street. In the surrounding area, you will find many shops, restaurants, pubs, theatres and nightclubs. Temple Bar and Trinity College are just a short stroll away. All rooms are en suite, with colourful modern décor. Full Irish breakfast available every morning. Hotel direct Tel line (01) 874 9202.

***An IHF Quality Employer***

Member of Days Hotels Ireland

*Bookable on www.irelandhotels.com*
*Special Offer: www.irelandhotels.com/offers*

*Room Rate from €69.00 to €220.00*

*Paul Dempsey*
*Group Operations Manager*

60

**Closed 24 - 28 December**

## Dergvale Hotel

HOTEL ★★ MAP 8 O 11

4 Gardiner Place,
Dublin 1

Tel: 01-874 4753 Fax: 01-874 8276
Email: dergvale@indigo.ie
Web: www.dergvalehotel.com

The Dergvale Hotel is located within walking distance of all principal shopping areas, cinemas, museums, Trinity College, Dublin Castle and airport bus. Most bedrooms with showers en suite, colour TV and direct dial telephone. Fully licensed. A courteous and efficient staff are on hand to make your stay an enjoyable one. The hotel is under the personal supervision of Gerard and Nancy Nolan.

*Bookable on www.irelandhotels.com*
*Special Offer: www.irelandhotels.com/offers*

*B&B from €40.00 to €70.00*

*Gerard Nolan*
*Owner*

17

3

**Closed 24 December - 07 January**

## Donnybrook Hall

GUESTHOUSE ★★★ MAP 8 O 11

6 Belmont Avenue,
Donnybrook,
Dublin 4

Tel: 01-269 1633 Fax: 01-269 2649
Email: info@donnybrookhall.com
Web: www.donnybrookhall.com

Centrally located to University College Dublin, RDS Showgrounds, Lansdowne Rugby Grounds and Dublin City centre. Located on a quiet, restful street yet only a few minutes walk to pubs, shops and restaurants. Our fine Victorian building features an intimate garden, with tea/coffee facilities in our conservatory for your convenience, Each en suite room is individually decorated and has TV, hairdryers and DD telephone, broadband access. Cleanliness, quality and a warm welcome. Please enquire about Facilities for Persons with Mobility Impairment.

Member of Premier Guesthouses

*Bookable on www.irelandhotels.com*
*Special Offer: www.irelandhotels.com/offers*

*B&B from €45.00 to €75.00*

*Terry & Rosemary Masterson*
*Owners*

9

**Open All Year**

## Dublin City

### Donnybrook Lodge

GUESTHOUSE ★★★ MAP 8 O 11

131 Stillorgan Road,
Donnybrook,
Dublin 4

Tel: 01-283 7333 Fax: 01-443 0550
Email: info@donnybrooklodge.net
Web: www.donnybrooklodge.com

Relax in comfortable surroundings in the heart of Dublin's most exclusive area. Ideally situated close to city centre, ferryports & adjacent to RDS, Lansdowne, UCD and RTE. We are located aprox 7 mins walk to St. Vincents Hospital. A short stroll from a host of restaurants & entertainment. Recently refurbished, our well-appointed rooms feature en suite bathrooms, direct dial phone & TV. Private parking available. Enjoy a leisurely breakfast in our elegant dining room, overlooking gardens. A relaxed atmosphere & warm welcome awaits you. info@donnybrooklodge.net / www.donnybrooklodge.net

*Bookable on www.irelandhotels.com*

**B&B from €35.00 to €75.00**

*Pat Butler*

7

Open All Year

### Drury Court Hotel

HOTEL ★★★ MAP 8 O 11

28-30 Lower Stephen Street,
Dublin 2

Tel: 01-475 1988 Fax: 01-478 5730
Email: reservations@drurycourthotel.com
Web: www.drurycourthotel.com

Located in the heart of Dublin, beside Stephen's Green and Grafton Street. Convenient to the hotel are theatres, galleries, museums, Trinity College and Temple Bar. The hotel comprises 42 luxurious bedrooms all en suite with direct dial phone, free wireless internet service available, multi-channel TV/Radio and tea/coffee facilities. There is also the Bia Bar, a lively bar serving sumptuous food all day. The hotel is adjacent to secure public parking, just perfect for the leisure or business visitor. Please enquire about Facilities for Persons with Mobility Impairment.

***An IHF Quality Employer***

Member of MinOtel Ireland Hotel Group

*Bookable on www.irelandhotels.com*
*Special Offer: www.irelandhotels.com/offers*

**B&B from €60.00 to €155.00**

*Paul Hand*
*General Manager*

42

Closed 22 - 27 December

### Dublin Citi Hotel

HOTEL MAP 8 O 11

46-49 Dame Street,
Dublin 2

Tel: 01-679 4455 Fax: 01-679 4496
Email: reservations@dublincitihotel.com
Web: www.dublincitihotel.com

Built to a 3*** specification. This hotel lies in the heart of Dublin city on the edge of Temple Bar. Boasting 26 guest rooms that have been designed with comfort and convenience in mind, the Dublin Citi Hotel offers great food and genuine Irish hospitality in a prime location. Attractions such as Trinity College, Grafton Street and Christ Church are right outside the door. Late bar Wed - Sat until 2:30am.

*Bookable on www.irelandhotels.com*
*Special Offer: www.irelandhotels.com/offers*

**B&B from €40.00 to €130.00**

*Philip Jaronski*
*Front Office Manager*

26

Closed 24 - 26 December



B&B Rates are per Person Sharing per Night incl. Breakfast. or Room Rates are per Room per Night - See also Page 8

## Dublin Skylon Hotel

HOTEL ★★★ MAP 8 O 11

Upper Drumcondra Road,
Dublin 9

Tel: 01-837 9121 Fax: 01-837 2778

Email: ahyland@dublinskylonhotel.com

Web: www.dublinskylonhotel.com

A smart hotel on the northern approach, ten minutes from the airport and five from the city centre. Dublin Skylon Hotel has just the right blend of style and informality to make your stay special. Its restaurant and bar are welcoming and just as popular in the neighbourhood as with guests. Please enquire about Facilities for Persons with Mobility Impairment.

***An IHF Quality Employer***

Member of Brian McEniff Hotels

*Bookable on www.irelandhotels.com*
*Special Offer: www.irelandhotels.com/offers*

*Room Rate from €79.00 to €549.00*

*Brian McEniff / Andrew Hyland*
*Proprietor / General Manager*

126

*Activities:*

**Closed 24 - 26 December**

## Dylan Hotel

HOTEL ★★★★★ MAP 8 O 11

Eastmoreland Place,
Dublin 2

Tel: 01-660 3000 Fax: 01-660 3005

Email: info@dylan.ie

Web: www.dylan.ie

By day the open plan lobby exudes warm & elegance by night Dylan is candles & champagne. Located on a leafy affluent residential street, Dylan is just minutes away from the heart of Dublin City Centre a short stroll over the canal along the historic Baggot Street leads to the city centre haven of St. Stephens Green & the world renowned Grafton Street, unrivalled for its top quality shopping and diverse Street entertainment. Please enquire about Facilities for Persons with Mobility Impairment.

***An IHF Quality Employer***

Member of Fylan Collection

*Bookable on www.irelandhotels.com*
*Special Offer: www.irelandhotels.com/offers*

*Room Rate from €295.00 to €800.00*

*Siobhan Delaney*
*Hotel General Manager*

44

**Closed 25 - 26 December**

## Egan's Guesthouse

GUESTHOUSE ★★★ MAP 8 O 11

7/9 Iona Park,
Glasnevin,
Dublin 9

Tel: 01-830 3611 Fax: 01-830 3312

Email: info@eganshouse.com

Web: www.eganshouse.com

Egan's House is an elegant terrace of Edwardian houses in a quiet area but only 1.7km from Dublin's city centre. All 23 guest rooms are en suite with television, telephone, hairdryer, electronic safe, ironing centre, power shower and tea/coffee facility. Free car parking. Dublin Airport is just 10 minutes by taxi and the car ferry is also close by, as is Croke Park, the Point Depot, RDS and championship golf courses. Broadband internet access available.

Member of Premier Guesthouses

*Bookable on www.irelandhotels.com*
*Special Offer: www.irelandhotels.com/offers*

*B&B from €30.00 to €90.00*

*Pat & Monica Finn*
*Proprietors*

23

**Open All Year**

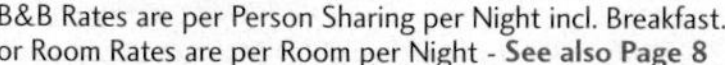
B&B Rates are per Person Sharing per Night incl. Breakfast.
or Room Rates are per Room per Night - **See also Page 8**

## Dublin City

### Ferryview House

GUESTHOUSE ★★★ MAP 8 O 11

96 Clontarf Road,
Clontarf,
Dublin 3

Tel: 01-833 5893 Fax: 01-853 2141
Email: ferryview@oceanfree.net
Web: www.ferryviewhouse.com

Ferryview House is located in the exclusive coastal suburb of Clontarf, 2.5 miles from the city centre on a regular bus route. The totally refurbished family-run guesthouse is also Selected ♦♦♦♦ with the Automobile Association. The house is close to Dublin Port, the Point Theatre, East Point Business Park (2km) and Dublin Airport is 15 minutes away. Local facilities include restaurants, coastal walks, Clontarf Rugby Club, tennis and 3 golf clubs.

*B&B from €45.00 to €55.00*

*Margaret Allister* — 8

Closed 21 December - 01 January

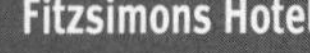

### Fitzsimons Hotel

HOTEL ★★★ MAP 8 O 11

21-22 Wellington Quay,
Temple Bar,
Dublin 2

Tel: 01-677 9315 Fax: 01-677 9387
Email: info@fitzsimonshotel.com
Web: www.fitzsimonshotel.com

Fitzsimons Hotel a boutique hotel situated on the banks of the River Liffey in the heart of Temple Bar. Its location offers the visitor doorstep access to this vibrant, exciting locale and all it has to offer, theatres, galleries, bars, restaurants, live music venues and alternative shops. Fitzsimons offers visitors a great place to socialise now with 4 floors of entertainment including our new open air Roof Terrace with bar, bars on all floors, restaurant and nightclub, seven nights a week. Please enquire about Facilities for Persons with Mobility Impairment.

*Bookable on www.irelandhotels.com*
*Special Offer: www.irelandhotels.com/offers*

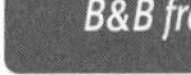

*B&B from €50.00 to €110.00*

*Edina Sallai*
*Reservations* — 22

Closed 24 - 25 December

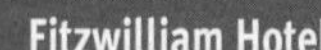

### Fitzwilliam Hotel

HOTEL ★★★★★ MAP 8 O 11

St. Stephen's Green,
Dublin 2

Tel: 01-478 7000 Fax: 01-478 7878
Email: enq@fitzwilliamhotel.com
Web: www.fitzwilliamhotel.com

This modern, 5***** Conran designed classic is uniquely positioned on St. Stephen's Green, paces away from Grafton Street, Ireland's premier shopping avenue. Understated luxury & impeccable service make it the perfect hotel for business and pleasure. Dine in the highly acclaimed Michelin Star Thornton's Restaurant or the fashionable Citron Brasserie. Complimentary broadband in all rooms, WiFi in public areas. State of the art AV equipment in all meeting rooms. Hair & Beauty Salon, Dublin's hippest & most stylish 2,000sq ft penthouse - the ultimate experience!

***An IHF Quality Employer***
Member of Summit Hotels & Resorts

*Bookable on www.irelandhotels.com*
*Special Offer: www.irelandhotels.com/offers*

*Room Rate from €230.00 to €380.00*
*Suites from €450.00 to €3,200.00*

*John Kavanagh*
*General Manager* — 139

*Activities:*

Open All Year



B&B Rates are per Person Sharing per Night incl. Breakfast.
or Room Rates are per Room per Night - See also Page 8

## Fleet Street Hotel (The)

HOTEL ★★★ MAP 8 O 11

19/20 Fleet Street,
Temple Bar,
Dublin 2

Tel: 01-670 8122 Fax: 01-670 8103

Email: reservations@fleethoteltemplebar.com

Web: www.fleethoteltemplebar.com

The Fleet Street Hotel is ideally located in the Temple Bar area of the city. We offer the finest traditions of quality and service. We are ideally based for both business and leisure, walking distance from Trinity College, Grafton Street and all the local bars and restaurants. All rooms are en suite with tea and coffee facilities, direct dial telephone, hairdryer and trouser press. TV in all bedrooms.

***An IHF Quality Employer***

*Bookable on www.irelandhotels.com*

*Special Offer: www.irelandhotels.com/offers*

*B&B from €60.00 to €120.00*

*Patrick Carney*
*General Manager*

71

**Closed 24 - 27 December**

## Four Seasons Hotel Dublin

HOTEL ★★★★★ MAP 8 O 11

Simmonscourt Road,
Dublin 4

Tel: 01-665 4000 Fax: 01-665 4099

Email: reservations.dublin@fourseasons.com

Web: www.fourseasons.com/dublin

The charm of Irish tradition & hospitality combine to provide the stage for Four Seasons Hotel Dublin. The hotel offers a location of cosmopolitan convenience in the prestigious embassy & residential district, bringing together exceptional guest rooms and suites with the finest facilities for business & leisure. Reflective of Dublin's architectural heritage, the hotel is just minutes from the cultural & entertainment options of the city centre. The hotel features 15,000 sq ft of meeting and banqueting space, fine dining in Seasons Restaurant, Ice Bar and an 11,000 sq ft full service spa.

***An IHF Quality Employer***

Member of Four Seasons Hotels & Resorts

*Room Rate from €315.00 to €405.00*
*Suites from €505.00 to €2,600.00*

*Jose Soriano*
*General Manager*

197

*Activities:*

**Open All Year**

## George Frederic Handel Hotel

HOTEL ★★ MAP 8 O 11

16-18 Fishamble Street,
Christchurch, Temple Bar,
Dublin 8

Tel: 01-670 9400 Fax: 01-670 9410

Email: info@handelshotel.com

Web: www.handelshotel.com

Our secret is out! Centrally located, while situated in the heart of Dublin's vibrant Temple Bar area, the George Frederic Handel Hotel is also within easy walking distance of the city's main tourist attractions and financial districts. We offer a high standard of accommodation combined with a warm Irish welcome - all at a great price. Live online booking system at www.handelshotel.com Please enquire about Facilities for Persons with Mobility Impairment.

*Room Rate from €75.00 to €240.00*

*Caroline Lamba*
*Operations Manager*

40

**Closed 24 - 27 December**

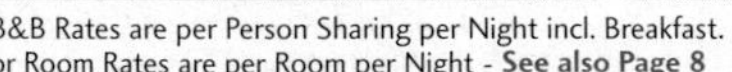

B&B Rates are per Person Sharing per Night incl. Breakfast.
or Room Rates are per Room per Night - **See also Page 8**

## Glenogra House

GUESTHOUSE ★★★★ MAP 8 O 11

64 Merrion Road,
Ballsbridge,
Dublin 4

Tel: 01-668 3661 Fax: 01-668 3698
Email: info@glenogra.com
Web: www.glenogra.com

Glenogra is a beautiful Edwardian guesthouse situated in Ballsbridge, 10 minutes from Dublin city centre. Opposite the RDS and Four Seasons Hotel, Glenogra is close to amenities including Sandymount DART station, bus routes, the Aircoach, car ferries, embassies and a range of excellent restaurants and traditional bars. Rated 4**** accommodation by Fáilte Ireland and ♦♦♦♦♦ by the AA. Glenogra is a non-smoking guesthouse. Free car park.

Member of Premier Guesthouses

*Bookable on www.irelandhotels.com*
*Special Offer: www.irelandhotels.com/offers*

*B&B from €59.50 to €99.50*

*Joseph Donohoe*
*Manager*

13

Closed 20 December - 10 January

## Grafton Capital Hotel

HOTEL ★★★ MAP 8 O 11

Stephens Street Lower,
Dublin 2

Tel: 01-648 1100 Fax: 01-648 1122
Email: info@graftoncapitalhotel.com
Web: www.capital-hotels.com

Grafton Capital Hotel is located in the heart of our effervescent city centre, paces from the core shopping, entertainment and cultural districts. Our traditional Georgian style guest rooms are bright and spacious and feature all modern conveniences to ensure a pleasant and memorable stay. Residents enjoy complimentary admission to a variety of popular nightclubs in the city centre, including the popular Break For The Border bar restaurant and nightclub adjacent. Now offering free wireless. Please enquire about Facilities for Persons with Mobility Impairment.

***An IHF Quality Employer***

Member of Capital Hotel Group

*Bookable on www.irelandhotels.com*
*Special Offer: www.irelandhotels.com/offers*

*B&B from €60.00 to €120.00*

*Rosemary Noone*
*General Manager*

75

Closed 24 - 26 December

## Grand Canal Hotel

HOTEL ★★★ MAP 8 O 11

Grand Canal Street,
Dublin 4

Tel: 01-646 1000 Fax: 01-646 1001
Email: sales@grandcanalhotel.com
Web: www.grandcanalhotel.com

Opened in 2004. 142 bedrooms offer a warm and friendly atmosphere and its excellent location in Georgian Dublin in the affluent Ballsbridge area makes the hotel the perfect base to discover Dublin. City Centre, Trinity College and the RDS are accessible on foot in only 15 minutes. Guests can enjoy breakfast in Epic Restaurant or a snack / beverage in the Gasworks Bar. Canal Express offers a variety of coffees. Free parking, DART station across the road. Please enquire about Facilities for Persons with Mobility Impairment.

***An IHF Quality Employer***

Member of Cara Hotels

*Bookable on www.irelandhotels.com*
*Special Offer: www.irelandhotels.com/offers*

*Room Rate from €99.00 to €229.00*

*Kirsty Fallis*
*General Manager*

142

*Activities:*

Closed 22 - 28 December



B&B Rates are per Person Sharing per Night incl. Breakfast.
or Room Rates are per Room per Night - **See also Page 8**

## Gresham (The)

HOTEL ★★★★ MAP 8 O 11

23 Upper O'Connell Street,
Dublin 1

Tel: 01-874 6881 Fax: 01-878 7175
Email: info@thegresham.com
Web: www.gresham-hotels.com

Elegant, sophisticated and offering unparalleled standards of hospitality and customer care. The Gresham has undergone an imaginative and tasteful transformation. Each room is equipped with air conditioning, complimentary WiFi and state of the art entertainment system. Other facilities include a renowned Class d'Or concierge service, two bars, and afternoon tea in the luxurious lobby. Car parking (charges apply). AA approved. Please enquire about Facilities for Persons with Mobility Impairment.

***An IHF Quality Employer***

Member of Gresham Hotel Group

*Bookable on www.irelandhotels.com*
*Special Offer: www.irelandhotels.com/offers*

*Room Rate from €200.00 to €650.00*
*Suites from €1,500.00 to €2,200.00*

*Paul McCracken*
*Operations Director*

288

*Activities:*

**Open All Year**

## Harcourt Hotel

HOTEL ★★★ MAP 8 O 11

60 Harcourt Street,
Dublin 2

Tel: 01-478 3677 Fax: 01-478 1557
Email: reservations@harcourthotel.ie
Web: www.harcourthotel.ie

The Harcourt Hotel's Georgian exterior conceals its contemporary interior. The boutique style hotel is famous for once being home to George Bernard Shaw. Facilities include a convivial Bar D-Two, a landscaped year-round beer garden (heated), restaurant "Little Caesers" & a nightclub from Wed - Sat (usually). It is best described as a lively hotel (some rooms can suffer from noise, particularly at the weekends). Local secure car parking available at under €5 per night. The hotel is located off the South West corner of St. Stephen's Green. It is one LUAS (tram) stop away from Grafton Street. The LUAS also services the new Dundrum Town Centre.

*Bookable on www.irelandhotels.com*
*Special Offer: www.irelandhotels.com/offers*

*Room Rate from €69.00 to €249.00*

*Danielle McGill*
*Operations Manager*

51

**Closed 24 - 26 December**

## Harding Hotel

HOTEL ★★ MAP 8 O 11

Copper Alley,
Fishamble Street,
Dublin 2

Tel: 01-679 6500 Fax: 01-679 6504
Email: info@hardinghotel.ie
Web: www.hardinghotel.ie

The Harding Hotel is a stylish city centre hotel located within Dublin's Temple Bar. All 53 en suite rooms have television, direct dial telephone, fridge, hairdryer, tea/coffee making facilities and WiFi access. Relax and enjoy a drink in Darkey Kelly's Bar or a wonderful meal in the new Copper Alley Bistro. Groups and individuals welcome. Please enquire about Facilities for Persons with Mobility Impairment.

*Bookable on www.irelandhotels.com*
*Special Offer: www.irelandhotels.com/offers*

*Room Rate from €65.00 to €190.00*

*Aine Hickey*
*Manager*

52

**Closed 24 - 26 December**

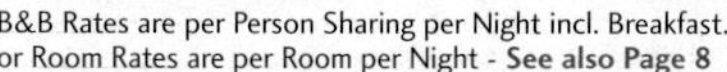

B&B Rates are per Person Sharing per Night incl. Breakfast.
or Room Rates are per Room per Night - **See also Page 8**

## Dublin City

### Harrington Hall

GUESTHOUSE ★★★★ MAP 8 O 11


70 Harcourt Street,
Dublin 2

Tel: 01-475 3497 Fax: 01-475 4544
Email: harringtonhall@eircom.net
Web: www.harringtonhall.com

Harrington Hall is centrally located on Harcourt St, just off the South West corner of St.Stephen's Green. It is convenient to the famous Shopping area of Grafton St. This boutique hotel features 28 magnificent bedrooms, including junior suites and family rooms. All bedrooms are equipped to today's exacting standards with en suite facilities, direct dial phone, wireless internet, TV and optional fax facilities.

Member of Manor House Hotels

*Bookable on www.irelandhotels.com*
*Special Offer: www.irelandhotels.com/offers*

*Room Rate from €130.00 to €180.00*

*Paul Glynn*

28

**Open All Year**

### Harvey's Guest House

GUESTHOUSE ★★★ MAP 8 O 11


11 Upper Gardiner Street,
Dublin 1

Tel: 01-874 8384 Fax: 01-874 5510
Email: info@harveysguesthouse.com
Web: www.harveysguesthouse.com

A family-run Georgian house with a friendly atmosphere. Located in the heart of Dublin City, 1km from O'Connell Bridge and (a 15 minute stroll to Temple Bar). We look forward to meeting you and guiding you through your stay in Dublin and in Ireland.

*B&B from €90.00 to €160.00*

*Robert Flood*
*Manager*

16

**Closed 22 - 28 December**

### Herbert Park Hotel

HOTEL ★★★★ MAP 8 O 11


Ballsbridge,
Dublin 4

Tel: 01-667 2200 Fax: 01-667 2595
Email: reservations@herbertparkhotel.ie
Web: www.herbertparkhotel.ie

The award-winning Herbert Park Hotel located in Ballsbridge is just five minutes from the city centre and adjacent to the RDS and Lansdowne Road DART station. The hotel offers cool, sleek surroundings with spectacular views over 48 acres of Herbert Park. Bedrooms are luxuriously appointed offering broadband, air-conditioning, mini-bar, safe, interactive television with playstation and pay per view movies. Facilities include the Pavilion Restaurant overlooking Herbert Park, Terrace Lounge, Bar, Gym, meeting rooms and car parking. Please enquire about Facilities for Persons with Mobility Impairment.

***An IHF Quality Employer***

Member of Supranational Hotels

*Room Rate from €125.00 to €295.00*
*Suites from €550.00 to €550.00*

*Ewan Plenderleith*
*Director / General Manager*

153

*Activities:*

**Open All Year**



B&B Rates are per Person Sharing per Night incl. Breakfast.
or Room Rates are per Room per Night - See also Page 8

## Hilton Dublin

HOTEL ★★★★ MAP 8 O 11

Charlemont Place,
Dublin 2

Tel: 01-402 9988 Fax: 01-402 9852

Email: reservations.dublin@hilton.com

Web: www.hilton.com

Overlooking the historic Grand Canal, the Hilton Dublin is perfectly placed to explore the city's main shopping areas and cultural quarters. Dublin's famous Grafton Street is just a 10 minute walk away or a 4 minute ride in the LUAS tram, which stops directly outside the hotel. Dundrum, Dublin's newest shopping centre, is just a 12 minute ride south on the LUAS tram. The Hilton Dublin can cater for up to 400 delegates in our Charlemont Suite. Our guests can relax in our canalside Waterfront Restaurant and Third Stop Bar. Please enquire about Facilities for Persons with Mobility Impairment.

***An IHF Quality Employer***

Member of Hilton International

**Room Rate from €150.00 to €280.00**

*Erwin Verhoog*
*Hotel Manager*

193

**Closed 24 - 27 December**

## Hilton Dublin Kilmainham

HOTEL MAP 8 O 11

Inchicore Road,
Kilmainham,
Dublin 8

Tel: 01-420 1800 Fax: 01-420 1866

Email: reservations.dublinkilmainham@hilton.com

Web: www.hilton.com/dublinkilmainham

Built to a 4**** specification. Hilton Dublin Kilmainham is located 10 minutes from the city centre and only 5 minutes from Heuston Train Station, taking you to the entire West of the country. Also located at the end of the M50 making this one of Ireland's most easily accessible hotels. We offer 120 bedrooms and a function room that caters for 80 people. 9 purpose built meeting rooms with a business centre, fitness centre, bar and restaurant. Please enquire about Facilities for Persons with Mobility Impairment.

***An IHF Quality Employer***

Member of Hilton Hotels Corporation

**Room Rate from €125.00 to €260.00**

*Meredith Bevan*
*Hotel Manager*

120

*Activities:*

**Closed 24-27 December**

## Holiday Inn Dublin City Centre

HOTEL ★★★ MAP 8 O 11

98-107 Pearse Street,
Dublin 2

Tel: 01-670 3666 Fax: 01-670 3636

Email: info@holidayinndublin.ie

Web: www.holidayinndublincitycentre.ie

Located in heart of the city centre with Dublin's main tourist attractions and principal shopping areas within walking distance of the IFSC, Point Depot, RDS, Lansdowne Road and Temple Bar. Featuring 101 en suite bedrooms, car parking, resident's gym and business centre. Conference facilities for up to 400. Our Green Bistro & Bar offers a full menu throughout the day helped along by one of the finest pints of Guinness in Dublin. Whether here for business or pleasure the Holiday Inn Dublin City Centre is the ideal location. Please enquire about Facilities for Persons with Mobility Impairment.

***An IHF Quality Employer***

Member of Intercontinental Hotels Group

**B&B from €55.00 to €150.00**

*Trevor Smith*
*General Manager*

101

*Activities:*

**Open All Year**

B&B Rates are per Person Sharing per Night incl. Breakfast.
or Room Rates are per Room per Night - **See also Page 8**

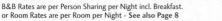

## Dublin City

### Hotel Isaacs

HOTEL ★★★ MAP 8 O 11

Store Street,
Dublin 1

Tel: 01-813 4700 Fax: 01-836 5390
Email: hotel@isaacs.ie
Web: www.hotelisaacs.com

Situated in the heart of Dublin City, Hotel Isaacs, a converted wine warehouse, is the perfect location for any visitor to Dublin. Only a short walk to the IFSC, Temple Bar, Point Depot, Croke Park, O'Connell Bridge and Busaras, this location cannot be beaten. All rooms are en suite with telephone, TV, tea/coffee, garment press, safe and hairdryer. Other facilities include Le Monde Café Bar, Il Vignardo Italian Restaurant and Beresford conference and meeting facilities.

*Bookable on www.irelandhotels.com*
*Special Offer: www.irelandhotels.com/offers*

*Room Rate from €60.00 to €250.00*
*Suites from €180.00 to €350.00*

*Justin Lowry*
*General Manager*

90

*Activities:*

**Closed 24 - 27 December**

### Hotel St. George

HOTEL ★★★ MAP 8 O 11

7 Parnell Square,
Dublin 1

Tel: 01-874 5611 Fax: 01-874 5582
Email: info@hotel-st-george.ie
Web: www.hotel-st-george.ie

The historical Hotel St. George is located on Parnell Square at the top of O'Connell Street, Dublin's principal thoroughfare. Within walking distance of the Abbey and the Gate Theatre, Municipal Art Gallery, Dublin's Writers Museum, principal shopping district and other major tourist attractions. Each bedroom is en suite, individually decorated with every modern comfort, including direct dial phone, colour multichannel TV and tea/coffee making facilities. Computer is available in the public area for internet use and there is WiFi throughout the hotel. Private car park and residents bar.

Member of Castle Hotel Group

*Bookable on www.irelandhotels.com*
*Special Offer: www.irelandhotels.com/offers*

*B&B from €54.00 to €130.00*

*Sinéad Costello*
*General Manager*

53

**Closed 24 - 27 December**

### IMI Residence

HOTEL MAP 8 O 11

Sandyford Road,
Dublin 16

Tel: 01-207 5900 Fax: 01-207 5962
Email: reservations@imires.ie
Web: www.imi.ie/res

Built to a 3*** specification. IMI residence is a tranquil haven on the edge of vibrant Dundrum Town. Built on 13 acres, it consists of 50 stylish bedrooms. IMI offers free parking, gym and all rooms have complimentary broadband access. Dundrum Town Centre is within close proximity for guests to enjoy shopping, bars and restaurants. The M50 and Luas are close by and the 44a bus to Dublin City is located at entrance to IMI. Please enquire about Facilities for Persons with Mobility Impairment.

Member of Prem Group

*Bookable on www.irelandhotels.com*
*Special Offer: www.irelandhotels.com/offers*

*Room Rate from €69.00 to €150.00*

*Pat Considine*
*General Manager*

50

*Activities:*

**Closed 24 December - 02 January**



B&B Rates are per Person Sharing per Night incl. Breakfast.
or Room Rates are per Room per Night - **See also Page 8**

## Jurys Croke Park Hotel

HOTEL ★★★★ MAP 8 O 11

Jones's Road,
Dublin 3

Tel: 01-871 4444 Fax: 01-871 4400
Email: crokepark@jurysdoyle.com
Web: www.jurysdoyle.com

Jurys Cork Hotel returns to the city steeped in luxury throughout - the elegant interior deftly exploiting its spectacular riverside backdrop. Designed to delight the eye and capitalise on its commanding location on the banks of the River Lee. The hotel bridges the gap between home and work by providing spacious, luxurious bedrooms and bathrooms with up to date entertainment systems, an excellent restaurant and bar serving fresh, healthy food, meeting rooms with state-of-the-art technology and leisure centre.

Member of Jurys Doyle Hotel Group

Bookable on www.irelandhotels.com
Special Offer: www.irelandhotels.com/offers

**Room Rate from €169.00 to €520.00**

*Edward Stephenson*
*General Manager*

232

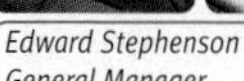

**Closed 25- 28 December**

## Jurys Inn Christchurch

HOTEL ★★★ MAP 8 O 11

Christchurch Place,
Dublin 8

Tel: 01-454 0000 Fax: 01-454 0012
Email: jurysinnchristchurch@jurysinns.com
Web: www.jurysinns.com

Located in Dublin's oldest quarter in the heart of the city just opposite the historical Christchurch Cathedral, Jurys Inn Christchurch is within easy strolling distance of Temple Bar, St. Patrick's Cathedral, Trinity College and fashionable Grafton Street. Please enquire about Facilities for Persons with Mobility Impairment.

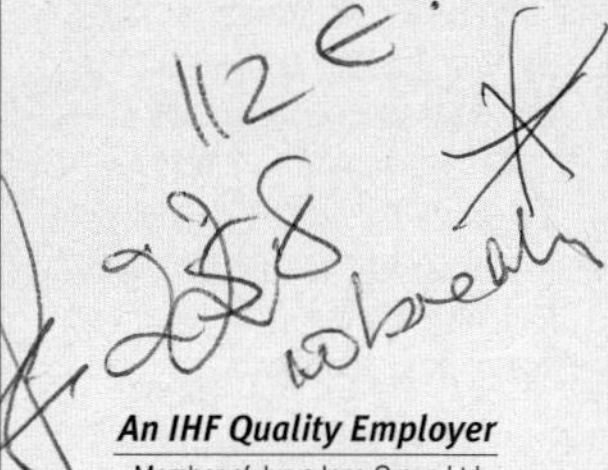

*An IHF Quality Employer*

Member of Jurys Inns Group Ltd

Bookable on www.irelandhotels.com
Special Offer: www.irelandhotels.com/offers

**Room Rate from €97.00 to €260.00**

*Brian O'Farrell*
*General Manager*

182

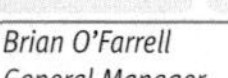

**Closed 24 - 26 December**

## Jurys Inn Custom House

HOTEL ★★★ MAP 8 O 11

Custom House Quay,
Dublin 1

Tel: 01-607 5000 Fax: 01-829 0400
Email: jurysinncustomhouse@jurysinns.com
Web: www.jurysinns.com

Jurys Inn Custom House is centrally and attractively located along the River Liffey in the International Financial Services Centre. Within easy walking distance are all of the city's main shopping districts and cultural attractions. Innfusion Restaurant - open for breakfast, lunch and dinner. The Inntro Bar is perfect for a quick lunch or drink and Il Barista serves gourmet coffee to go and fresh pastries. Please enquire about Facilities for Persons with Mobility Impairment.

*An IHF Quality Employer*

Member of Jurys Inns Group Ltd

Bookable on www.irelandhotels.com
Special Offer: www.irelandhotels.com/offers

**Room Rate from €97.00 to €260.00**

*Anna O'Dell*
*General Manager*

239

**Closed 24 - 26 December**

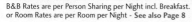

B&B Rates are per Person Sharing per Night incl. Breakfast.
or Room Rates are per Room per Night - See also Page 8

## Dublin City

### Jurys Inn Parnell Street

HOTEL ★★★ MAP 8 O 11

Parnell Street,
Dublin 1

Tel: 01-878 4900 Fax: 01-878 4999
Email: jurysinnparnellst@jurysinns.com
Web: www.jurysinns.com

Jurys Inn Parnell Street is ideally located in the heart of Dublin's City Centre, within a 2 minute walk from the main shopping, business and entertainment districts and within easy walking distance of Temple Bar and Trinity College. Please enquire about Facilities for Persons with Mobility Impairment.

Member of Jurys Inns Group Ltd

*Bookable on www.irelandhotels.com*
*Special Offer: www.irelandhotels.com/offers*

*Room Rate from €97.00 to €260.00*

*Bobby Fitzpatrick*
*General Manager*

253

Closed 24 - 26 December

### Kilronan Guesthouse

GUESTHOUSE ★★★ MAP 8 O 11

70 Adelaide Road,
Dublin 2

Tel: 01-475 5266 Fax: 01-478 2841
Email: info@kilronanhouse.com
Web: www.kilronanhouse.com

This exclusive AA RAC ♦♦♦♦ recommended Georgian house is in a secluded setting, within walking distance of St. Stephen's Green, Trinity College, National Concert Hall, Dublin Castle, St. Patrick's and Christchurch Cathedrals & most of Dublin's historic landmarks. Well appointed bedrooms with private shower, direct dial phone, flat screen TV's, hairdryers, tea/coffee facilities and quality orthopaedic beds. Free internet access is provided in the lounge, as is complimentary tea & coffee. Enjoy a delicious Irish breakfast. Commended by New York Times, Beth Bryant, Michelin Guide, Fodors, Frommer & Karen Browns.

Member of Premier Guesthouses

*Bookable on www.irelandhotels.com*
*Special Offer: www.irelandhotels.com/offers*

*B&B from €55.00 to €76.00*

*Leon Kinsella*
*Owner*

12

Closed 22 - 26 December

### La Stampa Hotel

HOTEL MAP 8 O 11

35/36 Dawson Street,
Dublin 2

Tel: 01-677 4444 Fax: 01-677 4411
Email: hotel@lastampa.ie
Web: www.lastampa.ie

Built to a 4**** specification. Situated in the heart of Dublin and centrally located within easy reach of its main shopping, dining, nightspots and heritage areas, La Stampa is a perfect combination of beautifully designed interiors, exquisite surroundings with a renowned reputation for top class food and luxury accommodation.

Member of Small Luxury Hotels

*Room Rate from €175.00 to €300.00*
*Suites from €250.00 to €700.00*

*Paul Davitt*
*Managing Director*

28

Closed 24 - 27 December



B&B Rates are per Person Sharing per Night incl. Breakfast.
or Room Rates are per Room per Night - See also Page 8

## Lansdowne Hotel

HOTEL ★★★ MAP 8 O 11

27-29 Pembroke Road,
Ballsbridge,
Dublin 4

Tel: 01-668 2522 Fax: 01-668 5585

Email: reception@lansdownehotel.ie

Web: www.lansdownehotel.ie

The Lansdowne Hotel is a boutique 3*** hotel set in the prestigious suburb of Ballsbridge. Minutes walk from Dublin City, Royal Dublin Society (RDS) and Lansdowne Road Rugby Stadium. Relax in our Den Bar where fine food is served daily or dine in Druids Restaurant which serves the finest local produce. Each bedroom is luxuriously appointed with multi-channel TVs, tea/coffee making facilities and en suite bathrooms. Private car parking for guests.

***An IHF Quality Employer***

*Bookable on www.irelandhotels.com*
*Special Offer: www.irelandhotels.com/offers*

*Room Rate from €99.00 to €189.00*
*Suites from €139.00 to €229.00*

*Vicky Bissonath*
*General Manager*

36

*Activities:*

T C P S I

**Closed 24 - 28 December**

## Leeson Inn Downtown

GUESTHOUSE ★★★ MAP 8 O 11

24 Lower Leeson Street,
Dublin 2

Tel: 01-662 2002 Fax: 01-662 1567

Email: info@leesoninndowntown.com

Web: www.leesoninndowntown.com

Located on the fashionable southside of the city centre on the Leeson Street side of St. Stephen's Green. Five minutes from Grafton Street, the capital's premier shopping street. Major attractions such as the National Concert Hall, National Gallery, National Museum, Oireachtas (Parliament), National Gallery, Trinity College, many government buildings and an abundance of restaurants, theatres, night clubs and bars are all within easy walking distance.

Member of Utell

*Bookable on www.irelandhotels.com*
*Special Offer: www.irelandhotels.com/offers*

*B&B from €45.00 to €110.00*

*Majella McGuane*
*General Manager*

30

T C P S I

**Closed 22 - 29 December**

## Lynam's Hotel

HOTEL MAP 12 O 11

63/64 O'Connell Street,
Dublin 1

Tel: 01-888 0856 Fax: 01-888 0890

Email: stay@lynams-hotel.com

Web: www.lynams-hotel.com

A boutique style 42 bedroomed hotel housed in two listed Georgian Townhouses. Superb city centre location on O'Connell Street facing Dublin's Spire, just minutes from the Temple Bar quarter and all of the city's top attractions. Decorated with elegance and individuality. Relax over a drink in the magnificently restored "O'Connell Room". Home to 'Café Carlo' offering a fusion of Irish and Italian cuisine. The Aircoach drops off and picks up opposite the hotel. A city centre haven.

*Bookable on www.irelandhotels.com*
*Special Offer: www.irelandhotels.com/offers*

*Room Rate from €85.00 to €189.00*

*James Brennan*
*General Manager*

42

T C S I

**Open All Year**

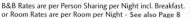

## Dublin City

### Lyndon Guesthouse

GUESTHOUSE ★★ MAP 8 O 11

26 Gardiner Place,
Dublin 1

Tel: 01-878 6950 Fax: 01-878 7420
Email: lyndonh@gofree.indigo.ie
Web: www.lyndonhouse.net

Lyndon House is an extremely popular newly refurbished Georgian guesthouse in the city centre of Dublin. The warm friendly atmosphere has helped to establish its reputation for hospitality. Rooms are mostly en suite with shower, toilet, central heating and TV. Situated within easy walking distance of main shopping areas of O'Connell Street and Henry Street. Also nearby are museums, cinemas, restaurants, train and bus services. Highly acclaimed AA. Please enquire about Facilities for Persons with Mobility Impairment.

*Bookable on www.irelandhotels.com*
*Special Offer: www.irelandhotels.com/offers*

*B&B from €35.00 to €70.00*

*Majella & Colm Hilliard*

9

T C S

**Closed 24 - 27 December**

### Maple Hotel

HOTEL ★★ MAP 8 O 11

75 Lower Gardiner Street,
Dublin 1

Tel: 01-874 0225 Fax: 01-874 5239
Email: info@maplehotel.com
Web: www.maplehotel.com

The Maple Hotel is situated in the heart of Dublin city centre, just off O'Connell Street beside all theatres, cinemas, galleries, museums, main railway and central bus station, with a direct link to Dublin Airport. The hotel has been upgraded in 2007. All bedrooms en suite with colour TV, direct dial phones, hairdryer, tea/coffee facilities. Private car parking. As stated in 'Time Out', "if you're after charm and comfort then you've hit the jackpot here".

*B&B from €35.00 to €65.00*

*Brian Moloney*
*Director*

12

T C P S I

**Closed 23 - 28 December**

### Maples House Hotel

HOTEL ★★★ MAP 8 O 11

Iona Road,
Glasnevin,
Dublin 9

Tel: 01-830 4227 Fax: 01-830 3874
Email: info@mapleshotel.com
Web: www.mapleshotel.com

The friendly and welcoming Maples House Hotel is a beautifully newly refurbished 20th century Edwardian building situated north of the city centre just 15 minutes from Temple Bar. Croke Park is just 1 mile while international football/rugby grounds, concert venues, airport and golf courses are easily accessible. Our 22 bedrooms are of high quality as is our restaurant, bar, lounge and function room. We also cater for conferences, weddings, funerals and banquets.

*Bookable on www.irelandhotels.com*
*Special Offer: www.irelandhotels.com/offers*

*B&B from €55.00 to €85.00*

*Patrica Butler*
*General Manager*

22

*Activities:*

T C S I

**Closed 24 - 29 December**



B&B Rates are per Person Sharing per Night incl. Breakfast.
or Room Rates are per Room per Night - See also Page 8

## Marian Guest House

GUESTHOUSE ★ MAP 8 O 11

21 Upper Gardiner Street,
Dublin 1

Tel: 01-874 4129
Email: enquiries@marianguesthouse.ie
Web: www.marianguesthouse.ie

The Marian Guesthouse is owned and run by the McElroy family. It is just off Mountjoy Square and five minutes walk from city centre and all principal shopping areas, cinemas, theatres and museums. Well appointed bedrooms some of which are en suite. Tea and coffee making facilities available and use of private car park.

**B&B from €30.00 to €45.00**

*McElroy Family*
*Owners*

5
1

C P

**Open All Year**

## Mercer Hotel

HOTEL ★★★ MAP 8 O 11

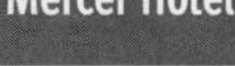

Mercer Street Lower,
Dublin 2

Tel: 01-478 2179 Fax: 01-475 6524
Email: info@mercerhotel.ie
Web: www.mercerhotel.ie

Luxurious, boutique style hotel located in the heart of Dublin City. Modern yet relaxed atmosphere; all rooms are beautifully appointed en suite & fully equipped with all you need: TV, CD player, wireless internet access, a fridge & complimentary mineral water. Indulge in Cusack's Bar & Restaurant with a variety of menus. Within easy walking distance of all city centre tourist attractions, Trinity College, Grafton St., St. Stephen's Green & Temple Bar, also restaurants, cafés & bars. Free overnight parking & discounted daily rate. Book on UTELL. Book online www.mercergroup.ie. Free broadband in conference rooms, WiFi in lobby & bar.

***An IHF Quality Employer***

Member of Mercer Accommodation Group

*Bookable on www.irelandhotels.com*
*Special Offer: www.irelandhotels.com/offers*

**B&B from €55.00 to €110.00**

*Danelle Van Jaarsveld*
*General Manager*

41

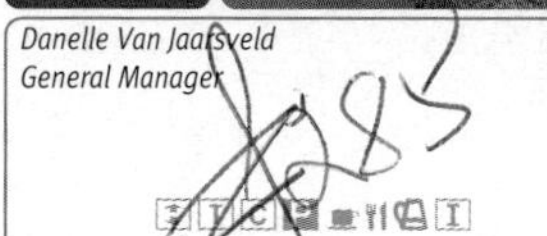

T C P

**Closed 22 - 29 December**

## Merrion Hall & Blakes Spa Suites

GUESTHOUSE ★★★★ MAP 8 O 11

54 Merrion Road,
Ballsbridge,
Dublin 4

Tel: 01-668 1426 Fax: 01-668 4280
Email: merrionhall@iol.ie
Web: www.halpinsprivatehotels.com

This luxury 4**** manor house has achieved many accolades, consistently classified as one of the Bridgestone Top 100 properties in Ireland. Classic & de luxe rooms are air-conditioned, spacious & elegant, some with four poster beds, spa baths & complimentary WiFi broadband. Spacious courtyard suites offer period furnishings, Irish linens & Herbal spa bath. For 2008 a private spa with sauna, steam & treatment rooms has been added. Beside Four Seasons Hotel & RDS. Close to city centre, airport & car ferry terminal by DART or bus. USA toll free 1800 617 3178. Global free phone +800 128 38155.

Member of Manor House Hotels

*Bookable on www.irelandhotels.com*
*Special Offer: www.irelandhotels.com/offers*

**B&B from €79.00 to €119.00**
**Suites from €260.00 to €350.00**

*Pat Halpin*
*Proprietor*

30

*Activities:*

T C P S

**Open All Year**

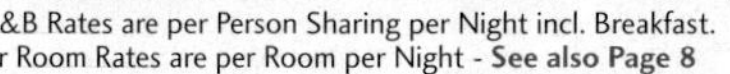

B&B Rates are per Person Sharing per Night incl. Breakfast.
or Room Rates are per Room per Night - See also Page 8

## Dublin City

### Merrion Hotel

HOTEL ★★★★★ MAP 8 O 11

Upper Merrion Street,
Dublin 2

Tel: 01-603 0600 Fax: 01-603 0700
Email: info@merrionhotel.com
Web: www.merrionhotel.com

Dublin's most stylish 5***** hotel, located in the city centre opposite Government Buildings and created from four restored Georgian Townhouses. Many of the 143 bedrooms and suites overlook 18th century gardens, including the luxurious Penthouse. Bars include The Cellar Bar and intimate cocktail bar, No. 23. The Cellar Restaurant serves traditional Irish cuisine, while Restaurant Patrick Guilbaud offers formal dining. Other features include an 18m pool, spa and private underground car park.

***An IHF Quality Employer***

Member of Leading Hotels of the World

***Bookable on www.irelandhotels.com***
*Special Offer: www.irelandhotels.com/offers*

*Room Rate from €295.00 to €595.00*
*Suites from €950.00 to €2,995.00*

*Peter MacCann*
*General Manager*

143

Open All Year

### Mespil Hotel

HOTEL ★★★ MAP 8 O 11

Mespil Road,
Dublin 4

Tel: 01-488 4600 Fax: 01-667 1244
Email: mespil@leehotels.com
Web: www.leehotels.com

The Mespil boasts an ideal city centre location overlooking the banks of the Grand Canal and just 15 minutes walk to St. Stephen's Green and the city's main shopping and cultural quarters, including the RDS and Ballsbridge district. All 255 guest bedrooms are bright, modern and spacious with restful color schemes. Relax in the Terrace Bar or enjoy some tempting dishes from the Glaze Bistro. WiFi access available in all bedrooms, meeting rooms, lobby and bar. Please enquire about Facilities for Persons with Mobility Impairment.

***An IHF Quality Employer***

Member of Lee Hotels

***Bookable on www.irelandhotels.com***
*Special Offer: www.irelandhotels.com/offers*

*Room Rate from €105.00 to €215.00*

*Martin Holohan*
*General Manager / Director*

255

Closed 24 - 27 December

### Montrose Hotel

HOTEL ★★★ MAP 8 O 11

Stillorgan Road,
Dublin 4

Tel: 01-269 3311 Fax: 01-269 3376
Email: info@montrosehotel.ie
Web: www.montrosehotel.ie

Ideally located in Dublin 4 next UCD and RTÉ, just 10 minutes from Dublin City Centre. Serviced by the Aircoach departs every 25 minutes. Spacious & relaxing rooms suites. Delicious food and a great selection of wines, beers and spirits in Belfield Bar & Restaurant. Lonnegan's traditional Irish Bar. Meeting rooms for large & small events. Live music. Ample free parking. Bookable on UTELL. Book on online www.montrosehotel.ie Please enquire about Facilities for Persons with Mobility Impairment.

***An IHF Quality Employer***

Member of Mercer Accommodation Group

***Bookable on www.irelandhotels.com***
*Special Offer: www.irelandhotels.com/offers*

*Room Rate from €49.50 to €175.00*

*Jerry Russell*
*General Manager*

178

Open All Year



B&B Rates are per Person Sharing per Night incl. Breakfast.
or Room Rates are per Room per Night - **See also Page 8**

## Morrison (The)

HOTEL ★★★★ MAP 8 O 11

Lower Ormond Quay,
Dublin 1

Tel: 01-887 2400 Fax: 01-874 4039

Email: reservations@morrisonhotel.ie

Web: www.morrisonhotel.ie

One of the most sophisticated hotel in Dublin, the Morrison is located in the heart of the city overlooking the River Liffey. The 138 individually styled guestrooms include 11 suites & the stunning penthouse. All rooms feature flat screen TV's, iPod docking stations/cd player and complimentary internet access. All suites feature apple Mac PC's. Halo restaurant is renowned for its charming service & modern European cuisine. The Café Bar is an exciting cocktail venue & the new meeting space can hold up to 240 delegates.

***An IHF Quality Employer***

Member of Preferred Boutique Hotels

***Bookable on www.irelandhotels.com***

*Room Rate from €195.00 to €355.00*
*Suites from €505.00 to €2,000.00*

*Sandra Doyle*
*General Manager*

138

**Closed 24 - 27 December**

## Mount Herbert Hotel

HOTEL ★★★ MAP 8 O 11

Herbert Road,
Lansdowne Road, Sandymount,
Dublin 4

Tel: 01-668 4321 Fax: 01-660 7077

Email: info@mountherberthotel.ie

Web: www.mountherberthotel.ie

Exclusive location, exceptional value. A rare gem of a hotel located in Sandymount beside Lansdowne Stadium and the RDS. Easy access to the city centre by train or bus. Guests can enjoy all of the hotels facilities including 172 bedrooms, Tritonville Bar, Cordyline Restaurant, conference and business centre and complimentary car park. Its outstanding value has made it one of Dublin's most popular hotels for many years. Please enquire about Facilities for Persons with Mobility Impairment.

***An IHF Quality Employer***

***Bookable on www.irelandhotels.com***

*Special Offer: www.irelandhotels.com/offers*

*Room Rate from €79.00 to €270.00*
*Suites from €150.00 to €400.00*

*Conor Doyle*
*General Manager*

172

*Activities:*

**Closed 23 - 30 December**



B&B Rates are per Person Sharing per Night incl. Breakfast.
or Room Rates are per Room per Night - See also Page 8

## Dublin City

### North Star Hotel

HOTEL ★★★ MAP 8 O 11

Amiens Street,
Dublin 1

Tel: 01-836 3136 Fax: 01-888 1711
Email: norths@regencyhotels.com
Web: www.northstarhoteldublin.ie

The North Star Hotel Dublin is located in the centre of Dublin city centre, Ireland, and it is a great starting point for every type of visitor to the city. Located in the heart of the city's transport hub with the main railway and tram station (Connolly Station) across the road, around the corner from the central bus station (Busarus) and the airport link bus stop outside the entrance to the hotel. Located a short walk away from some of Dublin's historical and cultural highlights, including Trinity College, Temple Bar (Dublin's "Left Bank") and the Custom House.

***An IHF Quality Employer***

Member of The Regency Hotel Group

*Bookable on www.irelandhotels.com*
*Special Offer: www.irelandhotels.com/offers*

*Room Rate from €90.00 to €200.00*
*Suites from €149.00 to €250.00*

*Brian McGettigan*
*General Manager*

140

*Activities:*

**Open All Year**

### Number 31

GUESTHOUSE ★★★★ MAP 8 O 11

31 Leeson Close,
Dublin 2

Tel: 01-676 5011 Fax: 01-676 2929
Email: info@number31.ie
Web: www.number31.ie

An award-winning guesthouse right in the heart of Georgian Dublin. The former home of Ireland's leading architect Sam Stephenson, just a few minutes walk from St. Stephen's Green and galleries. An oasis of tranquillity and greenery, where guests are encouraged to come back and relax and feel at home at any time of the day. Vast breakfasts are served in the dining room or in a sunny plant filled conservatory. Recommended by the Good Hotel Guide, Egon Ronay, Bridgestone 100 Best Places, Fodors. Fully refurbished in November 2006.

Member of Hidden Ireland

*B&B from €75.00 to €175.00*

*Deirdre & Noel Comer*
*Proprietors*

18

**Open All Year**

### O'Callaghan Alexander Hotel

HOTEL ★★★★ MAP 8 O 11

At Merrion Square,
Dublin 2

Tel: 01-607 3700 Fax: 01-661 5663
Email: info@ocallaghanhotels.com
Web: www.ocallaghanhotels.com

The O'Callaghan Alexander is a contemporary spacious hotel with large bay windows, spacious lobby area and round tower façade. Bedrooms fully refurbished in 2006. Located in city centre on a quite corner just off Merrion Square the hotel is within strolling distance of Trinity College, Grafton Street, and the financial district. State of the art conference facilities. Broadband throughout. Winners is a stylish cocktail bar. Caravaggio's Restaurant serves contemporary international cuisine. Gymnasium and business centre available. USA toll free reservations 1800 569 9983 or online at www.ocallaghanhotels.com

***An IHF Quality Employer***

Member of O'Callaghan Hotels

*Bookable on www.irelandhotels.com*

*Room Rate from €140.00 to €450.00*
*Suites from €190.00 to €500.00*

*Declan Fitzgerald*
*General Manager*

102

*Activities:*

**Closed 23 - 28 December**



B&B Rates are per Person Sharing per Night incl. Breakfast. or Room Rates are per Room per Night - See also Page 8

## O'Callaghan Davenport Hotel

HOTEL ★★★★ MAP 8 0 11

At Merrion Square, Dublin 2

Tel: 01-607 3500 Fax: 01-661 5663
Email: info@ocallaghanhotels.com
Web: www.ocallaghanhotels.com

The O'Callaghan Davenport is an elegant landmark Dublin hotel with a historic facade dating to 1863. Ideally located in the city centre beside Merrion Square within minutes walk of Trinity College and the main shopping and business districts. Fully installed with wired and wireless broadband, the O'Callaghan Davenport has excellent conference facilities. 115 air-conditioned de luxe bedrooms, discreet club like bar, fine dining restaurant, gymnasium facilities. USA Toll Free Reservations 1800 569 9983 and on line at www.ocallaghanhotels.com

***An IHF Quality Employer***

Member of O'Callaghan Hotels

*Bookable on www.irelandhotels.com*

*B&B from €140.00 to €450.00*
*Suites from €190.00 to €500.00*

*Declan Farrell*
*General Manager*

115

*Activities:*

**Open All Year**

## O'Callaghan Mont Clare Hotel

HOTEL ★★★ MAP 8 0 11

Merrion Square, Dublin 2

Tel: 01-607 3800 Fax: 01-661 5663
Email: info@ocallaghanhotels.com
Web: www.ocallaghanhotels.com

A traditional Dublin hotel, the O'Callaghan Mont Clare is centrally located on Dublin's Merrion Square, just a few minutes walk to all major attractions including Trinity College, museums, theatres, business and shopping areas. 74 newly refurbished bedrooms with air-conditioning, a charming lounge bar, Goldsmith's Restaurant, conference facilities and parking. Broadband available. Reservations via UTELL International Worldwide. USA Toll Free Reservations 1800 569 9983 and online at www.ocallaghanhotels.com

***An IHF Quality Employer***

Member of O'Callaghan Hotels

*Bookable on www.irelandhotels.com*

*Room Rate from €115.00 to €330.00*
*Suites from €165.00 to €380.00*

*Karen Donegan*
*General Manager*

74

*Activities:*

**Closed from 23 - 28 December**

## O'Callaghan Stephen's Green Hotel

HOTEL ★★★★ MAP 8 0 11

St. Stephen's Green, Dublin 2

Tel: 01-607 3600 Fax: 01-661 5663
Email: info@ocallaghanhotels.com
Web: www.ocallaghanhotels.com

The O'Callaghan Stephen's Green is a modern boutique style hotel, located within minutes walk of Grafton Street and the main shopping and business districts. The hotel beautifully combines two refurbished Georgian houses with a contemporary style four storey glass atrium overlooking St.Stephen's Green. 78 luxurious air-conditioned bedrooms, gymnasium, business centre, fashionable Magic Glasses Bar and Pie Dish Bistro. Wired and wireless broadband throughout and excellent meeting facilities. USA toll free reservations 1800 569 9983 or www.ocallaghanhotels.com

***An IHF Quality Employer***

Member of O'Callaghan Hotels

*Bookable on www.irelandhotels.com*

*B&B from €140.00 to €450.00*
*Suites from €190.00 to €500.00*

*Dara McEneaney*
*General Manager*

78

*Activities:*

**Closed 23 - 28 December**

B&B Rates are per Person Sharing per Night incl. Breakfast.
or Room Rates are per Room per Night - **See also Page 8**

## Dublin City

### O'Sheas Hotel

HOTEL ★ MAP 8 O 11

19 Talbot Street,
Dublin 1

Tel: 01-836 5670 Fax: 01-836 5214
Email: osheashotel@eircom.net
Web: www.osheashotel.com

O'Sheas Hotel - renowned the world over for its close association with Irish music, song & dance - it's this that provides the theme for the hotel, with its typical Irish pub and restaurant serving the best in Irish cuisine with a healthy sprinkling of international dishes. O'Sheas Hotel has 34 recently refurbished en suite bedrooms, the hotel also has function and conference room facilities for up to 180 people and provides live entertainment seven nights. We look forward to welcoming you.

*B&B from €60.00 to €80.00*

*John McCormack*
*Manager*

Rooms: 34

Closed 24 - 25 December

### Othello House

GUESTHOUSE ★★ MAP 8 O 11

74 Lower Gardiner Street,
Dublin 1

Tel: 01-855 5442 Fax: 01-855 7460
Email: othello1@eircom.net
Web: www.Athelloguesthouse.com

Othello is 150m from Abbey Theatre, 200m from Dublin's main O'Connell Street, 50m from central bus station. Number 41 bus direct from Dublin Airport stops outside door. 150m to Connolly Railway Station, 1 mile to ferry terminal, 800m to Point Theatre. Lock up secure car park. All rooms en suite with TV, telephone, tea/coffee making facilities. Trinity College, National Museum, National Library all within walking distance.

***Bookable on www.irelandhotels.com***
***Special Offer: www.irelandhotels.com/offers***

*B&B from €35.00 to €65.00*

*John Galloway*
*Manager*

Rooms: 22

Closed 23 - 27 December

### Palmerstown Lodge

GUESTHOUSE ★★★ MAP 8 O 11

Palmerstown Village,
Dublin 20

Tel: 01-623 5494 Fax: 01-623 6214
Email: info@palmerstownlodge.com
Web: www.palmerstownlodge.com

Prime location adjacent to all amenities and facilities this superb purpose-built property adjoins the N4/M50 motorway. Minutes from the city centre and a mere 12 minutes drive to the airport we offer all the features and standards of a hotel. Each elegant en suite bedroom has individual temperature control, ambient lighting, automated door locking system, phone, TV, etc. Separate tea/coffee and free internet area. Private car park. Golf packages available.

*B&B from €50.00 to €90.00*

*Gerry O'Connor*
*Owner*

Rooms: 19

Open All Year



B&B Rates are per Person Sharing per Night incl. Breakfast.
or Room Rates are per Room per Night - **See also Page 8**

## Paramount Hotel

HOTEL ★★★ MAP 8 O 11

Parliament Street & Essex Gate, Temple Bar, Dublin 2

Tel: 01-417 9900 Fax: 01-417 9904

Email: sales@paramounthotel.ie

Web: www.paramounthotel.ie

Set in Temple Bar's quieter west end, Paramount Hotel is one of the city's most trendy and cosmopolitan hotels. The hotel boasts 66 en suite bedrooms, tastefully decorated in the very elegant style of the 1930s. The hotel's bar, the Turks Head, is a stylish bar renowned for its extravagant design, and vibrant colours. Bistro dishes are served daily, and the bar turns into a late bar with club at the weekend. Email: info@turkshead.ie or Web: www.turkshead.ie. Please enquire about Facilities for Persons with Mobility Impairment.

***An IHF Quality Employer***

*Bookable on www.irelandhotels.com*

*Special Offer: www.irelandhotels.com/offers*

*B&B from €65.00 to €175.00*

*Rita Barcoe*
*General Manager*

66

*Activities:*

Closed 22 - 28 December

## Park Inn Dublin

HOTEL ★★★ MAP 8 O 11

Smithfield Village, Dublin 7

Tel: 01-817 3838 Fax: 01-817 3839

Email: info.dublin@rezidorparkinn.com

Web: www.dublin.parkinn.ie

Situated in the heart of Smithfield village, Park Inn Dublin is just a short walk from Dublin's main shopping, entertainment, business and sightseeing districts. With contemporary design each of the 73 en suite bedrooms is equipped with a CD/Hi-Fi player, cable TV, direct dial phone & tea/coffee facilities. One can also enjoy the spectacular views of Dublin from the Hotels Chimney Viewing Tower. Please enquire about Facilities for Persons with Mobility Impairment.

Member of Rezidor SAS

*Bookable on www.irelandhotels.com*

*Room Rate from €99.00 to €240.00*
*Suites from €180.00 to €240.00*

*Sally Hughes*
*General Manager*

73

*Activities:*

Open All Year

## Park Plaza Tyrrelstown

HOTEL ★★★★ MAP 8 O 11

Tyrrelstown, Dublin 15

Tel: 01-827 5600 Fax: 01-827 5601

Email: info@parkplazatyrrelstown.com

Web: www.parkplaza.com

Located in close proximity to both Dublin City centre & Dublin Airport, this magnificent contemporary hotel features 155 bedrooms including suites, with each room boasting complimentary broadband & state of the art entertainment systems. A self-contained conference area houses 11 meeting rooms with a capacity for over 450 delegates. Large gym for residents. Our Maya-Ché Restaurant & Hourglass Bar are tailored for your enjoyment. Complimentary extensive car parking is also provided. Please enquire about Facilities for Persons with Mobility Impairment.

Member of Park Plaza Hotels & Resorts

*Bookable on www.irelandhotels.com*

*Special Offer: www.irelandhotels.com/offers*

*Room Rate from €115.00 to €240.00*
*Suites from €165.00 to €340.00*

*Vincent O'Gorman*
*General Manager*

155

*Activities:*

Closed 24 - 26 December

B&B Rates are per Person Sharing per Night incl. Breakfast.
or Room Rates are per Room per Night - See also Page 8

## Dublin City

### Parliament Hotel

HOTEL ★★★ MAP 8 O 11

Lord Edward Street,
Temple Bar,
Dublin 2

Tel: 01-670 8777 Fax: 01-670 8787

Email: parl@regencyhotels.com

Web: www.parliamenthotel.ie

The Parliament Hotel is located directly opposite Dublin Castle at the gateway to Dublin's Temple Bar. Visitors have a superb choice of bars, restaurants, theatres and shops on the doorstep. Minutes from Trinity College and Grafton Street. The hotel has 63 totally renovated rooms, a new Italian restaurant offering the best in traditional Italian dishes and a traditional Irish Bar. Please call the hotel for superb theatre packages that include tickets to a show in the Olympia or Gaiety, pre-theatre meal and overnight accommodation with breakfast from just €99 per person.

Member of Regency Hotel Group

*Bookable on www.irelandhotels.com*
*Special Offer: www.irelandhotels.com/offers*

**B&B from €130.00 to €250.00**

*David Kiely*
*General Manager*

63

Activities:

**Open All Year**

### Phoenix Park House

GUESTHOUSE ★★ MAP 8 O 11

38-39 Parkgate Street,
Dublin 8

Tel: 01-677 2870 Fax: 01-679 9769

Email: info@dublinguesthouse.com

Web: www.dublinguesthouse.com

This friendly AA listed family-run guesthouse directly beside the Phoenix Park with its many facilities is ideally located 2 minutes walk from the new tram service and Heuston Station with direct bus service to ferry ports, Dublin Airport, Connolly Train Station and central bus station. Close to the Guinness Brewery, Whiskey Corner, the re-located National Museum and Kilmainham Museum of Modern Art, the popular Temple Bar and numerous pubs and restaurants. All rooms with tea/coffee making facilities.

*Bookable on www.irelandhotels.com*

**B&B from €36.00 to €80.00**

*Mary Smith & Emer Smith*
*Proprietors*

25

Activities:

**Closed 22 - 28 December**

### Plaza Hotel

HOTEL ★★★★ MAP 8 O 11

Belgard Road,
Tallaght,
Dublin 24

Tel: 01-462 4200 Fax: 01-462 4600

Email: reservations@plazahotel.ie

Web: www.plazahotel.ie

120 bedrooms, 2 suites. Convenient location on Belgard Road, just off the M50 motorway, 8 miles from the city centre. Secure underground car parking. LUAS Tallaght stop, direct tram link to the city centre is located 3 minutes from the Plaza Hotel. Extensive conference & banqueting facilities for up to 220 people. Floor One serving food from 9.00am - 10.00pm daily. Obar1 music bar. The Playhouse Nightclub. Grumpy McClafferty's traditional pub. 20 minutes from Dublin Airport. Please enquire about Facilities for Persons with Mobility Impairment.

*Bookable on www.irelandhotels.com*
*Special Offer: www.irelandhotels.com/offers*

**Room Rate from €99.00 to €285.00**

*Jim Lavery*
*General Manager*

122

Activities:

**Closed 24 - 31 December**



B&B Rates are per Person Sharing per Night incl. Breakfast. or Room Rates are per Room per Night - See also Page 8

## Portobello Hotel & Bar

HOTEL ★★ MAP 8 O 11

33 South Richmond Street,
Dublin 2

Tel: 01-475 2715 Fax: 01-478 5010
Email: portobellohotel@indigo.ie
Web: www.portobellohotel.ie

This landmark building is located in the heart of Dublin City along the Grand Canal. First opened in 1793, the Portobello Hotel & Bar boasts a long tradition in hospitality and provides guests with luxury en suite accommodation with tea/coffee making facilities, TV, radio, iron & board, direct dial phone and hairdryer. Rain Night Club popular with all ages. A friendly welcome and service is guaranteed. Please enquire about Facilities for Persons with Mobility Impairment.

*Bookable on www.irelandhotels.com*

*B&B from €25.00 to €125.00*

*Vali Popa*
*Front Office Manager*

24

**Closed 24 - 26 December**

## Quality Hotel Dublin City

HOTEL ★★★★ MAP 8 O 11

Cardiff Lane,
Sir John Rogerson's Quay,
Dublin 2

Tel: 01-643 9500 Fax: 01-643 9510
Email: info@qualityhoteldublin.com
Web: www.qualityhoteldublin.com

Superbly situated on Dublin's trendy South Bank, the hotel is perfectly placed in the heart of Dublin City, within a short walk of city centre shopping and tourist attractions. Features include 213 superior guestrooms, Lannigans Restaurant & Vertigo Bar. Club Vitae Health & Fitness Club incorporates a 22m swimming pool, sauna, steam room, jacuzzi, fully equipped gym and treatment suites. Please enquire about Facilities for Persons with Mobility Impairment.

Member of Choice Hotels Ireland

*Bookable on www.irelandhotels.com*
*Special Offer: www.irelandhotels.com/offers*

*Room Rate from €99.00 to €359.00*

*Conor O'Kane*
*General Manager*

213

**Closed 23 - 27 December**

## Radisson SAS Royal Hotel

HOTEL MAP 8 O 11

Golden Lane,
Dublin 8

Tel: 01-8982900 Fax: 01-8982901
Email: info.royal.dublin@radissonsas.com
Web: www.royal.dublin.radissonsas.com

Built to a 4**** specification. Located in the heart of Dublin City Centre, The Radisson SAS Royal Hotel is just five minutes walk from Dublin's shopping, business and theatre district. The Hotel has 150 bedrooms including a range of luxurious stylish suites. It has 15 meeting rooms, a conference room for up to 400 delegates, a roof top terrace ideal for BBQ's and an executive meeting room and bar on the 7th floor with panoramic views of the city. It has complimentary internet access for residents, is fully air conditioned & has 60 car spaces. Please enquire about Facilities for Persons with Mobility Impairment.

Member of Rezidor

*Room Rate from €159.00 to €350.00*

*Michel Schutzbach*
*General Manager*

150

*Activities:*

**Open All Year**

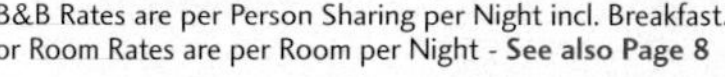

B&B Rates are per Person Sharing per Night incl. Breakfast.
or Room Rates are per Room per Night - **See also Page 8**

## Dublin City

### Radisson SAS St Helen's Hotel

HOTEL ★★★★★ MAP 8 O 11

Stillorgan Road,
Dublin 4

Tel: 01-218 6000 Fax: 01-218 6010
Email: info.dublin@radissonsas.com
Web: www.radissonsas.com

Luxurious is just one of the words used to describe the five star Radisson SAS St Helen's Hotel in Dublin. Sumptuous, relaxing and wonderfully historic are others. The hotel is situated just ten minutes outside the hustle and bustle of Dublin City centre, yet the peace and tranquillity you experience there means you could be hidden away in the countryside. Its amazing 4 acre formal gardens invite guests to wander around and admire the blooms or just sit on the raised terrace while sipping a glass of wine. Please enquire about Facilities for Persons with Mobility Impairment.

***An IHF Quality Employer***

Member of The Rezidor Hotel Group

*Bookable on www.irelandhotels.com*
*Special Offer: www.irelandhotels.com/offers*

*Room Rate from €165.00 to €350.00*
*Suites from €255.00 to €400.00*

*Neil Lane*
*General Manager*
151

*Activities:*

**Open All Year**

### Red Cow Moran Hotel

HOTEL ★★★★ MAP 8 O 11

Red Cow Complex,
Naas Road,
Dublin 22

Tel: 01-459 3650 Fax: 01-459 1588
Email: redcowres@moranhotels.com
Web: www.moranhotels.com

4**** Red Cow Moran Hotel combines classic elegance with modern design, situated at the gateway to the provinces, minutes drive from Dublin Airport. Easy access to the city centre via the LUAS light rail service! Bedrooms are fully air conditioned with flatscreen multi channel TV, fluffy duvets, DD telephone, WiFi, hairdryer, clothes care and tea/coffee making facilities. The complex also boasts two restaurants, a choice of lively bars also serving food, conference facilities and business centre. Night Club. Free carparking. AA 4****. A Moran Hotel. Please enquire about Facilities for Persons with Mobility Impairment.

***An IHF Quality Employer***

Member of Moran Hotels

*Bookable on www.irelandhotels.com*
*Special Offer: www.irelandhotels.com/offers*

*B&B from €65.00 to €195.00*
*Suites from €220.00 to €500.00*

*Tom Moran*
*Managing Director*
123

*Activities:*

**Closed 24 - 26 December**

### Regency Airport Hotel

HOTEL ★★★ MAP 8 O 11

Swords Road,
Dublin 9

Tel: 01-837 3544 Fax: 01-836 7121
Email: regency@regencyhotels.com
Web: www.regencyhotels.com

The Regency Airport Hotel is just three kilometres North of Dublin City Centre & 5 kilometres from Dublin Airport on the main Airport road. We have just opened a state of the art leisure centre with pool, sauna, steam room, jacuzzi & gym. In addition, 100 new executive rooms & a 600 guest banquet conference centre opened also. The perfect location for business & pleasure.

***An IHF Quality Employer***

Member of Regency Hotel Group

*Room Rate from €89.00 to €440.00*

*James McGettigan*
*Operations Manager*
300

*Activities:*

**Open All Year**



B&B Rates are per Person Sharing per Night incl. Breakfast.
or Room Rates are per Room per Night - **See also Page 8**

## River House Hotel

HOTEL ★★ MAP 8 O 11

23/24 Eustace Street,
Temple Bar,
Dublin 2

Tel: 01-670 7655 Fax: 01-670 7650

Email: reservations@riverhousehotel.com

Web: www.riverhousehotel.com

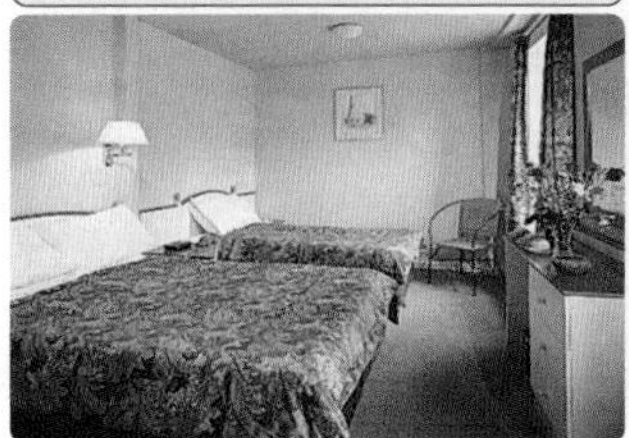

A city centre hotel located in Dublin's colourful and exciting Temple Bar area. With its cobbled streets, shops, art galleries, bars, restaurants and lively night life, Temple Bar has become a tourist attraction itself. All of our 29 bedrooms are en suite and have tea/coffee making facilities, remote control TV, radio, hairdryer and direct dial telephone. Hotel facilities include 'The Mezz' Bar and 'The Hub' Nightclub which is sound proofed, the best live music venues in Dublin.

*Bookable on www.irelandhotels.com*

*Special Offer: www.irelandhotels.com/offers*

*B&B from €50.00 to €95.00*

*Sheelagh Conway*
*Proprietor*

29

**Closed 24 - 27 December**

## Roxford Lodge Hotel

HOTEL ★★★ MAP 8 O 11

46 Northumberland Road,
Ballsbridge,
Dublin 4

Tel: 01-668 8572 Fax: 01-668 8158

Email: reservations@roxfordlodge.ie

Web: www.roxfordlodge.ie

Luxury family-run boutique style hotel located in Ballsbridge, Dublin's most exclusive area. Just 10 minutes walk from the city centre and all the major attractions such as Trinity College and Grafton Street. All of our en suite bedrooms have the added luxury of saunas, and most also have jacuzzi baths. All rooms have broadband internet access. Our executive suite offers the ultimate in luxury. Secure car parking. Public transport at front door. Please enquire about Facilities for Persons with Mobility Impairment.

*B&B from €65.00 to €125.00*
*Suites from €250.00 to €400.00*

*Desmond Killoran*
*Proprietor*

20

**Closed 24 - 27 December**

## Royal Dublin Hotel (The)

HOTEL ★★★ MAP 8 O 11

O'Connell Street,
Dublin 1

Tel: 01-873 3666 Fax: 01-873 3120

Email: enq@royaldublin.com

Web: www.royaldublin.com

The Royal Dublin Hotel is located on Dublin City's main thoroughfare, O'Connell Street, minutes from numerous shopping districts, theatres, museums, Temple Bar and Croke Park. Guests can enjoy the Georgian Lounge or Café Royale Restaurant or relax in the Traditional Raffles Bar. Complimentary secure car parking on site. A superb City Centre location at great value.

Member of Hotel Partners

*Room Rate from €89.00 to €240.00*

*Darrell Penney*
*General Manager*

117

*Activities:*

**Closed 24 - 26 December**

## Dublin City

### School House Hotel

HOTEL ★★★★ MAP 8 0 11

2-8 Northumberland Road,
Ballsbridge,
Dublin 4

Tel: 01-667 5014 Fax: 01-667 5015
Email: reservations@schoolhousehotel.com
Web: www.schoolhousehotel.com

Without doubt, one of the most unique and beautiful properties in the city. Do not miss an opportunity to stay at this charming 4**** hotel conversion. All 31 de luxe bedrooms are individually named and furnished to the highest international standard. The original classrooms now host the award-winning Canteen @ The Schoolhouse and the lively and popular Schoolhouse Bar. Just a short stroll to Grafton Street, Lansdowne Road, The RDS and all of Dublin's major visitor attractions.

*Bookable on www.irelandhotels.com*

*B&B from €54.50 to €250.00*

*Liz Carr*
*General Manager*
31

*Activities:*

**Closed 24 - 26 December**

### Shelbourne Hotel (The)

HOTEL ★★★★★ MAP 8 0 11

27 St. Stephen's Green,
Dublin 2

Tel: 01-663 4500 Fax: 01-661 6006
Email: annemarie.whelan@renaissancehotels.com
Web: www.theshelbourne.ie

Dublin's most distinguished address, The Shelbourne Dublin, a Renaissance Hotel is the ultimate in 5* luxury. The Shelbourne is Dublin's most famous hotel, located in the heart of Dublin overlooking St. Stephen's Green. With 265 luxury guestrooms including 19 suites, a Heritage Lounge, the Horseshoe Bar, Lord Mayor's Lounge, the Saddle Room & No.27 bar and lounge. The food & beverage outlets are the ultimate in elegance, innovative style and luxury. Banqueting facilities to accommodate 10 to 350 guests. New luxury state of the art spa opening in 2008. Managed by Marriott International.

***An IHF Quality Employer***

Member of Marriott International

*Room Rate from €265.00 to €485.00*
*Suites from €425.00 to €2,500.00*

*Liam Doyle*
*General Manager*
265

*Activities:*

**Open All Year**

### Stauntons on the Green

GUESTHOUSE ★★★ MAP 8 0 11

83 St. Stephen's Green,
Dublin 2

Tel: 01-478 2300 Fax: 01-478 2263
Email: info@stauntonsonthegreen.ie
Web: www.thecastlehotelgroup.com

Large Georgian house overlooking St. Stephen's Green, own private gardens. All rooms are en suite and fully equipped with direct dial telephone, TV and tea/coffee welcoming trays, trouser press and hairdryer. It is close to museums, galleries, Grafton Street shopping area and many other major tourist attractions. Stauntons On the Green occupies one of Dublin's most prestigious locations, close to many corporate headquarters and government buildings.

Member of Castle Hotel Group

*B&B from €70.00 to €95.00*

*Colette Winders*
*Manager*
30

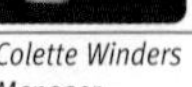

**Closed 24 - 26 December**



B&B Rates are per Person Sharing per Night incl. Breakfast. or Room Rates are per Room per Night - See also Page 8

## Stillorgan Park Hotel

HOTEL ★★★★ MAP 8 O 11

Stillorgan Road,
Stillorgan,
Dublin 18

Tel: 01-200 1800 Fax: 01-283 1610
Email: sales@stillorganpark.com
Web: www.stillorganpark.com

Dublin's premier city hotel, located only 3 miles from St. Stephen's Green, easily accessible from M50 motorway & all main city arteries. Boasting 150 en suite, contemporary rooms, fully air-conditioned. Outdoor courtyard. Purpose built conference area catering for 2-500 delegates & 8 new state of the art meeting rooms, video conference on request, traditional Irish bar with AA Rosette winning restaurant, White Pebble Spa & guest gym. Complimentary shuttle service, Aircoach airport transfer available. 300 car parking spaces. AA**** & Fáilte Ireland ****. Please enquire about Facilities for Persons with Mobility Impairment.

***An IHF Quality Employer***

Member of Talbot Hotel Group

*Bookable on www.irelandhotels.com*
*Special Offer: www.irelandhotels.com/offers*

*Room Rate from €99.00 to €298.00*
*Suites from €139.00 to €346.00*

*Pat Kenny*
*General Manager*

150

*Activities:*

Closed 25 - 26 December

## Tara Towers Hotel

HOTEL ★★★ MAP 8 O 11

Merrion Road,
Dublin 4

Tel: 01-269 4666 Fax: 01-269 1027
Email: info@taratowers.com
Web: www.taratowers.com

The Tara Towers Hotel is a well-established favourite, beside the sea on Merrion Road, just 3km south of Dublin City centre. Situated along the sweeping curves of Dublin Bay you can experience breathtaking views of sea & shore. Rooms are spacious, fully appointed & cater for comfort. You can relax & unwind in PJ Branagan's Pub or have a sumptuous dinner in Ocras Restaurant. Guests also have the bonus of ample free parking. Located close to UCD, RDS and RTE, a 10 minute drive to the city centre & within easy distance of Lansdowne Road. Bookable on UTELL. Book online at www.taratowers.com.

***An IHF Quality Employer***

Member of Mercer Accommodation Group

*Bookable on www.irelandhotels.com*
*Special Offer: www.irelandhotels.com/offers*

*B&B from €49.50 to €175.00*

*Catherine McGrath*
*General Manager*

111

Closed 23 - 27 December

## Tavistock House

GUESTHOUSE ★★★ MAP 8 O 11

64 Ranelagh Road,
Ranelagh,
Dublin 6

Tel: 01-498 8000 Fax: 01-498 8000
Email: info@tavistockhouse.com
Web: www.tavistockhouse.com

Magnificent Victorian house, tastefully converted retaining all its original plasterwork - very homely. Situated on the city side of Ranelagh Village, on the corner of Ranelagh / Northbrook Roads. We are only 7 minutes walk from Stephen's Green in the heart of Dublin, near Helen Dillon's world famous garden. All rooms have colour TV, direct dial phone, hairdryer and tea/coffee making facilities. Private parking. There is a wide variety of restaurants locally. Internet facilities.

*Bookable on www.irelandhotels.com*

*B&B from €45.00 to €90.00*

*Maureen & Brian Cusack*
*Co-Owners*

6

Open All Year

## Dublin City

### Temple Bar Hotel

HOTEL ★★★ MAP 8 0 11

Fleet Street,
Temple Bar,
Dublin 2

Tel: 01-677 3333 Fax: 01-677 3088
Email: reservations@tbh.ie
Web: www.templebarhotel.com

Located in the heart of Dublin's cultural quarter - Temple Bar Hotel is the ideal base from which to explore Dublin's numerous theatres, restaurants, shops and bars. Temple Bar Hotel combines modern comfort at affordable prices. The hotel features 129 newly refurbished bedrooms including 12 executive rooms. The Terrace Restaurant with its distinctive glass roof offers fine Irish Cuisine and a unique dining experience. 5 meeting rooms accommodating up to 70 guests including a dedicated boardroom are available. The hotel is located within easy access of train stations, airport Dublin Port & LUAS lines.

***An IHF Quality Employer***

Member of Tower Hotel Group

***Bookable on www.irelandhotels.com***
***Special Offer: www.irelandhotels.com/offers***

***B&B from €95.00 to €160.00***

*Guy Thompson*
*General Manager*

129

*Activities:*

Closed 23 - 25 December

### Tower Hotel

HOTEL ★★★ MAP 8 11 0

Whitestown Way,
Tallaght,
Dublin 24

Tel: 01-468 5400 Fax: 01-468 5411
Email: reservations@thdub.ie
Web: www.towerhoteldublin.com

This modern and stylish hotel is ideally located just minutes from the Tallaght LUAS stop & within easy reach of Dublin City centre. 120 bedroom hotel with four suites all with Wi-Fi, flat screen TV, tea/coffee making facilities & trouser press as standard. Extensive conference & banqueting facilities for up to 300 people & 9 individual meeting rooms including a superbly appointed boardroom. Located only a short drive from the M50 & 20 minutes from Dublin airport. Secure underground parking available. Special online offers available at www.towerhotelgroup.com.

Member of Tower Hotel Group

***Bookable on www.irelandhotels.com***
***Special Offer: www.irelandhotels.com/offers***

***B&B from €55.00 to €130.00***

*Nora Wyse*
*General Manager*

120

*Activities:*

Closed 23 - 25 December

### Trinity Capital Hotel

HOTEL ★★★ MAP 8 0 11

Pearse Street,
Dublin 2

Tel: 01-648 1000 Fax: 01-648 1010
Email: info@trinitycapitalhotel.com
Web: www.capital-hotels.com

Completely refurbished and extended in 2007 our boutique style hotel is located in the very heart of Dublin city centre, opposite Trinity College. Our relaxing bedrooms are dressed with oversize duvets and have been carefully designed with our guests comfort in mind. Café Cairo with its extensive food, drink and cocktail menu is the perfect place to relax while away. Please enquire about Facilities for Persons with Mobility Impairment.

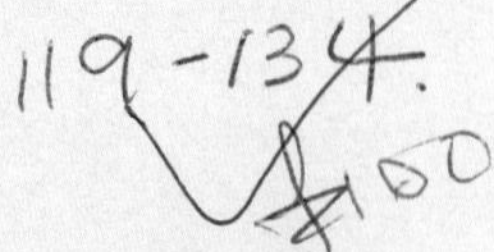


***An IHF Quality Employer***

Member of Capital Hotels

***Bookable on www.irelandhotels.com***
***Special Offer: www.irelandhotels.com/offers***

***Room Rate from €109.00 to €275.00***

*Denyse Campbell*
*General Manager*

158

Closed 24 - 26 December



B&B Rates are per Person Sharing per Night incl. Breakfast. or Room Rates are per Room per Night - See also Page 8

## Twelfth Lock Hotel (The)

HOTEL ★★★ MAP 8 O 11

Castleknock Marina,
Castleknock,
Dublin 15

Tel: 01-860 7400 Fax: 01-860 7401

Email: info@twelfthlock.com

Web: www.twelfthlock.com

Twelfth Lock Hotel is a pioneering example of European Café and hotel culture in Ireland inspired by the hotels, café and bars of Paris and Amsterdam. A cosmopolitan space positioned in a unique environment at Castleknock Marina on the banks of the Royal Canal. The Twelfth Lock is a feast for the senses, a feel good place. Please enquire about Facilities for Persons with Mobility Impairment.

*B&B from €40.00 to €62.50*

*Brian Clinton*
*General Manager*

10

Open All Year

## Uppercross House

HOTEL ★★★ MAP 8 O 11

26-30 Upper Rathmines Road,
Dublin 6

Tel: 01-497 5486 Fax: 01-497 5361

Email: reservations@uppercrosshousehotel.com

Web: www.uppercrosshousehotel.com

Uppercross House is a hotel providing 49 bedrooms of the highest standard of comfort. All with direct dial phone, TV, free WiFi internet access, tea/coffee maker, central heating and all bedrooms are en suite. Uppercross House has its own secure parking and is ideally situated in Dublin's south side 2km from St. Stephen's Green and R.D.S., with excellent public transport from directly outside the door. A fully licensed restaurant and bar opens nightly with a warm and friendly atmosphere.

***An IHF Quality Employer***

***Bookable on www.irelandhotels.com***
***Special Offer: www.irelandhotels.com/offers***

*B&B from €59.00 to €79.00*

*David Mahon*
*Proprietor*

49

Closed 23 - 30 December

## Waterloo House

GUESTHOUSE ★★★★ MAP 8 O 11

8-10 Waterloo Road,
Ballsbridge,
Dublin 4

Tel: 01-660 1888 Fax: 01-667 1955

Email: waterloohouse@eircom.net

Web: www.waterloohouse.ie

A warm welcome awaits you at this luxury guesthouse, in the heart of Georgian Dublin. It comprises 2 Georgian houses, refurbished to superb standard, retaining original features, offering unique atmosphere, style, elegance. Minutes from RDS, St. Stephen's Green, Grafton Street and city centre. Delicious breakfast is served in the dining room, overlooking conservatory & gardens. Lift & car park. WiFi available. Recommended: Bridgestone 100 Best Places, Alister Sawday's, Michelin Guide, Lonely Planet, Frommers and Karen Brown. Please enquire about Facilities for Persons with Mobility Impairment.

*B&B from €49.00 to €120.00*
*Suites from €110.00 to €220.00*

*Evelyn Corcoran*
*Proprietor*

17

Closed 23 - 28 December

## Dublin City

### West County Hotel

HOTEL ★★ MAP 8 O 11

Chapelizod,
Dublin 20

Tel: 01-626 4011 Fax: 01-623 1378
Email: info@westcountyhotel.ie
Web: www.westcountyhotel.ie

An established family-run hotel, located in the picturesque village of Chapelizod, just off the N4, close to M50 and Dublin International Airport, is convenient to Liffey Valley and Blanchardstown shopping centres. It comprises 50 en suite bedrooms equipped to 3*** standards (AA). Secure and free car parking. Extensive conference and banqueting facilities. The West County is also fully Wi-Fi enabled with coverage in all bedrooms and conference rooms. Part of the Colgan Group Hotels and sister of The Lucan Spa hotel. Special offers available Tel. 01 626 4647.

Member of The Colgan Group

*Bookable on www.irelandhotels.com*
*Special Offer: www.irelandhotels.com/offers*

*B&B from €55.00 to €80.00*

*Frank Colgan*
*Director*

50

*Activities:*

Closed 25 December

### Westbury (The)

HOTEL ★★★★★ MAP 8 O 11

Grafton Street,
Dublin 2

Tel: 01-679 1122 Fax: 01-679 7078
Email: westbury@jurysdoyle.com
Web: www.jurysdoyle.com

Smartly set just off Grafton Street in the very heart of the city, The Westbury can best be described as a truly international 5-star hotel; sophisticated, stylish and at the glamorous hub of Dublin life. Luxury, impeccable service and smart contemporary surroundings with the city at your feet.

***An IHF Quality Employer***

Member of Leading Hotels of the World

*Bookable on www.irelandhotels.com*
*Special Offer: www.irelandhotels.com/offers*

*Room Rate from €248.00 to €493.00*

*Paraic Doyle*
*General Manager*

205

Open All Year

### Westin Dublin

HOTEL ★★★★★ MAP 8 O 11

At College Green,
Westmoreland Street,
Dublin 2

Tel: 01-645 1000 Fax: 01-645 1234
Email: reservations.dublin@westin.com
Web: www.westin.com/dublin

Situated in the heart of the city, steps away from Grafton Street, overlooking Trinity College. One of Dublin's most luxurious five star hotels offers an ambience of warmth & Irish hospitality. Guestrooms feature the acclaimed Heavenly Bed and include 17 luxurious suites. A unique array of dining experiences awaits from the stylish Exchange Restaurant to the elegant Atrium Lounge or the popular Mint Bar. Flexible air-conditioned meeting rooms offer the latest in AV technology. Our largest room The Banking Hall has been restored to its original magnificent 19th century glory.

***An IHF Quality Employer***

*Bookable on www.irelandhotels.com*

*Room Rate from €189.00 to €489.00*
*Suites from €309.00 to €2,600.00*

*Enda M Mullin*
*General Manager*

163

*Activities:*

Open All Year



B&B Rates are per Person Sharing per Night incl. Breakfast. or Room Rates are per Room per Night - See also Page 8

## Kingston Hotel

HOTEL ★★ MAP 8 O 11

Adelaide St., (Off Georges St.),
Dun Laoghaire,
Co. Dublin

Tel: 01-280 1810 Fax: 01-280 1237

Email: reserv@kingstonhotel.com

Web: www.kingstonhotel.com

A delightful 45 bedroomed hotel with panoramic views of Dublin Bay, approximately 15 minutes from city centre. Beside ferryport and DART line. Situated convenient to R.D.S., Point Depot, Lansdowne Road and Leopardstown Racecourse. All rooms are en suite with direct dial phone, TV, tea/coffee making facilities. A family-run hotel serving food all day in our lounge/bar. Our Marconi Restaurant opens Friday and Saturday nights only. Carlisle Bar: lunch and evening dinners served 7 days a week. Please enquire about Facilities for Persons with Mobility Impairment.

***An IHF Quality Employer***

Member of Countrywide Hotels - MinOtel Ireland

*B&B from €80.00 to €95.00*

*Tom Murphy*
*General Manager*

45

**Closed 24 December - 07 January**

## Rochestown Lodge Hotel & Day Spa

HOTEL ★★★ MAP 8 O 11

Rochestown Avenue,
Killiney, Dun Laoghaire,
Co. Dublin

Tel: 01-285 3555 Fax: 01-285 3914

Email: info@rochestownlodge.com

Web: www.rochestownlodge.com

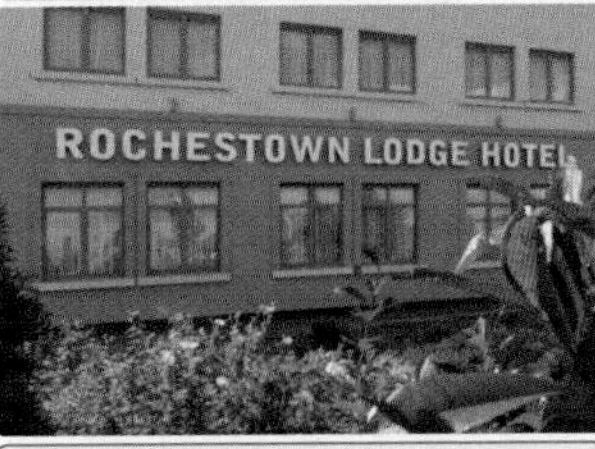


Whether you are staying for business or for leisure, Rochestown Lodge Hotel & Day Spa provides the perfect stylish modern setting to work or relax in complete comfort. Recently refurbished Rochestown Lodge Hotel & Day Spa, 90 executive rooms, suites and spacious family rooms, a stylish café, lounge and bistro restaurant. A luxurious day spa, with 9 treatment rooms, manicure and pedicure suite opened Summer '06. Fully equipped gym and 12m deck level pool. Ample car parking. Please enquire about Facilities for Persons with Mobility Impairment.

***Bookable on www.irelandhotels.com***
***Special Offer: www.irelandhotels.com/offers***

*B&B from €65.00 to €90.00*
*Suites from €149.00 to €189.00*

*Lisa Bradshaw*
*General Manager*

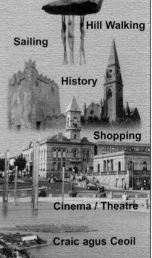

90

*Activities:*

**Closed 24 - 26 December**

# Dun Laoghaire / Howth

## Royal Marine Hotel

HOTEL MAP 8 O 11

Marine Road,
Dun Laoghaire,
Co. Dublin

Tel: 01-230 0030 Fax: 01-230 0029
Email: reservations@royalmarine.ie
Web: www.royalmarine.ie

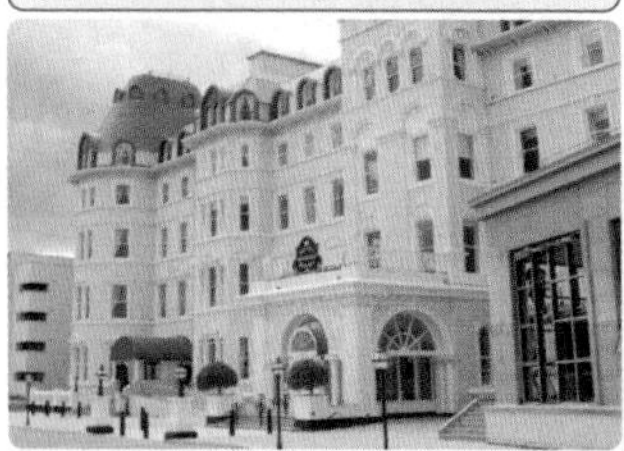

Built to a 4**** specification. The Royal Marine Hotel re-opened on the 22nd of June 2007 after undergoing extensive re-development. This superior Hotel has been fully restored to its former Victorian glory. The new look Royal Marine Hotel boasts 228 superior rooms, suites, presidential suites, business centre, 14 conference rooms with a maximum capacity of 800 delegates, which are all built to an international 4* standard. The Hotel's dining facilities comprise Hardy's Bar, Dún Bistro & Bay Lounge featuring the Pavillion Bar. sansanaSPA & The Pier Health Club opened Winter 2007.

***An IHF Quality Employer***

*Bookable on www.irelandhotels.com*

*Room Rate from €110.00 to €350.00*
*Suites from €500.00 to €2,000.00*

*Martin Mangan*
*General Manager*

228

*Activities:*

Open All Year

## Deer Park Hotel Golf & Spa

HOTEL ★★★ MAP 12 P 11

Howth,
Co. Dublin

Tel: 01-832 2624 Fax: 01-839 2405
Email: sales@deerpark.iol.ie
Web: www.deerpark-hotel.ie

14km from Dublin City/Airport on a quiet hillside overlooking the bay, Deer Park enjoys spectacular elevated sea views. Featuring Ireland's largest golf complex (5 courses), 18m swimming pool, sauna and steam room and two all-weather tennis courts. Whether on a golfing holiday or a visit to Dublin, you will find Deer Park the ideal choice. Easy access to Dublin city via DART rapid rail link. New spa and gym open. Please enquire about Facilities for Persons with Mobility Impairment.

Member of Irish Country Hotels

*Bookable on www.irelandhotels.com*
*Special Offer: www.irelandhotels.com/offers*

*B&B from €75.00 to €95.00*

*David & Antoinette Tighe*
*Managers*

75

*Activities:*

Closed 23 - 27 December

## King Sitric Fish Restaurant & Accommodation

GUESTHOUSE ★★★★ MAP 8 P 11

East Pier,
Howth,
Co. Dublin

Tel: 01-832 5235 Fax: 01-839 2442
Email: info@kingsitric.ie
Web: www.kingsitric.ie

Est. 1971, Aidan and Joan MacManus have earned an international reputation for fresh seafood in their harbour-side restaurant in the picturesque fishing village of Howth. Now with 8 guest rooms, all with sea views. Wine lovers will enjoy browsing in the atmospheric wine cellar. For leisure pursuits, Howth is the perfect location for golfing, walking and sailing. Dublin City is 25 minutes by DART; Dublin Airport 25 minutes driving.

Member of Ireland's Blue Book

*B&B from €75.00 to €102.50*

*Aidan & Joan MacManus*

8

*Activities:*

Closed Christmas & 16 -26 March



B&B Rates are per Person Sharing per Night incl. Breakfast. or Room Rates are per Room per Night - See also Page 8

## Fitzpatrick Castle Dublin

HOTEL ★★★★ MAP 8 P 10

Killiney,
Co. Dublin

Tel: 01-230 5400 Fax: 01-230 5466
Email: dublin@fitzpatricks.com
Web: www.fitzpatrickhotels.com

Fitzpatrick Castle Dublin is located in the fashionable suburbs of Killiney and Dalkey, overlooking Dublin Bay. Over 30 years of tradition in excellence has helped to create the perfect atmosphere at this family owned 18th century castle. Dining includes our award-winning restaurants, PJ's and Dungeon Bar & Grill. Full Leisure facilities including 20m pool and gym. Luxurious bedrooms, some with sea views and our recently renovated Castle Wing with sumptuous suites and authentic décor.

***An IHF Quality Employer***

*Bookable on www.irelandhotels.com*
*Special Offer: www.irelandhotels.com/offers*

**Room Rate from €140.00 to €350.00**
**Suites from €400.00 to €650.00**

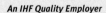

*Nicholas Logue*
*General Manager* — 113

*Activities:*

**Open All Year**

## Springfield Hotel

HOTEL ★★★ MAP 8 N 11

Leixlip,
Co. Dublin / Co. Kildare

Tel: 01-458 1100 Fax: 01-458 1142
Email: reception@springfieldhotel.ie
Web: www.springfieldhotel.ie

Our tastefully designed bedrooms are en suite, centrally heated with colour TV, satellite, hairdryer, tea/coffee courtesy tray, direct dial telephone, modem points, WiFi and broadband. Our restaurant offers menus to cater for all tastes. Guests return to enjoy our genuine hospitality. Our gym, which is well equipped with the latest machines, also has a sauna and steam room. Carton and Straffan golf courses within 6km. Dublin City centre 12km. Please enquire about Facilities for Persons with Mobility Impairment.

*Bookable on www.irelandhotels.com*
*Special Offer: www.irelandhotels.com/offers*

**B&B from €50.00 to €95.00**
**Suites from €105.00 to €185.00**

*Gerard Hannigan*
*Director / Manager* — 48

*Activities:*

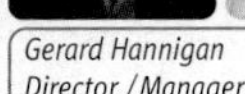

**Closed 25 - 26 December**

## Finnstown Country House Hotel

HOTEL ★★★ MAP 8 N 11

Newcastle Road,
Lucan,
Co. Dublin

Tel: 01-601 0700 Fax: 01-628 1088
Email: manager@finnstown-hotel.ie
Web: www.finnstown-hotel.ie

One of County Dublin's finest country house hotels. Set on 45 acres of private grounds it offers privacy, peace and seclusion yet is only twenty minutes drive from the bustling city centre of Dublin. If it's good old-fashioned hospitality you're after, great food and drink, a relaxed atmosphere and stylish surroundings, you're in the right place! Leisure facilities include gym, turkish bath, tennis court and indoor heated swimming pool. Please enquire about Facilities for Persons with Mobility Impairment.

***An IHF Quality Employer***

*Bookable on www.irelandhotels.com*
*Special Offer: www.irelandhotels.com/offers*

**B&B from €60.00 to €99.00**
**Suites from €140.00 to €216.00**

*Jenny Holmes*
*Hotel Manager* — 51

*Activities:*

**Closed 23 - 27 December**

B&B Rates are per Person Sharing per Night incl. Breakfast.
or Room Rates are per Room per Night - **See also Page 8**

## Lucan Spa Hotel

HOTEL ★★ MAP 8 N 11

Lucan,
Co. Dublin

Tel: 01-628 0494 Fax: 01-628 0841
Email: info@lucanspahotel.ie
Web: www.lucanspahotel.ie

Situated on the road to the West (N4) and close to the M50 and Dublin Airport, this elegant hotel offers its guests comfort and convenience in a country setting. All 70 bedrooms are equipped to 3 star standards (AA). Dine in the award-winning Honora D Restaurant (evenings daily & Sunday lunch) or The Earl Bistro (7.30am - 9.45pm). All conference and weddings catered for. The hotel is also Wi-Fi enabled. Special Offers available on 01-628 0494.

***An IHF Quality Employer***

Member of The Colgan Group

***Bookable on www.irelandhotels.com***
***Special Offer: www.irelandhotels.com/offers***

*B&B from €55.00 to €80.00*

*Frank Colgan*
*Director*

70

*Activities:*

**Closed 25 December**

## Moat Lodge

GUESTHOUSE ★★ MAP 8 N 11

Adamstown Road,
Lucan,
Co. Dublin

Tel: 01-624 1584 Fax: 01-628 1356
Email: info@moatlodge.ie
Web: www.moatlodge.ie

Exclusive 17th century house, convenient to buses for city centre, 200m walk to shops/pubs in the quaint Lucan Village. Ideal base for golf. Courses nearby include the K-Club, Carton House, Luttrellstown Castle, Hermitage and Lucan Golf Club. Off N4, near N7, N3 and M50. Private secure parking.

*B&B from €35.00 to €45.00*

*Astrid Scott*

10

**Open All Year**

## Hillview House

GUESTHOUSE MAP 12 O 12

Skerries Road,
Lusk,
Co. Dublin

Tel: 01-843 8218 Fax: 01-843 8218
Email: leofynes@eircom.net
Web: www.hillviewhouselusk.com

Built to a 3*** specification. A warm welcoming family home, set in a peaceful & tranquil area. Excellent spacious accommodation awaits all our guests, all rooms en suite, with TV, tea/coffee making facilities and hairdryer. Separate lounge. 15 minutes from Dublin Airport, 30 minutes from city centre. All amenities close by, 10 minutes from the picturesque town of Skerries with lots of pubs & restaurants. A warm welcome awaits you at Hillview House. Please enquire about Facilities for Persons with Mobility Impairment.

*B&B from €45.00 to €55.00*

*Leo & Kay Fynes*
*Proprietors*

8

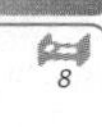

**Closed 20 December - 01 January**



B&B Rates are per Person Sharing per Night incl. Breakfast. or Room Rates are per Room per Night - See also Page 8

## Grand Hotel

HOTEL ★★★★ MAP 12 O 12

Malahide,
Co. Dublin

Tel: 01-845 0000 Fax: 01-845 0987

Email: booking@thegrand.ie

Web: www.thegrand.ie

The Grand Hotel is situated by the sea in the village of Malahide. Just 10 minutes drive from Dublin Airport and 30 minutes from the city centre, the hotel is ideally situated for guests staying for business or leisure. The conference and business centre is one of Ireland's largest and most successful. All 200 bedrooms have tea/coffee making facilities and fax/broadband lines. Most bedrooms have spectacular sea views. Leisure centre includes a 21 metre swimming pool, jacuzzi, fully equipped gymnasium, sauna and steam room. Please enquire about Facilities for Persons with Mobility Impairment.

***An IHF Quality Employer***

*Bookable on www.irelandhotels.com*

*Special Offer: www.irelandhotels.com/offers*

*B&B from €57.50 to €125.00*
*Suites from €130.00 to €600.00*

*Matthew Ryan*
*Managing Director*

200

Activities:

Closed 25 - 27 December

## Portmarnock Hotel & Golf Links

HOTEL ★★★★ MAP 12 O 11

Strand Road,
Portmarnock,
Co. Dublin

Tel: 01-846 0611 Fax: 01-846 2442

Email: res@portmarnock.com

Web: www.portmarnock.com

The Portmarnock Hotel & Golf Links sits on Ireland's east coast in the heart of Ireland's golfing region. A blend of the old & new, this elegant hotel was created from the former home of the famous Jameson Whiskey family. Luxurious modern accommodation alongside the lovingly restored public areas of the 19th century building. Set on 180 acres of seaside links terrain, the 138 rooms overlook the sea on one side with garden or golf course views on the other side. The Portmarknock Golf Links was designed by master champion Bernard Langer. Located 15 mins drive from Dublin Airport & 30 mins from the city centre.

***An IHF Quality Employer***

Member of Preferred Hotels and Resorts

*Bookable on www.irelandhotels.com*

*Special Offer: www.irelandhotels.com/offers*

*B&B from €75.00 to €175.00*
*Suites from €150.00 to €400.00*

*Edward Sweeney*
*General Manager*

138

Activities:

Open All Year

## White Sands Hotel

HOTEL ★★★ MAP 12 O 11

Coast Road,
Portmarnock,
Co. Dublin

Tel: 01-866 6000 Fax: 01-866 6006

Email: info@whitesandshotel.ie

Web: www.whitesandshotel.ie

De luxe 3 star family-run hotel overlooking the beautiful sandy beaches and spectacular sea views of north Co. Dublin. Situated within 4km of the M1 and M50 allowing easy access to Dublin Airport, Dublin City centre, all major golf courses and tourist attractions. All superbly appointed bedrooms are en suite with tea/coffee making facilities, DD telephone and some with air conditioning & safes. Our Business Centre with Internet access is also available. Lively Irish bar, Mad Fish Restaurant & carvery. Ample free coach & car parking. "With a view to impress" Please enquire about Facilities for Persons with Mobility Impairment.

*Bookable on www.irelandhotels.com*

*Special Offer: www.irelandhotels.com/offers*

*B&B from €60.00 to €120.00*
*Suites from €175.00 to €250.00*

*Georgina Higgins*
*General Manager*

58

Activities:

Closed 24 - 26 December

B&B Rates are per Person Sharing per Night incl. Breakfast.
or Room Rates are per Room per Night - See also Page 8

## Saggart / Skerries

### Citywest Hotel, Conference, Leisure & Golf Resort

HOTEL ★★★★ MAP 8 N 11

Saggart,
Co. Dublin

Tel: 01-401 0500 Fax: 01-458 8756
Email: sales@citywesthotel.com
Web: www.citywesthotel.com

Ireland's premier conference, leisure and golf resort and one of Europe's most popular international conference destinations. Dublin's most popular golf resort is just 15km from the city centre. This resort offers: luxurious rooms, lively bars, choice of restaurants, superb pool and leisure facilities. Imagine two of Ireland's finest golf courses in one magnificent setting designed by Christy O'Connor Junior. Enjoy all Dublin has to offer from this beautiful and tranquil setting. Please enquire about Facilities for Persons with Mobility Impairment.

*Bookable on www.irelandhotels.com*
*Special Offer: www.irelandhotels.com/offers*

**B&B from €50.00 to €100.00**
**Suites from €130.00 to €1,000.00**

*Bernard J. O'Byrne*
*Group Chief Executive*

492

Activities:

**Open All Year**

### Carroll's Pierhouse Hotel

HOTEL ★★ MAP 12 P 12

Harbour Road,
Skerries,
Co. Dublin

Tel: 01-849 1033 Fax: 01-849 4695
Email: info@pierhousehotel.ie
Web: www.pierhousehotel.ie

Carroll's Pierhouse Hotel is a family-run hotel, delightfully furnished & elegant in style. Situated on the Harbour Road of Skerries, a quaint fishing town about 15 mins from Dublin Airport & 30 mins from Dublin City centre. The idyllic location provides its guests with a wonderful panoramic view of the Irish Sea. Each of the hotel's executive en suite rooms has teletext TV, trouser press & tea/coffee making facilities. The restaurant provides Irish cuisine & an array of international dishes & in the main bar meals of similar content are available daily from 10am until 10pm. Our nightclub "Club Ocean" is open at weekends.

**B&B from €60.00 to €65.00**

*Mary & Michael Carroll*
*Proprietors*

11

**Closed 25 December**

### Redbank House Guesthouse & Restaurant

GUESTHOUSE ★★★★ MAP 12 P 12

5 - 7 Church Street,
Skerries,
Co. Dublin

Tel: 01-849 1005 Fax: 01-849 1598
Email: info@redbank.ie
Web: www.redbank.ie

Enjoy the extended hospitality of the McCoy's in Redbank House. The world famous seafood restaurant is the dining room of Redbank House. The 18 en suite rooms have the McCoys sense of style and elegance. The area is particularly rich in golf courses and a wide variety of leisure activities includes sea fishing, boat trips, sailing and horse riding. The Chef Proprietor Terry McCoy cooks the catch of the day landed at Skerries Pier specialising in the world famous Dublin Bay prawns. Just 20 minutes from Dublin Airport on the new M1. On-street parking Pay & Display, Mon - Sat: 8am - 6pm.

***An IHF Quality Employer***

Member of Premier Guesthouses, Private Ireland

*Bookable on www.irelandhotels.com*
*Special Offer: www.irelandhotels.com/offers*

**B&B from €50.00 to €70.00**

*Terry McCoy*
*Proprietor*

18

Activities:

**Open All Year**



B&B Rates are per Person Sharing per Night incl. Breakfast.
or Room Rates are per Room per Night - See also Page 8

## Marine Hotel

HOTEL ★★★ MAP 12 P 11

Sutton Cross,
Dublin 13

Tel: 01-839 0000 Fax: 01-839 0442
Email: info@marinehotel.ie
Web: www.marinehotel.ie

The Marine Hotel overlooks the north shore of Dublin Bay with its lawn sweeping down to the sea shore. All bedrooms are en suite and have trouser press, TV, direct dial phone and tea/coffee facilities. The city centre is 6km away and the airport 25 minutes drive. Close by is the DART rapid rail system. The hotel has a heated indoor swimming pool and sauna. Nearby are the Royal Dublin and Portmarnock championship golf courses. Please enquire about Facilities for Persons with Mobility Impairment.

***An IHF Quality Employer***

*Bookable on www.irelandhotels.com*
*Special Offer: www.irelandhotels.com/offers*

*B&B from €55.00 to €110.00*

*Matthew Ryan*
*Managing Director*

48

*Activities:*

**Closed 25 - 27 December**

## Carnegie Court Hotel

HOTEL ★★★ MAP 12 O 12

North Street,
Swords,
Co. Dublin

Tel: 01-840 4384 Fax: 01-840 4505
Email: info@carnegiecourt.com
Web: www.carnegiecourt.com

The Carnegie Court Hotel is a luxury accommodation hotel ideally situated in the town of Swords, 5 mins from Dublin Airport and 20 mins from the city centre. The hotel comprises 36 beautifully decorated and spacious bedrooms. A warm welcoming atmosphere makes it the perfect place of rest, be it business or pleasure. Enjoy our award-winning Courtyard Restaurant or indulge in a night out in one of our five bars. Other facilities include conference & banqueting services and an extensive secure car park. Please enquire about Facilities for Persons with Mobility Impairment.

***An IHF Quality Employer***

*B&B from €65.00 to €120.00*

*Allen Harrington*
*General Manager*

36

*Activities:*

**Closed 24 - 26 December**

B&B Rates are per Person Sharing per Night incl. Breakfast.
or Room Rates are per Room per Night - **See also Page 8**

## Swords / Athy

### Roganstown Golf & Country Club

HOTEL ★★★★ MAP 12 O 12

Roganstown,
Swords,
Co. Dublin

Tel: 01-843 3118 Fax: 01-843 3303

Email: info@roganstown.com

Web: www.roganstown.com

Converted from the original Roganstown House, the spectacular Roganstown Golf & Country Club is a destination of relaxation, fine food and exceptional golf set among circa 300 acres. To compliment the magnificent 52 bedroomed hotel, facilities also include leisure club, state of the art business and conference centre, and one of Ireland's most outstanding new golf courses. Located just 5 minutes from Dublin Airport and 25 minutes from city centre. Complimentary shuttle provided from Dublin Airport. Please enquire about Facilities for Persons with Mobility Impairment.

*Bookable on www.irelandhotels.com*
*Special Offer: www.irelandhotels.com/offers*

*B&B from €49.50 to €150.00*

*Ian McGuinness*
*Managing Director*

52

**Closed 24 - 26 December**

### Carlton Abbey Hotel & C Spa

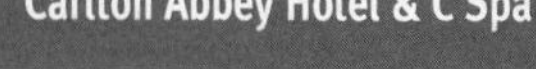

HOTEL ★★★★ MAP 7 M 9

Town Centre,
Athy,
Co. Kildare

Tel: 059-863 0100 Fax: 059-864 1786

Email: info@carltonabbeyhotel.com

Web: www.carlton.ie

New 4**** hotel, leisure club & C Spa. Carlton Abbey Hotel is situated in the heart of Athy, Co. Kildare. 50 minutes from Dublin. 49 luxurious bedrooms including junior/family suites along with conference & banqueting facilities for 300 guests. The Abbey Bar & Bistro, formerly an old church, is the centre piece of this restoration with Benedicts Restaurant offering an intimate fine dining experience. State of the art leisure club with 21m pool, sauna, jacuzzi, steam room & modern gym. C Spa with 6 treatment rooms is an oasis of calm for all guests to enjoy. Room Reservations
LoCall 1890 288 288.

Member of The Carlton Hotel Group

*B&B from €75.00 to €158.00*
*Suites from €250.00 to €390.00*

*Damien Mekitarian*
*General Manager*

49

*Activities:*

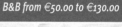

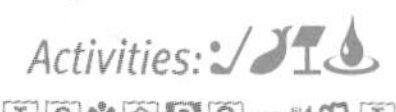

**Closed 24 - 27 December**

### Clanard Court Hotel

HOTEL ★★★★ MAP 7 M 9

Dublin Road,
Athy,
Co. Kildare

Tel: 059-864 0666 Fax: 059-864 0888

Email: sales@clanardcourt.ie

Web: www.clanardcourt.ie

Clanard Court Hotel is a delightful, boutique style 4**** with beautiful gardens situated just 1 hour from Dublin and 1km from Athy Town. It boasts 38 superbly appointed guest rooms complete with all modern conveniences including interactive TV and unlimited broadband. It is family-run with strong emphasis on customer service. Clanard Court specialises in tailor made banqueting and events. There are a choice of banqueting and conference rooms accommodating up to 450 pax. The ideal choice for superb food and genuine, warm hospitality - a leading wedding venue in Leinster.

*Bookable on www.irelandhotels.com*
*Special Offer: www.irelandhotels.com/offers*

*B&B from €50.00 to €130.00*

*Mary Fennin Byrne*
*Managing Director*

38

*Activities:*

**Closed 23 - 26 December**



B&B Rates are per Person Sharing per Night incl. Breakfast. or Room Rates are per Room per Night - See also Page 8

## Ardenode Hotel

HOTEL ★★★ MAP 8 N 10

Ballymore Eustace,
Co. Kildare

Tel: 045-864198 Fax: 045-864139
Email: info@ardenodehotel.com
Web: www.ardenodehotel.com

Beautiful holiday setting, located just outside the picturesque village of Ballymore Eustace, on 5 acres of landscaped gardens. The Ardenode Country House Hotel is a haven of tranquillity. Golf, fishing, shopping, horse racing all within 10 minutes drive. Stud Bar & Grill Restaurant serving modern food in contemporary surroundings. Private hire options available.

Member of Fitzers Catering LTD

*B&B from €75.00 to €100.00*

*Paul Crosby*
*General Manager*

17

Activities:

Closed 24 - 27 December

## Kilkea Castle

HOTEL ★★★★ MAP 7 M 8

Castledermot,
Co. Kildare

Tel: 059-914 5156 Fax: 059-914 5187
Email: reservations@kilkeacastle.ie
Web: www.kilkeacastle.ie

Kilkea Castle is the oldest inhabited castle in Ireland. Built in 1180, offering the best in modern comfort while the charm and elegance of the past has been retained. The facilities include de luxe accommodation, De Lacy's Restaurant, restful bar/lounge area, full banqueting and conference facilities and full on-site leisure centre with an indoor heated swimming pool, sauna, spa pool, steam room and fully equipped gym. 18 hole golf course encircles the castle. Please enquire about Facilities for Persons with Mobility Impairment.

Member of Manor House Hotels

*Bookable on www.irelandhotels.com*

*B&B from €115.00 to €140.00*

*Bríd Kearney*
*General Manager*

36

Activities:

Closed 23 - 27 December

## Celbridge / Clane / Curragh (The)

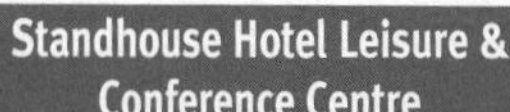

### Setanta House Hotel

HOTEL ★★★ MAP 8 N 11

Clane Road,
Celbridge,
Co. Kildare

Tel: 01-630 3200 Fax: 01-627 3387
Email: info@setantahousehotel.com
Web: www.setantahousehotel.com

Built in 1737, this former school, situated in the historic Heritage Town of Celbridge, combines elegance and tranquillity with modern facilities. Set in mature landscaped gardens with 65 newly refurbished spacious bedrooms including luxurious suites. Setanta House is ideal for business and leisure alike. Only 20 minutes from Dublin City and Airport with easy access off the N4 and M50. Renowned golf and race courses nearby. A warm welcome is always assured.

*Bookable on www.irelandhotels.com*
*Special Offer: www.irelandhotels.com/offers*

*Room Rate from €79.00 to €500.00*
*Suites from €160.00 to €500.00*

*Arthur McDaniel*
*General Manager*

65

Closed 24 -26 December

### Westgrove Hotel & Conference Centre

HOTEL ★★★★ MAP 8 N 11

Clane,
Co. Kildare

Tel: 045-989900 Fax: 045-989911
Email: reservations@westgrovehotel.com
Web: www.westgrovehotel.com

On the outskirts of Clane Village, this hotel combines accessibility with a feeling of getting away from the bustle of the city. Facilities to pamper the most discerning guest include Elemis Spa, leisure centre with 20m pool, a choice of 2 restaurants, 2 bars and a roof garden. An ideal base from which to play world class golf courses, attend exciting race meetings or enjoy many other activities. Flexible and comfortable conference spaces are available. Secure parking. Please enquire about Facilities for Persons with Mobility Impairment.

Member of Select Hotels of Ireland

*Bookable on www.irelandhotels.com*
*Special Offer: www.irelandhotels.com/offers*

*B&B from €50.00 to €150.00*
*Suites from €200.00 to €400.00*

*Ian Hyland*
*General Manager*

99

*Activities:*

Closed 24 - 26 December

### Standhouse Hotel Leisure & Conference Centre

HOTEL ★★★ MAP 7 M 10

Curragh (The),
Co. Kildare

Tel: 045-436177 Fax: 045-436180
Email: reservations@standhousehotel.com
Web: www.standhousehotel.ie

The Standhouse Hotel has a tradition which dates back to 1700. Situated at the Curragh Racecourse it has become synonymous with The Classics and offers a fine selection of quality restaurants, bars and leisure facilities which include 20 metre pool, gymnasium, jacuzzi, steam room, sauna and plunge pool. Conference facilities caters for 20 to 500 delegates. Phase one of the Grand Stand redevelopment has recently been completed.

*Bookable on www.irelandhotels.com*

*B&B from €70.00 to €145.00*

*Padraig Nolan*
*General Manager*

63

*Activities:*

Closed 25 - 26 December



B&B Rates are per Person Sharing per Night incl. Breakfast.
or Room Rates are per Room per Night - See also Page 8

## Derby House Hotel

HOTEL ★★ MAP 7 M 10

Dublin Road,
Kildare Town,
Co. Kildare

Tel: 045-522144 Fax: 045-521247

Email: enquiries@derbyhousehotel.ie

Web: www.derbyhousehotel.ie

A friendly and warm welcome awaits you at the Derby House Hotel. Conveniently located in the town centre, the hotel now incorporates Kingsland Restaurant offering Chinese and European cuisine. This 20 bedroomed hotel is conveniently located for racing, angling and numerous golf courses including the renowned K Club. Many attractions, including the Japanese Gardens, Irish National Stud and Kildare Village, are also nearby. Please enquire about Facilities for Persons with Mobility Impairment.

***Bookable on www.irelandhotels.com***

*Special Offer: www.irelandhotels.com/offers*

*B&B from €55.00 to €80.00*

*Sarah Chan*
*Proprietor*

20

Activities:

Open All Year

## Courtyard Hotel Leixlip

HOTEL ★★★★ MAP 8 N 11

Main Street,
Leixlip,
Co. Kildare

Tel: 01-629 5100 Fax: 01-629 5111

Email: info@courtyard.ie

Web: www.courtyard.ie

Opened in July 2005, The Courtyard Hotel is situated 20 mins from Dublin City and approx 20 mins from Dublin Airport. The hotel is situated on the site of the ancestral home of "Guinness" and features 40 tastefully appointed guest rooms. Dine in the "Riverbank Restaurant" overlooking the River Liffey and relax in "Arthur's Bar". The hotel is situated close to some of Ireland's best golf courses including the K Club and Carton House. Please enquire about Facilities for Persons with Mobility Impairment.

Member of The Moriarty Group

***Bookable on www.irelandhotels.com***

*Special Offer: www.irelandhotels.com/offers*

*B&B from €80.00 to €100.00*
*Suites from €260.00 to €500.00*

*Luke Moriarty*
*Owner*

40

Activities:

Open all year

## Leixlip House Hotel

HOTEL ★★★ MAP 8 N 11

Captain's Hill,
Leixlip,
Co. Kildare

Tel: 01-624 2268 Fax: 01-624 4177

Email: info@leixliphouse.com

Web: www.leixliphouse.com

A most elegant Georgian house hotel built in 1772. Leixlip House is a mere 20 minutes drive from Dublin City centre. The hotel has been lovingly restored and offers the discerning guest the highest standards of comfort and hospitality. It can cater for conferences of up to 70 people and our banqueting facilities can comfortably accommodate 140 people. Our signature restaurant "The Bradaun" has been awarded the prestigious AA Two Rosette 1996-2007.

***Bookable on www.irelandhotels.com***

*Special Offer: www.irelandhotels.com/offers*

*B&B from €75.00 to €140.00*

*Christian Schmelter*
*General Manager*

19

Closed 24 - 27 December

B&B Rates are per Person Sharing per Night incl. Breakfast.
or Room Rates are per Room per Night - **See also Page 8**

## Maynooth / Monasterevin

### Carton House

HOTEL ★★★★ MAP 12 N 11


Maynooth,
Co. Kildare

Tel: 01-505 2000 Fax: 01-651 7703

Email: reservations@cartonhouse.com

Web: www.cartonhouse.com

Carton House, one of Ireland's finest stately homes opened as a luxury 165 bedroomed hotel and includes 18 suites. It features 14 fully equipped conference and event facilities. It has 2 championship golf courses, The Montgomerie & The O'Meara, The Spa and a state of the art gym and leisure facilities. Carton House is located 14 miles west of Dublin City centre and 30 minutes' drive from Dublin Airport. Please enquire about Facilities for Persons with Mobility Impairment.

*Bookable on www.irelandhotels.com*
*Special Offer: www.irelandhotels.com/offers*

**B&B from €85.00 to €155.00**
**Suites from €360.00 to €2,500.00**

*David Webster*
*General Manager*

165

Activities:

**Open All Year**

### Glenroyal Hotel, Leisure Club & Conference Centre

HOTEL ★★★ MAP 8 N 11


Straffan Road,
Maynooth,
Co. Kildare

Tel: 01-629 0909 Fax: 01-629 0919

Email: info@glenroyal.ie

Web: www.glenroyal.ie

Located 20 minutes from Dublin off the M4, the Glenroyal Hotel has a well earned reputation for friendliness, informality and hospitality. Ideally located for the business or leisure traveller. With 112 en suite bedrooms, Saint's Bar & Bistro, Lemongrass Restaurant, extensive conference facilities, night club and free car parking. Our leisure facilities include two 20m pools, sauna, jacuzzi, steam room, solariums, gymnasium and beauty/spa. Carton and the K Club are minutes away. Please enquire about Facilities for Persons with Mobility Impairment.

*Bookable on www.irelandhotels.com*
*Special Offer: www.irelandhotels.com/offers*

**B&B from €49.50 to €75.00**

*Helen Courtney*
*General Manager*

112

Activities:

**Closed 24 - 25 December**

### Hazel Hotel

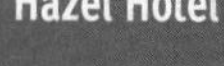

HOTEL ★★★ MAP 7 N 10


Dublin Road,
Monasterevin,
Co. Kildare

Tel: 045-525373 Fax: 045-525810

Email: sales@hazelhotel.com

Web: www.hazelhotel.com

The Hazel Hotel is a family-run country hotel on the main Dublin/Cork/Limerick road (N7). All bedrooms have bath/shower, colour TV and international direct dial telephone. The hotel's restaurant has extensive à la carte and table d'hôte menus. Ample car parking. Entertainment is provided. Ideal base for going to the Curragh, Naas or Punchestown racecourses. Several golf courses close by. National Stud and Japanese Gardens only 7 miles from hotel. No service charge. Please enquire about Facilities for Persons with Mobility Impairment.

***An IHF Quality Employer***

Member of Logis of Ireland

**B&B from €70.00 to €80.00**
**Suites from €130.00 to €150.00**

*Margaret Kelly*
*Proprietor*

24

Activities:

**Closed 24 - 26 December**



B&B Rates are per Person Sharing per Night incl. Breakfast. or Room Rates are per Room per Night - See also Page 8

## Moyvalley Hotel & Golf Resort

HOTEL ★★★★ MAP 7 M 11

Balyna Estate,
Moyvalley,
Co. Kildare

Tel: 046-954 8000 Fax: 046-954 8070

Email: info@moyvalley.com

Web: www.moyvalley.com

A fabulous resort set in the heart of the Irish countryside, only 60km from Dublin. Moyvalley is a modern country hotel with 54 superior rooms. Luxury 2 bedroomed courtyard cottages are fully furnished & ideal for families or just extra space. Balyna House is available for exclusive use & forms the perfect venue for private events or weddings. Moyvalley, home to the Darren Clarke designed champions club golf course available to members & resort guests only. Other activities include archery, bike hire & guided walks. Access to chauffeur drive vehicles & helipads is available. Please enquire about Facilities for Persons with Mobility Impairment.

*Bookable on www.irelandhotels.com*

*Special Offer: www.irelandhotels.com/offers*

**B&B from €109.00 to €250.00**

*Phillip Jones*
*General Manager*

54

*Activities:*

**Closed 25 December**

## Harbour Hotel & Restaurant

HOTEL ★★ MAP 8 N 10

Limerick Road,
Naas,
Co. Kildare

Tel: 045-879145 Fax: 045-874002

Email: mary@harbourhotel.ie

Web: www.harbourhotel.ie

Looking after the needs of our guests and providing quality service is a priority in this family-run hotel. All rooms have colour TV, direct dial telephone, hairdryer and teasmaid. We offer superb home-cooked food, extensive à la carte and table d'hôte menus and excellent wine list. Relax and enjoy a drink in our comfortable lounge. Conveniently situated to Dublin City, ferry, airport, Punchestown Racecourse, The Curragh and Mondello Park.

*Bookable on www.irelandhotels.com*

**B&B from €55.00 to €60.00**

*Mary Monaghan*
*Proprietor*

10

**Closed 24 - 27 December**

## Killashee House Hotel & Villa Spa

HOTEL ★★★★ MAP 8 N 10

Killashee,
Naas,
Co. Kildare

Tel: 045-879277 Fax: 045-879266

Email: reservations@killasheehouse.com

Web: www.killasheehouse.com

Killashee House Hotel & Villa Spa is ideally located on 80 acres of magnificent parkland and gardens, 45 minutes from Dublin and 1.5 miles from Naas. This 4 star Victorian manor house blends the dignity of a major business hotel with the casual atmosphere of a fine country resort. 141 luxurious guest rooms, including traditionally appointed suites. award-winning restaurant, traditional Irish Bar and residents lounge area. State of the art country club and villa spa with 18 treatment rooms. Located in close proximity to some of Ireland's Finest golf and race courses.

***An IHF Quality Employer***

*Bookable on www.irelandhotels.com*

*Special Offer: www.irelandhotels.com/offers*

**B&B from €99.00 to €175.00**
**Suites from €250.00 to €495.00**

*Deirdre Nix*
*General Manager*

141

*Activities:*

**Closed 24 - 25 December**

## Naas

### Lawlors Hotel

HOTEL ★★★ MAP 8 N 10

Popular Square,
Naas,
Co. Kildare

Tel: 045-906444 Fax: 045-906440
Email: info@lawlors.ie
Web: www.lawlors.ie

Lawlors Hotel is ideally located 25km from Dublin and central to Naas Town. This boutique hotel offers 28 luxurious guest rooms including executive suites with all modern conveniences combined with excellent service. Local amenities include horse racing, golf, fishing, Goffs Blood Stock Sales and motor racing. Meetings and private dining facilities also available.

*B&B from €79.00 to €199.00*

*Patrick Landy*
*General Manager*

28

Closed 25 December

### Maudlins House Hotel

HOTEL ★★★★ MAP 8 N 10

Dublin Road,
Naas,
Co. Kildare

Tel: 045-896999 Fax: 045-906411
Email: info@maudlinshousehotel.ie
Web: www.maudlinshousehotel.ie

Maudlins House Hotel is a restored luxury country house which opened in April 2006. Conveniently located less than 1km from Naas Town, 25km from Dublin and is ideal for those traveling to the south or west. The hotel comprises 20 luxury bedrooms, 5 private chalets, the Virginia Restaurant, Maudlins Bar and conference and banqueting facilities. Local amenities include Golf, Horse racing, Goffs Horse Sales, Japanese Gardens & National Stud, Shopping. A place to indulge yourself. Please enquire about Facilities for Persons with Mobility Impairment.

*B&B from €75.00 to €95.00*

*David Fagan*
*Director*

25

*Activities:*

Closed 24 - 26 December

### Osprey Hotel & Spa

HOTEL ★★★★ MAP 8 N 10

Devoy Quarter,
Naas,
Co. Kildare

Tel: 045-881111 Fax: 045-881112
Email: info@osprey.ie
Web: www.osprey.ie

The Osprey Complex, located in the heart of Kildare, is only 35 minutes from Dublin City and close to all major routes. It includes the Osprey Hotel, Osprey Spa, Life: health & leisure, Time: venue, Osprey Conference Centre, Osprey Business Campus and Osprey Nest Crèche. Osprey Hotel is of contemporary style with 104 bedrooms including two penthouse suites & has a dramatic foyer, glazed atria, Mash: Restaurant, Statler Bar and Waldorf Lounge and ballroom. It has been designed to cater for an entirely new lifestyle. Complimentary wireless connectivity throughout. Suites available up to €1,000 per night.

***Bookable on www.irelandhotels.com***
***Special Offer: www.irelandhotels.com/offers***

*Room Rate from €140.00 to €285.00*
*Suites from €485.00 to €1,000.00*

*John O'Connell*
*Proprietor*

104

*Activities:*

Closed 24 - 26 December



B&B Rates are per Person Sharing per Night incl. Breakfast. or Room Rates are per Room per Night - **See also Page 8**

## Newbridge / Straffan

### Gables Guesthouse & Leisure Centre

GUESTHOUSE ★★★ MAP 7 M 10

Ryston,
Newbridge,
Co. Kildare

Tel: 045-435330 Fax: 045-435355
Email: gablesguesthse@ireland.com

Set on the banks of the Liffey, our family-run guesthouse has 25 bedrooms with bath/shower, multi channel TV, direct dial telephone, hairdryer and teas maid. Our leisure centre includes a 14 metre indoor swimming pool, jacuzzi, steam room, large sauna, thermium, plunge pool and fully equipped gym. Horse racing, greyhound racing, golf and fishing are well catered for locally. A warm and friendly welcome awaits you at the Gables. Brochures available on request.

**B&B from €45.00 to €80.00**

*Ray Cribbin*
*Proprietor*

25

**Closed 23 December - 02 January**

### Keadeen Hotel

HOTEL ★★★★ MAP 7 M 10

Newbridge,
Co. Kildare

Tel: 045-431666 Fax: 045-434402
Email: info@keadeenhotel.ie
Web: www.keadeenhotel.ie

Kildare's longest family-run hotel, the Keadeen is ideally located on 9 acres of magnificent landscaped gardens, just 30 minutes from Dublin off the M7. This charming 4**** hotel offers unrivalled standards of service and facilities with a variety of 75 luxurious spacious bedrooms, a superb indoor health and fitness complex and 18 metre ozone pool. An extensive range of conference/banqueting suites for up to 1000 delegates. Dining facilities include the award-winning Derby Restaurant, the sophisticated 'Club Bar', the Drawing Room Lounge. Please enquire about Facilities for Persons with Mobility Impairment.

***An IHF Quality Employer***

**B&B from €125.00 to €140.00**

*Rose O'Loughlin*
*Proprietor*

75

Activities:

**Closed 24 December - 02 January**

### Barberstown Castle

HOTEL ★★★★ MAP 8 N 11

Straffan,
Co. Kildare

Tel: 01-628 8157 Fax: 01-627 7027
Email: info@barberstowncastle.ie
Web: www.barberstowncastle.ie

A member of Ireland's Blue Book, Barberstown Castle is a 4**** castle & country house hotel just a thirty minute drive from Dublin Airport and city centre. A visit to Dublin City, Newgrange, Glendalough, Kildare Village (chic outlet shopping) and the Japanese Gardens are just some of the trips to enjoy in a county famous for racing and golf (Ryder Cup 2006). Easily accessible from all major routes (M1, M50, M4, M7), make Barberstown Castle a very popular venue for romantic breaks for people from all parts of Ireland. Please enquire about Facilities for Persons with Mobility Impairment.

**B&B from €120.00 to €160.00**

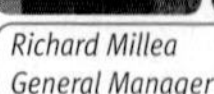

*Richard Millea*
*General Manager*

59

Activities:

**Closed 24 - 26 December & January**



B&B Rates are per Person Sharing per Night incl. Breakfast. or Room Rates are per Room per Night - See also Page 8

## Kildare Hotel, Spa and Country Club - The K Club

HOTEL ★★★★★ MAP 8 N 11

At Straffan,
Co. Kildare

Tel: 01-601 7200 Fax: 01-601 7297
Email: resortsales@kclub.ie
Web: www.kclub.ie

The K Club is Ireland's premier 5 red star resort, located 40 minutes from Dublin City Centre and Airport. Both river fishing & course fishing are available, the magnificent K Spa offers a chance to pamper yourself in style or work out before dining in one of our sumptuous restaurants. The Palmer Course was the host venue of the 2006 Ryder Cup Matches and The Smurfit Course is Home of The Smurfit Kappa European Open. The Kids Club allows you to relax while your children are well looked after & have fun while learning. Each weekend we offer tours of the wine cellar and art & history. Meeting facilities for up to 400 people.

Member of Preferred Hotel Group

*Bookable on www.irelandhotels.com*
*Special Offer: www.irelandhotels.com/offers*

*Room Rate from €385.00 to €600.00*
*Suites from €515.00 to €7,000.00*

*Michael Davern*
*Chief Executive*

92

*Activities:*

**Open All Year**

## Abbeyleix Manor Hotel

HOTEL ★★★ MAP 7 L 8

Abbeyleix,
Co. Laois

Tel: 057-873 0111 Fax: 057-873 0220
Email: info@abbeyleixmanorhotel.com
Web: www.abbeyleixmanorhotel.com

The Abbeyleix Manor Hotel boasts a prime location situated on the N8 halfway between Dublin and Cork, your perfect base for exploring the Midlands region. This family-run hotel has 46 luxurious bedrooms (23 newly built), restaurant, bar and a recently built state of the art conference centre. Surrounded by beautifully landscaped gardens it is ideal for your perfect wedding location. Already well established as a great place for breakfast, lunch or dinner, the friendly and professional staff will look after your every need. Please enquire about Facilities for Persons with Mobility Impairment.

*Bookable on www.irelandhotels.com*
*Special Offer: www.irelandhotels.com/offers*

*B&B from €55.00 to €65.00*
*Suites from €150.00 to €180.00*

*Michael Bennet, Eileen O'Connor*

46

*Activities:*

**Closed 25 - 26 December**

## Castle Arms Hotel

HOTEL ★ MAP 7 L 8

The Square,
Durrow,
Co. Laois

Tel: 057-873 6117 Fax: 057-873 6566
Email: info@castlearmshotel.ie
Web: www.castlearmshotel.ie

The Castle Arms Hotel is a family-run hotel situated in the award-winning picturesque village of Durrow. We are situated 1.5 hours from Dublin, two hours from Cork and three hours from Belfast. Our reputation is for good food, service and friendliness. Local amenities include fishing. Granstown Lake is described as being the best coarse fishing lake in Europe. Trout can be fished from the local Rivers Erkina and Nore, horse trekking and many golf courses within easy reach. Brand Central designer outlet is 10 minutes drive away. Ideal for a weekend away shopping. Please enquire about Facilities for Persons with Mobility Impairment.

*B&B from €65.00 to €65.00*

*Seosamh Murphy*
*General Manager*

14

**Open All Year**

B&B Rates are per Person Sharing per Night incl. Breakfast.
or Room Rates are per Room per Night - **See also Page 8**

## Killenard / Portlaoise

### Heritage Golf & Spa Resort (The)

HOTEL ★★★★★ MAP 7 L 10

Killenard,
Co. Laois

Tel: 057-864 5500 Fax: 057-864 2350
Email: info@theheritage.com
Web: www.theheritage.com

The Heritage Golf & Spa Resort is Ireland's most comprehensive leisure & lifestyle development. Situated in the village of Killenard just off the main Dublin - Cork motorway. We are just 40 miles from Dublin. A 98 guest room hotel, 20 therapy room resort Spa, the renowned Heritage Golf Course designed by Seve Ballesteros, Health Club, Walking & Jogging track, Ballesteros 'Natural' Golf School, Thatch Pub and Sol Oriens Italian Restaurant & Steakhouse, all provide a most comprehensive set of leisure & corporate offers at the highest quality. Superior, Junior & Penthouse Suites available.

***An IHF Quality Employer***

Member of Preferred Hotels & Resorts

*Bookable on www.irelandhotels.com*
*Special Offer: www.irelandhotels.com/offers*

*B&B from €162.50 to €237.50*
*Suites from €475.00 to €750.00*

*Donagh Davern*
*Resort General Manager*

98

*Activities:*

**Closed 23 - 27 December**

### Comfort Inn Portlaoise

HOTEL ★★★ MAP 7 L 9

Abbeyleix Road,
Portlaoise,
Co. Laois

Tel: 057-869 5900 Fax: 057-869 5901
Email: info.portlaoise@comfortinns.ie
Web: www.comfortinns.ie

This new superior 90 bedroomed hotel conveniently situated at the Tougher interchange (Dublin N7/ Cork N8 junction) and only 2kms from Portlaoise. All rooms are en suite with power showers, tea & coffee making facilities, broadband internet access and satellite television. The guests can make use of the hotel's Club Vitae Health & Fitness Club with a 20 metre swimming pool, treatment rooms and a gym. The hotel also has a bar & restaurant and 8 meeting suites. Please enquire about Facilities for Persons with Mobility Impairment.

Member of Quality Hotels & Comfort Inns

*Room Rate from €79.00 to €199.00*

*Mario Cassani*
*Regional Manager*

90

*Activities:*

**Closed 22 - 27 December**

### Killeshin (The)

HOTEL MAP 7 L 9

Dublin Road,
Portlaoise,
Co. Laois

Tel: 057-863 1200 Fax: 057-863 1205
Email: info@thekilleshin.com
Web: www.thekilleshin.com

Built to a 4**** specification. The Killeshin Portlaoise opened in May 2007. A 91 bedroomed contemporary styled property at the edge of Portlaoise Town, ideally located in the centre of Ireland, only 1/2 km from M7, N7, N8. Our facilities include Zest Health Club, the Cedar Rooms Bar and Restaurant, Forum at the Killeshin - offering 10 multi purpose meeting rooms, the Walnut Room - banqueting venue, with Piazza, our feature café bar completing this new vision in hospitality. The Killeshin Portlaoise - where all that remains the same is the name. Please enquire about Facilities for Persons with Mobility Impairment.

*Bookable on www.irelandhotels.com*
*Special Offer: www.irelandhotels.com/offers*

*B&B from €125.00 to €142.50*

*Greg Forrestal*
*General Manager*

91

*Activities:*

**Closed 23 - 27 December**



B&B Rates are per Person Sharing per Night incl. Breakfast.
or Room Rates are per Room per Night - **See also Page 8**

## O'Loughlins Hotel

HOTEL ★★ MAP 7 L 9

Main Street,
Portlaoise,
Co. Laois

Tel: 057-862 1305 Fax: 057-866 0883

Email: oloughlins@eircom.ie

Web: www.oloughlinshotel.ie

Our hotel is in the heart of Portlaoise Town. Dunamaise Theatre, cinema, shopping just minutes walk from the door. We have 18 fully refurbished bedrooms. Breakfast is served from 7.30am and a full à la carte menu until 9pm. We are family owned and operated. Particular attention is paid to service, home cooking, excellent beverages and a warm welcome. The hotel is famous for its G.A.A connections. You must experience the après match in O'Loughlin's and view the hall of fame. Club 23 Nite Club is open Thurs, Fri & Sat each week, the most reputable club in Leinster.

***An IHF Quality Employer***

*B&B from €60.00 to €80.00*

*Declan & Elizabeth O'Loughlin*
*Proprietors*

18

**Closed 25 - 26 December**

## Portlaoise Heritage Hotel

HOTEL ★★★★ MAP 7 L 9

Town Centre,
Portlaoise,
Co. Laois

Tel: 057-867 8588 Fax: 057-867 8577

Email: info@theheritagehotel.com

Web: www.theheritagehotel.com

The Portlaoise Heritage is one of the most sought after hotel in Ireland featuring superb facilities and a dedicated team. The hotel features 110 de luxe bedrooms & suites with a stylish difference, a choice of restaurants & bars, award-winning health & fitness Club with Ealu Spa & conference facilities for up to 500 delegates. A choice of 18 hole golf courses all within easy access of the hotel. Nestled in the heart of Portlaoise, the most accessible central location only 1 hour from Dublin, with direct rail access. Please enquire about Facilities for Persons with Mobility Impairment.

***An IHF Quality Employer***

*Bookable on www.irelandhotels.com*

*Special Offer: www.irelandhotels.com/offers*

*B&B from €85.00 to €120.00*
*Suites from €270.00 to €450.00*

*Jacinta Naughton*
*General Manager*

110

*Activities:*

**Closed 23 - 28 December**

## Richmond Inn Guesthouse

GUESTHOUSE ★★★ MAP 11 J 13

Clondra,
Co. Longford

Tel: 043-26126 Fax: 043-26166

Email: therichmondinn@eircom.net

Web: www.richmondinnireland.com

A family-run guesthouse and pub in the picturesque village of Clondra. 7km from Longford Town. The Richmond Inn occupies a prime position in this pretty village, standing on the banks of the Royal Canal overlooking the harbour. Your hosts are Des & Frances McPartland who assure their patrons of a warm welcome and fine home cooking. All rooms are en suite with TV, direct dial phone, tea/coffee making facilities. Local amenities include fishing, horse riding, golf, walking and cycling.

*Bookable on www.irelandhotels.com*

*B&B from €40.00 to €70.00*

*Des & Frances McPartland*
*Owners*

5

**Closed 16 December - 16 January**

## Longford Town / Carlingford

### Annaly Hotel

HOTEL ★★ MAP 11 J 13

57 Main Street,
Longford Town

Tel: 043-42058 Fax: 043-43690
Email: info@annalyhotel.ie
Web: www.annalyhotel.ie

Modern hotel located in the centre of Longford. Café bar in comfortable surroundings. Very competitive rates with a host of entertainment on site. 30 fully serviced stylish bedrooms. Full conference facilities. Large function room. Food available from 7am - 9pm including lunch and dinner.

**Room Rate from €69.00 to €129.00**

*Jonathan Naylor*
*General Manager*

30

*Activities:*

**Closed 24 - 26 December**

### Longford Arms Hotel

HOTEL ★★★ MAP 11 J 13

Main Street,
Longford Town,
Co. Longford

Tel: 043-46296 Fax: 043-46244
Email: longfordarms@eircom.net
Web: www.longfordarms.ie

Ideally located in the heart of the Midlands, this comfortable hotel, renovated to exacting standards, has a vibrant and relaxing atmosphere. The hotel boasts a state of the art conference centre, health and leisure centre, excellent restaurant and award-winning coffee shop where you can be assured of fine food, service and a warm welcome in relaxed, convivial surroundings. Free WiFi available to guests staying in executive bedrooms, also available in lobby & bar area. Available locally: 18 hole golf course, angling, equestrian centre and watersports on the Shannon.

***Bookable on www.irelandhotels.com***
***Special Offer: www.irelandhotels.com/offers***

**B&B from €70.00 to €100.00**

*Brendan Downes*
*General Manager*

57

*Activities:*

**Closed 24 - 26 December**

### Beaufort House

GUESTHOUSE ★★★★ MAP 12 O 15

Ghan Road,
Carlingford,
Co. Louth

Tel: 042-937 3879 Fax: 042-937 3878
Email: michaelcaine@beauforthouse.net
Web: www.beauforthouse.net

Beaufort House, AA ♦♦♦♦♦, listed in Bridgestone, Michelin BIB Hotel Award, Georgina Campbell, a magnificent shoreside residence with glorious sea and mountain views in mediaeval Carlingford Village. Your hosts, Michael & Glynnis Caine, Failte Ireland Award winners of Excellence, will ensure the highest standards. In-house activities include sailing school and yacht charter. Golfing arranged in any of five golf courses within 20 mins of Beaufort House. Private car parking. Dinner by prior arrangement. Small business conference facilities available. Please enquire about Facilities for Persons with Mobility Impairment.

**B&B from €45.00 to €60.00**

*Michael & Glynnis Caine*

5

**Open All Year**



B&B Rates are per Person Sharing per Night incl. Breakfast.
or Room Rates are per Room per Night - See also Page 8

## Four Seasons Hotel & Leisure Club Carlingford

HOTEL ★★★ MAP 12 O 15

Carlingford,
Co. Louth

Tel: 042-937 3530 Fax: 042-937 3531
Email: info@fshc.ie
Web: www.4seasonshotel.ie

Our 59 bedroomed hotel is located in the Heritage Village of Carlingford, overlooking Carlingford Lough and the dramatic Cooley Mountains. This is the ideal location of a relaxing break or an adventure filled activity weekend. We offer our guests a wide range of Conference and Banqueting Facilities and our Ballroom offers breathtaking views of the Lough. All our guests can relax and unwind in our extensive leisure facilities, including 18m swimming pool, gym, sauna, steam room and Jacuzzi and pamper themselves in our new spa, which openened in Sept. 2007.

*B&B from €90.00 to €130.00*

*Mairead McKenna*
*Operations Manager*

59

*Activities:*

**Open All Year**

## McKevitt's Village Hotel

HOTEL ★★ MAP 12 O 15

Market Square,
Carlingford,
Co. Louth

Tel: 042-937 3116 Fax: 042-937 3144
Email: mckevittshotel@yahoo.com
Web: www.mckevittshotel.com

McKevitt's Village Hotel is family owned and personally supervised by Kay & Terry McKevitt. At the hotel, pride of place is taken in the personal attention given to guests by owners and staff. Carlingford is one of Ireland's oldest and most interesting medieval villages. Beautifully situated on the shores of Carlingford Lough and half way between Dublin and Belfast.

*B&B from €55.00 to €85.00*

*Terry & Kay McKevitt*
*Owners*

17

*Activities:*

**Open All Year**

B&B Rates are per Person Sharing per Night incl. Breakfast.
or Room Rates are per Room per Night - **See also Page 8**

## Castlebellingham / Drogheda

### Bellingham Castle Hotel

HOTEL ★★ MAP 12 O 14

Castlebellingham,
Co. Louth

Tel: 042-937 2176 Fax: 042-937 2766
Email: bellinghamcastle@eircom.net
Web: www.bellinghamcastle.com

Bellingham Castle Hotel is situated close to the pleasant little village of Castlebellingham, Co. Louth, resting in countryside enveloped in history, legend and engaged in beautiful scenery. In the hotel itself, which is an elegant refurbished 17th century castle, you will find all the facilities of a modern hotel, harmonising beautifully with the antique décor and atmosphere of old world splendour.

*B&B from €65.00 to €80.00*

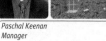

*Paschal Keenan*
*Manager*

19

Closed 24 - 26 December

### Boyne Valley Hotel & Country Club

HOTEL ★★★ MAP 12 O 13

Drogheda,
Co. Louth

Tel: 041-983 7737 Fax: 041-983 9188
Email: reservations@boyne-valley-hotel.ie
Web: www.boyne-valley-hotel.ie

Spacious country house in its own gardens of 16 acres on the edge of Drogheda. Full leisure complex, 2 tennis courts, Cellar Bistro and large and small conference facilities available. Wireless broadband and an internet computer room on site. Nearby are historical sites of Newgrange, Dowth, Knowth and medieval abbeys of Monasterboice, Melifont and Slane. Only 30 minutes from Dublin Airport on M1, turning off at Julianstown/Drogheda South. From Belfast - south on M1, turn off at Drogheda North. Please enquire about Facilities for Persons with Mobility Impairment.

Member of Best Western

*Bookable on www.irelandhotels.com*
*Special Offer: www.irelandhotels.com/offers*

*B&B from €90.00 to €90.00*
*Suites from €250.00 to €250.00*

*Michael McNamara*
*Proprietor / Manager*

72

*Activities:*

Open All Year

### D (The)

HOTEL ★★★★ MAP 12 O 13

Scotch Hall,
Drogheda,
Co. Louth

Tel: 041-987 7700 Fax: 041-987 7702
Email: reservethed@monogramhotels.ie
Web: www.monogramhotels.ie

A stylish hotel offering traditional hospitality and clean, contemporary design in the heart of one of the most historic areas of Ireland. Located on the south bank of the River Boyne in Drogheda, the d is just 25 minutes from Dublin Airport. Its 104 bedrooms are designed for guest comfort and the ground floor offers bright and spacious lounge areas and d bar and restaurant, opening onto a riverside terrace and promenade. The hotel has six air-conditioned meeting and event suites, equipped with the latest AV technology, making it ideal as a business retreat or for a leisurely short break.

Member of Monogram Hotels

*Bookable on www.irelandhotels.com*
*Special Offer: www.irelandhotels.com/offers*

*B&B from €65.00 to €180.00*
*Suites from €350.00 to €1,000.00*

*Rory Scott*
*General Manager*

104

*Activities:*

Closed 24 - 29 December



B&B Rates are per Person Sharing per Night incl. Breakfast.
or Room Rates are per Room per Night - **See also Page 8**

## Glenside Hotel

HOTEL ★★ MAP 12 O 13

Dublin Road,
Drogheda,
Co. Louth

Tel: 041-982 9185 Fax: 041-982 9049
Email: info@glensidehotel.ie
Web: www.glensidehotel.ie

The recently refurbished Glenside Hotel is situated 2km south of Drogheda and 20 mins from Dublin Airport on the N1. With 16 en suite rooms fitted to an exceptionally high standard, one master suite, à la carte restaurant and lounge bar, banquet facilities for up to 200 guests. The perfect setting for a special wedding day. Ideal base for golfing enthusiasts and touring Co. Louth/Meath. Ample car parking.

*B&B from €45.00 to €75.00*
*Suites from €175.00 to €250.00*

*Ronan McAuley*
*Proprietor*

16

**Open All Year**

## Westcourt Hotel

HOTEL ★★★ MAP 12 O 13

West Street,
Drogheda,
Co. Louth

Tel: 041-983 0965 Fax: 041-983 0970
Email: reservations@westcourt.ie
Web: www.westcourt.ie

Located in the heart of Drogheda gateway to the Boyne Valley. With easy access to popular business destinations top class shopping complexes and right on our doorstep you'll find the history that Drogheda & Co. Louth has to offer. Bedrooms tastefully decorated & en suite. Secure car parking. Enjoy a perfect pint at Barroco Bar Drogheda's newest hotspot. Modern Style Brasserie Menu. Earth Nightclub. Conference & Banqueting for up to 300 people

*B&B from €65.00 to €75.00*

*Valerie Sherlock*
*General Manager*

27

Activities:

**Closed 25 - 26 December**

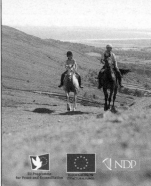

## Dundalk

### Ballymascanlon House Hotel

HOTEL ★★★★ MAP 12 O 14


Carlingford Road (R173), Dundalk, Co. Louth

Tel: 042-935 8200 Fax: 042-937 1598

Email: info@ballymascanlon.com

Web: www.ballymascanlon.com

Ballymascanlon House is a Fáilte Ireland, AA, RAC 4**** country house hotel just 45 mins by motorway from Dublin & Belfast. Just 8 miles from medieval Carlingford, it is set on 130 acres of parkland with its own Ruddy & Craddock designed 18 hole golf course. The beautifully appointed bedroom accommodation, award-winning Restaurant and Terrace Bar are complemented by modern leisure facilities including 20m deck level pool, sauna, jacuzzi, steam room, outdoor Canadian hot tub, gym and tennis courts. The perfect short break destination. New Function/Conference Centre now open.

***An IHF Quality Employer***

*Bookable on www.irelandhotels.com*

*Special Offer: www.irelandhotels.com/offers*

*B&B from €85.00 to €95.00*

*Suites from €250.00 to €325.00*

*Oliver Quinn*

*Managing Director*

90

Activities:

Open All Year

### Carrickdale Hotel & Leisure Complex

HOTEL ★★★ MAP 12 O 14


Carrickcarnon, Ravensdale, Dundalk, Co. Louth

Tel: 042-937 1397 Fax: 042-937 1740

Email: manager@carrickdale.com

Web: www.carrickdale.com

The hotel, conference, swimming and leisure complex is situated midway between Dublin and Belfast just take the left at junction 20 travelling from North or South. Our 119 en suite rooms include our newly open 68 de luxe tower block rooms containing 15 fully air-conditioned executive suites with mini bar facilities. Tastefully decorated bar and restaurant serve excellent food and wines. Ideal destination for touring Cooley, Carlingford and all of Northern Ireland's major tourist attractions. Please enquire about Facilities for Persons with Mobility Impairment.

*B&B from €70.00 to €82.50*

*John McParland*

*Proprietor*

119

Closed 25 - 26 December

### Crowne Plaza Dundalk

HOTEL MAP 12 O 14


Green Park, Inner Relief Road, Dundalk, Co. Louth

Tel: 042-9335453

Email: enquiries@crowneplazadundalk.ie

Web: www.cpdundalk.ie

Built to a 4**** specification. The Crowne Plaza Dundalk is a superb hotel, located within minutes walk of Dundalk Town. With amazing views of the county peninsula and of the Irish Sea, it is ideally located just off the M1 and exactly half way between Dublin and Belfast. All bedrooms are equipped to the highest international standards. Business & conference clients will enjoy 21st century technology in a ground floor conference centre offering 9 meeting rooms for 2 - 400 delegates. Please enquire about Facilities for Persons with Mobility Impairment.

Member of Intercontinental Hotels Group

*Room Rate from €200.00 to €250.00*

*Suites from €350.00 to €450.00*

*David Monks*

*General Manager*

129

Activities:

Open All Year



B&B Rates are per Person Sharing per Night incl. Breakfast. or Room Rates are per Room per Night - **See also Page 8**

## Fairways Hotel & Conference Centre

HOTEL ★★★ MAP 12 O 14

Dublin Road,
Dundalk,
Co. Louth

Tel: 042-932 1500 Fax: 042-932 1511

Email: info@fairways.ie

Web: www.fairways.ie

The Fairways Hotel and Conference Centre is situated 3 miles south of Dundalk, approximately 45 minutes from Dublin Airport and an hour's drive from Belfast and 5 minutes from the seaside. Facilities include tastefully furnished bedrooms, a new fully equipped conference and banqueting centre, catering for up to 1,000 delegates. Carvery/grill and Walnut Restaurant serving full meals and snacks throughout the day. Please enquire about Facilities for Persons with Mobility Impairment.

***An IHF Quality Employer***

*Bookable on www.irelandhotels.com*

*Special Offer: www.irelandhotels.com/offers*

**B&B from €45.00 to €120.00**
**Suites from €130.00 to €165.00**

*Ken Byrne*
*General Manager*

100

Activities:

**Closed 24 - 26 December**

## Hotel Imperial

HOTEL ★★ MAP 12 O 14

Park Street,
Dundalk,
Co. Louth

Tel: 042-933 2241 Fax: 042-933 7909

Email: info@imperialhoteldundalk.com

40 bedroom hotel situated in the heart of Dundalk town, within walking distance to all major attractions. Under new ownership, the hotel is stylishly refurbished to the highest standard offering an exciting and stimulating atmosphere with first class customer service in its state of the art bars, nightclub, restaurant and coffee shop. Adjacent to Dundalk's newest shopping centre, The Marshes. Live music every weekend, secure free parking. Why not try our all new restaurant Radius preparing great dishes from around the world? Please enquire about Facilities for Persons with Mobility Impairment.

***An IHF Quality Employer***

**B&B from €70.00 to €140.00**

*Michelle Arkins*
*General Manager*

47

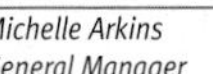

Activities:

**Closed 25 - 26 December**

## Keernaun House

GUESTHOUSE ★★★ MAP 12 O 14

Greengates,
Dublin Road, Dundalk,
Co. Louth

Tel: 042-932 1795 Fax: 042-932 1795

Email: nmcgn@eircom.net

Web: www.keernaunhouse.com

Theresa McGorrian and family would like to welcome you to their luxurious guesthouse which is just 1km from the picturesque village of Blackrock & 3km south of Dundalk. We are only 40 minutes from Dublin & Belfast Airports. Blackrock is a popular seaside village with award-winning restaurants, bars, beaches coffee shops & fantastic views. Local amenities include the Fairways Hotel & Conference Centre, golf courses, Dundalk Institute of Technology & Darver Castle. For directions see website. Awarded Guesthouse of the year 2006. Please enquire about Facilities for Persons with Mobility Impairment.

*Bookable on www.irelandhotels.com*

*Special Offer: www.irelandhotels.com/offers*

**B&B from €35.00 to €45.00**

*Rachel & Theresa McGorrian*
*Owner*

8

Activities:

**Closed 23 - 31 December**

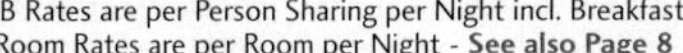

B&B Rates are per Person Sharing per Night incl. Breakfast.
or Room Rates are per Room per Night - **See also Page 8**

# Dundalk / Ashbourne

## Lismar Guesthouse & Serviced Apartments

GUESTHOUSE ★★★ MAP 12 O 14

8-9 Stapleton Place,
Dundalk,
Co. Louth

Tel: 042-935 7246 Fax: 042-935 7247
Email: lismar@iol.ie
Web: www.lismar.ie

Lismar is a superb family-run guesthouse only an hour from major airports and ferries, easily accessible from the M1 and within walking distance of bus and train stations. Situated on a quiet street, only minutes walk to Dundalk town centre and all amenities. Lismar is the ideal base for trips to the Cooley Peninsula, Carlingford, the Mournes, the Tain Trail, golf and race courses. Short let self-catering apartments and studio apartments also available. Michael and Elizabeth welcome you to enjoy all modern facilities and maximum comfort in their proudly refurbished Edwardian property.

***Bookable on www.irelandhotels.com***
***Special Offer: www.irelandhotels.com/offers***

*B&B from €42.50 to €50.00*
*Suites from €100.00 to €120.00*

*Michael & Elizabeth Smyth*

8

**Closed 24 - 28 December**

## Park Inn Dundalk

HOTEL ★★★ MAP 12 O 14

Carnbeg,
Armagh Road, Dundalk,
Co. Louth

Tel: 042-939 5700 Fax: 042-938 6788
Email: info.dundalk@rezidorparkinn.com
Web: www.dundalk.parkinn.ie

A warm, friendly welcome awaits you at Park Inn Dundalk. Ideally located within easy access of M1, 1hr drive from Dublin/Belfast. With many local attractions to discover, Park Inn is surrounded by magnificent views of Carnbeg 18 hole parkland golf course and Cooley Mountains. While in Dundalk, indulge yourself at our Major's Restaurant and avail of a variety of local flavours and international dishes, complemented by our extensive selection of fine wines. Also home to a fully equipped health & leisure club as well as conference facilities, unique bbq venue and a superb wedding location.

Member of Rezidor Hotel Group

***Bookable on www.irelandhotels.com***

*B&B from €60.00 to €75.00*
*Suites from €190.00 to €210.00*

*Gerard Kelly*
*General Manager*

84

*Activities:*

**Closed 24 - 26 December**

## Ashbourne Marriott Hotel

HOTEL ★★★★ MAP 12 O 12

The Rath,
Ashbourne,
Co. Meath

Tel: 01-835 0800 Fax: 01-801 0301
Email: info@marriottashbourne.com
Web: www.marriottashbourne.com

Ashbourne Marriott Hotel brings a new concept in luxury, ideally located in Ashbourne, Co.Meath, within close proximity to Dublin. Designed to an exceptionally high four star standard, this contemporary hotel offers 148 luxurious bedrooms and 8 meeting rooms featuring over 10,000 sq ft of meeting space. This property boasts a modern contemporary restaurant Grill Twenty One, funky upbeat lounge and bar, Red and Clann, fitness and leisure centre. Please enquire about Facilities for Persons with Mobility Impairment.

*Room Rate from €75.00 to €175.00*
*Suites from €175.00 to €350.00*

*Tom Devaney*
*General Manager*

148

*Activities:*

**Closed 24 - 26 December**



B&B Rates are per Person Sharing per Night incl. Breakfast.
or Room Rates are per Room per Night - **See also Page 8**

## Broadmeadow Country House & Equestrian Centre

GUESTHOUSE ★★★★ MAP 12 O 12

Bullstown,
Ashbourne,
Co. Meath

Tel: 01-835 2823 Fax: 01-835 2819

Email: info@irishcountryhouse.com

Web: www.irishcountryhouse.com

A stunning family-run country house surrounded by mature gardens, tennis court, private parking, modern equestrian centre. Located 15 minutes from Dublin Airport, 20 minutes Dublin City. All rooms en suite and designed for maximum guest comfort. Close to numerous golf courses, race courses, clay pigeon shooting. Enjoy the tranquillity of the countryside, yet minutes from the capital. Wine/supper menu available. On route R125. Members of Georgina Campbell and Hidden Places of Ireland.

Member of Michelin Guide

*Bookable on www.irelandhotels.com*

*Special Offer: www.irelandhotels.com/offers*

*B&B from €50.00 to €75.00*

*Sandra Duff*
*Owner/Manager*

8

**Closed 23 December - 02 January**

B&B Rates are per Person Sharing per Night incl. Breakfast.
or Room Rates are per Room per Night - **See also Page 8**

## Athboy / Bettystown

### Old Darnley Lodge Hotel

HOTEL ★★ MAP 11 M 12

Main Street,
Athboy,
Co. Meath

Tel: 046-943 2283 Fax: 046-943 2255

Email: info@olddarnley.com

Web: www.olddarnley.com

The Old Darnley Lodge Hotel is steeped in heritage, charm and character. A warm, friendly welcome awaits you, offering traditional hospitality in one of the most historic areas of Ireland. The Old Darnley Lodge Hotel is the ideal location for Weddings and Functions. The Hotel is close to Meath's finest Golf Clubs, which makes it the ideal retreat for a leisurely short break.

*B&B from €65.00 to €70.00*
*Suites from €140.00 to €160.00*

*Sean Mangan*
*General Manager*

14

*Activities:*

Closed 25 - 26 December

### Bettystown Court Conference & Leisure Hotel

HOTEL ★★★★ MAP 12 O 13

Bettystown,
Co. Meath

Tel: 041-981 2900 Fax: 041-981 2939

Email: info@bettystowncourthotel.com

Web: www.bettystowncourthotel.com

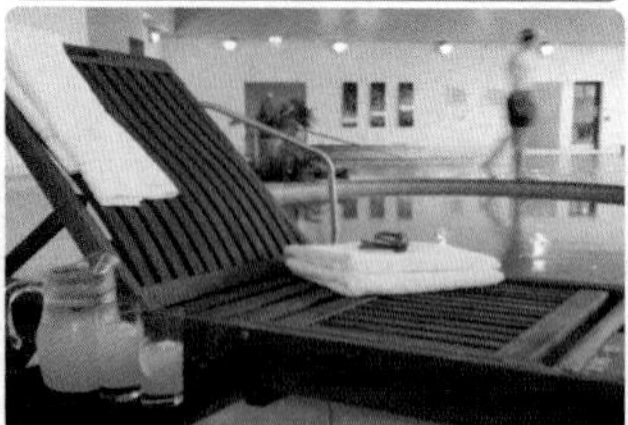

New 4**** property in the coastal town of Bettystown. Bettystown Court is located within walking distance of the stunning beach and Laytown Golf Course, only 25 minutes from Dublin Airport & 10 minutes from Drogheda. The hotel has a cool modern stylish feel - with guest comfort paramount. Extensive free car parking,a full leisure centre is available at the hotel with sauna, steam room, pool, jacuzzi, bar, restaurant, conference and banqueting for up to 450 people. Please enquire about Facilities for Persons with Mobility Impairment.

***An IHF Quality Employer***

Member of Brennan Hotels

***Bookable on www.irelandhotels.com***
***Special Offer: www.irelandhotels.com/offers***

*B&B from €90.00 to €110.00*
*Suites from €290.00 to €310.00*

*Emer Walsh*
*General Manager*

120

*Activities:*

Open All Year

### Neptune Beach Hotel & Leisure Club

HOTEL ★★★ MAP 12 O 13

Bettystown,
Co. Meath

Tel: 041-982 7107 Fax: 041-982 7412

Email: info@neptunebeach.ie

Web: www.neptunebeach.ie

Located 25 mins north of Dublin Airport in a spectacular setting overlooking Bettystown Beach. All 44 rooms are elegantly furnished to provide the comfort and facilities expected of a leading hotel. Enjoy the cosy Winter Garden Restaurant or a relaxing drink in the Neptune Bar. The leisure club facilities include 20m swimming pool, jacuzzi, sauna and fitness suite. Local golf courses: Laytown & Bettystown, Seapoint and Co. Louth. 6 new luxury suites now available. Please contact hotel for suite rates. Please enquire about Facilities for Persons with Mobility Impairment.

*Room Rate from €140.00 to €170.00*
*Suites from €250.00 to €250.00*

*Nuala McDonald &*
*Marina Redden*
*Managers*

44

*Activities:*

Open All Year



B&B Rates are per Person Sharing per Night incl. Breakfast. or Room Rates are per Room per Night - See also Page 8

## Dunboyne Castle Hotel & Spa

HOTEL ★★★★ MAP 12 N 11

Dunboyne,
Co. Meath

Tel: 01-801 3500 Fax: 01-436 6801

Email: info@dunboynecastlehotel.com

Web: www.dunboynecastlehotel.com

Set in the historical village of Dunboyne, you will find Dunboyne Castle Hotel & Spa, a 4**** hotel with 145 bedrooms, magnificent gardens, large conference and banquet facilities for up to 1,500 delegates. In addition, Seoid, our state of the art spa, is spread over 3 floors with 18 treatment rooms. Dunboyne Castle Hotel is just 12 miles from Dublin Airport and 10 miles from Dublin City centre. The "Heritage Capital" is just on your doorstep with tours to historical Newgrange and Hill of Tara. Please enquire about Facilities for Persons with Mobility Impairment.

***An IHF Quality Employer***

Member of Fylan Collection

*Bookable on www.irelandhotels.com*

*Special Offer: www.irelandhotels.com/offers*

*B&B from €125.00 to €340.00*
*Suites from €600.00 to €1,500.00*

*Shane Cookman*
*Director & Group General Manager*

145

*Activities:*

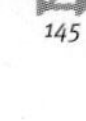

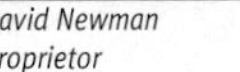

**Open All Year**

## Dunsany Lodge

GUESTHOUSE ★★★ MAP 11 M 12

Batterjohn Cross,
Kiltale, Dunsany,
Co. Meath

Tel: 046-902 6339 Fax: 046-902 6342

Email: info@dunsanylodge.ie

Web: www.dunsanylodge.ie

Nestled within the Heritage Region of Co. Meath, this unique boutique styled premises comprises 10 tastefully designed bedrooms. Intimate 50 seater restaurant & relaxed café/bar. Modern Irish & European menu with food served all day until 9pm most evenings. All situated along main Dublin to Trim road on 3 acres. Travel time to M50 is only 20 minutes. Fairyhouse Racecourse 10 mins drive. Ideal location to discover Hill of Tara, Trim & Killeen Castles plus many golf courses and equestrian options within short distance. Ideal for romantic getaway or family occassion. Please enquire about Facilities for Persons with Mobility Impairment.

*B&B from €40.00 to €50.00*

*David Newman*
*Proprietor*

10

**Open All Year**

## Marriott Johnstown House Hotel & Spa

HOTEL ★★★★ MAP 11 M 11

Enfield,
Co. Meath

Tel: 046-954 0000 Fax: 046-954 0001

Email: info@johnstownhouse.com

Web: www.marriottjohnstownhouse.com

Located off the Dublin to Galway M4 motorway, 40 mins from Dublin Airport & 45 mins from Dublin City. Luxurious rooms with modern features. Enjoy a choice of eating experiences - Pavilion Restaurant, Atrium Brasserie & Coach House Bar. Fully equipped meeting rooms catering for 2-900 people. 40 two bedroomed executive suites opened Sept. '06. Spa facilities: 25m swimming pool, 17 spa therapy rooms, hot thermal suites, climbing wall & golf simulator. On-site corporate activity centre with off road driving, hovercraft flying & clay target shooting. Please enquire about Facilities for Persons with Mobility Impairment.

***An IHF Quality Employer***

*Bookable on www.irelandhotels.com*

*Special Offer: www.irelandhotels.com/offers*

*B&B from €85.00 to €135.00*
*Suites from €240.00 to €400.00*

*Ann Gill*
*General Manager*

126

*Activities:*

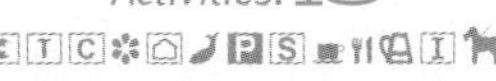

**Open All Year**

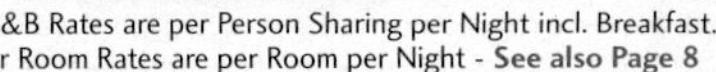

B&B Rates are per Person Sharing per Night incl. Breakfast.
or Room Rates are per Room per Night - **See also Page 8**

## Gormanston / Johnstownbridge / Kells

### City North Hotel

HOTEL ★★★★ MAP 12 O 13

Gormanston,
Co. Meath

Tel: 01-690 6666 Fax: 01-690 6677

Email: info@citynorthhotel.com

Web: www.citynorthhotel.com

Conveniently located along the M1 motorway just 15 mins north of Dublin Airport, M50 & Dublin port tunnel, this stylish new hotel is an exceptional choice for your stay along the East coast. Visit the local bustling towns, quaint craft shops, stylish boutiques and superb restaurants and bars. Take in the famous Boyne Valley Region, Newgrange or a relaxing coastal stroll. Golf, horse racing, hill walking, karting, falconry, clay pigeon shooting - all on your doorstep. Superb conference facilities for 650. Please enquire about Facilities for Persons with Mobility Impairment.

Member of Tullamore Court Hotel Group

***Bookable on www.irelandhotels.com***

***Special Offer: www.irelandhotels.com/offers***

***B&B from €49.00 to €80.00***
***Suites from €200.00 to €240.00***

*Aogan Dunne*
*General Manager*

128

Activities:

**Closed 24 - 26 December**

### Hamlet Court Hotel

HOTEL ★★★ MAP 11 M 11

Johnstownbridge,
Enfield,
Co. Meath

Tel: 046-954 1200 Fax: 046-954 1704

Email: info@thehamlet.ie

Web: www.thehamlet.ie

Nestled in the village of Johnstownbridge, 1km from Enfield, 30 minutes from Dublin on the new M4. This contemporary hotel was designed to provide you with all the latest features that modern Irish hotels have to offer. Winner of The Best Irish Wedding Venue and our award-winning Chef, Mr. John Conmy, are just a taste of what the Hamlet Court has to offer. Where "Customer Service" was invented before the word.

***Bookable on www.irelandhotels.com***

***Special Offer: www.irelandhotels.com/offers***

***B&B from €75.00 to €110.00***
***Suites from €180.00 to €250.00***

*John O'Neill*
*Owner*

30

Activities:

**Open All Year**

### Headfort Arms Hotel

HOTEL ★★★ MAP 11 M 13

Kells,
Co. Meath

Tel: 0818-222 800 Fax: 046-924 0587

Email: info@headfortarms.ie

Web: www.headfortarms.ie

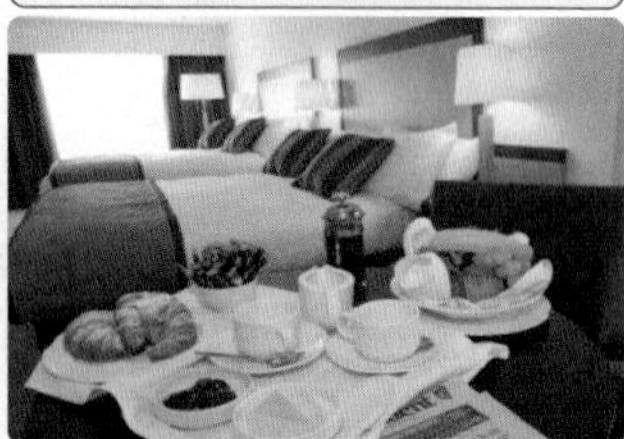

A regional landmark, the Headfort Arms Hotel has been run and managed by the Duff family for the past 35 years. Located in the Heritage Town of Kells, only one hour from Dublin City centre on the main route to Donegal. 45 bedrooms with de luxe facilities, Wellness Spa and private guest car park. Adjoining is the award-winning Vanilla Pod Restaurant. Sporting packages are a speciality, Headfort Golf Club is on the doorstep, with equestrian, fishing and heritage trips all close by. Please enquire about Facilities for Persons with Mobility Impairment.

Member of Irish Country Hotels

***Bookable on www.irelandhotels.com***

***Special Offer: www.irelandhotels.com/offers***

***B&B from €60.00 to €95.00***
***Suites from €195.00 to €275.00***

*Peggy, Vincent & Olivia Duff*
*Proprietors*

45

Activities:

**Closed 25 December**



B&B Rates are per Person Sharing per Night incl. Breakfast.
or Room Rates are per Room per Night - See also Page 8

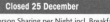

## Station House Hotel and Signal Restaurant

HOTEL ★★★ MAP 12 N 12

Kilmessan,
Co. Meath

Tel: 046-902 5239 Fax: 046-902 5588
Email: info@thestationhousehotel.com
Web: www.thestationhousehotel.com

Step off the fast track into a relaxed rural setting, where peace and tranquillity exude. Set on 12 acres of landscaped gardens and woodlands, this first class hotel offers many amenities we appreciate today, not forgetting yesterday's charm. The Signal Suite is a unique, exclusive haven with four poster bed and whirlpool bath. The Signal Restaurant, which has won numerous awards, is open daily for breakfast, lunch & fine dining. Bar food served daily. 20 miles from Dublin. Special offers online: www.thestationhousehotel.com. Please enquire about Facilities for Persons with Mobility Impairment.

*Bookable on www.irelandhotels.com*
*Special Offer: www.irelandhotels.com/offers*

*B&B from €55.00 to €120.00*
*Suites from €180.00 to €280.00*

*Denise & Paul Slattery*
*Managers*

20

*Activities:*

**Open All Year**

## Ardboyne Hotel

HOTEL ★★★ MAP 12 N 13

Dublin Road,
Navan,
Co. Meath

Tel: 046-902 3119 Fax: 046-902 2355
Email: info@ardboynehotel.com
Web: www.ardboynehotel.com

The Ardboyne Hotel Navan is set amidst a treasure trove of Irish historical sites in County Meath. Our warm and comfortable atmosphere coupled with our extensive gardens make the Ardboyne Hotel a perfect haven to unwind after an eventful day. Located just 2 minutes outside Navan Town, and just 40 minutes from Dublin. The hotel offers guests a wide range of facilities, including 29 tastefully decorated bedrooms. The Kells Bar, La Mezzanine Restaurant and extensive conference and banqueting facilities for up to 500 people. Please enquire about Facilities for Persons with Mobility Impairment.

***An IHF Quality Employer***

Member of Cusack Hotels

*Bookable on www.irelandhotels.com*
*Special Offer: www.irelandhotels.com/offers*

*B&B from €70.00 to €100.00*

*Mary Murphy*
*General Manager*

29

*Activities:*

**Open All Year**

## Ma Dwyers Guesthouse

GUESTHOUSE ★★★ MAP 12 N 13

Dublin Road,
Navan,
Co. Meath

Tel: 046-907 7992 Fax: 046-907 7995

Ma Dwyers Guesthouse possesses many of the qualities of a high class hotel, along with a cosy homely feel which is so vitally important. 9 beautiful en suite rooms with a direct dial telephone, TV, hairdryer and tea/coffee facilities with fax and photocopying services available. Ideally located just minutes walk from the town centre and plenty of historic landmarks to see and activities to enjoy including golf, fishing, boating and horse riding. 13 new bedrooms will open during 2008. Please enquire about Facilities for Persons with Mobility Impairment.

*B&B from €50.00 to €50.00*

*Joan O'Brien*

9

**Open All Year**

## Navan / Newgrange / Oldcastle

### Newgrange Hotel

HOTEL ★★★ MAP 12 N 13

Bridge Street,
Navan,
Co. Meath

Tel: 046-907 4100 Fax: 046-907 3977
Email: info@newgrangehotel.ie
Web: www.newgrangehotel.ie

Centrally located in Navan town only 40 mins from Dublin, The Newgrange is a modern hotel, designed and inspired by the ancient history of the area. In addition to 62 elegantly decorated en suite bedrooms, the hotel boasts extensive conference and banqueting facilities, 3 bars, a fine dining restaurant, café and daily lunchtime carvery. Local attractions include The Hill of Tara, Newgrange & Trim Castle. Activities in the area include salmon fishing, golfing, horse racing and horse riding. Please enquire about Facilities for Persons with Mobility Impairment.

***An IHF Quality Employer***

Member of Cusack Hotels

***Bookable on www.irelandhotels.com***
***Special Offer: www.irelandhotels.com/offers***

***B&B from €75.00 to €125.00***

*Noel J O'Mahony*
*General Manager*

62

*Activities:*

**Closed 24 - 26 December**

### Newgrange Lodge

GUESTHOUSE MAP 12 N 13

Staleen,
Donore (near Newgrange),
Co. Meath

Tel: 041-988 2478 Fax: 041-988 2479
Email: info@newgrangelodge.com
Web: www.newgrangelodge.com

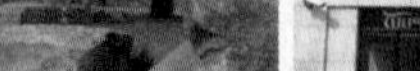

Built to a 3*** specification. Newgrange Lodge is a unique venue, built on 7 acres of Boyne Valley land overlooking the magical and mythical sites of Newgrange, Knowth and Dowth. Amenities include well appointed en suite bedrooms, free internet access, 2 outdoor decking & BBQ areas, a central courtyard, meals for groups on request. We also provide on-site outdoor activities on request for groups. We are located just off the M1 only 25 minutes from Dublin Airport.

***Bookable on www.irelandhotels.com***
***Special Offer: www.irelandhotels.com/offers***

***B&B from €28.50 to €55.00***

*Leon Kinsella*

20

*Activities:*

**Closed 15 - 26 December**

### Oldcastle House Hotel

HOTEL ★★★ MAP 11 L 13

Cogan Street,
Oldcastle,
Co. Meath

Tel: 049-854 2400 Fax: 049-854 1700
Email: stay@oldcastlehotel.com
Web: www.oldcastlehousehotel.com

Oldcastle House Hotel combines traditional values with a modern décor and facilities to create an original and memorable experience for our guests. We guarantee a personal touch and an attention to detail second to none, in either our Céili House Bar, Lush Italian Bistro or in any of our conference rooms. Just one hour from Dublin, the Oldcastle House Hotel provides an ideal base to explore the historic and scenic local area. Please enquire about Facilities for Persons with Mobility Impairment. Please enquire about Facilities for Persons with Mobility Impairment.

***B&B from €60.00 to €75.00***
***Suites from €180.00 to €210.00***

*Tom Curran*
*General Manager*

12

*Activities:*

**Closed 25 December**



B&B Rates are per Person Sharing per Night incl. Breakfast.
or Room Rates are per Room per Night - **See also Page 8**

## Millhouse (The)

HOTEL MAP 12 N 13

Slane,
Co. Meath

Tel: 041-982 0723 Fax: 041-982 0723
Email: info@themillhouse.ie
Web: www.themillhouse.ie

Built to a 3*** specification. Beautiful Romantic Private Boutique Hotel in the heart of Ireland's richest historical counties. Fantastic fishing walks, historical monuments, gourmet cooking and modern luxuries. Please enquire about Facilities for Persons with Mobility Impairment.

**Room Rate from €200.00 to €240.00**

*Janey Quigley*

11

**Open All Year**

## Castle Arch Hotel

HOTEL ★★★ MAP 11 M 12

Trim,
Co. Meath

Tel: 046-943 1516 Fax: 046-943 6002
Email: info@castlearchhotel.com
Web: www.castlearchhotel.com

Located in the heart of Trim, Co. Meath, just 30 miles from Dublin. The Castle Arch Hotel is a charming boutique style hotel with 23 beautifully decorated bedrooms. Locally renowned for traditional home cooked foods with daily cavery and bar food. The hotel is minutes walk from the historically famous Trim Castle and a short drive from Kells, Newgrange and the Hill of Tara. Other local attractions include angling, horse racing and horse riding. There are also 9 local golf courses with special discounted packages available. Please enquire about Facilities for Persons with Mobility Impairment.

***An IHF Quality Employer***

Member of Cusack Hotels

***Bookable on www.irelandhotels.com***
***Special Offer: www.irelandhotels.com/offers***

**B&B from €70.00 to €160.00**

*Billy O'Connell*
*General Manager*

23

*Activities:*

**Closed 24 - 26 December**

## Knightsbrook Hotel & Golf Resort

HOTEL ★★★★ MAP 11 M 12

Dublin Road,
Trim,
Co. Meath

Tel: 046-948 2110 Fax: 046-943 7428
Email: info@knightsbrook.com
Web: www.cusackhotels.com

Built to an exceptionally high 4**** standard, this hotel offers a unique experience in luxury and opulence combined with modern sophistication. 131 de luxe rooms with all the facilities a discerning guest requires. Guests will enjoy an extensive leisure centre with swimming pool, jacuzzi, sauna, steam room and health & beauty spa. 18 hole championship golf course designed by Christy O'Connor Jnr on site. Conference facilities for up to 1,000 delegates. Please enquire about Facilities for Persons with Mobility Impairment.

***An IHF Quality Employer***

Member of Cusack Hotels

**B&B from €85.00 to €105.00**

*Patrick Curran*
*General Manager*

131

*Activities:*

**Open All Year**

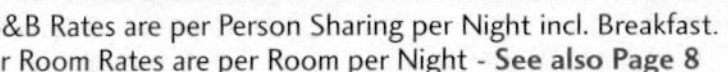

## Trim / Carrickmacross / Glaslough

### Trim Castle Hotel

HOTEL ★★★★ MAP 11 M 12

Trim,
Co. Meath

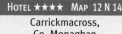

Tel: 046-948 3000 Fax: 046-948 3077
Email: info@trimcastlehotel.com
Web: www.trimcastlehotel.com

Overlooking the mystical Trim Castle, our hotel features 68 luxury guest rooms, The Bailey Bar, Barista Café and Jules Restaurant. Trim Castle Hotel is just 40 minutes from Dublin and is an ideal touring base for the Boyne Valley, golf, angling, equestrian and heritage activities. Conference facilities for up to 850 delegates. Please enquire about Facilities for Persons with Mobility Impairment.

Member of Hotel Partners

*Bookable on www.irelandhotels.com*
*Special Offer: www.irelandhotels.com/offers*

**Room Rate from €90.00 to €220.00**

*Noel Comer*
*General Manager*

68

Activities:

**Closed 24 - 26 December**

### Nuremore Hotel & Country Club

HOTEL ★★★★ MAP 12 N 14

Carrickmacross,
Co. Monaghan

Tel: 042-966 1438 Fax: 042-966 1853
Email: info@nuremore.com
Web: www.nuremore.com

Set in tranquil and beautiful surroundings, amidst a championship 18-hole golf course, the Nuremore offers unrivalled standards of service and sporting, leisure and conference facilities. The Country Club boasts an 18m swimming pool, whirlpool, sauna, steam room, gym, tennis courts & a beauty treatment spa. There is a wide range of spacious rooms and demi-suites on offer and our award-winning restaurant serves superb cuisine in idyllic surroundings, cooked by Ireland's Chef of the Year 2005 and Ulster's Chef of the Year 2006, Raymond McArdle. Only 1 hour from Dublin, take the M1 & then the N2.

***An IHF Quality Employer***

*Bookable on www.irelandhotels.com*
*Special Offer: www.irelandhotels.com/offers*

**B&B from €125.00 to €160.00**

*Julie Gilhooly*
*Proprietor*

72

Activities:

**Open All Year**

### Hunting Lodge (The)

HOTEL ★★★★ MAP 11 M 16

Castle Leslie Estate,
Glaslough,
Co. Monaghan

Tel: 047-88100 Fax: 047-88256
Email: info@castleleslie.com
Web: www.castleleslie.com

Located on 1,000 acres of undulating Irish countryside in County Monaghan, The Hunting Lodge on The Castle Leslie Estate is the perfect getaway. Stay in one of the 30 beautiful bedrooms, enjoy a delicious meal in Snaffles Restaurant before enjoying a pint in Conors Bar. Choose to explore the estate on horseback with our Equestrian Centre, improve your culinary expertise in the Cookery School or indulge in the Organic Victorian Spa. Just 70 minutes from Belfast and 90 minutes from Dublin Airport. Please enquire about Facilities for Persons with Mobility Impairment.

**B&B from €95.00 to €115.00**

*Samantha Leslie*

30

**Closed 25 - 26 December**



B&B Rates are per Person Sharing per Night incl. Breakfast.
or Room Rates are per Room per Night - See also Page 8

## Four Seasons Hotel & Leisure Club

HOTEL ★★★ MAP 11 M 16

Coolshannagh,
Monaghan Town,
Co. Monaghan

Tel: 047-81888 Fax: 047-83131

Email: info@4seasonshotel.ie

Web: www.4seasonshotel.ie

Elegance without extravagance!! Enjoy the excellent service, warmth and luxury of this family-run hotel. Relax by the turf fire in the Still Bar or savour the food in the informal setting of the Range Restaurant or the fine dining Avenue Restaurant. The rooms have all modern facilities and residents have unlimited use of our leisure facilities, 18m pool, jacuzzi, steam room, sauna, gym and outdoor hot tub. Also available massage & sunbed. Available locally: 18-hole golf course, angling, equestrian centre and water sports. Activity packages available.

**B&B from €50.00 to €120.00**

Frank McKenna
Managing Director

59

Activities:

**Closed 25 - 26 December**

## Hillgrove Hotel Leisure & Spa

HOTEL ★★★★ MAP 11 M 16

Old Armagh Road,
Monaghan Town,
Co. Monaghan

Tel: 047-81288 Fax: 047-84951

Email: info@hillgrovehotel.com

Web: www.hillgrovehotel.com

A majestic and magical setting awaits you, minutes walk from Monaghan Town. Luxurious bedrooms, including suites with jacuzzis. Exquisite restaurant and bars. State of the art conference centre. Leisure club with swimming pool, jacuzzi, steam room, sauna, gym, hot tub, tanning rooms, hair salon & nail bar. Spa & wellness centre, with rasul, herbal sauna, hydrotherapy pool, floatation bed, monsoon showers, pedi spas, relaxation room, extensive therapies and treatments for mind, body and soul. Please enquire about Facilities for Persons with Mobility Impairment.

***An IHF Quality Employer***

*Bookable on www.irelandhotels.com*
*Special Offer: www.irelandhotels.com/offers*

**B&B from €45.00 to €120.00**
**Suites from €95.00 to €150.00**

Colm & Audri Herron
Proprietors

87

Activities:

**Open All Year**

## Brosna Lodge Hotel

HOTEL ★★ MAP 7 J 10

Banagher-on-the-Shannon,
Co. Offaly

Tel: 057-915 1350 Fax: 057-915 1521

Email: info@brosnalodge.com

Web: www.brosnalodge.com

A family owned country hotel, close to the River Shannon, welcomes guests with superb hospitality and relaxed elegance. Mature gardens surround the hotel. With unique peat bogs, mountains, the River Shannon and Clonmacnois, you will delight in this gentle, little known part of Ireland. Fishing, golf, nature and historical tours arranged locally. Enjoy beautiful food in our restaurant, The Fields, and drinks in Pat's Olde Bar. Dining Pub of the Year Award 2003/2004/2005/2006/2007. Please enquire about Facilities for Persons with Mobility Impairment.

*Bookable on www.irelandhotels.com*
*Special Offer: www.irelandhotels.com/offers*

**B&B from €50.00 to €70.00**

Pat & Della Horan
Proprietors

14

Activities:

**Closed 20 - 28 December**

## Birr

### County Arms Hotel & Leisure Club

HOTEL ★★★★ MAP 7 J 9

Moorpark,
Birr,
Co. Offaly

Tel: 057-912 0791 Fax: 057-912 1234

Email: info@countyarmshotel.com

Web: www.countyarmshotel.com

Popular Family-Run Hotel since 1962, refurbished for 2007. Leisure Club & Wellness Suites with Elemis Spa Treatments. Suites and spacious Family Rooms with bunk-beds. Large bedrooms with Free High Speed Internet. Conference facilities now offer AC, Free WiFi and modern AV. Award-Winning Restaurant 2002-2007, lively Bar & Cosy Lounge, Georgian walled garden. Website constantly updated with Special Offers - Golf, Spa, Midweek, Weekend. Central location within 90 minutes of Dublin, Galway, Limerick. Please enquire about Facilities for Persons with Mobility Impairment.

Member of www.familyhotels.ie

***Bookable on www.irelandhotels.com***

***Special Offer: www.irelandhotels.com/offers***

***B&B from €60.00 to €160.00***
***Suites from €300.00 to €780.00***

*The Loughnane Family*

70

*Activities:*

**Open All Year**

### Doolys Hotel

HOTEL ★★ MAP 7 J 9

Emmet Square,
Birr,
Co. Offaly

Tel: 057-912 0032 Fax: 057-912 1332

Email: info@doolyshotel.ie

Web: www.doolyshotel.ie

Doolys Hotel - a gem of a hotel in the very heart of Georgian Birr. The hotel, which has just undergone major refurbishment, is one of the oldest coaching inns in the country, dating back to 1747. Our guests receive a warm welcome and traditional hospitality and professional service. Our coach house lounge is a favourite among locals and is very welcoming with great food served all day. Weddings are our speciality. Now with our own private customer car park. Please enquire about Facilities for Persons with Mobility Impairment.

***An IHF Quality Employer***

***B&B from €65.00 to €85.00***

*Sharon Grant / Jo Duignan*
*Proprietor / General Manager*

18

*Activities:*

**Closed 24 - 26 December**

### Enroute Bistro, Guesthouse & Bar

GUESTHOUSE ★★★ MAP 7 J 9

Fivealley,
Birr,
Co. Offaly

Tel: 057-913 3976 Fax: 057-913 3974

Email: info@guesthouse.ie

Web: www.guesthouse.ie

Located in the heart of Ireland, central to the region's top visitor attractions. Accessible by public bus. Extensive free car parking. Full bar and licensed bistro. All rooms en suite, guest lounge and rooftop patio. Facilities for the infirm/physically impaired. Guests have a choice of bistro or casual dining in the bar where food is available throughout the day. A warm welcome awaits you at this family-owned and run premises. Please enquire about Facilities for Persons with Mobility Impairment.

Member of Slieve Bloom Rural Development

***B&B from €45.00 to €55.00***

*Joe and Rita Guinan*

7

**Closed 24 - 28 December**



B&B Rates are per Person Sharing per Night incl. Breakfast. or Room Rates are per Room per Night - **See also Page 8**

## Maltings Guesthouse

GUESTHOUSE ★★★ MAP 7 J 9

Castle Street,
Birr,
Co. Offaly

Tel: 057-912 1345 Fax: 057-912 2073
Email: themaltingsbirr@eircom.net

Secluded on a picturesque riverside setting beside Birr Castle, in the centre of Ireland's finest Georgian town. Built circa 1810 to store malt for Guinness, and converted in 1994 to a 13 bedroomed guesthouse with full bar and restaurant. All bedrooms are comfortably furnished with bath/shower en suite, colour TV and phones.

B&B from €40.00 to €45.00

Maeve Garry
Manageress

13

Closed 22 - 29 December

## Bridge House Hotel, Leisure Club & Spa

HOTEL ★★★★ MAP 7 K 10

Tullamore,
Co. Offaly

Tel: 057-932 5600 Fax: 057-932 5690
Email: info@bridgehouse.com
Web: www.bridgehouse.com

A warm welcome awaits you at the Bridge House Hotel. Enjoy the best of Irish hospitality renowned for good food, service & great atmosphere. Two restaurants in town centre location. State of the art leisure club & swimming pool & a unique outdoor hot spa. New spa & wellness centre. Play golf in the virtual reality golf facility. Five mins away to two of Ireland's golfing treasures, Esker Hill & Tullamore Golf Club, both 18 hole golf courses. Winner of the Best Hotel Bar in Ireland. One of Ireland's most luxurious hotels with 70 rooms incl. 4 executive suites & superb presidential suite. Reservations Lo-Call 1850 312312.

***An IHF Quality Employer***

*Bookable on www.irelandhotels.com*
*Special Offer: www.irelandhotels.com/offers*

B&B from €65.00 to €140.00
Suites from €140.00 to €500.00

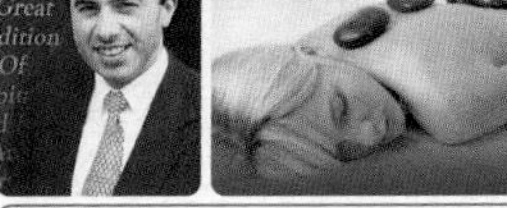

Colm McCabe
Manager

70

Activities:

Closed 24 - 26 December

## Tullamore

### Days Hotel Tullamore

HOTEL ★★★ MAP 7 K 10

Main Street,
Tullamore,
Co. Offaly

Tel: 1890-329329 Fax: 057-932 0350
Email: info@dayshoteltullamore.com
Web: www.dayshoteltullamore.com

Newly opened in 2005, Days Hotel is located in the town centre, close to bars, restaurants and great shopping. 62 superior rooms, all with pay per view movies, safe, tea/coffee station, iron/ironing board. Executive rooms offer extra space with designated work desk and jacuzzi bath. Our stylish bistro and bar are open throughout the day. Conference facilities include 2 air-conditioned meeting rooms, with capacity for up to 50 delegates. Specialised audio/visual facilities on site. Hotel direct Tel line: 057 936 0034. Please enquire about Facilities for Persons with Mobility Impairment.

Member of Days Hotels Ireland

*Bookable on www.irelandhotels.com*
*Special Offer: www.irelandhotels.com/offers*

*B&B from €45.00 to €99.00*

*Robert Fleming*
*General Manager*

62

*Activities:*

**Closed 24 - 27 December**

### Grennans Country House

GUESTHOUSE ★★★ MAP 7 K 10

Aharney,
Tullamore,
Co. Offaly

Tel: 057-935 5893 Fax: 057-935 5893
Email: deirdregrennan5@eircom.net
Web: www.grennanscountryhouse.ie

Situated in the heart of the Midlands 1 mile off N.80, 1.5 hours from Dublin Airport, Grennans Country House is a purpose built luxury guesthouse; a golfer's paradise - 10 golf courses within 1/2 hour's drive. Rural setting, ample car parking. All rooms are en suite & tastefully furnished, with super king beds, DD phone, TV, tea/coffee facilities, spring water, clock radio, hairdryer, iron/ironing board. Guest TV lounge, home-baking. Access for wheelchair user. Ideal touring base, golfing, fishing, equestrian, walking - your choice is our pleasure. Please enquire about Facilities for Persons with Mobility Impairment.

*B&B from €40.00 to €55.00*

*Deirdre & Pat Grennan*

6

**Open All Year**

### Moorhill House Hotel and Garden Suites

HOTEL MAP 7 K 10

Clara Road,
Tullamore,
Co. Offaly

Tel: 057-932 1395 Fax: 057-935 2424
Email: info@moorhill.ie
Web: www.moorhill.ie

UNDER REFURBISHMENT - RE-OPENING JUNE 2008

This registered hotel is being refurbished to a 4 star specification and will re-open June 2008. Moorhill is a unique experience in the best possible way. Combining the classic quality of a Victorian country house with the informal ambience of a modern hotel. In Moorhill, we have placed particular emphasis on marrying the elegant surroundings and atmosphere of the hotel with a warm Irish welcome and friendly efficient service. Centrally located and ideal for a relaxing break from daily life or to conduct business at a quiet and efficient pace. Please enquire about Facilities for Persons with Mobility Impairment.

*B&B from €75.00 to €145.00*
*Suites from €190.00 to €325.00*

*Alan Duffy*
*Managing Director*

10

*Activities:*

**Open All Year**



B&B Rates are per Person Sharing per Night incl. Breakfast.
or Room Rates are per Room per Night - **See also Page 8**

## Sea Dew Guesthouse

GUESTHOUSE ★★★ MAP 7 K 10

Clonminch Road,
Tullamore,
Co. Offaly

Tel: 057-935 2054 Fax: 057-935 2054
Email: enquiries@seadewguesthouse.com
Web: www.seadewguesthouse.com

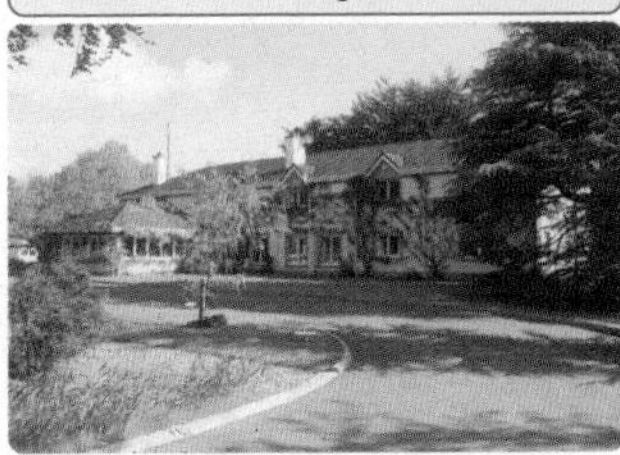

Set in a mature garden of trees, Sea Dew is a purpose-built guesthouse, providing guests with a high standard of comfort, only 5 mins walk from the town centre. The conservatory breakfast room will give you a bright start to the day, where there is an excellent selection of fresh produce. All breakfasts are cooked to order. Bedrooms are spacious with en suite, TV & DD phones, hairdryer, iron/ironing board, tea/coffee making facilities. Private car park. Golfing, fishing, horse riding, bowling & shooting nearby. Complimentary broadband. Please enquire about Facilities for Persons with Mobility Impairment.

*B&B from €40.00 to €65.00*

*Claire Gilsenan*
*Proprietor*

12

**Closed 22 - 27 December**

## Tullamore Court Hotel Conference & Leisure Centre

HOTEL ★★★★ MAP 7 K 10

Tullamore,
Co. Offaly

Tel: 057-934 6666 Fax: 057-934 6677
Email: info@tullamorecourthotel.ie
Web: www.tullamorecourthotel.ie

Luxury, elegance and style are the distinguishing qualities of this contemporary hotel. A wonderfully relaxed ambience in plush surroundings with friendly professional staff and superb food and wines is just the tonic you need to enjoy your next short break. So why drive for hours when you can enjoy unrivalled standards of service at the Tullamore Court Hotel? Tullamore itself is a vibrant town offering visitors a whole host of amenities, activities, pubs, restaurants and shopping. Check our website regularly for last minute special offers. Please enquire about Facilities for Persons with Mobility Impairment.

***An IHF Quality Employer***

*Bookable on www.irelandhotels.com*
*Special Offer: www.irelandhotels.com/offers*

*B&B from €85.00 to €170.00*
*Suites from €125.00 to €210.00*

*Philip O'Brien*
*General Manager*

104

*Activities:*

**Closed 24 - 26 December**

B&B Rates are per Person Sharing per Night incl. Breakfast.
or Room Rates are per Room per Night - **See also Page 8**

## Athlone

### Athlone Springs Hotel

HOTEL ★★★★ MAP 11 J 11

Monksland,
Athlone,
Co. Westmeath

Tel: 090-644 4444 Fax: 090-649 0711
Email: info@athlonespringshotel.com
Web: www.athlonespringshotel.com

Welcome to the Athlone Springs Hotel, a brand new 'lifestyle hotel' in the heart of Ireland. Standing on the west edge of Athlone town tucked away in its own oasis, Athlone Springs is ideally situated - just off the main Dublin to Galway road and only minutes from the river Shannon. Enjoy cutting edge design that has been translated into its conference facilities and a state of the art leisure complex. The hotel is equipped with all of the contemporary luxuries & technology that 21st century visitors can expect. Whatever the occasion, we look forward to welcoming you.

***Bookable on www.irelandhotels.com***
***Special Offer: www.irelandhotels.com/offers***

***B&B from €55.00 to €100.00***
***Suites from €250.00 to €310.00***

*Chris Pollier*
*General Manager*

*68*

*Activities:*

**Open All Year**

### Creggan Court Hotel

HOTEL ★★★ MAP 7 J 11

Kilmartin N6 Centre,
N6 Roundabout, Athlone,
Co. Westmeath

Tel: 090-647 7777 Fax: 090-647 7111
Email: info@creggancourt.com
Web: www.creggancourt.com

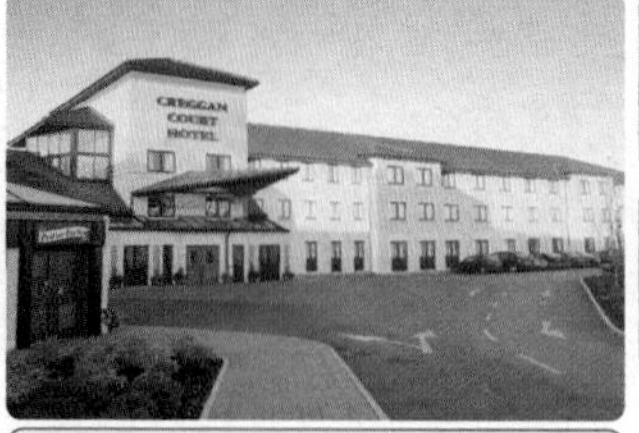

The Creggan Court Hotel is located just off the N6 in Athlone, midway between Dublin and Galway. The ideal base to explore Clonmacnoise, Ely O'Carroll Country and the Shannon Basin. Athlone is a golfer's paradise, surrounded by local championship golf courses such as Glasson, Mount Temple, Esker Hills and many more. The Creggan Court Hotel offers spacious en suite rooms and ample car parking. Conference rooms also available. Please enquire about Facilities for Persons with Mobility Impairment.

***Bookable on www.irelandhotels.com***
***Special Offer: www.irelandhotels.com/offers***

***B&B from €55.00 to €120.00***

*Catherine Daly*
*General Manager*

*69*

*Activities:*

**Closed 23 - 30 December**

### Glasson Golf Hotel and Country Club

HOTEL ★★★★ MAP 11 J 11

Glasson,
Athlone,
Co. Westmeath

Tel: 090-648 5120 Fax: 090-648 5444
Email: info@glassongolf.ie
Web: www.glassongolf.ie

"Glorious Glasson, a treat for all the senses" is what C. Kinny, a past guest has to say. The views are magnificent, the welcome the warmest, the most spacious and sumptuous rooms and of course, championship Golf. Enjoy Sauna, Steam Room, Massage, Boat Trips and rural country walks during your stay. "The holes range from good to great and the setting is at every turn little short of enthralling" James W. Finegan, Golf Journalist. The hotel is suited to both the discerning golfer and those looking for peace and relaxation in beautiful surroundings.

***Bookable on www.irelandhotels.com***
***Special Offer: www.irelandhotels.com/offers***

***B&B from €60.00 to €150.00***
***Suites from €160.00 to €440.00***

*Chris Vos*
*Manager*

*65*

*Activities:*

**Closed 25 - 26 December**



B&B Rates are per Person Sharing per Night incl. Breakfast.
or Room Rates are per Room per Night - **See also Page 8**

## Hodson Bay Hotel

HOTEL ★★★★ MAP 11 J 11

Athlone,
Co. Westmeath

Tel: 090-644 2000 Fax: 090-644 2020
Email: info@hodsonbayhotel.com
Web: www.hodsonbayhotel.com

This luxurious hotel and spa is located on the picturesque shores of Lough Ree in the Heart of Ireland. The hotel is renowned for its plush accommodation, fine cuisine and a warm, welcoming atmosphere. Leisure facilities includes a 20m pool and gym with steam room and sauna, while the spa offers a superb array of pampering treatments and a unique thermal spa. The hotel is adjacent to Athlone Golf Club and a marina. Please enquire about Facilities for Persons with Mobility Impairment.

***An IHF Quality Employer***

*Bookable on www.irelandhotels.com*
*Special Offer: www.irelandhotels.com/offers*

*B&B from €65.00 to €230.00*
*Suites from €270.00 to €460.00*

*Timothy Hayes*
*General Manager*

182

Activities:

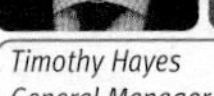

**Open All Year**

## Prince of Wales Hotel

HOTEL ★★★★ MAP 11 J 11

Church Street,
Athlone,
Co. Westmeath

Tel: 090-647 6666 Fax: 090-649 1750
Email: info@theprinceofwales.ie
Web: www.theprinceofwales.ie

Positioned in the very centre of Athlone, the Prince of Wales Hotel offers the very highest standards of comfort & service. The hotel has 46 stylish modern rooms comprised of classic, executive and 6 junior suites. Soothingly simple in black marble, chocolate & cream, each room is a tranquil haven of understated luxury, equipped with television, DVD players, multi-port modern connection & digital climate control. The new Corvus Restaurant offers a fusion of Contemporary & Traditional Irish Cuisine and Mediteranean influences. Please enquire about Facilities for Persons with Mobility Impairment.

***An IHF Quality Employer***

Member of Callanan Hotels

*Bookable on www.irelandhotels.com*
*Special Offer: www.irelandhotels.com/offers*

*B&B from €65.00 to €95.00*

*Neil Cummins*
*Operations Manager*

46

**Closed 23 - 30 December**

## Athlone

### Radisson SAS Hotel

HOTEL ★★★★ MAP 11 J 11


Northgate Street,
Athlone,
Co. Westmeath

Tel: 090-644 2600 Fax: 090-644 2655

Email: info.athlone@radissonsas.com

Web: www.athlone.radissonsas.com

The Radisson SAS Hotel, Athlone is centrally located overlooking the River Shannon with magnificent views of the marina, the historical cathedral and Athlone Castle. Within walking distance of the train & bus station. 127 stylish bedrooms/suites in an urban & ocean theme. Elements Restaurant offers the finest contemporary food in a trendy environment. Quayside Bar and Lounge with riverside terrace is the perfect location for guests to relax and enjoy the panoramic views across the town and the river. Synergy Health & Leisure Club offers a 16.5m indoor pool, sauna, steam room & fully equipped gym. Car parking is available.

*Bookable on www.irelandhotels.com*

*Special Offer: www.irelandhotels.com/offers*

*B&B from €87.50 to €107.50*
*Suites from €255.00 to €345.00*

*Geir Sikko*
*General Manager*

127

*Activities:*

**Open All Year**

### Shamrock Lodge Hotel and Conference Centre

HOTEL ★★★ MAP 11 J 11


Clonown Road,
Athlone,
Co. Westmeath

Tel: 090-649 2601 Fax: 090-649 2737

Email: info@shamrocklodgehotel.ie

Web: www.shamrocklodgehotel.ie

Set amongst its green leafy gardens, the Shamrock Lodge Hotel is highly acclaimed for its excellent food and service where a warm welcome awaits you. New development of 40 executive bedrooms and 12 apartments, several conference and banqueting rooms. Minutes walk from town centre. Free car parking with 300 spaces. Please enquire about Facilities for Persons with Mobility Impairment.

*Bookable on www.irelandhotels.com*

*Special Offer: www.irelandhotels.com/offers*

*B&B from €65.00 to €85.00*
*Suites from €295.00 to €350.00*

*Paddy McCaul*
*Proprietor*

70

*Activities:*

**Closed 24 - 27 December**

### Sheraton Athlone Hotel

HOTEL MAP 11 J 11


Athlone,
Co. Westmeath

Tel: 090-645 1000 Fax: 090-645 1001

Email: info.athlone@sheraton.com

Web: www.sheraton.com/athlone

UNDER CONSTRUCTION - OPENING APRIL 2008

Built to a 4**** specification. Located in the heart of the thriving town of Athlone, the distinctive 12 storey glazed tower of the Athlone Town Centre Hotel affords breathtaking views over this historic town, the River Shannon and its callowland together with the four counties of Westmeath, Roscommon, Longford and Offaly. The hotel offers 167 superbly appointed deluxe bedrooms with 2 opulent penthouse suites and 1 stunning presidential suite, elegant restaurant, casual dining brasserie, lively bar, spacious leisure centre and contemporary urban spa. Please enquire about Facilities for Persons with Mobility Impairment.

*B&B from €80.00 to €250.00*

*Shirley Delahunt*
*Business Development Manager*

167

*Activities:*

**Open All Year**



B&B Rates are per Person Sharing per Night incl. Breakfast. or Room Rates are per Room per Night - See also Page 8

## Wineport Lodge

GUESTHOUSE ★★★★ MAP 11 J 11

Glasson,
Athlone,
Co. Westmeath

Tel: 090-643 9010 Fax: 090-648 5471

Email: lodge@wineport.ie

Web: www.wineport.ie

Wineport Lodge is blissfully located on the edge of Ireland's peaceful Inland Waterways. It is the perfect place to dine and stay, either for business or pleasure, in an easily accessible destination. In the restaurant, Eurotoques Chef Feargal O'Donnell's delicious food is matched by genuinely friendly and expert service. An always interesting menu changes seasonally, and the freshest local produce regularly appears as a daily special. If you're looking for the ideal hideaway to escape to, then Wineport Lodge is the right place to drop in and revive your jaded soul.

Member of Ireland's Blue Book

*B&B from €97.50 to €125.00*

*Ray Byrne & Jane English*

30

**Closed 24 - 26 December**

## Hilamar Hotel

HOTEL ★★★ MAP 11 L 11

Main Street,
Kinnegad,
Westmeath

Tel: 044-939 1719 Fax: 044-939 1718

Email: info@hilamarhotel.com

Web: www.hilamarhotel.com

Arrive and feel immediately 'at home' in The Hilamar Hotel. The all new luxurious hotel is ideally located in Kinnegad, crossroads of Ireland and just a 40 minute drive from Dublin City centre, ideal for the business commuter and leisure travellers alike. All of our 45 luxuriously appointed bedrooms, decorated in modern contemporary style provide our guests the perfect retreat, with the ultimate in comfort and luxury. Our lively Spirit Bar & Bistro serve food all day. WiFi access. Complimentary parking for all our guests. Please enquire about Facilities for Persons with Mobility Impairment.

*Bookable on www.irelandhotels.com*
*Special Offer: www.irelandhotels.com/offers*

*Room Rate from €89.00 to €180.00*

*Brian Pierson*
*General Manager*

45

*Activities:*

**Closed 25 December**

## Temple Country Retreat & Spa

GUESTHOUSE ★★ MAP 11 J 11

Horseleap,
Moate,
Co. Westmeath

Tel: 057-933 5118 Fax: 057-933 5008

Email: reservations@templespa.ie

Web: www.templespa.ie

An oasis of calm, Temple Country Retreat and Spa is Ireland's original destination spa for adults only. Located just over an hour from Dublin, Temple creates a total spa experience. You can join in a daily activity program of yoga, walks, fitness and relaxation classes, and with over 80 different spa treatments you're spoilt for choice, not forgetting the vitality suite with hydrotherapy pool, sauna, steam room and experience showers. 23 luxurious bedrooms, including two suites, all with panoramic countryside views. Please enquire about Facilities for Persons with Mobility Impairment.

*B&B from €125.00 to €175.00*
*Suites from €350.00 to €550.00*

*Declan & Bernadette Fagan*
*Owners*

23

*Activities:*

**Closed 22- 27 December**

## Mullingar

### Annebrook House

HOTEL MAP 11 L 12


Pearse St,
Mullingar,
Co Westmeath

Tel: 044-935 3300 Fax: 044-935 3333

Email: info@annebrook.ie

Web: www.annebrook.ie

Built to a 4**** specification. The Annebrook House Hotel is steeped in history and enjoys the enviable advantage of being on of the most centrally located hotels in Mullingar town. This unique venue will make an impression on guests and conference delegates alike. The hotel boasts 30 executive hotel rooms and apartment suites and ample onsite car parking facilities. Please enquire about Facilities for Persons with Mobility Impairment.

*B&B from €95.00 to €270.00*

*Liam Corr*
*General Manager*

30

**Closed 24 - 27 December**

### Bloomfield House Hotel

HOTEL ★★★ MAP 11 L 12


Belvedere,
Mullingar,
Co. Westmeath

Tel: 044-934 0894 Fax: 044-934 3767

Email: reservations@bloomfieldhouse.com

Web: www.bloomfieldhouse.com

Located in the beautiful countryside of central Ireland, historic Bloomfield House nestles on the shores of Lough Ennell surrounded by magnificent parkland and gently sloping meadows. Easy travelling distance from all regions and just 75 minutes from Dublin, Bloomfield House blends tradition and elegance with the latest amenities. Combining comfort, hospitality and service with an excellent leisure & spa facility, neighbouring the golf club and Belvedere House, relaxation proves effortless at Bloomfield House Hotel. Please enquire about Facilities for Persons with Mobility Impairment.

***Bookable on www.irelandhotels.com***

*B&B from €85.00 to €120.00*
*Suites from €300.00 to €350.00*

*Lorraine O'Leary*
*General Manager*

111

*Activities:*

**Closed 23 - 26 December**

### Greville Arms Hotel

HOTEL ★★★ MAP 11 L 12


Mullingar,
Co. Westmeath

Tel: 044-934 8563 Fax: 044-934 8052

Email: grevillearmshotel@eircom.net

Web: www.grevillearms.com

In the heart of Mullingar town, the Greville Arms Hotel is a home from home where customers and their comfort is our main concern. Recently refurbished, the hotel offers 39 luxuriously appointed rooms. The Greville Restaurant is renowned for its cuisine and fine wines. No visit to Mullingar would be complete without a visit to our Ulysses Bar with its life-sized wax figure of James Joyce and other memorabilia. Local attractions include Belvedere House and Gardens, golf, fishing and horse riding.

***An IHF Quality Employer***

*B&B from €60.00 to €90.00*

*John Cochrane*
*General Manager*

39

*Activities:*

**Closed 25 December**



B&B Rates are per Person Sharing per Night incl. Breakfast.
or Room Rates are per Room per Night - **See also Page 8**

## McCormacks Guesthouse

GUESTHOUSE ★★★ MAP 11 L 12

Old Dublin Road,
Mullingar,
Co. Westmeath

Tel: 044-934 1483
Email: info@mccormacksbandb.com
Web: www.mccormacksbandb.com

One mile from Mullingar Town and across the road from Mullingar Park Hotel. All rooms are en suite including large family rooms. Situated in a peaceful farm setting and yet within walking distance of town. Facilities for fishermen and tennis court and picnic area on grounds. Internet broadband access available to guests. Three specially adapted wheelchair accessible rooms. Numerous golf courses and fishing lakes nearby. Located just off Mullingar bypass (N4) at junction with N52 bypass. Sauna and hot tub cabin available at reasonable rates. Please enquire about Facilities for Persons with Mobility Impairment.

*Bookable on www.irelandhotels.com*
*Special Offer: www.irelandhotels.com/offers*

**B&B from €45.00 to €70.00**

*Tom & Margaret Mc Cormack*
*Proprietors*

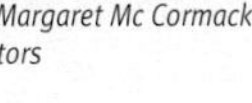

10

**Open All Year**

## Mullingar Park Hotel

HOTEL ★★★★ MAP 11 L 12

Dublin Road,
Mullingar,
Co. Westmeath

Tel: 044-933 7500 Fax: 044-933 5937
Email: info@mullingarparkhotel.com
Web: www.mullingarparkhotel.com

Contemporary in design and developed to 4**** specification, this stylish hotel is a modern classic. The hotel brings together 95 exceptional guest rooms with premium conference and banqueting facilities, the finest leisure and health spa, splendid choices for dining experiences and magnificent bars and lounges. Guests are within easy distance of championship golf courses, a range of equestrian activities, including major race meetings, and some of the best fishing in Ireland. Please enquire about Facilities for Persons with Mobility Impairment.

*Bookable on www.irelandhotels.com*
*Special Offer: www.irelandhotels.com/offers*

**B&B from €90.00 to €150.00**
**Suites from €300.00 to €600.00**

*Joesphine Hughes*
*Proprietor*

95

*Activities:*

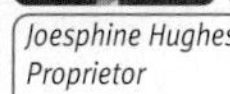

**Closed 24 - 25 December**

## Feerick's Hotel

HOTEL MAP 11 K 13

Rathowen,
Co. Westmeath

Tel: 043-76960 Fax: 043-76961
Email: info@feericks.ie
Web: www.ferricks.ie

Built to a 2** specification. Feerick's Hotel was established by John Feerick, a native of Ballinrobe, Co. Mayo. Recently, extensive renovation has transformed it into a very successful Hotel, Pub & Restaurant with 13 en suite rooms & large function/meeting rooms. Situated on the busy N4 in the village of Rathowen between Mullingar & Longford & 1 hour from Dublin, it has become a popular coach stop on the N4 with a reputation for good reasonably priced food. Food served from 7am till late, steaks a specialty but the menu contains choices for all. Please enquire about Facilities for Persons with Mobility Impairment.

**B&B from €40.00 to €60.00**

*John Feerick*

13

**Closed 25 December**

## Arklow / Ashford

### Arklow Bay Conference, Leisure & Spa Hotel

HOTEL ★★★ MAP 8 O 8

Arklow,
Co. Wicklow

Tel: 0402-32309 Fax: 0402-32300
Email: reservations@arklowbay.com
Web: www.brennanhotels.com

Among the hills and by the sea, Arklow is a unique destination for a leisure break. The 92 bedroomed Arklow Bay Hotel offers an elegant and comfortable setting for business or pleasure. Arklow Bay Hotel is part of Brennan Hotels. Please enquire about Facilities for Persons with Mobility Impairment.

***An IHF Quality Employer***

Member of Brennan Hotels

***Bookable on www.irelandhotels.com***
***Special Offer: www.irelandhotels.com/offers***

**B&B from €90.00 to €160.00**

*Tina O'Sullivan*
*General Manager*

92

**Open All Year**

### Bridge Hotel

HOTEL ★★ MAP 8 O 8

Bridge Street,
Arklow,
Co. Wicklow

Tel: 0402-31666 Fax: 0402-31666
Email: hbridge@eircom.net

The Bridge hotel is family owned and run, with 14 en suite bedrooms, TV and car parking. The hotel is situated at the bridge in Arklow Town, approximately 1 hour from Dublin and Rosslare. There is a wide choice of local golf courses as well as fine beaches nearby. Arklow is an ideal base from which to see the beautiful scenery of Wicklow.

**B&B from €55.00 to €70.00**

*Jim Hoey*
*Proprietor*

14

1

**Closed 25 December**

### Ballyknocken House & Cookery School

GUESTHOUSE ★★★★ MAP 8 P 9

Glenealy,
Ashford,
Co. Wicklow

Tel: 0404-44627 Fax: 0404-44696
Email: reservations@ballyknocken.com
Web: www.ballyknocken.com

1850's charming farmhouse, elegantly furnished with antiques. Individually styled bedrooms, most with claw feet baths offer lovely views over gardens and forest. Pre-dinner sherry by the Drawing Room's log fire before the splendid dinner using garden and local produce. Ballyknocken Cookery School on site. Superb breakfasts. Near to Wicklow Mountains, Glendalough, Powerscourt. Excellent golf, e.g. Druid's Glen. Lovely walks. Dublin 29 miles. Bridgestone 100 Best Places to Stay. Gift vouchers.

***An IHF Quality Employer***

***Bookable on www.irelandhotels.com***
***Special Offer: www.irelandhotels.com/offers***

**B&B from €59.00 to €68.00**

*Catherine Fulvio*
*Chef / Proprietor*

7

**Closed 12 December - 31 January**



B&B Rates are per Person Sharing per Night incl. Breakfast.
or Room Rates are per Room per Night - **See also Page 8**

## Bel-Air Hotel

HOTEL ★ MAP 8 P 9

Ashford,
Co. Wicklow

Tel: 0404-40109 Fax: 0404-40188

Email: belairhotel@eircom.net

Web: www.holidaysbelair.com

Bel-Air Hotel is a family-run country hotel situated in the centre of 81 hectares of farm and parkland. The lovely gardens have a breathtaking view to the sea. The traditional family atmosphere and rich history make the hotel a popular venue, a good restaurant, rooms en suite with tea making facilities, TV and hairdryers. Adjacent Equestrian Centre specialises in cross country riding and jumping for experienced riders. Family-run since 1937.

Member of Equestrian Holidays Ireland

**B&B from €57.00 to €65.00**

*William Freeman*
*Owner*

10

Closed 23 December - 11 January

## Chester Beatty Inn

HOTEL ★★ MAP 8 P 9

Ashford Village,
Co. Wicklow

Tel: 0404-40206 Fax: 0404-49003

Email: hotelchesterbeatty@eircom.net

Web: www.hotelchesterbeatty.ie

Charming Country Inn Family-run hotel with 12 luxury en suite rooms. Award-winning restaurant, lounge, traditional Irish bar with open log fires. Enjoy true Irish hospitality. We are located 35 minutes south of Dublin on route N11. Ideal spot for touring Wicklow, the Garden of Ireland. Mount Usher Gardens just 3 minutes walk away. Close to Glendalough, Powerscourt and many other tourist attractions. Numerous golf courses close by including Druids Glen and the European Golf Club. 1st Class Equestrian facilities, Hill walking. Private Car Parking.

*Bookable on www.irelandhotels.com*
*Special Offer: www.irelandhotels.com/offers*

**B&B from €50.00 to €100.00**

*Kitty & Paul Caprani*

12

*Activities:*

Closed 23 - 26 December and Good Friday

## BrookLodge and Wells Spa

HOTEL ★★★★ MAP 8 O 8

Macreddin Village,
Near Aughrim,
Co. Wicklow

Tel: 0402-36444 Fax: 0402-36580

Email: brooklodge@macreddin.ie

Web: www.brooklodge.com

Situated in a spectacular Wicklow Valley, 50 minutes from South Dublin. Home to The Strawberry Tree, Ireland's only certified organic restaurant and The Wells - a designated "Resort Spa". Macreddin Village also hosts Acton's Country Pub & Brewery, the Orchard Café, an organic bakery and smokehouse, the Store Rooms, Macreddin Stables, 4x4 driving and Macreddin Golf Club an 18 hole championship golf course designed by Paul McGinley.

*An IHF Quality Employer*

Member of Manor House Hotels

*Bookable on www.irelandhotels.com*

**B&B from €180.00 to €270.00**
**Suites from €250.00 to €390.00**

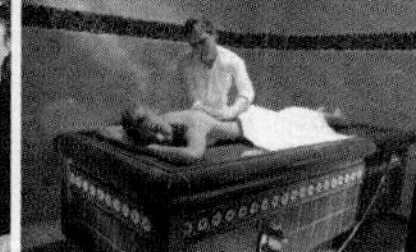

*Joe Kelly & Evan Doyle*
*Hosts*

66

*Activities:*

Open All Year

# Blessington / Bray

## Avon Rí

HOLIDAY VILLAGE MAP 8 N 10

Blessington Lakeshore,
Burgage, Blessington,
Co. Wicklow

Tel: 045-900670 Fax: 045-857756

Email: info@avonri.com

Web: www.avonri.com

Avon Rí is a wonderfully unique holiday, sporting and event resort spectacularly located on shores of The Blessington Lakes in Co.Wicklow, Ireland, only 40 minutes drive from the City Centre of Dublin. Glorious views of the lake and the surrounding mountains and glens: a thrilling list of professionally organised and supervised outdoor activities and a leisure centre and restaurant and luxury accommodation amount to a truly outstanding offering of a five star hotel standard in an unforgettable location.

**Room Rate from €100.00 to €300.00**

*James Stanley*
*Proprietor* 39

Activities:

**Closed 23- 26 December**

## Crofton Bray Head Inn

GUESTHOUSE ★★ MAP 8 P 10

Strand Road,
Bray,
Co. Wicklow

Tel: 01-286 7182 Fax: 01-286 7182

This 140 year old building is situated on the seafront, under the Bray Head Mountain. A 10 minute walk away from an excellent commuter train to Dublin, but also ideally located for touring Wicklow - The Garden of Ireland. The Bray Head Inn has ample car parking and is fully licensed. It has a lift, en suite bedrooms with TV and telephone. Our prices include full Irish breakfast.

**B&B from €50.00 to €60.00**

*Ena Regan Cummins* 30

**Closed 01 October - 01 June**

## Esplanade Hotel

HOTEL ★★★ MAP 8 P 10

Strand Road,
Bray,
Co. Wicklow

Tel: 01-286 2056 Fax: 01-286 6496

Email: info@esplanadehotel.ie

Web: www.esplanadehotel.ie

Stylish hotel with magnificent views, 12 miles from Dublin. Located on the seafront in Bray, the hotel retains many of its splendid Victorian features whilst offering modern day luxury and comfort. Comfortable lounges, excellent menu choices and exceptional value for money. Fully equipped and staffed fitness centre. Close to Bray DART station. A member of the Strandwood Hotel Group. Please enquire about Facilities for Persons with Mobility Impairment.

Member of Strandwood Hotel Group

*Bookable on www.irelandhotels.com*
*Special Offer: www.irelandhotels.com/offers*

**B&B from €45.00 to €90.00**

*Daniel Corbett*
*Area General Manager* 94

**Closed 24 - 26 December**



B&B Rates are per Person Sharing per Night incl. Breakfast. or Room Rates are per Room per Night - See also Page 8

## Heather House Hotel

HOTEL ★★ MAP 8 P 10

Strand Road,
Bray,
Co. Wicklow

Tel: 01-286 8000 Fax: 01-286 4254

Email: info@heatherhousehotel.com

Web: www.heatherhousehotel.com

A family-run hotel with spectacular seaviews. Catering for the business or leisure guest, with well appointed en suite accommodation, as well as self-catering apartments. The Martello Bar offers a superb carvery and bar food menu or dine in the Tower Bistro from our select menu and fine wines. Conference and banqueting facilities. Ideally located for touring Dublin City and County Wicklow. Located 5 minutes from all public transport and N11 Motorway. Please enquire about Facilities for Persons with Mobility Impairment.

*B&B from €60.00 to €70.00*

*John Duggan*
*General Manager*

25

Activities:

**Closed 24 - 26 December**

## Porterhouse Inn (The)

HOTEL ★★ MAP 8 P 10

Strand Road,
Bray,
Co. Wicklow

Tel: 01-286 0668 Fax: 01-286 1171

Email: tracy@theporterhouse.ie

Web: www.porterhousebrewco.com

Boutique Style Inn over busy bar/nightclub. Sea view rooms available. 40" LCD TV available in selected rooms. Located on Bray seafront, 10 mins from Main St., 5 mins walk from DART. Close to all local amenities including golf, angling & hill-walking. Group bookings taken.

*Room Rate from €75.00 to €150.00*

*Tracy & Lyndsey Kelly*

15

**Closed 24 - 25 December & Good Friday**

## Ramada Hotel Bray

HOTEL ★★★ MAP 8 P 10

Southern Cross,
Bray,
Co. Wicklow

Tel: 01-276 0258 Fax: 01-276 0298

Email: info@woodlandcourthotel.com

Web: www.woodlandcourthotel.com

The recently extended and refurbished 86 bedroomed hotel is situated just 12 miles south of Dublin City centre off the M11 / M50 link road. Located in private grounds with ample free parking, the Ramada Hotel Bray is the ideal base for touring County Wicklow and Dublin City. Only minutes away from both the LUAS (Sandyford) or DART (Bray), commuting to and from the hotel could not be easier. Please enquire about Facilities for Persons with Mobility Impairment.

***An IHF Quality Employer***

Member of Ramada Worldwide

***Bookable on www.irelandhotels.com***
***Special Offer: www.irelandhotels.com/offers***

*Room Rate from €75.00 to €99.00*

*Nikki McHugh*
*General Manager*

86

Activities:

**Closed 24 - 26 December**

B&B Rates are per Person Sharing per Night incl. Breakfast.
or Room Rates are per Room per Night - **See also Page 8**

## Dunlavin / Enniskerry

### Rathsallagh House, Golf and Country Club

GUESTHOUSE ★★★★ MAP 8 N 9

Dunlavin,
(West Wicklow),
Co. Wicklow

Tel: 045-403112 Fax: 045-403343
Email: info@rathsallagh.com
Web: www.rathsallagh.com

Winner of the Best Restaurant in Leinster Award 2007, the Supreme Irish Breakfast Awards and the AA Five Diamond Award for Guest Accommodation, Rathsallagh is a large Country House on 570 acres one hour south of Dublin airport. With its own 18 hole Championship Golf Course, rated in Irelands top 30 ( John Redmond 2007) , Rathsallagh is close to the K Club home of the 2006 Ryder Cup. Rathsallagh is an ideal venue for conferences, weddings & incentive outings. It is also available for private parties & rental.

***An IHF Quality Employer***

Member of Ireland's Blue Book

*Bookable on www.irelandhotels.com*
*Special Offer: www.irelandhotels.com/offers*

**B&B from €145.00 to €195.00**

*The O'Flynn Family*
*Proprietors*

29

*Activities:*

Closed 04 January - 28 February

### Summerhill House Hotel

HOTEL ★★★ MAP 8 O 10

Enniskerry,
Co. Wicklow

Tel: 01-286 7928 Fax: 01-286 7929
Email: info@summerhillhousehotel.com
Web: www.summerhillhousehotel.com

This charming hotel is just a short walk to the quaint village of Enniskerry, and the famous Powerscourt Gardens. Located on the N11, 19km south of Dublin City and 15km to Dunlaoire Ferryport. 55 spacious bedrooms, private free car parking, traditional Irish breakfast, hill walking and nature trails, local golf courses, family rooms (2 adults and 3 children). Enjoy a rare blend of the Wicklow countryside close to Dublin City. A member of the Strandwood Hotel Group. Please enquire about Facilities for Persons with Mobility Impairment.

***An IHF Quality Employer***

Member of Strandwood Hotel Group

*Bookable on www.irelandhotels.com*
*Special Offer: www.irelandhotels.com/offers*

**B&B from €45.00 to €90.00**

*Daniel Corbett*
*Area General Manager*

55

*Activities:*

Closed 24 - 26 December

B&B Rates are per Person Sharing per Night incl. Breakfast.
or Room Rates are per Room per Night - See also Page 8

## The Ritz-Carlton, Powerscourt

HOTEL ★★★★★ MAP 8 O 10

Powerscourt Estate,
Enniskerry,
Co. Wicklow

Tel: 01-274 8888 Fax: 01-274 9999

Email: powerscourtinquiries@ritzcarlton.com

Web: www.ritzcarlton.com

Nestled among the breathtaking glens and mountain foothills south of Dublin, The Ritz-Carlton, Powerscourt offers guests a glorious golf and spa experience enriched by magnificent scenic views and historic elegance. Visitors will enjoy impeccable service and a wealth of comforting amenities including dining at Gordon Ramsay at Powerscourt, The Sugar Loaf Lounge and McGill's traditional Irish Pub. For meeting and special events, the hotels includes extensive function space and private dining facilities

Member of The Ritz-Carlton Hotel Company L.L.C

*Room Rate from €490.00 to €490.00*
*Suites from €550.00 to €5,000.00*

*Andrew Nasskau*
*General Manager*

200

*Activities:*

**Open All Year**

## Glendalough Hotel

HOTEL ★★★ MAP 8 O 9

Glendalough,
Co. Wicklow

Tel: 0404-45135 Fax: 0404-45142

Email: info@glendaloughhotel.ie

Web: www.glendaloughhotel.com

The Casey family-owned Glendalough Hotel is a 40 bedroom hotel set in the heart of the Wicklow Mountains National Park and Ireland's most scenic valley, Glendalough. Located with easy access to walking trails, golf courses, outdoor pursuits and yet only 45km from Dublin City centre. Combining our location with excellent food and beverage fare available in our restaurant, bar or banqueting room and conference facilities, makes us the ideal location for that special event or occasion. Please enquire about Facilities for Persons with Mobility Impairment.

*B&B from €75.00 to €102.00*

*John Kelly*
*General Manager*

40

*Activities:*

**Closed 01 - 31 January**

## Lynham's Hotel

HOTEL ★★★ MAP 8 O 9

Laragh,
Glendalough,
Co. Wicklow

Tel: 0404-45345 Fax: 0404-45514

Email: info@lynhamsoflaragh.ie

Web: www.lynhamsoflaragh.ie

Family owned Lynham's Hotel Laragh is situated in the heart of Wicklow National Park, just a few minutes from the beautiful historic Glendalough. The warm welcoming atmosphere of Jake's Bar lends a traditional air to Lynham's. Famous for its superb bar food, you can also enjoy candlelight dining in our old world restaurant. Lynham's also offer special concessions to the world famous Druids Glen and Druids Heath Golf Courses. Please enquire about Facilities for Persons with Mobility Impairment.

*B&B from €65.00 to €150.00*

*John & Anne Lynham*
*Managers*

14

**Closed 21 - 28 December**

## Glen-O-The-Downs / Newtownmountkennedy / Rathnew

### Glenview Hotel

HOTEL ★★★★ MAP 8 O 10

Glen-O-The-Downs,
Delgany,
Co. Wicklow

Tel: 01-287 3399 Fax: 01-287 7511

Email: sales@glenviewhotel.com

Web: www.glenviewhotel.com

Situated on a magnificent panoramic site overlooking the garden of Ireland. The Glenview Hotel offers 70 de luxe bedrooms, the unrivalled Penthouse Suite, the award-winning Woodlands Restaurant, Conservatory Bar, 8 meeting rooms for up to 220 delegates and a magnificent leisure club. From the moment you walk through the door you will experience a warm welcome, gracious hospitality and personal service. Relax and unwind in the Haven Beauty salons where calm and peace replace stress and tension. Please enquire about Facilities for Persons with Mobility Impairment.

***An IHF Quality Employer***

*Bookable on www.irelandhotels.com*
*Special Offer: www.irelandhotels.com/offers*

**B&B from €70.00 to €135.00**

*Pat Hevey*
*General Manager*

70

Activities:

**Open All Year**

### Parkview Hotel

HOTEL ★★★ MAP 8 P 9

Main Street,
Newtownmountkennedy,
Co. Wicklow

Tel: 01-201 5600 Fax: 01-201 5699

Email: info@parkviewhotel.ie

Web: www.parkviewhotel.ie

Parkview Hotel, Newtownmountkennedy is located south of Dublin and approximately 1 hour from Dublin Airport. The hotel has a unique atmosphere that combines country comfort and city sophistication. The Hotel facilities include 60 tastefully furnished bedrooms equipped to the highest standards, banqueting and conference centre, dedicated meeting room and our Parkview Bar & Synnott's Restaurant are the perfect place for some relaxing time out. We look forward to welcoming you to the Parkview Hotel. Please enquire about Facilities for Persons with Mobility Impairment.

*Bookable on www.irelandhotels.com*
*Special Offer: www.irelandhotels.com/offers*

**B&B from €47.50 to €105.00**

*Lisa Bradshaw*
*General Manager*

60

Activities:

**Open All Year**

### Hunter's Hotel

HOTEL ★★★ MAP 8 P 9

Newrath Bridge,
Rathnew,
Co. Wicklow

Tel: 0404-40106 Fax: 0404-40338

Email: reception@hunters.ie

Web: www.hunters.ie

Ireland's oldest coaching inn, its award-winning gardens along River Vartry provide a haven from the world at large. Restaurant provides the very best of Irish food and fresh fish. Local amenities include golf, horse riding and fishing. Beautiful sandy beaches and sightseeing in the Garden of Ireland. Dublin 44.8km. Rosslare 115.2km. Off N11 at Rathnew or Ashford. Irish Country Houses and Restaurant Association.

***An IHF Quality Employer***

Member of Ireland's Blue Book

**B&B from €95.00 to €110.00**

*Gelletlie Family*
*Proprietors*

16

Activities:

**Closed 24 - 26 December**



B&B Rates are per Person Sharing per Night incl. Breakfast. or Room Rates are per Room per Night - See also Page 8

## Tinakilly House Hotel

HOTEL ★★★★ MAP 8 P 9

Wicklow,
(Rathnew),
Co. Wicklow

Tel: 0404-69274 Fax: 0404-67806

Email: reservations@tinakilly.ie

Web: www.tinakilly.ie

This Victorian mansion was built for Captain Halpin, who laid the world's telegraph cables. The bedrooms, some with 4 posters, are furnished in period style and most overlook the Irish Sea. Award-winning cuisine is prepared from garden vegetables, local fish and Wicklow lamb. The warm welcome ensures a relaxing, memorable stay. Available locally - golf, horse riding, Powerscourt, Mount Usher Gardens and Wicklow Mountains. Dublin 46km.

***An IHF Quality Employer***

***Bookable on www.irelandhotels.com***

***Special Offer: www.irelandhotels.com/offers***

***B&B from €114.00 to €141.00***
***Suites from €284.00 to €354.00***

*Conrad Robinson*
*General Manager*

51

*Activities:*

**Closed 24 - 27 December**

## Stoops Guesthouse

GUESTHOUSE MAP 8 N 8

Stoops, Coolattin,
Shillelagh,
Co. Wicklow

Tel: 053-9429903

Email: info@stoopsguesthouse.ie

Web: www.stoopsguesthouse.ie

Built to a 3*** specification. This beautiful constructed residence blends modern facilities with traditional architecture. Nestling in landscaped garden & surrounded by forestry with spectacular views of the Wicklow Hills, it is only a short walk to Coolattin Village and Golf club. Facilities for patrons include a large dining area for reading, TV and general relaxation. All bedrooms are spacious with LCD TV, coffee & full en suite. Please enquire about Facilities for Persons with Mobility Impairment.

***Room Rate from €50.00 to €100.00***

*Mr. Christopher Mulhall*

8

*Activities:*

**Closed 20 December - 3 January**

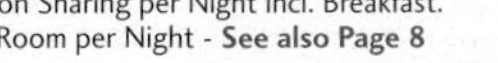

B&B Rates are per Person Sharing per Night incl. Breakfast.
or Room Rates are per Room per Night - **See also Page 8**

## Wicklow Town / Woodenbridge

### Grand Hotel

HOTEL ★★★ MAP 8 P 9

Wicklow Town,
Co. Wicklow

Tel: 0404-67337 Fax: 0404-69607
Email: reservations@grandhotel.ie
Web: www.grandhotel.ie

The Grand Hotel has been welcoming guests to the picturesque seaside town of Wicklow since 1896. Centrally located in the heart of "The Garden of Ireland", it's the perfect relaxing base for exploring Wicklow. Facilities include: 33 luxurious rooms, lively main bar and cosy lounge, food served all day, excellent conferencing and banqueting facilities and secure parking. Stunning scenery, golf, walking, historic houses and gardens all nearby. Dublin 48km.

**B&B from €52.50 to €85.00**

*Adrian Flynn*
*Hotel Director*

33

Activities:

**Closed 24 - 26 December**

### Woodenbridge Hotel

HOTEL ★★★ MAP 8 O 8

Vale Of Avoca,
Arklow,
Co. Wicklow

Tel: 0402-35146 Fax: 0402-35573
Email: info@woodenbridgehotel.com
Web: www.woodenbridgehotel.com

Family owned and run with 23 en suite rooms, including rooms with balconies overlooking Woodenbridge golf course. Dating from 1608 the hotel is the oldest in Ireland. Our restaurant and bar serve quality Irish food: Bord Bia accredited. Tourism Menu award-winner, bar food served all day. Horse riding, fishing, golfing, fine beaches and walking available locally. Near Avoca film location for Ballykissangel. Please enquire about Facilities for Persons with Mobility Impairment.

***An IHF Quality Employer***

Member of Best Western

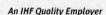

***Bookable on www.irelandhotels.com***
***Special Offer: www.irelandhotels.com/offers***

**B&B from €45.00 to €85.00**

*Esther O'Brien & Bill O'Brien*
*Proprietors*

23

Activities:

**Open All Year**

### Woodenbridge Lodge

HOTEL ★★★ MAP 8 O 8

Vale Of Avoca,
Arklow,
Co. Wicklow

Tel: 0402-35146 Fax: 0402-35573
Email: info@woodenbridgehotel.com
Web: www.woodenbridgehotel.com

Woodenbridge Lodge is sheltered by Wicklow's rolling hills and is in the picturesque Vale of Avoca. Situated on the banks of the Aughrim River, with 40 bedrooms. A perfect setting for golfing breaks, family reunions, or relaxing, peaceful weekends for two. Il Ruscello Italian restaurant is located here, with authentic Italian cuisine recommended by Paolo Tullio. Please enquire about Facilities for Persons with Mobility Impairment.

***An IHF Quality Employer***

Member of Best Western

**B&B from €45.00 to €85.00**

*Esther O'Brien & Bill O'Brien*
*Proprietors*

40

Activities:

**Open All Year**



B&B Rates are per Person Sharing per Night incl. Breakfast.
or Room Rates are per Room per Night - **See also Page 8**

# NORTHERN IRELAND

**For Detailed Maps of this Region See Pages 477-492**

**Each Hotel or Guesthouse has a Map Reference to these detailed maps under their photograph.**

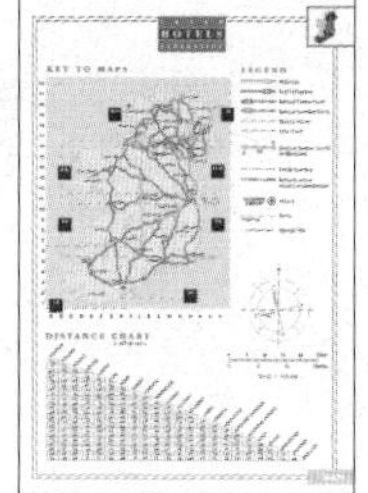

**See page 477 for map with access points and driving distances**

# northern ireland is a place steeped in history, myth and legend, waiting to be discovered....

**Start with the Giant's Causeway, formed 60 million years ago by the cooling and shrinking of unusually shaped basalt columns, or as legend would have it, built by the giant Finn MacCool to enable him to cross over to Scotland. Set on the stunning Antrim Coast amongst golden beaches and the dramatic Antrim Glens.**

Move onto Belfast, once an industrial powerhouse and birthplace of the most famous ship of all – Titanic. Take the Titanic Tour in a burgeoning and modern Belfast City bursting with city life. From Titanic's birthplace to Saint Patrick's resting place in Downpatrick.

Take the Saint Patrick's Trail following Saint Patrick's footsteps across the historic counties of Down and Armagh.

The mighty Mourne Mountains in the south of County Down are said to be the inspiration behind the landscape of CS Lewis' Chronicles of Narnia. Born in Belfast in 1898, the great author visited the 'turbulent democracy of little hills' many times.

In the west, Northern Ireland has its own Venice in the Lakelands of Fermanagh, with wide stretches of island dotted waterway and secluded bays surrounded by a patchwork of green fields and the island town of Enniskillen with its 15th century castle.

The Walled City of Derry is one of the few remaining completely walled cities in the world. The city is home to a number of museums, galleries and theatres, as well as thriving musical and literary scenes.

Best of all, Northern Ireland is easy to get to and easy to get around.

We're only an hour from Dublin and with transatlantic routes from the US and Canada and low cost flights from all over Europe into our three airports, there's never been a better time to discover Northern Ireland for yourself.

So come to Northern Ireland and meet the people with the warmest hospitality who'll show you history in the making, call us on: **+44 (0) 28 9024 6609**

**discovernorthernireland.com**

## Bushmills

### Bayview Hotel

HOTEL ★★★ MAP 14 N 21

2 Bayhead Road,
Portballintrae, Bushmills,
Co. Antrim BT57 8RZ

Tel: 028-2073 4100 Fax: 028-2073 4330

Email: info@bayviewhotelni.com

Web: www.bayviewhotelni.com

Opened 2001, the Bayview Hotel is situated in the heart of the picturesque village of Portballintrae, one mile from Bushmills. Overlooking the Atlantic Ocean and close to the Giant's Causeway and Old Bushmills Distillery, with 25 luxurious bedrooms, standard, superior, premier, interlinking and ambulant disabled rooms available. Excellent conference facilities, Porthole Restaurant and Bar. Lift and private car park. This small luxury hotel is the ideal destination for conferencing, golfing, business, incentive travel and leisure.

Member of North Coast Hotels Ltd.

***Bookable on www.irelandhotels.com***
***Special Offer: www.irelandhotels.com/offers***

***B&B from £40.00 to £95.00***

*Mary O'Neill*
*Group Marketing Manager*

25

*Activities:*

**Open All Year**

### Bushmills Inn Hotel

HOTEL ★★★ MAP 14 N 21

9 Dunluce Road,
Bushmills,
Co. Antrim BT57 8QG

Tel: 028-2073 3000 Fax: 028-2073 2048

Email: mail@bushmillsinn.com

Web: www.bushmillsinn.com

A "living museum of Ulster Hospitality". In the village that is home to the world's oldest distillery between the Giant's Causeway and Royal Portrush Golf Club, this multi award-winning hotel, on the banks of the River Bush, with turf fires, oil lamps, nooks, crannies and even a secret room presents an extensive range of intriguing bedrooms, an atmospheric restaurant (new Irish cuisine), a turf-fired old kitchen and a Victorian bar still lit by gas light - you're welcome.

Member of Ireland's Blue Book

***Bookable on www.irelandhotels.com***
***Special Offer: www.irelandhotels.com/offers***

***B&B from £69.00 to £84.00***

*Alan Dunlop*
*General Manager*

32

*Activities:*

**Open All Year**

### Causeway Hotel

HOTEL ★★ MAP 14 N 21

40 Causeway Road,
Bushmills,
Co. Antrim BT57 8SU

Tel: 028-2073 1226 Fax: 028-2073 2552

Email: reception@giants-causeway-hotel.co.uk

Web: www.giants-causeway-hotel.com

Situated on the North Antrim Coast at the entrance to the world famous Giant's Causeway. This old family hotel established in 1836 has been tastefully renovated and restored to provide modern facilities while retaining its old grandeur and charm. The 28 centrally heated bedrooms have TV, tea/coffee making facilities and bathrooms en suite.

***B&B from £35.00 to £40.00***

*Darrel Stevenson*
*Manager*

28

**Open All Year**



B&B Rates are per Person Sharing per Night incl. Breakfast.
or Room Rates are per Room per Night - **See also Page 8**

## Londonderry Arms Hotel

HOTEL ★★★ MAP 15 P 20

Glens Of Antrim, 20 Harbour Rd, Carnlough, Co. Antrim BT44 0EU

Tel: 028-2888 5255 Fax: 028-2888 5263

Email: lda@glensofantrim.com

Web: www.glensofantrim.com

This beautiful Georgian hotel was built in 1847. Once owned by Sir Winston Churchill, it is now owned and managed by Mr. Frank O'Neill. With its open log fires, private lounges and award-winning restaurant, this premier hotel in the Glens of Antrim is the perfect place to stay and discover the north eastern part of Ireland. Member of Irish Country Hotels. Ideal for incentive travel, close to the Giant's Causeway. Suits tour parties, conferences and weddings. Please enquire about Facilities for Persons with Mobility Impairment.

Member of Irish Country Hotels

**Bookable on www.irelandhotels.com**
**Special Offer: www.irelandhotels.com/offers**

**B&B from £40.00 to £85.00**

Frank O'Neill
Proprietor
35

Activities:

Closed 24 - 25 December

## Clarion Hotel

HOTEL ★★★ MAP 15 P 18

75 Belfast Road, Carrickfergus, Co. Antrim BT38 8PH

Tel: 028-9336 4556 Fax: 028-9335 1620

Email: info@clarioncarrick.com

Web: www.clarioncarrick.com

Situated 15 minutes from Belfast City centre at the gateway to the Antrim Coastal Route. Boasting 68 luxurious bedrooms including 2 suites, each room offers multi-channel TV with in-house movie channels, DD telephone, executive desk, internet connection, trouser press, hairdryer and complimentary tea/coffee. Bar 75 offers informal dining options where you can watch your favourite team on the wide screen TV. The Red Pepper Restaurant caters for breakfast & dinner. Please enquire about Facilities for Persons with Mobility Impairment.

Member of Choice Hotels Europe

**Bookable on www.irelandhotels.com**
**Special Offer: www.irelandhotels.com/offers**

**B&B from £40.00 to £55.00**
**Suites from £125.00 to £175.00**

Stephen Carson
General Manager
68

Activities:

Closed 25 December

## Ramada Portrush

HOTEL ★★★ MAP 14 N 21

73 Main Street, Portrush, Co. Antrim BT56 8BN

Tel: 028-7082 6100 Fax: 028-7082 6160

Email: info@ramadaportrush.com

Web: www.ramadaportrush.com

Hotel of the Year 2004/5 (Northern Ireland Tourism Awards) - the award-winning Ramada Portrush is situated overlooking the Atlantic Ocean in the centre of Portrush. 69 en suite bedrooms with internet access, safe and lift. Ideal base for golfing, walking, cycling, angling, sightseeing, (Giant's Causeway), tour parties, conferences and functions. Golf at Royal Portrush, Portstewart, Castlerock, Ballycastle, Gracehill, Bushfoot and Galgorm Castle Golf Courses. Sister hotel "Bayview Hotel Portballintrae, Bushmills". Please enquire about Facilities for Persons with Mobility Impairment.

Member of Ramada Worldwide

**Bookable on www.irelandhotels.com**
**Special Offer: www.irelandhotels.com/offers**

**B&B from £40.00 to £80.00**

Ann Donaghy
Group General Manager
69

Activities:

Open All Year

## Stoneyford / Templepatrick / Armagh City

### Ballymac

HOTEL ★★ MAP 15 O 18

7a Rock Road,
Stoneyford,
Co. Antrim BT28 3SU

Tel: 028-9264 8313 Fax: 028-9264 8312

Email: info@ballymachotel.co.uk

Web: www.ballymac.com

The Ballymac Hotel set amid tranquil surroundings. Spectacularly reincarnated, the contemporarily designed 15 en suite bedrooms with excellent facilities including DD phones, modem facilities, hairdryers, TVs and hospitality trays. Our Grill Bar/Lounge and à la carte restaurant feature outstanding cuisine along with an extensive wine list. The Ballymac also boasts well-equipped function suites suitable for weddings, parties, trade shows and conferences. Extensive private parking is available in our grounds.

**B&B from £45.00 to £55.00**
**Suites from £90.00 to £100.00**

*Ciaran Cunningham*
*General Manager*

15

*Activities:*

**Closed 25 December**

### Templeton Hotel

HOTEL ★★★ MAP 15 O 18

882 Antrim Rd, Templepatrick,
Ballyclare,
Co. Antrim BT39 0AH

Tel: 028-9443 2984 Fax: 028-9443 3406

Email: reception@templetonhotel.com

Web: www.templetonhotel.com

This privately owned hotel, 5 minutes from Belfast International Airport, 20 minutes from Belfast City centre and Belfast and Larne Ports, offers total quality for all tastes. With the choice of Raffles à la carte restaurant, the Upton Grill Room and the spacious lounge bar, you are guaranteed an enjoyable dining experience. Sam's Bar hosts a pub quiz every Monday evening and offers a late bar at weekends. Our 24 en suite bedrooms, including executive suites, are ideal for a relaxing and comfortable stay. Please enquire about Facilities for Persons with Mobility Impairment.

**B&B from £42.50 to £62.50**
**Suites from £125.00 to £145.00**

*Alison McCombe / Claire Kerr*
*General Manager /*
*Marketing Manager*

24

**Closed 25 - 26 December**

### Armagh City Hotel

HOTEL ★★★ MAP 14 N 16

2 Friary Road,
Armagh,
Co. Armagh BT60 4FR

Tel: 028-3751 8888 Fax: 028-3751 2777

Email: info@armaghcityhotel.com

Web: www.armaghcityhotel.com

Featuring imposing views over Ireland's oldest city, The Armagh City Hotel is a popular choice for local & international guests. Situated only one hour from Belfast and 1 hour 30 mins from Dublin, it's a natural meeting place for national conferences where the capacity is up to 1,000 delegates. Hospitality and friendly service enhance the comfortable, spacious bedrooms and extensive leisure facilities. Please enquire about Facilities for Persons with Mobility Impairment.

Member of Mooney Hotel Group

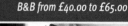

***Bookable on www.irelandhotels.com***
***Special Offer: www.irelandhotels.com/offers***

**B&B from £40.00 to £65.00**

*Zoe Millar*
*General Manager*

99

*Activities:*

**Closed 24 - 25 December**



B&B Rates are per Person Sharing per Night incl. Breakfast.
or Room Rates are per Room per Night - See also Page 8

## Charlemont Arms Hotel

HOTEL ★★ MAP 14 N 16

57-65 English Street,
Armagh City,
Co. Armagh BT61 7LB
Tel: 028-3752 2028 Fax: 028-3752 6979
Email: info@charlemontarmshotel.com
Web: www.charlemontarmshotel.com

A family-run hotel set in the city centre, offering the best of both worlds, traditional and modern. Convenient to shops, 18 hole golf course, leisure centre and all major tourist attractions including the 2 Cathedrals and other places of interest. 30 en suite bedrooms including one for the disabled, a 60 seat restaurant, 80 seat lounge bar, Turner's theme bar and Basement Bistro/Winebar that offers a unique dining experience for Armagh.

**B&B from £42.50 to £45.00**

*The Forster Family*

30

**Closed 25 - 26 December**

## Days Hotel, Belfast

HOTEL ★★★ MAP 15 P 18

40 Hope Street,
Belfast,
Co. Antrim BT12 5EE
Tel: 028-9024 2494 Fax: 028-9024 2495
Email: mail@dayshotelbelfast.co.uk
Web: www.dayshotelbelfast.co.uk

Days Hotel Belfast offers great value for money in a prime city centre location. Many of the city's shops, restaurants, attractions and nightlife are right on your doorstep. The hotel is also ideally located for all transport links. Facilities include hotel bar, restaurant, meeting room and 300 on-site car parking spaces. Parking is free for residents. Please enquire about Facilities for Persons with Mobility Impairment.

Member of Andras House

*Bookable on www.irelandhotels.com*

**Room Rate from £65.00 to £105.00**

*Gary Gaynor*
*General Manager*

250

**Open All Year**

## Dunadry Hotel

HOTEL ★★★★ MAP 15 O 18

2 Islandreagh Drive,
Dunadry,
Co. Antrim BT41 2HA
Tel: 028-9443 4343 Fax: 028-9443 3389
Email: info@dunadry.com
Web: www.dunadry.com

A truly magical atmosphere awaits guests at this hotel where the warmth of yesterday meets the style of today. Built on the site of an ancient fort and once home to both paper and linen mills, the Dunadry is rich with stories of times past. Only 20 minutes from Belfast and an hour from The Giant's Causeway. It's a perfect location to spend a relaxing break. Private car park and leisure facilities with beauty therapies. Please enquire about Facilities for Persons with Mobility Impairment.

Member of Mooney Hotel Group

*Bookable on www.irelandhotels.com*
*Special Offer: www.irelandhotels.com/offers*

**Room Rate from £90.00 to £152.00**

*Conor Collery*
*General Manager*

83

*Activities:*

**Closed 24 - 26 December**

## Belfast City

### Jurys Inn Belfast

HOTEL ★★★ MAP 15 P 18

Fisherwick Place,
Great Victoria St.,
Belfast BT2 7AP

Tel: 028-9053 3500 Fax: 028-9053 3511

Email: jurysinnbelfast@jurysdoyle.com

Web: www.jurysinns.com

Located in City Centre of Belfast, adjacent to the Opera House, City Hall and the cities main commercial district. Just a few minutes walk away are the prime shopping areas of Donegal Place, Castlecourt Centre and the new Victoria square while the cities Golden mile and Cathedral Quarter with their myriad of bars and restaurants are also a short distance from the Odyssey and Waterfront Hall. Please enquire about Facilities for Persons with Mobility Impairment.

Member of Jurys Inns Group Ltd

**Bookable on www.irelandhotels.com**
**Special Offer: www.irelandhotels.com/offers**

**Room Rate from £69.00 to £120.00**

*Rachel Strange*
*General Manager*

190

**Closed 23 - 26 December**

### La Mon Hotel & Country Club

HOTEL ★★★★ MAP 15 P 18

41 Gransha Road,
Castlereagh,
Belfast BT23 5RF

Tel: 028-9044 8631 Fax: 028-9044 8026

Email: info@lamon.co.uk

Web: www.lamon.co.uk

This modern 4 star hotel offers 88 en suite bedrooms, excellent banqueting & conference facilities in a tranquil setting just 8 miles south east of Belfast City centre. Guests will enjoy the superb luxury leisure facilities including 15 metre swimming pool, childrens' pool, sauna, jacuzzi, steam room, gymnasium, hair studio & beauty salon. A wide range of dining options is also available with table d'hôte and à la carte menus in the Shakespeare Restaurant. Casual dining with a cosmopolitan flavour is also available in our lively bistro. An ideal venue for business or leisure.

**Bookable on www.irelandhotels.com**

**B&B from £62.50 to £70.00**
**Suites from £155.00 to £200.00**

*Francis Brady*
*Managing Director*

88

*Activities:*

**Closed 24 - 26 December**

### Malone Lodge Hotel & Apartments

HOTEL ★★★★ MAP 15 P 18

60 Eglantine Avenue,
Malone Road,
Belfast BT9 6DY

Tel: 028-9038 8000 Fax: 028-9038 8088

Email: info@malonelodgehotel.com

Web: www.malonelodgehotelbelfast.com

In the leafy suburbs of the university area of South Belfast, discover one of Northern Ireland's finest 4**** hotels. The centre piece of a beautiful Victorian terrace, the Malone Lodge Hotel offers you an oasis of calm and quiet elegance. The hotel offers luxury en suite accommodation, an award-winning restaurant, bar with big screen, conference & banqueting facilities and a fitness suite & sauna.

Member of Select Hotels of Ireland

**Bookable on www.irelandhotels.com**
**Special Offer: www.irelandhotels.com/offers**

**B&B from £55.00 to £100.00**
**Suites from £150.00 to £250.00**

*Mary & Brian Macklin*

51

*Activities:*

**Open All Year**



B&B Rates are per Person Sharing per Night incl. Breakfast.
or Room Rates are per Room per Night - See also Page 8

## Park Avenue Hotel

HOTEL ★★★ MAP 15 P 18

158 Holywood Road,
Belfast BT4 1PB

Tel: 028-9065 6520 Fax: 028-9047 1417
Email: frontdesk@parkavenuehotel.co.uk
Web: www.parkavenuehotel.co.uk

The Park Avenue Hotel is closest to George Best Belfast City Airport & situated a few minutes from city centre. Close to Odyssey, Belfast's Waterfront Hall and Titanic Quarter. Excellent road, rail and air links. A cinema complex and an array of shops are steps away. All 56 bedrooms are modern, bright, spacious and provide full en suite facilities. Free on site car parking. Griffin Restaurant & Gelston's Corner Bar both serve meals daily. Conference & banqueting for up to 600. Please enquire about Facilities for Persons with Mobility Impairment.

Member of The Independents

***Bookable on www.irelandhotels.com***
***Special Offer: www.irelandhotels.com/offers***

***B&B from £39.50 to £62.50***

*Mandy Martin*
*Director*

56

**Closed 25 December**

## Wellington Park Hotel

HOTEL ★★★★ MAP 15 P 18

21 Malone Road,
Belfast BT9 6RU

Tel: 028-9038 1111 Fax: 028-9066 5410
Email: info@wellingtonparkhotel.com
Web: www.mooneyhotelgroup.com

Located on the Malone Road close to Queen's University, this premier hotel enjoys a great location, 15 minutes walk from the city centre and the Belfast Waterfront hall. Better still, it is close to Belfast's best shopping on the Lisburn Road; home to fashionable shops such as Space NK, Hobbs, the top interior designers and magnificent Galleries. Stroll from this popular, lively hotel and enjoy some of the best cafés, restaurants and bars in the city. Please enquire about Facilities for Persons with Mobility Impairment.

Member of Best Western Hotels

***Bookable on www.irelandhotels.com***
***Special Offer: www.irelandhotels.com/offers***

***Room Rate from £90.00 to £144.00***
***Suites from £192.00 to £192.00***

*Malachy Toner*
*General Manager*

75

**Closed 24 - 26 December**

## Brown Trout Golf & Country Inn

HOTEL ★★★ MAP 14 N 20

209 Agivey Road,
Aghadowey, Coleraine,
Co. Derry BT51 4AD

Tel: 028-7086 8209 Fax: 028-7086 8878
Email: bill@browntroutinn.com
Web: www.browntroutinn.com

The Brown Trout Golf and Country Inn nestles near the River Bann only 12.8km from the picturesque Causeway Coast. This old inn with 15 rooms and four 5 star cottages, is Northern Ireland's first golf hotel. Gerry, Jane or Joanna will happily organise golf and fishing packages with professional tuition if required, or you can just enjoy a relaxing break and the craic with the locals. The warm hospitality and 'Taste of Ulster' restaurant will make your stay enjoyable. Please enquire about Facilities for Persons with Mobility Impairment.

Member of Irish Country Hotels

***Bookable on www.irelandhotels.com***
***Special Offer: www.irelandhotels.com/offers***

***B&B from £40.00 to £55.00***

*Jane O'Hara*
*Owner*

15

**Open All Year**

B&B Rates are per Person Sharing per Night incl. Breakfast.
or Room Rates are per Room per Night - **See also Page 8**

## Derry City

### Beech Hill Country House Hotel

HOTEL ★★★★ MAP 14 L 20

32 Ardmore Road,
Derry BT47 3QP

Tel: 028-7134 9279 Fax: 028-7134 5366
Email: info@beech-hill.com
Web: www.beech-hill.com

Beech Hill is a privately owned country house hotel, 2 miles from Londonderry. It retains the elegance of country living & has been restored to create a hotel of charm, character & style. Its ambience is complemented by the surrounding grounds, planted with a myriad trees, including beech. Superb cuisine using local produce and homemade specialties. NITB Highly Commended Marketing Excellence Award 2004 & Flavour of Northern Ireland 2005. Sauna, steam room, jacuzzi & gym available. Relaxation weekends, aromatherapy, reiki, massage & beauty therapies. Booking advisable.

Member of Manor House Hotels

*Bookable on www.irelandhotels.com*
*Special Offer: www.irelandhotels.com/offers*

*B&B from £55.00 to £65.00*
*Suites from £170.00 to £200.00*

*Seamus Donnelly*
*Proprietor*

27

Closed 24 - 26 December

### Best Western White Horse Hotel

HOTEL ★★★ MAP 14 L 20

68 Clooney Road,
Derry BT47 3PA

Tel: 028-7186 0606 Fax: 028-7186 1438
Email: sales@whitehorsehotel.biz
Web: www.whitehorsehotel.biz

A luxury family-run hotel with 57 bedrooms, incl. 16 executive rooms, and leisure complex. The hotel is ideal for pleasure and business with 4 conference suites. The leisure complex consists of 22m swimming pool, childrens' pool, sauna, steam room, jacuzzi, aerobics studio and state of the art gymnasium. Only 10 minutes from the historic city of Londonderry and on the main route to the Giant's Causeway. Award-winning restaurant and bar. Very keen room rates. AA selected. Horse riding, golf and fishing close by. Free WiFi. Children welcome. Please enquire about Facilities for Persons with Mobility Impairment.

Member of Best Western

*Bookable on www.irelandhotels.com*
*Special Offer: www.irelandhotels.com/offers*

*B&B from £35.00 to £50.00*
*Suites from £90.00 to £130.00*

*Keith Baldrick*
*General Manager*

57

Open All Year

### City Hotel

HOTEL MAP 14 L 20

Queens Quay,
Derry BT48 7AS

Tel: 028-7136 5800 Fax: 028-7136 5801
Email: reservations@cityhotelderry.com
Web: www.cityhotelderry.com

Stylish modern NITB certified hotel in the heart of the city centre. Located on Queen's Quay, overlooking the River Foyle, offering fabulous river & city views, within a minute's walk of the spectacular 17th century city walls. 145 guest rooms, including de luxe, family & suites. Full leisure centre with swimming pool. Our restaurant Thompson's On The River is one of Derry's finest, offering a range of traditional Irish fare with a modern twist. Conferences & weddings are spectacular affairs from our first floor ballroom, with the River Foyle & historical Guildhall providing the perfect backdrop.

*Bookable on www.irelandhotels.com*
*Special Offer: www.irelandhotels.com/offers*

*Room Rate from £60.00 to £140.00*
*Suites from £180.00 to £350.00*

*Sean Murray*
*General Manager*

145

Closed 24 - 27 December



B&B Rates are per Person Sharing per Night incl. Breakfast.
or Room Rates are per Room per Night - See also Page 8

## Ramada Da Vinci's Hotel

HOTEL ★★★ MAP 14 L 20

15 Culmore Road,
Derry BT48 8JB

Tel: 028-7127 9111 Fax: 028-7127 9222
Email: info@davincishotel.com
Web: www.davincishotel.com

Stylish sophistication comes as standard in this uniquely designed & impeccably managed hotel. With high standards, fine facilities and imaginative design, accommodation within this complex will certainly impress. With different bedroom types, we guarantee a range of options to suit the most discerning travellers. Home to the award-winning Grillroom Restaurant, the Main Bar, Spirit Bar and Style Bar, we have all types of entertainment under one roof. Ideally located only one mile from the city centre with a delightful riverside walk way directly to the main shopping district. Private Car Parking Available.

Member of Ramada

***Bookable on www.irelandhotels.com***
***Special Offer: www.irelandhotels.com/offers***

***Room Rate from £49.95 to £99.00***
***Suites from £120.00 to £150.00***

*Ciaran O'Neill*
*General Manager*

65

**Closed 24 - 26 December**

## Radisson SAS Roe Park Resort

HOTEL ★★★★ MAP 14 M 20

Roe Park,
Limavady,
Co. Londonderry BT49 9LB

Tel: 028-7772 2222 Fax: 028-7772 2313
Email: reservations@radissonroepark.com
Web: www.radissonroepark.com

The north coast's only 4**** de luxe resort, offers 118 spacious en suite bedrooms, Fairways Leisure Club with indoor pool and fitness suite, the Roe Spa with 12 treatment rooms offering Elemis treatments in brand new spa facilities. Greens Restaurant offers international cuisine with local ingredients served in an elegant atmosphere and the Coach House Brasserie is perfect for the more informal occasion overlooking the 18 hole parkland golf course. Please enquire about Facilities for Persons with Mobility Impairment.

Member of Radisson SAS Hotels & Resorts

***Bookable on www.irelandhotels.com***
***Special Offer: www.irelandhotels.com/offers***

***B&B from £60.00 to £80.00***

*John O' Carroll*

118

*Activities:*

**Open All Year**

## Ardtara Country House

GUESTHOUSE ★★★★ MAP 14 N 19

8 Gorteade Rd, Upperlands,
Maghera,
Co. Londonderry BT46 5SA

Tel: 028-7964 4490 Fax: 028-7964 5080
Email: valerie_ferson@ardtara.com
Web: www.ardtara.com

Ardtara is a charming and substantial 19th century house, located in the little village of Upperlands in the south of Londonderry. Ardtara is a splendid Victorian house full of atmosphere and character, where the warmth of your surroundings will be matched only by the warmth of the welcome, and the high quality of our restaurant which has been awarded 2 AA rosettes. Please enquire about Facilities for Persons with Mobility Impairment.

Member of Ireland's Blue Book

***B&B from £65.00 to £75.00***

*Valerie Ferson*
*General Manager*

9

**Open All Year**

## Portstewart / Bangor

### Anchorage Inn (The)

GUESTHOUSE ★★★ MAP 14 M 21

87-89 The Promenade,
Portstewart,
Co. Londonderry BT55 7AG

Tel: 028-7083 2003 Fax: 028-7083 4508
Email: info@theanchorbar.co.uk
Web: www.theanchorbar.co.uk

Situated within easy access to Portstewart's picturesque promenade and all of the town's amenities. The Anchorage Inn has twenty newly re-furbished modern en suite bedrooms which offer contempory comfortable & relaxed accommodation. It also has a state of the art conference suite & The Inn is known throughout Ireland for its convivial atmosphere, friendliness, fantastic live entertainment, great food and great Guinness. We are also close to all major attractions & great golf courses. Please enquire about Facilities for Persons with Mobility Impairment.

***B&B from £37.50 to £45.00***

*Danny Coyles*
*General Manager*

20

*Activities:*

**Closed 25 - 26 December**

### Clandeboye Lodge Hotel

HOTEL ★★★★ MAP 15 Q 18

10 Estate Road,
Bangor,
Co. Down BT19 1UR

Tel: 028-9185 2500 Fax: 028-9185 2772
Email: info@clandeboyelodge.co.uk
Web: www.clandeboyelodge.com

With its tranquil location adjacent to the historic Clandeboye Estate and sweeping fairways of Blackwood Golf Centre, just 15 minutes from Belfast city centre, the 4**** Clandeboye Lodge Hotel offers an innovative contemporary style, gracious hospitality and exacting service standards. 43 recently refurbished standard and executive guestrooms, with LCD wide screen TVs and DVD library, extensive dining options for a relaxing night in the Lodge Restaurant & Lobby Bar, both noted for outstanding cuisine. Free wireless internet access and access to business suite.

Member of Belfast Visitor & Convention Bureau

***Bookable on www.irelandhotels.com***
***Special Offer: www.irelandhotels.com/offers***

***B&B from £55.00 to £75.00***
***Suites from £120.00 to £175.00***

*Pim Dalm*
*Proprietor*

43

**Closed 24 - 27 December**

### Shelleven House

GUESTHOUSE ★★★ MAP 15 Q 18

61 Princetown Road,
Bangor,
Co. Down BT20 3TA

Tel: 028-9127 1777 Fax: 028-9127 1777
Email: shellevenhouse@aol.com
Web: www.shellevenhouse.com

Victorian townhouse with great charm, providing luxurious accommodation in a warm, relaxing atmosphere. Situated in a quiet conservation area of Bangor, close to the Marina, the Promenade and the town centre, Shelleven is set back from the road with gardens and private parking to the front. 11 en suite rooms, some with sea views. Train/bus station 5 minutes away, with direct link to Dublin service and to Belfast City Airport. Several golf courses nearby. Top rating of 4**** from AA. Please enquire about Facilities for Persons with Mobility Impairment.

Member of Kingdoms of Down

***B&B from £35.00 to £40.00***

*Mary Weston*

11

**Open All Year**



B&B Rates are per Person Sharing per Night incl. Breakfast.
or Room Rates are per Room per Night - **See also Page 8**

## Old Inn (The)

HOTEL ★★★ MAP 15 Q 18

15 - 19 Main Street,
Crawfordsburn,
Co. Down BT19 1JH

Tel: 028-9185 3255 Fax: 028-9185 2775

Email: info@theoldinn.com

Web: www.theoldinn.com

Situated in the village of Crawfordsburn beside Crawfordsburn Country Park and only 9 miles from Belfast City centre, this picturesque hotel, complete with thatched roof, is the perfect location from which to explore. Popular for tourists, families and couples staying on a short break or over - night stay. The Old Inn offers superbly decorated feature bedrooms, excellent cuisine and the warmest of welcomes. "2007 Hotel of The Year" as awarded by the Northern Ireland Tourist Board. Please enquire about Facilities for Persons with Mobility Impairment.

***B&B from £52.50 to £52.50***
***Suites from £150.00 to £150.00***

*Brendan McCann*
*General Manager*

31

**Closed 25 December**

## Burrendale Hotel and Country Club

HOTEL ★★★ MAP 12 P 16

51 Castlewellan Road,
Newcastle,
Co. Down BT33 0JY

Tel: 028-4372 2599 Fax: 028-4372 2328

Email: reservations@burrendale.com

Web: www.burrendale.com

At the foot of the Mournes, the Burrendale is the ideal location for your family or golfing holiday, short break. The hotel comprises a Country Club, Health & Beauty Clinic, à la carte Vine Restaurant, bistro style Cottage Kitchen Restaurant, Cottage Bar and excellent banqueting / conference facilities. In close proximity are 15 golf courses including Royal County Down, golden beaches, nature walks, forest parks and pony trekking. Superb hospitality awaits you.

***B&B from £60.00 to £75.00***
***Suites from £150.00 to £150.00***

*Denis Orr*
*General Manager*

69

*Activities:*

**Open All Year**

## Canal Court Hotel

HOTEL ★★★★ MAP 12 O 15

Merchants Quay,
Newry,
Co. Down BT35 8HF

Tel: 028-3025 1234 Fax: 028-3025 1177

Email: manager@canalcourthotel.com

Web: www.canalcourthotel.com

This fabulous 4 star hotel is located in the heart of Newry City. The perfect location for a special break. With 112 beautiful bedrooms and suites and an extensive leisure complex, it is the ideal location to relax and unwind. Enjoy the shopping opportunities or visit the wealth of visitor and tourist attractions this city has to offer. Great weekend and midweek breaks available and guests can book online for all packages. This wonderful hotel has won many awards including Best Customer Service for 2 consecutive years, Eat Safe Award and NITB Hotel of the Year award twice also.

***Bookable on www.irelandhotels.com***
***Special Offer: www.irelandhotels.com/offers***

***B&B from £65.00 to £90.00***
***Suites from £150.00 to £300.00***

*Michelle Barrett*
*General Manager*

112

*Activities:*

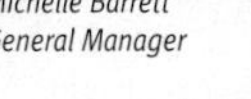

**Closed 25 December**

## Belcoo / Enniskillen

### Customs House Country Inn

GUESTHOUSE ★★★★ MAP 11 J 16

25 - 27 Main Street,
Belcoo,
Co. Fermanagh BT93 5FB
Tel: 028-6638 6285 Fax: 028-6638 6936
Email: info@customshouseinn.com
Web: www.customshouseinn.com

Situated in the award-winning village of Belcoo, overlooking Lough McNean, is The Customs House Country Inn. A visit to the Customs House will not disappoint with luxurious accommodation, cuisine that excels and service that emphasises the personal atmosphere of this family-run inn. Marble Arch Caves, Belleek Pottery and Florencecourt House are close by. Ideal for golfing, walking, cycling and fishing. AA♦♦♦♦, RAC♦♦♦♦ and RAC Dining Award plus RAC Warm Welcome Award.

*Bookable on www.irelandhotels.com*
*Special Offer: www.irelandhotels.com/offers*

**B&B from £40.00 to £50.00**

*John Roche*
*General Manager*
9

**Closed 24 - 27 December**

### Killyhevlin Hotel

HOTEL ★★★★ MAP 11 K 16

Killyhevlin,
Enniskillen,
Co. Fermanagh BT74 6RW
Tel: 028-6632 3481 Fax: 028-6632 4726
Email: info@killyhevlin.com
Web: www.killyhevlin.com

Killyhevlin Hotel and chalets are situated on the shores of scenic Lough Erne yet only 1km from the historic town of Enniskillen. All 70 spacious bedrooms, including suites, have been finished to an exceptional standard. Silks Restaurant and the Boathouse Grill offer a wide variety of menus daily. The Health Club and Elemis Spa are complete with pool, gym, outdoor hot tub and four treatment suites. Broadband Internet access available throughout the hotel. Please enquire about Facilities for Persons with Mobility Impairment.

Member of Irish Country Hotels

*Bookable on www.irelandhotels.com*
*Special Offer: www.irelandhotels.com/offers*

**B&B from £65.00 to £75.00**
**Suites from £185.00 to £225.00**

*Rodney J. Watson*
*Managing Director*
70

**Closed 24 - 26 December**

### Lough Erne Golf Resort

HOTEL MAP 11 K 16

Belleek Road,
Enniskillen,
Co. Fermanagh BT93 7ED
Tel: 028-6632 0613 Fax: 028-6632 0613
Email: info@loughernegolfresort.com
Web: www.loughernegolfresort.com

Built to a 4**** specification. Located on a peninsula of breathtaking scenery, the resort is one of Europe's most anticipated developments, offering guests a unique experience. The resort has a total of 120 bedrooms, including lodges, and Thai Spa offering the ultimate in relaxation. The Nick Faldo-designed championship golf course opens late 2008. "I've played golf on every continent and I can honestly say that I am overwhelmed by the location and beauty of The Lough Erne Golf Resort". Please enquire about Facilities for Persons with Mobility Impairment.

Member of Preferred Hotel Group

**B&B from £50.00 to £80.00**
**Suites from £200.00 to £260.00**

*Penny Thornberry*
*Director of Sales & Marketing*
95

Activities:

**Closed 24 - 26 December**



B&B Rates are per Person Sharing per Night incl. Breakfast.
or Room Rates are per Room per Night - **See also Page 8**

## Mahons Hotel

HOTEL ★★★ MAP 13 K 17

Enniskillen Road,
Irvinestown,
Co. Fermanagh BT94 1GS

Tel: 028-6862 1656 Fax: 028-6862 8344

Email: info@mahonshotel.co.uk

Web: www.mahonshotel.co.uk

Situated in the heart of the Fermanagh Lakeland. Ideal for visiting all major tourist attractions: Belleek Pottery 20 mins, Marble Arch Caves 30 mins, Necarne Equestrian Centre 5 mins, Lough Erne 5 mins, Donegal 20 mins. All rooms en suite, TV, tea making facilities. Bushmills Bar of the Year winner, entertainment at weekends, private car park. Family-run since 1883. Visit us in our third century. Cycling, horse riding, tennis & golf all available. Hotel has been upgraded to three star NITB and AA. Bedrooms have modem access, DVD and WiFi. Please enquire about Facilities for Persons with Mobility Impairment.

Member of Fermanagh Lakeland Hotels

**B&B from £42.50 to £55.00**

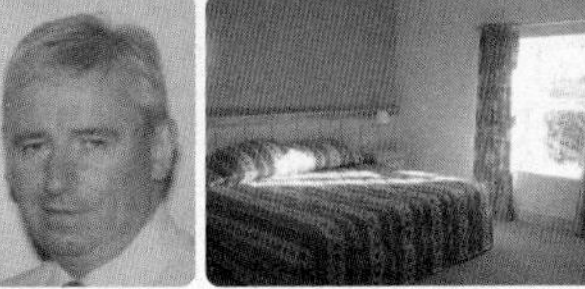

*Joe Mahon*
*Manager*

15

Activities:

**Closed 25 - 26 December**

## Corick House & Licensed Restaurant

GUESTHOUSE ★★★ MAP 14 L 17

20 Corick Rd,
Clogher,
Co. Tyrone BT76 0BZ

Tel: 028-8554 8216 Fax: 028-8554 9531

Email: reservations@corickcountryhouse.com

Web: www.corickcountryhouse.com

The only privately owned and managed 17th century country house with extensive gardens in Mid-Ulster. Meander through the walled garden and manicured lawns and savour the beauty of the Clogher Valley. Close to many tourist attractions for sightseeing and 8-mile fishing rights in River Blackwater. Carleton Licensed Restaurant: Major industry awards for imaginative menus, good service and hospitality, complemented by our Blackwater Bar and Conservatory. Garden Suite: Conference/private events for 200 delegates. Wedding Receptions at affordable prices.

**B&B from £55.00 to £60.00**

*Jean Beacom*
*Proprietor*

19

Activities:

**Open All Year**

## Tullylagan Country House Hotel

HOTEL ★★ MAP 14 M 18

40b Tullylagan Road,
Cookstown,
Co. Tyrone BT80 8UP

Tel: 028-8676 5100 Fax: 028-8676 1715

Email: info@tullylagan.com

Web: www.tullylagan.com

This 19th century style manor is set in 30 acres of mature grounds and plantation, situated in the heart of Mid-Ulster. The rural setting lends itself to being the ideal place for a relaxing meal, short breaks, venue for a wedding or a business conference. This family-run hotel offers 15 en suite country style bedrooms. The hotel restaurant with its warm & relaxed atmosphere, offers high quality food and friendly service in gracious surroundings. A welcome addition to the estate is our newly opened wine bar. Certainly worth a visit! Suites available upon request. Taste of Ulster 2007 award.

Member of The Good Food Circle

**B&B from £55.00 to £75.00**

*Adrian & Paul Martin*
*Proprietors*

15

**Closed 24 - 27 December**

B&B Rates are per Person Sharing per Night incl. Breakfast.
or Room Rates are per Room per Night - See also Page 8

## Fivemiletown / Omagh

### Valley Hotel (The)

HOTEL ★★ MAP 14 L 16

60 Main St,
Fivemiletown,
Co. Tyrone BT75 0PW
Tel: 028-8952 1505 Fax: 028-8952 1688
Email: info@thevalleyhotel.com
Web: www.thevalleyhotel.com

This magnificent family-run hotel has just been awarded the prestigious AA three star rating. The hotel boasts 22 newly refurbished bedrooms to include trouser press & Iron Board, Complimentary Broadband, 30 inch flat screen TV and hairdryer. On the ground floor guests are entertained with 2 bars with contrasting themes, "Flavour of Tyrone" recommended restaurant and entertainment for guest every weekend in our bar. Please enquire about Facilities for Persons with Mobility Impairment.

*Bookable on www.irelandhotels.com*
*Special Offer: www.irelandhotels.com/offers*

***B&B from £45.00 to £55.00***
***Suites from £90.00 to £100.00***

*Greg Williamson*
*General Manager*

22

**Closed 25 December**

### Silverbirch Hotel

HOTEL ★★★ MAP 14 L 18

5 Gortin Road,
Omagh,
Co. Tyrone BT79 7DH
Tel: 028-8224 2520 Fax: 028-8224 9061
Email: info@silverbirchhotel.com
Web: www.silverbirchhotel.com

Hotel is located on outskirts of Omagh on the B48 leading to the Gortin Glens, Sperrins and the Ulster American Folk Park. Set in its own spacious and mature grounds, the hotel has 40 bedrooms furnished to a 3*** standard. Other facilities include a newly refurbished Bar & Restaurant and also a new Business Centre complimenting our existing banqueting facilities. Now book online via our website providing a secure real-time booking with automated confirmation. Please enquire about Facilities for Persons with Mobility Impairment.

***B&B from £42.50 to £51.00***

*Allan Duncan*
*Manager*

40

**Closed 25 December**

B&B Rates are per Person Sharing per Night incl. Breakfast.
or Room Rates are per Room per Night - See also Page 8

We invite you to sample the golf, the countryside and the friendship of the Irish people and then to stay in some of Ireland's most charming accommodation. We have listed a range of hotels and guesthouses which are either situated on or close to a golf course. Your host will assist you if necessary in arranging your golfing requirements including tee reservations and green fee charges. A full description of the hotels and guesthouses can be had by looking up the appropriate page number. ***Premises are listed in Alphabetical Order in each County.***

# Ireland West

## Co. Clare

### Aran View House Hotel & Restaurant
Doolin, Co. Clare
Tel: 065-707 4061 ....................Page 39
**Arrangements with Golf Courses:**
*Lahinch Links Course, Lahinch Castle Course, Doonbeg Greg Norman Course, Woodstock, Ennis Golf Club*
**Green Fees From:** *€150.00*
**Facilities available:**
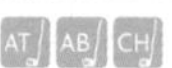


### Atlantic Hotel
Lahinch, Co. Clare
Tel: 065-708 1049 ....................Page 47
**Arrangements with Golf Courses:**
*Lahinch Golf Course, Doonbeg, Spanish Point, Kilkee, Kilrush*
**Green Fees From:** *€35.00*
**Facilities available:**

### Ballinalacken Castle Country House & Restaurant
Doolin, Co. Clare
Tel: 065-707 4025 ....................Page 39
**Arrangements with Golf Courses:**
*Lahinch, Lahinch Castle, Woodstock, Galway Bay, Dromoland Castle, Doonbeg*
**Facilities available:**

### Bellbridge House Hotel
Milltown Malbay, Co. Clare
Tel: 065-708 4038 ....................Page 52
**Arrangements with Golf Courses:**
*Spanish Point, Lahinch, Doonbeg, Kilkee, Kilrush*
**Green Fees From:** *€30.00*
**Facilities available:**

### Best Western West County Hotel
Ennis, Co. Clare
Tel: 065-682 8421 ....................Page 42
**Arrangements with Golf Courses:**
*Ennis Golf Course*
**Facilities available:**

### Bunratty Manor Hotel
Bunratty, Co. Clare
Tel: 061-707984 ......................Page 38
**Arrangements with Golf Courses:**
*Dromoland, Adare Manor, Shannon, Lahinch, Doonbeg, Ballybunion*
**Green Fees From:** *€55.00*
**Facilities available:**

### Dough Mor Lodge
Lahinch, Co. Clare
Tel: 065-708 2063 ....................Page 47
**Arrangements with Golf Courses:**
*Lahinch Golf Club (36 holes), Doonbeg Golf Club, Kilrush, Kilkee, East Clare, Shannon, Dromoland Castle*
**Facilities available:**

### Greenbrier Inn Guesthouse
Lahinch, Co. Clare
Tel: 065-708 1242 ....................Page 47
**Arrangements with Golf Courses:**
*Lahinch Championship Links, Lahinch Castle Links, Doonbeg Championship Links, Woodstock (Ennis), Dromoland Castle GC*
**Green Fees From:** *€50.00*
**Facilities available:**

### Grovemount House
Ennistymon, Co. Clare
Tel: 065-707 1431 ....................Page 44
**Arrangements with Golf Courses:**
*Lahinch, Spanish Point, Doonbeg, Ennis, Dromoland*
**Green Fees From:** *€50.00*
**Facilities available:**
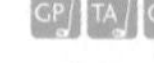

### Halpin's Townhouse Hotel
Kilkee, Co. Clare
Tel: 065-905 6032 ....................Page 45
**Arrangements with Golf Courses:**
*Ballybunion, Lahinch, Kilkee, Doonbeg, Woodstock, Shannon*
**Green Fees From:** *€40.00*
**Facilities available:**

### Kilkee Bay Hotel
Kilkee, Co. Clare
Tel: 065-906 0060 ....................Page 45
**Arrangements with Golf Courses:**
*Kilkee, Kilrush, Lahinch, Doonbeg*
**Green Fees From:** *€15.00*
**Facilities available:**

### Lahinch Golf & Leisure Hotel
Lahinch, Co. Clare
Tel: 065-708 1100 ....................Page 48
**Arrangements with Golf Courses:**
*Lahinch Golf Course, Doonbeg Golf Course*
**Green Fees From:** *€50.00*
**Facilities available:**

### Lynch Clare Inn & Suites
Ennis, Co. Clare
Tel: 061-368 161........................Page 42
**Arrangements with Golf Courses:**
*Ennis GC, Woodstock GC*
**Facilities available:**

### Mountshannon Hotel
Mountshannon, Co. Clare
Tel: 061-927162........................Page 52
**Arrangements with Golf Courses:**
*Bodyke - East Clare Golf Club, Portumna*
**Green Fees From:** *€25.00*
**Facilities available:**

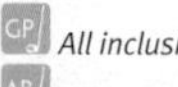
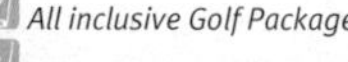
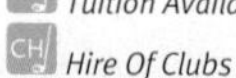
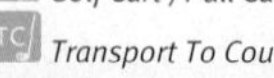
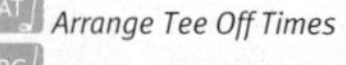

GP *All inclusive Golf Package* · TA *Tuition Available* · GC *Golf Cart / Pull Cart* · AT *Arrange Tee Off Times* · HC *Hire Of Caddy*
AB *Advance Golf Booking Made* · CH *Hire Of Clubs* · TC *Transport To Course* · PG *Preferential Green Fees*

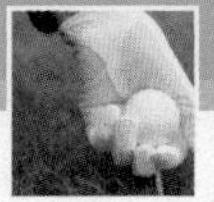

**Oakwood Arms Hotel**
Shannon Airport, Co. Clare
Tel: 061-361500 ........................Page 53
**Arrangements with Golf Courses:**
*Shannon Golf Club, Dromoland Golf Club*
**Green Fees From:** *€50.00*
**Facilities available:**

**Old Ground Hotel**
Ennis, Co. Clare
Tel: 065-682 8127 ....................Page 43
**Arrangements with Golf Courses:**
*Doonbeg, Lahinch, Woodstock, Ennis, Dromoland, Shannon, East Clare*
**Green Fees From:** *€25.00*
**Facilities available:**

**Sancta Maria Hotel**
Lahinch, Co. Clare
Tel: 065-708 1041 ....................Page 48
**Arrangements with Golf Courses:**
*Lahinch Championship Golf Links, Lahinch Castle, Doonbeg, Woodstock, Dromoland, Spanish Point*
**Green Fees From:** *€40.00*
**Facilities available:**

**Temple Gate Hotel**
Ennis, Co. Clare
Tel: 065-682 3300 ....................Page 43
**Arrangements with Golf Courses:**
*Woodstock, Ennis, Lahinch, East Clare, Doonbeg, Dromoland*
**Facilities available:**

**Vaughan Lodge and Seafood Restaurant**
Lahinch, Co. Clare
Tel: 065-708 1111 ....................Page 49
**Arrangements with Golf Courses:**
*Lahinch, Doonbeg, Spanish Point, Dromoland, Kilrush, Ennis*
**Green Fees From:** *€160.00*
**Facilities available:**

## Co. Donegal

**Arnolds Hotel**
Dunfanaghy, Co. Donegal
Tel: 074-913 6208 ....................Page 60
**Arrangements with Golf Courses:**
*Dunfanaghy 18 Hole Links, Cloughaneely 9 Hole, Parkland, Rosapenna 36 Hole Links, Cruit Island 9 Hole Links, Portsalon 18 Hole Links, Letterkenny 18 Hole Parkland*
**Green Fees From:** *€26.00*
**Facilities available:**

GP GC AT AB CH TC PG HC

**Ballyliffin Lodge & Spa**
Ballyliffin, Co. Donegal
Tel: 074-937 8200 ....................Page 56
**Arrangements with Golf Courses:**
*Ballyliffin Golf Club*
**Facilities available:**

**Carlton Redcastle Hotel & C Spa**
Moville, Co. Donegal
Tel: 074-938 5555 ....................Page 66
**Golf Course(s) On Site:**
*9 Hole Golf Course*
**Arrangements with Golf Courses:**
*Ballyliffin, Greencastle, Castlerock, Portstewart, Royal Portrush*
**Green Fees From:** *€20.00*
**Facilities available:**

**Castle Grove Country House Hotel**
Letterkenny, Co. Donegal
Tel: 074-915 1118 ....................Page 63
**Arrangements with Golf Courses:**
*Portsalon, Letterkenny, Rosapenna, Ballyliffin*
**Green Fees From:** *€50.00*
**Facilities available:**

GP GC AT AB CH PG HC

**Dorrians Imperial Hotel**
Ballyshannon, Co. Donegal
Tel: 071-985 1147 ....................Page 56
**Arrangements with Golf Courses:**
*Murvagh (Donegal), Bundoran*
**Green Fees From:** *€50.00*
**Facilities available:**

TA GC AT AB CH PG HC

**Downings Bay Hotel**
Letterkenny, Co. Donegal
Tel: 074-915 5586 ....................Page 63
**Arrangements with Golf Courses:**
*Rosapenna Links, Dunfanaghy, Portsalon, Letterkenny*
**Green Fees From:** *€30.00*
**Facilities available:**

**Fort Royal Hotel**
Rathmullan, Co. Donegal
Tel: 074-915 8100 ....................Page 66
**Golf Course(s) On Site:**
*Par 3 Golf Course*
**Arrangements with Golf Courses:**
*Portsalon, Letterkenny, Otway*
**Green Fees From:** *€40.00*
**Facilities available:**

**Great Northern Hotel**
Bundoran, Co. Donegal
Tel: 071-984 1204 ....................Page 58
**Golf Course(s) On Site:**
*18 Hole Golf Course*
**Arrangements with Golf Courses:**
*Donegal, Strandhill, Rosses Point*
**Green Fees From:** *€30.00*
**Facilities available:**

**Highlands Hotel**
Glenties, Co. Donegal
Tel: 074-955 1111 ....................Page 61
**Arrangements with Golf Courses:**
*Narin Portnoo Golf Club*
**Green Fees From:** *€35.00*
**Facilities available:**

**Inishowen Gateway Hotel**
Buncrana, Co. Donegal
Tel: 074-936 1144 ....................Page 57
**Arrangements with Golf Courses:**
*Buncrana, North West Golf Course, Ballyliffin Old Course, Ballyliffin Glashedy Course*
**Green Fees From:** *€30.00*
**Facilities available:**

**Jackson's Hotel, Conference & Leisure Centre**
Ballybofey, Co. Donegal
Tel: 074-913 1021 ....................Page 54
**Arrangements with Golf Courses:**
*Ballybofey, Stranorlar, Murvagh, Donegal Town, Portsalon, Portnoo, Ballyliffin*
**Green Fees From:** *€25.00*
**Facilities available:**

GP *All inclusive Golf Package*
AB *Advance Golf Booking Made*
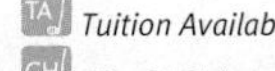
TA *Tuition Available*
CH *Hire Of Clubs*
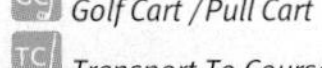
GC *Golf Cart / Pull Cart*
TC *Transport To Course*
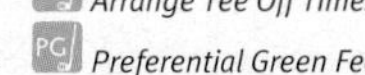
AT *Arrange Tee Off Times*
PG *Preferential Green Fees*
HC *Hire Of Caddy*

## Co. Donegal CONTINUED

**Lake House Hotel**
Portnoo, Co. Donegal
Tel: 074-954 5123 ....................Page 66
Arrangements with Golf Courses:
*Narin Portnoo Golf Club*
Green Fees From: *€30.00*
Facilities available:

**Malin Hotel**
Malin, Co. Donegal
Tel: 074-937 0606 ....................Page 65
Arrangements with Golf Courses:
*Ballyliffin Golf Club - Glashedy Links, The Old Course, Greencastle Golf Club, North West Golf Club*
Green Fees From: *€70.00*
Facilities available:

**McGrorys of Culdaff**
Culdaff, Co. Donegal
Tel: 074-937 9104 ....................Page 58
Arrangements with Golf Courses:
*Ballyliffin Golf Club*
Facilities available:

**Milford Inn Hotel**
Milford, Co. Donegal
Tel: 074-915 3313 ....................Page 65
Arrangements with Golf Courses:
*Portsalon, Rosapenna, Letterkenny, Dunfanaghy, Ballyliffin, Letterkenny*
Green Fees From: *€35.00*
Facilities available:

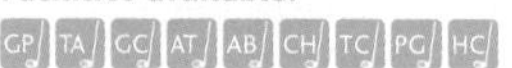

**Nesbitt Arms Hotel**
Ardara, Co. Donegal
Tel: 074-954 1103 ....................Page 54
Arrangements with Golf Courses:
*Narin, Portnoo, Murvagh*
Green Fees From: *€30.00*
Facilities available:

**Rosapenna Hotel and Golf Resort**
Downings, Co. Donegal
Tel: 074-915 5301 ....................Page 60
Golf Course(s) On Site:
*2 x 18 Hole Golf Courses*
Green Fees From: *€60.00*
Facilities available:
GP TA GC AT AB CH PG HC

**Sandhouse Hotel**
Rossnowlagh, Co. Donegal
Tel: 071-985 1777 ....................Page 67
Arrangements with Golf Courses:
*Donegal Murvagh, Bundoran, Rosses Point, Castle Hume, Ballyliffin, Portnoo*
Green Fees From: *€45.00*
Facilities available:
GP TA GC AT AB CH TC PG HC

**Waters Edge (The)**
Rathmullan, Co. Donegal
Tel: 074-915 8182 ....................Page 67
Arrangements with Golf Courses:
*Portsalon, Letterkenny, Rosapenna, Dunfanaghy, Ballyliffin*
Green Fees From: *€30.00*
Facilities available:

## Co. Galway

**Adare Guest House**
Galway City, Co. Galway
Tel: 091-582638 ....................Page 79
Arrangements with Golf Courses:
*Galway Bay, Oughterard*
Green Fees From: *€50.00*
Facilities available:

**Alcock and Brown Hotel**
Clifden, Co. Galway
Tel: 095-21206 ....................Page 73
Arrangements with Golf Courses:
*Connemara GC, Oughterard GC, Westport GC*
Green Fees From: *€35.00*
Facilities available:
TA GC AT AB CH PG HC

**Anno Santo Hotel**
Galway City, Co. Galway
Tel: 091-523011 ....................Page 79
Arrangements with Golf Courses:
*Glenlo, Athenry, Galway, Oughterard, Galway Bay, Barna*
Facilities available:
GP TA AB CH TC PG HC

**Ben View House**
Clifden, Co. Galway
Tel: 095-21256 ....................Page 74
Arrangements with Golf Courses:
*Connemara*
Green Fees From: *€60.00*
Facilities available:
AT AB CH TC

**Carlton Shearwater Hotel & C Spa**
Ballinasloe, Co. Galway
Tel: 0909-630400 ....................Page 70
Arrangements with Golf Courses:
*Ballinasloe, Portumna, Athlone, Glasson, Athenry*
Green Fees From: *€25.00*
Facilities available:
GP TA GC AT AB CH PG HC

**Cashel House Hotel**
Cashel, Co. Galway
Tel: 095-31001....................Page 72
Arrangements with Golf Courses:
*Ballyconneely (Clifden)*
Facilities available:
TA GC AT AB CH HC

**Connemara Country Lodge**
Clifden, Co. Galway
Tel: 095-22122 ....................Page 76
Arrangements with Golf Courses:
*Connemara GC, Ballyconneely, Hazel Wood, Oughterard, Westport*
Green Fees From: *€30.00*
Facilities available:

**Fairhill House Hotel**
Clonbur (An Fháirche), Co. Galway
Tel: 094-954 6176 ....................Page 78
Arrangements with Golf Courses:
*Ballinrobe 18 Hole GC (15 mins), Westport 18 Hole GC (25 mins), Claremorris 18 Hole GC (25 mins), Galway 18 Hole GC (40 mins)*
Green Fees From: *€30.00*
Facilities available:

**Galway Bay Hotel, Conference & Leisure Centre**
Galway City, Co. Galway
Tel: 091-520520 ....................Page 83
Arrangements with Golf Courses:
*Galway, Galway Bay, Athenry, Bearna, Gort, Connemara Championship Links, Oughterard Golf Course*
Green Fees From: *€35.00*
Facilities available:

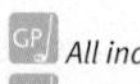 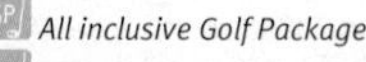 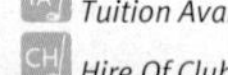 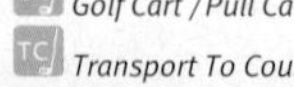 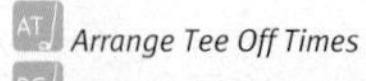

GP *All inclusive Golf Package* | TA *Tuition Available* | GC *Golf Cart / Pull Cart* | AT *Arrange Tee Off Times* | HC *Hire Of Caddy*
AB *Advance Golf Booking Made* | CH *Hire Of Clubs* | TC *Transport To Course* | PG *Preferential Green Fees*

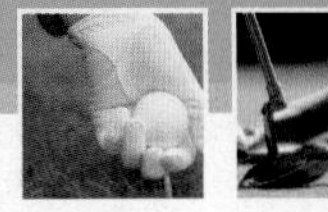

**Glenlo Abbey Hotel**
Galway City, Co. Galway
Tel: 091-526666 ........................ Page 84
Golf Course(s) On Site:
*18 Hole Golf Course*
Arrangements with Golf Courses:
*Glenlo Abbey, Galway, Bearna, Oughterard, Galway Bay, Connemara*
Green Fees From: *€20.00*
Facilities available:

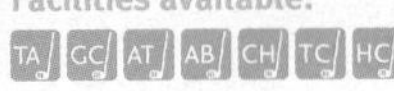

**Harbour Hotel**
Galway City, Co. Galway
Tel: 091-569466 ........................ Page 84
Arrangements with Golf Courses:
*Oughterrard, Barna Golf Club*
Green Fees From: *€25.00*
Facilities available:

**Inishmore Guesthouse**
Galway City, Co. Galway
Tel: 091-582639 ........................ Page 86
Arrangements with Golf Courses:
*Barna, Galway Bay, Oughterard, Athenry, Galway, Gort*
Green Fees From: *€35.00*
Facilities available:

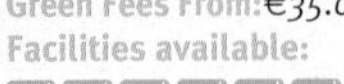

**Lady Gregory Hotel, Conference & Leisure Club**
Gort, Co. Galway
Tel: 091-632333 ........................ Page 92
Arrangements with Golf Courses:
*Gort*
Green Fees From: *€30.00*
Facilities available:

**O'Deas Hotel**
Loughrea, Co. Galway
Tel: 091-841611 ........................ Page 96
Arrangements with Golf Courses:
*Loughrea, Curragh, Gort, Galway Bay*
Green Fees From: *€20.00*
Facilities available:

**Raheen Woods Hotel & Spa**
Athenry, Co. Galway
Tel: 091-875888 ........................ Page 69
Arrangements with Golf Courses:
*Athenry Golf Club, Tuam Golf Club*
Green Fees From: *€30.00*
Facilities available:

**Rock Glen Country House Hotel**
Clifden, Co. Galway
Tel: 095-21035 ........................ Page 77
Arrangements with Golf Courses:
*Connemara GC*
Green Fees From: *€45.00*
Facilities available:

**Shannon Oaks Hotel & Country Club**
Portumna, Co. Galway
Tel: 090-974 1777 ........................ Page 98
Arrangements with Golf Courses:
*Portumna, Galway Bay, Birr, Glasson, Gort, Lahinch*
Green Fees From: *€25.00*
Facilities available:

**St. Clerans Manor House**
Craughwell, Co. Galway
Tel: 091-846555 ........................ Page 78
Arrangements with Golf Courses:
*Athenry, Lahinch, Gort, Loughrea, Doonbeg, Gregmore Golf Resort*
Green Fees From: *€30.00*
Facilities available:

**Westwood (The)**
Galway City, Co. Galway
Tel: 091-521442 ........................ Page 91
Arrangements with Golf Courses:
*Barna, Oughterard, Ballyconneely, Galway Bay Golf and Country Club, Galway Golf Club*
Facilities available:

## Co. Leitrim

**Flynns Shannon Key West Hotel**
Rooskey, Co. Leitrim
Tel: 071-963 8800 ........................ Page 104
Arrangements with Golf Courses:
*Longford, Carrick-on-Shannon, Roscommon*
Green Fees From: *€30.00*
Facilities available:

**Kilbrackan Arms Hotel**
Carrigallen, Co. Leitrim
Tel: 049-433 9737 ........................ Page 102
Arrangements with Golf Courses:
*Slieve Russell, Cavan, Longford, Ballinamore, Carrick-on-Shannon, Sligo*
Green Fees From: *€20.00*
Facilities available:

**Lough Rynn Castle**
Mohill, Co. Leitrim
Tel: 071-963 2700 ........................ Page 103
Golf Course(s) On Site:
*9 Hole Golf Course*
Arrangements with Golf Courses:
*Carrick-on-Shannon*
Green Fees From: *€30.00*
Facilities available:

## Co. Limerick

**Adare Manor Hotel & Golf Resort**
Adare, Co. Limerick
Tel: 061-396566 ........................ Page 104
Golf Course(s) On Site:
*18 Hole Golf Course*
Green Fees From: *€75.00*
Facilities available:

**Carriage House (The)**
Limerick City, Co. Limerick
Tel: 061-396566 ........................ Page 106
Golf Course(s) On Site:
*18 Hole Golf Course*
Green Fees From: *€75.00*
Facilities available:

**Courtenay Lodge Hotel**
Newcastle West, Co. Limerick
Tel: 069-62244 ........................ Page 112
Arrangements with Golf Courses:
*Newcastle West, Adare Manor Golf & Country Club, Adare Golf Club, Ballybunion, Charleville, Dingle (Ceann Sibeal)*
Green Fees From: *€35.00*
Facilities available:

**Fitzgeralds Woodlands House Hotel, Health and Leisure Spa**
Adare, Co. Limerick
Tel: 061-605100 ........................ Page 105
Arrangements with Golf Courses:
*Adare Manor Golf Club, Adare Golf Club, Newcastle West, Charleville, Limerick County Golf Club, Castletroy Golf Club*
Green Fees From: *€32.00*
Facilities available:

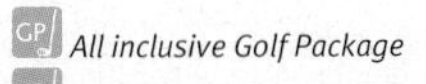
*GP All inclusive Golf Package*

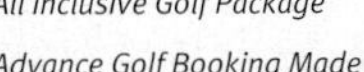
*AB Advance Golf Booking Made*

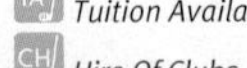
*TA Tuition Available*
*CH Hire Of Clubs*

*GC Golf Cart / Pull Cart*
*TC Transport To Course*

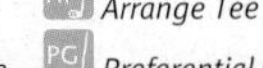
*AT Arrange Tee Off Times*
*PG Preferential Green Fees*

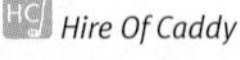
*HC Hire Of Caddy*

## Co. Limerick CONTINUED

### George Boutique Hotel (The)
Limerick City, Co. Limerick
Tel: 065-682 3000 ..................Page 108
Arrangements with Golf Courses:
*Adare Manor Hotel Golf Course, Limerick Golf & Country Club, Limerick Golf Club*
Facilities available:

### Lynch South Court And Suites
Limerick City, Co. Limerick
Tel: 061-487487 ......................Page 110
Arrangements with Golf Courses:
*Adare Manor Hotel Golf Club, Limerick Golf Club*
Facilities available:

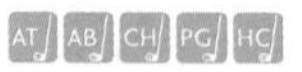

### Radisson SAS Hotel & Spa
Limerick City, Co. Limerick
Tel: 061-456200 ......................Page 111
Arrangements with Golf Courses:
*Shannon Golf Club, Dromoland Golf Club, Adare Golf Club, Doonbeg, Lahinch*
Green Fees From: *€35.00*
Facilities available:

### Rathkeale House Hotel
Rathkeale, Co. Limerick
Tel: 069-63333........................Page 113
Arrangements with Golf Courses:
*Adare, Adare Manor, Newcastle West, Charleville, Ballybunion*
Green Fees From: *€35.00*
Facilities available:

## Co. Mayo

### Ashford Castle
Cong, Co. Mayo
Tel: 094-954 6003 ..................Page 119
Golf Course(s) On Site:
*9 Hole Golf Course*
Arrangements with Golf Courses:
*Ballyconneely GC, Ballinrobe GC, Galway Bay GC, Rosses Point GC, Enniscrone GC, Westport GC*
Green Fees From: *€60.00*
Facilities available:

### Breaffy International Sports Hotel
Castlebar, Co. Mayo
Tel: 094-9022033 ....................Page 117
Arrangements with Golf Courses:
*Castle Golf Course*
Facilities available:

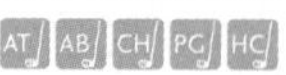

### Carlton Atlantic Coast Hotel
Westport, Co. Mayo
Tel: 098-29000 ......................Page 124
Arrangements with Golf Courses:
*Ballinrobe, Westport, Castlebar*
Green Fees From: *€20.00*
Facilities available:

### Castlecourt Hotel Conference and Leisure Centre
Westport, Co. Mayo
Tel: 098-55088 ......................Page 125
Arrangements with Golf Courses:
*Westport, Ballinrobe, Castlebar, Belmullet, Clew Bay, Enniscrone*
Green Fees From: *€30.00*
Facilities available:

### Clew Bay Hotel
Westport, Co. Mayo
Tel: 098-28088 ......................Page 125
Arrangements with Golf Courses:
*Westport, Castlebar, Ballinrobe, Belmullet, Enniscrone, Claremorris, Clew Bay, Ballyglass*
Green Fees From: *€25.00*
Facilities available:

### Downhill House Hotel & Eagles Leisure Club
Ballina, Co. Mayo
Tel: 096-21033 ........................Page 114
Arrangements with Golf Courses:
*Ballina, Enniscrone, Carne (Belmullet), Rosses Point, Strandhill, Westport, Claremorris, Ballinrobe, Castlebar, Tubbercurry, Swinford*
Green Fees From: *€35.00*
Facilities available:

### Healys Restaurant & Country House
Pontoon, Co. Mayo
Tel: 094-925 6443 ..................Page 122
Arrangements with Golf Courses:
*Castlebar, Ballina, Westport, Enniscrone, Carne, Swinford, Ballinrobe, Mulranny, Belmullet, Rosses Point, Strandhill*
Green Fees From: *€50.00*
Facilities available:

### Hotel Westport leisure - spa - conference
Westport, Co. Mayo
Tel: 098-25122........................Page 126
Arrangements with Golf Courses:
*Westport, Castlebar, Ballinrobe, Carne (Belmullet), Enniscrone, Clew Bay*
Green Fees From: *€25.00*
Facilities available:

### Kelly's Gateway Hotel
Swinford, Co. Mayo
Tel: 094-925 2156 ..................Page 123
Arrangements with Golf Courses:
*Swinford, Westport, Enniscrone, Ballinrobe, Claremorris, Carne*
Green Fees From: *€20.00*
Facilities available:

### Knockranny House Hotel & Spa
Westport, Co. Mayo
Tel: 098-28600 ......................Page 126
Arrangements with Golf Courses:
*Westport, Castlebar, Ballinrobe, Clew Bay, Mulranny*
Green Fees From: *€35.00*
Facilities available:

### Lynch Breaffy House Hotel And Spa
Castlebar, Co. Mayo
Tel: 094-902 2033 ..................Page 118
Arrangements with Golf Courses:
*Castlebar Golf Course*
Facilities available:

### McWilliam Park Hotel (The)
Claremorris, Co. Mayo
Tel: 094-937 3333 ..................Page 119
Arrangements with Golf Courses:
*Claremorris, Ballinrobe, Tuam*
Green Fees From: *€30.00*
Facilities available:

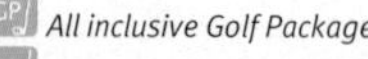
GP All inclusive Golf Package
AB Advance Golf Booking Made

TA Tuition Available
CH Hire Of Clubs
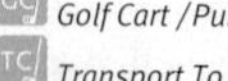
GC Golf Cart / Pull Cart
TC Transport To Course
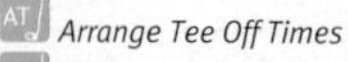
AT Arrange Tee Off Times
PG Preferential Green Fees
HC Hire Of Caddy

**Mount Falcon Country House Hotel**
Ballina, Co. Mayo
Tel: 096-74472 ........................ Page 115
Arrangements with Golf Courses:
*Enniscrone, Ballina, Carne, Rosses Point, Strandhill*
Green Fees From: *€55.00*
Facilities available:

**Ostán Oileán Acla**
Achill Island, Co. Mayo
Tel: 098-45138 ........................ Page 114
Arrangements with Golf Courses:
*Achill, Mulranny, Westport, Castlebar, Ballinrobe, Carne*
Green Fees From: *€15.00*
Facilities available:

**Park Inn Mulranny**
Mulranny, Co. Mayo
Tel: 098-36000 ...................... Page 122
Arrangements with Golf Courses:
*Westport, Carne, Ballinrobe, Mulranny*
Green Fees From: *€20.00*
Facilities available:

**Sea Rod Inn**
Belmullet, Co. Mayo
Tel: 097-86767 ........................ Page 116
Arrangements with Golf Courses:
*Carne, Belmullet, New Doohoma Par 3*
Green Fees From: *€50.00*
Facilities available:

**Western Strands Hotel**
Belmullet, Co. Mayo
Tel: 097-81096 ........................ Page 117
Arrangements with Golf Courses:
*Carne Golf Course*
Facilities available:

**Westport Plaza Hotel**
Westport, Co. Mayo
Tel: 098-51166 ........................ Page 127
Arrangements with Golf Courses:
*Westport, Ballinrobe, Belmullet, Clew Bay, Enniscrone, Castlebar*
Green Fees From: *€30.00*
Facilities available:

**Westport Woods Hotel & Spa**
Westport, Co. Mayo
Tel: 098-25811 ........................ Page 127
Arrangements with Golf Courses:
*Westport, Castlebar, Ballinrobe, Clew Bay, Carne (Belmullet)*
Green Fees From: *€25.00*
Facilities available:

**Wyatt Hotel**
Westport, Co. Mayo
Tel: 098-25027 ...................... Page 128
Arrangements with Golf Courses:
*Westport Golf Club, Castlebar Golf Club, Ballinrobe Golf Club, Carne Golf Links*
Green Fees From: *€20.00*
Facilities available:

## Co. Roscommon

**Abbey Hotel, Conference and Leisure Centre**
Roscommon Town, Co. Roscommon
Tel: 090-666 6200 .................. Page 129
Arrangements with Golf Courses:
*Glasson 18 hole, Carrick-on-Shannon 18 hole, Ballinasloe 18 hole, Longford 18 hole, Roscommon 18 hole*
Green Fees From: *€30.00*
Facilities available:

**Gleesons Townhouse & Restaurant**
Roscommon Town, Co. Roscommon
Tel: 090-662 6954 .................. Page 129
Arrangements with Golf Courses:
*Roscommon, Ballinasloe, Athlone, Carrick-on-Shannon, Longford, Glasson*
Green Fees From: *€25.00*
Facilities available:

**O'Gara's Royal Hotel**
Roscommon Town, Co. Roscommon
Tel: 090-662 6317 .................. Page 130
Arrangements with Golf Courses:
*Roscommon, Glasson, Longford, Athlone*
Green Fees From: *€30.00*
Facilities available:

## Co. Sligo

**Castle Dargan Golf Hotel Wellness**
Ballygawley, Co. Sligo
Tel: 071-911 8080 .................... Page 130
Golf Course(s) On Site:
*18 Hole Golf Course*
Green Fees From: *€40.00*
Facilities available:

**Glasshouse Hotel (The)**
Sligo Town, Co. Sligo
Tel: 071-919 4300.................... Page 133
Arrangements with Golf Courses:
*Enniscrone Golf Club, County Sligo Golf Club, Strandhill Golf Club*
Green Fees From: *€25.00*
Facilities available:

**Kingsfort Country House**
Ballintogher, Co. Sligo
Tel: 071-911 5111...................... Page 130
Arrangements with Golf Courses:
*Co. Sligo, Strandhill, Enniscrone, Murvagh, Bundoran, Castle Dargan*
Green Fees From: *€45.00*
Facilities available:

**Sligo City Hotel**
Sligo Town, Co. Sligo
Tel: 071-914 4000.................... Page 134
Arrangements with Golf Courses:
*Strandhill, Enniscrone, Rosses Point (Sligo), Murvagh, Bundoran (Donegal)*
Green Fees From: *€40.00*
Facilities available:

**Sligo Southern Hotel & Leisure Centre**
Sligo Town, Co. Sligo
Tel: 071-916 2101 .................... Page 134
Arrangements with Golf Courses:
*Rosses Point, Strandhill, Bundoran, Enniscrone*
Green Fees From: *€45.00*
Facilities available:

---

GP *All inclusive Golf Package* 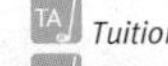 TA *Tuition Available*  GC *Golf Cart / Pull Cart*  AT *Arrange Tee Off Times* 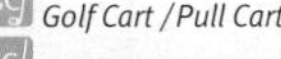 HC *Hire Of Caddy* 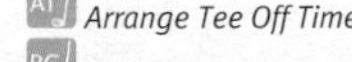
AB *Advance Golf Booking Made* CH *Hire Of Clubs* TC *Transport To Course* PG *Preferential Green Fees*

## Co. Sligo CONTINUED

**Yeats Country Hotel, Spa & Leisure Club**
Rosses Point, Co. Sligo
Tel: 071-917 7211 ....................Page 132
**Arrangements with Golf Courses:**
*Co. Sligo, Strandhill, Enniscrone, Bundoran, Castle Dargan*
**Facilities available:**
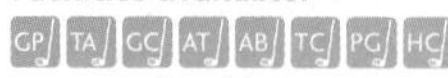

# Ireland South

## Co. Carlow

**Mount Wolseley Hotel Spa & Country Club**
Tullow, Co. Carlow
Tel: 059-918 0100....................Page 142
**Golf Course(s) On Site:**
*18 Hole Golf Course*
**Green Fees From:***€45.00*
**Facilities available:**
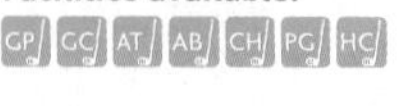

**Ramada Hotel & Suites at Killerig Golf Resort**
Carlow Town, Co. Carlow
Tel: 059-916 3050 ..................Page 140
**Golf Course(s) On Site:**
*18 Hole Golf Course*
**Arrangements with Golf Courses:**
*Kilkea Castle Golf Course, Mount Wolsley Tullow, Carlow Golf Course*
**Green Fees From:***€30.00*
**Facilities available:**

**Seven Oaks Hotel**
Carlow Town, Co. Carlow
Tel: 059-913 1308 ....................Page 141
**Arrangements with Golf Courses:**
*Mount Wolseley, Kilkea Castle, Killerig Castle, Carlow, Gowran Park*
**Facilities available:**

**Talbot Hotel Carlow**
Carlow Town, Co. Carlow
Tel: 059-915 3000....................Page 141
**Arrangements with Golf Courses:**
*Carlow Golf Club, Mount Juilet, Gowran, The Heritage*
**Green Fees From:***€60.00*
**Facilities available:**
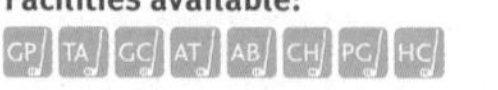

## Co. Cork

**Actons Hotel**
Kinsale, Co. Cork
Tel: 021-477 9900 ..................Page 166
**Arrangements with Golf Courses:**
*Kinsale, Old Head of Kinsale, Fota Island, Bandon, Harbour Point, Little Island*
**Green Fees From:***€30.00*
**Facilities available:**

**Ashlee Lodge**
Blarney, Co. Cork
Tel: 021-438 5346 ..................Page 147
**Arrangements with Golf Courses:**
*Lee Valley, Harbour Point, Fota Island, Muskerry, Cork, Mallow*
**Green Fees From:***€30.00*
**Facilities available:**

**Blarney Castle Hotel**
Blarney, Co. Cork
Tel: 021-438 5116 ....................Page 147
**Arrangements with Golf Courses:**
*Muskerry, Lee Valley, Fota Island, Harbour Point, Mallow, Monkstown, Blarney*
**Green Fees From:***€30.00*
**Facilities available:**
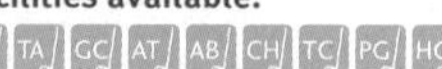

**Blarney Golf Resort**
Blarney, Co. Cork
Tel: 021-438 4477 ..................Page 147
**Golf Course(s) On Site:**
*18 Hole Golf Course*
**Arrangements with Golf Courses:**
*Lee Valley, Cork Club*
**Green Fees From:***€50.00*
**Facilities available:**

**Blue Haven Kinsale (The)**
Kinsale, Co. Cork
Tel: 021-477 2209 ..................Page 166
**Arrangements with Golf Courses:**
*Kinsale Golf Club, Old Head Golf Club*
**Green Fees From:***€50.00*
**Facilities available:**

**Capella Castlemartyr**
Castlemartyr, Co. Cork
Tel: 021-464 4050 ..................Page 149
**Golf Course(s) On Site:**
*18 Hole Golf Course*
**Facilities available:**

**Carlton Kinsale Hotel & C Spa**
Kinsale, Co. Cork
Tel: 021-470 6000 ..................Page 167
**Arrangements with Golf Courses:**
*Old Head of Kinsale, Ringenane Golf Course (9 Hole), Farrangalway Golf Course (18 Hole)*
**Green Fees From:***€45.00*
**Facilities available:**

**Casey's Hotel**
Glengarriff, Co. Cork
Tel: 027-63010........................Page 164
**Arrangements with Golf Courses:**
*Glengarriff GC*
**Facilities available:**

**Celtic Ross Hotel Conference & Leisure Centre**
Rosscarbery, Co. Cork
Tel: 023-48722 ......................Page 174
**Arrangements with Golf Courses:**
*Skibbereen, Bandon, Lisselan, Bantry, Kinsale, Dunmore*
**Facilities available:**

**Commodore Hotel**
Cobh, Co. Cork
Tel: 021-481 1277 ....................Page 152
**Arrangements with Golf Courses:**
*East Cork, Midleton - 18 Hole Course, Cobh - 9 Hole Course*
**Facilities available:**

**Dunmore House Hotel**
Clonakilty, Co. Cork
Tel: 023-33352 ......................Page 150
**Golf Course(s) On Site:**
*9 Hole Golf Course*
**Arrangements with Golf Courses:**
*Macroom, Bandon, Skibbereen, Old Head of Kinsale, The Island and Fota Island*
**Facilities available:**

**Emmet Hotel**
Clonakilty, Co. Cork
Tel: 023-33394 ......................Page 150
**Arrangements with Golf Courses:**
*Dunmore, Lisselan Estate, Bandon, Skibbereen*
**Facilities available:**

---

GP *All inclusive Golf Package*
AB *Advance Golf Booking Made*
TA *Tuition Available*
CH *Hire Of Clubs*
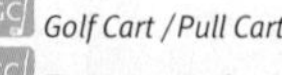
GC *Golf Cart / Pull Cart*
TC *Transport To Course*

AT *Arrange Tee Off Times*
PG *Preferential Green Fees*
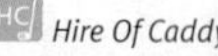
HC *Hire Of Caddy*

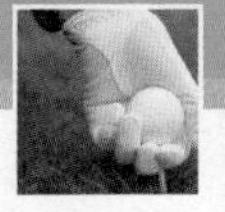

**Fernhill Carrigaline Hotel, Golf & Health Club**
Carrigaline, Co. Cork
Tel: 021-437 2226 ..................Page 149
**Golf Course(s) On Site:**
*18 Hole Golf Course*
**Arrangements with Golf Courses:**
*Douglas, Monkstown, Harbour Point, Kinsale - Old Head, Cork, Fota*
**Green Fees From:**€20.00
**Facilities available:**

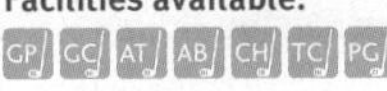

**Fitzgeralds Vienna Woods Hotel Cork**
Cork City, Co. Cork
Tel: 021-455 6800 ..................Page 157
**Arrangements with Golf Courses:**
*Cork, Fota Island, Old Head of Kinsale, Water Rock, Harbour Point, Mahon*
**Green Fees From:**€40.00
**Facilities available:**

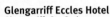

**Glengarriff Eccles Hotel**
Glengarriff, Co. Cork
Tel: 027-63003 ......................Page 165
**Arrangements with Golf Courses:**
*Bantry Bay, Glengarriff, Ring of Kerry*
**Green Fees From:**€30.00
**Facilities available:**

**Glengarriff Park Hotel**
Glengarriff, Co. Cork
Tel: 027-63000 ......................Page 165
**Arrangements with Golf Courses:**
*Bantry Bay, Glengarriff, Ring of Kerry, Kenmare Golf Club*
**Green Fees From:**€25.00
**Facilities available:**

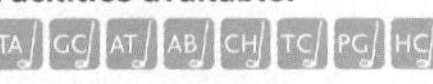

**Gresham Metropole**
Cork City, Co. Cork
Tel: 021-464 3789 ..................Page 158
**Arrangements with Golf Courses:**
*Fota Island, Little Island, Harbour Point, Muskerry, Kinsale*
**Facilities available:**

**Harbour Lodge**
Kinsale, Co. Cork
Tel: 021-477 2376 ..................Page 168
**Arrangements with Golf Courses:**
*Old Head of Kinsale, Fota Island, Little Island, Kinsale Golf Club, Faithlegg, Ballybunion*
**Facilities available:**

**Hayfield Manor Hotel**
Cork City, Co. Cork
Tel: 021-484 5900 ..................Page 158
**Arrangements with Golf Courses:**
*Harbour Point, Fota Island, Cork Golf Club, Old Head, Muskerry, Frankfield, Killarney Golf & Fishing, Douglas Golf Club*
**Green Fees From:**€35.00
**Facilities available:**

**Hibernian Hotel and Leisure Centre**
Mallow, Co. Cork
Tel: 022-58200 ......................Page 172
**Arrangements with Golf Courses:**
*Mallow, Lee Valley, Charleville, Fota Island, Kanturk, Blarney*
**Green Fees From:**€35.00
**Facilities available:**

**Hotel Isaacs**
Cork City, Co. Cork
Tel: 021-450 0011 ....................Page 159
**Arrangements with Golf Courses:**
*Lee Valley, Harbour Point, Cork Golf Club, Fota Golf Course*
**Facilities available:**

**Long Quay House**
Kinsale, Co. Cork
Tel: 021-477 4563 ..................Page 169
**Arrangements with Golf Courses:**
*Kinsale Golf Club, Old Head Golf Links, Ringenane Golf Club (Kinsale)*
**Green Fees From:**€30.00
**Facilities available:**

**Maryborough Hotel & Spa**
Cork City, Co. Cork
Tel: 021-436 5555....................Page 161
**Arrangements with Golf Courses:**
*Douglas, Fota Island, Cork, Kinsale Old Head, Harbour Point, Monkstown*
**Green Fees From:**€45.00
**Facilities available:**

**Midleton Park Hotel**
Midleton, Co. Cork
Tel: 021-463 5100....................Page 173
**Arrangements with Golf Courses:**
*Fota, Harbour Point, East Cork Golf Club, Water Rock Golf Club, Cork Golf Club, Lismore Golf Club*
**Green Fees From:**€35.00
**Facilities available:**

**Old Bank House**
Kinsale, Co. Cork
Tel: 021-477 4075 ..................Page 169
**Arrangements with Golf Courses:**
*Old Head of Kinsale, Kinsale - Farrangalway, Fota Golf Course, Cork Golf Club, Ballybunion, Waterville*
**Facilities available:**

**Oriel House Hotel, Leisure Club & Spa**
Ballincollig, Co. Cork
Tel: 021-420 8400 ..................Page 143
**Arrangements with Golf Courses:**
*Lee Valley, Killarney, Muskerry, Fota Island, Cork, Harbour Point*
**Green Fees From:**€30.00
**Facilities available:**

**Quality Hotel & Leisure Centre Clonakilty**
Clonakilty, Co. Cork
Tel: 023-36400 ......................Page 152
**Arrangements with Golf Courses:**
*Lisselan, Dunmore, Kinsale, Bandon, Skibbereen, Bantry*
**Green Fees From:**€25.00
**Facilities available:**

**Quality Hotel and Leisure Centre Youghal**
Youghal, Co. Cork
Tel: 024-93050 ......................Page 177
**Arrangements with Golf Courses:**
*Youghal, West Waterford, Dungarvan, Water Rock, Little Island, Fota*
**Green Fees From:**€25.00
**Facilities available:**

**Radisson SAS Hotel & Spa, Cork**
Cork City, Co. Cork
Tel: 021-429 7000 ..................Page 162
**Arrangements with Golf Courses:**
*Cork GC, Harbour Point GC*
**Green Fees From:**€35.00
**Facilities available:**

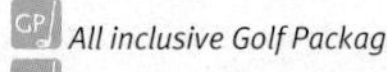

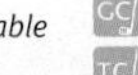
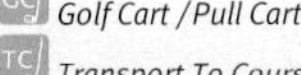
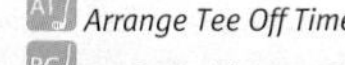

GP *All inclusive Golf Package* TA *Tuition Available* GC *Golf Cart / Pull Cart* AT *Arrange Tee Off Times* HC *Hire Of Caddy*
AB *Advance Golf Booking Made* CH *Hire Of Clubs* TC *Transport To Course* PG *Preferential Green Fees*

## Co. Cork CONTINUED

**Sheraton Fota Island Hotel & Spa (The)**
Fota Island, Co. Cork
Tel: 021-467 3000 ..................Page 164
**Golf Course(s) On Site:**
*18 Hole Golf Course*
*9 Hole Golf Course*
**Green Fees From:** *€62.00*
**Facilities available:**

**Trident Hotel**
Kinsale, Co. Cork
Tel: 021-477 9300 ..................Page 170
**Arrangements with Golf Courses:**
*Old Head Golf Links, Kinsale Golf Club, Lisselan Golf Club, Fota Island, Lee Valley*
**Green Fees From:** *€30.00*
**Facilities available:**

**Walter Raleigh Hotel**
Youghal, Co. Cork
Tel: 024-92011 ........................Page 177
**Arrangements with Golf Courses:**
*Youghal GC, Fota Island GC, Water Rock GC, West Waterford GC, Harbour Point GC, Little Island*
**Green Fees From:** *€30.00*
**Facilities available:**

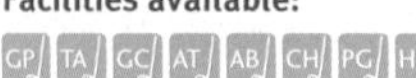

**WatersEdge Hotel**
Cobh, Co. Cork
Tel: 021-481 5566....................Page 152
**Arrangements with Golf Courses:**
*Fota Island, Harbour Point, Cobh, Water Rock, East Cork, Old Head of Kinsale, Cork*
**Green Fees From:** *€35.00*
**Facilities available:**

**West Cork Hotel**
Skibbereen, Co. Cork
Tel: 028-21277........................Page 176
**Arrangements with Golf Courses:**
*Skibbereen, West Carbery*
**Green Fees From:** *€25.00*
**Facilities available:**

**Westlodge Hotel**
Bantry, Co. Cork
Tel: 027-50360 ......................Page 146
**Arrangements with Golf Courses:**
*Bantry Bay Golf Club - guaranteed times, 18 hole Championship Course*
**Green Fees From:** *€45.00*
**Facilities available:**

**White House**
Kinsale, Co. Cork
Tel: 021-477 2125....................Page 170
**Arrangements with Golf Courses:**
*Kinsale (18 Hole) and (9 Hole), Old Head, Bandon, Carrigaline, Muskerry*
**Green Fees From:** *€25.00*
**Facilities available:**

## Co. Kerry

**Aghadoe Heights Hotel & Spa**
Killarney, Co. Kerry
Tel: 064-31766........................Page 193
**Arrangements with Golf Courses:**
*Waterville, Ballybunion, Kenmare, Killarney, Beaufort, Tralee, Dooks*
**Green Fees From:** *€80.00*
**Facilities available:**

**Arbutus Hotel**
Killarney, Co. Kerry
Tel: 064-31037........................Page 193
**Arrangements with Golf Courses:**
*Killarney, Ballybunion, Waterville, Dooks, Tralee, Ring of Kerry*
**Facilities available:**

**Ard-Na-Sidhe**
Caragh Lake, Co. Kerry
Tel: 066-976 9105 ..................Page 180
**Arrangements with Golf Courses:**
*Dooks, Killorglin, Waterville, Beaufort, Killarney, Tralee*
**Green Fees From:** *€80.00*
**Facilities available:**

**Ballygarry House Hotel & Spa**
Tralee, Co. Kerry
Tel: 066-712 3322 ..................Page 215
**Arrangements with Golf Courses:**
*Tralee, Castleisland, Ballybunion, Killarney, Listowel, Ballyheigue, Dooks*
**Green Fees From:** *€60.00*
**Facilities available:**

**Ballyroe Heights Hotel**
Tralee, Co. Kerry
Tel: 066-712 6796 ..................Page 215
**Arrangements with Golf Courses:**
*Barrow (Tralee Golf Club), Ardfert, Castleisland, Ballyheigue, Ballybunion*
**Green Fees From:** *€50.00*
**Facilities available:**

**Best Western Eviston House Hotel**
Killarney, Co. Kerry
Tel: 064-31640........................Page 194
**Arrangements with Golf Courses:**
*Killarney, Ballybunion, Beaufort, Waterville, Dooks, Tralee*
**Green Fees From:** *€50.00*
**Facilities available:**

**Bianconi**
Killorglin, Co. Kerry
Tel: 066-976 1146....................Page 212
**Arrangements with Golf Courses:**
*Killarney, Beaufort, Dunloe, Killorglin, Dooks, Waterville, Tralee, Ballybunion, Dingle*
**Green Fees From:** *€50.00*
**Facilities available:**

**Brehon (The)**
Killarney, Co. Kerry
Tel: 064-30700 ......................Page 194
**Arrangements with Golf Courses:**
*Ross, Beaufort, Dooks, Mahonys, Killeen, Lackabane (Killarney)*
**Green Fees From:** *€55.00*
**Facilities available:**

**Brookhaven Country House**
Waterville, Co. Kerry
Tel: 066-947 4431 ..................Page 219
**Arrangements with Golf Courses:**
*Skellig Bay, Waterville Links Course, Ring of Kerry, Dooks, Tralee, Kilarney*
**Green Fees From:** *€70.00*
**Facilities available:**

**Butler Arms Hotel**
Waterville, Co. Kerry
Tel: 066-947 4144 ..................Page 219
**Arrangements with Golf Courses:**
*Waterville, Dooks, Killarney, Tralee, Ballybunion, Ring of Kerry, Skellig Bay*
**Green Fees From:** *€60.00*
**Facilities available:**

---

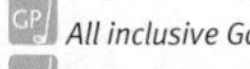 *All inclusive Golf Package*
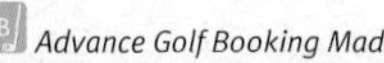 *Advance Golf Booking Made*
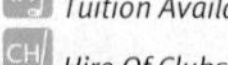 *Tuition Available* / *Hire Of Clubs*
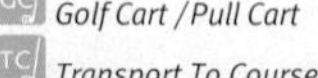 *Golf Cart / Pull Cart* / *Transport To Course*
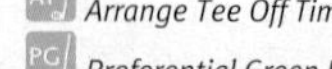 *Arrange Tee Off Times* / *Hire Of Caddy*
 *Preferential Green Fees*

**Carrig Country House**
Caragh Lake, Co. Kerry
Tel: 066-976 9100 ..................Page 180
**Arrangements with Golf Courses:**
*Dooks, Killarney, Beaufort, Killorglin, Waterville, Tralee, Ring Of Kerry*
**Green Fees From:** *€35.00*
**Facilities available:**

**Castlerosse Hotel and Golf Resort**
Killarney, Co. Kerry
Tel: 064-31144 ........................Page 196
**Golf Course(s) On Site:**
*9 Hole Golf Course*
**Arrangements with Golf Courses:**
*Killarney's Mahony's Point, Killeen, Lackabane, Dooks, Beaufort*
**Green Fees From:** *€18.00*
**Facilities available:**

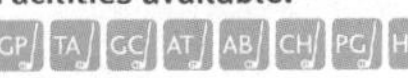

**Derrynane Hotel**
Caherdaniel, Co. Kerry
Tel: 066-947 5136 ..................Page 178
**Arrangements with Golf Courses:**
*Skellig Bay, Ring of Kerry*
**Facilities available:**

**Dingle Benners Hotel**
Dingle (An Daingean), Co. Kerry
Tel: 066-915 1638....................Page 184
**Arrangements with Golf Courses:**
*Dingle Golf Links, Ceann Sibéal, Castlegregory Golf Club*
**Green Fees From:** *€45.00*
**Facilities available:**

**Dingle Skellig Hotel & Peninsula Spa**
Dingle (An Daingean), Co. Kerry
Tel: 066-915 0200 .................Page 185
**Arrangements with Golf Courses:**
*Dingle Golf Links, Ceann Sibéal, Castlegregory*
**Green Fees From:** *€29.00*
**Facilities available:**

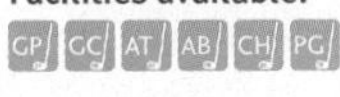

**Dromhall Hotel**
Killarney, Co. Kerry
Tel: 064-39300 ......................Page 197
**Arrangements with Golf Courses:**
*Killarney Golf & Fishing Club, Tralee, Ballybunion, Waterville, Dooks, Ring of Kerry*
**Green Fees From:** *€50.00*
**Facilities available:**

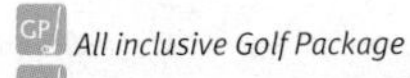

**Failte Hotel**
Killarney, Co. Kerry
Tel: 064-33404 ......................Page 198
**Arrangements with Golf Courses:**
*Lackabane, O'Mahony's Point, Beaufort, Ross, Castlerosse, Killeen*
**Facilities available:**

**Fairview Guesthouse**
Killarney, Co. Kerry
Tel: 064-34164........................Page 198
**Arrangements with Golf Courses:**
*Killarney, Waterville, Tralee, Dooks, Ballybunion, Beaufort*
**Green Fees From:** *€60.00*
**Facilities available:**

**Fels Point Hotel**
Tralee, Co. Kerry
Tel: 066-711 9986....................Page 217
**Arrangements with Golf Courses:**
*Tralee, Ballybunion, Killarney, Castleisland*
**Green Fees From:** *€40.00*
**Facilities available:**

**Foley's Townhouse & Restaurant**
Killarney, Co. Kerry
Tel: 064-31217 ........................Page 199
**Arrangements with Golf Courses:**
*Killarney, Barrow, Beaufort, Dooks, Ballybunion, Waterville*
**Facilities available:**

**Fuchsia House**
Killarney, Co. Kerry
Tel: 064-33743 ......................Page 200
**Arrangements with Golf Courses:**
*Killarney, Tralee, Ballybunion, Waterville, Dooks, Beaufort*
**Green Fees From:** *€50.00*
**Facilities available:**

**Gleann Fia Country House**
Killarney, Co. Kerry
Tel: 064-35035 ......................Page 200
**Arrangements with Golf Courses:**
*Killarney, Beaufort, Tralee, Ballybunion, Dooks, Waterville, Ring of Kerry Golf Course, Kenmare, Old Head, Kinsale, Skellig Bay*
**Green Fees From:** *€70.00*
**Facilities available:**

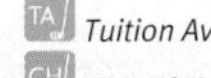

**Gleneagle Hotel**
Killarney, Co. Kerry
Tel: 064-36000 ......................Page 201
**Arrangements with Golf Courses:**
*Killarney, Ross, Beaufort, Ring of Kerry, Dooks, Ballybunion*
**Green Fees From:** *€55.00*
**Facilities available:**

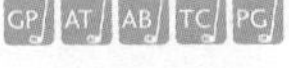

**Grand Hotel**
Tralee, Co. Kerry
Tel: 066-712 1499....................Page 218
**Arrangements with Golf Courses:**
*Tralee, Ballybunion, Waterville, Dingle, Dooks, Killarney*
**Green Fees From:** *€75.00*
**Facilities available:**

**Grove Lodge Riverside Guesthouse**
Killorglin, Co. Kerry
Tel: 066-976 1157....................Page 212
**Arrangements with Golf Courses:**
*Waterville, Tralee, Ballybunion, Beaufort, Killarney, Killorglin, Dooks, Gap of Dunloe, Dingle*
**Green Fees From:** *€35.00*
**Facilities available:**

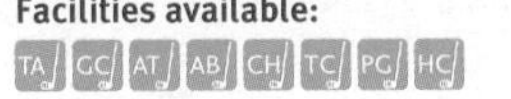

**Heights Hotel - Killarney (The)**
Killarney, Co. Kerry
Tel: 064-31158 ........................Page 201
**Arrangements with Golf Courses:**
*Killarney Golf & Fishing Club, Beaufort, Dooks, Waterville*
**Green Fees From:** *€45.00*
**Facilities available:**

**Hotel Dunloe Castle**
Killarney, Co. Kerry
Tel: 064-44111 ........................Page 202
**Arrangements with Golf Courses:**
*Dunloe, Dooks, Beaufort, Killarney, Ross, Killorglin*
**Green Fees From:** *€80.00*
**Facilities available:**

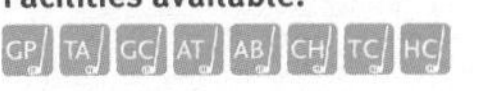

**Hotel Europe**
Killarney, Co. Kerry
Tel: 064-71300 ......................Page 202
**Arrangements with Golf Courses:**
*Killarney, Mahony's Point, Killeen, Lackabane, Beaufort, Dooks, Killorglin*
**Green Fees From:** *€80.00*
**Facilities available:**

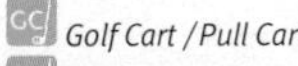

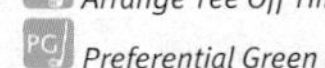

GP *All inclusive Golf Package* · TA *Tuition Available* · GC *Golf Cart / Pull Cart* · AT *Arrange Tee Off Times* · HC *Hire Of Caddy*
AB *Advance Golf Booking Made* · CH *Hire Of Clubs* · TC *Transport To Course* · PG *Preferential Green Fees*

## Co. Kerry CONTINUED

**Inveraray Farm Guesthouse**
Killarney, Co. Kerry
Tel: 064-44224 .....................Page 203
**Arrangements with Golf Courses:**
*Beaufort, Dunloe, Killarney, Ross, Killorglin, Dooks*
**Green Fees From:** *€35.00*
**Facilities available:**

**Kathleens Country House**
Killarney, Co. Kerry
Tel: 064-32810 .....................Page 203
**Arrangements with Golf Courses:**
*Killarney, Waterville, Tralee, Dooks, Ballybunion, Ring of Kerry*
**Green Fees From:** *€50.00*
**Facilities available:**

**Killarney Lodge**
Killarney, Co. Kerry
Tel: 064-36499 .....................Page 204
**Arrangements with Golf Courses:**
*Killarney GC, Tralee, Waterville, Dooks, Old Head, Beaufort*
**Green Fees From:** *€80.00*
**Facilities available:**

**Killarney Park Hotel**
Killarney, Co. Kerry
Tel: 064-35555 .....................Page 205
**Arrangements with Golf Courses:**
*Killarney, Ballybunion, Tralee, Waterville, Dooks, Ring of Kerry*
**Green Fees From:** *€70.00*
**Facilities available:**
TA GC AT AB CH TC PG

**Killarney Plaza Hotel & Spa**
Killarney, Co. Kerry
Tel: 064-21111 .....................Page 205
**Arrangements with Golf Courses:**
*Killarney Golf & Fishing Club, Waterville, Ballybunion, Dooks, Tralee, Old Head of Kinsale*
**Green Fees From:** *€55.00*
**Facilities available:**
GP AT AB CH TC HC

**Killarney Royal**
Killarney, Co. Kerry
Tel: 064-31853 .....................Page 206
**Arrangements with Golf Courses:**
*Killarney, Tralee, Dooks, Waterville, Beaufort, Ross*
**Green Fees From:** *€60.00*
**Facilities available:**
TA GC AT AB CH TC PG

**Kingfisher Lodge Guesthouse**
Killarney, Co. Kerry
Tel: 064-37131.......................Page 206
**Arrangements with Golf Courses:**
*Beaufort, Killarney, Killorglin, Waterville, Ballybunion, Tralee*
**Green Fees From:** *€20.00*
**Facilities available:**

**Lake Hotel**
Killarney, Co. Kerry
Tel: 064-31035 .....................Page 207
**Arrangements with Golf Courses:**
*Killarney (3 courses), Beaufort, Dooks, Ballybunion, Waterville, Tralee, Ross, Castlerosse, Ring of Kerry*
**Green Fees From:** *€30.00*
**Facilities available:**
GP TA GC AT AB CH TC PG HC

**Lakelands Farm Guesthouse**
Waterville, Co. Kerry
Tel: 066-947 4303 .................Page 220
**Arrangements with Golf Courses:**
*Waterville, Skelligs Bay, Dooks, Ring of Kerry, Killarney*
**Green Fees From:** *€60.00*
**Facilities available:**

**Lansdowne Arms Hotel**
Kenmare, Co. Kerry
Tel: 064-41368.......................Page 189
**Arrangements with Golf Courses:**
*Ring of Kerry, Kenmare*
**Green Fees From:** *€40.00*
**Facilities available:**
GP TA GC AT AB CH TC PG HC

**Manor West Hotel, Spa & Leisure Club**
Tralee, Co. Kerry
Tel: 066-719 4500 .................Page 218
**Arrangements with Golf Courses:**
*Tralee, Ring of Kerry, Castleisland, Ballybunion, Dooks*
**Green Fees From:** *€35.00*
**Facilities available:**
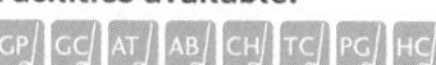

**McSweeney Arms Hotel**
Killarney, Co. Kerry
Tel: 064-31211 .......................Page 208
**Arrangements with Golf Courses:**
*Killarney, Waterville, Tralee, Ballybunion, Ring of Kerry, Dooks*
**Green Fees From:** *€80.00*
**Facilities available:**
GP TA GC AT AB CH TC PG HC

**Meadowlands Hotel**
Tralee, Co. Kerry
Tel: 066-718 0444 .................Page 218
**Arrangements with Golf Courses:**
*Ballybunion, Tralee (Barrow), Killarney, Dooks, Killorglin, Waterville*
**Facilities available:**

**Muckross Park Hotel & Cloisters Spa**
Killarney, Co. Kerry
Tel: 064-23400 .....................Page 208
**Arrangements with Golf Courses:**
*Waterville, O'Mahony's Point, Tralee, Dooks, Ring of Kerry Golf & Country Club, Killarney Golf & Fishing Club*
**Green Fees From:** *€80.00*
**Facilities available:**

**Old Weir Lodge**
Killarney, Co. Kerry
Tel: 064-35593 .....................Page 209
**Arrangements with Golf Courses:**
*Killarney, Waterville, Ballybunion, Tralee, Dooks, Beaufort*
**Green Fees From:** *€80.00*
**Facilities available:**

**Randles Court Clarion Hotel**
Killarney, Co. Kerry
Tel: 064-35333 .....................Page 210
**Arrangements with Golf Courses:**
*Killarney, Tralee, Beaufort, Dooks, Ring of Kerry, Ballybunion, Waterville*
**Green Fees From:** *€50.00*
**Facilities available:**

**Ring of Kerry Hotel**
Cahersiveen, Co. Kerry
Tel: 066-947 2543 .................Page 179
**Arrangements with Golf Courses:**
*Skellig Bay Golf Course*
**Green Fees From:** *€60.00*
**Facilities available:**
GP TA GC AT AB CH TC HC

**Rivermere**
Killarney, Co. Kerry
Tel: 064-37933 .....................Page 210
**Arrangements with Golf Courses:**
*Killarney (O'Mahony's Point and Killeen), Dooks, Ballybunion, Waterville, Tralee, Ring of Kerry*
**Green Fees From:** *€25.00*
**Facilities available:**

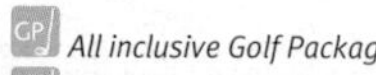
GP *All inclusive Golf Package*
AB *Advance Golf Booking Made*
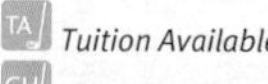
TA *Tuition Available*
CH *Hire Of Clubs*
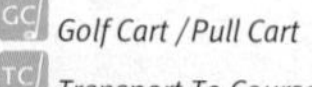
GC *Golf Cart / Pull Cart*
TC *Transport To Course*
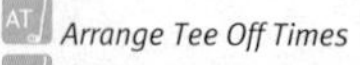
AT *Arrange Tee Off Times*
PG *Preferential Green Fees*
HC *Hire Of Caddy*

**Ross (The)**
Killarney, Co. Kerry
Tel: 064-31855 ........................Page 210
**Arrangements with Golf Courses:**
*Killarney, Ballybunion, Tralee, Waterville, Dooks, Ring of Kerry*
**Green Fees From:** *€70.00*
**Facilities available:**
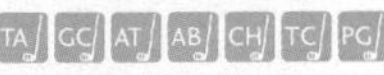

**Scotts Hotel**
Killarney, Co. Kerry
Tel: 064-31060 ........................Page 211
**Arrangements with Golf Courses:**
*Killarney, Ross, Beaufort, Ring of Kerry, Dooks, Ballybunion*
**Green Fees From:** *€40.00*
**Facilities available:**

**Sheen Falls Lodge**
Kenmare, Co. Kerry
Tel: 064-41600 ........................Page 191
**Arrangements with Golf Courses:**
*Kenmare, Ring of Kerry*
**Green Fees From:** *€45.00*
**Facilities available:**

**Smerwick Harbour Hotel**
Dingle (An Daingean), Co. Kerry
Tel: 066-915 6470 .................Page 188
**Arrangements with Golf Courses:**
*Dingle Golf Course (18 hole golf links, par 72)*
**Green Fees From:** *€55.00*
**Facilities available:**
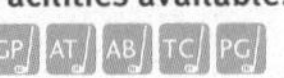

**Smugglers Inn**
Waterville, Co. Kerry
Tel: 066-947 4330 .................Page 220
**Arrangements with Golf Courses:**
*Waterville (2 Courses), Killarney (2 Courses), Dooks, Tralee, Ballybunion, Kenmare, Parknasilla*
**Green Fees From:** *€65.00*
**Facilities available:**

**Sneem Hotel**
Sneem, Co. Kerry
Tel: 064-75100........................Page 214
**Arrangements with Golf Courses:**
*Ring of Kerry Golf Course, Waterville, Parknasilla, Killeen & O'Mahonys Golf Courses Killarney, Old Head Golf Links Kinsale*
**Green Fees From:** *€50.00*
**Facilities available:**

**Valley Suites (The)**
Killarney, Co. Kerry
Tel: 064-23600........................Page 211
**Arrangements with Golf Courses:**
*Killarney GC, Dooks GC, Beaufort GC*
**Green Fees From:** *€55.00*
**Facilities available:**

## Co. Kilkenny

**Butler House**
Kilkenny City, Co. Kilkenny
Tel: 056-776 5707 .................Page 222
**Arrangements with Golf Courses:**
*Kilkenny, Mount Juliet, Carlow, Killerig Castle, Kilkea Castle, Gowran Park*
**Green Fees From:** *€30.00*
**Facilities available:**

**Glendine Inn**
Kilkenny City, Co. Kilkenny
Tel: 056-772 1069 .................Page 223
**Arrangements with Golf Courses:**
*Kilkenny, Mount Juliet, Callan, Castlecomer, Pococke, Gowran*
**Facilities available:**

**Kilkenny Hibernian Hotel**
Kilkenny City, Co. Kilkenny
Tel: 056-777 1888 .................Page 224
**Arrangements with Golf Courses:**
*Gowran Park, Mount Juliet, Rosslare GC, The European Club*
**Green Fees From:** *€30.00*
**Facilities available:**

**Kilkenny River Court**
Kilkenny City, Co. Kilkenny
Tel: 056-772 3388 .................Page 226
**Arrangements with Golf Courses:**
*Gowran Park, Kilkenny*
**Green Fees From:** *€30.00*
**Facilities available:**

**Langton House Hotel**
Kilkenny City, Co. Kilkenny
Tel: 056-776 5133 .................Page 226
**Arrangements with Golf Courses:**
*Mount Juliet, Kilkenny Golf Club, Gowran Park, Castlecomer Golf Club*
**Green Fees From:** *€90.00*
**Facilities available:**
GP AT AB CH TC

**Lyrath Estate Hotel, Spa & Convention Centre**
Kilkenny City, Co. Kilkenny
Tel: 056-776 0088 .................Page 227
**Arrangements with Golf Courses:**
*Gowran Park, Kilkenny*
**Green Fees From:** *€30.00*
**Facilities available:**
GP AT AB CH TC PG HC

**Mount Juliet Conrad**
Thomastown, Co. Kilkenny
Tel: 056-777 3000 .................Page 230
**Golf Course(s) On Site:**
*18 Hole Golf Course*
**Green Fees From:** *€85.00*
**Facilities available:**

**Springhill Court Hotel, Conference, Leisure & Spa Hotel**
Kilkenny City, Co. Kilkenny
Tel: 056-772 1122 .................Page 229
**Arrangements with Golf Courses:**
*Castlecomer, Callan, Gowran, Kilkenny*
**Green Fees From:** *€25.00*
**Facilities available:**

## Co. Tipperary

**Abbey Court Hotel, Lodges & Trinity Leisure Spa**
Nenagh, Co. Tipperary
Tel: 067-41111 ........................Page 237
**Arrangements with Golf Courses:**
*Nenagh, Roscrea, Birr, Portumna, Thurles, Castletroy*
**Green Fees From:** *€25.00*
**Facilities available:**
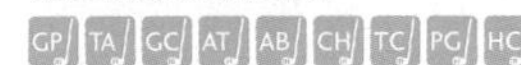

**Ach Na Sheen Guesthouse**
Tipperary Town, Co. Tipperary
Tel: 062-51298 ......................Page 238
**Arrangements with Golf Courses:**
*Tipperary, Ballykisteen, Cahir, Dundrum*
**Green Fees From:** *€30.00*
**Facilities available:**

**Anner Hotel & Leisure Centre**
Thurles, Co. Tipperary
Tel: 0504-21799......................Page 238
**Arrangements with Golf Courses:**
*Thurles, Dundrum, Templemore*
**Facilities available:**

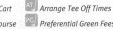

GP *All inclusive Golf Package* TA *Tuition Available* GC *Golf Cart / Pull Cart* AT *Arrange Tee Off Times* HC *Hire Of Caddy*
AB *Advance Golf Booking Made* CH *Hire Of Clubs* TC *Transport To Course* PG *Preferential Green Fees*

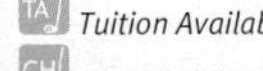
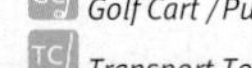
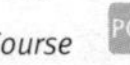
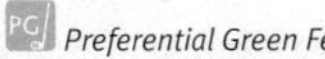

## Co. Tipperary CONTINUED

### Ballykisteen Hotel & Golf Resort
Tipperary Town, Co. Tipperary
Tel: 062-33333 ......................Page 239
**Golf Course(s) On Site:**
*18 Hole Golf Course*
**Green Fees From:***€35.00*
**Facilities available:**

### Cahir House Hotel
Cahir, Co. Tipperary
Tel: 052-43000 ......................Page 231
**Arrangements with Golf Courses:**
*Cahir Park, Carrick-on-Suir, Clonmel, Ballykisteen, Dundrum, Tipperary, Thurles*
**Green Fees From:***€30.00*
**Facilities available:**

### Dundrum House Hotel
Cashel, Co. Tipperary
Tel: 062-71116 ........................Page 233
**Golf Course(s) On Site:**
*18 Hole Golf Course*
**Green Fees From:***€45.00*
**Facilities available:**

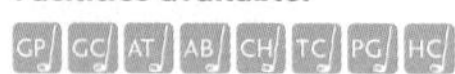

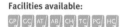

### Kilcoran Lodge Hotel, Lodges & Leisure Centre
Cahir, Co. Tipperary
Tel: 052-41288........................Page 231
**Arrangements with Golf Courses:**
*Cahir GC, Clonmel GC, Tipperary GC, Mitchelstown GC*
**Green Fees From:***€30.00*
**Facilities available:**

### Racket Hall Country House Golf & Conference Hotel
Roscrea, Co. Tipperary
Tel: 0505-21748......................Page 237
**Arrangements with Golf Courses:**
*Roscrea, Birr, Mountrath, Rathdowney, Portumna, The Heritage*
**Green Fees From:***€25.00*
**Facilities available:**

## Co. Waterford

### Athenaeum House Hotel
Waterford City, Co. Waterford
Tel: 051-833999......................Page 246
**Arrangements with Golf Courses:**
*Waterford, Faithlegg, Waterford Castle, Tramore, Mount Juliet*
**Green Fees From:***€45.00*
**Facilities available:**

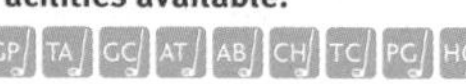

### Days Hotel Waterford
Waterford City, Co. Waterford
Tel: 1890-329 329 .................Page 248
**Arrangements with Golf Courses:**
*Waterford Castle, Faithlegg, Waterford Golf Club, Dunmore East, Gold Coast, New Ross, West Waterford*
**Green Fees From:***€35.00*
**Facilities available:**

### Dooley's Hotel
Waterford City, Co. Waterford
Tel: 051-873531......................Page 249
**Arrangements with Golf Courses:**
*Waterford, Tramore, Faithlegg, Waterford Castle, Mount Juliet, Carrick-on-Suir*
**Green Fees From:***€55.00*
**Facilities available:**

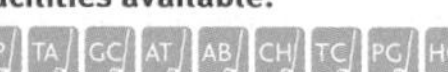

### Faithlegg House Hotel and Golf Club
Faithlegg, Co. Waterford
Tel: 051-382000......................Page 244
**Golf Course(s) On Site:**
*18 Hole Golf Course*
**Arrangements with Golf Courses:**
*Waterford Castle, Tramore, Waterford Golf Club, Faithlegg Golf Course, Mount Juliet*
**Green Fees From:***€50.00*
**Facilities available:**

### Granville Hotel
Waterford City, Co. Waterford
Tel: 051-305555......................Page 249
**Arrangements with Golf Courses:**
*Waterford, Faithlegg, Waterford Castle, Tramore, Dunmore East*
**Green Fees From:***€25.00*
**Facilities available:**

### Lismore House Hotel
Lismore, Co. Waterford
Tel: 058-72966 ......................Page 244
**Arrangements with Golf Courses:**
*Gold Coast Golf Club, Dungarvan Golf Club*
**Green Fees From:***€25.00*
**Facilities available:**

### Majestic Hotel
Tramore, Co. Waterford
Tel: 051-381761 ......................Page 245
**Arrangements with Golf Courses:**
*Tramore, Waterford, Faithlegg, Waterford Castle, Mount Juliet, Dunmore East*
**Green Fees From:***€40.00*
**Facilities available:**

### Ocean Hotel
Dunmore East, Co. Waterford
Tel: 051-383136......................Page 243
**Arrangements with Golf Courses:**
*Waterford, Waterford Castle, Faithlegg, Dunmore East, Tramore*
**Green Fees From:***€35.00*
**Facilities available:**

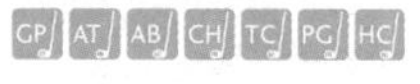

### O'Shea's Hotel...by the sea
Tramore, Co. Waterford
Tel: 051-381246......................Page 245
**Arrangements with Golf Courses:**
*Tramore, Faithlegg, Waterford Castle, Waterford, Dungarvan*
**Green Fees From:***€45.00*
**Facilities available:**

### Park Hotel, Leisure Centre & Holiday Homes
Dungarvan, Co. Waterford
Tel: 058-42899 ......................Page 242
**Arrangements with Golf Courses:**
*Dungarvan Golf Club, West Waterford Golf Club, Gold Coast Golf Club*
**Green Fees From:***€25.00*
**Facilities available:**

### Ramada Viking Hotel
Waterford City, Co. Waterford
Tel: 051-336933......................Page 249
**Arrangements with Golf Courses:**
*Tramore, Mount Juliet, Waterford Castle, Faithlegg, Waterford*
**Green Fees From:***€40.00*
**Facilities available:**

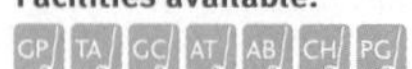

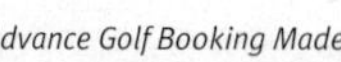
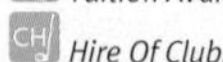

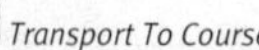

GP *All inclusive Golf Package* · TA *Tuition Available* · GC *Golf Cart / Pull Cart* · AT *Arrange Tee Off Times* · HC *Hire Of Caddy* · AB *Advance Golf Booking Made* · CH *Hire Of Clubs* · TC *Transport To Course* · PG *Preferential Green Fees*

### Rhu Glenn Country Club Hotel
Waterford City, Co. Waterford
Tel: 051-832242......................Page 250
**Arrangements with Golf Courses:**
*Waterford, New Ross, Faithlegg, Waterford Castle, Tramore, Dunmore East, Mount Juillet*
**Green Fees From:** *€40.00*
**Facilities available:**

### Rice Guesthouse & Batterberry's Bar
Waterford City, Co. Waterford
Tel: 051-371606......................Page 250
**Arrangements with Golf Courses:**
*Dunmore East, Faithlegg, Waterford Castle, Tramore, Waterford*
**Green Fees From:** *€40.00*
**Facilities available:**

### Tower Hotel & Leisure Centre
Waterford City, Co. Waterford
Tel: 051-862300......................Page 251
**Arrangements with Golf Courses:**
*Waterford Castle, Waterford, Faithlegg, Tramore*
**Green Fees From:** *€50.00*
**Facilities available:**

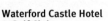

### Waterford Castle Hotel & Golf Club
Waterford City, Co. Waterford
Tel: 051-878203......................Page 251
**Golf Course(s) On Site:**
*18 Hole Golf Course*
**Arrangements with Golf Courses:**
*Waterford Castle Golf Club, Faithlegg, Tramore, Waterford Golf Club, Mount Juliet*
**Green Fees From:** *€62.00*
**Facilities available:**

## Co. Wexford

### Amber Springs Hotel and Health Spa
Gorey, Co. Wexford
Tel: 053-948 4000 ..................Page 256
**Arrangements with Golf Courses:**
*Seafield, Courtown, Coollattin, Ballymoney*
**Green Fees From:** *€36.00*
**Facilities available:**

### Ashdown Park Hotel Conference & Leisure Centre
Gorey, Co. Wexford
Tel: 053-948 0500 ..................Page 256
**Arrangements with Golf Courses:**
*Seafield, Courtown, Ballymoney, Coolattin, Enniscorthy, Woodenbridge*
**Green Fees From:** *€40.00*
**Facilities available:**

### Carlton Millrace Hotel & C Spa
Bunclody, Co. Wexford
Tel: 053-937 5100 ..................Page 252
**Golf Course(s) On Site:**
*18 Hole Golf Course*
**Arrangements with Golf Courses:**
*Enniscorthy Golf Club, Seafield Golf Club, Killerig Golf Course, Bunclody Golf & Fishing Club*
**Green Fees From:** *€25.00*
**Facilities available:**

### Crosbie Cedars Hotel
Rosslare, Co. Wexford
Tel: 053-913 2124 ..................Page 259
**Arrangements with Golf Courses:**
*Rosslare 18 Hole Links, Rosslare 12 Hole Links, St. Helen's Golf & Country Club, Wexford Golf Course*
**Green Fees From:** *€40.00*
**Facilities available:**

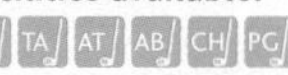

### Danby Lodge Hotel
Rosslare, Co. Wexford
Tel: 053-915 8191....................Page 259
**Arrangements with Golf Courses:**
*St. Helens & Rosslare Golf Links*
**Green Fees From:** *€50.00*
**Facilities available:**

### Kelly's Resort Hotel & Spa
Rosslare, Co. Wexford
Tel: 053-913 2114....................Page 259
**Arrangements with Golf Courses:**
*Rosslare Golf Club, St. Helen's Bay Golf & Country Club, Wexford Golf Club*
**Green Fees From:** *€40.00*
**Facilities available:**

### Pines Country House Hotel
Enniscorthy, Co. Wexford
Tel: 053-938 3600 ..................Page 254
**Arrangements with Golf Courses:**
*Ballymoney Golf Club, Courtown, Seafield*
**Green Fees From:** *€27.50*
**Facilities available:**

GP TA AT AB TC PG HC

### Quality Hotel & Leisure Club Wexford
Wexford Town, Co. Wexford
Tel: 053-917 2000 ..................Page 262
**Arrangements with Golf Courses:**
*St Helen's GC, Wexford GC, Rosslare GC, Scarke GC*
**Facilities available:**

### Riverside Park Hotel and Leisure Club
Enniscorthy, Co. Wexford
Tel: 053-923 7800 ..................Page 255
**Arrangements with Golf Courses:**
*Enniscorthy Golf Club, Rosslare Golf Club, Wexford Golf Club, New Ross Golf Club, Seafield Golf Club, St. Helen's Golf Club*
**Green Fees From:** *€35.00*
**Facilities available:**

### Seafield Hotel
Gorey, Co. Wexford
Tel: 053-942 4000 ..................Page 257
**Golf Course(s) On Site:**
*18 Hole Golf Course*
**Green Fees From:** *€50.00*
**Facilities available:**

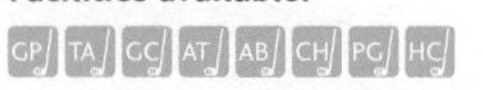

### Talbot Hotel Conference and Leisure Centre
Wexford Town, Co. Wexford
Tel: 053-912 2566 ..................Page 263
**Arrangements with Golf Courses:**
*St. Helen's, Wexford, Rosslare, Enniscorthy, Courtown*
**Green Fees From:** *€25.00*
**Facilities available:**

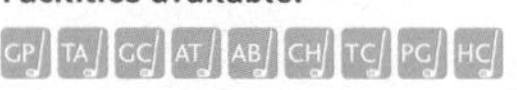

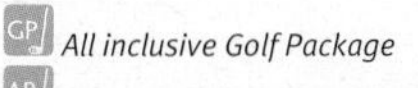
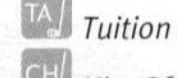
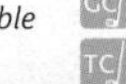
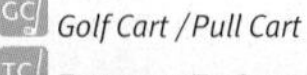
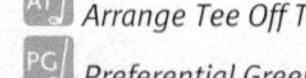

GP *All inclusive Golf Package* TA *Tuition Available* GC *Golf Cart / Pull Cart* AT *Arrange Tee Off Times* HC *Hire Of Caddy*
AB *Advance Golf Booking Made* CH *Hire Of Clubs* TC *Transport To Course* PG *Preferential Green Fees*

# Dublin & Ireland East

## Co. Cavan

**Cavan Crystal Hotel**
Cavan Town, Co. Cavan
Tel: 049-436 0600 ..................Page 270
**Arrangements with Golf Courses:**
*Co. Cavan Golf Club, Clones, Headfort Golf Club, Kells*
**Green Fees From:** *€35.00*
**Facilities available:**

**Crover House Hotel & Golf Club**
Mountnugent, Co. Cavan
Tel: 049-854 0206 ..................Page 272
**Golf Course(s) On Site:**
*9 Hole Golf Course*
**Arrangements with Golf Courses:**
*Headfort GC*
**Green Fees From:** *€15.00*
**Facilities available:**

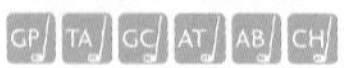

**Park Manor House Hotel & Estate**
Virginia, Co. Cavan
Tel: 049-854 6100 ..................Page 273
**Golf Course(s) On Site:**
*9 Hole Golf Course*
**Arrangements with Golf Courses:**
*Cavan Golf Club, Headfort Golf Club, Kells*
**Green Fees From:** *€9.00*
**Facilities available:**

**Radisson SAS Farnham Estate Hotel**
Cavan Town, Co. Cavan
Tel: 049-437 7700 ..................Page 271
**Golf Course(s) On Site:**
*18 Hole Golf Course*
**Green Fees From:** *€50.00*
**Facilities available:**

**Slieve Russell Hotel Golf & Country Club**
Ballyconnell, Co. Cavan
Tel: 049-952 6444 ..................Page 270
**Golf Course(s) On Site:**
*18 Hole Golf Course*
*9 Hole Golf Course*
*Par 3 Golf Course*
**Green Fees From:** *€50.00*
**Facilities available:**

## Co. Dublin

**Aberdeen Lodge**
Dublin City, Co. Dublin
Tel: 01-283 8155 ....................Page 279
**Arrangements with Golf Courses:**
*St. Margarets, Portmarnock, K Club, Elm Park, Carton House, Druids Glen*
**Green Fees From:** *€60.00*
**Facilities available:**

**Airportview Hotel & Spa**
Blakes Cross, Co. Dublin
Tel: 01-843 8756 ....................Page 273
**Arrangements with Golf Courses:**
*Rush Golf Club, Skerries Golf Club, Balbriggan Golf Club, Swords Open, Donabate Golf Club, Portmarnock Links*
**Green Fees From:** *€25.00*
**Facilities available:**

**Bracken Court Hotel**
Balbriggan, Co. Dublin
Tel: 01-841 3333 ....................Page 273
**Arrangements with Golf Courses:**
*Balbriggan, Seapoint, Co. Louth, Bellewstown, Rush, Portmarnock, St. Margaret's*
**Green Fees From:** *€50.00*
**Facilities available:**

**Cassidys Hotel**
Dublin City, Co. Dublin
Tel: 01-878 0555 ....................Page 289
**Arrangements with Golf Courses:**
*Roganstown, St Margaret's, Portmarnock Links, Royal Dublin, Clontarf, St. Anne's*
**Green Fees From:** *€40.00*
**Facilities available:**

TA GC AT AB CH TC PG

**Castleknock Hotel and Country Club**
Dublin City, Co. Dublin
Tel: 01-640 6300 ....................Page 290
**Golf Course(s) On Site:**
*18 Hole Golf Course*
**Arrangements with Golf Courses:**
*Luttrellstown, Carton House, Citywest, Castleknock Golf Course*
**Green Fees From:** *€60.00*
**Facilities available:**

GP GC AT AB CH PG HC

**Charleville Lodge**
Dublin City, Co. Dublin
Tel: 01-838 6633 ....................Page 290
**Arrangements with Golf Courses:**
*St. Margaret's, Luttrellstown, The Links, Portmarnock, The Island Golf Links*
**Green Fees From:** *€70.00*
**Facilities available:**

**Citywest Hotel, Conference, Leisure & Golf Resort**
Saggart, Co. Dublin
Tel: 01-401 0500 ....................Page 330
**Golf Course(s) On Site:**
*2 x 18 Hole Golf Courses*
**Arrangements with Golf Courses:**
*Palmerstown House Golf Club*
**Green Fees From:** *€25.00*
**Facilities available:**

**Clontarf Castle Hotel**
Dublin City, Co. Dublin
Tel: 01-833 2321 ....................Page 292
**Arrangements with Golf Courses:**
*Royal Dublin, St. Margaret's, Portmarnock, St. Anne's, Clontarf, Malahide*
**Green Fees From:** *€70.00*
**Facilities available:**

**Deer Park Hotel Golf & Spa**
Howth, Co. Dublin
Tel: 01-832 2624 ....................Page 326
**Golf Course(s) On Site:**
*18 Hole Golf Course*
*2 x 9 Hole Golf Courses*
*Par 3 Golf Course*
**Green Fees From:** *€20.00*
**Facilities available:**

**Grand Hotel**
Malahide, Co. Dublin
Tel: 01-845 0000 ....................Page 329
**Arrangements with Golf Courses:**
*Portmarnock GC, Malahide GC, The Island GC, Swords GC, St. Margarets, Royal Dublin*
**Green Fees From:** *€60.00*
**Facilities available:**

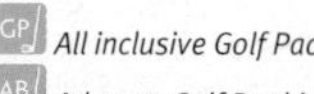 *All inclusive Golf Package* / *Advance Golf Booking Made*
 *Tuition Available* / *Hire Of Clubs*
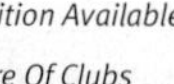 *Golf Cart / Pull Cart* / *Transport To Course*
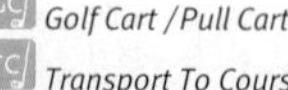 *Arrange Tee Off Times* / *Preferential Green Fees*
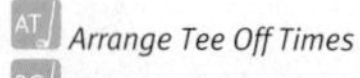 *Hire Of Caddy*

**Gresham (The)**
Dublin City, Co. Dublin
Tel: 01-874 6881......................Page 301
**Arrangements with Golf Courses:**
*Royal Dublin, Portmarnock, St. Margaret's, The Island, St. Anne's, Malahide*
**Facilities available:**

**Hilton Dublin Airport**
Dublin Airport, Co. Dublin
Tel: 01-866 1800 ....................Page 277
**Arrangements with Golf Courses:**
*St. Margaret's, Donabate, Malahide, Portmarnock*
**Green Fees From:** *€50.00*
**Facilities available:**

**King Sitric Fish Restaurant & Accommodation**
Howth, Co. Dublin
Tel: 01-832 5235 ....................Page 326
**Arrangements with Golf Courses:**
*Deerpark, Howth, Royal Dublin, Portmarnock, St. Margaret's, The Island*
**Green Fees From:** *€15.00*
**Facilities available:**

**Lansdowne Hotel**
Dublin City, Co. Dublin
Tel: 01-668 2522 ....................Page 307
**Arrangements with Golf Courses:**
*St. Anne's, Deerpark, Elmgreen, Leopardstown*
**Green Fees From:** *€45.00*
**Facilities available:**

**Lucan Spa Hotel**
Lucan, Co. Dublin
Tel: 01-628 0494 ....................Page 328
**Arrangements with Golf Courses:**
*Carton House, Hermitage, Citywest, Lucan, The K Club*
**Green Fees From:** *€80.00*
**Facilities available:**

**Marine Hotel**
Sutton, Co. Dublin
Tel: 01-839 0000 ....................Page 331
**Arrangements with Golf Courses:**
*Portmarnock Hotel & Golf Links, Howth GC, Sutton GC, Royal Dublin GC, St. Anne's*
**Green Fees From:** *€60.00*
**Facilities available:**

**Merrion Hall & Blakes Spa Suites**
Dublin City, Co. Dublin
Tel: 01-668 1426 ....................Page 309
**Arrangements with Golf Courses:**
*Portmarnock, Royal Dublin, Elm Park, Castle, K Club, Druid's Glen*
**Green Fees From:** *€60.00*
**Facilities available:**

**Phoenix Park House**
Dublin City, Co. Dublin
Tel: 01-677 2870 ....................Page 316
**Arrangements with Golf Courses:**
*Carton House GC*
**Green Fees From:** *€90.00*
**Facilities available:**

**Portmarnock Hotel & Golf Links**
Portmarnock, Co. Dublin
Tel: 01-846 0611......................Page 329
**Golf Course(s) On Site:**
*18 Hole Golf Course*
**Arrangements with Golf Courses:**
*Portmarnock, St. Margaret's, Royal Dublin, Malahide, The Island*
**Green Fees From:** *€90.00*
**Facilities available:**

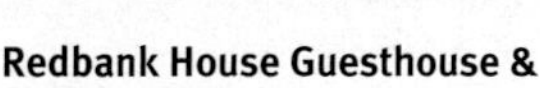


**Redbank House Guesthouse & Restaurant**
Skerries, Co. Dublin
Tel: 01-849 1005 ....................Page 330
**Arrangements with Golf Courses:**
*Skerries, Laytown, Bettystown, Baltray, Portmarnock, St. Margaret's, Donabate*
**Green Fees From:** *€40.00*
**Facilities available:**

**Regency Airport Hotel**
Dublin City, Co. Dublin
Tel: 01-837 3544 ....................Page 318
**Arrangements with Golf Courses:**
*St. Margarets, Deer Park, Howth Golf Club*
**Green Fees From:** *€45.00*
**Facilities available:**

TA AT AB PG

**Rochestown Lodge Hotel & Day Spa**
Dun Laoghaire, Co. Dublin
Tel: 01-285 3555 ....................Page 325
**Arrangements with Golf Courses:**
*Powerscourt GC, Woodbrook GC, Druids Glen GC, The European GC*
**Green Fees From:** *€95.00*
**Facilities available:**

GP AT AB CH PG

**Springfield Hotel**
Leixlip, Co. Dublin
Tel: 01-458 1100......................Page 327
**Arrangements with Golf Courses:**
*K Club, Carton, Hermitage, Lucan, Westmanston*
**Green Fees From:** *€50.00*
**Facilities available:**

**Tower Hotel**
Dublin City, Co. Dublin
Tel: 01-468 5400 ....................Page 322
**Arrangements with Golf Courses:**
*Castleknock Golf Club*
**Facilities available:**

**Waterside House Hotel (The)**
Donabate, Co. Dublin
Tel: 01-843 6153 ....................Page 274
**Arrangements with Golf Courses:**
*Donabate, Turvey, Beaverstown, Balcarrick, The Island Links, St. Margaret's*
**Green Fees From:** *€35.00*
**Facilities available:**

**White Sands Hotel**
Portmarnock, Co. Dublin
Tel: 01-866 6000 ....................Page 329
**Arrangements with Golf Courses:**
*Malahide, St. Margaret's, Portmarnock Golf Links, Donabate, Balcarrick, St. Anne's Golf Club*
**Green Fees From:** *€32.00*
**Facilities available:**

## Did you know ?

Soft studs are now required at many golf courses. If your shoes have metal studs the professional's shop will usually be able to change them to soft for you for a small charge.

GP *All inclusive Golf Package* · AB *Advance Golf Booking Made*

TA *Tuition Available* · CH *Hire Of Clubs*
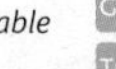
GC *Golf Cart / Pull Cart* · TC *Transport To Course*
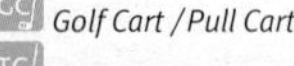
AT *Arrange Tee Off Times* · PG *Preferential Green Fees*
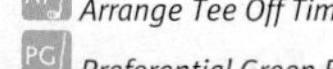
HC *Hire Of Caddy*

## Co. Kildare

**Barberstown Castle**
Straffan, Co. Kildare
Tel: 01-628 8157 ....................Page 340
**Arrangements with Golf Courses:**
*K Club, Carton House*
**Green Fees From:** *€140.00*
**Facilities available:**

**Carlton Abbey Hotel & C Spa**
Athy, Co. Kildare
Tel: 059-863 0100 ..................Page 332
**Arrangements with Golf Courses:**
*Coollattin, Killerig, Athy, Carlow*
**Green Fees From:** *€25.00*
**Facilities available:**

**Carton House**
Maynooth, Co. Kildare
Tel: 01-505 2000 ....................Page 336
**Golf Course(s) On Site:**
*18 Hole Golf Course*
*Par 3 Golf Course*
**Arrangements with Golf Courses:**
*The K Club, PGA*
**Green Fees From:** *€115.00*
**Facilities available:**
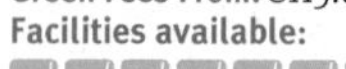

**Clanard Court Hotel**
Athy, Co. Kildare
Tel: 059-864 0666 ..................Page 332
**Arrangements with Golf Courses:**
*Athy Golf Club, Cardenton Par 3*
**Green Fees From:** *€6.00*
**Facilities available:**

**Courtyard Hotel Leixlip**
Leixlip, Co. Kildare
Tel: 01-629 5100 ....................Page 335
**Arrangements with Golf Courses:**
*K Club - 2 x 18 Hole Courses,*
*Carton - 2 x 18 Hole Courses,*
*Heritage - 18 Hole Course*
**Green Fees From:** *€75.00*
**Facilities available:**
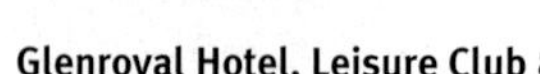

**Glenroyal Hotel, Leisure Club & Conference Centre**
Maynooth, Co. Kildare
Tel: 01-629 0909 ....................Page 336
**Arrangements with Golf Courses:**
*Knockanally, K Club, Killeen, Castlewarden, Bodenstown, Citywest, Carton*
**Facilities available:**

**Hazel Hotel**
Monasterevin, Co. Kildare
Tel: 045-525373 ....................Page 336
**Arrangements with Golf Courses:**
*Cill Dara, Portarlington, Curragh, The Heath, Athy, The Heritage at Killenard*
**Facilities available:**

**Kildare Hotel, Spa and Country Club - The K Club**
Straffan, Co. Kildare
Tel: 01-601 7200......................Page 341
**Golf Course(s) On Site:**
*2 x 18 Hole Golf Courses*
**Arrangements with Golf Courses:**
*Luttrellstown Castle, Druid's Glen, Portmarnock Links, Rathsallagh, Hermitage, Heritage*
**Green Fees From:** *€165.00*
**Facilities available:**

**Kilkea Castle**
Castledermot, Co. Kildare
Tel: 059-914 5156 ..................Page 333
**Golf Course(s) On Site:**
*18 Hole Golf Course*
**Green Fees From:** *€45.00*
**Facilities available:**

**Moyvalley Hotel & Golf Resort**
Moyvalley, Co. Kildare
Tel: 046-954 8000 ..................Page 337
**Golf Course(s) On Site:**
*18 Hole Golf Course*
**Arrangements with Golf Courses:**
*New Forest*
**Green Fees From:** *€95.00*
**Facilities available:**

**Westgrove Hotel & Conference Centre**
Clane, Co. Kildare
Tel: 045-989900 ....................Page 334
**Arrangements with Golf Courses:**
*The K Club, Carton House GC, Millicent GC, Killeen GC, Naas GC, PGA National Naas*
**Facilities available:**

## Co. Laois

**Heritage Golf & Spa Resort (The)**
Killenard, Co. Laois
Tel: 057-864 5500 ..................Page 342
**Golf Course(s) On Site:**
*18 Hole Golf Course*
*9 Hole Golf Course*
*Par 3 Golf Course*
**Green Fees From:** *€115.00*
**Facilities available:**

**Killeshin (The)**
Portlaoise, Co. Laois
Tel: 057-863 1200 ..................Page 342
**Arrangements with Golf Courses:**
*Abbeyleix, Rathdowney, Heath, Mountrath, Portarlington*
**Green Fees From:** *€25.00*
**Facilities available:**

**Portlaoise Heritage Hotel**
Portlaoise, Co. Laois
Tel: 057-867 8588 ..................Page 343
**Arrangements with Golf Courses:**
*The Heritage, The Heath, Abbeyleix, Esker Hills*
**Green Fees From:** *€40.00*
**Facilities available:**

## Co. Longford

**Annaly Hotel**
Longford Town, Co. Longford
Tel: 043-42058 ......................Page 344
**Arrangements with Golf Courses:**
*Longford, Ballyconnell, Glasson, Mullingar, Roscommon*
**Facilities available:**

**Longford Arms Hotel**
Longford Town, Co. Longford
Tel: 043-46296 ......................Page 344
**Arrangements with Golf Courses:**
*Longford, Glasson, Ballyconnell, Carrick-on-Shannon, Roscommon, Mullingar*
**Facilities available:**

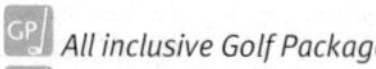
*All inclusive Golf Package* · *Advance Golf Booking Made*
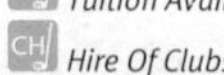
*Tuition Available* · *Hire Of Clubs*
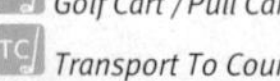
*Golf Cart / Pull Cart* · *Transport To Course*

*Arrange Tee Off Times* · *Preferential Green Fees* · *Hire Of Caddy*

## Co. Louth

**Ballymascanlon House Hotel**
Dundalk, Co. Louth
Tel: 042-935 8200 ..................Page 348
**Golf Course(s) On Site:**
*18 Hole Golf Course*
**Green Fees From:** *€30.00*
**Facilities available:**

**Boyne Valley Hotel & Country Club**
Drogheda, Co. Louth
Tel: 041-983 7737 ..................Page 346
**Arrangements with Golf Courses:**
*Baltray - Seapoint, Laytown/Bettystown, Dundalk, Headfort (2 courses), Kells, Ardee, St. Margaret's*
**Green Fees From:** *€50.00*
**Facilities available:**

**D (The)**
Drogheda, Co. Louth
Tel: 041-987 7700 ..................Page 346
**Arrangements with Golf Courses:**
*County Louth (Baltray), Seapoint, Laytown, Bettystown*
**Green Fees From:** *€60.00*
**Facilities available:**

**Fairways Hotel & Conference Centre**
Dundalk, Co. Louth
Tel: 042-932 1500 ..................Page 349
**Arrangements with Golf Courses:**
*Ballymascalon, Carnbeg, Killeen, Dundalk, Seapoint, Greenore*
**Facilities available:**

**Four Seasons Hotel & Leisure Club Carlingford**
Carlingford, Co. Louth
Tel: 042-937 3530 ..................Page 345
**Arrangements with Golf Courses:**
*Greenore Golf Club, County Louth, Ballymac Golf Club, Dundalk, Warrenpoint, Cloverhill*
**Green Fees From:** *€40.00*
**Facilities available:**

**Hotel Imperial**
Dundalk, Co. Louth
Tel: 042-933 2241 ..................Page 349
**Arrangements with Golf Courses:**
*Ballymascanlon, Dundalk, Greenore, Carnbeg*
**Green Fees From:** *€15.00*
**Facilities available:**

GP GC AT AB CH PG HC

**Keernaun House**
Dundalk, Co. Louth
Tel: 042-932 1795 ..................Page 349
**Arrangements with Golf Courses:**
*Dundalk, Killin, Greenore, Mannan Castle, Carnbeg*
**Green Fees From:** *€35.00*
**Facilities available:**

GP AT AB CH TC

**McKevitt's Village Hotel**
Carlingford, Co. Louth
Tel: 042-937 3116 ..................Page 345
**Arrangements with Golf Courses:**
*Greenore*
**Green Fees From:** *€45.00*
**Facilities available:**

GP GC AT AB CH PG HC

**Park Inn Dundalk**
Dundalk, Co. Louth
Tel: 042-939 5700 ..................Page 350
**Golf Course(s) On Site:**
*18 Hole Golf Course*
**Arrangements with Golf Courses:**
*Park Inn Golf Course*
**Green Fees From:** *€28.00*
**Facilities available:**

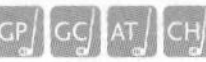

## Co. Meath

**Bettystown Court Conference & Leisure Hotel**
Bettystown, Co. Meath
Tel: 041-981 2900 ..................Page 352
**Arrangements with Golf Courses:**
*Bettystown, Seapoint*
**Facilities available:**

**Castle Arch Hotel**
Trim, Co. Meath
Tel: 046-943 1516 ..................Page 357
**Arrangements with Golf Courses:**
*Knightsbrook Hotel and Golf Resort Trim*
**Green Fees From:** *€50.00*
**Facilities available:**

**Hamlet Court Hotel**
Johnstownbridge, Co. Meath
Tel: 046-954 1200 ..................Page 354
**Arrangements with Golf Courses:**
*Knockanally GC, Rathcore GC, Carton House, K Club, Highfield, Edenderry, Trim*
**Green Fees From:** *€20.00*
**Facilities available:**

GP TA GC AT AB CH TC PG HC

**Headfort Arms Hotel**
Kells, Co. Meath
Tel: 0818-222 800 ..................Page 354
**Arrangements with Golf Courses:**
*Headfort Golf Course - 36 Holes, Royal Tara, Navan Race Course, Delvin Castle, Ballinlough Castle*
**Green Fees From:** *€35.00*
**Facilities available:**

**Knightsbrook Hotel & Golf Resort**
Trim, Co. Meath
Tel: 046-948 2110 ..................Page 357
**Golf Course(s) On Site:**
*18 Hole Golf Course*
**Arrangements with Golf Courses:**
*Headfort GC, Co. Meath GC, Navan GC*
**Green Fees From:** *€50.00*
**Facilities available:**

**Neptune Beach Hotel & Leisure Club**
Bettystown, Co. Meath
Tel: 041-982 7107 ..................Page 352
**Arrangements with Golf Courses:**
*Laytown & Bettystown, Sea Point, County Louth/Baltray, Royal Tara, Bellewstown*
**Facilities available:**

**Old Darnley Lodge Hotel**
Athboy, Co. Meath
Tel: 046-943 2283 ..................Page 352
**Arrangements with Golf Courses:**
*Ballinlough Castle, Delvin Castle, Headfort, The Glebe, Royal Meath*
**Green Fees From:** *€50.00*
**Facilities available:**

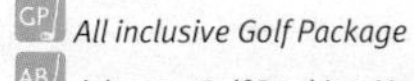

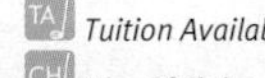

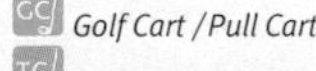

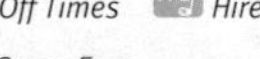

GP *All inclusive Golf Package* TA *Tuition Available* GC *Golf Cart / Pull Cart* AT *Arrange Tee Off Times* HC *Hire Of Caddy*
AB *Advance Golf Booking Made* CH *Hire Of Clubs* TC *Transport To Course* PG *Preferential Green Fees*

## Co. Meath CONTINUED

**Station House Hotel and Signal Restaurant**
Kilmessan, Co. Meath
Tel: 046-902 5239 ..................Page 355
**Arrangements with Golf Courses:**
*Royal Tara, Blackbush, Headfort, The K Club, The Island Links, Carton House*
**Green Fees From:** *€35.00*
**Facilities available:**

**Trim Castle Hotel**
Trim, Co. Meath
Tel: 046-948 3000 ..................Page 358
**Arrangements with Golf Courses:**
*Royal Tara, Headfort Old and New, Rathcore*
**Green Fees From:** *€45.00*
**Facilities available:**

## Co. Monaghan

**Four Seasons Hotel & Leisure Club**
Monaghan Town, Co. Monaghan
Tel: 047-81888 ......................Page 359
**Arrangements with Golf Courses:**
*Rossmore, Nuremore, Armagh, Clones, Slieve Russell*
**Facilities available:**

**Hillgrove Hotel Leisure & Spa**
Monaghan Town, Co. Monaghan
Tel: 047-81288 ......................Page 359
**Arrangements with Golf Courses:**
*Rossmore GC, Clones GC, Nuremore Country Club, Castle Hume GC, Mannan Castle GC, Co. Armagh GC*
**Green Fees From:** *€30.00*
**Facilities available:**

**Nuremore Hotel & Country Club**
Carrickmacross, Co. Monaghan
Tel: 042-966 1438 ..................Page 358
**Golf Course(s) On Site:**
*18 Hole Golf Course*
**Arrangements with Golf Courses:**
*Nuremore, Baltray, Headfort, Dundalk, Greenore, Royal County Down*
**Green Fees From:** *€35.00*
**Facilities available:**

## Co. Offaly

**Bridge House Hotel, Leisure Club & Spa**
Tullamore, Co. Offaly
Tel: 057-932 5600 ..................Page 361
**Arrangements with Golf Courses:**
*Esker Hills & Tullamore Golf Club both 5 minutes away, Castle Barna Golf Club 12km away, Glasson, Virtual Reality Golf Facility on site*
**Green Fees From:** *€35.00*
**Facilities available:**

**Brosna Lodge Hotel**
Banagher, Co. Offaly
Tel: 057-915 1350 ..................Page 359
**Arrangements with Golf Courses:**
*Birr, Esker Hills, Tullamore, Roscrea, Portumna, Ballinasloe*
**Green Fees From:** *€35.00*
**Facilities available:**

**County Arms Hotel & Leisure Club**
Birr, Co. Offaly
Tel: 057-912 0791 ..................Page 360
**Arrangements with Golf Courses:**
*Birr, Portumna, Roscrea, Esker Hills, Castle Barna, Glasson*
**Green Fees From:** *€20.00*
**Facilities available:**

**Days Hotel Tullamore**
Tullamore, Co. Offaly
Tel: 1890-329329...................Page 362
**Arrangements with Golf Courses:**
*Esker Hills GC, Tullamore GC, Glasson GC*
**Facilities available:**

**Doolys Hotel**
Birr, Co. Offaly
Tel: 057-912 0032 ..................Page 360
**Arrangements with Golf Courses:**
*Birr, Roscrea, Esker Hills, Mount Temple, Tullamore*
**Green Fees From:** *€35.00*
**Facilities available:**

**Moorhill House Hotel and Garden Suites**
Tullamore, Co. Offaly
Tel: 057-932 1395 ..................Page 362
**Arrangements with Golf Courses:**
*Esker Hills, Tullamore, Castle Barna, Mount Temple, Birr, Glasson, Mullingar, The Heritage*
**Green Fees From:** *€20.00*
**Facilities available:**

**Tullamore Court Hotel Conference & Leisure Centre**
Tullamore, Co. Offaly
Tel: 057-934 6666 ..................Page 363
**Arrangements with Golf Courses:**
*Tullamore, Esker Hills, Castle Barna, Mount Temple, Glasson, Birr, The Heritage at Killenard*
**Green Fees From:** *€35.00*
**Facilities available:**

## Co. Westmeath

**Bloomfield House Hotel**
Mullingar, Co. Westmeath
Tel: 044-934 0894 ..................Page 368
**Arrangements with Golf Courses:**
*Mullingar, Glasson, Mount Temple, Esker Hills, Athlone, Tullamore*
**Green Fees From:** *€40.00*
**Facilities available:**

**Creggan Court Hotel**
Athlone, Co. Westmeath
Tel: 090-647 7777 ..................Page 364
**Arrangements with Golf Courses:**
*Glasson, Mount Temple, Esker Hills, Athlone, Mullingar*
**Green Fees From:** *€40.00*
**Facilities available:**

**Glasson Golf Hotel and Country Club**
Athlone, Co. Westmeath
Tel: 090-648 5120 ..................Page 364
**Golf Course(s) On Site:**
*18 Hole Golf Course*
**Arrangements with Golf Courses:**
*Glasson Golf Hotel and Country Club, Athlone Golf Club, Mount Temple Golf Club, Esker Hills, Moate Golf Club, Tullamore*
**Green Fees From:** *€60.00*
**Facilities available:**

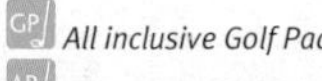
*All inclusive Golf Package* / *Advance Golf Booking Made*
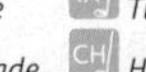
*Tuition Available* / *Hire Of Clubs*

*Golf Cart / Pull Cart* / *Transport To Course*
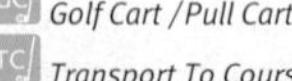
*Arrange Tee Off Times* / *Preferential Green Fees*
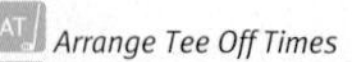
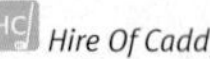
*Hire Of Caddy*

**Greville Arms Hotel**
Mullingar, Co. Westmeath
Tel: 044-934 8563 ..................Page 368
**Arrangements with Golf Courses:**
*Mullingar, Glasson, Mount Temple, Tullamore, Longford, Esker Hills*
**Green Fees From:** *€30.00*
**Facilities available:**

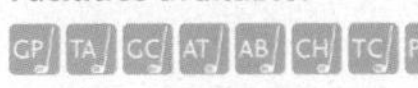

**Hilamar Hotel**
Kinnegad, Co. Westmeath
Tel: 044-939 1719 ..................Page 367
**Arrangements with Golf Courses:**
*Mullingar, New Forest Tyrrellspass, Trim, Mount Temple, Edenderry*
**Green Fees From:** *€45.00*
**Facilities available:**

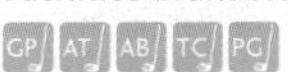

**Hodson Bay Hotel**
Athlone, Co. Westmeath
Tel: 090-644 2000 ..................Page 365
**Golf Course(s) On Site:**
*18 Hole Golf Course*
**Arrangements with Golf Courses:**
*Athlone, Glasson, Mount Temple, Ballinasloe, Roscommon, Esker Hills*
**Green Fees From:** *€30.00*
**Facilities available:**

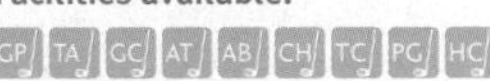

**Mullingar Park Hotel**
Mullingar, Co. Westmeath
Tel: 044-933 7500 ..................Page 369
**Arrangements with Golf Courses:**
*Mullingar, Glasson, Tullamore, Delvin, Mount Temple, Athlone, Highfield, Rathcore*
**Green Fees From:** *€35.00*
**Facilities available:**

**Temple Country Retreat & Spa**
Moate, Co. Westmeath
Tel: 057-933 5118 ..................Page 367
**Arrangements with Golf Courses:**
*New Forest, Glasson, Esker Hills, Mount Temple, Mullingar, Athlone*
**Green Fees From:** *€60.00*
**Facilities available:**

## Co. Wicklow

**Arklow Bay Conference, Leisure & Spa Hotel**
Arklow, Co. Wicklow
Tel: 0402-32309 ....................Page 370
**Arrangements with Golf Courses:**
*European, Arklow, Woodenbridge, Blainroe, Seafield*
**Green Fees From:** *€40.00*
**Facilities available:**

**Avon Ri**
Blessington, Co. Wicklow
Tel: 045-900670 ....................Page 372
**Arrangements with Golf Courses:**
*Tulfaris, Citywest*
**Green Fees From:** *€60.00*
**Facilities available:**

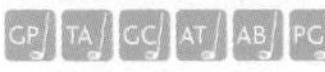

**BrookLodge and Wells Spa**
Aughrim, Co. Wicklow
Tel: 0402-36444......................Page 371
**Golf Course(s) On Site:**
*18 Hole Golf Course*
**Green Fees From:** *€120.00*
**Facilities available:**

**Chester Beatty Inn**
Ashford, Co. Wicklow
Tel: 0404-40206......................Page 371
**Arrangements with Golf Courses:**
*Druid's Glen, Woodenbridge, Blainroe, European, Powerscourt, Wicklow Golf Club*
**Facilities available:**

**Glendalough Hotel**
Glendalough, Co. Wicklow
Tel: 0404-45135......................Page 375
**Arrangements with Golf Courses:**
*The European Club, Woodenbridge, Charlesland, Druid's Glen, Blainroe, Roundwood*
**Green Fees From:** *€35.00*
**Facilities available:**

**Glenview Hotel**
Glen-O-The-Downs, Co. Wicklow
Tel: 01-287 3399 ....................Page 376
**Arrangements with Golf Courses:**
*Glen O' The Downs, Powerscourt, Druid's Glen, The European Club, Charlesland, Delgany, Greystones*
**Green Fees From:** *€55.00*
**Facilities available:**

**Grand Hotel**
Wicklow Town, Co. Wicklow
Tel: 0404-67337 ....................Page 377
**Arrangements with Golf Courses:**
*Blainroe, Wicklow, Druid's Glen, European Golf Course, Woodenbridge, Powerscourt*
**Green Fees From:** *€35.00*
**Facilities available:**

**Heather House Hotel**
Bray, Co. Wicklow
Tel: 01-286 8000 ....................Page 373
**Arrangements with Golf Courses:**
*Bray, Woodbrook, Old Conna, Powerscourt, Greystones, Druid's Glen*
**Green Fees From:** *€50.00*
**Facilities available:**

**Hunter's Hotel**
Rathnew, Co. Wicklow
Tel: 0404-40106......................Page 376
**Arrangements with Golf Courses:**
*Druid's Glen, European, Blainroe, Powerscourt, Woodenbridge, Delgany*
**Green Fees From:** *€40.00*
**Facilities available:**

**Rathsallagh House, Golf and Country Club**
Dunlavin, Co. Wicklow
Tel: 045-403112 ......................Page 374
**Golf Course(s) On Site:**
*18 Hole Golf Course*
**Arrangements with Golf Courses:**
*Mount Juliet, Druid's Glen, Powerscourt, Portmarnock, Mount Wolseley, The Heritage*
**Green Fees From:** *€55.00*
**Facilities available:**

**Stoops Guesthouse**
Shillelagh, Co. Wicklow
Tel: 053-9429903 ..................Page 377
**Arrangements with Golf Courses:**
*Coolattin*
**Green Fees From:** *€35.00*
**Facilities available:**

**Summerhill House Hotel**
Enniskerry, Co. Wicklow
Tel: 01-286 7928 ....................Page 374
**Arrangements with Golf Courses:**
*Powerscourt, Druid's Glen, Kilternan, Old Conna*
**Green Fees From:** *€35.00*
**Facilities available:**

---

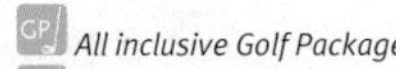
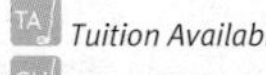
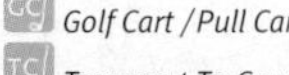
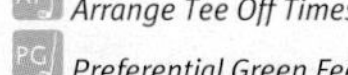

GP *All inclusive Golf Package* · TA *Tuition Available* · GC *Golf Cart / Pull Cart* · AT *Arrange Tee Off Times* · HC *Hire Of Caddy*
AB *Advance Golf Booking Made* · CH *Hire Of Clubs* · TC *Transport To Course* · PG *Preferential Green Fees*

## Co. Wicklow CONTINUED

**The Ritz-Carlton, Powerscourt**
Enniskerry, Co. Wicklow
Tel: 01-274 8888 ....................Page 375
**Golf Course(s) On Site:**
*2 x 18 Hole Golf Courses*
**Green Fees From:** *€74.25*
**Facilities available:**

**Tinakilly House Hotel**
Rathnew, Co. Wicklow
Tel: 0404-69274 ....................Page 377
**Arrangements with Golf Courses:**
*European Club, Druid's Glen, Blainroe, Woodenbridge, Wicklow, Delgany*
**Green Fees From:** *€50.00*
**Facilities available:**

**Woodenbridge Hotel**
Woodenbridge, Co. Wicklow
Tel: 0402-35146......................Page 378
**Arrangements with Golf Courses:**
*Woodenbridge, Blainroe, Arklow, European Club, Coollattin, Seafield*
**Green Fees From:** *€30.00*
**Facilities available:**

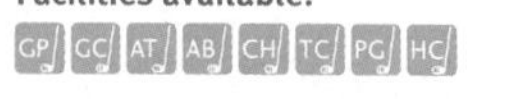

**Woodenbridge Lodge**
Woodenbridge, Co. Wicklow
Tel: 0402-35146......................Page 378
**Arrangements with Golf Courses:**
*Woodenbridge GC, Arklow GC, Seafield GC, Coollattin GC, Blainroe GC, European Club*
**Green Fees From:** *€30.00*
**Facilities available:**

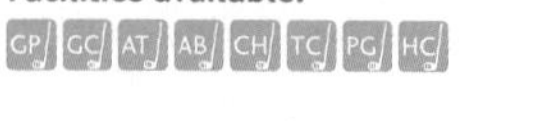

# Northern Ireland

## Co. Antrim

**Bayview Hotel**
Bushmills, Co. Antrim
Tel: 028-2073 4100 ................Page 382
**Arrangements with Golf Courses:**
*Royal Portrush, Portstewart, Castlerock, Ballycastle, Bushfoot, Gracehill, Galgorm Castle*
**Green Fees From:** *£50.00*
**Facilities available:**

GP TA GC AT AB CH TC PG HC

**Bushmills Inn Hotel**
Bushmills, Co. Antrim
Tel: 028-2073 3000 ................Page 382
**Arrangements with Golf Courses:**
*Royal Portrush, Portstewart, Castlerock, Ballycastle, Bushfoot, Gracehill*
**Facilities available:**

**Londonderry Arms Hotel**
Carnlough, Co. Antrim
Tel: 028-2888 5255 ................Page 383
**Arrangements with Golf Courses:**
*Cairndhu GC (18 Hole, 7 miles), Galgorm GC (18 Hole, 14 miles), Ballycastle (18 Hole, 26 miles), Cushendall (9 Hole, 12 miles)*
**Facilities available:**

**Ramada Portrush**
Portrush, Co. Antrim
Tel: 028-7082 6100 ................Page 383
**Arrangements with Golf Courses:**
*Royal Portrush, Portstewart, Castlerock, Ballycastle, Bushfoot, Gracehill, Galgorm Castle*
**Green Fees From:** *£50.00*
**Facilities available:**

## Co. Derry

**Radisson SAS Roe Park Resort**
Limavady, Co. Derry
Tel: 028-7772 2222 ................Page 389
**Golf Course(s) On Site:**
*18 Hole Golf Course*
**Arrangements with Golf Courses:**
*Roe Park Golf Club, Radisson SAS Roe Park Resort*
**Facilities available:**

## Co. Down

**Burrendale Hotel and Country Club**
Newcastle, Co. Down
Tel: 028-4372 2599 ................Page 391
**Arrangements with Golf Courses:**
*Royal County Down, Kilkeel, Downpatrick, Ardglass, Spa, Bright*
**Facilities available:**

## Co. Fermanagh

**Lough Erne Golf Resort**
Enniskillen, Co. Fermanagh
Tel: 028-6632 0613 ................Page 392
**Arrangements with Golf Courses:**
*Castle Hume*
**Green Fees From:** *£25.00*
**Facilities available:**

GP TA GC AT AB CH TC

**Mahons Hotel**
Irvinestown, Co. Fermanagh
Tel: 028-6862 1656 ................Page 393
**Arrangements with Golf Courses:**
*Castle Hume Golf Course*
**Facilities available:**

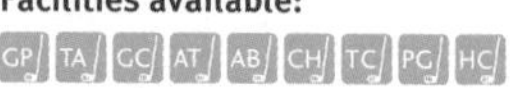

### Did you know ?

Year round golfing in Ireland is perfectly feasible - provided you have suitable wet weather gear! - but conditions are best between April and October.

During these months you can expect to be able to play up to 7pm in the evening at least, with many courses playable until 10pm or 11pm. During the months of June-August you may even fit two games into a single day.

For best value, aim to play as early as possible in the day and preferrably on a week day. In many golf clubs there are few if any tee times available to visitors at weekends during the summer, so if you must play at the weekend book well in advance.

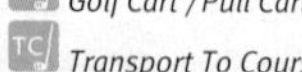
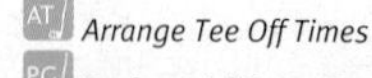
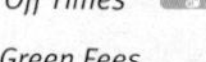

GP *All inclusive Golf Package* — TA *Tuition Available* — GC *Golf Cart / Pull Cart* — AT *Arrange Tee Off Times* — HC *Hire Of Caddy*
AB *Advance Golf Booking Made* — CH *Hire Of Clubs* — TC *Transport To Course* — PG *Preferential Green Fees*

# ANGLING - IRELAND 2008

Ireland is accepted as being the outstanding angling holiday resort in Europe. Whether you are a competition angler, a serious specimen hunter, or just fishing while on holiday, you are sure to enjoy yourself here. With over 14,000km of rivers feeding over 4,000 lakes and with no part of Ireland over 112km from the sea, Ireland can, in truth, be called an angler's dream!

*.....So come on and get hooked!*

We invite you to sample the fishing, the countryside and the friendship of the Irish people and then to stay in some of Ireland's most charming accommodation. We have listed a range of hotels and guesthouses which are either situated with or near angling facilities. Your host will assist you in arranging your angling itinerary. A full description of the hotels and guesthouses can be had by looking up the appropriate page number.

***Premises are listed in Alphabetical Order in each County.***

# Ireland West

## Co. Clare

**Ardilaun Guesthouse**
Ennis, Co. Clare
Tel: 065-682 2311 ...................... Page 41
Coarse Angling:
*Pike, Perch, Trout*
Game Angling:
*Trout, Salmon*
Facilities available:
BT DR TR FR

**Falls Hotel & Spa**
Ennistymon, Co. Clare
Tel: 065-707 1004 .................... Page 44
Coarse Angling:
*Bream, Tench, Pike*
Facilities available:

**Grovemount House**
Ennistymon, Co. Clare
Tel: 065-707 1431 ...................... Page 44
Coarse Angling:
*Roach*
Game Angling:
*Trout*
Facilities available:

**Mountshannon Hotel**
Mountshannon, Co. Clare
Tel: 061-927162 ........................ Page 52
Coarse Angling:
*Bream, Perch, Pike*
Game Angling:
*Salmon, Trout*
Facilities available:
BT BH DR PL GI TR FR PR

## Co. Donegal

**Downings Bay Hotel**
Letterkenny, Co. Donegal
Tel: 074-915 5586 .................... Page 63
Sea Angling:
*Pollock, Mackerel, Tuna, Ling, Skate, Cod, Haddock*
Facilities available:

**Highlands Hotel**
Glenties, Co. Donegal
Tel: 074-955 1111 ...................... Page 61
Game Angling:
*Salmon, Trout*
Sea Angling:
*Mackerel, Pollock, Ling*
Facilities available:
DR PL FR PR

## Co. Galway

**Alcock and Brown Hotel**
Clifden, Co. Galway
Tel: 095-21206 .......................... Page 73
Coarse Angling:
*Perch, Pike, Tench, Roach*
Game Angling:
*Trout, Salmon, Brown Trout*
Sea Angling:
*Pollock, Cod, Sea Bass, Mackerel*
Facilities available:
BT BH DR PL GI FR PR

**Anglers Rest Hotel**
Headford, Co. Galway
Tel: 093-35528 ........................ Page 93
Coarse Angling:
*Pike, Perch*
Game Angling:
*Salmon, Trout*
Facilities available:
BT BH DR PL GI FR

**Ballynahinch Castle Hotel**
Ballynahinch, Co. Galway
Tel: 095-31006 .......................... Page 70
Game Angling:
*Salmon, Brown Trout, Sea Trout*
Sea Angling:
*Charter Available*
Facilities available:
BT BH DR PL GI TR FR PR

**Ben View House**
Clifden, Co. Galway
Tel: 095-21256 .......................... Page 74
Game Angling:
*Salmon, Trout*
Sea Angling:
*Cod, Herring, Whiting, Pollock, Plaice*
Facilities available:
BT BH DR FR PR

**Carlton Shearwater Hotel & C Spa**
Ballinasloe, Co. Galway
Tel: 0909-630400 ...................... Page 70
Coarse Angling:
*Pike, Perch, Bream, Roach, Tench, Rudd*
Game Angling:
*Trout, Salmon*
Facilities available:
BT BH PL GI PR

**Cashel House Hotel**
Cashel, Co. Galway
Tel: 095-31001 .......................... Page 72
Coarse Angling:
*Pike*
Game Angling:
*Trout, Salmon*
Facilities available:
BT BH PL GI FR

**Corrib Wave Guest House**
Oughterard, Co. Galway
Tel: 091-552147 ........................ Page 96
Coarse Angling:
*Pike, Perch*
Game Angling:
*Brown Trout, Salmon*
Facilities available:
BT BH DR PL GI TR FR

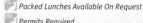

BT *Bait & Tackle* BH *Boats For Hire* DR *Drying Room* PL *Packed Lunches Available On Request*
GI *Gillie* TR *Tackle Room* FR *Freezer For Storage Of Catch* PR *Permits Required*

**Doonmore Hotel**
Inishbofin Island, Co. Galway
Tel: 095-45804 ........................Page 93
Sea Angling:
*Pollock, Mackerel, Plaice*
Facilities available:

**Fairhill House Hotel**
Clonbur (An Fháirche), Co. Galway
Tel: 094-954 6176 ....................Page 78
Coarse Angling:
*Pike, Roach, Perch, Bream, Eel*
Game Angling:
*Salmon, Wild Brown Trout*
Sea Angling:
*Dogfish, Cod, Ray, Shark, Pollock*
Facilities available:

**Galway Bay Hotel, Conference & Leisure Centre**
Galway City, Co. Galway
Tel: 091-520520........................Page 83
Coarse Angling:
*Bream, Roach, Perch, Rudd*
Game Angling:
*Salmon, Brown Trout*
Sea Angling:
*Blue Shark, Cod, Ling, Pollock, Ray*
Facilities available:

**Glenlo Abbey Hotel**
Galway City, Co. Galway
Tel: 091-526666........................Page 84
Coarse Angling:
*Pike, Bream, Roach*
Game Angling:
*Trout, Salmon*
Sea Angling:
*Shark, Cod, Mackerel*
Facilities available:

**Harbour Hotel**
Galway City, Co. Galway
Tel: 091-569466........................Page 84
Coarse Angling:
*Pike, Perch, Rudd, Tench, Carp*
Game Angling:
*Salmon, Trout, Sea Trout*
Sea Angling:
*Mackerel, Shark, Skate, Ray*
Facilities available:

**Inishbofin House Hotel**
Inishbofin Island, Co. Galway
Tel: 095-45809 ........................Page 93
Sea Angling:
*Pollock, Ray, Plaice, Mackerel, Gurnard, Tope*
Facilities available:

**Lough Inagh Lodge**
Recess, Co. Galway
Tel: 095-34706 ........................Page 98
Game Angling:
*Salmon, Brown Trout, Sea Trout*
Sea Angling:
*Sea Trout*
Facilities available:

**O'Deas Hotel**
Loughrea, Co. Galway
Tel: 091-841611 ........................Page 96
Coarse Angling:
*Pike, Perch*
Game Angling:
*Trout*
Facilities available:

**Portfinn**
Leenane, Co. Galway
Tel: 095-42265 ........................Page 95
Coarse Angling:
*Pike, Roach, Perch*
Game Angling:
*Trout, Salmon*
Sea Angling:
*Cod, Shark, Pollock, Mackerel*
Facilities available:

**Shannon Oaks Hotel & Country Club**
Portumna, Co. Galway
Tel: 090-974 1777 ....................Page 98
Coarse Angling:
*Pike, Bream, Eel, Roach, Perch*
Facilities available:

## Co. Leitrim

**Flynns Shannon Key West Hotel**
Rooskey, Co. Leitrim
Tel: 071-963 8800....................Page 104
Coarse Angling:
*Bream, Rudd, Pike, Perch, Brown Trout*
Facilities available:

**Kilbrackan Arms Hotel**
Carrigallen, Co. Leitrim
Tel: 049-433 9737 ..................Page 102
Coarse Angling:
*Tench, Bream, Roach, Rudd, Perch, Pike*
Game Angling:
*Salmon, Trout*
Facilities available:

**Lough Rynn Castle**
Mohill, Co. Leitrim
Tel: 071-963 2700....................Page 103
Coarse Angling:
*Trench, Bream, Pike*
Facilities available:

## Co. Limerick

**Adare Manor Hotel & Golf Resort**
Adare, Co. Limerick
Tel: 061-396566 ......................Page 104
Game Angling:
*Salmon, Trout*
Facilities available:

**Carriage House (The)**
Limerick City, Co. Limerick
Tel: 061-396566 ......................Page 106
Game Angling:
*Salmon, Trout*
Facilities available:

**Fitzgeralds Woodlands House Hotel, Health and Leisure Spa**
Adare, Co. Limerick
Tel: 061-605100 ......................Page 105
Coarse Angling:
*Pike*
Game Angling:
*Trout, Salmon*
Facilities available:

## Co. Mayo

**Ashford Castle**
Cong, Co. Mayo
Tel: 094-954 6003....................Page 119
Coarse Angling:
*Perch, Pike*
Game Angling:
*Trout, Salmon*
Sea Angling:
*Pollock, Mackerel*
Facilities available:

---

*Bait & Tackle*
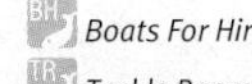
*Boats For Hire*
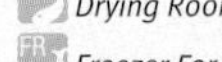
*Drying Room*

*Packed Lunches Available On Request*
*Gillie*
*Tackle Room*
*Freezer For Storage Of Catch*
*Permits Required*

## Co. Mayo CONTINUED

### Carlton Atlantic Coast Hotel
Westport, Co. Mayo
Tel: 098-29000........................Page 124
Sea Angling:
*Ray, Bull Huss, Monkfish, Dogfish, Conger, Pollock, Tope*
Facilities available:

### Castlecourt Hotel Conference and Leisure Centre
Westport, Co. Mayo
Tel: 098-55088........................Page 125
Coarse Angling:
*Pike, Perch, Roach, Bream, Tench, Hybrids*
Game Angling:
*Trout, Salmon*
Sea Angling:
*Cod, Shark, Pollock, Plaice, Dogfish, Conger Eels, Whiting, Monkfish*
Facilities available:
BT BH DR PL GI FR PR

### Clew Bay Hotel
Westport, Co. Mayo
Tel: 098-28088........................Page 125
Coarse Angling:
*Pike, Bream, Perch, Tench, Roach*
Game Angling:
*Trout, Salmon*
Sea Angling:
*Sea Trout, Mackerel, Pollock, Ray, Herring*
Facilities available:

### Healys Restaurant & Country House
Pontoon, Co. Mayo
Tel: 094-925 6443 ..................Page 122
Coarse Angling:
*Pike, Perch*
Game Angling:
*Salmon, Brown Trout, Rainbow Trout, Sea Trout*
Sea Angling:
*Blue Shark, Pollock, Mackerel, Cod, Sole, Brill, Turbot, Plaice, Conger Eel*
Facilities available:

### Hotel Westport leisure - spa - conference
Westport, Co. Mayo
Tel: 098-25122 ........................Page 126
Coarse Angling:
*Pike, Perch, Bream, Eel, Roach, Tench*
Game Angling:
*Salmon, Trout*
Sea Angling:
*Cod, Whiting, Sea Trout, Mackerel, Monkfish*
Facilities available:
BT BH DR PL GI TR FR PR

### Kelly's Gateway Hotel
Swinford, Co. Mayo
Tel: 094-925 2156....................Page 123
Coarse Angling:
*Pike, Bream, Tench*
Game Angling:
*Salmon, Sea Trout, Brown Trout*
Facilities available:

### Knockranny House Hotel & Spa
Westport, Co. Mayo
Tel: 098-28600........................Page 126
Game Angling:
*Salmon, Trout, Sea Trout*
Sea Angling:
*Cod, Whiting, Skate, Ray, Monkfish*
Facilities available:

### McWilliam Park Hotel (The)
Claremorris, Co. Mayo
Tel: 094-937 3333....................Page 119
Coarse Angling:
*Rudd, Bream, Roach, Pike*
Game Angling:
*Brown Trout, Salmon*
Sea Angling:
*Mackerel, Plaice, Flounder, Ray, Tope*
Facilities available:

### Mount Falcon Country House Hotel
Ballina, Co. Mayo
Tel: 096-74472 ........................Page 115
Coarse Angling:
*Pike, Perch, Roach, Bream*
Game Angling:
*Salmon, Trout, Sea Trout*
Sea Angling:
*Sea Trout, Bass, Shark, Turbot, Ray*
Facilities available:
BT BH DR PL GI FR PR

### Ostán Oileán Acla
Achill Island, Co. Mayo
Tel: 098-45138 ........................Page 114
Game Angling:
*Trout*
Sea Angling:
*Cod, Ling, Conger Eel, Shark, Mackerel, Sea Trout, Brill, Whiting, Ray, Tuna*
Facilities available:
BT BH PL GI FR PR

### Western Strands Hotel
Belmullet, Co. Mayo
Tel: 097-81096 ........................Page 117
Sea Angling:
*Mackerel, Pollock, Glasson, Turbot, Halibut*
Facilities available:

### Westport Plaza Hotel
Westport, Co. Mayo
Tel: 098-51166 ........................Page 127
Coarse Angling:
*Pike, Perch, Roach, Bream, Tench, Hybrids*
Sea Angling:
*Cod, Shark, Pollock, Plaice, Dogfish, Conger Eels, Whiting, Monkfish*
Facilities available:

## Co. Roscommon

### Gleesons Townhouse & Restaurant
Roscommon Town, Co. Roscommon
Tel: 090-662 6954 ..................Page 129
Coarse Angling:
*Pike, Trout, Bream, Roach, Hybrids*
Facilities available:
DR PL FR

### Royal Hotel
Boyle, Co. Roscommon
Tel: 071-966 2016 ....................Page 129
Coarse Angling:
*Pike, Trout, Bream, Roach, Perch*
Game Angling:
*Salmon, Trout*
Sea Angling:
*Pollock, Mackerel*
Facilities available:
BT BH DR PL GI FR

*Bait & Tackle*
*Gillie*

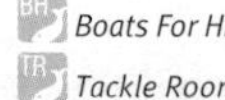


*Boats For Hire*
*Tackle Room*

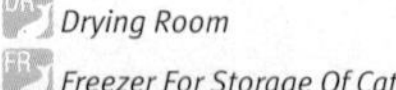


*Drying Room*
*Freezer For Storage Of Catch*

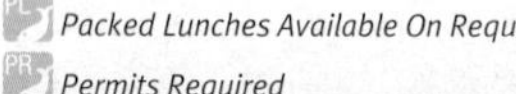


*Packed Lunches Available On Request*
*Permits Required*

**Whitehouse Hotel**
Ballinlough, Co. Roscommon
Tel: 094-964 0112 ....................Page 128
**Coarse Angling:**
*Pike, Perch, Rudd, Bream, Tench*
**Game Angling:**
*Brown Trout*
**Facilities available:**

## Co. Sligo

**Beach Hotel and Leisure Club**
Mullaghmore, Co. Sligo
Tel: 071-916 6103 ....................Page 132
**Sea Angling:**
*Shark, Tuna, Cod, Mackerel, Pollock*
**Facilities available:**

**Kingsfort Country House**
Ballintogher, Co. Sligo
Tel: 071-911 5111 ....................Page 130
**Coarse Angling:**
*Pike*
**Game Angling:**
*Sea Trout, Salmon*
**Sea Angling:**
*Mackerel, Pollock, Ling, Sea Bass*
**Facilities available:**

**Sligo City Hotel**
Sligo Town, Co. Sligo
Tel: 071-914 4000 ....................Page 134
**Coarse Angling:**
*Bream, Pike, Perch, Hybrids*
**Game Angling:**
*Salmon, Sea Trout, Trout*
**Sea Angling:**
*Cod, Ling, Mackerel, Pollock, Sea Bass, Shark*
**Facilities available:**

# Ireland South

## Co. Carlow

**Seven Oaks Hotel**
Carlow Town, Co. Carlow
Tel: 059-913 1308 ....................Page 141
**Coarse Angling:**
*Bream, Perch, Roach, Pike, Eel*
**Game Angling:**
*Salmon, Trout*
**Facilities available:**

## Co. Cork

**Carlton Kinsale Hotel & C Spa**
Kinsale, Co. Cork
Tel: 021-470 6000....................Page 167
**Coarse Angling:**
*Salmon*
**Sea Angling:**
*Shark, Makerel, Cod, Pollock*
**Facilities available:**

**Celtic Ross Hotel Conference & Leisure Centre**
Rosscarbery, Co. Cork
Tel: 023-48722 ........................Page 174
**Coarse Angling:**
*Bream, Roach, Tench*
**Game Angling:**
*Trout, Salmon*
**Sea Angling:**
*Cod, Shark, Wrasse, Flat Fish*
**Facilities available:**
BT BH DR PL GI FR PR

**Commodore Hotel**
Cobh, Co. Cork
Tel: 021-481 1277 ....................Page 152
**Sea Angling:**
*Ling, Cod, Pollock, Conger, Blue Shark*
**Facilities available:**

**Coolcower House**
Macroom, Co. Cork
Tel: 026-41695 ........................Page 171
**Coarse Angling:**
*Bream, Rudd, Pike, Perch*
**Game Angling:**
*Trout*
**Facilities available:**

**Dunmore House Hotel**
Clonakilty, Co. Cork
Tel: 023-33352........................Page 150
**Sea Angling:**
*Bass, Cod, Mackerel, Skate, Whiting, Ling*
**Facilities available:**

**Fitzgeralds Vienna Woods Hotel Cork**
Cork City, Co. Cork
Tel: 021-455 6800....................Page 157
**Coarse Angling:**
*Trout, Pike, Perch, Bream*
**Game Angling:**
*Salmon*
**Sea Angling:**
*Shark, Ling, Cod, Ray, Pollock*
**Facilities available:**
BT BH DR PL GI TR FR PR

**Harbour Lodge**
Kinsale, Co. Cork
Tel: 021-477 2376....................Page 168
**Sea Angling:**
*Cod, Shark, Mackerel, Pollock, Conger Eel*
**Facilities available:**

**Hibernian Hotel and Leisure Centre**
Mallow, Co. Cork
Tel: 022-58200........................Page 172
**Coarse Angling:**
*Bream, Pike, Perch, Tench*
**Game Angling:**
*Trout, Salmon*
**Facilities available:**
DR PL FR PR

**Longueville House Hotel**
Mallow, Co. Cork
Tel: 022-47156 ........................Page 172
**Game Angling:**
*Brown Trout, Salmon*
**Facilities available:**
BT DR PL GI FR PR

**Maryborough Hotel & Spa**
Cork City, Co. Cork
Tel: 021-436 5555 ....................Page 161
**Coarse Angling:**
*Bream, Perch, Pike, Trout, Rudd, Eel*
**Game Angling:**
*Salmon*
**Sea Angling:**
*Shark, Ling, Conger, Pollock, Cod, Ray, Wrasse*
**Facilities available:**
BT BH PL GI PR

**Midleton Park Hotel**
Midleton, Co. Cork
Tel: 021-463 5100 ....................Page 173
**Sea Angling:**
*Mackerel, Cod, Shark, Pollock, Skate, Turbot*
**Facilities available:**

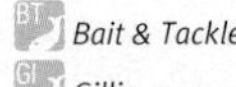
BT *Bait & Tackle*
GI *Gillie*

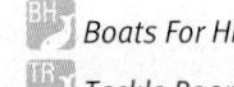
BH *Boats For Hire*
TR *Tackle Room*

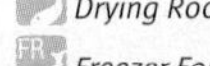
DR *Drying Room*

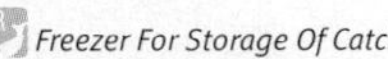
FR *Freezer For Storage Of Catch*

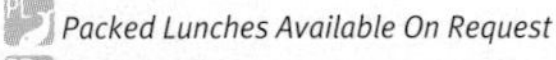
PL *Packed Lunches Available On Request*
PR *Permits Required*

## Co. Cork CONTINUED

**Riverside Park Hotel (The)**
Macroom, Co. Cork
Tel: 026-20090 ........................Page 171
**Coarse Angling:**
*Bream, Pike, Rudd, Perch*
**Game Angling:**
*Trout*
**Facilities available:**

**Trident Hotel**
Kinsale, Co. Cork
Tel: 021-477 9300....................Page 170
**Game Angling:**
*Salmon, Brown Trout*
**Sea Angling:**
*Shark, Ling, Conger Eel, Mackerel, Pollock, Sea Trout*
**Facilities available:**

**WatersEdge Hotel**
Cobh, Co. Cork
Tel: 021-481 5566....................Page 152
**Sea Angling:**
*Plaice, Cod, Monkfish, Bass, Turbot*
**Facilities available:**

**Whispering Pines Hotel**
Crosshaven, Co. Cork
Tel: 021-483 1843....................Page 164
**Sea Angling:**
*Blue Shark, Conger, Ling, Pollock, Coalfish*
**Facilities available:**

## Co. Kerry

**Ard-Na-Sidhe**
Caragh Lake, Co. Kerry
Tel: 066-976 9105....................Page 180
**Game Angling:**
*Salmon, Trout*
**Facilities available:**

**Butler Arms Hotel**
Waterville, Co. Kerry
Tel: 066-947 4144....................Page 219
**Game Angling:**
*Salmon, Trout*
**Sea Angling:**
*Bass, Pollock, Cod, Shark, Mackerel, Whiting*
**Facilities available:**

**Dingle Benners Hotel**
Dingle (An Daingean), Co. Kerry
Tel: 066-915 1638....................Page 184
**Game Angling:**
*Salmon, Trout*
**Sea Angling:**
*Pollock, Garfish, Blue Shark, Tope, Dogfish, Ling, Whiting, Ray*
**Facilities available:**

**Dingle Skellig Hotel & Peninsula Spa**
Dingle (An Daingean), Co. Kerry
Tel: 066-915 0200....................Page 185
**Sea Angling:**
*Pollock, Garfish, Blue Shark, Tope, Dogfish, Ling, Whiting, Ray*
**Facilities available:**

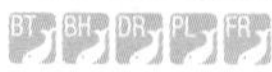

**Harbour House & Leisure Centre**
Castlegregory, Co. Kerry
Tel: 066-713 9292....................Page 181
**Game Angling:**
*Salmon, Brown Trout, White Trout*
**Sea Angling:**
*Cod, Ray, Mackerel, Shark*
**Facilities available:**

**Hotel Dunloe Castle**
Killarney, Co. Kerry
Tel: 064-44111 ........................Page 202
**Game Angling:**
*Salmon, Trout*
**Facilities available:**

**Inveraray Farm Guesthouse**
Killarney, Co. Kerry
Tel: 064-44224 ......................Page 203
**Game Angling:**
*Brown Trout, Salmon*
**Sea Angling:**
*Sea Trout*
**Facilities available:**

**Killarney Plaza Hotel & Spa**
Killarney, Co. Kerry
Tel: 064-21111 ........................Page 205
**Coarse Angling:**
*Perch, Tench*
**Game Angling:**
*Wild Brown Trout, Wild Salmon*
**Sea Angling:**
*Sole, Mackerel, Cod*
**Facilities available:**

**Killarney Royal**
Killarney, Co. Kerry
Tel: 064-31853........................Page 206
**Game Angling:**
*Brown Trout, Salmon*
**Facilities available:**

**Lake Hotel**
Killarney, Co. Kerry
Tel: 064-31035........................Page 207
**Game Angling:**
*Salmon, Brown Trout*
**Facilities available:**

**Lakelands Farm Guesthouse**
Waterville, Co. Kerry
Tel: 066-947 4303 .................Page 220
**Game Angling:**
*Salmon, Sea Trout, Brown Trout*
**Sea Angling:**
*Bass, Mackerel, Whiting, Pollock, Cod, Plaice*
**Facilities available:**

**Lansdowne Arms Hotel**
Kenmare, Co. Kerry
Tel: 064-41368 ........................Page 189
**Game Angling:**
*Salmon, Wild Trout*
**Sea Angling:**
*Sea Trout, Sole, Mackerel, Plaice, Pollock*
**Facilities available:**

**Ring of Kerry Hotel**
Cahersiveen, Co. Kerry
Tel: 066-947 2543 .................Page 179
**Game Angling:**
*Salmon, Trout*
**Sea Angling:**
*Bass, Pollock, Conger Wrasse, Mackerel*
**Facilities available:**

**Sheen Falls Lodge**
Kenmare, Co. Kerry
Tel: 064-41600 ........................Page 191
**Game Angling:**
*Salmon, Trout*
**Sea Angling:**
*Shark, Mackerel, Pollock, Skate, Conger Eel, Dogfish*
**Facilities available:**

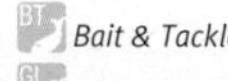
*Bait & Tackle*
*Gillie*

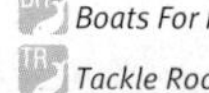
*Boats For Hire*
*Tackle Room*

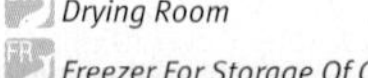
*Drying Room*
*Freezer For Storage Of Catch*

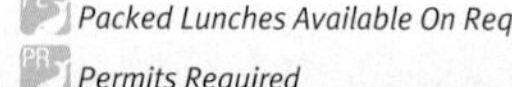
*Packed Lunches Available On Request*
*Permits Required*

**Smugglers Inn**
Waterville, Co. Kerry
Tel: 066-947 4330 ..................Page 220
**Game Angling:**
*Salmon*
**Sea Angling:**
*Cod, Bass, Mackerel, Tuna, Plaice, Sole*
**Facilities available:**

**Sneem Hotel**
Sneem, Co. Kerry
Tel: 064-75100 ........................Page 214
**Game Angling:**
*Rainbow Trout, Brown Trout, Salmon*
**Sea Angling:**
*Conger, Pollock, Ray*
**Facilities available:**

## Co. Kilkenny

**Butler House**
Kilkenny City, Co. Kilkenny
Tel: 056-776 5707 ..................Page 222
**Game Angling:**
*Brown Trout, Salmon*
**Facilities available:**

**Kilkenny River Court**
Kilkenny City, Co. Kilkenny
Tel: 056-772 3388 ..................Page 226
**Coarse Angling:**
*Shad, Bream*
**Game Angling:**
*Trout, Salmon*
**Facilities available:**

**Lyrath Estate Hotel, Spa & Convention Centre**
Kilkenny City, Co. Kilkenny
Tel: 056-776 0088 ..................Page 227
**Coarse Angling:**
*Shad, Bream*
**Game Angling:**
*Salmon, Trout*
**Facilities available:**

**Mount Juliet Conrad**
Thomastown, Co. Kilkenny
Tel: 056-777 3000 ..................Page 230
**Game Angling:**
*Salmon, Trout*
**Facilities available:**

**Waterside**
Graiguenamanagh, Co. Kilkenny
Tel: 059-972 4246 ..................Page 220
**Coarse Angling:**
*Bream, Dace, Pike, Perch, Rudd, Shark*
**Game Angling:**
*Trout, Salmon*
**Facilities available:**

## Co. Tipperary

**Cahir House Hotel**
Cahir, Co. Tipperary
Tel: 052-43000........................Page 231
**Coarse Angling:**
*Perch, Pike*
**Game Angling:**
*Trout, Salmon*
**Facilities available:**

**Cashel Palace Hotel**
Cashel, Co. Tipperary
Tel: 062-62707 ......................Page 233
**Coarse Angling:**
*Perch*
**Game Angling:**
*Salmon, Brown Trout, Grilse*
**Facilities available:**

**Kilcoran Lodge Hotel, Lodges & Leisure Centre**
Cahir, Co. Tipperary
Tel: 052-41288 ........................Page 231
**Coarse Angling:**
*Salmon, Brown Trout*
**Facilities available:**

**Racket Hall Country House Golf & Conference Hotel**
Roscrea, Co. Tipperary
Tel: 0505-21748......................Page 237
**Coarse Angling:**
*Pike, Perch, Roach, Bream, Tench*
**Game Angling:**
*Trout, Carp*
**Facilities available:**

## Co. Waterford

**Lismore House Hotel**
Lismore, Co. Waterford
Tel: 058-72966 ......................Page 244
**Game Angling:**
*Salmon,Sea Trout,*
**Facilities available:**

## Co. Wexford

**Carlton Millrace Hotel & C Spa**
Bunclody, Co. Wexford
Tel: 053-937 5100 ..................Page 252
**Game Angling:**
*Small Wild Brown Trout*
**Sea Angling:**
*Bass, Sea Trout*
**Facilities available:**

**Hotel Saltees**
Kilmore Quay, Co. Wexford
Tel: 053-912 9601....................Page 257
**Sea Angling:**
*Tope, Cod, Pollock, Ray, Ling*
**Facilities available:**

# Dublin & Ireland East

## Co. Cavan

**Crover House Hotel & Golf Club**
Mountnugent, Co. Cavan
Tel: 049-854 0206 ..................Page 272
**Coarse Angling:**
*Pike*
**Game Angling:**
*Trout*
**Facilities available:**

**Lakeside Manor Hotel**
Virginia, Co. Cavan
Tel: 049-854 8200 ..................Page 272
**Coarse Angling:**
*Bream, Hybrids, Roach, Perch, Pike*
**Game Angling:**
*Trout*
**Facilities available:**

## Co. Kildare

**Carlton Abbey Hotel & C Spa**
Athy, Co. Kildare
Tel: 059-863 0100 ..................Page 332
**Coarse Angling:**
*Pike*
**Game Angling:**
*Trout, Salmon*
**Facilities available:**

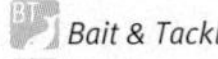
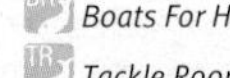
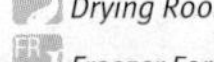
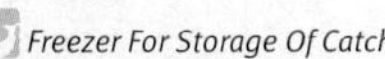

*Bait & Tackle* — *Boats For Hire* — *Drying Room* — *Packed Lunches Available On Request*
*Gillie* — *Tackle Room* — *Freezer For Storage Of Catch* — *Permits Required*

## Co. Kildare CONTINUED

**Carton House**
Maynooth, Co. Kildare
Tel: 01-505 2000 ....................Page 336
**Game Angling:**
*Trout, Salmon*
**Facilities available:**
BT BH PL GI TR FR

**Hazel Hotel**
Monasterevin, Co. Kildare
Tel: 045-525373 ....................Page 336
**Coarse Angling:**
*Pike, Rudd, Roach, Eel, Tench, Perch*
**Game Angling:**
*Salmon, Trout*
**Facilities available:**
BT PL FR PR

**Kildare Hotel, Spa and Country Club - The K Club**
Straffan, Co. Kildare
Tel: 01-601 7200......................Page 341
**Coarse Angling:**
*Carp, Bream, Rudd, Roach, Perch*
**Game Angling:**
*Salmon, Brown Trout*
**Facilities available:**
BT DR PL GI TR FR

**Moyvalley Hotel & Golf Resort**
Moyvalley, Co. Kildare
Tel: 046-954 8000 ..................Page 337
**Coarse Angling:**
*Rainbow Trout, Brown Trout*
**Facilities available:**

## Co. Meath

**Hamlet Court Hotel**
Johnstownbridge, Co. Meath
Tel: 046-954 1200 ..................Page 354
**Coarse Angling:**
*Tench, Bream, Pike, Roach, Carp*
**Game Angling:**
*Trout, Salmon*
**Facilities available:**

**Knightsbrook Hotel & Golf Resort**
Trim, Co. Meath
Tel: 046-948 2110....................Page 357
**Coarse Angling:**
*Bream*
**Game Angling:**
*Trout, Salmon*
**Facilities available:**

## Co. Offaly

**Moorhill House Hotel and Garden Suites**
Tullamore, Co. Offaly
Tel: 057-932 1395 ..................Page 362
**Coarse Angling:**
*Bream, Roach, Perch, Brown Trout, Pike*
**Facilities available:**
BT BH DR PL FR

## Co. Westmeath

**Glasson Golf Hotel and Country Club**
Athlone, Co. Westmeath
Tel: 090-648 5120 ..................Page 364
**Coarse Angling:**
*Pike, Perch, Roach, Bream*
**Game Angling:**
*Brown Trout*
**Facilities available:**
BT BH DR PL GI FR PR

**Greville Arms Hotel**
Mullingar, Co. Westmeath
Tel: 044-934 8563 ..................Page 368
**Coarse Angling:**
*Roach, Pike, Bream*
**Game Angling:**
*Brown Trout*
**Facilities available:**

**Hilamar Hotel**
Kinnegad, Co. Westmeath
Tel: 044-939 1719....................Page 367
**Coarse Angling:**
*Pike, Perch*
**Game Angling:**
*Brown Trout*
**Facilities available:**

**Hodson Bay Hotel**
Athlone, Co. Westmeath
Tel: 090-644 2000 ..................Page 365
**Coarse Angling:**
*Bream, Perch, Pike*
**Game Angling:**
*Brown Trout*
**Facilities available:**
BT BH PL GI FR PR

## Co. Wicklow

**Avon Ri**
Blessington, Co. Wicklow
Tel: 045-900670 ....................Page 372
**Coarse Angling:**
*Trout*
**Game Angling:**
*Pike, Perch, Roache*
**Facilities available:**
BH PL GI FR PR

# Northern Ireland

## Co. Fermanagh

**Lough Erne Golf Resort**
Enniskillen, Co. Fermanagh
Tel: 028-6632 0613 ................Page 392
**Coarse Angling:**
*Carp, Bream, Pike*
**Game Angling:**
*Salmon, Trout*
**Facilities available:**
BT BH DR PL GI TR

### Did you know ?

Ireland is recognised as being the outstanding angling destination in Europe. The vast variety & quality of our fishing has given the country a reputation of which we are justly proud.

The Irish climate is well suited to sport angling. It is temperate and kind to the angler with moderate summers, mild winters and adequate rainfall throughout the year.

The warm waters of the North Atlantic Drift lap the south and west coasts, giving us a milder climate than our geographical location would indicate. The result is a fabulous mixture of cold and warm water fish species, capable of exciting the specialist or casual angler on the annual family holiday.



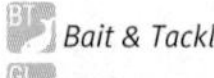

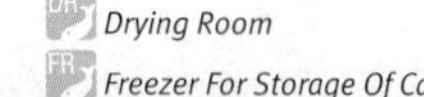

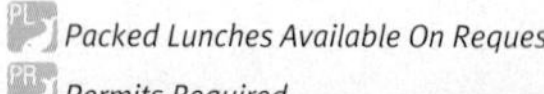

# CONFERENCE - IRELAND 2008

Small meetings or large conferences are part and parcel of life in Irish hotels and guesthouses. What makes Ireland special as a venue is the warmth of the welcome you will receive, coupled with excellent facilities which can be tailored to your needs.

*.....Our venues will tick all your boxes!*

irelandhotels.com

Official Website of the Irish Hotels Federation

# Conference Facilities ...Select A Venue For your Agenda!

We will be glad to see you and work with you to make your meeting or conference a successful one. Choose from the wide selection of special facilities throughout the country as shown here. A full description of the hotels and guesthouses can be had by looking up the appropriate page number.

***Premises are listed in Alphabetical Order in each County.***

# Ireland West

## Co. Clare

### Best Western West County Hotel
Ennis, Co. Clare
Tel: 065-682 8421 ....................Page 42
Contact Person:
C & B Coordinator
Seating Capacity of Meeting Rooms:
+500: 3 +300: 1 +50: 2 -50: 3
Facilities available:
BO AC IEH AVH

### Bunratty Castle Hotel & Angsana Spa
Bunratty, Co. Clare
Tel: 061-478700 ......................Page 38
Contact Person:
Marguerite Curran
Seating Capacity of Meeting Rooms:
+100: 1 +50: 1 -50: 2
Facilities available:
BO AC IEH AVO AVH

### Falls Hotel & Spa
Ennistymon, Co. Clare
Tel: 065-707 1004 ...................Page 44
Contact Person:
Joanne Clancy
Seating Capacity of Meeting Rooms:
+300: 1 +50: 1 -50: 3
Facilities available:
AC IEH AVO

### Lynch Clare Inn & Suites
Ennis, Co. Clare
Tel: 061-368 161 ......................Page 42
Contact Person:
C & B Coordinator
Seating Capacity of Meeting Rooms:
+400: 1 +100: 1 +50: 1 -50: 1
Facilities available:
BO AC IEH AVH

### Mountshannon Hotel
Mountshannon, Co. Clare
Tel: 061-927162 ......................Page 52
Contact Person:
Pauline Madden
Seating Capacity of Meeting Rooms:
+200: 1
Facilities available:

### Oakwood Arms Hotel
Shannon Airport, Co. Clare
Tel: 061-361500 ......................Page 53
Contact Person:
Yvonne McNamara
Seating Capacity of Meeting Rooms:
+300: 1 +200: 1 +100: 1 +50: 2
-50: 5
Facilities available:

### Park Inn Shannon Airport
Shannon Airport, Co. Clare
Tel: 061-471122 ........................Page 53
Contact Person:
Louise O'Hara
Seating Capacity of Meeting Rooms:
+200: 1 -50: 3
Facilities available:
BO AC IEH AVO

### Temple Gate Hotel
Ennis, Co. Clare
Tel: 065-682 3300 ...................Page 43
Contact Person:
Paul Madden
Seating Capacity of Meeting Rooms:
+200: 1 +100: 1 +50: 2 -50: 4
Facilities available:

## Co. Donegal

### An Chúirt, Gweedore Court Hotel
Gweedore, Co. Donegal
Tel: 074-953 2900 ....................Page 61
Contact Person:
Conference Manager
Seating Capacity of Meeting Rooms:
+200: 1 -50: 3
Facilities available:

### Ballyliffin Lodge & Spa
Ballyliffin, Co. Donegal
Tel: 074-937 8200 ...................Page 56
Contact Person:
Breda McGonigle
Seating Capacity of Meeting Rooms:
+300: 1 +50: 1 -50: 1
Facilities available:
AC AVO

### Carlton Redcastle Hotel & C Spa
Moville, Co. Donegal
Tel: 074-938 5555 ...................Page 66
Contact Person:
Cathryn Baldrick
Seating Capacity of Meeting Rooms:
+300: 1 +200: 1 +100: 2 -50: 2
Facilities available:
BO AC IEH AVO

### Castle Grove Country House Hotel
Letterkenny, Co. Donegal
Tel: 074-915 1118 ...................Page 63
Contact Person:
Mary Sweeney
Seating Capacity of Meeting Rooms:
-50: 1
Facilities available:

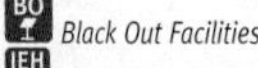
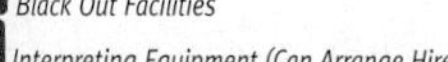

BO *Black Out Facilities*
IEH *Interpreting Equipment (Can Arrange Hire)*
AC *Air-Conditioning*
AVO *Audio Visual (Available On Premises)*
IEO *Interpreting Equipment (Available On Premises)*
AVH *Audio Visual (Can Arrange Hire)*

**Downings Bay Hotel**
Letterkenny, Co. Donegal
Tel: 074-915 5586 .................... Page 63
Contact Person:
Eileen Rock
Seating Capacity of Meeting Rooms:
+300: 1 +100: 1 +50: 1 -50: 1
Facilities available:

**Great Northern Hotel**
Bundoran, Co. Donegal
Tel: 071-984 1204 .................... Page 58
Contact Person:
Philip McGlynn
Seating Capacity of Meeting Rooms:
+500: 1 +400: 1 +300: 1 +200: 1 +100: 1 +50: 1 -50: 1
Facilities available:

**Inishowen Gateway Hotel**
Buncrana, Co. Donegal
Tel: 074-936 1144 .................... Page 57
Contact Person:
Sales/Marketing Manager, Michelle Simpson
Seating Capacity of Meeting Rooms:
+500: 1 +100: 1 -50: 1
Facilities available:

**Jackson's Hotel, Conference & Leisure Centre**
Ballybofey, Co. Donegal
Tel: 074-913 1021 .................... Page 54
Contact Person:
Margaret Jackson
Seating Capacity of Meeting Rooms:
+500: 3 +200: 1 +50: 1 -50: 5
Facilities available:
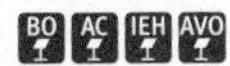


**Mill Park Hotel, Conference Centre & Leisure Club**
Donegal Town, Co. Donegal
Tel: 074-972 2880.................... Page 59
Contact Person:
Karen Slevin
Seating Capacity of Meeting Rooms:
+300: 1 -50: 4
Facilities available:
BO AC AVO

**Radisson SAS Hotel**
Letterkenny, Co. Donegal
Tel: 074-919 4444 .................... Page 64
Contact Person:
Debra Magill
Seating Capacity of Meeting Rooms:
+400: 1 +50: 1 -50: 4
Facilities available:

**Sandhouse Hotel**
Rossnowlagh, Co. Donegal
Tel: 071-985 1777 .................... Page 67
Contact Person:
Paul Diver
Seating Capacity of Meeting Rooms:
+50: 1 -50: 3
Facilities available:
BO AC IEH AVH

**Silver Tassie Hotel**
Letterkenny, Co. Donegal
Tel: 074-912 5619 .................... Page 65
Contact Person:
Rose Blaney
Seating Capacity of Meeting Rooms:
+300: 1 +200: 1 +100: 1 +50: 2 -50: 3
Facilities available:

## Co. Galway

**Anglers Rest Hotel**
Headford, Co. Galway
Tel: 093-35528 .................... Page 93
Contact Person:
Frank Heneghan
Seating Capacity of Meeting Rooms:
+100: 1
Facilities available:

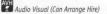

**Ardilaun Hotel, Conference Centre & Leisure Club**
Galway City, Co. Galway
Tel: 091-521433 .................... Page 80
Contact Person:
Orla Dolan
Seating Capacity of Meeting Rooms:
+500: 1 +400: 1 +300: 1 +200: 1 +100: 2 +50: 4 -50: 6
Facilities available:
BO AC IEH AVO

**Best Western Flannery's Hotel**
Galway City, Co. Galway
Tel: 091-755111 .................... Page 81
Contact Person:
Emma Mooney
Seating Capacity of Meeting Rooms:
+50: 3 -50: 3
Facilities available:
BO AC IEH AVH

**Carlton Shearwater Hotel & C Spa**
Ballinasloe, Co. Galway
Tel: 0909-630400 .................... Page 70
Contact Person:
Mairead Geehan
Seating Capacity of Meeting Rooms:
+500: 1 +400: 1 +300: 1 +200: 2 +100: 3 +50: 5 -50: 10
Facilities available:

**Connemara Coast Hotel**
Furbo, Co. Galway
Tel: 091-592108 .................... Page 78
Contact Person:
Karl Reinhardt / Claire Leahy
Seating Capacity of Meeting Rooms:
+400: 1 +300: 1 +200: 2 +100: 2 +50: 5 -50: 8
Facilities available:
BO IEH AVO

**Days Hotel Galway**
Galway City, Co. Galway
Tel: 1890-329329 .................... Page 82
Contact Person:
Karen Barrett
Seating Capacity of Meeting Rooms:
+100: 1 +50: 1 -50: 7
Facilities available:
BO AC IEH AVO

**Doonmore Hotel**
Inishbofin Island, Co. Galway
Tel: 095-45804 .................... Page 93
Contact Person:
Aileen Murray
Seating Capacity of Meeting Rooms:
+50: 2
Facilities available:
BO IEH AVH

BO *Black Out Facilities*
IEH *Interpreting Equipment (Can Arrange Hire)*
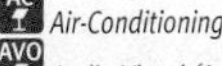
AC *Air-Conditioning*
AVO *Audio Visual (Available On Premises)*
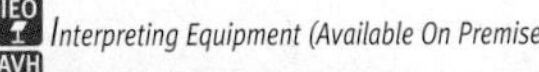
IEO *Interpreting Equipment (Available On Premises)*
AVH *Audio Visual (Can Arrange Hire)*

## Co. Galway CONTINUED

**G (The)**
Galway City, Co. Galway
Tel: 091-865200 ......................Page 83
Contact Person:
Colm O'Sullivan
Seating Capacity of Meeting Rooms:
+100: 1 -50: 5
Facilities available:
BO AC IEH AVO

**Galway Bay Hotel, Conference & Leisure Centre**
Galway City, Co. Galway
Tel: 091-520520 ......................Page 83
Contact Person:
Sinead Geoghegan
Seating Capacity of Meeting Rooms:
+500: 1 +400: 1 +300: 2 +200: 2
+100: 2 +50: 5 -50: 12
Facilities available:
BO AC IEH AVO

**Glenlo Abbey Hotel**
Galway City, Co. Galway
Tel: 091-526666 ......................Page 84
Contact Person:
Brian Bourke
Seating Capacity of Meeting Rooms:
+100: 1 +50: 2 -50: 9
Facilities available:
BO AC IEH AVH

**Harbour Hotel**
Galway City, Co. Galway
Tel: 091-569466 ......................Page 84
Contact Person:
Sales Department
Seating Capacity of Meeting Rooms:
+100: 1 +50: 1 -50: 4
Facilities available:
BO AC IEH AVO

**Hotel Meyrick**
Galway City, Co. Galway
Tel: 091-564041 ......................Page 85
Contact Person:
Duty Manager
Seating Capacity of Meeting Rooms:
+200: 1 +100: 1 -50: 3
Facilities available:
BO AC IEH AVO

**Inishbofin House Hotel**
Inishbofin Island, Co. Galway
Tel: 095-45809 ......................Page 93
Contact Person:
C&B Coordinator
Seating Capacity of Meeting Rooms:
+100: 1 +50: 2 -50: 1
Facilities available:
BO AC AVO

**Kilmurvey House**
Aran Islands, Co. Galway
Tel: 099-61218 ......................Page 68
Contact Person:
Treasa Joyce
Seating Capacity of Meeting Rooms:
+50: 1
Facilities available:
BO IEH AVH

**Lady Gregory Hotel, Conference & Leisure Club**
Gort, Co. Galway
Tel: 091-632333 ......................Page 92
Contact Person:
Brian Morrissey
Seating Capacity of Meeting Rooms:
+300: 1 -50: 2
Facilities available:
BO AC IEH AVO AVH

**Meadow Court Hotel**
Loughrea, Co. Galway
Tel: 091-841051......................Page 95
Contact Person:
Tom Corbett Jnr
Seating Capacity of Meeting Rooms:
+300: 1 -50: 1
Facilities available:
BO AC AVH

**Oranmore Lodge Hotel, Conference & Leisure Centre**
Galway City
Tel: 091-794400 ......................Page 88
Contact Person:
Mary O'Higgins / Shirley Kilduff
Seating Capacity of Meeting Rooms:
+300: 1 +100: 1 +50: 1 -50: 1
Facilities available:
BO AC IEH AVO AVH

**Park Lodge Hotel**
Spiddal, Co. Galway
Tel: 091-553159......................Page 100
Contact Person:
Jane Marie Foyle
Seating Capacity of Meeting Rooms:
+50: 1 -50: 1
Facilities available:
AC AVO

**Racing Lodge (The)**
Galway City, Co. Galway
Tel: 091-746666 ......................Page 89
Contact Person:
Conor Fleming
Seating Capacity of Meeting Rooms:
+50: 1
Facilities available:
AC IEH AVH

**Radisson SAS Hotel & Spa Galway**
Galway City, Co. Galway
Tel: 091-538300 ......................Page 89
Contact Person:
James Dilleen
Seating Capacity of Meeting Rooms:
+500: 1 +100: 3 -50: 8
Facilities available:
BO AC IEH AVO

**Raheen Woods Hotel & Spa**
Athenry, Co. Galway
Tel: 091-875888 ......................Page 69
Contact Person:
Carmel Barrett
Seating Capacity of Meeting Rooms:
+300: 1 -50: 3
Facilities available:
BO AC IEH AVO

**Salthill Hotel**
Galway City, Co. Galway
Tel: 091-522711......................Page 89
Contact Person:
Pauline Griffin
Seating Capacity of Meeting Rooms:
+500: 1 +50: 4
Facilities available:
BO AC IEH AVO

BO *Black Out Facilities*
IEH *Interpreting Equipment (Can Arrange Hire)*
AC *Air-Conditioning*
AVO *Audio Visual (Available On Premises)*
IEO *Interpreting Equipment (Available On Premises)*
AVH *Audio Visual (Can Arrange Hire)*

**Shannon Oaks Hotel & Country Club**
Portumna, Co. Galway
Tel: 090-974 1777 ....................Page 98
Contact Person:
Mary Broder
Seating Capacity of Meeting Rooms:
+500: 1 +100: 1 +50: 1 -50: 2
Facilities available:

**Twelve (The)**
Barna, Co. Galway
Tel: 091-597000 ......................Page 70
Contact Person:
Sorcha Murray/Fergus O'Halloran
Seating Capacity of Meeting Rooms:
+100: 1 +50: 1 -50: 2
Facilities available:

**Victoria Hotel**
Galway City, Co. Galway
Tel: 091-567433 ......................Page 90
Contact Person:
Reception
Seating Capacity of Meeting Rooms:
-50: 1
Facilities available:
AC IEH AVH

**Westwood (The)**
Galway City, Co. Galway
Tel: 091-521442........................Page 91
Contact Person:
David Kelly
Seating Capacity of Meeting Rooms:
+300: 1 +200: 1 +100: 1 +50: 3 -50: 3
Facilities available:
BO AC IEH AVO

## Co. Leitrim

**Bush Hotel**
Carrick-on-Shannon, Co. Leitrim
Tel: 071-967 1000 .................Page 102
Contact Person:
Joseph Dolan
Seating Capacity of Meeting Rooms:
+300: 1 +100: 2 +50: 3 -50: 5
Facilities available:
BO AC IEH AVO

**Flynns Shannon Key West Hotel**
Rooskey, Co. Leitrim
Tel: 071-963 8800 .................Page 104
Contact Person:
Joe O'Gorman
Seating Capacity of Meeting Rooms:
+500: 1 +300: 1 -50: 1
Facilities available:
BO AC AVO

**Lough Rynn Castle**
Mohill, Co. Leitrim
Tel: 071-963 2700 .................Page 103
Contact Person:
Tara Regan/Ruth Conlon
Seating Capacity of Meeting Rooms:
+300: 1
Facilities available:
BO AC IEO IEH AVO AVH

## Co. Limerick

**Adare Manor Hotel & Golf Resort**
Adare, Co. Limerick
Tel: 061-396566 ...................Page 104
Contact Person:
Maura Lee
Seating Capacity of Meeting Rooms:
+200: 1 +100: 1 +50: 1 -50: 4
Facilities available:
BO IEH AVO

**Carriage House (The)**
Limerick City, Co. Limerick
Tel: 061-396566 ...................Page 106
Contact Person:
Maura Lee
Seating Capacity of Meeting Rooms:
-50: 2
Facilities available:
BO IEO IEH

**Castletroy Park Hotel**
Limerick City, Co. Limerick
Tel: 061-335566 ...................Page 107
Contact Person:
Ursula Cullen
Seating Capacity of Meeting Rooms:
+400: 1 +300: 2 +200: 2 +100: 2 +50: 2 -50: 9
Facilities available:
BO AC IEH AVO

**Clarion Hotel Limerick**
Limerick City, Co. Limerick
Tel: 061-444100......................Page 107
Contact Person:
Lisa Toomey
Seating Capacity of Meeting Rooms:
+200: 1 +100: 1 +50: 3 -50: 3
Facilities available:
BO AC IEH AVO AVH

**Deebert House Hotel**
Kilmallock, Co. Limerick
Tel: 063-31200 ......................Page 105
Contact Person:
Margaret Atalla
Seating Capacity of Meeting Rooms:
+50: 1 -50: 1
Facilities available:
BO AC IEH AVO

**Dunraven Arms Hotel**
Adare, Co. Limerick
Tel: 061-605 900 ....................Page 104
Contact Person:
Louis Murphy
Seating Capacity of Meeting Rooms:
+300: 1 +200: 1 +100: 2 +50: 3 -50: 4
Facilities available:
BO AC IEH AVO AVH

**Fitzgeralds Woodlands House Hotel, Health and Leisure Spa**
Adare, Co. Limerick
Tel: 061-605100......................Page 105
Contact Person:
David or Bríd
Seating Capacity of Meeting Rooms:
+400: 1 +300: 1 +200: 1 +100: 2 +50: 3 -50: 3
Facilities available:
BO AC IEH AVH

**George Boutique Hotel (The)**
Limerick City, Co. Limerick
Tel: 065-682 3000 .................Page 108
Contact Person:
C&B Coordinator
Seating Capacity of Meeting Rooms:
-50: 2
Facilities available:
BO AC IEH AVH

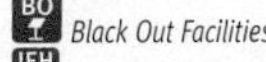

*Black Out Facilities*

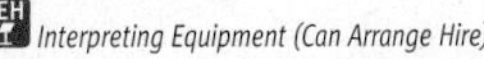

*Interpreting Equipment (Can Arrange Hire)*

AC *Air-Conditioning*
AVO *Audio Visual (Available On Premises)*
IEO *Interpreting Equipment (Available On Premises)*
AVH *Audio Visual (Can Arrange Hire)*

## Co. Limerick CONTINUED

### Hilton Limerick
Limerick City, Co. Limerick
Tel: 061-421800 ...................... Page 109
Contact Person:
Olivia Curran
Seating Capacity of Meeting Rooms:
+400: 1 +100: 3 +50: 5 -50: 10
Facilities available:
BO AC IEH AVO

### Kilmurry Lodge Hotel
Limerick City, Co. Limerick
Tel: 061-331133 ...................... Page 109
Contact Person:
Elaine Murphy
Seating Capacity of Meeting Rooms:
+300: 1 +100: 1 +50: 2 -50: 7
Facilities available:
AC IEH AVO

### Limerick Marriott Hotel
Limerick City, Co. Limerick
Tel: 061-448700 ...................... Page 110
Contact Person:
Claire Kennedy
Seating Capacity of Meeting Rooms:
+200: 2 +100: 2 +50: 3 -50: 11
Facilities available:
BO AC IEH AVO

### Lynch South Court And Suites
Limerick City, Co. Limerick
Tel: 061-487487 ...................... Page 110
Contact Person:
C & B Coordinator
Seating Capacity of Meeting Rooms:
+500: 1 +100: 4 +50: 1 -50: 1
Facilities available:
BO AC IEH AVH

### Quality Hotel & Leisure Centre Limerick
Limerick City, Co. Limerick
Tel: 061-436100 ...................... Page 111
Contact Person:
Aisling Moore
Seating Capacity of Meeting Rooms:
-50: 12
Facilities available:

### Radisson SAS Hotel & Spa
Limerick City, Co. Limerick
Tel: 061-456200 ...................... Page 111
Contact Person:
Suzanne O'Dwyer
Seating Capacity of Meeting Rooms:
+500: 1 +100: 1 -50: 4
Facilities available:
BO AC IEH AVO AVH

### Rathkeale House Hotel
Rathkeale, Co. Limerick
Tel: 069-63333 ...................... Page 113
Contact Person:
Gerry O'Connor
Seating Capacity of Meeting Rooms:
+300: 1 +100: 1 -50: 1
Facilities available:
BO AC IEH AVO

## Co. Mayo

### Ashford Castle
Cong, Co. Mayo
Tel: 094-954 6003 .................. Page 119
Contact Person:
Regina O'Donoghue
Seating Capacity of Meeting Rooms:
+100: 1
Facilities available:
IEH AVH

### Belmont Hotel
Knock, Co. Mayo
Tel: 094-938 8122 .................. Page 121
Contact Person:
Evelyn Fleming
Seating Capacity of Meeting Rooms:
+300: 1 -50: 1
Facilities available:
AC AVO

### Carlton Atlantic Coast Hotel
Westport, Co. Mayo
Tel: 098-29000 ...................... Page 124
Contact Person:
Deirdre Drenna
Seating Capacity of Meeting Rooms:
+100: 1 -50: 3
Facilities available:
AC IEH AVO

### Castlecourt Hotel Conference and Leisure Centre
Westport, Co. Mayo
Tel: 098-55088 ...................... Page 125
Contact Person:
Sinead Hopkins
Seating Capacity of Meeting Rooms:
+500: 1 +400: 1 +300: 2 +200: 3
+100: 4 +50: 6 -50: 8
Facilities available:
BO AC IEH AVO

### Hotel Westport leisure - spa - conference
Westport, Co. Mayo
Tel: 098-25122 ...................... Page 126
Contact Person:
Gerry Walshe / Eithne McDonnell / Rhona Chambers
Seating Capacity of Meeting Rooms:
+500: 1 +400: 1 +300: 1 +200: 2
+100: 2 +50: 5 -50: 1
Facilities available:
BO AC IEH AVO AVH

### Kelly's Gateway Hotel
Swinford, Co. Mayo
Tel: 094-925 2156 .................. Page 123
Contact Person:
Cathal Kelly
Seating Capacity of Meeting Rooms:
+100: 1 +50: 1 -50: 1
Facilities available:
BO AC AVO

### Knock House Hotel
Knock, Co. Mayo
Tel: 094-938 8088 .................. Page 121
Contact Person:
Brian Crowley
Seating Capacity of Meeting Rooms:
+100: 1 +50: 1 -50: 1
Facilities available:

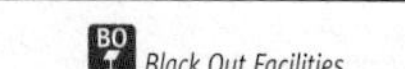

*Black Out Facilities*
*Interpreting Equipment (Can Arrange Hire)*

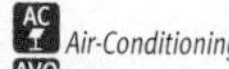

*Air-Conditioning*
*Audio Visual (Available On Premises)*

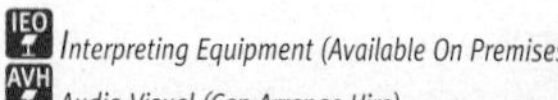

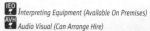

*Interpreting Equipment (Available On Premises)*
*Audio Visual (Can Arrange Hire)*

**Knockranny House Hotel & Spa**
Westport, Co. Mayo
Tel: 098-28600 ...................... Page 126
Contact Person:
Patricia Crowley / Fergal Harte
Seating Capacity of Meeting Rooms:
+500: 1 +400: 1 +300: 1 +200: 2
+100: 3 +50: 4 -50: 3
Facilities available:
BO AC IEH AVO AVH

**Lynch Breaffy House Hotel And Spa**
Castlebar, Co. Mayo
Tel: 094-902 2033 .................. Page 118
Contact Person:
C & B Co-ordinator
Seating Capacity of Meeting Rooms:
+500: 2 +200: 1 -50: 2
Facilities available:
BO AC IEH AVH

**McWilliam Park Hotel (The)**
Claremorris, Co. Mayo
Tel: 094-937 3333 .................. Page 119
Contact Person:
Virginia Connolly
Seating Capacity of Meeting Rooms:
+500: 1 +400: 1 +300: 1 +200: 1
+100: 1 +50: 3 -50: 5
Facilities available:
BO AC IEH AVO

**Mount Falcon Country House Hotel**
Ballina, Co. Mayo
Tel: 096-74472 ...................... Page 115
Contact Person:
Shane Maloney
Seating Capacity of Meeting Rooms:
+200: 1 +50: 2 -50: 1
Facilities available:
BO AC AVO AVH

**Ostán Oileán Acla**
Achill Island, Co. Mayo
Tel: 098-45138........................ Page 114
Contact Person:
Michael McLoughlin
Seating Capacity of Meeting Rooms:
+300: 1 +50: 1 -50: 1
Facilities available:
BO AC IEO AVO

**Park Hotel Kiltimagh**
Kiltimagh, Co. Mayo
Tel: 094-937 4922 .................. Page 121
Contact Person:
Noel Lafferty
Seating Capacity of Meeting Rooms:
+300: 1 -50: 2
Facilities available:
BO AC IEH AVO

**Park Inn Mulranny**
Mulranny, Co. Mayo
Tel: 098-36000 ...................... Page 122
Contact Person:
Tara O'Brien
Seating Capacity of Meeting Rooms:
+300: 1 +50: 2
Facilities available:
BO AC IEH AVO

**Pontoon Bridge Hotel**
Pontoon, Co. Mayo
Tel: 094-925 6120 .................. Page 123
Contact Person:
Breeta Geary / Sean O'Keeffe
Seating Capacity of Meeting Rooms:
+200: 1 +100: 1 +50: 1 -50: 3
Facilities available:
BO AC IEH AVH

**TF Royal Hotel & Theatre**
Castlebar, Co. Mayo
Tel: 094-902 3111.................... Page 118
Contact Person:
Donnacha Roche
Seating Capacity of Meeting Rooms:
+500: 1 +400: 1 +300: 2 +200: 2
+100: 3 +50: 3 -50: 4
Facilities available:
BO AC IEH AVO

**Westport Plaza Hotel**
Westport, Co. Mayo
Tel: 098-51166........................ Page 127
Contact Person:
Sinead Hopkins
Seating Capacity of Meeting Rooms:
+50: 1
Facilities available:
BO AC IEH AVO

**Westport Woods Hotel & Spa**
Westport, Co. Mayo
Tel: 098-25811........................ Page 127
Contact Person:
Michelle McKenna
Seating Capacity of Meeting Rooms:
+200: 1 +100: 2 +50: 1 -50: 2
Facilities available:
BO AC IEH AVO AVH

**Wyatt Hotel**
Westport, Co. Mayo
Tel: 098-25027 ...................... Page 128
Contact Person:
Chris McGauley / Maire Brid Ni Ghionnain
Seating Capacity of Meeting Rooms:
+400: 1 +100: 2 +50: 3
Facilities available:
BO AC IEH AVO AVH

## Co. Roscommon

**Abbey Hotel, Conference and Leisure Centre**
Roscommon Town, Co. Roscommon
Tel: 090-666 6200 .................. Page 129
Contact Person:
Alma Farrell
Seating Capacity of Meeting Rooms:
+200: 2 +50: 1 -50: 3
Facilities available:
BO AC AVH

**O'Gara's Royal Hotel**
Roscommon Town, Co. Roscommon
Tel: 090-662 6317 .................. Page 130
Contact Person:
Larry O'Gara
Seating Capacity of Meeting Rooms:
+500: 1 +400: 1 +300: 1 +200: 1
+100: 1 +50: 2 -50: 1
Facilities available:
BO AC AVO

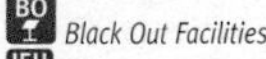

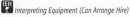

BO *Black Out Facilities*
IEH *Interpreting Equipment (Can Arrange Hire)*
AC *Air-Conditioning*
AVO *Audio Visual (Available On Premises)*
IEO *Interpreting Equipment (Available On Premises)*
AVH *Audio Visual (Can Arrange Hire)*

## Co. Roscommon CONTINUED

### Whitehouse Hotel
Ballinlough, Co. Roscommon
Tel: 094-964 0112 .................Page 128
**Contact Person:**
Conference Co-Ordinator Hannah Muldoon
**Seating Capacity of Meeting Rooms:**
+300: 1 -50: 2
**Facilities available:**
BO AC IEO AVO

## Co. Sligo

### Castle Dargan Golf Hotel Wellness
Ballygawley, Co. Sligo
Tel: 071-911 8080 .................Page 130
**Contact Person:**
Phil Wilkinson
**Seating Capacity of Meeting Rooms:**
+300: 1 +50: 3 -50: 4
**Facilities available:**
BO AC AVO

### Sligo City Hotel
Sligo Town, Co. Sligo
Tel: 071-914 4000 .................Page 134
**Contact Person:**
Sales & Marketing Manager
**Seating Capacity of Meeting Rooms:**
+200: 1 +100: 1 -50: 2
**Facilities available:**

AC IEH AVO

### Sligo Park Hotel & Leisure Club
Sligo Town, Co. Sligo
Tel: 071-919 0400 .................Page 134
**Contact Person:**
Manager on Duty
**Seating Capacity of Meeting Rooms:**
+500: 1 +400: 1 +300: 1 +200: 1
+100: 3 +50: 3 -50: 5
**Facilities available:**
BO AC IEH AVO

### Sligo Southern Hotel & Leisure Centre
Sligo Town, Co. Sligo
Tel: 071-916 2101...................Page 134
**Contact Person:**
Kevin McGlynn
**Seating Capacity of Meeting Rooms:**
+300: 1 +200: 1 +100: 1 +50: 2
-50: 4
**Facilities available:**
AC IEH AVH

### Yeats Country Hotel, Spa & Leisure Club
Rosses Point, Co. Sligo
Tel: 071-917 7211...................Page 132
**Contact Person:**
Breda O'Dwyer
**Seating Capacity of Meeting Rooms:**
+100: 1 +50: 2 -50: 3
**Facilities available:**

IEH AVH

# Ireland South

## Co. Carlow

### Dolmen Hotel and River Court Lodges
Carlow Town, Co. Carlow
Tel: 059-914 2002 .................Page 140
**Contact Person:**
Alison Fitzharris
**Seating Capacity of Meeting Rooms:**
+500: 1 +400: 1 +300: 2 +200: 2
+100: 2 +50: 3 -50: 7
**Facilities available:**
AC AVH

### Lord Bagenal Inn
Leighlinbridge, Co. Carlow
Tel: 059-977 4000 .................Page 142
**Contact Person:**
Sue Baldwin
**Seating Capacity of Meeting Rooms:**
+300: 1 -50: 4
**Facilities available:**
BO AC AVO

### Mount Wolseley Hotel Spa & Country Club
Tullow, Co. Carlow
Tel: 059-918 0100 .................Page 142
**Contact Person:**
Ann Rafftery
**Seating Capacity of Meeting Rooms:**
+500: 1 +200: 1 +100: 1 +50: 2
-50: 6
**Facilities available:**
BO AC IEH AVO

### Ramada Hotel & Suites at Killerig Golf Resort
Carlow Town, Co. Carlow
Tel: 059-916 3050 .................Page 140
**Contact Person:**
Ivanna Lopez
**Seating Capacity of Meeting Rooms:**
+400: 1 -50: 2
**Facilities available:**
BO AC IEH AVO AVH

### Seven Oaks Hotel
Carlow Town, Co. Carlow
Tel: 059-913 1308 .................Page 141
**Contact Person:**
Kathleen Dooley / Michael Walsh
**Seating Capacity of Meeting Rooms:**
+400: 1 +200: 1 +50: 1 -50: 2
**Facilities available:**
BO AC AVO

### Talbot Hotel Carlow
Carlow Town, Co. Carlow
Tel: 059-915 3000 .................Page 141
**Contact Person:**
Josephine Hutton
**Seating Capacity of Meeting Rooms:**
+300: 1 +100: 1 +50: 1 -50: 2
**Facilities available:**
BO AC IEH AVO AVH

---

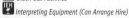

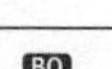
BO *Black Out Facilities*
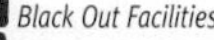
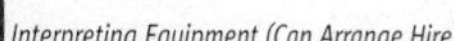
IEH *Interpreting Equipment (Can Arrange Hire)*
AC *Air-Conditioning*
AVO *Audio Visual (Available On Premises)*
IEO *Interpreting Equipment (Available On Premises)*
AVH *Audio Visual (Can Arrange Hire)*

## Co. Cork

### Abbey Hotel
Ballyvourney, Co. Cork
Tel: 026-45324 ....................Page 144
**Contact Person:**
John Buckley
**Seating Capacity of Meeting Rooms:**
+200: 1 +50: 1 -50: 1
**Facilities available:**

AVO

### Actons Hotel
Kinsale, Co. Cork
Tel: 021-477 9900 .................Page 166
**Contact Person:**
Mary Kirby
**Seating Capacity of Meeting Rooms:**
+300: 1 -50: 2
**Facilities available:**
BO AC IEH AVH

### Ambassador Hotel
Cork City, Co. Cork
Tel: 021-453 9000 .................Page 154
**Contact Person:**
Jim Maher / John McCarthy
**Seating Capacity of Meeting Rooms:**
+200: 1 +100: 2 +50: 2 -50: 1
**Facilities available:**
BO AC IEH AVO AVH

### Blarney Golf Resort
Blarney, Co. Cork
Tel: 021-438 4477 .................Page 147
**Contact Person:**
Michelle Queally
**Seating Capacity of Meeting Rooms:**
+200: 1 +100: 1 +50: 2 -50: 5
**Facilities available:**
BO AC IEH AVO

### Carlton Kinsale Hotel & C Spa
Kinsale, Co. Cork
Tel: 021-470 6000 .................Page 167
**Contact Person:**
Andy Greenslade
**Seating Capacity of Meeting Rooms:**
+200: 1
**Facilities available:**
BO AC IEH AVH

### Carrigaline Court Hotel & Leisure Centre
Carrigaline, Co. Cork
Tel: 021-485 2100 .................Page 148
**Contact Person:**
Helen Murphy / Sinead Gillen
**Seating Capacity of Meeting Rooms:**
+300: 1 +200: 1 +100: 2 +50: 4
-50: 5
**Facilities available:**
BO AC IEH AVH

### Celtic Ross Hotel Conference & Leisure Centre
Rosscarbery, Co. Cork
Tel: 023-48722 ....................Page 174
**Contact Person:**
Norma McNamara / Steven Ward
**Seating Capacity of Meeting Rooms:**
+200: 1 +50: 1 -50: 1
**Facilities available:**
BO AC IEH AVH

### Clarion Hotel
Cork City, Co. Cork
Tel: 021-422 4900 .................Page 156
**Contact Person:**
Dora Romicsne Kiss
**Seating Capacity of Meeting Rooms:**
+300: 1 +50: 4 -50: 2
**Facilities available:**
BO AC IEH AVH

### Commodore Hotel
Cobh, Co. Cork
Tel: 021-481 1277 .................Page 152
**Contact Person:**
Robert Fitzpatrick
**Seating Capacity of Meeting Rooms:**
+300: 1 -50: 1
**Facilities available:**
IEH AVO

### Commons Inn
Cork City, Co. Cork
Tel: 021-421 0300 .................Page 156
**Contact Person:**
Ashley Colson
**Seating Capacity of Meeting Rooms:**
+300: 1 +50: 1 -50: 3
**Facilities available:**
BO AC AVO

### Fernhill House Hotel
Clonakilty, Co. Cork
Tel: 023-33258 ....................Page 151
**Contact Person:**
Teresa O'Neill
**Seating Capacity of Meeting Rooms:**
+300: 1 +50: 2 -50: 3
**Facilities available:**
BO AC IEH AVO

### Fitzgeralds Vienna Woods Hotel Cork
Cork City, Co. Cork
Tel: 021-455 6800 .................Page 157
**Contact Person:**
C&B Coordinator
**Seating Capacity of Meeting Rooms:**
+300: 1 +200: 1 +100: 3 +50: 3
-50: 3
**Facilities available:**
BO AC IEH AVH

### Glengarriff Eccles Hotel
Glengarriff, Co. Cork
Tel: 027-63003 ....................Page 165
**Contact Person:**
Geraldine Owens
**Seating Capacity of Meeting Rooms:**
+300: 1 +50: 1 -50: 1
**Facilities available:**
BO AC AVH

### Glengarriff Park Hotel
Glengarriff, Co. Cork
Tel: 027-63000 ....................Page 165
**Contact Person:**
Paul Cullinan
**Seating Capacity of Meeting Rooms:**
+50: 1 -50: 1
**Facilities available:**
BO AVH

### Gresham Metropole
Cork City, Co. Cork
Tel: 021-464 3789 .................Page 158
**Contact Person:**
Fiona Keohane
**Seating Capacity of Meeting Rooms:**
+500: 1 +400: 1 +300: 1 +200: 2
+100: 2 +50: 6 -50: 11
**Facilities available:**
BO AC IEH AVH

---

BO *Black Out Facilities*
IEH *Interpreting Equipment (Can Arrange Hire)*
AC *Air-Conditioning*
AVO *Audio Visual (Available On Premises)*
IEO *Interpreting Equipment (Available On Premises)*
AVH *Audio Visual (Can Arrange Hire)*

## Co. Cork CONTINUED

### Harbour Lodge
Kinsale, Co. Cork
Tel: 021-477 2376 .................Page 168
**Contact Person:**
Siun Tiernan
**Seating Capacity of Meeting Rooms:**
-50: 2
**Facilities available:**

AVO AVH

### Hibernian Hotel and Leisure Centre
Mallow, Co. Cork
Tel: 022-58200 ......................Page 172
**Contact Person:**
Catherine Gyves
**Seating Capacity of Meeting Rooms:**
+300: 1 +100: 1 +50: 2 -50: 4
**Facilities available:**
BO AC IEH AVO

### Hotel Isaacs
Cork City, Co. Cork
Tel: 021-450 0011 .................Page 159
**Contact Person:**
Paula Lynch
**Seating Capacity of Meeting Rooms:**
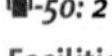
-50: 2
**Facilities available:**
BO AC AVH

### Imperial Hotel with Escape Salon and Spa
Cork City, Co. Cork
Tel: 021-427 4040 .................Page 159
**Contact Person:**
Jodi Cronin
**Seating Capacity of Meeting Rooms:**
+300: 1 +200: 1 +100: 2 +50: 5 -50: 1
**Facilities available:**
BO AC IEH AVH

### Inchydoney Island Lodge & Spa
Clonakilty, Co. Cork
Tel: 023-33143.......................Page 151
**Contact Person:**
Peter Lehoybe
**Seating Capacity of Meeting Rooms:**
+300: 1 -50: 4
**Facilities available:**
BO AC IEH AVO

### Kingsley Hotel & Residences
Cork City, Co. Cork
Tel: 021-480 0500 .................Page 160
**Contact Person:**
Julie Crowley
**Seating Capacity of Meeting Rooms:**
+200: 1 +100: 2 +50: 1 -50: 7
**Facilities available:**
BO AC IEH AVO AVH

### Lancaster Lodge
Cork City, Co. Cork
Tel: 021-425 1125...................Page 161
**Contact Person:**
Susan Leahy
**Seating Capacity of Meeting Rooms:**
-50: 1
**Facilities available:**
BO AC AVH

### Longueville House Hotel
Mallow, Co. Cork
Tel: 022-47156 ......................Page 172
**Contact Person:**
Aisling O'Callaghan
**Seating Capacity of Meeting Rooms:**
-50: 1
**Facilities available:**
BO IEH AVH

### Maryborough Hotel & Spa
Cork City, Co. Cork
Tel: 021-436 5555 .................Page 161
**Contact Person:**
Mary Bernard
**Seating Capacity of Meeting Rooms:**
+400: 1 +300: 1 +100: 2 +50: 2 -50: 5
**Facilities available:**
BO AC IEH AVO AVH

### Midleton Park Hotel
Midleton, Co. Cork
Tel: 021-463 5100 .................Page 173
**Contact Person:**
Ms. Maria O' Riordan
**Seating Capacity of Meeting Rooms:**
+300: 1 +50: 1
**Facilities available:**
IEH AVH

### Oriel House Hotel, Leisure Club & Spa
Ballincollig, Co. Cork
Tel: 021-420 8400 .................Page 143
**Contact Person:**
Ann Shanahan
**Seating Capacity of Meeting Rooms:**
+300: 2 +100: 2 -50: 2
**Facilities available:**
BO AC IEH AVO

### Quality Hotel & Leisure Centre Clonakilty
Clonakilty, Co. Cork
Tel: 023-36400 ......................Page 152
**Contact Person:**
Raymond Kelleher
**Seating Capacity of Meeting Rooms:**
+100: 1 +50: 1 -50: 1
**Facilities available:**
BO IEH AVO AVH

### Quality Hotel & Leisure Centre, Cork
Cork City, Co. Cork
Tel: 021-452 9200 .................Page 162
**Contact Person:**
Lucy Murphy
**Seating Capacity of Meeting Rooms:**
+50: 1
**Facilities available:**
BO IEH AVH

### Quality Hotel and Leisure Centre Youghal
Youghal, Co. Cork
Tel: 024-93050 ......................Page 177
**Contact Person:**
Raymond Kelleher
**Seating Capacity of Meeting Rooms:**
+50: 1 -50: 1
**Facilities available:**
BO IEH AVO AVH

---

BO *Black Out Facilities*
IEH *Interpreting Equipment (Can Arrange Hire)*
AC *Air-Conditioning*
AVO *Audio Visual (Available On Premises)*
IEO *Interpreting Equipment (Available On Premises)*
AVH *Audio Visual (Can Arrange Hire)*

### Radisson SAS Hotel & Spa, Cork
Cork City, Co. Cork
Tel: 021-429 7000 .................. Page 162
**Contact Person:**
Anne Dugdale
**Seating Capacity of Meeting Rooms:**
*+400: 1 +200: 2 +100: 2 +50: 2 -50: 11*
**Facilities available:**
BO AC IEH AVO

### Radisson SAS Hotel, Cork Airport
Cork Airport, Co. Cork
Tel: 021-494 7500 .................. Page 153
**Contact Person:**
Agnes Hennessy
**Seating Capacity of Meeting Rooms:**
*+200: 1 -50: 5*
**Facilities available:**
BO AC IEH AVO

### Rochestown Park Hotel
Cork City, Co. Cork
Tel: 021-489 0800 .................. Page 163
**Contact Person:**
Shay Livingstone
**Seating Capacity of Meeting Rooms:**
*+500: 2 +400: 2 +300: 2 +200: 2 +100: 4 +50: 9 -50: 9*
**Facilities available:**
BO AC IEH AVH

### Sheraton Fota Island Hotel & Spa (The)
Fota Island, Co. Cork
Tel: 021-467 3000 .................. Page 164
**Contact Person:**
Events Department
**Seating Capacity of Meeting Rooms:**
*+300: 1*
**Facilities available:**
BO AC IEH AVO AVH

### Silver Springs Moran Hotel
Cork City, Co. Cork
Tel: 021-450 7533 .................. Page 163
**Contact Person:**
Sales & Conference Co-Ordinator
**Seating Capacity of Meeting Rooms:**
*+500: 2 +400: 2 +300: 4 +200: 4 +100: 4 +50: 4 -50: 7*
**Facilities available:**
BO AC IEO IEH AVO AVH

### Springfort Hall Hotel
Mallow, Co. Cork
Tel: 022-21278 ...................... Page 172
**Contact Person:**
Theresa O'Sullivan
**Seating Capacity of Meeting Rooms:**
*+300: 1 +200: 1 +100: 1 +50: 1 -50: 3*
**Facilities available:**
IEH AVO

### Trident Hotel
Kinsale, Co. Cork
Tel: 021-477 9300 .................. Page 170
**Contact Person:**
Hal McElroy / Una Wren
**Seating Capacity of Meeting Rooms:**
*+200: 1 -50: 4*
**Facilities available:**
BO AC IEH AVO AVH

### West Cork Hotel
Skibbereen, Co. Cork
Tel: 028-21277 ...................... Page 176
**Contact Person:**
Sharon Cleary
**Seating Capacity of Meeting Rooms:**
*+200: 1 -50: 2*
**Facilities available:**
AC AVO

### Westlodge Hotel
Bantry, Co. Cork
Tel: 027-50360 ...................... Page 146
**Contact Person:**
Eileen M. O'Shea
**Seating Capacity of Meeting Rooms:**
*+300: 1 +200: 1 +100: 1 +50: 1 -50: 1*
**Facilities available:**
BO AC IEH AVH

## Co. Kerry

### Abbey Gate Hotel
Tralee, Co. Kerry
Tel: 066-712 9888 .................. Page 215
**Contact Person:**
Tom O'Connor
**Seating Capacity of Meeting Rooms:**
*+300: 1*
**Facilities available:**
BO AC AVH

### Aghadoe Heights Hotel & Spa
Killarney, Co. Kerry
Tel: 064-31766 ...................... Page 193
**Contact Person:**
Thérèse Kenneally
**Seating Capacity of Meeting Rooms:**
*+100: 1 -50: 2*
**Facilities available:**
BO AC IEH AVO

### Ballyroe Heights Hotel
Tralee, Co. Kerry
Tel: 066-712 6796 .................. Page 215
**Contact Person:**
Mark Sullivan
**Seating Capacity of Meeting Rooms:**
*+400: 1 +300: 1 +200: 1 +100: 3 +50: 3 -50: 4*
**Facilities available:**
BO AC IEH AVO

### Brandon Hotel Conference and Leisure Centre
Tralee, Co. Kerry
Tel: 066-712 3333 .................. Page 216
**Contact Person:**
Aine Brosnan
**Seating Capacity of Meeting Rooms:**
*+500: 1 +400: 1 +300: 2 +200: 3 +100: 4 +50: 7 -50: 8*
**Facilities available:**
BO AC IEH AVO

---

BO *Black Out Facilities*
AC *Air-Conditioning*
IEO *Interpreting Equipment (Available On Premises)*
IEH *Interpreting Equipment (Can Arrange Hire)*
AVO *Audio Visual (Available On Premises)*
AVH *Audio Visual (Can Arrange Hire)*

## Co. Kerry CONTINUED

**Brehon (The)**
Killarney, Co. Kerry
Tel: 064-30700 ......................Page 194
**Contact Person:**
Cara Fuller
**Seating Capacity of Meeting Rooms:**
*+200: 1 +100: 1 -50: 4*
**Facilities available:**
BO AC IEH AVO

**Dingle Skellig Hotel & Peninsula Spa**
Dingle (An Daingean), Co. Kerry
Tel: 066-915 0200 ..................Page 185
**Contact Person:**
Karen Byrnes
**Seating Capacity of Meeting Rooms:**
*+200: 1 -50: 1*
**Facilities available:**
BO AC IEH AVH

**Dromhall Hotel**
Killarney, Co. Kerry
Tel: 064-39300 ......................Page 197
**Contact Person:**
Bernadette Randles
**Seating Capacity of Meeting Rooms:**
*+300: 1 +200: 1 +100: 1 +50: 1 -50: 1*
**Facilities available:**
BO AC IEH AVH

**Fels Point Hotel**
Tralee, Co. Kerry
Tel: 066-711 9986 ..................Page 217
**Contact Person:**
Jacqui Dowling / Peter McDermott
**Seating Capacity of Meeting Rooms:**
*+300: 1 +100: 1 -50: 5*
**Facilities available:**
BO AC AVO

**Gleneagle Hotel**
Killarney, Co. Kerry
Tel: 064-36000 ......................Page 201
**Contact Person:**
Cara Fuller
**Seating Capacity of Meeting Rooms:**
*+500: 2 +400: 2 +300: 3 +200: 3 +100: 4 +50: 4 -50: 4*
**Facilities available:**
BO AC IEH AVO

**Grand Hotel**
Tralee, Co. Kerry
Tel: 066-712 1499 ..................Page 218
**Contact Person:**
Eileen Egan
**Seating Capacity of Meeting Rooms:**
*+200: 1 +100: 1 +50: 6 -50: 6*
**Facilities available:**
BO AC IEH AVH

**Hillgrove (The)**
Dingle (An Daingean), Co. Kerry
Tel: 066-915 1131...................Page 186
**Contact Person:**
Kieran Ashe
**Seating Capacity of Meeting Rooms:**
*+500: 1 +300: 2 -50: 3*
**Facilities available:**
BO AC IEH AVH

**Hotel Dunloe Castle**
Killarney, Co. Kerry
Tel: 064-44111........................Page 202
**Contact Person:**
Gerry Browne
**Seating Capacity of Meeting Rooms:**
*+200: 1 +100: 2 +50: 4 -50: 4*
**Facilities available:**
BO AC IEH AVH

**Hotel Europe**
Killarney, Co. Kerry
Tel: 064-71300 ......................Page 202
**Contact Person:**
Gerry Browne
**Seating Capacity of Meeting Rooms:**
*+500: 1 +400: 1 +300: 1 +200: 2 +100: 3 +50: 6 -50: 8*
**Facilities available:**
BO AC IEH AVO AVH

**Killarney Park Hotel**
Killarney, Co. Kerry
Tel: 064-35555 ......................Page 205
**Contact Person:**
Aoife Hickey
**Seating Capacity of Meeting Rooms:**
*+100: 1 +50: 1 -50: 3*
**Facilities available:**
BO AC IEH AVO

**Killarney Plaza Hotel & Spa**
Killarney, Co. Kerry
Tel: 064-21111........................Page 205
**Contact Person:**
Mary Hartnett
**Seating Capacity of Meeting Rooms:**
*+200: 1 +50: 2*
**Facilities available:**
BO AC AVO

**Killarney Royal**
Killarney, Co. Kerry
Tel: 064-31853 ......................Page 206
**Contact Person:**
Gillian O'Dea
**Seating Capacity of Meeting Rooms:**
*+50: 1*
**Facilities available:**
BO AC IEH AVH

**Lake Hotel**
Killarney, Co. Kerry
Tel: 064-31035 ......................Page 207
**Contact Person:**
Heather MacIver / Martina McKenna
**Seating Capacity of Meeting Rooms:**
*+50: 1 -50: 2*
**Facilities available:**
BO AC IEO IEH AVO AVH

**Malton (The)**
Killarney, Co. Kerry
Tel: 064-38000 ......................Page 208
**Contact Person:**
Emer Smith
**Seating Capacity of Meeting Rooms:**
*+500: 1 +200: 1 +50: 2 -50: 2*
**Facilities available:**
BO AC IEH AVH

---

BO *Black Out Facilities*
IEH *Interpreting Equipment (Can Arrange Hire)*
AC *Air-Conditioning*
AVO *Audio Visual (Available On Premises)*
IEO *Interpreting Equipment (Available On Premises)*
AVH *Audio Visual (Can Arrange Hire)*

**Manor West Hotel, Spa & Leisure Club**
Tralee, Co. Kerry
Tel: 066-719 4500 ..................Page 218
**Contact Person:**
Hazel Boyle
**Seating Capacity of Meeting Rooms:**
*+200: 1 +50: 2 -50: 3*
**Facilities available:**
BO AC IEH AVO

**Meadowlands Hotel**
Tralee, Co. Kerry
Tel: 066-718 0444 ..................Page 218
**Contact Person:**
Dawn Fitzell
**Seating Capacity of Meeting Rooms:**
*+200: 1 +100: 2 +50: 1 -50: 2*
**Facilities available:**
BO AC IEH AVO AVH

**Muckross Park Hotel & Cloisters Spa**
Killarney, Co. Kerry
Tel: 064-23400 .......................Page 208
**Contact Person:**
Annie Byrne
**Seating Capacity of Meeting Rooms:**
*+300: 1 +200: 1 +100: 2 +50: 4*
**Facilities available:**
BO AC IEH AVO AVH

**Randles Court Clarion Hotel**
Killarney, Co. Kerry
Tel: 064-35333 .......................Page 210
**Contact Person:**
Tom Randles
**Seating Capacity of Meeting Rooms:**
*+100: 1 +50: 1*
**Facilities available:**
BO AC IEH AVO

**Sheen Falls Lodge**
Kenmare, Co. Kerry
Tel: 064-41600........................Page 191
**Contact Person:**
Sheila King
**Seating Capacity of Meeting Rooms:**
*+100: 1 +50: 1 -50: 3*
**Facilities available:**
BO AC IEH AVO

**Smerwick Harbour Hotel**
Dingle (An Daingean), Co. Kerry
Tel: 066-915 6470 ..................Page 188
**Contact Person:**
Fionnbar Walsh
**Seating Capacity of Meeting Rooms:**
*+100: 1 +50: 1 -50: 1*
**Facilities available:**
BO IEH AVH

**Sneem Hotel**
Sneem, Co. Kerry
Tel: 064-75100 .......................Page 214
**Contact Person:**
Nicola Duggan
**Seating Capacity of Meeting Rooms:**
*+200: 1 +50: 2*
**Facilities available:**
BO AC IEH AVO

**Watermarque Boutique Hotel**
Cahersiveen, Co. Kerry
Tel: 066-947 2222 ..................Page 179
**Contact Person:**
Deirdre Lynch
**Seating Capacity of Meeting Rooms:**
*+100: 1*
**Facilities available:**
BO IEH AVH

## Co. Kilkenny

**Butler House**
Kilkenny City, Co. Kilkenny
Tel: 056-776 5707..................Page 222
**Contact Person:**
Gabrielle Hickey
**Seating Capacity of Meeting Rooms:**
*+100: 1 +50: 2 -50: 2*
**Facilities available:**
IEH AVO

**Days Hotel Kilkenny**
Kilkenny City, Co. Kilkenny
Tel: 1890-329329 ..................Page 222
**Contact Person:**
Clement Gleeson / Angela Doyle
**Seating Capacity of Meeting Rooms:**
*+50: 1 -50: 4*
**Facilities available:**
BO AC IEH AVO

**Hotel Kilkenny**
Kilkenny City, Co. Kilkenny
Tel: 056-776 2000..................Page 224
**Contact Person:**
Margaret Coughlan
**Seating Capacity of Meeting Rooms:**
*+500: 1 +400: 2 +300: 2 +200: 2 +100: 2 +50: 1 -50: 3*
**Facilities available:**
BO AC IEH AVO

**Kilkenny Hibernian Hotel**
Kilkenny City, Co. Kilkenny
Tel: 056-777 1888..................Page 224
**Contact Person:**
Michael Reuter
**Seating Capacity of Meeting Rooms:**
*-50: 1*
**Facilities available:**
BO AC IEO IEH AVO AVH

**Kilkenny House Hotel**
Kilkenny City, Co. Kilkenny
Tel: 056-777 0711 ..................Page 225
**Contact Person:**
Ted Dore
**Seating Capacity of Meeting Rooms:**
*+50: 1 -50: 1*
**Facilities available:**

BO AVH

**Kilkenny Inn Hotel**
Kilkenny City, Co. Kilkenny
Tel: 056-777 2828..................Page 225
**Contact Person:**
Linda Simpson / Eileen Quealy
**Seating Capacity of Meeting Rooms:**
*-50: 1*
**Facilities available:**

AVH

**Kilkenny Ormonde Hotel**
Kilkenny City, Co. Kilkenny
Tel: 056-772 3900..................Page 225
**Contact Person:**
Sheena McCanny
**Seating Capacity of Meeting Rooms:**
*+500: 1 +300: 1 +50: 2 -50: 6*
**Facilities available:**
BO AC IEH AVO

---

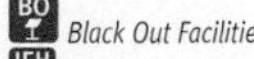
BO *Black Out Facilities*
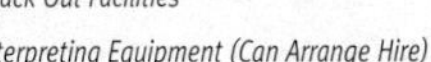
IEH *Interpreting Equipment (Can Arrange Hire)*
AC *Air-Conditioning*
AVO *Audio Visual (Available On Premises)*
IEO *Interpreting Equipment (Available On Premises)*
AVH *Audio Visual (Can Arrange Hire)*

## Co. Kilkenny CONTINUED

### Kilkenny River Court
Kilkenny City, Co. Kilkenny
Tel: 056-772 3388..................Page 226
**Contact Person:**
Elaine Brennan
**Seating Capacity of Meeting Rooms:**
+200: 1 +100: 1 +50: 1 -50: 2
**Facilities available:**
AC IEH AVH

### Langton House Hotel
Kilkenny City, Co. Kilkenny
Tel: 056-776 5133..................Page 226
**Contact Person:**
Sinead Bolger
**Seating Capacity of Meeting Rooms:**
+500: 1 +50: 1 -50: 1
**Facilities available:**
BO AC IEO IEH AVH

### Lyrath Estate Hotel, Spa & Convention Centre
Kilkenny City, Co. Kilkenny
Tel: 056-776 0088..................Page 227
**Contact Person:**
Dervala, Elaine, Mary Áine
**Seating Capacity of Meeting Rooms:**
+500: 2 +400: 3 +300: 3 +200: 3 +100: 4 +50: 6 -50: 10
**Facilities available:**
BO AC IEH AVO AVH

### Mount Juliet Conrad
Thomastown, Co. Kilkenny
Tel: 056-777 3000..................Page 230
**Contact Person:**
Evelyn Hohla
**Seating Capacity of Meeting Rooms:**
+100: 1 +50: 3 -50: 2
**Facilities available:**
BO AC IEH AVO

### Newpark Hotel
Kilkenny City, Co. Kilkenny
Tel: 056-776 0500..................Page 228
**Contact Person:**
Trish Condon
**Seating Capacity of Meeting Rooms:**
+500: 1 +400: 1 +200: 1 +100: 1 +50: 3 -50: 9
**Facilities available:**
BO AC IEH AVH

### Rising Sun
Mullinavat, Co. Kilkenny
Tel: 051-898173 ....................Page 230
**Contact Person:**
Kathrena O'Connor
**Seating Capacity of Meeting Rooms:**
+100: 1 -50: 1
**Facilities available:**
BO AC IEH AVH

### Springhill Court Hotel, Conference, Leisure & Spa Hotel
Kilkenny City, Co. Kilkenny
Tel: 056-772 1122 ..................Page 229
**Contact Person:**
Eimear Tiernan
**Seating Capacity of Meeting Rooms:**
+500: 1 +100: 2 -50: 2
**Facilities available:**
BO AC IEH AVO

## Co. Tipperary

### Abbey Court Hotel, Lodges & Trinity Leisure Spa
Nenagh, Co. Tipperary
Tel: 067-41111........................Page 237
**Contact Person:**
Imelda Connolly
**Seating Capacity of Meeting Rooms:**
+400: 1 +300: 1 +200: 1 +100: 3 +50: 7 -50: 4
**Facilities available:**
BO AC IEH AVH

### Anner Hotel & Leisure Centre
Thurles, Co. Tipperary
Tel: 0504-21799 ....................Page 238
**Contact Person:**
Noelle Troy
**Seating Capacity of Meeting Rooms:**
+400: 1 +300: 1 +200: 1 +100: 2 +50: 3
**Facilities available:**
AC AVO

### Ballykisteen Hotel & Golf Resort
Tipperary Town, Co. Tipperary
Tel: 062-33333 ......................Page 239
**Contact Person:**
Aileen Hoyne
**Seating Capacity of Meeting Rooms:**
+200: 1 +50: 3 -50: 3
**Facilities available:**
BO AC IEH AVO

### Cahir House Hotel
Cahir, Co. Tipperary
Tel: 052-43000 ......................Page 231
**Contact Person:**
Colette O'Dwyer
**Seating Capacity of Meeting Rooms:**
+400: 1 +300: 1 +200: 1 +100: 1 +50: 1 -50: 3
**Facilities available:**
BO AC IEH AVH

### Cashel Palace Hotel
Cashel, Co. Tipperary
Tel: 062-62707 ......................Page 233
**Contact Person:**
Tracy Wallace
**Seating Capacity of Meeting Rooms:**
+50: 1 -50: 2
**Facilities available:**
BO IEH AVO

### Dundrum House Hotel
Cashel, Co. Tipperary
Tel: 062-71116........................Page 233
**Contact Person:**
Leo Egan
**Seating Capacity of Meeting Rooms:**
+400: 1 +50: 2 -50: 2
**Facilities available:**
BO AC IEH AVO

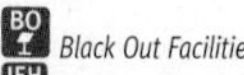
BO *Black Out Facilities*

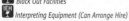

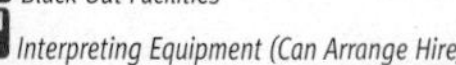
IEH *Interpreting Equipment (Can Arrange Hire)*

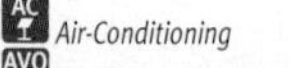
AC *Air-Conditioning*
AVO *Audio Visual (Available On Premises)*

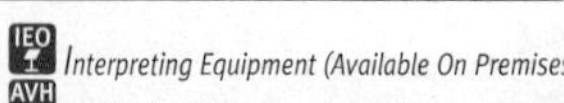
IEO *Interpreting Equipment (Available On Premises)*
AVH *Audio Visual (Can Arrange Hire)*

**Horse and Jockey Hotel**
Horse and Jockey, Co. Tipperary
Tel: 0504-44192 ....................Page 236
**Contact Person:**
Caroline Egan
**Seating Capacity of Meeting Rooms:**
*+200: 1 +100: 1 +50: 2 -50: 7*
**Facilities available:**
BO AC IEH AVO

**Hotel Minella & Leisure Club**
Clonmel, Co. Tipperary
Tel: 052-22388 ......................Page 235
**Contact Person:**
John Nallen
**Seating Capacity of Meeting Rooms:**
*+500: 1 +400: 1 +300: 1 +200: 2*
*+100: 2 +50: 4 -50: 5*
**Facilities available:**
BO AC IEH AVO AVH

**Racket Hall Country House Golf & Conference Hotel**
Roscrea, Co. Tipperary
Tel: 0505-21748 ....................Page 237
**Contact Person:**
Susan Sugrue
**Seating Capacity of Meeting Rooms:**
*+300: 1 +200: 1 +100: 2 +50: 4*
*-50: 3*
**Facilities available:**
BO AC IEH AVO

**Templemore Arms Hotel**
Templemore, Co. Tipperary
Tel: 0504-31423 ....................Page 237
**Contact Person:**
Julie Tarrant
**Seating Capacity of Meeting Rooms:**
*+200: 1 +50: 1 -50: 1*
**Facilities available:**
AC AVH

## Co. Waterford

**Cliff House Hotel**
Ardmore, Co. Waterford
Tel: +44 (0)-207 259 3621 ......Page 239
**Contact Person:**
Kristina Heinze
**Seating Capacity of Meeting Rooms:**
*+50: 1 -50: 2*
**Facilities available:**
BO AC IEH AVH

**Dooley's Hotel**
Waterford City, Co. Waterford
Tel: 051-873531 ....................Page 249
**Contact Person:**
Mareike Eccleston / Niamh Darcy
**Seating Capacity of Meeting Rooms:**
*+300: 1 +200: 1 +100: 2 +50: 1*
*-50: 3*
**Facilities available:**
BO AC IEH AVO

**Faithlegg House Hotel and Golf Club**
Faithlegg, Co. Waterford
Tel: 051-382000 ....................Page 244
**Contact Person:**
Suzanne Molloy
**Seating Capacity of Meeting Rooms:**
*+200: 1 +50: 1 -50: 3*
**Facilities available:**
BO AC IEH AVO

**Granville Hotel**
Waterford City, Co. Waterford
Tel: 051-305555 ....................Page 249
**Contact Person:**
Richard Hurley
**Seating Capacity of Meeting Rooms:**
*+100: 1 +50: 2 -50: 1*
**Facilities available:**
BO IEH AVH

**Lismore House Hotel**
Lismore, Co. Waterford
Tel: 058-72966 ......................Page 244
**Contact Person:**
Elaine Ahern
**Seating Capacity of Meeting Rooms:**
*+100: 1 -50: 1*
**Facilities available:**
BO AC IEH AVO AVH

**Park Hotel, Leisure Centre & Holiday Homes**
Dungarvan, Co. Waterford
Tel: 058-42899 ......................Page 242
**Contact Person:**
Geoff Dawson
**Seating Capacity of Meeting Rooms:**
*+500: 1 +400: 1 +300: 1 +200: 1*
*+100: 1 +50: 4 -50: 19*
**Facilities available:**
BO AC IEH AVO AVH

**Ramada Viking Hotel**
Waterford City, Co. Waterford
Tel: 051-336933 ....................Page 249
**Contact Person:**
Clodagh O'Connell
**Seating Capacity of Meeting Rooms:**
*+100: 1 +50: 2 -50: 7*
**Facilities available:**
BO AC AVO

**Rhu Glenn Country Club Hotel**
Waterford City, Co. Waterford
Tel: 051-832242 ....................Page 250
**Contact Person:**
Anne / Rita
**Seating Capacity of Meeting Rooms:**
*+400: 1 +300: 1 +200: 1 +100: 1*
*+50: 2 -50: 2*
**Facilities available:**
AC IEH AVH

**Tower Hotel & Leisure Centre**
Waterford City, Co. Waterford
Tel: 051-862300 ....................Page 251
**Contact Person:**
Catherina Hurley
**Seating Capacity of Meeting Rooms:**
*+400: 1 +100: 3 +50: 1 -50: 2*
**Facilities available:**
BO AC AVH

**Waterford Marina Hotel**
Waterford City, Co. Waterford
Tel: 051-856600 ....................Page 251
**Contact Person:**
Linda Bennett
**Seating Capacity of Meeting Rooms:**
*-50: 3*
**Facilities available:**
BO AVH

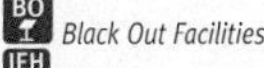
BO *Black Out Facilities*
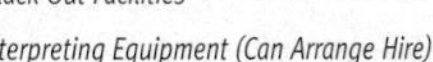
IEH *Interpreting Equipment (Can Arrange Hire)*
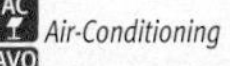
AC *Air-Conditioning*
AVO *Audio Visual (Available On Premises)*
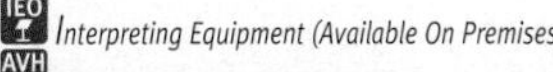
IEO *Interpreting Equipment (Available On Premises)*
AVH *Audio Visual (Can Arrange Hire)*

## Co. Waterford CONTINUED

### Woodlands Hotel
Waterford City, Co. Waterford
Tel: 051-304574 ....................Page 252
**Contact Person:**
Billy Brenner
**Seating Capacity of Meeting Rooms:**
+500: 1 +100: 4 +50: 5 -50: 6
**Facilities available:**
BO AC IEH AVO

## Co. Wexford

### Amber Springs Hotel and Health Spa
Gorey, Co. Wexford
Tel: 053-948 4000..................Page 256
**Contact Person:**
Jo Denby
**Seating Capacity of Meeting Rooms:**
+500: 1 +100: 1 -50: 6
**Facilities available:**

BO AC IEH AVO

### Ashdown Park Hotel Conference & Leisure Centre
Gorey, Co. Wexford
Tel: 053-948 0500..................Page 256
**Contact Person:**
Conference Co-ordinator
**Seating Capacity of Meeting Rooms:**
+500: 1 +50: 2 -50: 2
**Facilities available:**
BO AC IEH AVO

### Brandon House Hotel, Health Club & Spa
New Ross, Co. Wexford
Tel: 051-421703 ....................Page 258
**Contact Person:**
Susan Caulfield
**Seating Capacity of Meeting Rooms:**
+300: 1 -50: 3
**Facilities available:**
AC IEH AVO

### Carlton Millrace Hotel & C Spa
Bunclody, Co. Wexford
Tel: 053-937 5100 ..................Page 252
**Contact Person:**
Louise Hall
**Seating Capacity of Meeting Rooms:**
+300: 1
**Facilities available:**
BO AC IEO IEH AVO AVH

### Crosbie Cedars Hotel
Rosslare, Co. Wexford
Tel: 053-913 2124 ..................Page 259
**Contact Person:**
Anthony Spencer
**Seating Capacity of Meeting Rooms:**
+200: 1 +50: 1 -50: 2
**Facilities available:**
AC IEH AVH

### Danby Lodge Hotel
Rosslare, Co. Wexford
Tel: 053-915 8191 ..................Page 259
**Contact Person:**
Gavin McGuire
**Seating Capacity of Meeting Rooms:**
+400: 1
**Facilities available:**
BO AC IEO IEH AVH

### Ferrycarrig Hotel
Wexford Town, Co. Wexford
Tel: 053-912 0999 ..................Page 261
**Contact Person:**
Siobhán O'Rourke
**Seating Capacity of Meeting Rooms:**
+300: 1
**Facilities available:**
BO AC IEH AVO

### Quality Hotel & Leisure Club Wexford
Wexford Town, Co. Wexford
Tel: 053-917 2000 ..................Page 262
**Contact Person:**
Catherina Sharkey
**Seating Capacity of Meeting Rooms:**
-50: 4
**Facilities available:**

BO AC AVH

### Riverside Park Hotel and Leisure Club
Enniscorthy, Co. Wexford
Tel: 053-923 7800..................Page 255
**Contact Person:**
Hazel Shaw - Conference & Banqueting Manager
**Seating Capacity of Meeting Rooms:**
+500: 1 +200: 1 +100: 1 +50: 2 -50: 1
**Facilities available:**
AC AVO

### Seafield Hotel
Gorey, Co. Wexford
Tel: 053-942 4000..................Page 257
**Contact Person:**
Barbara Bailey
**Seating Capacity of Meeting Rooms:**
+500: 1 +100: 1 +50: 2 -50: 2
**Facilities available:**
BO AC IEH AVO

### St. Helens Hotel (formerly Great Southern Hotel)
Rosslare Harbour, Co. Wexford
Tel: 053-913 3233 ..................Page 261
**Contact Person:**
Eoin O'Sullivan
**Seating Capacity of Meeting Rooms:**
+200: 1 -50: 1
**Facilities available:**
BO AC IEH AVH

### Stanville Lodge Hotel
Barntown, Co. Wexford
Tel: 053-913 4300 ..................Page 252
**Contact Person:**
Martina Berney
**Seating Capacity of Meeting Rooms:**
+300: 1 +200: 1 +100: 1 +50: 2 -50: 2
**Facilities available:**
AC IEH AVO

### Talbot Hotel Conference and Leisure Centre
Wexford Town, Co. Wexford
Tel: 053-912 2566 ..................Page 263
**Contact Person:**
Niamh Lambert
**Seating Capacity of Meeting Rooms:**
+300: 1 +200: 1 +100: 2 +50: 3 -50: 8
**Facilities available:**
BO AC IEH AVO

*BO Black Out Facilities*
*IEH Interpreting Equipment (Can Arrange Hire)*
*AC Air-Conditioning*
*AVO Audio Visual (Available On Premises)*
*IEO Interpreting Equipment (Available On Premises)*
*AVH Audio Visual (Can Arrange Hire)*

**Whites of Wexford**
Wexford Town, Co. Wexford
Tel: 053-912 2311 ..................Page 263
**Contact Person:**
Liz Sinnott
**Seating Capacity of Meeting Rooms:**
*+500: 1 +400: 2 +300: 2 +200: 2 +100: 3 +50: 4 -50: 6*
**Facilities available:**
BO AC IEH AVO AVH

# Dublin & Ireland East

## Co. Cavan

**Cavan Crystal Hotel**
Cavan Town, Co. Cavan
Tel: 049-436 0600..................Page 270
**Contact Person:**
Sharon McCarron
**Seating Capacity of Meeting Rooms:**
*+500: 1 +400: 2 +300: 2 +200: 2 +100: 2 +50: 6 -50: 8*
**Facilities available:**
BO AC IEH AVO

**Crover House Hotel & Golf Club**
Mountnugent, Co. Cavan
Tel: 049-854 0206..................Page 272
**Contact Person:**
Pauline Kehoe
**Seating Capacity of Meeting Rooms:**
*+500: 1 +50: 1 -50: 2*
**Facilities available:**
AC AVO

**Hotel Kilmore**
Cavan Town, Co. Cavan
Tel: 049-433 2288 ..................Page 271
**Contact Person:**
Sharon McLaughlin
**Seating Capacity of Meeting Rooms:**
*+500: 1 +200: 2 +100: 2 +50: 3 -50: 4*
**Facilities available:**
BO AC IEH AVO

**Lakeside Manor Hotel**
Virginia, Co. Cavan
Tel: 049-854 8200..................Page 272
**Contact Person:**
Breda Traynor
**Seating Capacity of Meeting Rooms:**
*+400: 1 +200: 1 +50: 1 -50: 2*
**Facilities available:**
BO AC AVO

**Park Manor House Hotel & Estate**
Virginia, Co. Cavan
Tel: 049-854 6100 ..................Page 273
**Contact Person:**
Laura Burns
**Seating Capacity of Meeting Rooms:**
*+100: 2 +50: 2 -50: 2*
**Facilities available:**
BO IEH AVO

**Radisson SAS Farnham Estate Hotel**
Cavan Town, Co. Cavan
Tel: 049-437 7700 ..................Page 271
**Contact Person:**
Bridie Gallagher
**Seating Capacity of Meeting Rooms:**
*+300: 1 +100: 4 +50: 7 -50: 8*
**Facilities available:**
BO AC IEH AVO AVH

**Slieve Russell Hotel Golf & Country Club**
Ballyconnell, Co. Cavan
Tel: 049-952 6444..................Page 270
**Contact Person:**
Clodagh Pryce
**Seating Capacity of Meeting Rooms:**
*+500: 2 +400: 2 +300: 3 +200: 4 +100: 4 +50: 4 -50: 7*
**Facilities available:**
BO AC IEH AVO

## Co. Dublin

**Airportview Hotel & Spa**
Blakes Cross, Co. Dublin
Tel: 01-843 8756....................Page 273
**Contact Person:**
Gerry / Annie
**Seating Capacity of Meeting Rooms:**
*+50: 1 -50: 2*
**Facilities available:**
BO IEH AVH

**Ardmore Hotel**
Dublin City, Co. Dublin
Tel: 01-864 8300 ....................Page 281
**Contact Person:**
Donna Curry
**Seating Capacity of Meeting Rooms:**
*+100: 1 +50: 2*
**Facilities available:**
AC AVO

**Ashling Hotel**
Dublin City, Co. Dublin
Tel: 01-677 2324....................Page 282
**Contact Person:**
C&B Coordinator
**Seating Capacity of Meeting Rooms:**
*+200: 1 +100: 1 +50: 2 -50: 10*
**Facilities available:**
BO AC IEH AVH

**Ballymun Plaza Hotel**
Dublin City, Co. Dublin
Tel: 01-842 2000....................Page 284
**Contact Person:**
Kolvi Rutz
**Seating Capacity of Meeting Rooms:**
*+100: 1 +50: 2 -50: 1*
**Facilities available:**
BO AC IEH AVO AVH

**Best Western Academy Plaza Hotel**
Dublin City, Co. Dublin
Tel: 01-817 4141 ....................Page 284
**Contact Person:**
Conor Dean
**Seating Capacity of Meeting Rooms:**
*+50: 1 -50: 4*
**Facilities available:**
BO AC IEH AVO

BO *Black Out Facilities*
IEH *Interpreting Equipment (Can Arrange Hire)*
AC *Air-Conditioning*
AVO *Audio Visual (Available On Premises)*
IEO *Interpreting Equipment (Available On Premises)*
AVH *Audio Visual (Can Arrange Hire)*

## Co. Dublin CONTINUED

**Bracken Court Hotel**
Balbriggan, Co. Dublin
Tel: 01-841 3333 ....................Page 273
**Contact Person:**
Gavin O'Shea
**Seating Capacity of Meeting Rooms:**
+300: 1 +200: 1 +100: 1 +50: 3
-50: 6
**Facilities available:**
BO AC IEH AVH

**Brooks Hotel**
Dublin City, Co. Dublin
Tel: 01-670 4000 ....................Page 287
**Contact Person:**
Mark O'Sullivan/Brian Rooney
**Seating Capacity of Meeting Rooms:**
-50: 3
**Facilities available:**
BO AC IEH AVH

**Brownes Dublin**
Dublin City, Co. Dublin
Tel: 01-638 3939 ....................Page 287
**Contact Person:**
Jennifer Abelsen
**Seating Capacity of Meeting Rooms:**
-50: 1
**Facilities available:**
BO AC IEH AVH

**Buswells Hotel**
Dublin City, Co. Dublin
Tel: 01-614 6500 ....................Page 288
**Contact Person:**
Dee McCabe
**Seating Capacity of Meeting Rooms:**
+50: 1 -50: 5
**Facilities available:**
AC AVO

**Camden Court Hotel**
Dublin City, Co. Dublin
Tel: 01-475 9666 ....................Page 288
**Contact Person:**
Denise Corboy
**Seating Capacity of Meeting Rooms:**
+100: 1 +50: 3 -50: 7
**Facilities available:**
BO AC IEH AVH

**Carlton Dublin Airport Hotel**
Dublin Airport, Co. Dublin
Tel: 01-866 7500 ....................Page 275
**Contact Person:**
Aisling Carrick
**Seating Capacity of Meeting Rooms:**
+400: 1 +300: 1 +200: 1 +100: 2
+50: 3 -50: 17
**Facilities available:**
BO AC IEH AVO AVH

**Carnegie Court Hotel**
Swords, Co. Dublin
Tel: 01-840 4384 ....................Page 331
**Contact Person:**
Teresa Long
**Seating Capacity of Meeting Rooms:**
+200: 1 +100: 1 +50: 1 -50: 2
**Facilities available:**
BO AC IEH AVO

**Cassidys Hotel**
Dublin City, Co. Dublin
Tel: 01-878 0555 ....................Page 289
**Contact Person:**
Maeve Sankey
**Seating Capacity of Meeting Rooms:**
+50: 2 -50: 4
**Facilities available:**
BO AC IEH AVO

**Castleknock Hotel and Country Club**
Dublin City, Co. Dublin
Tel: 01-640 6300 ....................Page 290
**Contact Person:**
Dearbhla Sheridon, Events Manager
**Seating Capacity of Meeting Rooms:**
+500: 1 +400: 1 +300: 1 +200: 2
+100: 4 +50: 4 -50: 6
**Facilities available:**
BO AC IEH AVO

**Citywest Hotel, Conference, Leisure & Golf Resort**
Saggart, Co. Dublin
Tel: 01-401 0500 ....................Page 330
**Contact Person:**
Gillian Prendergast
**Seating Capacity of Meeting Rooms:**
+500: 4 +400: 5 +300: 5 +200: 9
+100: 12 +50: 16 -50: 9
**Facilities available:**
BO AC IEH AVH

**Clarence (The)**
Dublin City, Co. Dublin
Tel: 01-407 0800 ....................Page 291
**Contact Person:**
Denise Bevan
**Seating Capacity of Meeting Rooms:**
+50: 1 -50: 3
**Facilities available:**
BO AC IEH AVH

**Clarion Hotel Dublin IFSC**
Dublin City, Co. Dublin
Tel: 01-433 8800 ....................Page 291
**Contact Person:**
Christina Connolly
**Seating Capacity of Meeting Rooms:**
+50: 3 -50: 5
**Facilities available:**
BO AC IEH AVO

**Clarion Hotel Dublin Liffey Valley**
Dublin City, Co. Dublin
Tel: 01-625 8000 ....................Page 291
**Contact Person:**
Tara Byrne
**Seating Capacity of Meeting Rooms:**
+300: 1 +200: 1 +100: 2 +50: 4
-50: 16
**Facilities available:**
BO AC IEH AVO

**Clontarf Castle Hotel**
Dublin City, Co. Dublin
Tel: 01-833 2321 ....................Page 292
**Contact Person:**
Orla O'Brien
**Seating Capacity of Meeting Rooms:**
+500: 1 +400: 1 +300: 1 +200: 1
+100: 3 +50: 2 -50: 5
**Facilities available:**
BO AC IEH AVH

BO *Black Out Facilities*
IEH *Interpreting Equipment (Can Arrange Hire)*
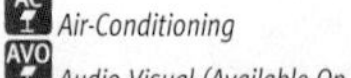
AC *Air-Conditioning*
AVO *Audio Visual (Available On Premises)*
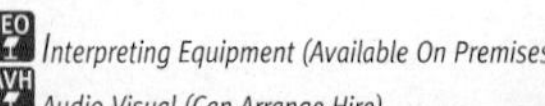
IEO *Interpreting Equipment (Available On Premises)*
AVH *Audio Visual (Can Arrange Hire)*

**Conrad Dublin**
Dublin City, Co. Dublin
Tel: 01-602 8900 .................... Page 294
**Contact Person:**
Orla Lee
**Seating Capacity of Meeting Rooms:**
+200: 1 +100: 1 +50: 4 -50: 9
**Facilities available:**
BO AC IEH AVH

**Crowne Plaza Dublin Northwood**
Dublin Airport, Co. Dublin
Tel: 01-862 8888 .................... Page 276
**Contact Person:**
Judith Graham
**Seating Capacity of Meeting Rooms:**
+500: 1 +200: 3 +50: 3 -50: 25
**Facilities available:**
BO AC IEH AVO AVH

**Days Hotel Dublin Airport**
Dublin Airport, Co. Dublin
Tel: 1890-329 329 .................. Page 276
**Contact Person:**
Mark Williams
**Seating Capacity of Meeting Rooms:**
+50: 1 -50: 3
**Facilities available:**
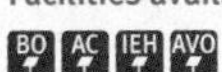


**Dublin Skylon Hotel**
Dublin City, Co. Dublin
Tel: 01-837 9121 .................... Page 297
**Contact Person:**
Andrew Hyland
**Seating Capacity of Meeting Rooms:**
+50: 2 -50: 5
**Facilities available:**
BO AC IEH AVH

**Finnstown Country House Hotel**
Lucan, Co. Dublin
Tel: 01-601 0700 .................... Page 327
**Contact Person:**
Edwina King
**Seating Capacity of Meeting Rooms:**
+200: 1 +100: 1 +50: 1 -50: 3
**Facilities available:**
AC AVO AVH

**Fitzpatrick Castle Dublin**
Killiney, Co. Dublin
Tel: 01-230 5400 .................... Page 327
**Contact Person:**
Eilish Kealy
**Seating Capacity of Meeting Rooms:**
+500: 1 +400: 2 +300: 2 +200: 2 +100: 4 +50: 6 -50: 14
**Facilities available:**
BO AC IEH AVO

**Fitzwilliam Hotel**
Dublin City, Co. Dublin
Tel: 01-478 7000 .................... Page 298
**Contact Person:**
Orna Eiffe, Events Manager
**Seating Capacity of Meeting Rooms:**
+50: 1 -50: 2
**Facilities available:**
BO AC IEH AVO AVH

**Four Seasons Hotel Dublin**
Dublin City, Co. Dublin
Tel: 01-665 4000 .................... Page 299
**Contact Person:**
John O'Leary
**Seating Capacity of Meeting Rooms:**
+500: 1 +200: 1 +50: 3 -50: 1
**Facilities available:**
BO AC IEH AVH

**Grand Canal Hotel**
Dublin City, Co. Dublin
Tel: 01-646 1000 .................... Page 300
**Contact Person:**
Sarah Barry
**Seating Capacity of Meeting Rooms:**
+100: 2 +50: 3 -50: 6
**Facilities available:**
BO AC IEH AVH

**Grand Hotel**
Malahide, Co. Dublin
Tel: 01-845 0000 .................... Page 329
**Contact Person:**
Hilary Fogarty
**Seating Capacity of Meeting Rooms:**
+400: 1 +200: 1 +100: 1 +50: 6 -50: 6
**Facilities available:**
BO AC IEH AVO

**Gresham (The)**
Dublin City, Co. Dublin
Tel: 01-874 6881 .................... Page 301
**Contact Person:**
Michelle Costelloe
**Seating Capacity of Meeting Rooms:**
+300: 1 +200: 2 +100: 3 +50: 8 -50: 22
**Facilities available:**
BO AC IEH AVH

**Herbert Park Hotel**
Dublin City, Co. Dublin
Tel: 01-667 2200 .................... Page 302
**Contact Person:**
Sorcha Moore
**Seating Capacity of Meeting Rooms:**
+100: 2 +50: 1 -50: 2
**Facilities available:**
BO AC IEH AVH

**Hilton Dublin Airport**
Dublin Airport, Co. Dublin
Tel: 01-866 1800 .................... Page 277
**Contact Person:**
Estefania Garcia
**Seating Capacity of Meeting Rooms:**
+300: 1 -50: 9
**Facilities available:**
BO AC IEH AVO

**Hilton Dublin Kilmainham**
Dublin City, Co. Dublin
Tel: 01-420 1800 .................... Page 303
**Contact Person:**
Sonja Schmitz
**Seating Capacity of Meeting Rooms:**
+100: 1 -50: 9
**Facilities available:**
BO AC IEH AVO AVH

**Holiday Inn Dublin City Centre**
Dublin City, Co. Dublin
Tel: 01-670 3666 .................... Page 303
**Contact Person:**
Sales Department
**Seating Capacity of Meeting Rooms:**
+400: 1 +300: 1 +200: 1 +100: 2 +50: 5 -50: 6
**Facilities available:**
BO AC IEH AVO

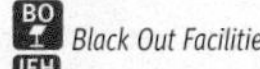


BO *Black Out Facilities*
IEH *Interpreting Equipment (Can Arrange Hire)*
AC *Air-Conditioning*
AVO *Audio Visual (Available On Premises)*
IEO *Interpreting Equipment (Available On Premises)*
AVH *Audio Visual (Can Arrange Hire)*

## Co. Dublin CONTINUED

**Hotel Isaacs**
Dublin City, Co. Dublin
Tel: 01-813 4700 ....................Page 304
**Contact Person:**
Jeannette Mee
**Seating Capacity of Meeting Rooms:**
*+100: 1 -50: 6*
**Facilities available:**
BO AC AVO AVH

**IMI Residence**
Dublin City, Co. Dublin
Tel: 01-207 5900....................Page 304
**Contact Person:**
Adrienne Hughes
**Seating Capacity of Meeting Rooms:**
*+300: 1 +200: 2 +100: 3 +50: 10 -50: 30*
**Facilities available:**
BO AC IEO AVO

**Lansdowne Hotel**
Dublin City, Co. Dublin
Tel: 01-668 2522....................Page 307
**Contact Person:**
Vicky Bissonath
**Seating Capacity of Meeting Rooms:**
*+100: 1 +50: 1*
**Facilities available:**
BO IEH AVO

**Lucan Spa Hotel**
Lucan, Co. Dublin
Tel: 01-628 0494....................Page 328
**Contact Person:**
Betty Dolan / Stephen Foran
**Seating Capacity of Meeting Rooms:**
*+500: 1 +400: 1 +300: 1 +200: 1 +100: 1 +50: 1 -50: 2*
**Facilities available:**
BO AC IEH AVO

**Maples House Hotel**
Dublin City, Co. Dublin
Tel: 01-830 4227....................Page 308
**Contact Person:**
June O'Hara
**Seating Capacity of Meeting Rooms:**
*+50: 1 -50: 1*
**Facilities available:**
AC AVH

**Marine Hotel**
Sutton, Co. Dublin
Tel: 01-839 0000 ....................Page 331
**Contact Person:**
Leslee Ann Glennon
**Seating Capacity of Meeting Rooms:**
*+100: 1 -50: 6*
**Facilities available:**
BO AC IEH AVH

**Merrion Hall & Blakes Spa Suites**
Dublin City, Co. Dublin
Tel: 01-668 1426 ....................Page 309
**Contact Person:**
Pat Halpin
**Seating Capacity of Meeting Rooms:**
*+50: 1 -50: 2*
**Facilities available:**
BO AC IEH AVH

**Mount Herbert Hotel**
Dublin City, Co. Dublin
Tel: 01-668 4321 ....................Page 311
**Contact Person:**
Niamh Flynn
**Seating Capacity of Meeting Rooms:**
*+50: 2 -50: 7*
**Facilities available:**
BO AC IEH AVO

**North Star Hotel**
Dublin City, Co. Dublin
Tel: 01-836 3136 ....................Page 312
**Contact Person:**
Deirdre McGettigan
**Seating Capacity of Meeting Rooms:**
*+50: 1 -50: 2*
**Facilities available:**
AC IEH AVO

**O'Callaghan Alexander Hotel**
Dublin City, Co. Dublin
Tel: 01-607 3700 ....................Page 312
**Contact Person:**
Claire Walker
**Seating Capacity of Meeting Rooms:**
*+400: 1 +300: 1 +200: 2 +100: 4 +50: 5 -50: 1*
**Facilities available:**
BO AC IEH AVO

**O'Callaghan Davenport Hotel**
Dublin City, Co. Dublin
Tel: 01-607 3500 ....................Page 313
**Contact Person:**
Gemma Nolan
**Seating Capacity of Meeting Rooms:**
*+300: 1 +200: 2 +100: 2 +50: 2 -50: 7*
**Facilities available:**
BO AC IEH AVO

**O'Callaghan Mont Clare Hotel**
Dublin City, Co. Dublin
Tel: 01-607 3800 ....................Page 313
**Contact Person:**
Katy Rothchild
**Seating Capacity of Meeting Rooms:**
*+100: 1 +50: 2 -50: 9*
**Facilities available:**
BO AC IEH AVH

**O'Callaghan Stephen's Green Hotel**
Dublin City, Co. Dublin
Tel: 01-607 3600 ....................Page 313
**Contact Person:**
Claire Walker
**Seating Capacity of Meeting Rooms:**
*-50: 6*
**Facilities available:**
BO AC IEH AVO

**Paramount Hotel**
Dublin City, Co. Dublin
Tel: 01-417 9900 ....................Page 315
**Contact Person:**
Bernadette Monaghan
**Seating Capacity of Meeting Rooms:**
*-50: 1*
**Facilities available:**

AC AVH

**Park Inn Dublin**
Dublin City, Co. Dublin
Tel: 01-817 3838 ....................Page 315
**Contact Person:**
Vedrina Damjanic
**Seating Capacity of Meeting Rooms:**
*+200: 1 +100: 2 +50: 3 -50: 2*
**Facilities available:**
BO IEH AVH

---

BO *Black Out Facilities*
IEH *Interpreting Equipment (Can Arrange Hire)*

AC *Air-Conditioning*
AVO *Audio Visual (Available On Premises)*
IEO *Interpreting Equipment (Available On Premises)*
AVH *Audio Visual (Can Arrange Hire)*

**Park Plaza Tyrrelstown**
Dublin City, Co. Dublin
Tel: 01-827 5600 ....................Page 315
**Contact Person:**
Louise Maguire
**Seating Capacity of Meeting Rooms:**
*+400: 1 +300: 1 +200: 2 +100: 4 +50: 7 -50: 7*
**Facilities available:**
BO AC IEH AVO AVH

**Parliament Hotel**
Dublin City, Co. Dublin
Tel: 01-670 8777 ....................Page 316
**Contact Person:**
Carol Nulty
**Seating Capacity of Meeting Rooms:**
*-50: 1*
**Facilities available:**
AC AVH

**Plaza Hotel**
Dublin City, Co. Dublin
Tel: 01-462 4200 ....................Page 316
**Contact Person:**
Claire Coleman
**Seating Capacity of Meeting Rooms:**
*+200: 1 +100: 2 +50: 2 -50: 11*
**Facilities available:**
AC IEH AVO AVH

**Radisson SAS Hotel, Dublin Airport**
Dublin Airport, Co. Dublin
Tel: 01-844 6000 ....................Page 277
**Contact Person:**
Anne Hickey
**Seating Capacity of Meeting Rooms:**
*+300: 1 +200: 1 +100: 3 -50: 8*
**Facilities available:**
BO AC IEH AVO AVH

**Radisson SAS Royal Hotel**
Dublin City, Co. Dublin
Tel: 01-8982900 ....................Page 317
**Contact Person:**
Conference Co-ordinator, Jean Bermingham
**Seating Capacity of Meeting Rooms:**
*+400: 1 +100: 1 +50: 2 -50: 6*
**Facilities available:**
BO AC IEH AVO AVH

**Radisson SAS St Helen's Hotel**
Dublin City, Co. Dublin
Tel: 01-218 6000 ....................Page 318
**Contact Person:**
Laura Shurie
**Seating Capacity of Meeting Rooms:**
*+300: 1 +50: 7 -50: 5*
**Facilities available:**
BO AC IEH AVH

**Red Cow Moran Hotel**
Dublin City, Co. Dublin
Tel: 01-459 3650 ....................Page 318
**Contact Person:**
Karen Moran
**Seating Capacity of Meeting Rooms:**
*+500: 1 +400: 1 +300: 1 +200: 2 +100: 5 +50: 10 -50: 16*
**Facilities available:**
BO AC IEH AVO AVH

**Regency Airport Hotel**
Dublin City, Co. Dublin
Tel: 01-837 3544 ....................Page 318
**Contact Person:**
Catherine McGettigan
**Seating Capacity of Meeting Rooms:**
*+500: 1 +300: 2 -50: 4*
**Facilities available:**
BO AC IEH AVO AVH

**Rochestown Lodge Hotel & Day Spa**
Dun Laoghaire, Co. Dublin
Tel: 01-285 3555 ....................Page 325
**Contact Person:**
Reservations
**Seating Capacity of Meeting Rooms:**
*+50: 1 -50: 4*
**Facilities available:**
BO AC IEH AVO AVH

**Royal Dublin Hotel (The)**
Dublin City, Co. Dublin
Tel: 01-873 3666 ....................Page 319
**Contact Person:**
Darrell Penney, General Manager
**Seating Capacity of Meeting Rooms:**
*+300: 1 +200: 1 +100: 2 +50: 3 -50: 3*
**Facilities available:**
IEH

**Royal Marine Hotel**
Dun Laoghaire, Co. Dublin
Tel: 01-230 0030 ....................Page 326
**Contact Person:**
Adrianne Molloy
**Seating Capacity of Meeting Rooms:**
*+500: 1 +100: 5 +50: 6 -50: 12*
**Facilities available:**
BO AC IEO IEH AVO AVH

**School House Hotel**
Dublin City, Co. Dublin
Tel: 01-667 5014 ....................Page 320
**Contact Person:**
Liz Carr
**Seating Capacity of Meeting Rooms:**
*-50: 1*
**Facilities available:**
BO AC AVH

**Shelbourne Hotel (The)**
Dublin City, Co. Dublin
Tel: 01-663 4500 ....................Page 320
**Contact Person:**
Anne-Marie Whelan
**Seating Capacity of Meeting Rooms:**
*+400: 1 +100: 2 +50: 2 -50: 6*
**Facilities available:**
BO AC IEH AVH

**Springfield Hotel**
Leixlip, Co. Dublin
Tel: 01-458 1100 ....................Page 327
**Contact Person:**
Barry, Kathleen or Padraig
**Seating Capacity of Meeting Rooms:**
*+300: 1 +200: 1 +100: 1 +50: 2 -50: 3*
**Facilities available:**
AC IEH AVO

**Stillorgan Park Hotel**
Dublin City, Co. Dublin
Tel: 01-200 1800 ....................Page 321
**Contact Person:**
Catherine Redmond
**Seating Capacity of Meeting Rooms:**
*+500: 1 +400: 1 +300: 1 +200: 3 +100: 6 +50: 7 -50: 19*
**Facilities available:**
BO AC IEO IEH AVO AVH

BO *Black Out Facilities*
IEH *Interpreting Equipment (Can Arrange Hire)*
AC *Air-Conditioning*
AVO *Audio Visual (Available On Premises)*
IEO *Interpreting Equipment (Available On Premises)*
AVH *Audio Visual (Can Arrange Hire)*

## Co. Dublin CONTINUED

**Temple Bar Hotel**
Dublin City, Co. Dublin
Tel: 01-677 3333 ....................Page 322
**Contact Person:**
Sally Spearman
**Seating Capacity of Meeting Rooms:**
+50: 1 -50: 4
**Facilities available:**
BO IEH AVH

**Tower Hotel**
Dublin City, Co. Dublin
Tel: 01-468 5400 ....................Page 322
**Contact Person:**
Louise Whitehead
**Seating Capacity of Meeting Rooms:**
+200: 1 -50: 7
**Facilities available:**
BO AC IEH AVO AVH

**Waterside House Hotel (The)**
Donabate, Co. Dublin
Tel: 01-843 6153 ....................Page 274
**Contact Person:**
Paul Slattery / Sharon Jackson
**Seating Capacity of Meeting Rooms:**
+300: 1 +200: 1 +100: 1 +50: 2 -50: 3
**Facilities available:**
AC IEH AVO AVH

**West County Hotel**
Dublin City, Co. Dublin
Tel: 01-626 4011 ....................Page 324
**Contact Person:**
Gary Spain
**Seating Capacity of Meeting Rooms:**
+100: 1 +50: 1 -50: 2
**Facilities available:**
BO AC IEH AVO

**Westin Dublin**
Dublin City, Co. Dublin
Tel: 01-645 1000 ....................Page 324
**Contact Person:**
Marlene Buckridge
**Seating Capacity of Meeting Rooms:**
+200: 1 +100: 2 +50: 2 -50: 8
**Facilities available:**
BO AC IEH AVO

## Co. Kildare

**Ardenode Hotel**
Ballymore Eustace, Co. Kildare
Tel: 045-864198 ....................Page 333
**Contact Person:**
Paul Crosby
**Seating Capacity of Meeting Rooms:**
+500: 1 +400: 1 +300: 1 +200: 1 +100: 2 +50: 3 -50: 3
**Facilities available:**
BO AVO AVH

**Barberstown Castle**
Straffan, Co. Kildare
Tel: 01-628 8157 ....................Page 340
**Contact Person:**
Gretchen Ridgeway / Lee-Ann Mc-Carthy
**Seating Capacity of Meeting Rooms:**
+200: 1 +100: 2 +50: 2 -50: 4
**Facilities available:**
BO IEH AVO

**Carlton Abbey Hotel & C Spa**
Athy, Co. Kildare
Tel: 059-863 0100 ....................Page 332
**Contact Person:**
Lisa Murphy
**Seating Capacity of Meeting Rooms:**
+300: 1 +200: 1 +100: 1 +50: 1 -50: 4
**Facilities available:**
BO AC IEH AVO

**Carton House**
Maynooth, Co. Kildare
Tel: 01-505 2000 ....................Page 336
**Contact Person:**
Fiona Mullin
**Seating Capacity of Meeting Rooms:**
+500: 1 +400: 1 +300: 1 +200: 1 +100: 5 +50: 7 -50: 14
**Facilities available:**
BO AC IEH AVO

**Clanard Court Hotel**
Athy, Co. Kildare
Tel: 059-864 0666 ....................Page 332
**Contact Person:**
Sandra Foy
**Seating Capacity of Meeting Rooms:**
+400: 1 +200: 1 +100: 1 +50: 1 -50: 3
**Facilities available:**
BO AC IEH AVO

**Courtyard Hotel Leixlip**
Leixlip, Co. Kildare
Tel: 01-629 5100 ....................Page 335
**Contact Person:**
Gavin O'Shea
**Seating Capacity of Meeting Rooms:**
+100: 2 +50: 4 -50: 4
**Facilities available:**
BO AC IEO IEH AVO AVH

**Derby House Hotel**
Kildare Town, Co. Kildare
Tel: 045-522144 ....................Page 335
**Contact Person:**
Stephanie Lau
**Seating Capacity of Meeting Rooms:**
+200: 1 -50: 1
**Facilities available:**
IEO IEH AVH

**Glenroyal Hotel, Leisure Club & Conference Centre**
Maynooth, Co. Kildare
Tel: 01-629 0909 ....................Page 336
**Contact Person:**
Kate Voice
**Seating Capacity of Meeting Rooms:**
+500: 1 +400: 2 +300: 4 +200: 4 +100: 6 +50: 6 -50: 12
**Facilities available:**
BO AC IEH AVO

**Hazel Hotel**
Monasterevin, Co. Kildare
Tel: 045-525373 ....................Page 336
**Contact Person:**
John Kelly
**Seating Capacity of Meeting Rooms:**
+300: 1 +200: 1 +100: 1 +50: 1 -50: 1
**Facilities available:**
BO AC AVO

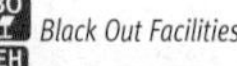
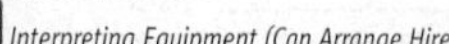

BO *Black Out Facilities*
IEH *Interpreting Equipment (Can Arrange Hire)*
AC *Air-Conditioning*
AVO *Audio Visual (Available On Premises)*
IEO *Interpreting Equipment (Available On Premises)*
AVH *Audio Visual (Can Arrange Hire)*

**Keadeen Hotel**
Newbridge, Co. Kildare
Tel: 045-431666 ....................Page 340
**Contact Person:**
Pauline Barry
**Seating Capacity of Meeting Rooms:**
*+500: 1 +400: 1 +300: 1 +200: 1*
*+100: 3 +50: 4 -50: 7*
**Facilities available:**
BO AC IEH AVO

**Kildare Hotel, Spa and Country Club - The K Club**
Straffan, Co. Kildare
Tel: 01-601 7200 ....................Page 341
**Contact Person:**
Anne Marie Hogan
**Seating Capacity of Meeting Rooms:**
*+400: 1 +300: 1 +200: 2 +100: 2*
*+50: 3 -50: 8*
**Facilities available:**
BO AC IEH AVO

**Kilkea Castle**
Castledermot, Co. Kildare
Tel: 059-914 5156 ..................Page 333
**Contact Person:**
Liz Mahon / Paula Jamal
**Seating Capacity of Meeting Rooms:**
*+300: 1 +200: 1 +100: 1 +50: 1 -50: 2*
**Facilities available:**
AVO AVH

**Killashee House Hotel & Villa Spa**
Naas, Co. Kildare
Tel: 045-879277 ....................Page 337
**Contact Person:**
Anne-Marie Hayes
**Seating Capacity of Meeting Rooms:**
*+500: 1 +400: 2 +300: 2 +200: 2*
*+100: 4 +50: 5 -50: 14*
**Facilities available:**
BO AC IEH AVO AVH

**Maudlins House Hotel**
Naas, Co. Kildare
Tel: 045-896999 ....................Page 338
**Contact Person:**
Tom Ryan / Darren Lynch
**Seating Capacity of Meeting Rooms:**
*+50: 1 -50: 4*
**Facilities available:**
BO AC IEH AVO

**Moyvalley Hotel & Golf Resort**
Moyvalley, Co. Kildare
Tel: 046-954 8000..................Page 337
**Contact Person:**
Yolande Bell / Antoinette Tyrell
**Seating Capacity of Meeting Rooms:**
*+200: 1 +100: 1 +50: 2 -50: 4*
**Facilities available:**
BO AC AVO

**Osprey Hotel & Spa**
Naas, Co. Kildare
Tel: 045-881111 ......................Page 338
**Contact Person:**
Sharon Deegan
**Seating Capacity of Meeting Rooms:**
*+300: 1 +200: 1 +100: 2 +50: 3*
*-50: 12*
**Facilities available:**
BO AC AVH

**Standhouse Hotel Leisure & Conference Centre**
Curragh (The), Co. Kildare
Tel: 045-436177 ....................Page 334
**Contact Person:**
Helen O'Donnell/Deirdre O'Callaghan
**Seating Capacity of Meeting Rooms:**
*+500: 1 +400: 1 +300: 1 +200: 1*
*+100: 1 +50: 2 -50: 5*
**Facilities available:**
BO AC IEH AVO AVH

**Westgrove Hotel & Conference Centre**
Clane, Co. Kildare
Tel: 045-989900 ....................Page 334
**Contact Person:**
Clodagh McDonnell
**Seating Capacity of Meeting Rooms:**
*+500: 1 +400: 2 +50: 4 -50: 5*
**Facilities available:**
BO AC IEH AVO

## Co. Laois

**Abbeyleix Manor Hotel**
Abbeyleix, Co. Laois
Tel: 057-873 0111 ..................Page 341
**Contact Person:**
Eileen O'Connor
**Seating Capacity of Meeting Rooms:**
*+500: 1 +300: 1 +200: 1 +100: 1*
*+50: 1 -50: 2*
**Facilities available:**
BO AC IEH AVH

**Comfort Inn Portlaoise**
Portlaoise, Co. Laois
Tel: 057-869 5900..................Page 342
**Contact Person:**
Martina Yearsley
**Seating Capacity of Meeting Rooms:**
*+50: 2 -50: 6*
**Facilities available:**
BO AC IEH AVO

**Heritage Golf & Spa Resort (The)**
Killenard, Co. Laois
Tel: 057-864 5500..................Page 342
**Contact Person:**
David Haniffy
**Seating Capacity of Meeting Rooms:**
*+400: 1 +50: 2 -50: 4*
**Facilities available:**
BO AC IEH AVO

**Killeshin (The)**
Portlaoise, Co. Laois
Tel: 057-863 1200 ..................Page 342
**Contact Person:**
Roisin Lawlor
**Seating Capacity of Meeting Rooms:**
*+100: 1 +50: 4 -50: 11*
**Facilities available:**
BO AC IEH AVO

**Portlaoise Heritage Hotel**
Portlaoise, Co. Laois
Tel: 057-867 8588..................Page 343
**Contact Person:**
Nollaig Baker
**Seating Capacity of Meeting Rooms:**
*+500: 1 +400: 1 +300: 1 +200: 1*
*+100: 2 +50: 4 -50: 9*
**Facilities available:**
BO AC IEH AVO

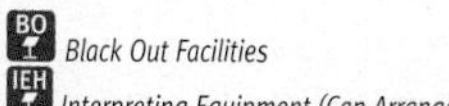

BO *Black Out Facilities*
IEH *Interpreting Equipment (Can Arrange Hire)*

AC *Air-Conditioning*
AVO *Audio Visual (Available On Premises)*

IEO *Interpreting Equipment (Available On Premises)*
AVH *Audio Visual (Can Arrange Hire)*

## Co. Longford

**Annaly Hotel**
Longford Town, Co. Longford
Tel: 043-42058 ....................... Page 344
**Contact Person:**
Jonathan Naylor
**Seating Capacity of Meeting Rooms:**
*+200: 1*
**Facilities available:**
BO IEO IEH AVO AVH

**Longford Arms Hotel**
Longford Town, Co. Longford
Tel: 043-46296 ....................... Page 344
**Contact Person:**
Duty Manager
**Seating Capacity of Meeting Rooms:**
*+500: 1 +100: 2 +50: 3*
**Facilities available:**
BO AC IEH AVH

## Co. Louth

**Ballymascanlon House Hotel**
Dundalk, Co. Louth
Tel: 042-935 8200 .................. Page 348
**Contact Person:**
Chris Brayden
**Seating Capacity of Meeting Rooms:**
*+300: 1 +100: 1 -50: 6*
**Facilities available:**
BO AC IEH AVO

**Boyne Valley Hotel & Country Club**
Drogheda, Co. Louth
Tel: 041-983 7737 .................. Page 346
**Contact Person:**
Peter McNamara
**Seating Capacity of Meeting Rooms:**
*+500: 2 +400: 2 +300: 1 +200: 2 +100: 1 +50: 2 -50: 4*
**Facilities available:**
BO AC IEH AVO AVH

**Crowne Plaza Dundalk**
Dundalk, Co. Louth
Tel: 042-9335453 .................. Page 348
**Contact Person:**
Amanda Finlay
**Seating Capacity of Meeting Rooms:**
*+400: 1 +100: 2 +50: 2 -50: 4*
**Facilities available:**
BO AC IEH AVO

**D (The)**
Drogheda, Co. Louth
Tel: 041-987 7700 .................. Page 346
**Contact Person:**
Martina Hannigan
**Seating Capacity of Meeting Rooms:**
*-50: 5*
**Facilities available:**
BO AC IEH AVO AVH

**Fairways Hotel & Conference Centre**
Dundalk, Co. Louth
Tel: 042-932 1500 .................. Page 349
**Contact Person:**
Ken Byrne / Karen Taggart / Eva Bernie
**Seating Capacity of Meeting Rooms:**
*+500: 1 +400: 1 +300: 2 +200: 2 +100: 2 +50: 5 -50: 10*
**Facilities available:**
BO AC IEH AVO

**Four Seasons Hotel & Leisure Club Carlingford**
Carlingford, Co. Louth
Tel: 042-937 3530 .................. Page 345
**Contact Person:**
Elaine / Lorraine
**Seating Capacity of Meeting Rooms:**
*+500: 1 +400: 1 +300: 1 +200: 2 +100: 4 +50: 4 -50: 4*
**Facilities available:**
BO AC IEH AVO

**Hotel Imperial**
Dundalk, Co. Louth
Tel: 042-933 2241 .................. Page 349
**Contact Person:**
Conference Co-Ordinator
**Seating Capacity of Meeting Rooms:**
*-50: 1*
**Facilities available:**
BO AC AVO AVH

**McKevitt's Village Hotel**
Carlingford, Co. Louth
Tel: 042-937 3116 .................. Page 345
**Contact Person:**
Terry and Kay McKevitt
**Seating Capacity of Meeting Rooms:**
*+100: 1 -50: 1*
**Facilities available:**
BO AC AVH

**Park Inn Dundalk**
Dundalk, Co. Louth
Tel: 042-939 5700 .................. Page 350
**Contact Person:**
Anja Schroeder
**Seating Capacity of Meeting Rooms:**
*+400: 1 +50: 2 -50: 2*
**Facilities available:**
BO AC AVH

**Westcourt Hotel**
Drogheda, Co. Louth
Tel: 041-983 0965 .................. Page 347
**Contact Person:**
Thomas Gavan
**Seating Capacity of Meeting Rooms:**
*+200: 1 +100: 1 +50: 2*
**Facilities available:**
AC AVH

## Co. Meath

**Ardboyne Hotel**
Navan, Co. Meath
Tel: 046-902 3119 .................. Page 355
**Contact Person:**
Michelle Gilbane
**Seating Capacity of Meeting Rooms:**
*+300: 1 +100: 2 +50: 3 -50: 4*
**Facilities available:**
BO AC IEH AVH

**Ashbourne Marriott Hotel**
Ashbourne, Co. Meath
Tel: 01-835 0800 .................. Page 350
**Contact Person:**
Laura Mulvaney
**Seating Capacity of Meeting Rooms:**
*+500: 1 +200: 1 +50: 6 -50: 2*
**Facilities available:**
BO AC IEH AVO

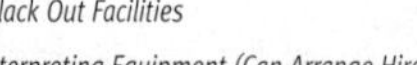
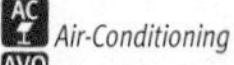

BO *Black Out Facilities*
IEH *Interpreting Equipment (Can Arrange Hire)*
AC *Air-Conditioning*
AVO *Audio Visual (Available On Premises)*
IEO *Interpreting Equipment (Available On Premises)*
AVH *Audio Visual (Can Arrange Hire)*

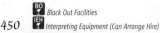

**Bettystown Court Conference & Leisure Hotel**
Bettystown, Co. Meath
Tel: 041-981 2900 ..................Page 352
**Contact Person:**
Amanda Nulty
**Seating Capacity of Meeting Rooms:**
*+400: 1 +200: 2 +100: 3*
**Facilities available:**
BO AC AVO AVH

**City North Hotel**
Gormanston, Co. Meath
Tel: 01-690 6666 ....................Page 354
**Contact Person:**
Susan Roddy
**Seating Capacity of Meeting Rooms:**
*+500: 1 +100: 1 -50: 12*
**Facilities available:**
BO AC AVO

**Dunboyne Castle Hotel & Spa**
Dunboyne, Co. Meath
Tel: 01-801 3500 ....................Page 353
**Contact Person:**
Sinead Codd
**Seating Capacity of Meeting Rooms:**
*+400: 1 +300: 1 -50: 8*
**Facilities available:**
BO AC IEH AVH

**Hamlet Court Hotel**
Johnstownbridge, Co. Meath
Tel: 046-954 1200 ..................Page 354
**Contact Person:**
Michelle Bolger
**Seating Capacity of Meeting Rooms:**
*+400: 1 +300: 1 +200: 1 +100: 2 +50: 2*
**Facilities available:**
BO AC IEO AVO

**Knightsbrook Hotel & Golf Resort**
Trim, Co. Meath
Tel: 046-948 2110 ..................Page 357
**Contact Person:**
Conference & Banqueting Manager
**Seating Capacity of Meeting Rooms:**
*+500: 2 +400: 2 +300: 2 +200: 4 +100: 4 +50: 5 -50: 10*
**Facilities available:**
BO AC IEH AVO AVH

**Marriott Johnstown House Hotel & Spa**
Enfield, Co. Meath
Tel: 046-954 0000..................Page 353
**Contact Person:**
Camille Ward
**Seating Capacity of Meeting Rooms:**
*+500: 1 +400: 1 +300: 2 +200: 2 +100: 2 +50: 2 -50: 13*
**Facilities available:**
BO AC IEH AVO

**Neptune Beach Hotel & Leisure Club**
Bettystown, Co. Meath
Tel: 041-982 7107 ..................Page 352
**Contact Person:**
Nuala McDonnell
**Seating Capacity of Meeting Rooms:**
*+200: 1 -50: 2*
**Facilities available:**
BO IEH AVO

**Newgrange Hotel**
Navan, Co. Meath
Tel: 046-907 4100 ..................Page 356
**Contact Person:**
Caroline Hegarty
**Seating Capacity of Meeting Rooms:**
*+500: 1 +300: 1 +200: 2 +50: 1 -50: 2*
**Facilities available:**
BO AC IEH AVO

**Newgrange Lodge**
Newgrange, Co. Meath
Tel: 041-988 2478 ..................Page 356
**Contact Person:**
Tina O'Reilly
**Seating Capacity of Meeting Rooms:**
*-50: 1*
**Facilities available:**
BO AVH

**Old Darnley Lodge Hotel**
Athboy, Co. Meath
Tel: 046-943 2283..................Page 352
**Contact Person:**
Séan Mangan
**Seating Capacity of Meeting Rooms:**
*+300: 1 +200: 1 +100: 1 +50: 1 -50: 1*
**Facilities available:**
BO

**Oldcastle House Hotel**
Oldcastle, Co. Meath
Tel: 049-854 2400..................Page 356
**Contact Person:**
Tom Curran
**Seating Capacity of Meeting Rooms:**
*+200: 1 +100: 1 -50: 1*
**Facilities available:**

AC AVO

**Station House Hotel and Signal Restaurant**
Kilmessan, Co. Meath
Tel: 046-902 5239..................Page 355
**Contact Person:**
Denise Slattery
**Seating Capacity of Meeting Rooms:**
*+300: 1 +200: 1 +100: 1 +50: 1 -50: 1*
**Facilities available:**
BO AC IEH AVO

**Trim Castle Hotel**
Trim, Co. Meath
Tel: 046-948 3000..................Page 358
**Contact Person:**
Alan Clare
**Seating Capacity of Meeting Rooms:**
*+500: 1 +400: 1 +300: 1 +200: 1 +100: 1 +50: 1 -50: 6*
**Facilities available:**
BO AC IEH AVO AVH

---

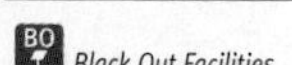
BO *Black Out Facilities*
IEH *Interpreting Equipment (Can Arrange Hire)*
AC *Air-Conditioning*
AVO *Audio Visual (Available On Premises)*
IEO *Interpreting Equipment (Available On Premises)*
AVH *Audio Visual (Can Arrange Hire)*

## Co. Monaghan

**Four Seasons Hotel & Leisure Club**
Monaghan Town, Co. Monaghan
Tel: 047-81888 ......................Page 359
**Contact Person:**
Orla McKenna
**Seating Capacity of Meeting Rooms:**
*+400: 2 +300: 3 +200: 3 +100: 3 +50: 7 -50: 7*
**Facilities available:**
BO AC IEH AVO

**Hillgrove Hotel Leisure & Spa**
Monaghan Town, Co. Monaghan
Tel: 047-81288 ......................Page 359
**Contact Person:**
Mike Nolan
**Seating Capacity of Meeting Rooms:**
*+500: 2 +400: 2 +300: 3 +200: 3 +100: 5 +50: 8 -50: 15*
**Facilities available:**
BO AC IEO IEH AVO AVH

**Nuremore Hotel & Country Club**
Carrickmacross, Co. Monaghan
Tel: 042-966 1438 ..................Page 358
**Contact Person:**
Sinead Rock
**Seating Capacity of Meeting Rooms:**
*+500: 1 +400: 1 +300: 1 +200: 2 +100: 3 +50: 3 -50: 6*
**Facilities available:**
BO AC IEH AVO

## Co. Offaly

**Bridge House Hotel, Leisure Club & Spa**
Tullamore, Co. Offaly
Tel: 057-932 5600 ..................Page 361
**Contact Person:**
Colm McCabe
**Seating Capacity of Meeting Rooms:**
*+500: 1 +400: 1 +300: 2 +200: 2 +100: 3 +50: 4 -50: 9*
**Facilities available:**
BO AC IEH AVO

**County Arms Hotel & Leisure Club**
Birr, Co. Offaly
Tel: 057-912 0791 ..................Page 360
**Contact Person:**
Peter Loughnane
**Seating Capacity of Meeting Rooms:**
*+500: 1 +400: 1 +300: 1 +200: 1 +100: 3 +50: 6 -50: 12*
**Facilities available:**
BO AC IEH AVO

**Days Hotel Tullamore**
Tullamore, Co. Offaly
Tel: 1890-329329 ..................Page 362
**Contact Person:**
Sinead Byrne
**Seating Capacity of Meeting Rooms:**
*+50: 1 -50: 1*
**Facilities available:**
BO AC IEH AVO

**Kinnitty Castle Demesne**
Birr, Co. Offaly
Tel: 057-913 7318 ..................Page 361
**Contact Person:**
Sales & Marketing Dept.
**Seating Capacity of Meeting Rooms:**
*+100: 1 -50: 2*
**Facilities available:**
BO IEH AVO AVH

**Moorhill House Hotel and Garden Suites**
Tullamore, Co. Offaly
Tel: 057-932 1395 ..................Page 362
**Contact Person:**
Alan Duffy
**Seating Capacity of Meeting Rooms:**
*+100: 1 +50: 2 -50: 2*
**Facilities available:**
BO AC IEO IEH AVO AVH

**Tullamore Court Hotel Conference & Leisure Centre**
Tullamore, Co. Offaly
Tel: 057-934 6666..................Page 363
**Contact Person:**
Ann Lynch
**Seating Capacity of Meeting Rooms:**
*+500: 1 +400: 1 +300: 2 +200: 2 +100: 4 +50: 8 -50: 17*
**Facilities available:**
BO AC IEH AVO

## Co. Westmeath

**Athlone Springs Hotel**
Athlone, Co. Westmeath
Tel: 090-644 4444..................Page 364
**Contact Person:**
Caroline Spollen
**Seating Capacity of Meeting Rooms:**
*+400: 1 -50: 6*
**Facilities available:**
BO AC IEH AVO

**Bloomfield House Hotel**
Mullingar, Co. Westmeath
Tel: 044-934 0894..................Page 368
**Contact Person:**
Conference & Banqueting Co-Ordinator
**Seating Capacity of Meeting Rooms:**
*+300: 1 +200: 2 +100: 4 +50: 5 -50: 8*
**Facilities available:**
BO AC IEH AVO

**Creggan Court Hotel**
Athlone, Co. Westmeath
Tel: 090-647 7777..................Page 364
**Contact Person:**
Paulette Daly
**Seating Capacity of Meeting Rooms:**
*+50: 1 -50: 4*
**Facilities available:**
BO AC IEH AVO AVH

**Glasson Golf Hotel and Country Club**
Athlone, Co. Westmeath
Tel: 090-648 5120 ..................Page 364
**Contact Person:**
Gareth Jones / Fidelma Reid
**Seating Capacity of Meeting Rooms:**
*+100: 1 +50: 1 -50: 3*
**Facilities available:**
BO AC IEH AVO

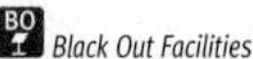
*BO Black Out Facilities*
*IEH Interpreting Equipment (Can Arrange Hire)*

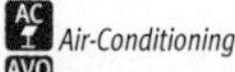
*AC Air-Conditioning*
*AVO Audio Visual (Available On Premises)*

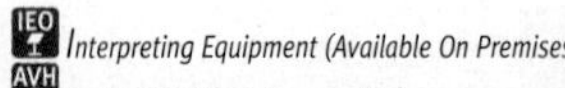
*IEO Interpreting Equipment (Available On Premises)*
*AVH Audio Visual (Can Arrange Hire)*

**Greville Arms Hotel**
Mullingar, Co. Westmeath
Tel: 044-934 8563..................Page 368
**Contact Person:**
John Cochrane
**Seating Capacity of Meeting Rooms:**
+200: 1 +100: 2 +50: 1 -50: 2
**Facilities available:**

**Hilamar Hotel**
Kinnegad, Co. Westmeath
Tel: 044-939 1719 ..................Page 367
**Contact Person:**
Patrice Whelehan
**Seating Capacity of Meeting Rooms:**
+200: 1 -50: 2
**Facilities available:**

**Hodson Bay Hotel**
Athlone, Co. Westmeath
Tel: 090-644 2000..................Page 365
**Contact Person:**
Christina Melican
**Seating Capacity of Meeting Rooms:**
+500: 1 +400: 1 +300: 1 +200: 2
+100: 3 +50: 6 -50: 13
**Facilities available:**

**Mullingar Park Hotel**
Mullingar, Co. Westmeath
Tel: 044-933 7500..................Page 369
**Contact Person:**
Ita Kerrigan
**Seating Capacity of Meeting Rooms:**
+500: 2 +400: 2 +300: 3 +200: 4
+100: 7 +50: 14 -50: 9
**Facilities available:**
BO AC IEH AVO AVH

**Radisson SAS Hotel**
Athlone, Co. Westmeath
Tel: 090-644 2600..................Page 366
**Contact Person:**
Meetings and Events Department
**Seating Capacity of Meeting Rooms:**
+500: 1 +400: 1 +300: 1 +200: 2
+100: 4 +50: 4 -50: 6
**Facilities available:**
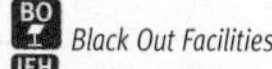


**Shamrock Lodge Hotel and Conference Centre**
Athlone, Co. Westmeath
Tel: 090-649 2601 ..................Page 366
**Contact Person:**
Fiona Claffey / Pamela Egan
**Seating Capacity of Meeting Rooms:**
+200: 1 +100: 2 +50: 3 -50: 3
**Facilities available:**
AC AVH

**Sheraton Athlone Hotel**
Athlone, Co. Westmeath
Tel: 090-645 1000 ..................Page 366
**Contact Person:**
Shirley Delahunt
**Seating Capacity of Meeting Rooms:**
+500: 1 +400: 1 +300: 1 +200: 2
+100: 4 +50: 10 -50: 11
**Facilities available:**
BO AC IEH AVO AVH

**Temple Country Retreat & Spa**
Moate, Co. Westmeath
Tel: 057-933 5118 ..................Page 367
**Contact Person:**
Bernadette Fagan
**Seating Capacity of Meeting Rooms:**
-50: 3
**Facilities available:**
BO AC AVO

## Co. Wicklow

**Arklow Bay Conference, Leisure & Spa Hotel**
Arklow, Co. Wicklow
Tel: 0402-32309 ....................Page 370
**Contact Person:**
Rachel Merrigan
**Seating Capacity of Meeting Rooms:**
+500: 1 +400: 1 +300: 1 +200: 2
+100: 2 +50: 4 -50: 5
**Facilities available:**
BO AC IEH AVO AVH

**Avon Ri**
Blessington, Co. Wicklow
Tel: 045-900670 ....................Page 372
**Contact Person:**
Siobhan Kendrick / Michaela O'Neill
**Seating Capacity of Meeting Rooms:**
+200: 1 +50: 2 -50: 1
**Facilities available:**
BO AC IEH AVH

**Glendalough Hotel**
Glendalough, Co. Wicklow
Tel: 0404-45135 ....................Page 375
**Contact Person:**
John Kelly
**Seating Capacity of Meeting Rooms:**
+100: 1 -50: 2
**Facilities available:**
BO AC IEH AVO

**Glenview Hotel**
Glen-O-The-Downs, Co. Wicklow
Tel: 01-287 3399 ....................Page 376
**Contact Person:**
Fiona O'Regan
**Seating Capacity of Meeting Rooms:**
+200: 1 +100: 1 +50: 2 -50: 4
**Facilities available:**
BO AC IEH AVO

**Grand Hotel**
Wicklow Town, Co. Wicklow
Tel: 0404-67337 ....................Page 377
**Contact Person:**
Jenny Byrne
**Seating Capacity of Meeting Rooms:**
+300: 1 +100: 1 -50: 2
**Facilities available:**
BO AC AVO AVH

**Heather House Hotel**
Bray, Co. Wicklow
Tel: 01-286 8000 ....................Page 373
**Contact Person:**
Frances Lamb / Donal Byrne
**Seating Capacity of Meeting Rooms:**
+50: 1
**Facilities available:**
BO AVH

---

BO *Black Out Facilities*
IEH *Interpreting Equipment (Can Arrange Hire)*
AC *Air-Conditioning*
AVO *Audio Visual (Available On Premises)*
IEO *Interpreting Equipment (Available On Premises)*
AVH *Audio Visual (Can Arrange Hire)*

## Co. Wicklow CONTINUED

**Hunter's Hotel**
Rathnew, Co. Wicklow
Tel: 0404-40106 ....................Page 376
**Contact Person:**
Maragret Thompson
**Seating Capacity of Meeting Rooms:**
*-50: 3*
**Facilities available:**
BO IEH AVH

**Parkview Hotel**
Newtownmountkennedy, Co. Wicklow
Tel: 01-201 5600 ....................Page 376
**Contact Person:**
Roslle Pabillano
**Seating Capacity of Meeting Rooms:**
*+300: 1 +50: 1 -50: 1*
**Facilities available:**
BO AC AVO AVH

**Ramada Hotel Bray**
Bray, Co. Wicklow
Tel: 01-276 0258....................Page 373
**Contact Person:**
Nikki McHugh
**Seating Capacity of Meeting Rooms:**
*+200: 1 +100: 1 +50: 5 -50: 1*
**Facilities available:**
BO AC IEH AVO

**Rathsallagh House, Golf and Country Club**
Dunlavin, Co. Wicklow
Tel: 045-403112 ....................Page 374
**Contact Person:**
Catherine Lawlor
**Seating Capacity of Meeting Rooms:**
*-50: 4*
**Facilities available:**
BO IEH AVO

**The Ritz-Carlton, Powerscourt**
Enniskerry, Co. Wicklow
Tel: 01-274 8888....................Page 375
**Contact Person:**
Tobias Schoch
**Seating Capacity of Meeting Rooms:**
*+400: 1 +300: 1 +200: 3 +100: 2 +50: 6 -50: 6*
**Facilities available:**
BO AC IEH AVO AVH

**Tinakilly House Hotel**
Rathnew, Co. Wicklow
Tel: 0404-69274 ....................Page 377
**Contact Person:**
Denise Stockdale
**Seating Capacity of Meeting Rooms:**
*+50: 1 -50: 3*
**Facilities available:**
BO AC IEH AVO

**Woodenbridge Hotel**
Woodenbridge, Co. Wicklow
Tel: 0402-35146 ....................Page 378
**Contact Person:**
Gerard O'Brien
**Seating Capacity of Meeting Rooms:**
*+100: 1 +50: 2 -50: 5*
**Facilities available:**
AC IEH AVO

# Northern Ireland

## Co. Antrim

**Ballymac**
Stoneyford, Co. Antrim
Tel: 028-9264 8313 ................Page 384
**Contact Person:**
Gaile McCarthy
**Seating Capacity of Meeting Rooms:**
*+100: 1 -50: 1*
**Facilities available:**
BO AVO

**Bayview Hotel**
Bushmills, Co. Antrim
Tel: 028-2073 4100 ................Page 382
**Contact Person:**
Mary O'Neill
**Seating Capacity of Meeting Rooms:**
*+50: 1 -50: 1*
**Facilities available:**
BO AC IEH AVH

**Clarion Hotel**
Carrickfergus, Co. Antrim
Tel: 028-9336 4556................Page 383
**Contact Person:**
Karen Balloch
**Seating Capacity of Meeting Rooms:**
*+500: 1 +100: 1 +50: 2 -50: 3*
**Facilities available:**
BO AC IEH AVO AVH

**Londonderry Arms Hotel**
Carnlough, Co. Antrim
Tel: 028-2888 5255................Page 383
**Contact Person:**
Frank O'Neill & Maureen Morrow
**Seating Capacity of Meeting Rooms:**
*+100: 1 +50: 2 -50: 2*
**Facilities available:**
BO IEH AVH

**Ramada Portrush**
Portrush, Co. Antrim
Tel: 028-7082 6100 ................Page 383
**Contact Person:**
Mary O'Neill
**Seating Capacity of Meeting Rooms:**
*+100: 1 +50: 1 -50: 3*
**Facilities available:**
BO AC IEH AVH

## Co. Armagh

**Armagh City Hotel**
Armagh City, Co. Armagh
Tel: 028-3751 8888 ................Page 384
**Contact Person:**
Garrett McElearney
**Seating Capacity of Meeting Rooms:**
*+500: 2 +400: 2 +300: 2 +200: 4 +100: 4 +50: 5 -50: 10*
**Facilities available:**
BO AC IEH AVO

## Belfast City

**Dunadry Hotel**
Belfast City
Tel: 028-9443 4343................Page 385
**Contact Person:**
Sheree Davis
**Seating Capacity of Meeting Rooms:**
*+300: 1 +200: 1 +100: 1 +50: 3 -50: 4*
**Facilities available:**
BO AC AVO

**La Mon Hotel & Country Club**
Belfast City
Tel: 028-9044 8631 ................Page 386
**Contact Person:**
Duty Manager
**Seating Capacity of Meeting Rooms:**
*+500: 1 +400: 2 +300: 2 +200: 2 +100: 5 +50: 12 -50: 17*
**Facilities available:**
BO AC AVH

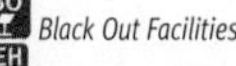

BO *Black Out Facilities*
IEH *Interpreting Equipment (Can Arrange Hire)*
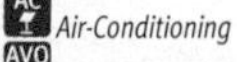
AC *Air-Conditioning*
AVO *Audio Visual (Available On Premises)*
IEO *Interpreting Equipment (Available On Premises)*
AVH *Audio Visual (Can Arrange Hire)*

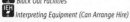

**Malone Lodge Hotel & Apartments**
Belfast City
Tel: 028-9038 8000................Page 386
**Contact Person:**
Conference Co-Ordinator
**Seating Capacity of Meeting Rooms:**
*+100: 1 +50: 1 -50: 4*
**Facilities available:**
BO AC IEH AVO AVH

## Co. Derry

**Anchorage Inn (The)**
Portstewart, Co. Derry
Tel: 028-7083 2003................Page 390
**Contact Person:**
Carolyn McKeown
**Seating Capacity of Meeting Rooms:**
*-50: 1*
**Facilities available:**
BO AC AVO

## Co. Down

**Burrendale Hotel and Country Club**
Newcastle, Co. Down
Tel: 028-4372 2599 ................Page 391
**Contact Person:**
Fiona O'Hare
**Seating Capacity of Meeting Rooms:**
*+200: 1 +100: 1 -50: 6*
**Facilities available:**
BO AC IEH AVO

**Canal Court Hotel**
Newry, Co. Down
Tel: 028-3025 1234 ................Page 391
**Contact Person:**
Conference & Banqueting Office
**Seating Capacity of Meeting Rooms:**
*+400: 1 +300: 1 +200: 2 +100: 3 +50: 5 -50: 4*
**Facilities available:**
AC IEH AVO

## Co. Fermanagh

**Lough Erne Golf Resort**
Enniskillen, Co. Fermanagh
Tel: 028-6632 0613 ................Page 392
**Contact Person:**
Joanne Walsh
**Seating Capacity of Meeting Rooms:**
*+400: 1 +300: 1 +200: 1 +100: 2 +50: 3 -50: 4*
**Facilities available:**
BO AC IEH AVO AVH

## Co. Tyrone

**Corick House & Licensed Restaurant**
Clogher, Co. Tyrone
Tel: 028-8554 8216 ................Page 393
**Contact Person:**
Paula Farry
**Seating Capacity of Meeting Rooms:**
*+200: 1 +50: 1*
**Facilities available:**
AVO AVH

 *Black Out Facilities*
IEH *Interpreting Equipment (Can Arrange Hire)*
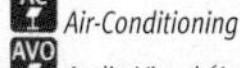

*Air-Conditioning*
*Audio Visual (Available On Premises)*
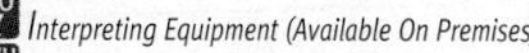
*Interpreting Equipment (Available On Premises)*
*Audio Visual (Can Arrange Hire)*

# SPA & LEISURE - IRELAND 2008

Ireland is rapidly developing its spa market, with a selection of destination, day, health and resort spas to choose from, as well as superb leisure facilities - all in the wonderful surroundings that make Ireland a unique holiday destination. The following pages will provide a flavour of some of the facilities and treatments on offer in many of the hotels and guesthouses featured in this guide.

*.....So come on and get pampered!*

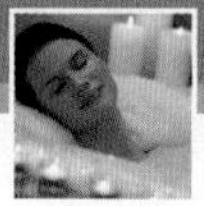

We invite you to Ireland to enhance your precious leisure time. Relax in the perfect sanctuary of the oasis that is Ireland! Our philosophy is to enable you to leave us fully refreshed and restored by experiencing some of the wonderful spa & leisure treatments available in the unique and warm facilities on offer in the hotels and guesthouses listed in this section. A full description of the hotels and guesthouses can be had by looking up the appropriate page number.

***Premises are listed in Alphabetical Order in each County.***

# Ireland West

## Co. Clare

### Bunratty Castle Hotel & Angsana Spa

Bunratty, Co. Clare
Tel: 061-478700 ........................Page 38
Name of Spa:
**Angsana Spa**
Treatments:20 ........Treatment Rooms:5
Type of Treatments:
*Massage, Body Polish, Facial, Indian Head Massage, Skin Enhancer, Hands Paraffin, Feet Paraffin, 1/2 Day & Full Day Pamper Packages*
Type of Facilities:
*Sauna, Steam Room, Vitality Pool, Relaxation Balcony, Relaxation Suite, Jacuzzi, Fully Equipped Gym, Personal Training Facilities*

### Falls Hotel & Spa

Ennistymon, Co. Clare
Tel: 065-707 1004 ....................Page 44
Name of Spa:
**River Spa**
Treatments:50 ......Treatment Rooms:12
Type of Treatments:
*Elemis Facials, Rasul Mud Treatment, Hydrobath, Dry Floats, Hammam, Kings Bath, Relaxation Room, Massage*
Type of Facilities:
*20m Swimming Pool, Outdoor Hot Tub, Jacuzzi, Steam Room, Sauna, Gymnasium, 12 Treatment Rooms*

### Kilkee Bay Hotel

Kilkee, Co. Clare
Tel: 065-906 0060....................Page 45
Name of Spa:
**Sentosa Spa**
Treatments:40 ........Treatment Rooms:4
Type of Treatments:
*Aromatis Facial, De Luxe Pedicure, Total Youth Facial Treatment, Matis Body Polish, Sports Massage*
Type of Facilities:
*15m Indoor Pool, Gym, Sauna, Jacuzzi, Steam Room*

### Thomond Guesthouse & Kilkee Thalassotherapy Centre

Kilkee, Co. Clare
Tel: 065-905 6742....................Page 46
Name of Spa:
**Kilkee Thalassotherapy Centre**
Treatments:18 ........Treatment Rooms:6
Type of Treatments:
*Natural Seaweed Baths, Balneotherapy, Swedish Massage, Body Scrub, Seaweed Body Wrap, Frigi-Thalgo, Facials, Manicures, Pedicures, Aromatherapy, Massage*
Type of Facilities:
*Sauna, Steam Room, Manicure/Pedicure room, 6 Treatment rooms. Relaxation area. Winner, Best Day Spa 2004 (Irish Beauty Industry)*

### Did you know ?

**Thalassotherapy**
*This is a traditional, holistic marine-based therapy that uses natural ocean elements to restore wellness and to unveil one's pure, natural beauty.*

**Pressotherapy**
*This is an exclusive detoxifying treatment, which through effective lymphatic drainage, helps to promote the body's natural toxin clearing functions. The revitalization and oxygenation of the tissue helps to slim and redefine the legs, stomach and arms while enhancing skin tone.*

**Hammam**
*It means "spreader of warmth". It is the word given to the sensual bathing retreat that evolved over thousands of years and traces its roots back to the Roman Thermae.*

## Co. Donegal

### Ballyliffin Lodge & Spa

Ballyliffin, Co. Donegal
Tel: 074-937 8200....................Page 56
Name of Spa:
**The Rock Crystal Spa**
Treatments:10 ........Treatment Rooms:8
Type of Treatments:
*Massage (Hot Stone), Facial (Thalgo & USPA), Hand & Foot Care, Beauty Treatments, Male Grooming, 1/2 Day Packages, Full Day Packages, Dry Floatation*
Type of Facilities:
*Relaxation Room, 17m Pool, Steam Room, Sauna, Jacuzzi, Gym, Children's Pool, Aerobics Studio*

### Carlton Redcastle Hotel & C Spa

Moville, Co. Donegal
Tel: 074-938 5555....................Page 66
Name of Spa:
**The C Spa**
Treatments:35 ......Treatment Rooms:12
Type of Treatments:
*Chromotherapy Bath, Rasul, Balneotherapy Bath, Affusion Shower, Hydrojet Massage, Pressotherapy, Cryotherapy, Thalasso Body Wrapping, Marine Body Polish, Elemis Facials massages and body Wraps*
Type of Facilities:
*Gymnasium, Thalasso Spa Relaxation Room, Thalassotherapy Pool*

### Downings Bay Hotel

Letterkenny, Co. Donegal
Tel: 074-915 5586 ....................Page 63
Name of Spa:
**Secrets Beauty Salon**
Treatments:25 ........Treatment Rooms:2
Type of Treatments:
*Manicure/Pedicure, Waxing, Eye Treatments, Nail Extensions, Facials - Absolute Hydrating Facial, Cold Marine Facial, Body Treatments - Marine Prelude Treatment, Thalgobodytherm Wrap, Spray Tan*
Type of Facilities:
*Beauty Salon, 20m Pool, Kids' Pool, Jacuzzi, Sauna, Gym*

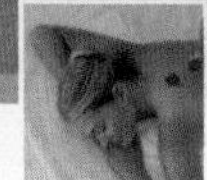

### Inishowen Gateway Hotel
Buncrana, Co. Donegal
Tel: 074-936 1144 ....................Page 57
Name of Spa:
**Seagrass Wellbeing Centre**
Treatments:50 ........Treatment Rooms:6
Type of Treatments:
*Aroma Stone Massage, Body Wraps, Hydrotherapy, Indian Head Massage, Reiki, Aromatherapy Massage, Facials, Pedicures, Manicures, Reflexology*
Type of Facilities:
*Relaxation Room, Herbal Teas & Juice Bar, Showers & Changing Rooms, Towelling Robes and Slippers provided, Hydrotherapy Bath*

### Jackson's Hotel, Conference & Leisure Centre
Ballybofey, Co. Donegal
Tel: 074-913 1021 ....................Page 54
Name of Spa:
**Health Suite**
Treatments:10 ........Treatment Rooms:3
Type of Treatments:
*Full Body Massage, Indian Head Massage, Reflexology, Facials, Manicures, Pedicures*
Type of Facilities:
*22m Swimming Pool, Jacuzzi, Steam Cabin, Sauna, Massage Rooms, Spa Bath, Sun Beds, Hot Tub, Aqua Lounger*

### Mill Park Hotel, Conference Centre & Leisure Club
Donegal Town, Co. Donegal
Tel: 074-972 2880....................Page 59
Name of Spa:
**The Wellness Centre**
Treatments:20 ........Treatment Rooms:4
Type of Treatments:
*Massage, Waxing, Make up, Manicure, Pedicure, Facials, Body Wraps, Holistic Treatments, Hopi Candle, Hot Stone Therapy Treatments*
Type of Facilities:
*Massage Room, Beauty Treatment Room, Nail Bar, Heated Swimming Pool, Fitness Room, Steam Room, Jacuzzi, Solarium*

### Sandhouse Hotel
Rossnowlagh, Co. Donegal
Tel: 071-985 1777 ....................Page 67
Name of Spa:
**The Marine Spa**
Treatments:25 ........Treatment Rooms:8
Type of Treatments:
*Manicure, Pedicure, Facials, Massage, Hydrotherapy, Body Wraps, Tinting, Waxing, Electrolysis, Tanning*
Type of Facilities:
*Jacuzzi, Steam Room, 8 Treatment Rooms, Relaxation Room*

### Shandon Hotel Spa and Wellness
Dunfanaghy, Co. Donegal
Tel: 074-913 6137 ....................Page 60
Name of Spa:
**Shandon Spa and Wellness**
Treatments:41 ........Treatment Rooms:8
Type of Treatments:
*Balneotherapy, Dry Floatation, Hot & Cold Stone Therapy, Swedish Massage, Reflexology, Aromatherapy, Indian Head Massage & many more*
Type of Facilities:
*10,000 sq feet of Total Spa with Executive Lounge, Male & Female Changing Rooms, Relaxation Room, Exercise Room, Vitality Pool, Heated Slabs, Foot Spa, Outdoor Hot Tub, Salt Grotto, Ice Fountain, Aromatherapy Showers*

### Villa Rose Hotel & V - Spa
Ballybofey, Co. Donegal
Tel: 074-913 2266 ....................Page 55
Name of Spa:
**V-Spa**
Treatments:43 ........Treatment Rooms:7
Type of Treatments:
*Cosmetic Demo Abrasion & Timexpert Facials (Germaine de Capuccini), Selection of Spa Wrap Sensations & Spa Exfoliations, Germaine de Capuccini Stone body Therapy, Hand and Foot care (Jessana), Full & Half day Spa Experiences & Bridal Packages*
Type of Facilities:
*Luxurious Foot Spa's, Hydrotherapy Spa, Crystal Steam Room, Ice Fountain, Tropical Showers & Razul*

## Co. Galway

### Carlton Shearwater Hotel & C Spa
Ballinasloe, Co. Galway
Tel: 0909-630400 ....................Page 70
Name of Spa:
**C.Spa**
Treatments:25 ........Treatment Rooms:8
Type of Treatments:
*Hydrotherapy Bath, Dry Floatation Tank, Couples Massage, Elemis Facial, Elemis Massage*
Type of Facilities:
*20 meter pool, Sauna, Jacuzzi, Childrens Pool, Steam Room, Gym*

### G (The)
Galway City, Co. Galway
Tel: 091-865200 ......................Page 83
Name of Spa:
**ESPA at the g**
Treatments:45 ........Treatment Rooms:8
Type of Treatments:
*Detoxifying Day, Pure Time - Pure Indulgence, Holistic Back, Face, Scalp Massage & Hot Stones, Chakra Balancing With Hot Stones, ESPA Ayurvedic Rituals, ESPA Facials, ESPA Body Wraps, Anti-Aging Rejuvenator, ESPA Body Massage, ESPA Holistic Hand & Foot Treatments*
Type of Facilities:
*8 Treatment Rooms, 4 Beauty Suites, Crystal Steam Room, Vitality Pool, Rock Sauna, Rain Shower, Fitness Centre, Ice Fountain, Tepidariums, Relaxation Rooms overlooking a Zen rooftop garden*

### Galway Bay Hotel, Conference & Leisure Centre
Galway City, Co. Galway
Tel: 091-520520 ......................Page 83
Name of Spa:
**Calmer Waters Health & Beauty**
Treatments:29 ........Treatment Rooms:2
Type of Treatments:
*Hot Stone Massage, Aromatherapy Massage, Indian Head Massage, Swedish Massage, Reflexology, Reiki and Seichem, Thalgo Facial, Thalgodermy Facial, Oxygen Facial, Cold Marine Facial*
Type of Facilities:
*Swimming Pool, Steam Room, Sauna, Treatment Rooms, Gymnasium, Aqua Aerobics Classes*

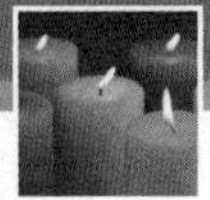

## Co. Galway CONTINUED

### Harbour Hotel
Galway City, Co. Galway
Tel: 091-569466........................Page 84
Name of Spa:
**Haven Health and Beauty**
Treatments:21 ........Treatment Rooms:2
Type of Treatments:
*The Repechage Four Layer Facial, Seaweed "on the go" Facial, Aromatherapy Purifying Facial, Back Facial, Repechage Sea Body Treat, Repechage New York Experience, Peppermint Sea Twist, Seaweed Body Treatment, Honey & Almond Body Polish, Manicure/Pedicure*
Type of Facilities:
*Jacuzzi, Gym, Steam Room*

### Hotel Meyrick
Galway City, Co. Galway
Tel: 091-564041 ......................Page 85
Name of Spa:
**The Square Spa and Health Club**
Treatments:20 ........Treatment Rooms:3
Type of Treatments:
*Hydrotherapy Baths, Waxing Treatments (various), Massage (various), Facials (various), Hand & Feet Treatments, Aromatherapy*
Type of Facilities:
*Fitness Suite, Steam Room, Jacuzzi, Outdoor Canadian Hot Tub, Hydrotherapy Baths*

### Inishbofin House Hotel
Inishbofin Island, Co. Galway
Tel: 095-45809 ........................Page 93
Treatments:12 ........Treatment Rooms:7
Type of Treatments:
*Variety of Treatments and Beauty Therapy available*

### Radisson SAS Hotel & Spa Galway
Galway City, Co. Galway
Tel: 091-538300 ......................Page 89
Name of Spa:
**Spirit One Spa**
Treatments:60 ......Treatment Rooms:16
Type of Treatments:
*Massage, Facials, Hand Treatments, Foot Treatments, Floats, Wraps, Waxing, Reflexology, Exfoliation, Eye Teatments*
Type of Facilities:
*Indoor Swimming Pool, Hot Tub, Gym, Slipper, Laconium, Sabia Med, Heated Loungers, Rock Sauna, Hammam, Snail Showers*

### Raheen Woods Hotel & Spa
Athenry, Co. Galway
Tel: 091-875888 .....................Page 69
Name of Spa:
**Tranquillity**
Treatments:50 ........Treatment Rooms:6
Type of Treatments:
*Germaine De Cappucini Facials, Dermalogica Facial, Body Wraps including Chocolate Wrap, Massage, Waxing, Pedicures, Manicures, Spa Days, Spray Tan, Make Up*
Type of Facilities:
*20m Heated Indoor Pool, Gymnasium, Sauna and Steam Room, Hydrotherapy Bath, Jacuzzi, Kiddies Pool, Crèche*

## Co. Leitrim

### Lough Rynn Castle
Mohill, Co. Leitrim
Tel: 071-963 2700 .................Page 103
Name of Spa:
**Spa Opening September 2008**
Treatment Rooms:15
Type of Treatments:
*Please Enquire about Treatments Available*
Type of Facilities:
*Please Enquire about Facilities Available*

### Ramada Hotel & Suites at Lough Allen
Drumshanbo, Co. Leitrim
Tel: 071-964 0100 .................Page 103
Name of Spa:
**Oshadi**
Treatments:25 ........Treatment Rooms:4
Type of Treatments:
*Manicure, Salt & Oil Body Scrub, Back, Neck & Shoulder Massage, Indian Head Massage, Aromatherapy Facial Massage, Sports & Fitness Massage etc*
Type of Facilities:
*15m Indoor Pool, Gym, Steam Room, Sauna, Outdoor Hot Tub, Kiddies' Pool*

## Did you know ?

**Reflexology**
*The physical act of applying pressure to the feet & hands without the use of oil or lotion. It is based on a system of zones & reflex areas that reflect an image of the body on the feet and hands with a premise that such work effects a physical change to the body.*

## Co. Limerick

### Adare Manor Hotel & Golf Resort
Adare, Co. Limerick
Tel: 061-396566 ...................Page 104
Name of Spa:
**The Spa at Adare Manor**
Treatments:24 ........Treatment Rooms:6
Type of Treatments:
*Elemis Deep Tissue Massage, Elemis Aromatherapy Massage, Elemis Skin Specific Facials, Elemis Visible Brilliance Facial, Elemis Pro Collagen Facial, Lime & Ginger Salt Glow, Elemis Coconut & Milk Body Wrap, Frangipani Body Nourish Wrap, Elemis Pregnancy Massage, Elemis Hydrotherapy Baths*
Type of Facilities:
*Guest Shower Rooms, Hydrotherapy Bath*

### Carriage House (The)
Limerick City, Co. Limerick
Tel: 061-396566 ...................Page 106
Name of Spa:
**The Spa at Adare Manor**
Treatments:24 ........Treatment Rooms:6
Type of Treatments:
*Elemis Deep Tissue Massage, Elemis Aromatherapy Massage, Elemis Skin Specific Facial, Elemis Visable Brilliance Facial, Elemis Pro Collagen Facial, Lime & Ginger Salt Glow. Elemis Coconut & Milk Body Wrap, Frangipani Body Nourish Wrap.*
Type of Facilities:
*Guest Shower Rooms, Hydrotherapy Bath*

### Fitzgeralds Woodlands House Hotel, Health and Leisure Spa
Adare, Co. Limerick
Tel: 061-605100.....................Page 105
Name of Spa:
**Revas Hair Salon, Beauty & Relaxation Spa**
Treatments:100......Treatment Rooms:15
Type of Treatments:
*Hot Stone Massage Therapy, Body Polish, Platinum Detox, Non-Surgical Lyposculpture, Ocean Chleir Seaweed Envelopment Wrap, Genesis Inch Loss Wrap, Stimulating & Oxygenerating Facial, GM Collin Skin Care*
Type of Facilities:
*Thermal Suite, Herb Sauna, Crystal Steam Room, Experience Showers, Rasul Mud Chamber, Foot Baths, Relaxation Area, Rock Pool, Hair Salon, Balneotherapy Bath*

### Hilton Limerick
Limerick City, Co. Limerick
Tel: 061-421800......................Page 109
Name of Spa:
**Livingwell Health Club & Zigomi Spa**
Treatments:30 ........Treatment Rooms:5
Type of Treatments:
*Facial, Body Massage, Pedicure, Manicure, Head Massage, Waxing, Beauty Treatments, Range of Body & Facial Treatments*
Type of Facilities:
*20m Swimming Pool, Hydrotherapy Pool, Jacuzzi, Kids Pool, Sauna, Gym, Fitness Room, Family Changing Rooms, Ladies & Gents Changing Rooms, Aerobics Room*

### Radisson SAS Hotel & Spa
Limerick City, Co. Limerick
Tel: 061-456200......................Page 111
Name of Spa:
**Renaissance**
Treatments:71 ........Treatment Rooms:9
Type of Treatments:
*Hot Stone, Reflexology, Elemis Tahitian Bloom, Elemis Bathing Experiences, Elemis Skin Specific Facials, Exotic Lime & Ginger Salt Glow, Sole Delight Foot Treamtment, Elemis Massage Therapies*
Type of Facilities:
*Hydrotherapy Bath, Dry Floatation Bed, Beauty Suite, Thermal Suite, Outdoor Canadian Hot Tub, Relaxation Suite, Swimming Pool, Saunas*

## Co. Mayo

### Ashford Castle
Cong, Co. Mayo
Tel: 094-954 6003 ..................Page 119
Name of Spa:
**Health & Beauty Rooms at Ashford Castle**
Treatments:27 ........Treatment Rooms:3
Type of Treatments:
*Aroma - Stone Massage, Gommage Marin, Soins Velours, Hydralessence Corps, Phyto Marine, Secret De Beaute*
Type of Facilities:
*Jacuzzi, Sauna, Steam Room, Gym, Sun Room*

### Belmont Hotel
Knock, Co. Mayo
Tel: 094-938 8122 ..................Page 121
Name of Spa:
**The Health Suite**
Treatments:9 ..........Treatment Rooms:3
Type of Treatments:
*Reiki, Aromatherapy, Reflexology, Swedish Massage, Indian Head Massage, Stress Management, Hydrotherapy Bath*
Type of Facilities:
*Sauna, Steam Room, Sun Bed, Gym, Hydrotherapy Bath*

### Carlton Atlantic Coast Hotel
Westport, Co. Mayo
Tel: 098-29000 ......................Page 124
Name of Spa:
**The C Spa**
Treatments:48 ........Treatment Rooms:9
Type of Treatments:
*Tri-Enzyme Resurfacing Facial, Elemis Fruit Active Glow, Exotic Lime & Ginger Salt Glow, Exotic Frangipani Body Nourish Wrap, Elemis Cellutox Ocean Spa Wrap, Swedish Full Body Massage, Jessana Spa Manicure, Jessana Spa Pedicure, Carlton Man (Elemis Skin IQ Facial, Complete Spa Detox, De-stress for the Carlton Man), Spa Days*
Type of Facilities:
*9 State of the Art Treatment Rooms, Hydrotherapy Bath, Dry Floatation Tank, Swimming Pool, Sauna, Steam Room, Fitness Suite*

### Castlecourt Hotel Conference and Leisure Centre
Westport, Co. Mayo
Tel: 098-55088 ......................Page 125
Name of Spa:
**Resort Spa**
Treatments:32 ........Treatment Rooms:9
Type of Treatments:
*Rasul Mud Treatment, Dry Floatation Bath, Hydrotherapy Bath, Aromatherapy, Reflexology & Indian Head Massage, Body Treatments, Facials*
Type of Facilities:
*Thermal Suites, Rasul Mud Chamber, Dry Floatation, Outdoor Hot Tub, Rock Sauna, Relaxation Area*

### Hotel Westport leisure - spa - conference
Westport, Co. Mayo
Tel: 098-25122 ......................Page 126
Name of Spa:
**Ocean Spirit Spa**
Treatments:35 ......Treatment Rooms:10
Type of Treatments:
*Aromatherapy Massage, Body Exfoliant Treatments, Body Moisturising Peels & Wraps, Facials, Pedicure/Manicure, Turkish Hammam Massage & Body Treatments, Hot Stone Massage, Homeopathic Aromatherapy Massage, Golfers Tonic, Combined Treatments / Orange Zest, Chocolate Dream*
Type of Facilities:
*Cleopatra Bath, Serail Mud Chamber, Relaxation Suite, Swimming Pools, Jacuzzi, Steam Room, Sauna, Hammam Heated Ceramic Table, Pedicure & Manicure Room, California Spray Tan Room*

### Knockranny House Hotel & Spa
Westport, Co. Mayo
Tel: 098-28600 ......................Page 126
Name of Spa:
**Spa Salveo**
Treatments:30 ......Treatment Rooms:12
Type of Treatments:
*Deep Tissue Muscle Massage, Deep Tissue Back Massage, Kerstin Florian Anti-ageing Facials, Kerstin Florian Aroma Hand Treatment, Kerstin Florian Moor Mud Foot Treatment, Kerstin Florian Aromatherapy Facial, Kerstin Florian Turkish Salt Scrub*
Type of Facilities:
*Vitality Pool, Thermal Suite, 12 Treatment Rooms, Serail, Hammam Massage, Dry Floatation, Relaxation Areas, Fitness Suite*

### Mount Falcon Country House Hotel
Ballina, Co. Mayo
Tel: 096-74472 ......................Page 115
Treatments:12 ........Treatment Rooms:4
Type of Treatments:
*Advanced Performance Facials, Oil Massages, Indian Head Massage, Reflexology, Body Maintenance, Hand and Foot*
Type of Facilities:
*17m Swimming Pool, Jacuzzi, Sauna, Steam Room, Gym*

## Co. Mayo CONTINUED

### Westport Plaza Hotel
Westport, Co. Mayo
Tel: 098-51166 ........................Page 127
Name of Spa:
**Resort Spa**
Treatments:32 ........Treatment Rooms:9
Type of Treatments:
*Rasul Mud Treatment, Dry Floatation Bath, Hydrotherapy Bath, Aromatherapy, Reflexology & Indian Head Massage, Body Treatments, Facials*
Type of Facilities:
*Thermal Suites, Rasul Mud Chamber, Dry Floatation, Outdoor Hot Tub, Rock Sauna, Relaxation Area*

### Westport Woods Hotel & Spa
Westport, Co. Mayo
Tel: 098-25811........................Page 127
Name of Spa:
**Westport Woods Hotel & Spa**
Treatments:36 ........Treatment Rooms:5
Type of Treatments:
*Swedish Massage, Aromatherapy Massage, Reflexology, Indian Head Massage, Le Grand Classique Facial, Hydralessence Visage Facial, Mud & Seaweed Body Polishes, Jessica Nails, St. Tropez Tanning, Hot Stone Massage*
Type of Facilities:
*Sauna, Steam Room, Jacuzzi, Relaxation Suite, Outdoor Hot Tub*

## Co. Roscommon

### Abbey Hotel, Conference and Leisure Centre
Roscommon Town, Co. Roscommon
Tel: 090-666 6200 ..................Page 129
Name of Spa:
**Abbey Health & Fitness**
Treatments:5 ..........Treatment Rooms:1
Type of Treatments:
*Massage, Reflexology, Indian Head Massage, Swedish Massage, Aromatherapy Massage, Sports Massage*
Type of Facilities:
*Sauna, Jacuzzi, Steam Room, Plunge Pool, 20m Swimming Pool, Fully Equipped Gymnasium*

## Co. Sligo

### Castle Dargan Golf Hotel Wellness
Ballygawley, Co. Sligo
Tel: 071-911 8080 .................Page 130
Name of Spa:
**Icon Spa**
Treatments:47 ........Treatment Rooms:8
Type of Treatments:
*Venus Beauty Med Medi-Spa & Aesthetic Treatments, Kerstin Florian Facials, Body Wraps & Scrubs, Microdermabrasion, Balneotherapy, Floatation Therapy, Beauty Treatments, Men's Treatments, Touch Therapies, Mother-To-Be Treatments, Venus Beauty Med.*
Type of Facilities:
*HydroSpa, Oxygen Steam Room, Ice Fountain, Herb Sauna, Hydrotherapy Pool/Suite, Relaxation Suite, Touch Therapy Suite, Nail Bar*

### Pier Head Hotel, Spa and Leisure Centre
Mullaghmore, Co. Sligo
Tel: 071-916 6171....................Page 132
Name of Spa:
**Pier Head Spa & Leisure Centre**
Treatment Rooms:2
Type of Treatments:
*Dermalogica Facials (Men & Women), Waxing, Manicure/Pedicures, Art Deco Make-Up, Eye Treatments, Hot Stone Therapy, Beauty Packages*
Type of Facilities:
*2 Seaweed Baths & Steam Showers, Outdoor Canadian Hot Tub, Indoor Heated Swimming Pool, Sea-Facing Gym, Sauna & Massage Room*

### Yeats Country Hotel, Spa & Leisure Club
Rosses Point, Co. Sligo
Tel: 071-917 7211....................Page 132
Name of Spa:
**Eros Health Spa**
Treatments:35 ........Treatment Rooms:6
Type of Treatments:
*Seaweed Baths, Hydrotherapy Bath, Reiki, Reflexology, Aromatherapy, Swedish Massage, Hot Stone Treatments, Yon-ka Paris Beauty Treatments, Manicure, Waxing*
Type of Facilities:
*Relaxation Suite, Double Treatment Room, Single Treatment Room, Double Seaweed Bath Suite, Single Seaweed Bath Suite, Hydrotherapy Suite, Day Packages & Vouchers available*

# Ireland South

## Co. Carlow

### Mount Wolseley Hotel Spa & Country Club
Tullow, Co. Carlow
Tel: 059-918 0100 .................Page 142
Name of Spa:
**Sanctuary Spa**
Treatments:52 ......Treatment Rooms:14
Type of Treatments:
*Facials: De Luxe Collagen Face, Eyes & Neck Treatment, Total Rehydration Treatment*
*Body Therapies: Total Body Polish, Balneotherapy, Cellutox Ocean Wrap Specialist Therapies: Thalgomince Pregancy Therapy*
Type of Facilities:
*Oval Spa Pool with Waterfalls, Experience Showers, Rasul Room, Steam Room & Dry Air Room, Floatation Chambers, Sabiamed Light Treatment, Relaxation Room*

### Ramada Hotel & Suites at Killerig Golf Resort
Carlow Town, Co. Carlow
Tel: 059-916 3050 ..................Page 140
Name of Spa:
**Sentosa**
Treatments:5 ..........Treatment Rooms:3
Type of Treatments:
*Swedish Massage, De Luxe Jessana Manicure, Deep Pore Cleansing Facial, Eye Crystal Treatment, Matis Body Polish*
Type of Facilities:
*Sauna, Steam Room, Jacuzzi, Pool, Gym*

### Seven Oaks Hotel
Carlow Town, Co. Carlow
Tel: 059 913 1308 ..................Page 141
Name of Spa:
**Greenbank Health and Leisure Club**
Treatments:10 ........Treatment Rooms:2
Type of Treatments:
*Indian Head Massage, Aerobics, Massage, Reflexology*
Type of Facilities:
*20m Deck Level Pool, Childrens' Pool, Jacuzzi, Steam Room & Sauna, Solarium, Massage & Sports Injury Clinic, Gymnasium - Cardiovascular Resistance, Free Weights, Aerobic Studio, Disabled Facilities*

**Talbot Hotel Carlow**
Carlow Town, Co. Carlow
Tel: 059-915 3000 .................Page 141
**Name of Spa:**
**Essence Nail & Beauty Therapy**
**Treatments:**25 .......**Treatment Rooms:**4
**Type of Treatments:**
*Bodywraps, Aromatherapy Massage, Manicure, Pedicure, Mens Skincare Treatment, Dermalogica Customised Facial, Multi-Vitamin Power Facial, Skin Brightening Treatment, Intensive Moisture Facial, Revitalising Eye Rescue Treatment*
**Type of Facilities:**
*Treatment Rooms, Nail Bar, Make Up Room, Sauna, Spa Pool, Steam Room*

## Co. Cork

**Blarney Golf Resort**
Blarney, Co. Cork
Tel: 021-438 4477 .................Page 147
**Name of Spa:**
**Blarney Golf Resort Spa**
**Treatments:**40 ........**Treatment Rooms:**3
**Type of Treatments:**
*Hot Stone Massage, Deep Pore Cleansing Facial, Eye Crystal Treatment, De Luxe Manicure, Seaweed Wrap, Yonka & Matis Products*
**Type of Facilities:**
*Sauna, 20m Swimming Pool, Gym, Jacuzzi, Steam Room, Childrens' Pool*

**Capella Castlemartyr**
Castlemartyr, Co. Cork
Tel: 021-464 4050 .................Page 149
**Name of Spa:**
**Auriga**
**Treatments:**30 ......**Treatment Rooms:**10
**Type of Treatments:**
*4 signature Auriga treatments, Golfers treatments, Special treatments according to Lunar cycles, Facials, Body Wraps*
**Type of Facilities:**
*Vitality Pools, Indoor 20m Ozone Pool, Saunas, Steam Rooms, Yoga Studio, Pilates Studio, V.I.P Suites, Spa Café*

**Carlton Kinsale Hotel & C Spa**
Kinsale, Co. Cork
Tel: 021-470 6000 .................Page 167
**Name of Spa:**
**The C Spa**
**Treatments:**10........**Treatment Rooms:**10
**Type of Treatments:**
*Balneotherapy Bath, Tranquillity Massage, Indulgence Scalp Massage, Tension Relief Back Massage, Reflexology, Spa Manicure, Spa Pedicure, Body Exfoliation, Body Wraps, Spa Facials*
**Type of Facilities:**
*3 Wet Treatment Rooms, 7 Dry Treatment Rooms*

**Clarion Hotel**
Cork City, Co. Cork
Tel: 021-422 4900 .................Page 156
**Name of Spa:**
**The Spa at Essence**
**Treatments:**61 ........**Treatment Rooms:**5
**Type of Treatments:**
*Carita Rénovateur Lift Fermeté, Hot Stone Massage, Massotherm-Detox Tunnel, Aroma Enveloppement, Aroma Man, Rénovateur Revitalising Corps, The Full Body Balance, Fountain of Youth, Body Maintenance Treatments, Re-energising and Exfoliating Treatment*
**Type of Facilities:**
*18m Pool, Sauna, Steam Room, Jacuzzi, Gymnasium, Aerobics Studio, Spa*

**Hayfield Manor Hotel**
Cork City, Co. Cork
Tel: 021-484 5900 .................Page 158
**Name of Spa:**
**The Beautique**
**Treatments:**20 ........**Treatment Rooms:**9
**Type of Treatments:**
*Skin Specific Facial, Deep Tissue Massage, OPI Manicures*
**Type of Facilities:**
*Indoor Heated Pool, Nail Bar, Hair Salon, 9 Treatment Rooms, Relaxation Rooms*

**Imperial Hotel with Escape Salon and Spa**
Cork City, Co. Cork
Tel: 021-427 4040 .................Page 159
**Name of Spa:**
**Escape Salon & Spa**
**Treatments:**80 ......**Treatment Rooms:**10
**Type of Treatments:**
*Full range of Aveda Signature Salon Treatments, Spa & Beauty Treatments, Facials, Massages, Body Treatments, Body Wraps, Aveda Make-Up, Spa Rituals, State of the Art Cutting and Styling*
**Type of Facilities:**
*Hair Salon, 10 Treatment Rooms, Serail, Vitality Suite, Relaxation Suite, Manicure Room, Retail Area*

**Inchydoney Island Lodge & Spa**
Clonakilty, Co. Cork
Tel: 023-33143 .......................Page 151
**Name of Spa:**
**Island Spa**
**Treatments:**25 ......**Treatment Rooms:**17
**Type of Treatments:**
*Rasul, Sea Mist, Slimming Algotherapy, Spa Manicure, Facial, Cryotherapy, Chocolate Ritual, Aroma Stone Massage*
**Type of Facilities:**
*Thalassotherapy Pool, Hammam, Sauna, Relaxation Room, Gymnasium, Seawater Pool*

**Kingsley Hotel & Residences**
Cork City, Co. Cork
Tel: 021-480 0500 .................Page 160
**Name of Spa:**
**Yauvana Spa Ayurvedic**
**Treatments:**60 ......**Treatment Rooms:**12
**Type of Treatments:**
*Shirodhara (mind de-stressing, hair nourishing oil stream), Pizhicilli (revitalisng oil stream massage), Hydrating Facials, Swedish Massage, Deep Cleansing Facials, Aromatherapy Massage, Specific Facials for Men, Reflexology, Facials for Mums-to-be, Indian Head Massage, Deep Bath Cleanse, Targeted Eye Treatments, Ayurvedic Treatments*
**Type of Facilities:**
*20m Swimming Pool, Sauna, Steam Room, Jacuzzi, Outdoor Hydro Pool, Gymnasium, Aerobics Suite, Spa, Thermal Suite, Spinning, Pilates, Kinesis, Health Checks*

## Did you know ?

**Reiki**
*Reiki practitioners channel energy in a particular pattern to heal and harmonize. Unlike other healing therapies based on the premise of a human energy field, Reiki seeks to restore order to the body whose vital energy has become unbalanced. It brings about deep relaxation, destroys energy blockages, detoxifies the system.*

## Co. Cork CONTINUED

### Maryborough Hotel & Spa
Cork City, Co. Cork
Tel: 021-436 5555 .................Page 161
**Name of Spa:**
**Maryborough Spa**
**Treatments:**38 ......**Treatment Rooms:**10
**Type of Treatments:**
*Hot Stone Therapy, Massage, Ayurvedic Rituals, Facials, Body Wraps, Full & 1/2 Day Programmes*
**Type of Facilities:**
*Relaxation Rooms, Vitality (Male & Female), Thermal Suites, 10 Treatment Rooms, Spa Café, Finishing Touches Studio*

### Oriel House Hotel, Leisure Club & Spa
Ballincollig, Co. Cork
Tel: 021-420 8400 .................Page 143
**Name of Spa:**
**The Oriel Spa**
**Treatments:**30 ........**Treatment Rooms:**8
**Type of Treatments:**
*Please call for treatments available*
**Type of Facilities:**
*25m Swimming Pool, Infinity Pool, Spa Jet Station, 8 Seater Jacuzzi, Steam Room, Sauna, Shallow Childrens' Pool, 16 Cardiovascular Machines, Fitness Studio*

### Quality Hotel & Leisure Centre, Cork
Cork City, Co. Cork
Tel: 021-452 9200 .................Page 162
**Name of Spa:**
**Beauty Treatment Room**
**Treatments:**5 ..........**Treatment Rooms:**1
**Type of Treatments:**
*Therapeutic Massage, Reflexology, Reiki, Indian Head Massage, Hopi Ear Candling*
**Type of Facilities:**
*20m Swimming Pool, Sauna, Steam room, Jacuzzi, Children's Pool, Aerobic Studio, Comprehensively Equipped Fitness Studio, Exclusive Treatment Room, Assessment & Programme Packages*

### Quality Hotel and Leisure Centre Youghal
Youghal, Co. Cork
Tel: 024-93050 .....................Page 177
**Name of Spa:**
**The Spa @ Club Vitae**
**Treatments:**30 ........**Treatment Rooms:**4
**Type of Treatments:**
*Eye Care, Make Up, Pamper Package, Waxing, Mens Grooming Treatments, Therapeutic Treatments, Body Treatments, Facials, Hand & Foot Treatments*
**Type of Facilities:**
*Treatment Rooms, Hydrotherapy Bath Suite, Relaxation Area with Sea View*

### Radisson SAS Hotel & Spa, Cork
Cork City, Co. Cork
Tel: 021-429 7000 .................Page 162
**Name of Spa:**
**The Retreat Spa**
**Treatments:**28 ........**Treatment Rooms:**9
**Type of Treatments:**
*Balneotherapy, Body Wraps, Body Polish, Vichy Massage, Elemis Deep Tissue Massage, Classic Rasul, Advanced Elemis Facials Mother To Be Massage, Reflexology, Jessica Manicure/Pedicure*
**Type of Facilities:**
*9 Treatment Rooms, Rasul Room, Relaxation Suite, Hydrotherapy Pool*

### Sheraton Fota Island Hotel & Spa (The)
Fota Island, Co. Cork
Tel: 021-467 3000 .................Page 164
**Name of Spa:**
**Fota Island Spa**
**Treatments:**60 ......**Treatment Rooms:**18
**Type of Treatments:**
*Cold Marine Leg Wrap, Spa Packages, Hot Stones, Marine Body Polish, Chocolate Sensualite Wrap, Green Tea Silhouette Therapy, Lushly Polynesian Hand/Foot Ritual, Comfort Zone Facials*
**Type of Facilities:**
*Sheraton Fitness Gym, Indoor Swimming Pool, 18 Treatment Rooms, Hydrotherapy Area, Thermal Area, Juice Bar, Relaxation Area Garden*

### Westlodge Hotel
Bantry, Co. Cork
Tel: 027-50360 .....................Page 146
**Treatments:**7 ..........**Treatment Rooms:**2
**Type of Treatments:**
*Reflexology, Full Body Massage, Aromatherapy Massage, Indian Head Massage, Sports Massage, Reiki, Top'n'Tail*
**Type of Facilities:**
*Heated Swimming Pool, Sauna, Steam Room, Jacuzzi, Fully equipped Gym, Squash Court*

## Co. Kerry

### Aghadoe Heights Hotel & Spa
Killarney, Co. Kerry
Tel: 064-31766 .....................Page 193
**Name of Spa:**
**The Spa at The Heights**
**Treatments:**58 ......**Treatment Rooms:**10
**Type of Treatments:**
*Futuresse Face & Body Treatments, Biodroga Wraps, Aveda Face & Body Treatments, Manicure, Pedicure, Indian Head Massage, Reflexology & Thermal Suite*
**Type of Facilities:**
*Hammam, Rock Sauna, Laconium, Aroma Grotto, Tropical Rain Shower, Cold Fog Shower, Heated Loungers, Relaxation Room, Slipper Bath, Serail, Swimming Pool, Jacuzzi, Fitness Suite, Tennis Court, Yoga, Pilates, Hair Salon*

### Ballygarry House Hotel & Spa
Tralee, Co. Kerry
Tel: 066-712 3322 .................Page 215
**Name of Spa:**
**Nádúr**
**Treatments:**40 ........**Treatment Rooms:**7
**Type of Treatments:**
*Hydrotherapy, Bamboo & Ginseng Body Polish, USPA Concept Facial Treatments, Holistic Therapy, Herbal & Mud Body Wrap, Hot Stone Massage, Ritual Body Massage, Beauty, many other treatments available*
**Type of Facilities:**
*Beauty Suite, Relaxing Room, Glass Sauna, Crystal Steam Room, Outdoor Canadian Hot Tub, Vitality Showers, Tanning Suite, Hydrotherapy Suite*

## Did you know ?

**Rasul:** *An Oriental ceremony for body care involving a cleansing seaweed soap shower, medicinal muds and an invigorating herbal steam bath.*

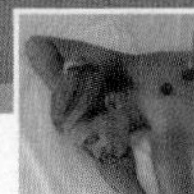

### Brandon Hotel Conference and Leisure Centre

Tralee, Co. Kerry

Tel: 066-712 3333 ..................Page 216

**Name of Spa:**

**The Sanctuary Spa**

**Treatments:**15 ........**Treatment Rooms:**8

**Type of Treatments:**

*Decleor Facials (Aromaplasty, Harmonie & Evidence), Exfoliating Body Polish, Sea Algae Body Wraps, Aromaceane Sea Mud & Sea Salt Wrap, Marine Prelude, Balneotherapy, Aroma Spa Envelopement Programme, Body Massage, Carita Hot Stone Therapy Massage, Carita Progressive Lift Facial, Olys Anti Ageing Facial, Endermologie, Ellipse Light Hair Removal, Photorejuvenation, Manicures, Pedicures, All Grooming Treatments*

**Type of Facilities:**

*17m Indoor Swimming Pool, Sauna, Steam Room, Jacuzzi, Full Gym, Hydrobath, Solarium and Laser Treatments*

### Brehon (The)

Killarney, Co. Kerry

Tel: 064-30700 ......................Page 194

**Name of Spa:**

**Angsana Spa**

**Treatments:**23 ........**Treatment Rooms:**6

**Type of Treatments:**

*Rain Shower, Massage, Body Polish, Facial, Foot Soak, Rasul, Indian Head Massage, Skin Enhancer, Signature Angsana Massage, Manicure*

**Type of Facilities:**

*Herb Sauna, Crystal Steam Room, Salt Grotto, Rasul, Foot Spa, Tropical Shower, Ice Fountain, Kubeldusche, Vitality Pool, Hot & Cold Spa*

### Castlerosse Hotel and Golf Resort

Killarney, Co. Kerry

Tel: 064-31144........................Page 196

**Treatments:**18 ........**Treatment Rooms:**2

**Type of Treatments:**

*Lenache Purifying and Balance Control, Hydra Plus, Dr Grandle Special Care, Dr Grandle A.C.E., Mens Executive Facial, Swedish Massage, Indian Head Massage, Reflexology, Reiki, Luxury Spa Body Treatments*

### Dingle Skellig Hotel & Peninsula Spa

Dingle (An Daingean), Co. Kerry

Tel: 066-915 0200 ..................Page 185

**Name of Spa:**

**The Peninsula Spa**

**Treatments:**55 ........**Treatment Rooms:**7

**Type of Treatments:**

*Yon-ka Aroma Stone, Yon-ka Face & Body Treatments, Peninsula Spa Face & Body Treatments, Massage, Hydrotherapy, Body Wraps, Sports Injury, Tanning, Nail Treatments, Makeovers, Selection of unique "Irish" treatments from local Organic Products & Ingredients*

**Type of Facilities:**

*Outdoor Hot Tub overlooking Dingle Harbour, Relaxation Suite with Refreshments Bar, Hydrotherapy Suite, Sauna, Steam Room, Beauty Salon, Outdoor Relaxation Balcony, 17m Pool, Childrens' pool, Jacuzzi in Leisure Club*

### Hotel Europe

Killarney, Co. Kerry

Tel: 064-71300 ......................Page 202

**Name of Spa:**

**Espa at the Europe**

**Treatments:**11 ........**Treatment Rooms:**16

**Type of Treatments:**

*Espa Total Luxury, Espa Total Balance, Espa Purely Holistic, Espa New Beginnings, Espa Total Relaxation, Espa Body Cleansing Programme, Espa Ritual, Espa Face, Espa Body, Espa Mini Rituals*

**Type of Facilities:**

*Treatment Rooms, Couples Suite, Express Suites, Indoor / Outdoor Pools, Saunas, Gymnasium, Pilates Room, Restaurant, Relaxation Rooms, Thermal Suites*

### Killarney Park Hotel

Killarney, Co. Kerry

Tel: 064-35555 ......................Page 205

**Name of Spa:**

**The Spa at the Killarney Park Hotel**

**Treatments:**45 ........**Treatment Rooms:**8

**Type of Treatments:**

*Eve Lom Facial, Elemis Aroma Stone Therapy, Elemis Japanese Silk Booster Facial, Elemis Well Being Massage, Elemis Fennel Cleansing Cellulite and Colon Therapy, Healing Bath Ceremony, Elemis Aromapure Facial, Reflexology, Elemis Musclease Aroma Spa Ocean Wrap*

**Type of Facilities:**

*8 Custom-built Private Treatment Suites, A specially designed Relaxation Room, Hydrotherapy Suite, Caldarium, Couples Suite, Juice Bar*

### Killarney Plaza Hotel & Spa

Killarney, Co. Kerry

Tel: 064-21111 ........................Page 205

**Name of Spa:**

**Molton Brown Spa**

**Treatments:**20 ........**Treatment Rooms:**8

**Type of Treatments:**

*Spring, Summer, Autumn and Winter Facial and Massage, Cloud Walking, Palm Pressure, Earth, Fire and Water Serail*

**Type of Facilities:**

*Gulf Stream Pool, Sauna, Steam Room, Jacuzzi, Earth, Fire & Water Serail*

### Lake Hotel

Killarney, Co. Kerry

Tel: 064-31035 ......................Page 207

**Name of Spa:**

**Muckross Fitness Centre**

**Treatments:**10 ........**Treatment Rooms:**3

**Type of Treatments:**

*Massages, Facials, Manicures, Pedicures, Wraps*

**Type of Facilities:**

*Gym, Sauna, Steam Room, Outdoor Hot Tub, Spa Sensations Treatment Centre*

## Did you know ?

**Balneotherapy**

*The term Balneology refers to the study of the art and science of bathing. Balneotherapy refers to the use of balneology in the treatment of disease. The aim of these treatments is to enhance the immune system, stimulate circulatory process including lymph and blood circulation, accelerate cell activity, dilating tissue and vessels activating the self healing potential naturally.*

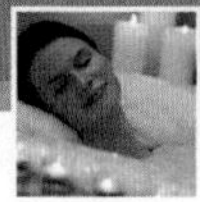
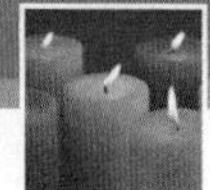

## Co. Kerry CONTINUED

### Malton (The)
Killarney, Co. Kerry
Tel: 064-38000 .....................Page 208
**Name of Spa:**
**Innisfallen Health & Beauty Rooms**
**Treatments:**20 ........**Treatment Rooms:**3
**Type of Treatments:**
*Hydrotherapy Bath, Waxing Treatments, Massage (various), Seaweed Treatments (various), Aromatherapy, Body Polishing, Facials, Manicures & Pedicures, Hot Stone Massage*
**Type of Facilities:**
*Hydrotherapy Baths, Indoor Heated Swimming Pool, Jacuzzi, Steam Room, Monsoon Shower, Gym, Sauna, Tennis Courts*

### Manor West Hotel, Spa & Leisure Club
Tralee, Co. Kerry
Tel: 066-719 4500 ..................Page 218
**Name of Spa:**
**Harmony Wellness Suites & Leisure Club**
**Treatments:**20 ........**Treatment Rooms:**2
**Type of Treatments:**
*Treatments & therapies from the ELEMIS range. Call today for full list of treatments and packages*
**Type of Facilities:**
*18m Swimming Pool, Therapy Pool, Underwater Loungers, Swan Jets, Sauna, Steam Room, Jacuzzi, state-of-the-art Gymnasium, 2 Wellness Suites*

### Muckross Park Hotel & Cloisters Spa
Killarney, Co. Kerry
Tel: 064-23400 ......................Page 208
**Name of Spa:**
**Cloisters Spa**
**Treatments:**50 ......**Treatment Rooms:**12
**Type of Treatments:**
*Massage, Facials, Microdermabrasion, Manicure, Pedicure, Hot Shaves, Hydrotherapy Baths, Energy Healing, Reflexology*
**Type of Facilities:**
*Thermal Suite, Vitality Pool, Herb Sauna, Ice Fountain, Salt Grotto, Eucalyptus Mist, Mud Rasul, Relaxation Suite, Heated Loungers, UV Sonacare Camera*

### Park Hotel Kenmare
Kenmare, Co. Kerry
Tel: 064-41200 ......................Page 190
**Name of Spa:**
**SAMAS**
**Treatments:**30 ........**Treatment Rooms:**8
**Type of Treatments:**
*Full Spa Facilities with Treatments - Ayurvedic, Deep Tissue, Aromatherapy, etc.*
**Type of Facilities:**
*Laconium, Rock Sauna, Steam, Tropical Mist Showers, Vitality Pool, Relaxation Rooms, Tai Chi, Chi Kung Pilates*

### Randles Court Clarion Hotel
Killarney, Co. Kerry
Tel: 064-35333 ......................Page 210
**Name of Spa:**
**Zen Day Spa**
**Treatments:**40 ........**Treatment Rooms:**6
**Type of Treatments:**
*Lavender Dreams Ultimate Experience by Kerstin Florian, Absolute Sheer Bliss, Golfers Stress Relief, Ritual for Mother To Be, Gentleman's Time Out, Warm Mud Body Wrap, Therapeutic Swedish Massage, Aromatherapy Ritual, Hydrotherapy Treatments, Facials by Kerstin Florian & G.M. Collin*
**Type of Facilities:**
*6 Custom-Built Private Treatment Rooms including our Hydrotherapy Suite. Guests can also avail of Club Santé Swimming Pool, Sauna & Steam Room*

### Ross (The)
Killarney, Co. Kerry
Tel: 064-31855 ......................Page 210
**Name of Spa:**
**The Spa at The Killarney Park Hotel (Adjacent - Sister Hotel)**
**Treatments:**45 ........**Treatment Rooms:**8
**Type of Treatments:**
*Eve Lom Facial, Elemis Aroma Stone Therapy, Elemis Japanese Silk Booster Facial, Elemis Well Being Massage, Elemis Fennel Cleansing Cellulite and Colon Therapy, Healing Bath Ceremony, Elemis Aromapure Facial, Reflexology, Elemis Musclease Aroma Spa Ocean Wrap*
**Type of Facilities:**
*8 Custom-built Private Treatment Suites, A specially designed Relaxation Room, Hydrotherapy Suite, Caldarium, Couples Suite, Juice Bar*

### Sheen Falls Lodge
Kenmare, Co. Kerry
Tel: 064-41600........................Page 191
**Name of Spa:**
**The Health Club**
**Treatments:**30 ........**Treatment Rooms:**3
**Type of Treatments:**
*Facial, Body Wrap, Manicure, Massage, Aromastone, Pedicure, Indian Head Massage, Reiki, Body Detox Wrap, Seaweed Wrap*
**Type of Facilities:**
*Jacuzzi, Sauna, Steam Room, Swimming Pool, Gymnasium, Sun Deck, Tennis, Jogging Trail*

### Watermarque Boutique Hotel
Cahersiveen, Co. Kerry
Tel: 066-947 2222 ..................Page 179
**Name of Spa:**
**The Quays Therapy Spa**
**Treatments:**20 ........**Treatment Rooms:**2
**Type of Treatments:**
*Elemis Treatments: Skin Specific Facials, Skin Solutions Facials, Advanced Anti Ageing Facials, Time for Men Facials, Deep Tissue Muscle Massage, Aroma Spa Ocean Wraps, Body Sculpting Cellulite & Colon Therapy, Absolute Spa Ritual & Total Timeout, Exotic Lime & Ginger Salt Glow, Exotic Hand Ritual/Sole Delight Foot Treatment*
**Type of Facilities:**
*Two Therapy Treatment Rooms, One Relaxation Room, Swimming Pool, Sauna, Jacuzzi, Gym*

## Did you know ?

**Ayurvedic**

*Ayurveda, the "science of life," is the traditional medicine and the natural healing system of India and its cultural sphere. It is probably the oldest health care system in the world, with roots going back over 500 years into the Vedic era. Not surprisingly, it has been called the "Mother of all healing".*

*Ayurveda is one of the most comprehensive healing systems in the world, dealing integrally with body, mind and spirit. Given its antiquity, we could say that it is the original medical system of which the modern medical systems are either derivations or deviations.*

## Co. Kilkenny

### Hotel Kilkenny
Kilkenny City, Co. Kilkenny
Tel: 056-776 2000.................Page 224
**Name of Spa:**
**Lilac Lodge Spa**
**Treatments:**40 ........**Treatment Rooms:**4
**Type of Treatments:**
*Dermalogica Facial Treatments, Yon-ka Facial Treatments, Aroma Hot Stone Massage, Phyto-Marine Slimming Treatment, Reflexology, Sports Therapy Massage, Waxing, Tanning, Body Treatments*
**Type of Facilities:**
*Luxury Relaxation Room, 4 Treatment Rooms, Complimentary off-street Parking*

### Kilkenny River Court
Kilkenny City, Co. Kilkenny
Tel: 056-772 3388.................Page 226
**Treatments:**10 ........**Treatment Rooms:**4
**Type of Treatments:**
*Aromaplasty, Nutri-Gain Moisture, Harmony Epidermis, Anti-Ageing Eye Treatment, Fitness Essential Massage, Reiki, Reflexology*
**Type of Facilities:**
*Treatment Rooms, Gymnasium, 17m Swimming Pool, Geyser Pool, Jacuzzi, Sauna*

### Lyrath Estate Hotel, Spa & Convention Centre
Kilkenny City, Co. Kilkenny
Tel: 056-776 0088.................Page 227
**Name of Spa:**
**Oasis Spa**
**Treatments:**47 ........**Treatment Rooms:**8
**Type of Treatments:**
*Sea Results Facial, Seaweed Smoothing Treatment, Slimming Warm Hibiscus Petal Treatment, Reflexology, Reiki, Caviar Facial, Indian Head Massage, Rasul, Hot Stones*
**Type of Facilities:**
*Male Relaxation Area, Female Relaxation Area, Hydro Pool - both indoor & outdoor, Sauna, Steam Room, Gym, Tropical Showers, Couples Suite, 15m Swimming Pool*

### Mount Juliet Conrad
Thomastown, Co. Kilkenny
Tel: 056-777 3000.................Page 230
**Name of Spa:**
**The Spa at Mount Juliet Conrad**
**Treatments:**70 ........**Treatment Rooms:**7
**Type of Treatments:**
*Reiki, La Stone Therapy, Floatation Therapy Treatment, Reflexology, Radiance Facial, Body Polish, Deep Cleansing Back Treatment, ESPA Facials, Matis Facials*
**Type of Facilities:**
*Swimming Pool, Steam Room, Sauna, Gym, Floatation Tank, Relaxation Rooms*

### Newpark Hotel
Kilkenny City, Co. Kilkenny
Tel: 056-776 0500.................Page 228
**Name of Spa:**
**Newpark Health Spa**
**Treatments:**30 ........**Treatment Rooms:**6
**Type of Treatments:**
*Swedish Body Massage, Hot Stone Therapy, Seaweed Body Wraps, Collagen Hydro Lifting Facial, Hydrotherapy Massage Bath, Hand and Foot Treatments, Nails/Manicures, all Related Beauty Treatments*
**Type of Facilities:**
*Six Wet & Dry Treatment Rooms, Nail & Manicure Bar, Hydrotherapy Massage Bath, Relaxation Area & Kieran O'Gorman Hair Salon*

### Springhill Court Hotel, Conference, Leisure & Spa Hotel
Kilkenny City, Co. Kilkenny
Tel: 056-772 1122 .................Page 229
**Name of Spa:**
**AquaSpa**
**Treatments:**50 ........**Treatment Rooms:**7
**Type of Treatments:**
*Floatation Therapy, Balneotherapy, Dermalogical Facials & Body Wraps, Phytomer Body Wraps, Luxury Spa Pedicure & Manicure, Mens Skincare & De Luxe Body Treaments*
**Type of Facilities:**
*Relaxation Room, Sauna, Steam Room, Floatation Therapy, Chromatherapy Bath*

## Co. Tipperary

### Abbey Court Hotel, Lodges & Trinity Leisure Spa
Nenagh, Co. Tipperary
Tel: 067-41111.......................Page 237
**Name of Spa:**
**Trinity Leisure Spa**
**Treatments:**20 ........**Treatment Rooms:**8
**Type of Treatments:**
*Swedish Massage, Decleor Facials, Jessica Pedicure, Manicure, Make-up, Waxing, Self-Tan, Universal Contour Wrap*
**Type of Facilities:**
*Stand Up Balneotherapy Bath, Sun Room*

### Ballykisteen Hotel & Golf Resort
Tipperary Town, Co. Tipperary
Tel: 062-33333 .....................Page 239
**Name of Spa:**
**Beauty Suite**
**Treatments:**40 ........**Treatment Rooms:**4
**Type of Treatments:**
*De Luxe Pedicure, Matis Body Polish, Hot Stone Massage, Signature Facial, Crystal Eye Treatment*
**Type of Facilities:**
*Swimming Pool, Sauna, Jacuzzi, Gym*

### Cahir House Hotel
Cahir, Co. Tipperary
Tel: 052-43000 .....................Page 231
**Name of Spa:**
**Cahir House Hotel Health & Beauty Spa**
**Treatments:**36 ........**Treatment Rooms:**4
**Type of Treatments:**
*Facials, Manicure, Pedicure, Hot Stone Massage, Hydrotherapy Bath, Ear Candling, Body Treatments, Sunbeds, Multi Gym, Pamper Days*
**Type of Facilities:**
*Steam Room,Treadmill, Sauna, Air Strider, Exercise Bike, Sun Beds*

## Co. Tipperary CONTINUED

### Horse and Jockey Hotel
Horse and Jockey, Co. Tipperary
Tel: 0504-44192 ......................Page 236
**Treatments:**30 ........**Treatment Rooms:**7
**Type of Treatments:**
*Massage, Make Up, Facial, Body Wrap, Hydrotherapy, Waxing, Manicure, Pedicure, Treatments for Men, Relaxation/Exercise Classes*
**Type of Facilities:**
*Relaxation, Sauna, Steam Room, Jacuzzi, 21m Pool with Relaxing Features, Private Spa Changing Rooms, Gym*

### Hotel Minella & Leisure Club
Clonmel, Co. Tipperary
Tel: 052-22388 ......................Page 235
**Name of Spa:**
**Club Minella**
**Treatments:**14 ........**Treatment Rooms:**2
**Type of Treatments:**
*Massage, Reflexology, Micronized Marine Algae Wrap, Toning Body Wrap, Marine Facial, Waxing, Manicure, Body Polish*
**Type of Facilities:**
*Treatment Rooms, Jacuzzi, Relaxation Room, Outdoor Hot Tub, 20m Pool, Outdoor Tennis Court, Sauna, Steam Room, Gym, Gardens*

## Co. Waterford

### Cliff House Hotel
Ardmore, Co. Waterford
Tel: +44 (0)-207 259 3621 ......Page 239
**Treatment Rooms:**4
**Type of Treatments:**
*Various Treatments Available*
**Type of Facilities:**
*Indoor Pool, Steam Room, Sauna, Jacuzzi, Fully Equipped Gym, 4 Treatment Rooms*

### Faithlegg House Hotel and Golf Club
Faithlegg, Co. Waterford
Tel: 051-382000 ....................Page 244
**Name of Spa:**
**Estuary Club**
**Treatments:**40 ........**Treatment Rooms:**5
**Type of Treatments:**
*Aromatherapy Massage, Reflexology, Reiki, Deep Sea Mud Treatment, Facials*
**Type of Facilities:**
*Swimming Pool, Jacuzzi, Steam Room, Gym, Sauna*

### Park Hotel, Leisure Centre & Holiday Homes
Dungarvan, Co. Waterford
Tel: 058-42899 ......................Page 242
**Name of Spa:**
**The Park Hotel & Leisure Centre**
**Treatments:**5 .........**Treatment Rooms:**2
**Type of Treatments:**
*Swedish & Deep Tissue Massage, Reflexology, Therapeutic Massage*
**Type of Facilities:**
*20m Swimming Pool, Gym, Sauna, Steam Room, Whirlpool, Jacuzzi, Kids Pool, Chartered Physiotherapist, Kids Club*

### Woodlands Hotel
Waterford City, Co. Waterford
Tel: 051-304574 ....................Page 252
**Name of Spa:**
**Caroline's Hair & Beauty**
**Treatments:**25 ........**Treatment Rooms:**6
**Type of Treatments:**
*Facials, Body Treatments, Pedicures, Manicures, Electrolysis, Waxing, Tinting, Eyebrow Shaping, Make Up, Nail Art*
**Type of Facilities:**
*Hair Salon, Pool, Jacuzzi, Steam Room, Sauna, Beauty and Health Treatment Rooms*

## Co. Wexford

### Amber Springs Hotel and Health Spa
Gorey, Co. Wexford
Tel: 053-948 4000..................Page 256
**Name of Spa:**
**Cocoon Health & Beauty Spa**
**Treatments:**9..........**Treatment Rooms:**11
**Type of Treatments:**
*Massage, Facials, Waxing, Manicure, Body Wraps, Balneo Treatment, Dry Floatation Tank, Relaxation Room*
**Type of Facilities:**
*18m Indoor Pool, Jacuzzi, Steam Room, Sauna, Hydro Therapy Pool, Fitness Centre, Kiddies Pool & Games Room, Playroom*

### Ashdown Park Hotel Conference & Leisure Centre
Gorey, Co. Wexford
Tel: 053-948 0500 Page 256
**Name of Spa:**
**Ashdown Club & Beauty Studio**
**Treatments:**36 ........**Treatment Rooms:**2
**Type of Treatments:**
*Facials, Men's Skincare, Glycolic Peels, Body Masks, Caci Quantum, Indian Head Massage, Reflexology, Hot Stone Massage, Grooming Treatments, Pamper Days*
**Type of Facilities:**
*18m Swimming Pool, Kids' Pool, Jacuzzi, Steam Room, Sauna, Gym*

### Brandon House Hotel, Health Club & Spa
New Ross, Co. Wexford
Tel: 051-421703 ...................Page 258
**Name of Spa:**
**Solas Croí**
**Treatments:**70 ......**Treatment Rooms:**10
**Type of Treatments:**
*Reiki, Reflexology, Marine Algae Bodywrap, Cold Marine, La Stone Massage, The Energiser, Swedish Massage*
**Type of Facilities:**
*20m Swimming Pool, Swimming Lessons, Sauna, Aerobics, Gym, Hydro Therapy Grotto, Kids Swimming Pool*

### Carlton Millrace Hotel & C Spa
Bunclody, Co. Wexford
Tel: 053-937 5100 ..................Page 252
**Name of Spa:**
**The C Spa**
**Treatments:**30 ......**Treatment Rooms:**10
**Type of Treatments:**
*Rasul, Back, Neck and Shoulder Massage, Skin specific Facials, Manicures and Pedicures, Salt Body Glow Exfoliation, Spray Tans*
**Type of Facilities:**
*Hydro Bath, Relaxation Room*

## Did you know ?

**'CACI' Quantum:** *Non-Surgical Face & Body Lifts*
*The CACI Quantum is the most advanced face and body treatment system available. Using specific facial techniques in conjunction with a combination of slimming and toning applications, it restores and re-defines facial muscles, reducing lines and wrinkles while simultaneously tightening body muscles.*

### Ferrycarrig Hotel
Wexford Town, Co. Wexford
Tel: 053-912 0999 ..................Page 261
**Name of Spa:**
**Health & Beauty @ Lodge**
**Treatments:**45 ........**Treatment Rooms:**4
**Type of Treatments:**
*Facials, Aromatherapy, Massage, Reflexology, Hot Stone Therapy, Indian Head Massage, Manicures & Pedicures, Makeovers, Body Treatments, Pamper Days, Bridal Packages*
**Type of Facilities:**
*Intense Pulsed Light, Platinum Detox, Relaxation and Reception Area*

### Kelly's Resort Hotel & Spa
Rosslare, Co. Wexford
Tel: 053-913 2114 ..................Page 259
**Name of Spa:**
**SeaSpa**
**Treatments:**34 ......**Treatment Rooms:**12
**Type of Treatments:**
*Aromatherapy & Holistic Massages, Body Wraps, Facials, Ayurvedic Hot Stone Treatments, Reflexology, Reiki, Sports Therapy Massage, Manicure & Pedicure, Thai Massage, Candling*
**Type of Facilities:**
*Serail Mud Room, Seaweed Baths, Rock Sauna, Heated Loungers, Sea Water Vitality Pool, Rain Forest Showers, Pebble Walk Way, Salt Infused Steam Rooms, Relaxation Rooms, Laconium Sauna*

### Quality Hotel & Leisure Club Wexford
Wexford Town, Co. Wexford
Tel: 053-917 2000 ..................Page 262
**Name of Spa:**
**The Salon Body & Soul @ Club Vitae**
**Treatments:**30 ........**Treatment Rooms:**2
**Type of Treatments:**
*Body Therapy Treatments, Skin Therapy Treatments, Facial Treatments, Nail Care, Grooming Treatments*
**Type of Facilities:**
*20m Swimming Pool, Sauna, Steam Room, Jacuzzi, Fitness Gym, Aerobics Studio, Dedicated Kids Pool*

### Seafield Hotel
Gorey, Co. Wexford
Tel: 053-942 4000..................Page 257
**Name of Spa:**
**Oceo Spa**
**Treatments:**66 ......**Treatment Rooms:**16
**Type of Treatments:**
*Payot Renewing Youth Smooth Facial, Firm Facial, Hot Stone Massage, Back Massage, Resource Mineral Body Wrap & Exfoliation Fitness Wrap, Aroma Algae Detox Wrap, Oceo Spa Manicure & Pedicure*
**Type of Facilities:**
*16 Metre Hydrotherapy Pool, Outdoor Vitality Pool, Rasul Suite, Hammam Table, Sauna, Saunarium, Ice Grotto, Couples Suite, Spa Café, Aromatherapy Room, Kaiser Gym*

### Talbot Hotel Conference and Leisure Centre
Wexford Town, Co. Wexford
Tel: 053-912 2566 ..................Page 263
**Name of Spa:**
**Essence Nail & Beauty Therapy**
**Treatments:**44 ........**Treatment Rooms:**3
**Type of Treatments:**
*Dermalogica Customised Facial, Multi Vitamin Power Plus Facial, Ultimate Spa Experience, Hydro-Mineral Salt Scrub, Enzymatic Sea Mud Wrap*
**Type of Facilities:**
*Treatment Rooms, Nail Bar, Make Up Room, Sports Massage Therapist*

### Whites of Wexford
Wexford Town, Co. Wexford
Tel: 053-912 2311 ..................Page 263
**Name of Spa:**
**Tranquillity Spa**
**Treatments:**45 ........**Treatment Rooms:**9
**Type of Treatments:**
*The Sundari Facial, Neem & Goty Kola Body Wrap, Abangya Massage (Ayurvedic), Shiro Dara, Sea Essentials Eye Treatment, Tranquillity Spa Experience, Heavenly Hands Manicure, Marine Thermal Mud Therapy, Sundari Gentlemens Facial, Reiki, Hot Stone Therapy*
**Type of Facilities:**
*9 Contemporary Treatment Rooms, Thermal Suite - Laconium / Sauna / Steam Room (Aroma Essence) / Tropical Showers / Ice Grotto / Stainless Steel Hydrospa Pool / Tepidarium / Cryotherapy Clinic, Wet & Dry Relaxation Room, Manicure Lounge*

# Dublin & Ireland East

## Co. Cavan

### Cavan Crystal Hotel
Cavan Town, Co. Cavan
Tel: 049-436 0600..................Page 270
**Name of Spa:**
**Utopia Health & Beauty Clinic**
**Treatments:**45 ........**Treatment Rooms:**5
**Type of Treatments:**
*Dermalogica Facials, Dermalogica Body Treatments, Swedish Body Massage, Hot Stone Body Massage, Creative Manicures & Pedicures, Make Up Application, Tinting, Waxing, Spray Tan, Body Wraps*
**Type of Facilities:**
*Facial Suites, Body Treatment Suites, Specifically Designed Spray Tanning Room, Nail Bar, Make Up Room, Spacious Reception / Relaxation Area*

### Radisson SAS Farnham Estate Hotel
Cavan Town, Co. Cavan
Tel: 049-437 7700 ..................Page 271
**Name of Spa:**
**Farnham Estate Health Spa**
**Treatments:**100......**Treatment Rooms:**19
**Type of Treatments:**
*Renew Rose Facial, Specialised Prescription Facial, Caviar Facial, Farnham Estate Cure, The Real Aromatherapy Experience, Trilogy Lavender Dreams*
**Type of Facilities:**
*Gymnasium, Indoor/Outdoor Infinity Pool, Thermal Suite, 19 Treatment Rooms, 7km of Walkways, Relaxation Rooms, Yoga Studio*

## Did you know ?

**Abhyanga**
*Abhyanga massage is a gentle but firm whole body massage from head to toe using warm medicated oils. Oils are chosen according to the prakruti (psychosomatic constitution) and the illness. The massage is done in a soft rhythmic way with one or two persons massaging at the same time for forty five to sixty minutes.*

## Co. Cavan CONTINUED

### Slieve Russell Hotel Golf & Country Club
Ballyconnell, Co. Cavan
Tel: 049-952 6444..................Page 270
**Name of Spa:**
**Ciúin Spa and Wellness Centre**
**Treatments:**30 ......**Treatment Rooms:**17
**Type of Treatments:**
*A wide selection of treatments available along with microdermabrasion and other beauty treatments*
**Type of Facilities:**
*Hammam (Traditional Turkish Bath), Herb Sauna, Salt Grotto, Floatation Tank, Relaxation Room, Rasul, Adventure and Health Showers, Hydrotherapy Pool, 17 Treatment rooms*

## Co. Dublin

### Airportview Hotel & Spa
Blakes Cross, Co. Dublin
Tel: 01-843 8756....................Page 273
**Name of Spa:**
**Airport View Spa**
**Treatments:**35 ......**Treatment Rooms:**10
**Type of Treatments:**
*Massages, Facial, Beauty Therapy, Body Treatments, Hydro Bath*
**Type of Facilities:**
*Pool, Saunas, Steam Room, Small Gym Area*

### Castleknock Hotel and Country Club
Dublin City, Co. Dublin
Tel: 01-640 6300....................Page 290
**Name of Spa:**
**Lavender Lane**
**Treatments:**19 ........**Treatment Rooms:**4
**Type of Treatments:**
*Facials, Massage, Reflexology, Body Treatments, Manicures, Pedicures, Waxing, False Tan Application, Beauty Treatments*
**Type of Facilities:**
*Sauna, Steam Room, Spa Jacuzzi, 18m Swimming Pool, Gymnasium, Aerobics Studio, Childrens' Pool*

### Clarence (The)
Dublin City, Co. Dublin
Tel: 01-407 0800 ....................Page 291
**Name of Spa:**
**Therapy Treatment Room**
**Treatments:**1 ..........**Treatment Rooms:**1
**Type of Treatments:**
*1 Hour Body Massage, Aromatherapy Massage 1.5 hours, Swedish Massage1.5 hours. Pre-Natal Massage 1 hour*
**Type of Facilities:**
*Fitness Room with running machine, cross-trainer & cycling machine*

### Clarion Hotel Dublin IFSC
Dublin City, Co. Dublin
Tel: 01-433 8800 ....................Page 291
**Name of Spa:**
**Medi Spa**
**Treatments:**5 ..........**Treatment Rooms:**5
**Type of Treatments:**
*Various Treatments Available*
**Type of Facilities:**
*Pool, Sauna, Steam Room, Jacuzzi, Gym, Aerobics Classes, Body Treatments, Face Treatments, massage within the 5 treatment rooms*

### Fitzwilliam Hotel
Dublin City, Co. Dublin
Tel: 01-478 7000....................Page 298
**Name of Spa:**
**Free Spirit @ The Fitzwilliam**
**Treatments:**7 ..........**Treatment Rooms:**1
**Type of Treatments:**
*Hot Stone Massage, Aromatherapy Massage, Reflexology, Body Wrap, Dermalogica Facials, Massage Treatments*
**Type of Facilities:**
*Treatment Room, Nail Bar, Hair Salon, Mist Tanning*

### Four Seasons Hotel Dublin
Dublin City, Co. Dublin
Tel: 01-665 4000....................Page 299
**Name of Spa:**
**The Spa**
**Treatments:**45 ........**Treatment Rooms:**4
**Type of Treatments:**
*La Prairie Facial, Caviar Body Treatment and Facial, Shirodhara and Abhyanga Massage, Gota Kola and Neem Wrap, Swiss Bliss, Four Seasons Massage*
**Type of Facilities:**
*Indoor Swimming Pool, Whirlpool, Sauna, Steam Room, Fitness Facilities*

### Merrion Hall & Blakes Spa Suites
Dublin City, Co. Dublin
Tel: 01-668 1426 ....................Page 309
**Name of Spa:**
**Merrion Hall & Blakes Spa Suites**
**Treatments:**6 ..........**Treatment Rooms:**4
**Type of Treatments:**
*Full Body Massage, Manual Lymphatic Drainage, Feet Reflexology Massage, Oil-Seasalt Massage, Shiatsu, La Stone-Therapy, Indian Head Massage, Beauty Treatments, Ayurvedic Treatment*
**Type of Facilities:**
*Aroma Steam Bath, Herbal Bath, Finnish Sauna, Laconium, Ice Fountain, Crystal Sound Meditation Room, Relaxation Area, Jacuzzi, Colour Therapy, Feet Reflexology Walk*

### Portmarnock Hotel & Golf Links
Portmarnock, Co. Dublin
Tel: 01-846 0611 ....................Page 329
**Name of Spa:**
**Oceana**
**Treatments:**10 ........**Treatment Rooms:**3
**Type of Treatments:**
*Facials, Body Treatments, Tanning, Nails, Pedicures, Waxing, De-stressing and Sports Physiotherapy, Balneotherapy*
**Type of Facilities:**
*Sauna, Gym, Steam Shower, Nail Bars, Treatment Rooms*

### Rochestown Lodge Hotel & Day Spa
Dun Laoghaire, Co. Dublin
Tel: 01-285 3555....................Page 325
**Name of Spa:**
**Replenish Day Spa**
**Treatments:**60 ........**Treatment Rooms:**9
**Type of Treatments:**
*Aroma Stone Therapy, Skin Specific Facials, Massage Rituals, Aroma Spa Wraps, Luxurious Manicures /Pedicures, Tinting, Waxing, Make Up*
**Type of Facilities:**
*9 Multi-functional Treatment Rooms, Hydrotherm Facilities, Consultation Area, Relaxation Suite, Pedicure /Manicure Suite, Ladies /Gents Changing Area, Juice Bar, Retail Area*

### Royal Marine Hotel
Dun Laoghaire, Co. Dublin
Tel: 01-230 0030 ..................Page 326
**Name of Spa:**
**Sansanaspa**
**Treatments:**40 ........**Treatment Rooms:**9
**Type of Treatments:**
*Uspa Face & Body Rituals, Dry Floatation, Hydrotherapy, Razul, Massage, Hot Stone Therapy, Tanning, Manicure & Pedicure, Body Wraps, Body Scrubs*
**Type of Facilities:**
*18m Infinity Pool, Jacuzzi, Treatment Rooms, Gymnasium, Rock Sauna, Aroma Steam, Drench Shower, Experience Shower, Ice Font, Aqua Relaxation Room*

### Shelbourne Hotel (The)
Dublin City, Co. Dublin
Tel: 01-663 4500 ..................Page 320
**Name of Spa:**
**Luxury Spa opening in 2008**
**Type of Treatments:**
*Various Treatments Available*
**Type of Facilities:**
*Indoor Pool, Jacuzzi, Gym, Steam Room, Sauna*

### Stillorgan Park Hotel
Dublin City, Co. Dublin
Tel: 01-200 1800 ..................Page 321
**Name of Spa:**
**White Pebble Spa**
**Treatments:**30 ........**Treatment Rooms:**7
**Type of Treatments:**
*8 Facials including Le Grand Classique & Alpha Vital, Tanning, Eyes, Hands & Feet, Reflexology, Body Treatments, Waxing, Stone Massage*
**Type of Facilities:**
*Relaxation Room, Steam Room, Changing Rooms, Gym*

## Did you know ?

**Hot Stone Massage**

*Is a specialty massage that uses smooth, heated stones. They are often basalt, a black volcanic rock that absorbs and retains heat well.*

*It is a deeply soothing, relaxing form of massage. The heat helps tight muscles release.*

## Co. Kildare

### Carlton Abbey Hotel & C Spa
Athy, Co. Kildare
Tel: 059-863 0100 ................Page 332
**Name of Spa:**
**The C Spa**
**Treatments:**30 ........**Treatment Rooms:**8
**Type of Treatments:**
*Hydro Bath, Sports Massage, Full Body Wraps, Anti-stress Package, Manicure & Pedicure, Body & Facial Massage, Gentlemen's Wellbeing Treatments*
**Type of Facilities:**
*Relaxation Room, Hydrotherapy Bath Pool, Sauna, Gym, Jacuzzi, Balneotherapy, Roof Top Relaxation Suite and Juice Bar*

### Carton House
Maynooth, Co. Kildare
Tel: 01-505 2000 ..................Page 336
**Name of Spa:**
**The Spa at Carton House**
**Treatments:**24 ........**Treatment Rooms:**7
**Type of Treatments:**
*Lifeforce Facial, De-Stressing Yuan Zhi Body Polish, Primalsource Facial, Celestial Maracuja Body Cocoon & Massage, Primal-Radiance Contouring Eye Therapy, Bodynurture Pregancy Massage, Energising Shiatswe Body Massage, Primal-Radiance Contouring Facial, Equillibrium Facial for Men, Regenerating Facial for Men, Full Range of Molton Brown Products*
**Type of Facilities:**
*7 Treatment Rooms, Including a Couples Treatment Room, Mud Rasul, Relaxation Area, Floatation Pool, Manicure/Pedicure Room*

### Glenroyal Hotel, Leisure Club & Conference Centre
Maynooth, Co. Kildare
Tel: 01-629 0909 ..................Page 336
**Name of Spa:**
**Ealú Spa**
**Treatments:**10 ........**Treatment Rooms:**6
**Type of Treatments:**
*Body Wraps, Hot Stone Massage, Waxing, Facials, Manicures, Pedicures, Spray Tans, Indian Head Massage, Tinting, Make up*
**Type of Facilities:**
*2 x 20m Pools, Sauna, Jacuzzi, Steam Room, Solariums, Hydro Spa, Gymnasium, Aerobics Studio, Spinning Room*

### Keadeen Hotel
Newbridge, Co. Kildare
Tel: 045-431666 ..................Page 340
**Name of Spa:**
**Keadeen Club**
**Treatments:**10..........**Treatment Rooms:**1
**Type of Treatments:**
*Massage Treatments, Beauty Treatments, Facials, Hot Stone Therapy, Face & Eye Treatment, Manicure, Pedicure, Waxing, Skin Performance Anti Ageing Treatment*
**Type of Facilities:**
*Swimming Pool, Gym, Sauna, Jacuzzi, Sun Bed*

### Kildare Hotel, Spa and Country Club - The K Club
Straffan, Co. Kildare
Tel: 01-601 7200 ..................Page 341
**Name of Spa:**
**The K Spa**
**Treatments:**100......**Treatment Rooms:**13
**Type of Treatments:**
*Body Wraps, Hot Stone Therapy, Waxing, Facials, Massage, Hair Salon, Reflexology, Manicure, Pedicure, Rasul, Pilates*
**Type of Facilities:**
*Rasul, Swimming Pool, Hot Tub, Hair Beauty & Pedicure Salon, Tanning System, Kings Bath, Vichy Shower, Hammam, Hot Stone Therapy*

### Killashee House Hotel & Villa Spa
Naas, Co. Kildare
Tel: 045-879277 ..................Page 337
**Name of Spa:**
**The Villa Spa**
**Treatments:**30 ......**Treatment Rooms:**18
**Type of Treatments:**
*Rasul, Elemis Visible Brilliance Facial, Balneotherapy, Indian Head Massage, Jessica Manicure & Pedicure, Hot Stones Massage, Swedish Massage, Elemis Exotic Lime & Ginger Salt Glow, Thalgo Frigi Wrap, Hammam*
**Type of Facilities:**
*Therapeutic Pool, Mud Chamber, Hair Salon, Juice Bar, Relaxation Rooms, Hydrojets, Floatation Rooms*

## Co. Kildare CONTINUED

### Osprey Hotel & Spa
Naas, Co. Kildare
Tel: 045-881111 ......................Page 338
**Name of Spa:**
**Osprey Spa**
**Treatments:**75 ........**Treatment Rooms:**8
**Type of Treatments:**
*Hydrofloat, Rasul Bath, Reflexology, Sports Massage, Hot Stone Massage, Aromatherapy, La Phyto Facial, Pedicure, Hammam Hot Massage, Tranquillity Face & Body Treatment*
**Type of Facilities:**
*Swimming Pool, Foot Baths, Sanarium, Relaxation Room, Salt Grotto, Snow Paradise, Hydro Jet Pool, Fitness Studio, Steam Room, Family Changing Room*

### Standhouse Hotel Leisure & Conference Centre
Curragh (The), Co. Kildare
Tel: 045-436177 ....................Page 334
**Name of Spa:**
**Decleor Beauty Salon**
**Treatments:**15 ........**Treatment Rooms:**2
**Type of Treatments:**
*Aromatherapy Facials, Body Massage, Reflexology, Dermalogica Treatments*
**Type of Facilities:**
*Sauna, Steam Room, Jacuzzi, Plunge Pool, Swimming Pool, Gymnasium*

### Westgrove Hotel & Conference Centre
Clane, Co. Kildare
Tel: 045-989900 ....................Page 334
**Name of Spa:**
**Spa Haven**
**Treatments:**20 ........**Treatment Rooms:**7
**Type of Treatments:**
*Elemis Facials, Deep Tissue Massage, Hot Stone Therapy, Elemis Body Wraps, Hydrotherapy Bath, Rasul Mud Chamber, Hammam Body Cleansing*
**Type of Facilities:**
*Fully Equipped Gym, 20m Pool, Sauna, Steam Room, Jacuzzi, Kids Pool, Aerobics Suite*

## Co. Laois

### Comfort Inn Portlaoise
Portlaoise, Co. Laois
Tel: 057-869 5900..................Page 342
**Name of Spa:**
**Club Vitae**
**Treatments:**5 ..........**Treatment Rooms:**4
**Type of Treatments:**
*Facials, Body Massage, Head Massage, Pedicure, Manicure*
**Type of Facilities:**
*20 Meter Swimming Pool, Sauna, Jacuzzi, Stream Room, Aerobic Suite, Free Weights, Cardio-Vascular Machines*

### Heritage Golf & Spa Resort (The)
Killenard, Co. Laois
Tel: 057-864 5500..................Page 342
**Name of Spa:**
**The Spa at the Heritage**
**Treatments:**70 ......**Treatment Rooms:**20
**Type of Treatments:**
*Massage, Wraps, Hydrotherapy, Facials, Mud Wraps, Stone Therapy, Manicure, Sports & Body Therapy, Mens Treatments, Eye/Lip Treatments*
**Type of Facilities:**
*Sanarium, Tepidarium, Hydrotherapy Pool, Tropical Showers, Hammam, Steam Bath, Sauna, Foot Bath, Mud Chamber, Ice Fountain*

### Portlaoise Heritage Hotel
Portlaoise, Co. Laois
Tel: 057-867 8588..................Page 343
**Name of Spa:**
**Ealu**
**Treatments:**25 ........**Treatment Rooms:**7
**Type of Treatments:**
*Full Body Wraps, Massages, Nail Treatments, Reflexology, Waxing, Footcare, Make-up, False Tan, General Grooming, Electrolysis, Skin Exfoliation Treatments, Slimming Treatments, Body Toning*
**Type of Facilities:**
*Swimming Pool, Sauna, Steam Room, Jacuzzi, Gymnasium, Relaxation Room, Balneotherapy Room*

## Co. Louth

### Boyne Valley Hotel & Country Club
Drogheda, Co. Louth
Tel: 041-983 7737 ..................Page 346
**Name of Spa:**
**Boyne Valley Health & Beauty Spa**
**Treatments:**30 ........**Treatment Rooms:**2
**Type of Treatments:**
*Hot Stone Full Body/Back Massage, Botox Facials, Royal Jelly Facials, Solglo Spray Tan, Spa Manicures, Spa Pedicures, Indian Head Massage, Make Up, Waxing, Inch Loss Wraps*
**Type of Facilities:**
*20m Swimming Pool with Jacuzzi, Sauna & Steam Room Facilities, Aerobic & Spinning Studios with Aqua, Body Board, Body Bar, Yoga and Boxercise, Powerplate, Lifestyle Checks, CV and Weight Equipment*

### Park Inn Dundalk
Dundalk, Co. Louth
Tel: 042-939 5700..................Page 350
**Name of Spa:**
**Park Inn Dundalk**
**Type of Treatments:**
*Various Treatments Available*
**Type of Facilities:**
*Sauna, Steam Room, Jacuzzi, swimming pool, gym, weight room*

## Co. Meath

### Ashbourne Marriott Hotel
Ashbourne, Co. Meath
Tel: 01-835 0800 ....................Page 350
**Name of Spa:**
**DayDream Spa**
**Treatments:**35 ......**Treatment Rooms:**12
**Type of Treatments:**
*Face, Body, Massage & Holistic Healing, Hair & Scalp, Hand & Feet, Waxing, Skin Repair, Himself, Power Plate*
**Type of Facilities:**
*Waxing Room, Treatment Rooms, Tanning Room, Hairdressers, Relaxation Room, Reception, Power Plate*

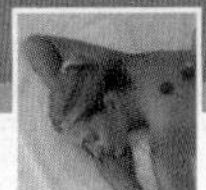

### Dunboyne Castle Hotel & Spa
Dunboyne, Co. Meath
Tel: 01-801 3500 ....................Page 353
**Name of Spa:**
**Seoid**
**Treatments:**80 ......**Treatment Rooms:**18
**Type of Treatments:**
*Balneotherapy, Hammam, Dry Floatation, Hydrojet Water Massage Bed, Thai Massage, Rasul, Thalgo Facial*
**Type of Facilities:**
*18 Treatment Rooms including Hydrotherapy Pool, Heat Rooms, Ice Rooms, Experience Showers, Fitness Suite*

### Knightsbrook Hotel & Golf Resort
Trim, Co. Meath
Tel: 046-948 2110 ..................Page 357
**Name of Spa:**
**The River Spa**
**Treatments:**8 ........**Treatment Rooms:**18
**Type of Treatments:**
*Holistic Therapies, Facials, Body Treatments, Rasual, Massage*
**Type of Facilities:**
*Gym, 16m Swimming Pool, Herb Sauna, Rasual Bath, Salt Grotto, Steam Room, Jacuzzi, Foot Spas, Spa Treatment Rooms*

### Marriott Johnstown House Hotel & Spa
Enfield, Co. Meath
Tel: 046-954 0000..................Page 353
**Name of Spa:**
**The Spa at Marriott Johnstown House**
**Treatments:**55 ......**Treatment Rooms:**17
**Type of Treatments:**
*Serail Mud /Milk Chamber, Hammam Therapies, Precious Stone Therapy, Floatation Room, Elemis Full Body Deep Tissue Muscle Massage, Elemis Aroma Hot Stone Therapy, Elemis Visible Brilliance Facial, Elemis Exotic Frangipani Body Nourish Wrap, Elemis Nurturing Massage for Mother-To-Be, The Male Must Have*
**Type of Facilities:**
*Indoor Heated Swimming Pool, Gymnasium, Hot Thermal Suite, Outdoor Hot Tub, Pilates Studio, 17 Spa Therapy Rooms, Climbing Wall, Golf Simulator, On Site Corporate Activity Centre*

## Co. Monaghan

### Hillgrove Hotel Leisure & Spa
Monaghan Town, Co. Monaghan
Tel: 047-81288 ......................Page 359
**Name of Spa:**
**Lir Spa & Wellness Centre**
**Treatments:**85 ........**Treatment Rooms:**8
**Type of Treatments:**
*Facials, Massage, Body Wraps, Exfoliation, Water Treatments, Alternative Therapies, Tanning Treatments, Beauty Treatments, Nail Bar & Hair Salon*
**Type of Facilities:**
*Thermal Spa Area, Rasul, Floatation Bed, Hydrotherapy Pool, Herbal Sauna, Pedi Spas, Ice Fountain, Monsoon Showers, Relaxation Room, Hair Salon*

### Nuremore Hotel & Country Club
Carrickmacross, Co. Monaghan
Tel: 042-966 1438..................Page 358
**Name of Spa:**
**Vida**
**Treatments:**40 ........**Treatment Rooms:**3
**Type of Treatments:**
*Aromatherapy, Full Body Massage, Detoxifying Algae Wrap, Reflexology, Indian Head Massage, Golfers Tonic, Luxury Eye Treatment, Sports and Fitness Massage, Facials*
**Type of Facilities:**
*Sauna, Steam Room, Whirlpool Swimming Pool, Gym, Tennis Courts, Jacuzzi*

## Co. Offaly

### Bridge House Hotel, Leisure Club & Spa
Tullamore, Co. Offaly
Tel: 057-932 5600 ..................Page 361
**Name of Spa:**
**Sanctuary Spa**
**Treatments:**25 ........**Treatment Rooms:**6
**Type of Treatments:**
*Swedish Holistic Massage, Spray Tan, Sports Massage, Indian Head Massage, Facials, Pilates, Hot Stone Therapy, Reflexology, Seaweed Treatments*
**Type of Facilities:**
*Sauna, Steam Room, Jacuzzi, Outdoor Hydrotherapy Pool, Swimming Pool, State of the Art Health Club, Fitness Studio, Power Plate Vibration Training System, Relaxation Chamber*

### County Arms Hotel & Leisure Club
Birr, Co. Offaly
Tel: 057-912 0791....................Page 360
**Name of Spa:**
**Springs Wellness Suites**
**Treatments:**30 ........**Treatment Rooms:**7
**Type of Treatments:**
*Elemis Spa Treatments Exclusively. Anti-Ageing Facials, Aromapure Facials, Absolute Spa Ritual, Aroma Spa Ocean Wrap, Well-Being Massage, Hot Stone Therapy, Spray Tanning, Manicure, Pedicure*
**Type of Facilities:**
*Jacuzzi, Kids Pool, Sauna, Steam Room, 20m Pool, Hydrotherapy Pool, Air-Conditioned Gym, Whirlpool*

### Kinnitty Castle Demesne
Birr, Co. Offaly
Tel: 057-913 7318 ..................Page 361
**Name of Spa:**
**The Gate Lodge Spa at Kinnitty Castle**
**Treatments:**40 ........**Treatment Rooms:**3
**Type of Treatments:**
*Hot Stone Massage, Aromatic Facials, Massor Exotic Wrap, Nails by Design, MAC Make-Up Design, Eye Treatments, Tanning Treatments*
**Type of Facilities:**
*Outdoor Hot Tub, Massor Hydrotherapy Baths, Sauna, Steam Room, Exotic Wrap, Hair Salon*

## Co. Westmeath

### Bloomfield House Hotel
Mullingar, Co. Westmeath
Tel: 044-934 0894..................Page 368
**Name of Spa:**
**Zoi Spa - Beauty**
**Treatments:**30 ........**Treatment Rooms:**8
**Type of Treatments:**
*Facials, Massage, Spa Wraps, Exfoliation, Nourishing Wraps, Pedicures, Manicures, Full Range of Grooming Treatments and Complementary Therapies*
**Type of Facilities:**
*Relaxation Room, Solarium, Sauna, Steam Room, Swimming Pool, Gymnasium, Jacuzzi, Aerobics Studio*

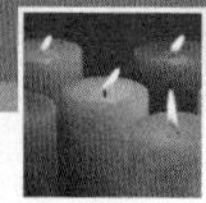

## Co. Westmeath CONTINUED

### Hodson Bay Hotel
Athlone, Co. Westmeath
Tel: 090-644 2000..................Page 365
**Name of Spa:**
**The Spa at Hodson Bay**
**Treatments:**60 ......**Treatment Rooms:**12
**Type of Treatments:**
*Aromatherapy Massage, Reflexology, Aroma Stone Therapy, Reiki, Full Body Polish, Watsu Treatments, Jet Douche Treatments, Bath Ceremony, Vichy Shower, Shiatsu*
**Type of Facilities:**
*Thermal Suite, Outdoor Hot Tub overlooking lake shore, Hair & Beauty Studios, Aerobics & Fitness Studios, Watsu Pool, Jet Douche, Rasul, Laconiums, 20m Pool with Hydrotherapy Features, Relaxation Suites*

### Mullingar Park Hotel
Mullingar, Co. Westmeath
Tel: 044-933 7500..................Page 369
**Name of Spa:**
**Azure Leisure and Spa**
**Treatments:**36 ........**Treatment Rooms:**7
**Type of Treatments:**
*Aromatherapy, Swedish Body Massage, Body Wraps, Facials, Paraffin Wax, Manicures, Pedicures, Fake Tan, Eye Masks and Tinting, Body Wax, La Stone Therapy*
**Type of Facilities:**
*Shower Facility for Body Treatments, Massage Room, Relaxation Room, Nail Bar, Linen Facility - Towels, Duvet, etc.*

### Sheraton Athlone Hotel
Athlone, Co. Westmeath
Tel: 090-645 1000..................Page 366
**Treatments:**50 ........**Treatment Rooms:**7
**Type of Treatments:**
*Body Wraps, Aromatherapy, Massage, Hot Stone Treatments, Full Body Polish, Head Massage, Facials, Hand & Foot Treatments*
**Type of Facilities:**
*Swimming Pool, Sauna, Steam Room, Relaxation Suite, Rasul, Laconium, Hair & Beauty Studios, Jacuzzi*

### Temple Country Retreat & Spa
Moate, Co. Westmeath
Tel: 057-933 5118 ..................Page 367
**Name of Spa:**
**Temple Country Retreat & Spa**
**Treatments:**80 ......**Treatment Rooms:**18
**Type of Treatments:**
*Massage, Reflexology, Hot Stone Massage, Detox Herbal Massage, Chocotherapy, Vinotherapy, Jessana Manicure, Jessana Pedicure, Floatation, Facials*
**Type of Facilities:**
*Vitality Pool, Sauna, Steam Room, Experience Showers, Foot Spa, Yoga Studio, Gym, Juice Bar, Tranquillity Room, Daily Programme of Yoga, Walking, Fitness & Relaxation Classes, One-to-One Personal Training, Nutritionist & Lifestyle Coach by Appointment*

## Co. Wicklow

### Arklow Bay Conference, Leisure & Spa Hotel
Arklow, Co. Wicklow
Tel: 0402-32309 ....................Page 370
**Name of Spa:**
**Rivendell Body & Beauty Spa**
**Treatments:**50 ........**Treatment Rooms:**6
**Type of Treatments:**
*Aromatherapy & Hot Stone Massage, Dermalogica Facials, Nail Bar, Pedicure, Waxing, Holistic Treatments, Fake Bake Tan Spray, Make-up for all occasions, Spa Packages*
**Type of Facilities:**
*6 Treatment Rooms plus Sauna, Steam Room, Jacuzzi, 20 metre level-deck Swimming Pool*

> ## Did you know ?
> **Body Wraps**
> *Improve elimination of toxins in the body while remineralizing the body with the nutrients it needs. Wraps can have toning, relaxing, or stimulating effects and can provide relief from pain due to improper removal of metabolic waste products.*

### BrookLodge and Wells Spa
Aughrim, Co. Wicklow
Tel: 0402-36444 ....................Page 371
**Name of Spa:**
**The Wells Spa at The BrookLodge Hotel**
**Treatments:**45 ......**Treatment Rooms:**14
**Type of Treatments:**
*Decleor Body and Facials including Envelopement, Carita Body and Facials including Renovateur, Floatation Therapy, Hammam Massage, Cleopatra and Thalassotherapy Baths, Mud Chamber*
**Type of Facilities:**
*Indoor to Outdoor Swimming Pool, Floatation Room, Serail Mud Chamber, Aroma Steam Room, Finnish Baths, Outdoor Hot Tub, Jacuzzi, Hammam Massage Room*

### Glenview Hotel
Glen-O-The-Downs, Co. Wicklow
Tel: 01-287 3399....................Page 376
**Name of Spa:**
**The Haven Beauty Salons**
**Treatments:**26 ........**Treatment Rooms:**3
**Type of Treatments:**
*Specialised Hot Stone Massage, Aromaplastie Facial, Tranquillity Back Massage, Vital Eyes Treatment, Aroma Relax Envelopement, De Luxe French Manicure & Pedicure, Perfect Contour, Swedish Massage, Reflexology*
**Type of Facilities:**
*Swimming Pool, Sauna, Steam Room, Jacuzzi, Outdoor Hot Tub, Fully Equipped Gymnasium*

### Rathsallagh House, Golf and Country Club
Dunlavin, Co. Wicklow
Tel: 045-403112 ....................Page 374
**Treatments:**5 ..........**Treatment Rooms:**2
**Type of Treatments:**
*Full Body Massage, Back and Leg Massage, Hand and Feet Massage, Anti-Cellulite Massage, All Beauty Treatments*
**Type of Facilities:**
*Jacuzzi, Steam Room*

**The Ritz-Carlton, Powerscourt**
Enniskerry, Co. Wicklow
Tel: 01-274 8888 .................... Page 375
**Name of Spa:**
**ESPA at The Ritz-Carlton, Powerscourt**
**Treatments:**50 ......**Treatment Rooms:**22
**Type of Treatments:**
*ESPA at Ritz-Carlton Treatments rituals, ESPA Ayurvedic influenced Treatments, ESPA Advanced Facials*
**Type of Facilities:**
*Fitness Suite includes Technologym, Chi Studio, Indoor Swimming Pool, Spa Café, 22 Treatment Rooms*

## Did you know ?

**Vinotherapy**
*Consists of skin care products and treatments derived from the by-products of grapes. It is up to 20 times more effective than vitamin C and up to 50 times more effective than vitamin E.*

# Northern Ireland

## Co. Derry

**Radisson SAS Roe Park Resort**
Limavady, Co. Derry
Tel: 028-7772 2222................ Page 389
**Name of Spa:**
**Roe Spa**
**Treatments:**1S........**Treatment Rooms:**12
**Type of Treatments:**
*Hot Stone Massage, Seaweed Body Wraps, Skin Specific Facials, Anti-Ageing & Advanced Performance Facials, Jessana Spa Pedicure & Manicure, Elemis Bathing Ceremonies, Exotic Rasul, Aqua Veda Exfoliation Treatment, Specific Men's Treatments, Glow Minerals Make Up*
**Type of Facilities:**
*Champagne Bath, Rasul Mud Chamber, Aqua Veda Exfoliation Table, Aromatherapy Steam Shower, Pedicure Suite & Nail Clinic, Aqua Meditation Chamber, Relaxation Suite, Refreshment Centre & Leisure Facilities*

## Co. Fermanagh

**Lough Erne Golf Resort**
Enniskillen, Co. Fermanagh
Tel: 028-6632 0613 ................ Page 392
**Treatments:**35 ........**Treatment Rooms:**8
**Type of Treatments:**
*Traditional Thai Massage, Botanical Wraps, Wet Treatments, Oriental Sole Foot Therapy, Open Mind Back Neck and Shoulder Relief, Purity Hand Detox, Thai Herbal Healer*
**Type of Facilities:**
*14 Meter Infinity Pool, Thermal Suite, Rock Sauna, Aroma Grotto, Jacuzzzi, Slipper Bath*

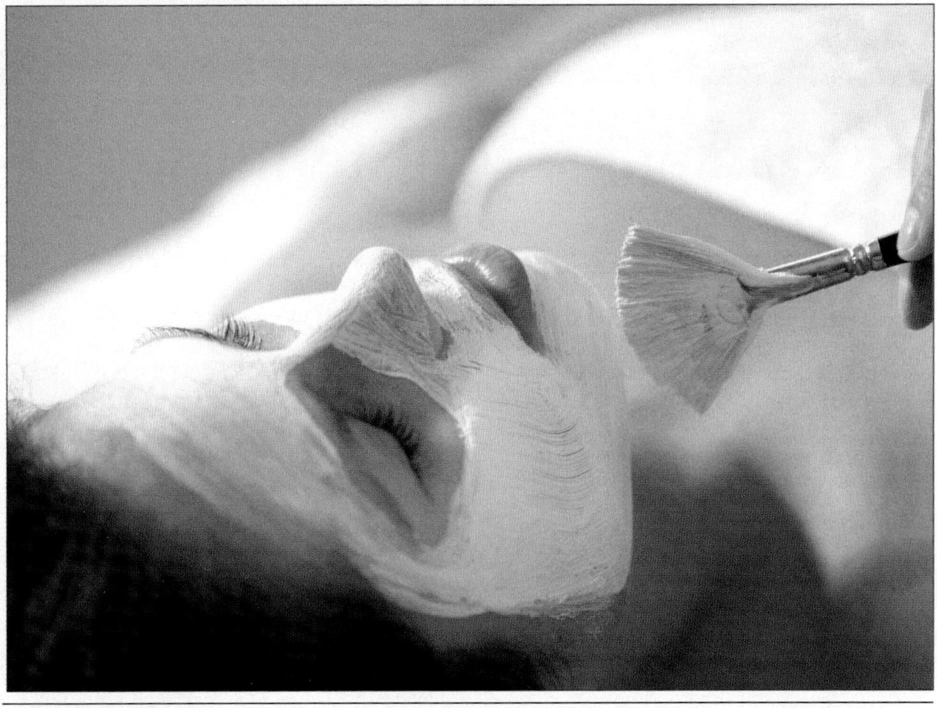

## KEY TO MAPS

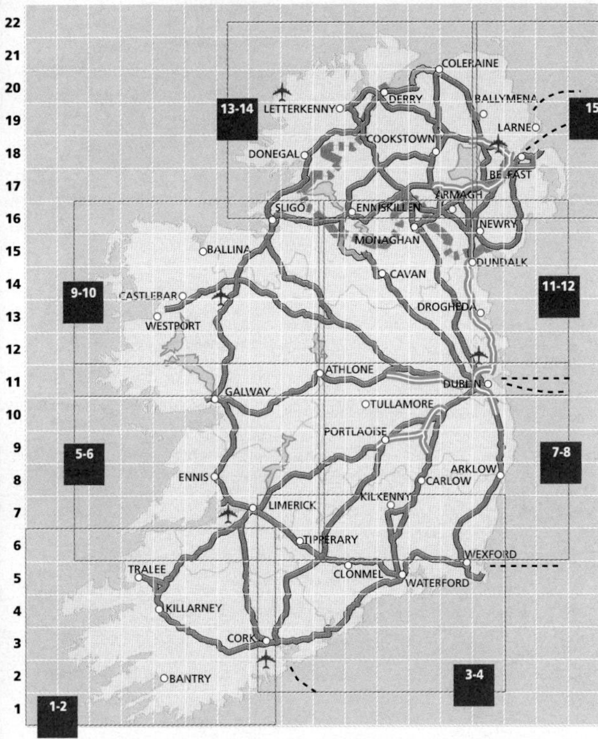


## LEGEND

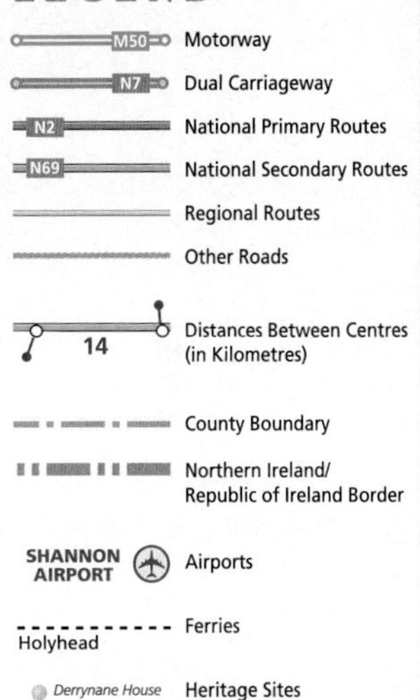


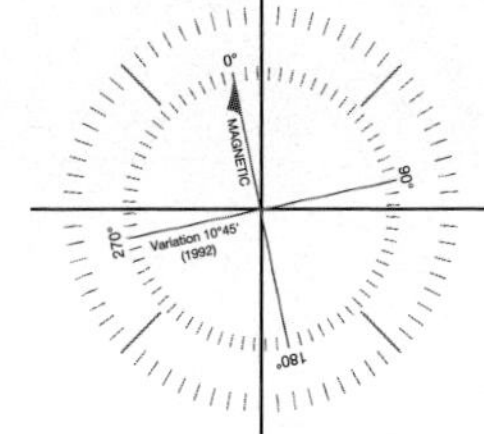


0 5 10 15 20 25km

0 5 10 15miles

SCALE 1 : 625 000

## DISTANCE CHART

in Kilometres

| | ARMAGH | ATHLONE | BELFAST | CARLOW | CLIFDEN | CORK | DERRY | DUBLIN | DUNDALK | ENNISKILLEN | GALWAY | KILKENNY | KILLARNEY | LARNE | LIMERICK | PORTLAOISE | ROSSLARE HARBOUR | SHANNON AIRPORT | SLIGO | TRALEE | WATERFORD | WEXFORD |
|---|---|---|---|---|---|---|---|---|---|---|---|---|---|---|---|---|---|---|---|---|---|---|
| ATHLONE | 159 | | | | | | | | | | | | | | | | | | | | | |
| BELFAST | 66 | 224 | | | | | | | | | | | | | | | | | | | | |
| CARLOW | 211 | 108 | 248 | | | | | | | | | | | | | | | | | | | |
| CLIFDEN | 316 | 171 | 370 | 256 | | | | | | | | | | | | | | | | | | |
| CORK | 380 | 219 | 423 | 187 | 287 | | | | | | | | | | | | | | | | | |
| DERRY | 114 | 225 | 118 | 309 | 303 | 460 | | | | | | | | | | | | | | | | |
| DUBLIN | 129 | 124 | 167 | 82 | 296 | 256 | 233 | | | | | | | | | | | | | | | |
| DUNDALK | 45 | 142 | 82 | 166 | 314 | 340 | 158 | 84 | | | | | | | | | | | | | | |
| ENNISKILLEN | 81 | 127 | 135 | 240 | 237 | 346 | 98 | 175 | 101 | | | | | | | | | | | | | |
| GALWAY | 238 | 92 | 303 | 177 | 79 | 206 | 277 | 216 | 233 | 192 | | | | | | | | | | | | |
| KILKENNY | 245 | 121 | 282 | 39 | 248 | 148 | 335 | 114 | 200 | 242 | 169 | | | | | | | | | | | |
| KILLARNEY | 388 | 229 | 430 | 235 | 295 | 89 | 480 | 303 | 348 | 356 | 214 | 196 | | | | | | | | | | |
| LARNE | 105 | 264 | 40 | 287 | 411 | 462 | 122 | 206 | 121 | 174 | 343 | 320 | 470 | | | | | | | | | |
| LIMERICK | 279 | 119 | 320 | 138 | 184 | 101 | 369 | 192 | 238 | 245 | 105 | 114 | 109 | 356 | | | | | | | | |
| PORTLAOISE | 208 | 71 | 250 | 37 | 229 | 174 | 287 | 82 | 167 | 192 | 150 | 50 | 221 | 285 | 109 | | | | | | | |
| ROSSLARE HARBOUR | 282 | 201 | 320 | 93 | 348 | 206 | 385 | 151 | 237 | 324 | 269 | 100 | 272 | 356 | 204 | 130 | | | | | | |
| SHANNON AIRPORT | 293 | 134 | 345 | 163 | 172 | 126 | 357 | 216 | 261 | 261 | 93 | 138 | 134 | 380 | 24 | 134 | 229 | | | | | |
| SLIGO | 148 | 116 | 203 | 224 | 167 | 336 | 134 | 213 | 171 | 68 | 142 | 237 | 345 | 240 | 235 | 187 | 319 | 224 | | | | |
| TRALEE | 382 | 222 | 423 | 242 | 288 | 121 | 472 | 296 | 341 | 349 | 208 | 216 | 32 | 460 | 103 | 213 | 291 | 127 | 338 | | | |
| WATERFORD | 285 | 167 | 324 | 74 | 296 | 126 | 383 | 156 | 240 | 290 | 217 | 48 | 192 | 359 | 124 | 97 | 81 | 148 | 283 | 211 | | |
| WEXFORD | 264 | 184 | 301 | 76 | 330 | 187 | 365 | 132 | 219 | 306 | 250 | 81 | 254 | 338 | 187 | 113 | 19 | 209 | 299 | 272 | 61 | |
| WICKLOW | 185 | 138 | 222 | 61 | 311 | 256 | 293 | 56 | 140 | 221 | 232 | 100 | 303 | 259 | 193 | 82 | 118 | 216 | 238 | 296 | 135 | 100 |

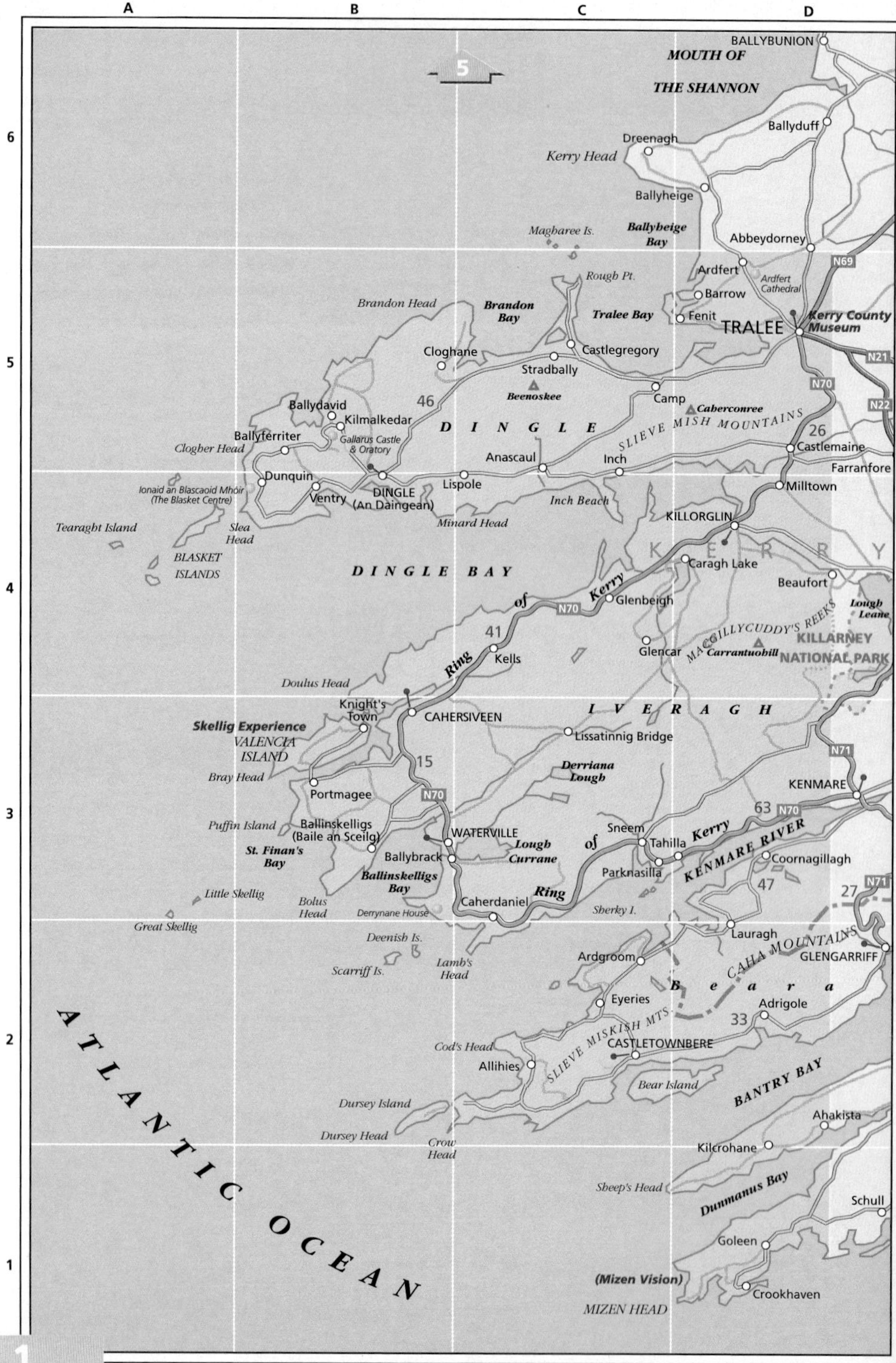

A
B
C
D
5
6
4
3
2
1
BALLYBUNION
MOUTH OF
THE SHANNON
Ballyduff
Dreenagh
Kerry Head
Ballyheige
Magharee Is.
Ballyheige Bay
Abbeydorney
N69
Ardfert
Ardfert Cathedral
Rough Pt.
Barrow
Brandon Head
Brandon Bay
Tralee Bay
Fenit
TRALEE
Kerry County Museum
Cloghane
Castlegregory
N21
Stradbally
Beenoskee
Camp
N70
46
N22
Ballydavid
Kilmalkedar
Caherconree
D I N G L E
SLIEVE MISH MOUNTAINS
26
Ballyferriter
Gallarus Castle & Oratory
Clogher Head
Castlemaine
Anascaul
Inch
Farranfore
Dunquin
Ionaid an Blascaoid Mhóir (The Blasket Centre)
Ventry
DINGLE (An Daingean)
Lispole
Milltown
Inch Beach
Minard Head
KILLORGLIN
Tearaght Island
Slea Head
BLASKET ISLANDS
K E R R Y
Caragh Lake
D I N G L E B A Y
Beaufort
Kerry
Glenbeigh
Lough Leane
of
N70
41
MACGILLYCUDDY'S REEKS
KILLARNEY NATIONAL PARK
Glencar
Carrantuohill
Kells
Ring
Doulus Head
Knight's Town
CAHERSIVEEN
I V E R A G H
Skellig Experience
VALENCIA ISLAND
Lissatinnig Bridge
15
N71
Bray Head
Derriana Lough
Portmagee
KENMARE
N70
63
N70
Puffin Island
Ballinskelligs (Baile an Sceilg)
Sneem
St. Finan's Bay
WATERVILLE
Lough Currane
of
Tahilla
Kerry
KENMARE RIVER
Ballybrack
Coornagillagh
Parknasilla
Ballinskelligs Bay
47
N71
Little Skellig
Ring
27
Bolus Head
Caherdaniel
Sherky I.
Derrynane House
Great Skellig
Lauragh
Deenish Is.
CAHA MOUNTAINS
GLENGARRIFF
Ardgroom
Scarriff Is.
Lamb's Head
B e a r a
Eyeries
Adrigole
SLIEVE MISKISH MTS
33
ATLANTIC OCEAN
Cod's Head
CASTLETOWNBERE
Allihies
Bear Island
BANTRY BAY
Dursey Island
Ahakista
Dursey Head
Crow Head
Kilcrohane
Sheep's Head
Dunmanus Bay
Schull
Goleen
(Mizen Vision)
Crookhaven
MIZEN HEAD
1

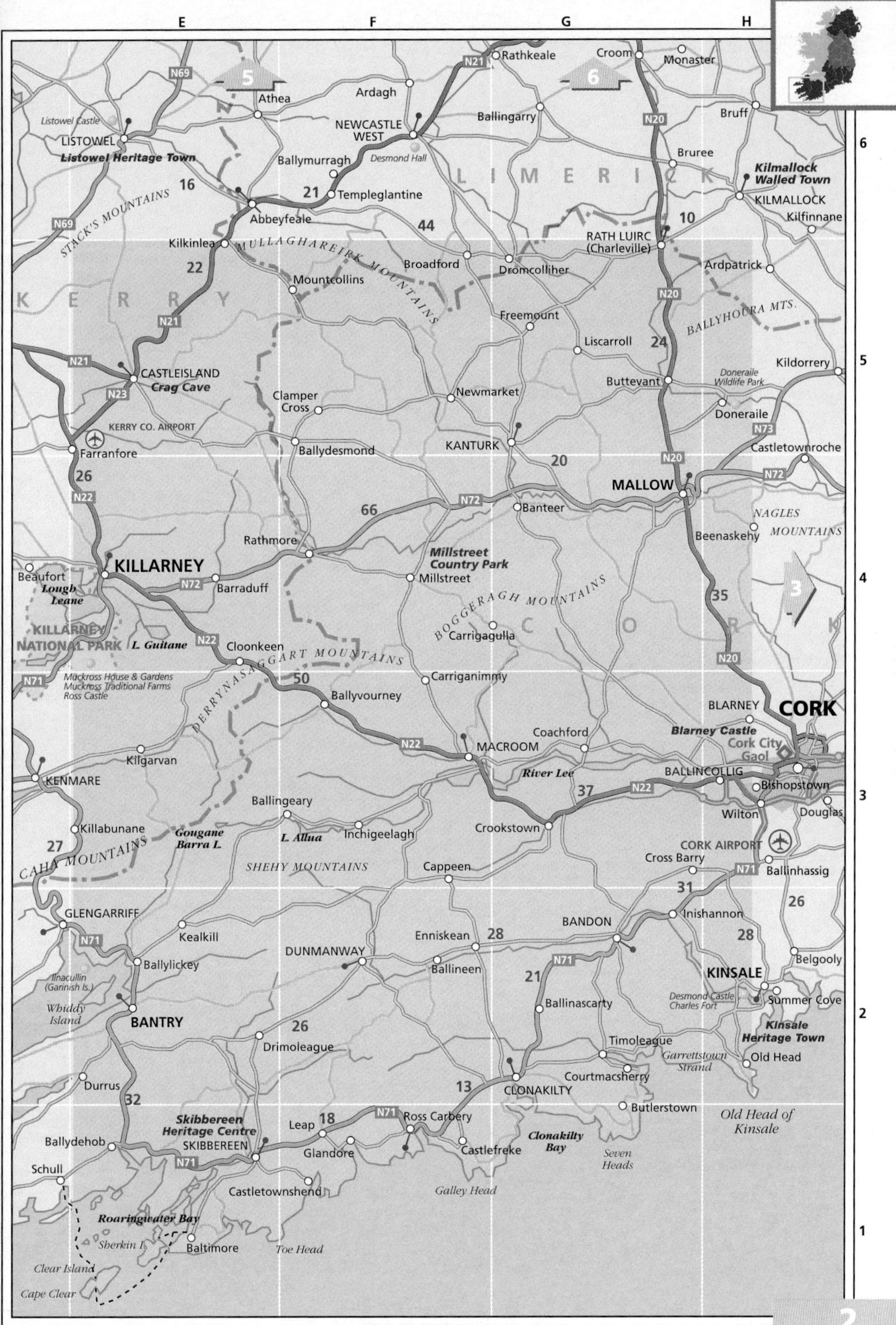
E
F
G
H
6
5
4
3
2
1
5
6
3
2
N69
N21
N20
N22
N23
N71
N72
N73
Athea
Ardagh
Rathkeale
Croom
Monaster
Ballingarry
Bruff
Listowel Castle
LISTOWEL
Listowel Heritage Town
NEWCASTLE WEST
Desmond Hall
Ballymurragh
Bruree
Kilmallock Walled Town
KILMALLOCK
Kilfinnane
16
21
Templeglantine
LIMERICK
STACK'S MOUNTAINS
Abbeyfeale
44
10
RATH LUIRC (Charleville)
Kilkinlea
MULLAGHAREIRK MOUNTAINS
22
Broadford
Dromcolliher
Ardpatrick
Mountcollins
KERRY
BALLYHOURA MTS.
Freemount
Liscarroll
24
Kildorrery
CASTLEISLAND
Crag Cave
Buttevant
Doneraile Wildlife Park
Clamper Cross
Newmarket
Doneraile
KERRY CO. AIRPORT
Farranfore
Ballydesmond
KANTURK
Castletownroche
26
20
MALLOW
66
Banteer
NAGLES MOUNTAINS
Beenaskehy
Rathmore
Millstreet Country Park
Beaufort
KILLARNEY
Barraduff
Millstreet
Lough Leane
35
BOGGERAGH MOUNTAINS
CORK
KILLARNEY NATIONAL PARK
L. Guitane
Cloonkeen
Carrigagulla
DERRYNASAGGART MOUNTAINS
Muckross House & Gardens
Muckross Traditional Farms
Ross Castle
50
Carriganimmy
Ballyvourney
BLARNEY
CORK
Blarney Castle
Coachford
Cork City Gaol
Kilgarvan
MACROOM
KENMARE
River Lee
BALLINCOLLIG
37
Bishopstown
Ballingeary
Wilton
Douglas
Killabunane
Gougane Barra L.
L. Allua
Inchigeelagh
Crookstown
27
CAHA MOUNTAINS
CORK AIRPORT
SHEHY MOUNTAINS
Cappeen
Cross Barry
Ballinhassig
31
26
GLENGARRIFF
Inishannon
BANDON
28
Kealkill
Enniskean
28
DUNMANWAY
Ballylickey
Ballineen
Belgooly
21
KINSALE
Ilnacullin (Garinish Is.)
Desmond Castle
Charles Fort
Summer Cove
Whiddy Island
Ballinascarty
BANTRY
26
Kinsale Heritage Town
Timoleague
Drimoleague
Garrettstown Strand
Old Head
Courtmacsherry
Durrus
13
CLONAKILTY
32
Butlerstown
Old Head of Kinsale
Skibbereen Heritage Centre
Leap
18
Ross Carbery
Clonakilty Bay
Ballydehob
SKIBBEREEN
Glandore
Castlefreke
Seven Heads
Schull
Castletownshend
Galley Head
Roaringwater Bay
Sherkin I.
Baltimore
Toe Head
Clear Island
Cape Clear

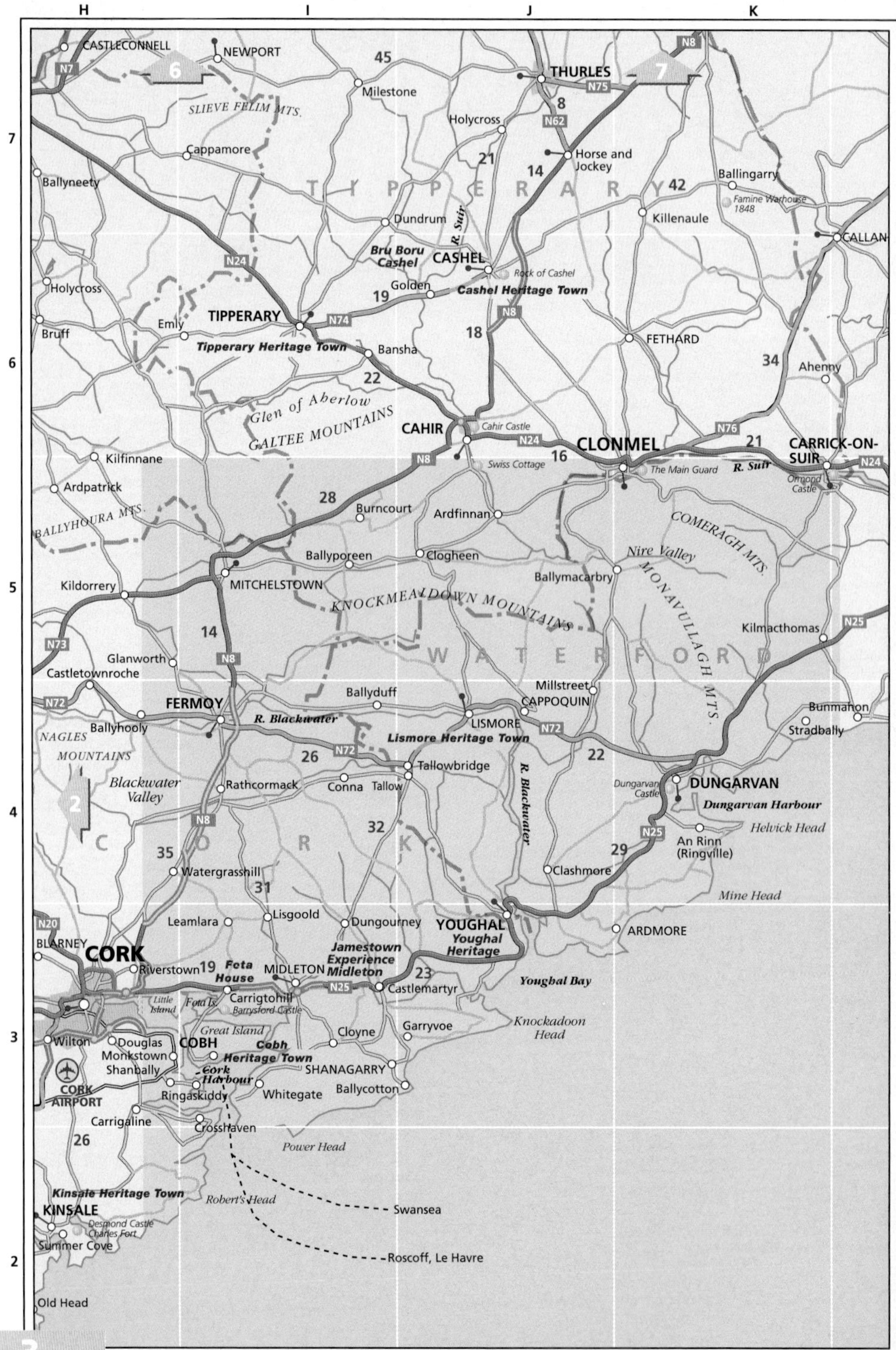
H
I
J
K
7
6
5
4
3
2
CASTLECONNELL
NEWPORT
N7
6
45
THURLES
7
N8
N75
Milestone
SLIEVE FELIM MTS.
8
Holycross
N62
Cappamore
21
Horse and
Jockey
14
Ballyneety
TIPPERARY
42
Ballingarry
Famine Warhouse 1848
Killenaule
Dundrum
R. Suir
CALLAN
Bru Boru
Cashel
CASHEL
N24
Rock of Cashel
Golden
Holycross
19
Cashel Heritage Town
TIPPERARY
N74
Emly
N8
Bruff
18
Tipperary Heritage Town
FETHARD
Bansha
34
Ahenny
22
Glen of Aherlow
GALTEE MOUNTAINS
CAHIR
Cahir Castle
N76
N24
CLONMEL
21
CARRICK-ON-SUIR
Kilfinnane
N8
16
Swiss Cottage
The Main Guard
R. Suir
N24
Ormond Castle
Ardpatrick
28
Burncourt
Ardfinnan
COMERAGH MTS.
BALLYHOURA MTS.
Ballyporeen
Clogheen
Nire Valley
Ballymacarbry
MONAVULLAGH MTS.
Kildorrery
MITCHELSTOWN
KNOCKMEALDOWN MOUNTAINS
14
Kilmacthomas
N25
N73
W A T E R F O R D
Glanworth
N8
Castletownroche
Millstreet
Ballyduff
CAPPOQUIN
N72
FERMOY
Bunmahon
R. Blackwater
LISMORE
Stradbally
Ballyhooly
N72
NAGLES
Lismore Heritage Town
22
MOUNTAINS
26
N72
Tallowbridge
R. Blackwater
2
Blackwater
Valley
Rathcormack
Conna
Tallow
DUNGARVAN
Dungarvan Castle
Dungarvan Harbour
Helvick Head
N8
32
N25
An Rinn
(Ringville)
C O R K
35
29
Watergrasshill
Clashmore
31
Mine Head
N20
Leamlara
Lisgoold
Dungourney
YOUGHAL
ARDMORE
BLARNEY
Youghal
Heritage
Jamestown
Experience
Midleton
CORK
Riverstown
19
Fota
House
MIDLETON
23
Youghal Bay
N25
Castlemartyr
Little Island
Fota Is.
Carrigtohill
Barrysford Castle
Knockadoon
Head
Great Island
Garryvoe
Wilton
Douglas
COBH
Cloyne
Monkstown
Cobh
Heritage Town
Shanbally
Cork
Harbour
SHANAGARRY
CORK
AIRPORT
Ringaskiddy
Whitegate
Ballycotton
Carrigaline
Crosshaven
26
Power Head
Kinsale Heritage Town
Robert's Head
KINSALE
Swansea
Desmond Castle
Charles Fort
Summer Cove
Roscoff, Le Havre
Old Head
3

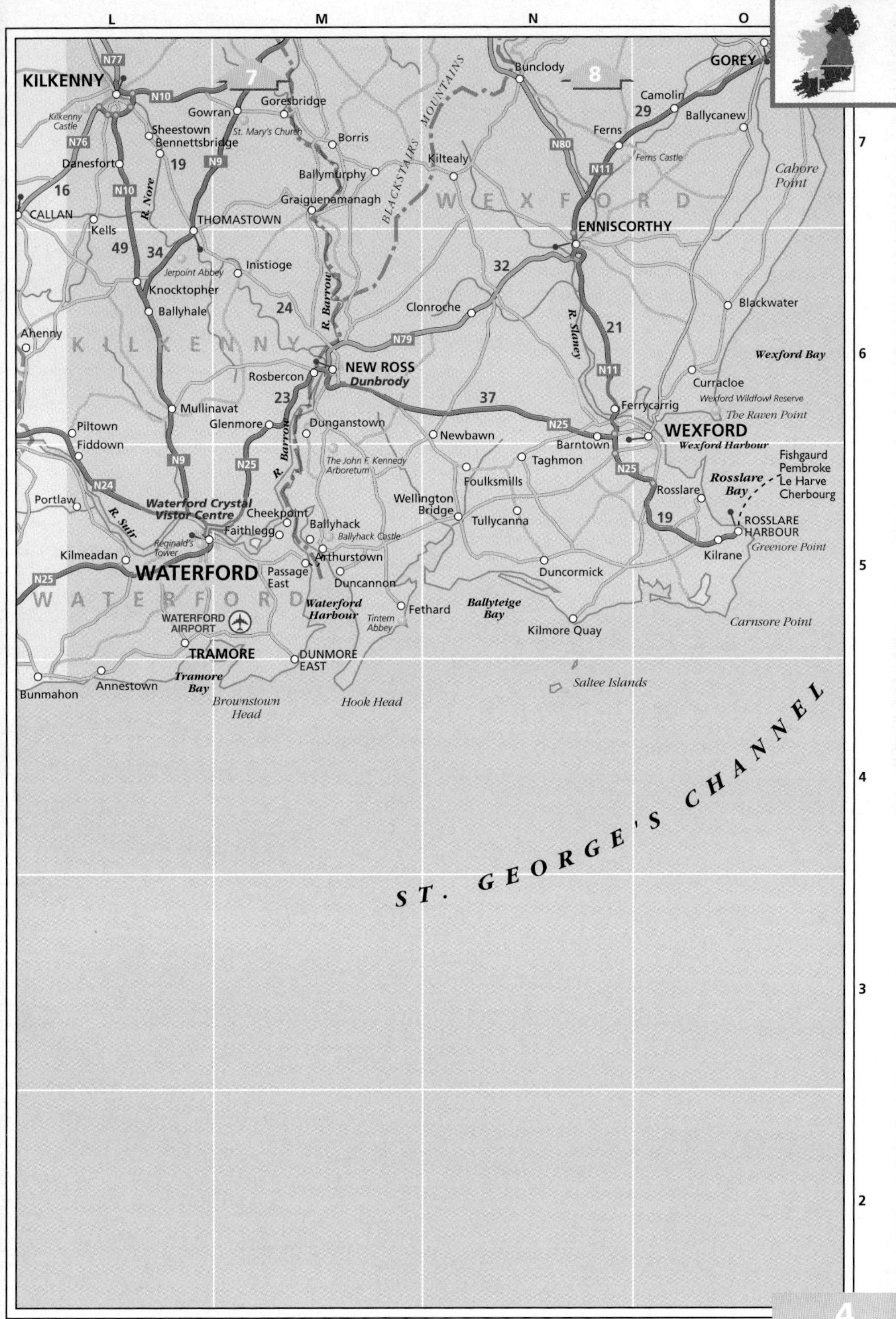

L
M
N
O
7
6
5
4
3
2
KILKENNY
Kilkenny Castle
Gowran
Goresbridge
Sheestown
Bennettsbridge
St. Mary's Church
Borris
Danesfort
Ballymurphy
Kiltealy
CALLAN
Kells
Graiguenamanagh
THOMASTOWN
Jerpoint Abbey
Inistioge
Knocktopher
Ballyhale
Ahenny
K I L K E N N Y
BLACKSTAIRS MOUNTAINS
R. Nore
R. Barrow
Bunclody
GOREY
Camolin
Ballycanew
Ferns
Ferns Castle
Cahore Point
W E X F O R D
ENNISCORTHY
Clonroche
R. Slaney
Blackwater
NEW ROSS
Dunbrody
Rosbercon
Wexford Bay
Curracloe
Wexford Wildfowl Reserve
The Raven Point
Ferrycarrig
WEXFORD
Wexford Harbour
Mullinavat
Glenmore
Dunganstown
Newbawn
Barntown
Taghmon
Piltown
Fiddown
The John F. Kennedy Arboretum
Foulksmills
Fishgaurd
Pembroke
Le Harve
Cherbourg
Rosslare
Rosslare Bay
Portlaw
R. Suir
Waterford Crystal Vistor Centre
Cheekpoint
Wellington Bridge
Tullycanna
ROSSLARE HARBOUR
Faithlegg
Ballyhack
Ballyhack Castle
Kilrane
Greenore Point
Kilmeadan
Reginald's Tower
Arthurstown
WATERFORD
Passage East
Duncannon
Duncormick
W A T E R F O R D
Waterford Harbour
Fethard
Ballyteige Bay
Tintern Abbey
Carnsore Point
Kilmore Quay
WATERFORD AIRPORT
TRAMORE
DUNMORE EAST
Saltee Islands
Bunmahon
Annestown
Tramore Bay
Brownstown Head
Hook Head
ST. GEORGE'S CHANNEL
N77
N10
N76
N9
N80
N11
N79
N25
N24
7
8
19
16
49
34
24
29
32
21
23
37
19
4

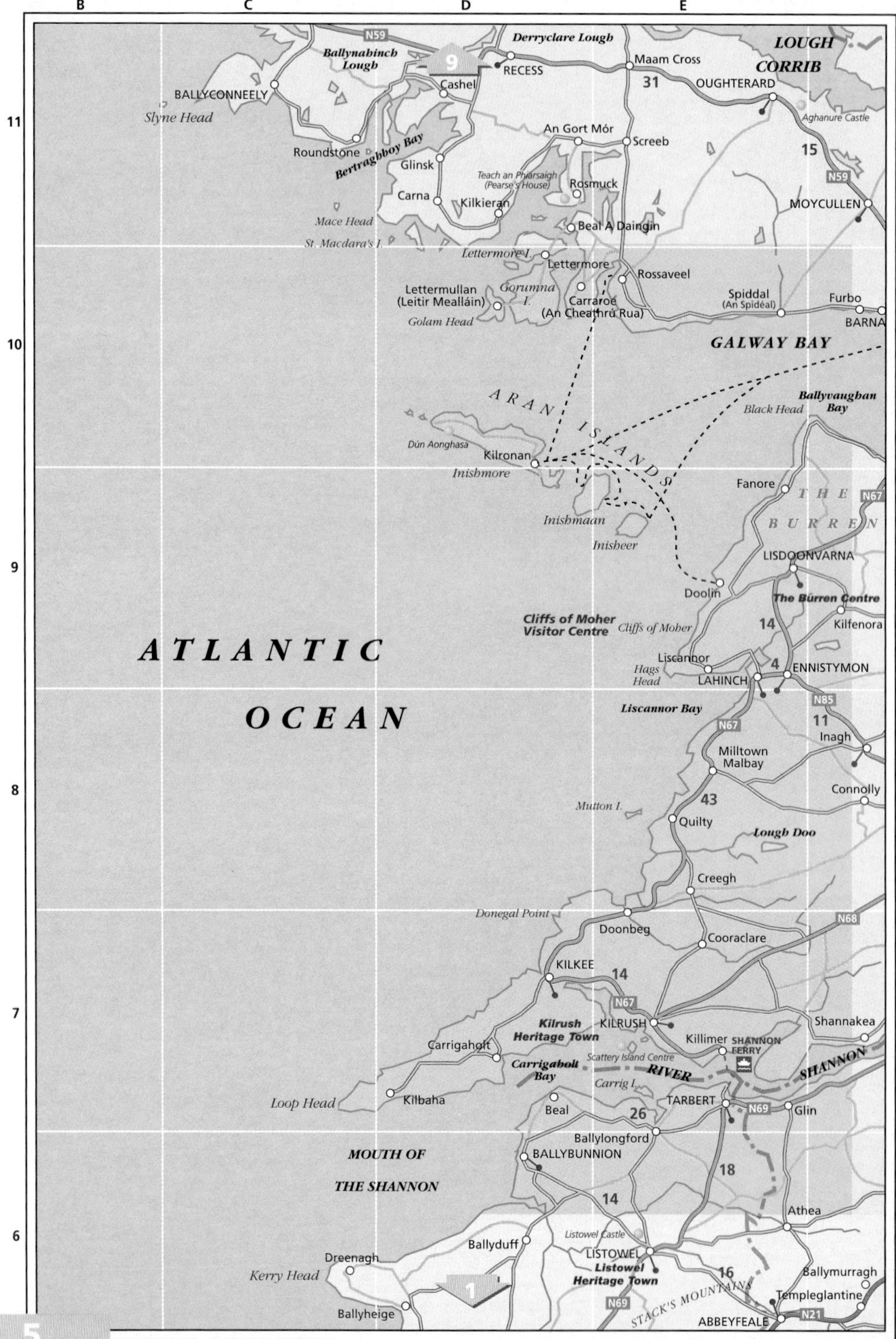
B
C
D
E
11
10
9
8
7
6
5
9
1
N59
Derryclare Lough
LOUGH
CORRIB
Ballynahinch
Lough
RECESS
Maam Cross
Cashel
31
OUGHTERARD
BALLYCONNEELY
Slyne Head
Aghanure Castle
An Gort Mór
Screeb
Roundstone
Bertragbboy Bay
15
Glinsk
Teach an Phiarsaigh
(Pearse's House)
Rosmuck
N59
Carna
Kilkieran
MOYCULLEN
Mace Head
Beal A Daingin
St. Macdara's I.
Lettermore I.
Lettermore
Rossaveel
Lettermullan
(Leitir Mealláin)
Gorumna
I.
Carraroe
(An Cheathrú Rua)
Spiddal
(An Spidéal)
Furbo
BARNA
Golam Head
GALWAY BAY
ARAN ISLANDS
Ballyvaughan
Bay
Black Head
Dún Aonghasa
Kilronan
Inishmore
Fanore
THE
BURREN
N67
Inishmaan
Inisheer
LISDOONVARNA
Doolin
The Burren Centre
Cliffs of Moher
Visitor Centre
Cliffs of Moher
14
Kilfenora
ATLANTIC
OCEAN
Liscannor
Hags
Head
4
ENNISTYMON
LAHINCH
N85
Liscannor Bay
11
N67
Inagh
Milltown
Malbay
Connolly
43
Mutton I.
Quilty
Lough Doo
Creegh
Donegal Point
N68
Doonbeg
Cooraclare
KILKEE
14
N67
Kilrush
Heritage Town
KILRUSH
Shannakea
Killimer
SHANNON
FERRY
Carrigaholt
Scattery Island Centre
Carrigaholt
Bay
RIVER
SHANNON
Carrig I.
Loop Head
Kilbaha
Beal
TARBERT
N69
Glin
26
Ballylongford
MOUTH OF
THE SHANNON
BALLYBUNNION
18
14
Athea
Listowel Castle
Ballyduff
LISTOWEL
Listowel
Heritage Town
Dreenagh
16
Ballymurragh
Kerry Head
STACK'S MOUNTAINS
Templeglantine
N69
N21
Ballyheige
ABBEYFEALE

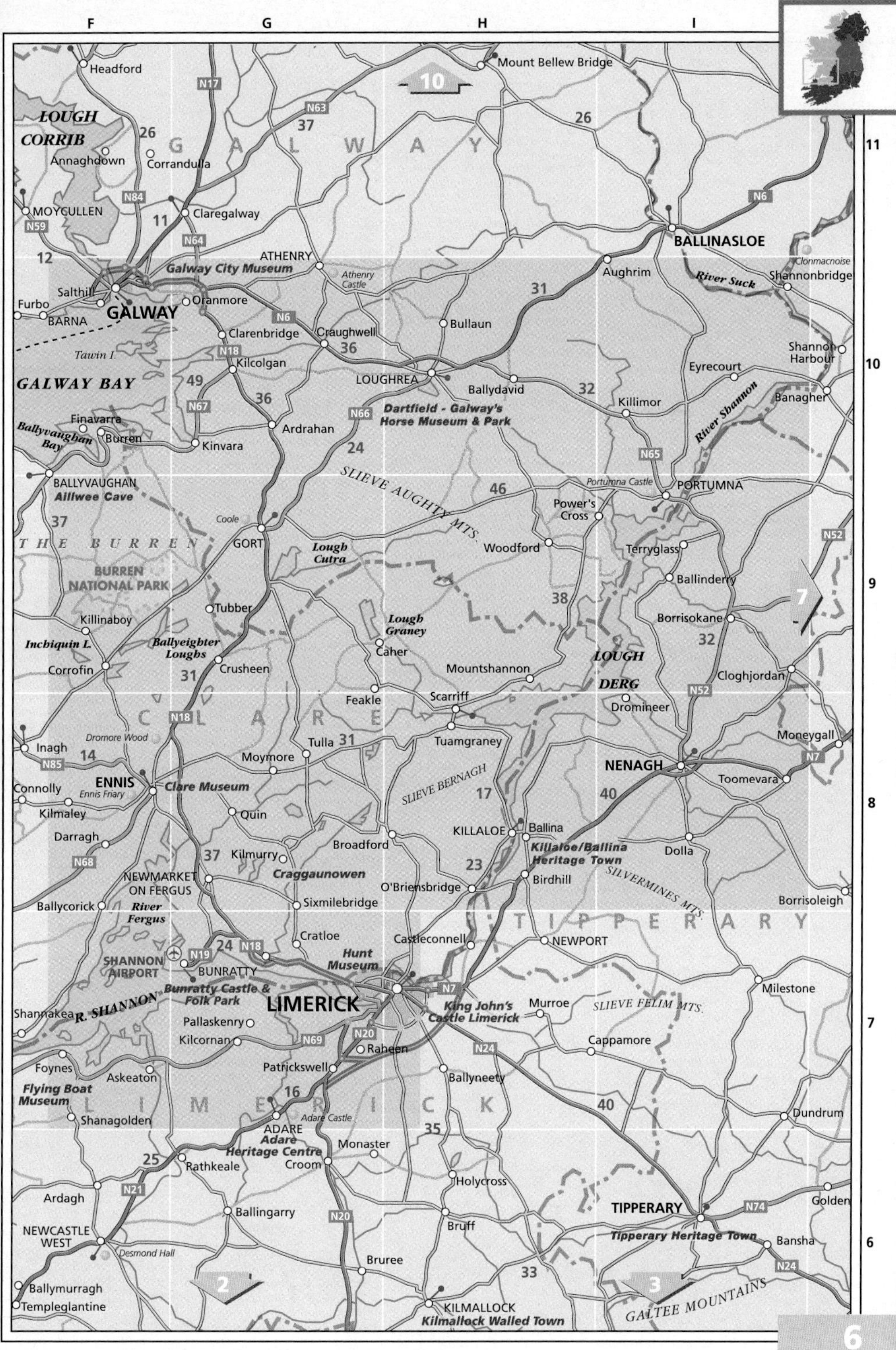

F
G
H
I
Headford
Mount Bellew Bridge
10
LOUGH CORRIB
Annaghdown
Corrandulla
GALWAY
MOYCULLEN
Claregalway
BALLINASLOE
ATHENRY
Galway City Museum
Athenry Castle
Aughrim
Clonmacnoise
River Suck
Shannonbridge
Salthill
Furbo
BARNA
GALWAY
Oranmore
Clarenbridge
Craughwell
Bullaun
Tawin I.
Kilcolgan
LOUGHREA
Ballydavid
Eyrecourt
Shannon Harbour
GALWAY BAY
Dartfield - Galway's Horse Museum & Park
Killimor
Banagher
River Shannon
Finavarra
Ballyvaughan Bay
Burren
Kinvara
Ardrahan
BALLYVAUGHAN
Aillwee Cave
SLIEVE AUGHTY MTS.
Portumna Castle
PORTUMNA
Power's Cross
Coole
GORT
THE BURREN
Woodford
Terryglass
Lough Cutra
BURREN NATIONAL PARK
Ballinderry
Tubber
Killinaboy
Lough Graney
Borrisokane
Inchiquin L.
Ballyeighter Loughs
Caher
LOUGH DERG
Corrofin
Crusheen
Mountshannon
Cloghjordan
Feakle
Scarriff
Dromineer
CLARE
Inagh
Dromore Wood
Tulla
Tuamgraney
Moneygall
Moymore
ENNIS
Ennis Friary
Clare Museum
SLIEVE BERNAGH
NENAGH
Toomevara
Connolly
Kilmaley
Quin
KILLALOE
Ballina
Darragh
Broadford
Killaloe/Ballina Heritage Town
Dolla
Kilmurry
Craggaunowen
NEWMARKET ON FERGUS
Birdhill
SILVERMINES MTS.
O'Briensbridge
Borrisoleigh
Ballycorick
River Fergus
Sixmilebridge
TIPPERARY
Cratloe
Castleconnell
NEWPORT
SHANNON AIRPORT
Hunt Museum
BUNRATTY
Milestone
Bunratty Castle & Folk Park
LIMERICK
King John's Castle Limerick
Murroe
SLIEVE FELIM MTS.
Shannakea
R. SHANNON
Pallaskenry
Kilcornan
Raheen
Cappamore
Foynes
Askeaton
Patrickswell
Ballyneety
Flying Boat Museum
LIMERICK
Shanagolden
ADARE
Adare Castle
Dundrum
Adare Heritage Centre
Monaster
Rathkeale
Croom
Holycross
Ardagh
Golden
Ballingarry
TIPPERARY
NEWCASTLE WEST
Bruff
Tipperary Heritage Town
Bansha
Desmond Hall
Bruree
Ballymurragh
Templeglantine
KILMALLOCK
Kilmallock Walled Town
GALTEE MOUNTAINS
2
3
7
6
11
10
9
8
7
6

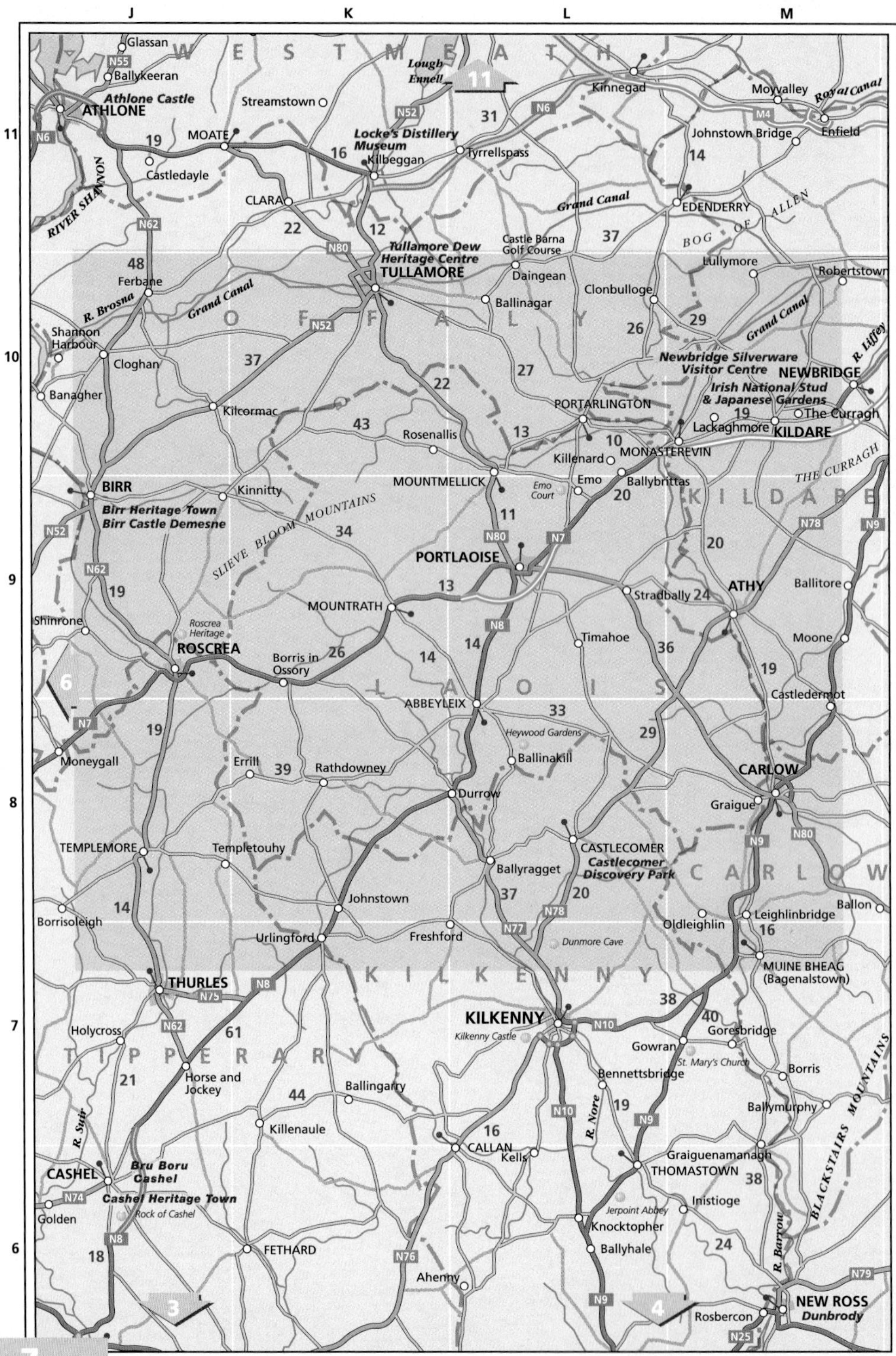
J
K
L
M
11
10
9
8
7
6
W E S T M E A T H
O F F A L Y
L A O I S
K I L K E N N Y
K I L D A R E
C A R L O W
T I P P E R A R Y
Glassan
Ballykeeran
Athlone Castle
ATHLONE
Lough Ennell
11
Streamstown
Kinnegad
Moyvalley
Royal Canal
Enfield
Johnstown Bridge
MOATE
Castledayle
Locke's Distillery Museum
Kilbeggan
Tyrrellspass
RIVER SHANNON
CLARA
Grand Canal
EDENDERRY
BOG OF ALLEN
Tullamore Dew Heritage Centre
TULLAMORE
Castle Barna Golf Course
Daingean
Lullymore
Robertstown
Ferbane
R. Brosna
Ballinagar
Clonbulloge
Shannon Harbour
Cloghan
Newbridge Silverware Visitor Centre
NEWBRIDGE
R. Liffey
Banagher
Irish National Stud & Japanese Gardens
Kilcormac
PORTARLINGTON
Lackaghmore
KILDARE
The Curragh
Rosenallis
Killenard
MONASTEREVIN
THE CURRAGH
MOUNTMELLICK
Emo
Emo Court
Ballybrittas
BIRR
Birr Heritage Town
Birr Castle Demesne
Kinnitty
SLIEVE BLOOM MOUNTAINS
PORTLAOISE
Stradbally
ATHY
Ballitore
MOUNTRATH
Shinrone
Roscrea Heritage
ROSCREA
Timahoe
Moone
Borris in Ossory
Castledermot
ABBEYLEIX
Heywood Gardens
Moneygall
Ballinakill
CARLOW
Erril
Rathdowney
Durrow
Graigue
TEMPLEMORE
Templetouhy
CASTLECOMER
Castlecomer Discovery Park
Ballyragget
Johnstown
Ballon
Borrisoleigh
Oldleighlin
Leighlinbridge
Urlingford
Freshford
Dunmore Cave
MUINE BHEAG (Bagenalstown)
THURLES
KILKENNY
Kilkenny Castle
Holycross
Goresbridge
Gowran
St. Mary's Church
Horse and Jockey
Bennettsbridge
Borris
Ballingarry
Ballymurphy
Killenaule
R. Nore
BLACKSTAIRS MOUNTAINS
R. Suir
Bru Boru Cashel
CALLAN
Kells
Graiguenamanagh
CASHEL
THOMASTOWN
Cashel Heritage Town
Rock of Cashel
Jerpoint Abbey
Inistioge
Golden
Knocktopher
R. Barrow
FETHARD
Ballyhale
Ahenny
NEW ROSS
Dunbrody
Rosbercon
3
4
6
N55
N6
N52
N62
N80
M4
N78
N9
N7
N8
N77
N78
N75
N10
N74
N76
N79
N25
7

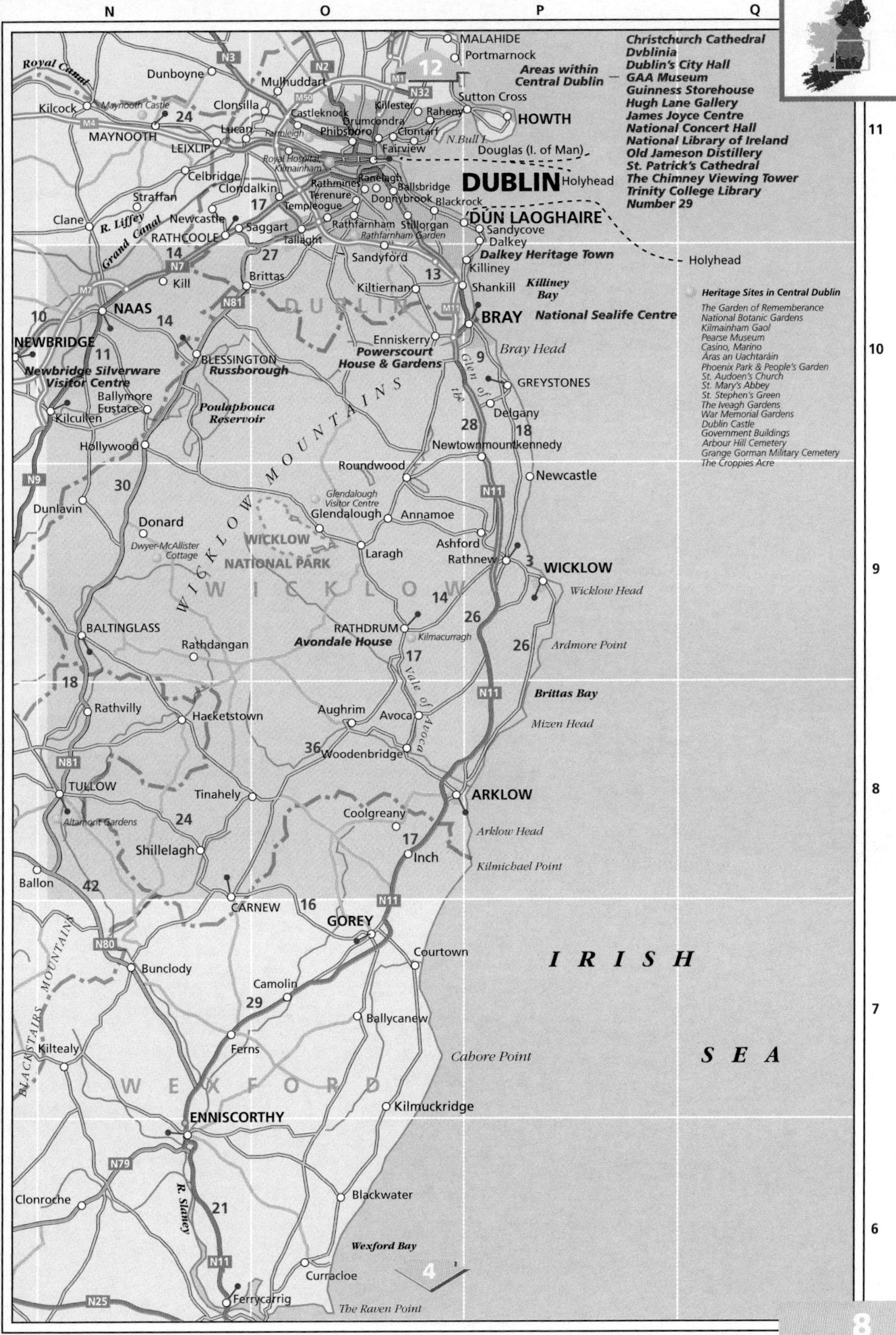
N
O
P
Q
11
10
9
8
7
6
8
Christchurch Cathedral
Dvblinia
Dublin's City Hall
GAA Museum
Guinness Storehouse
Hugh Lane Gallery
James Joyce Centre
National Concert Hall
National Library of Ireland
Old Jameson Distillery
St. Patrick's Cathedral
The Chimney Viewing Tower
Trinity College Library
Number 29
Areas within Central Dublin
12
Heritage Sites in Central Dublin
The Garden of Rememberance
National Botanic Gardens
Kilmainham Gaol
Pearse Museum
Casino, Marino
Áras an Uachtaráin
Phoenix Park & People's Garden
St. Audoen's Church
St. Mary's Abbey
St. Stephen's Green
The Iveagh Gardens
War Memorial Gardens
Dublin Castle
Government Buildings
Arbour Hill Cemetery
Grange Gorman Military Cemetery
The Croppies Acre
MALAHIDE
Portmarnock
Sutton Cross
HOWTH
N.Bull I.
Douglas (I. of Man)
DUBLIN
Holyhead
Holyhead
DÚN LAOGHAIRE
Sandycove
Dalkey
Dalkey Heritage Town
Killiney
Killiney Bay
Shankill
BRAY
National Sealife Centre
Bray Head
GREYSTONES
Delgany
Royal Canal
Dunboyne
Mulhuddart
Clonsilla
Kilcock
Maynooth Castle
MAYNOOTH
LEIXLIP
Lucan
Castleknock
Farmleigh
Phibsboro
Drumcondra
Killester
Raheny
Clontarf
Fairview
Royal Hospital Kilmainham
Celbridge
Clondalkin
Rathmines
Ranelagh
Ballsbridge
Terenure
Templeogue
Donnybrook
Blackrock
Straffan
Clane
R. Liffey
Grand Canal
Newcastle
Saggart
RATHCOOLE
Tallaght
Rathfarnham
Rathfarnham Garden
Stillorgan
Sandyford
Brittas
Kill
Kiltiernan
NAAS
NEWBRIDGE
Newbridge Silverware Visitor Centre
BLESSINGTON
Russborough
Enniskerry
Powerscourt House & Gardens
the Glen of
Ballymore Eustace
Kilcullen
Poulaphouca Reservoir
Hollywood
WICKLOW MOUNTAINS
DUBLIN
Newtownmountkennedy
Roundwood
Newcastle
Dunlavin
Glendalough Visitor Centre
Glendalough
Annamoe
Donard
Dwyer-McAllister Cottage
WICKLOW NATIONAL PARK
Laragh
Ashford
Rathnew
WICKLOW
Wicklow Head
WICKLOW
BALTINGLASS
Rathdangan
RATHDRUM
Avondale House
Kilmacurragh
Ardmore Point
Brittas Bay
Mizen Head
Vale of Avoca
Rathvilly
Hacketstown
Aughrim
Avoca
Woodenbridge
TULLOW
Tinahely
ARKLOW
Arklow Head
Coolgreany
Altamont Gardens
Shillelagh
Inch
Kilmichael Point
Ballon
CARNEW
GOREY
Courtown
BLACKSTAIRS MOUNTAINS
Bunclody
Camolin
IRISH SEA
Ballycanew
Kiltealy
Ferns
Cabore Point
WEXFORD
Kilmuckridge
ENNISCORTHY
Clonroche
R. Slaney
Blackwater
Wexford Bay
Curracloe
Ferrycarrig
The Raven Point
N3
N2
M1
N32
M50
M4
N7
M7
N81
M11
N9
N11
N80
N79
N25
4
10
11
13
14
17
18
21
24
26
27
28
29
30
36
42
3
9
16

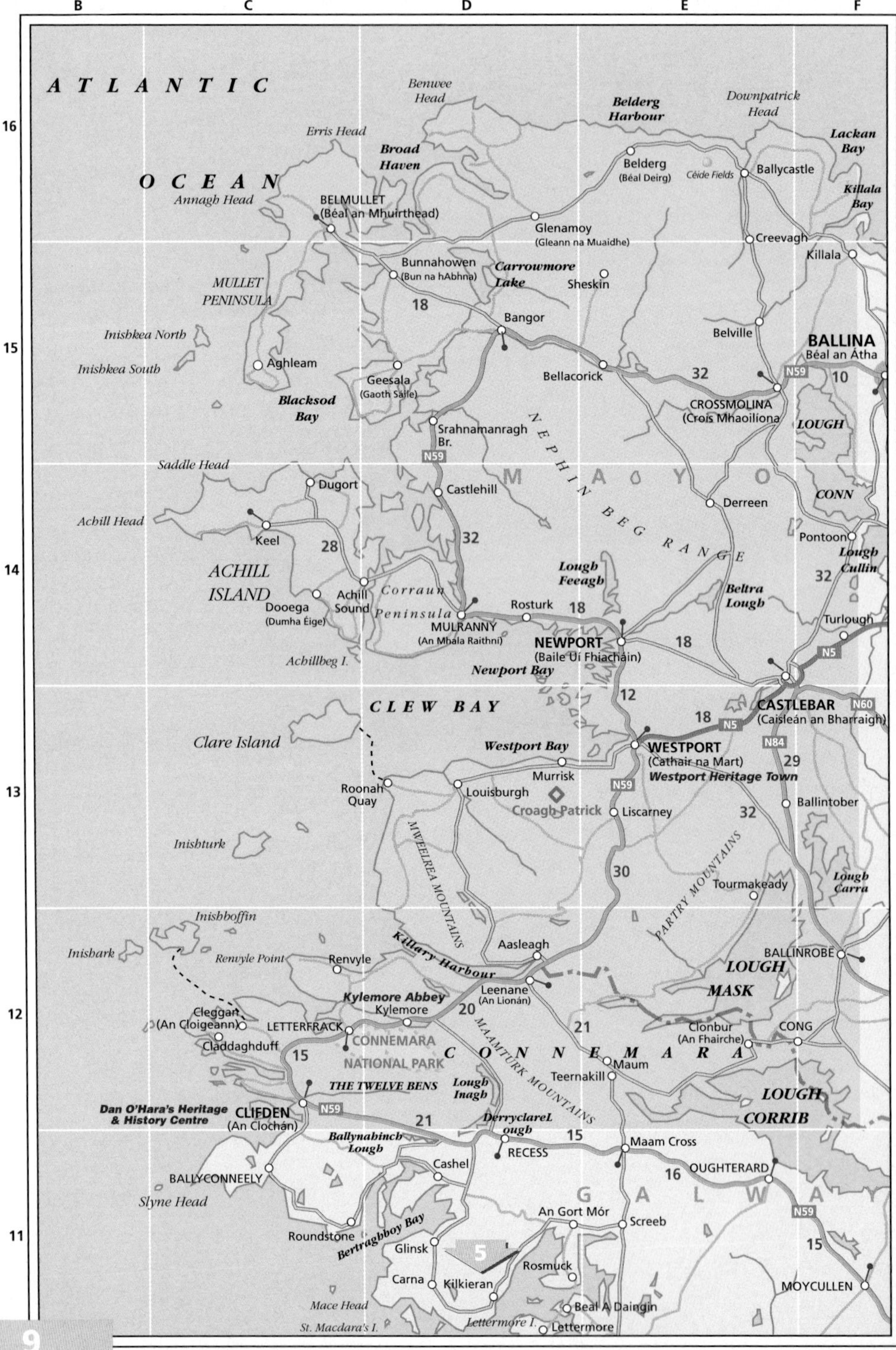

B
C
D
E
F
16
15
14
13
12
11
ATLANTIC
OCEAN
Benwee Head
Belderg Harbour
Downpatrick Head
Erris Head
Broad Haven
Lackan Bay
Belderg
(Béal Deirg)
Céide Fields
Ballycastle
Killala Bay
Annagh Head
BELMULLET
(Béal an Mhuirthead)
Glenamoy
(Gleann na Muaidhe)
Creevagh
Killala
Bunnahowen
(Bun na hAbhna)
Carrowmore Lake
Sheskin
MULLET PENINSULA
18
Bangor
Belville
BALLINA
Béal an Átha
Inishkea North
Inishkea South
Aghleam
Geesala
(Gaoth Sáile)
Bellacorick
32
N59
10
Blacksod Bay
Srahnamanragh Br.
CROSSMOLINA
(Crois Mhaoilíona)
LOUGH
NEPHIN BEG RANGE
Saddle Head
Dugort
MAYO
Castlehill
Derreen
CONN
Achill Head
Keel
28
32
Pontoon
Lough Cullin
ACHILL ISLAND
Lough Feeagh
Beltra Lough
Achill Sound
Corraun Peninsula
Dooega
(Dumha Éige)
Rosturk
18
Turlough
MULRANNY
(An Mhala Raithní)
NEWPORT
(Baile Uí Fhiacháin)
18
N5
Achillbeg I.
Newport Bay
12
CLEW BAY
CASTLEBAR
(Caisleán an Bharraigh)
N60
18
N5
Clare Island
Westport Bay
WESTPORT
(Cathair na Mart)
Westport Heritage Town
N84
29
Murrisk
Roonah Quay
Louisburgh
Croagh Patrick
N59
Liscarney
Ballintober
32
MWEELREA MOUNTAINS
PARTRY MOUNTAINS
Inishturk
30
Tourmakeady
Lough Carra
Inishbofin
Inishark
Renvyle Point
Renvyle
Killary Harbour
Aasleagh
BALLINROBE
LOUGH MASK
Kylemore Abbey
Leenane
(An Lionán)
Kylemore
20
MAAMTURK MOUNTAINS
Cleggan
(An Cloigeann)
LETTERFRACK
21
Clonbur
(An Fhairche)
CONG
Claddaghduff
CONNEMARA NATIONAL PARK
15
CONNEMARA
Maum
Teernakill
THE TWELVE BENS
Lough Inagh
LOUGH CORRIB
Dan O'Hara's Heritage & History Centre
CLIFDEN
(An Clochán)
N59
21
DerryclareLough
15
Ballynahinch Lough
RECESS
Maam Cross
Cashel
16
OUGHTERARD
BALLYCONNEELY
GALWAY
Slyne Head
An Gort Mór
Screeb
N59
Roundstone
Bertragbboy Bay
Glinsk
5
15
Rosmuck
Carna
Kilkieran
MOYCULLEN
Mace Head
Beal A Daingin
St. Macdara's I.
Lettermore I.
Lettermore

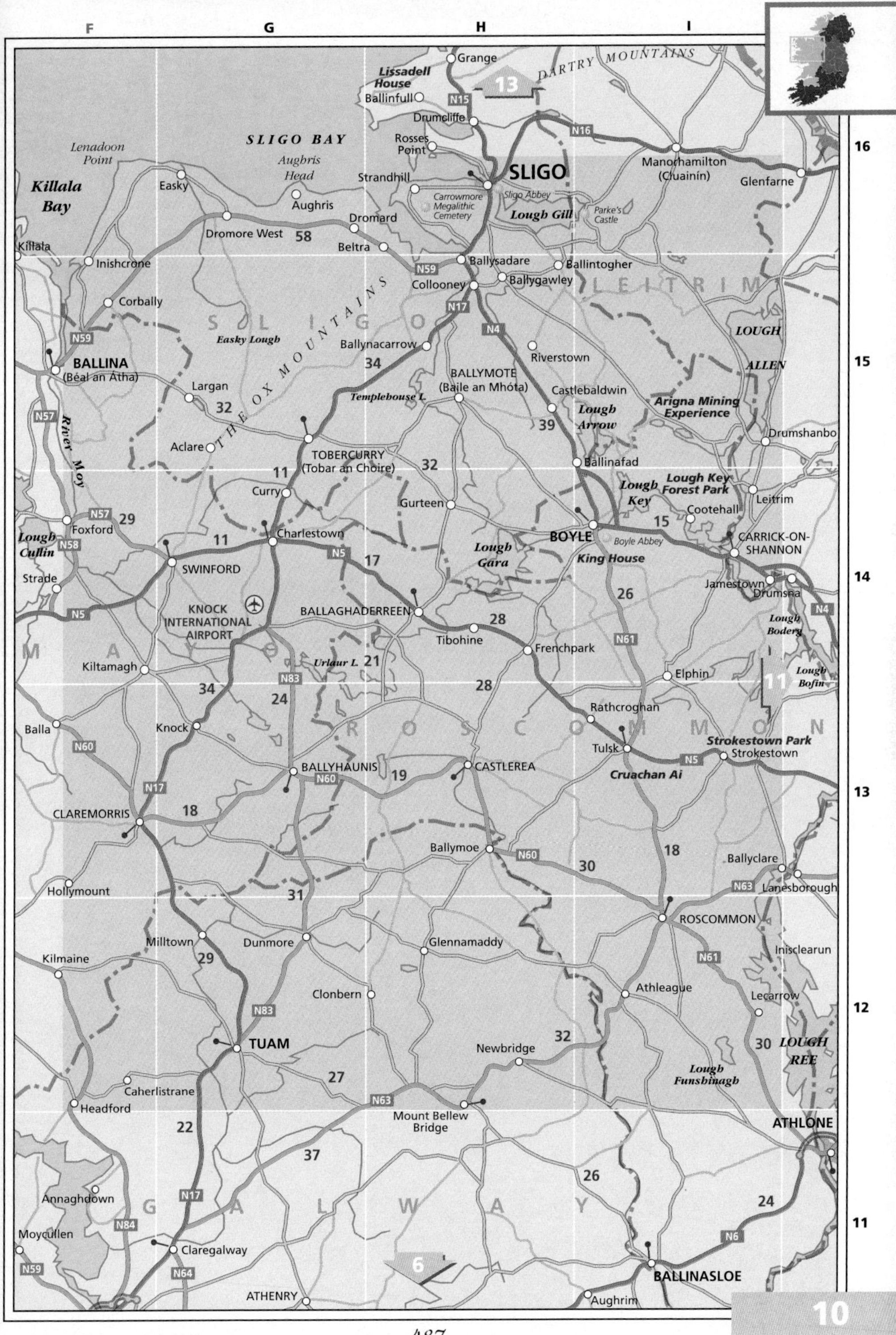
F
G
H
I
16
15
14
13
12
11
SLIGO BAY
Killala Bay
Lenadoon Point
Aughris Head
SLIGO
BALLINA
(Béal an Átha)
TOBERCURRY
(Tobar an Choire)
BALLYMOTE
(Baile an Mhóta)
BOYLE
CARRICK-ON-SHANNON
SWINFORD
KNOCK INTERNATIONAL AIRPORT
BALLAGHADERREEN
BALLYHAUNIS
CASTLEREA
CLAREMORRIS
ROSCOMMON
TUAM
ATHLONE
BALLINASLOE
ATHENRY
Manorhamilton
(Cluainín)
DARTRY MOUNTAINS
THE OX MOUNTAINS
LOUGH ALLEN
LOUGH REE
Lissadell House
Carrowmore Megalithic Cemetery
Sligo Abbey
Lough Gill
Parke's Castle
Lough Arrow
Arigna Mining Experience
Lough Key Forest Park
Lough Key
Boyle Abbey
King House
Lough Gara
Strokestown Park
Cruachan Ai
Easky Lough
Templehouse L.
Urlaur L.
Lough Cullin
River Moy
Lough Boderg
Lough Bofin
Lough Funshinagh
S L I G O
L E I T R I M
M A Y O
R O S C O M M O N
G A L W A Y
13
6
11
10

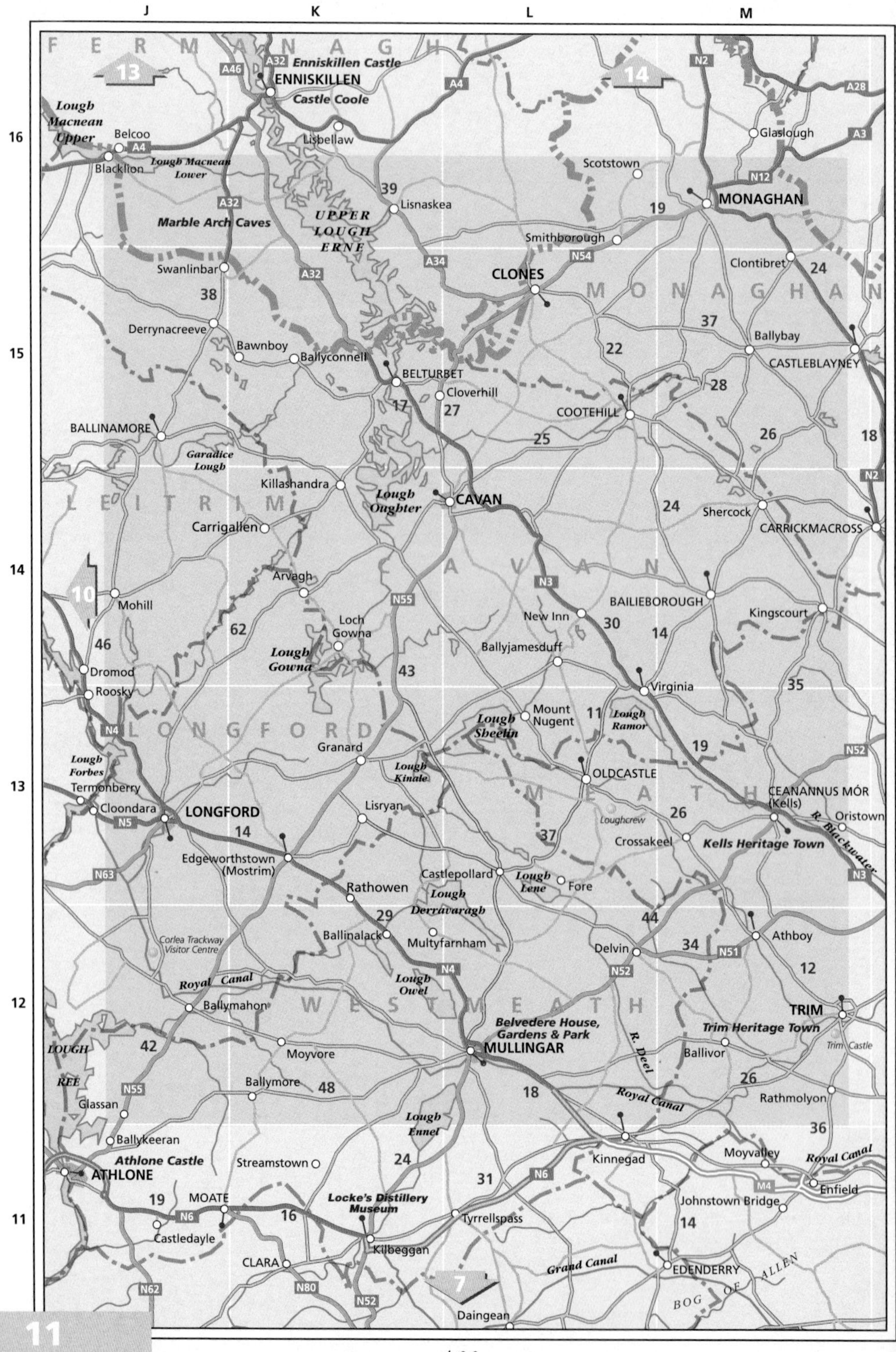

J
K
L
M
16
15
14
13
12
11
FERMANAGH
13
14
A46
A32
Enniskillen Castle
ENNISKILLEN
Castle Coole
A4
N2
A28
Lough Macnean Upper
Belcoo
Blacklion
A4
Lough Macnean Lower
Lisbellaw
Glaslough
A3
Scotstown
N12
MONAGHAN
19
39
Lisnaskea
A32
Marble Arch Caves
UPPER LOUGH ERNE
Smithborough
N54
A34
Swanlinbar
A32
CLONES
Clontibret
24
MONAGHAN
38
Derrynacreeve
37
Bawnboy
Ballyconnell
Ballybay
22
CASTLEBLAYNEY
BELTURBET
Cloverhill
28
17
27
COOTEHILL
BALLINAMORE
25
26
18
Garadice Lough
N2
Killashandra
Lough Oughter
CAVAN
24
Shercock
LEITRIM
Carrigallen
CARRICKMACROSS
CAVAN
10
Arvagh
N3
BAILIEBOROUGH
Mohill
N55
Kingscourt
New Inn
30
62
Loch Gowna
14
46
Lough Gowna
Ballyjamesduff
Dromod
43
35
Roosky
Virginia
Mount Nugent
11
Lough Ramor
Lough Sheelin
N4
LONGFORD
Granard
19
N52
Lough Forbes
Lough Kinale
OLDCASTLE
Termonberry
MEATH
CEANANNUS MÓR (Kells)
Cloondara
Lisryan
26
Oristown
LONGFORD
Loughcrew
N5
14
R. Blackwater
37
Crossakeel
Kells Heritage Town
Edgeworthstown (Mostrim)
N63
Castlepollard
Lough Lene
Fore
N3
Rathowen
Lough Derravaragh
29
44
Ballinalack
Multyfarnham
Athboy
Corlea Trackway Visitor Centre
Delvin
34
N51
N4
N52
12
Lough Owel
Royal Canal
WESTMEATH
Ballymahon
TRIM
Belvedere House, Gardens & Park
Trim Heritage Town
R. Deel
Trim Castle
LOUGH REE
42
Moyvore
MULLINGAR
Ballivor
Ballymore
48
18
26
N55
Royal Canal
Rathmolyon
Glassan
Lough Ennel
36
Ballykeeran
Kinnegad
Moyvalley
Athlone Castle
Streamstown
24
Royal Canal
ATHLONE
31
N6
M4
Enfield
19
MOATE
Locke's Distillery Museum
N6
16
Johnstown Bridge
Tyrrellspass
14
Castledayle
Kilbeggan
CLARA
Grand Canal
EDENDERRY
7
N80
BOG OF ALLEN
N62
N52
Daingean
11

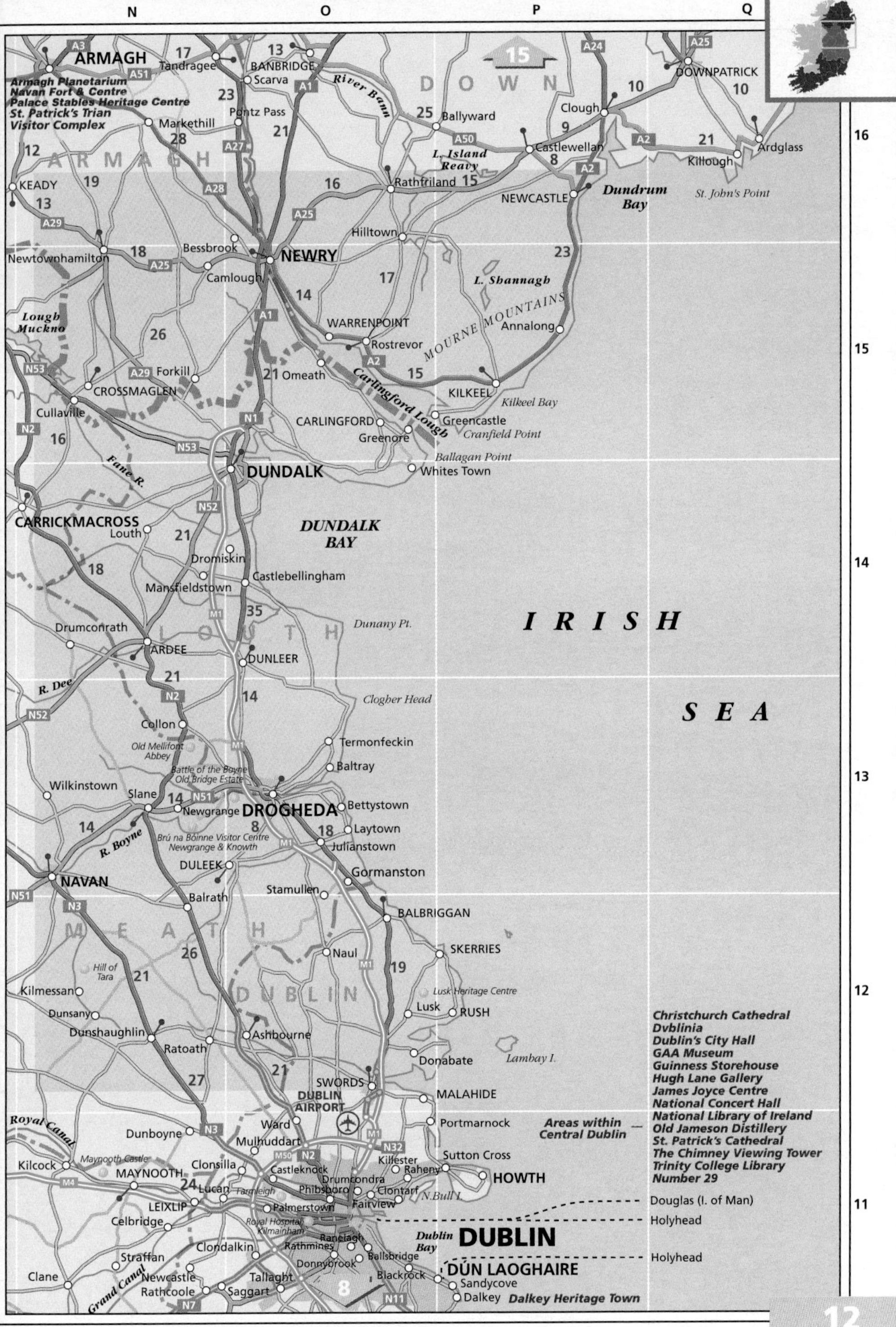

N
O
P
Q
16
15
14
13
12
11
12
15
ARMAGH
Tandragee
BANBRIDGE
Scarva
River Bann
D O W N
DOWNPATRICK
Armagh Planetarium
Navan Fort & Centre
Palace Stables Heritage Centre
St. Patrick's Trian
Visitor Complex
Markethill
Poyntz Pass
Ballyward
Clough
Castlewellan
Ardglass
Killough
A R M A G H
L. Island Reavy
KEADY
Rathfriland
NEWCASTLE
Dundrum Bay
St. John's Point
Hilltown
Newtownhamilton
Bessbrook
NEWRY
Camlough
L. Shannagh
MOURNE MOUNTAINS
Lough Muckno
WARRENPOINT
Rostrevor
Annalong
Forkill
Omeath
Carlingford Lough
CROSSMAGLEN
KILKEEL
Kilkeel Bay
Cullaville
CARLINGFORD
Greencastle
Greenore
Cranfield Point
Ballagan Point
Whites Town
Fane R.
DUNDALK
CARRICKMACROSS
Louth
DUNDALK BAY
Dromiskin
Castlebellingham
Mansfieldstown
L O U T H
Dunany Pt.
I R I S H
S E A
Drumconrath
ARDEE
DUNLEER
R. Dee
Clogher Head
Collon
Old Mellifont Abbey
Termonfeckin
Baltray
Battle of the Boyne Old Bridge Estate
Wilkinstown
Slane
Newgrange
DROGHEDA
Bettystown
Laytown
R. Boyne
Brú na Bóinne Visitor Centre Newgrange & Knowth
Julianstown
DULEEK
Gormanston
NAVAN
Stamullen
Balrath
BALBRIGGAN
M E A T H
SKERRIES
Naul
Hill of Tara
D U B L I N
Lusk Heritage Centre
Kilmessan
Lusk
RUSH
Dunsany
Dunshaughlin
Ashbourne
Ratoath
Donabate
Lambay I.
SWORDS
DUBLIN AIRPORT
MALAHIDE
Royal Canal
Ward
Portmarnock
Dunboyne
Mulhuddart
Areas within Central Dublin
Maynooth Castle
Kilcock
MAYNOOTH
Clonsilla
Castleknock
Killester
Raheny
Sutton Cross
HOWTH
Lucan
Farmleigh
Drumcondra
Phibsboro
Clontarf
N.Bull I.
LEIXLIP
Palmerstown
Fairview
Celbridge
Royal Hospital Kilmainham
Dublin Bay
DUBLIN
Clondalkin
Ranelagh
Rathmines
Ballsbridge
Straffan
Donnybrook
DÚN LAOGHAIRE
Clane
Grand Canal
Newcastle
Tallaght
Blackrock
Sandycove
Rathcoole
Saggart
Dalkey
Dalkey Heritage Town
Christchurch Cathedral
Dvblinia
Dublin's City Hall
GAA Museum
Guinness Storehouse
Hugh Lane Gallery
James Joyce Centre
National Concert Hall
National Library of Ireland
Old Jameson Distillery
St. Patrick's Cathedral
The Chimney Viewing Tower
Trinity College Library
Number 29
Douglas (I. of Man)
Holyhead
Holyhead
8

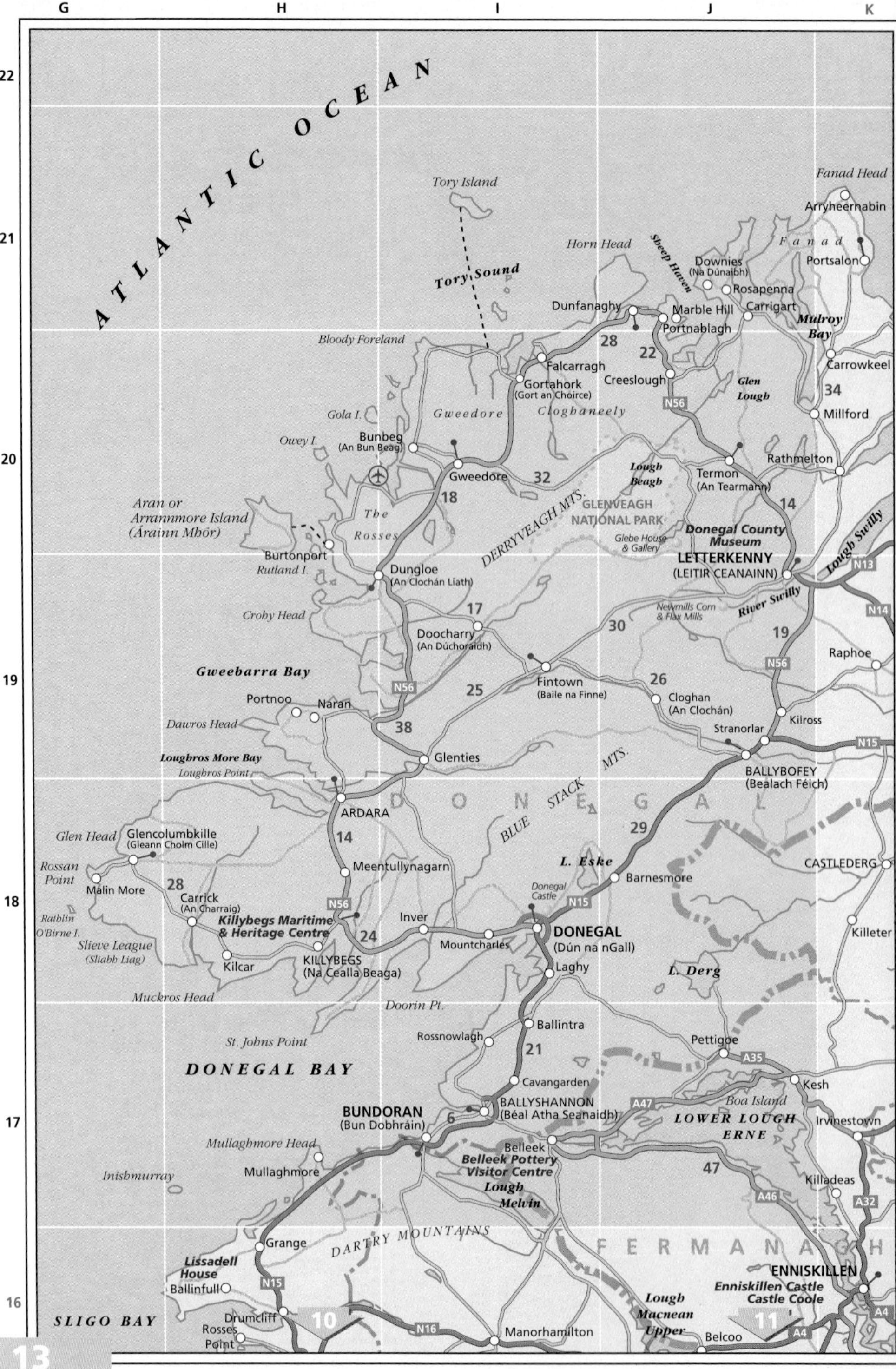
G
H
I
J
K
22
21
20
19
18
17
16
ATLANTIC OCEAN
Tory Island
Tory Sound
Fanad Head
Arryheernabin
Fanad
Portsalon
Horn Head
Sheep Haven
Downies
(Na Dúnaibh)
Rosapenna
Carrigart
Mulroy Bay
Dunfanaghy
Marble Hill
Portnablagh
Bloody Foreland
Falcarragh
Creeslough
Carrowkeel
Gortahork
(Gort an Choirce)
Glen Lough
Gola I.
Gweedore
Cloghaneely
Millford
Owey I.
Bunbeg
(An Bun Beag)
Gweedore
Lough Beagh
Termon
(An Tearmann)
Rathmelton
Aran or
Arrannmore Island
(Árainn Mhór)
The Rosses
DERRYVEAGH MTS.
GLENVEAGH
NATIONAL PARK
Glebe House
& Gallery
Donegal County
Museum
LETTERKENNY
(LEITIR CEANAINN)
Lough Swilly
Burtonport
Rutland I.
Dungloe
(An Clochán Liath)
Croby Head
Doocharry
(An Dúchoraidh)
Newmills Corn
& Flax Mills
River Swilly
Raphoe
Gweebarra Bay
Fintown
(Baile na Finne)
Cloghan
(An Clochán)
Portnoo
Naran
Kilross
Dawros Head
Stranorlar
Glenties
BALLYBOFEY
(Bealach Féich)
Loughbros More Bay
Loughbros Point
BLUE STACK MTS.
DONEGAL
ARDARA
Glen Head
Glencolumbkille
(Gleann Cholm Cille)
Rossan Point
Malin More
Meentullynagarn
L. Eske
Barnesmore
CASTLEDERG
Carrick
(An Charraig)
Donegal Castle
Rathlin O'Birne I.
Killybegs Maritime
& Heritage Centre
Inver
DONEGAL
(Dún na nGall)
Killeter
Slieve League
(Sliabh Liag)
Kilcar
KILLYBEGS
(Na Cealla Beaga)
Mountcharles
Laghy
L. Derg
Muckros Head
Doorin Pt.
Ballintra
St. Johns Point
Rossnowlagh
Pettigoe
DONEGAL BAY
Cavangarden
Kesh
BALLYSHANNON
(Béal Atha Seanaidh)
Boa Island
BUNDORAN
(Bun Dobhráin)
LOWER LOUGH ERNE
Irvinestown
Mullaghmore Head
Belleek
Belleek Pottery
Visitor Centre
Inishmurray
Mullaghmore
Lough Melvin
Killadeas
Grange
DARTRY MOUNTAINS
FERMANAGH
Lissadell House
Ballinfull
ENNISKILLEN
Enniskillen Castle
Castle Coole
Drumcliff
Lough Macnean Upper
SLIGO BAY
Rosses Point
Manorhamilton
Belcoo
N56
N13
N14
N15
N16
A35
A47
A46
A32
A4
10
11
28
22
34
32
18
14
17
30
19
25
26
38
29
24
21
6
47

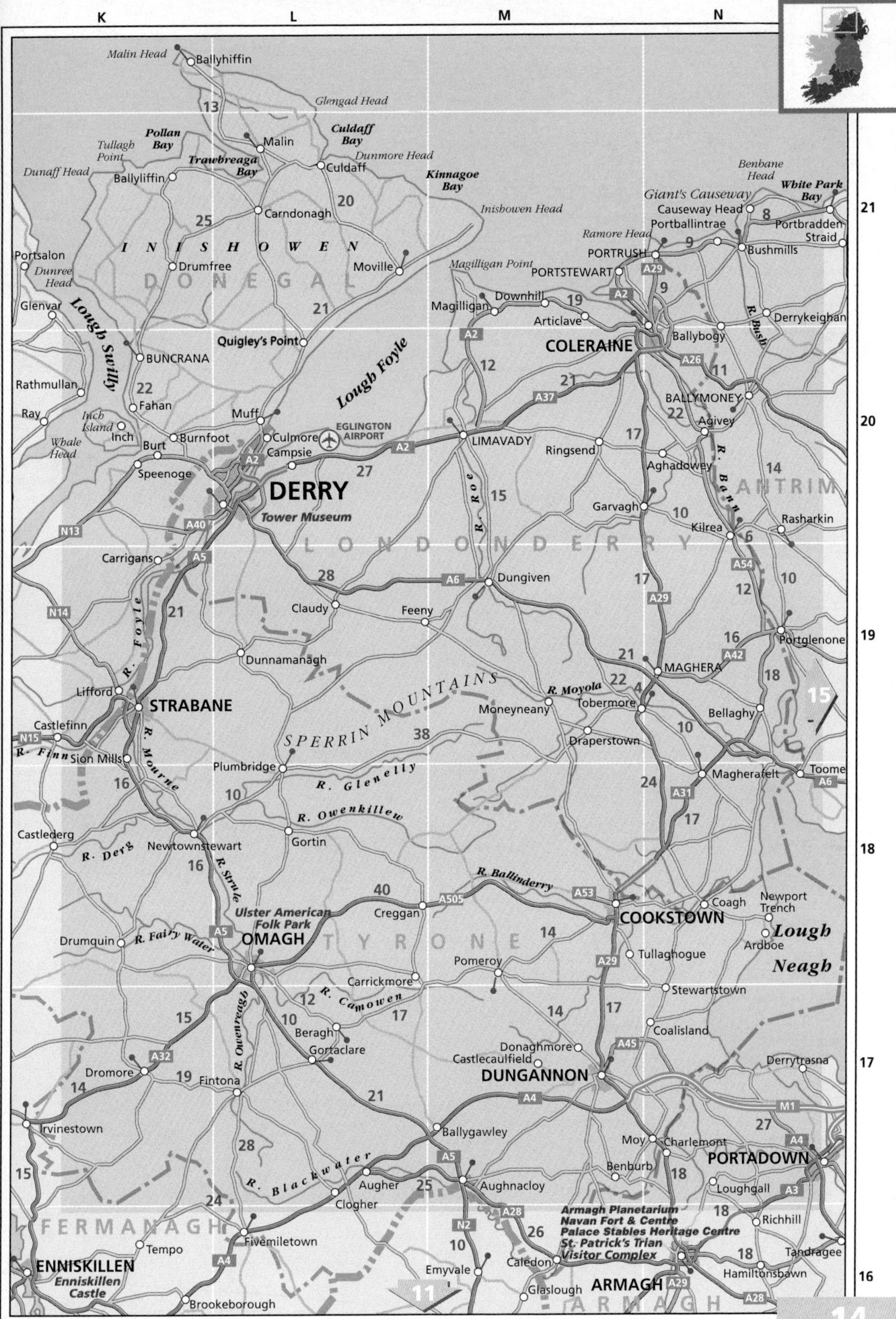
K
L
M
N
21
20
19
18
17
16
14
15
11
Malin Head
Ballyhiffin
Glengad Head
Pollan Bay
Culdaff Bay
Tullagh Point
Malin
Trawbreaga Bay
Dunmore Head
Dunaff Head
Ballyliffin
Culdaff
Kinnagoe Bay
Carndonagh
Inishowen Head
INISHOWEN
DONEGAL
Portsalon
Dunree Head
Drumfree
Moville
Glenvar
Lough Swilly
Quigley's Point
Lough Foyle
BUNCRANA
Rathmullan
Fahan
Ray
Inch Island
Inch
Muff
Whale Head
Burnfoot
Burt
Culmore
EGLINTON AIRPORT
Campsie
Speenoge
DERRY
Tower Museum
Carrigans
LONDONDERRY
Claudy
Feeny
Dungiven
Dunnamanagh
Lifford
STRABANE
Castlefinn
R. Finn
Sion Mills
R. Foyle
R. Mourne
SPERRIN MOUNTAINS
Plumbridge
R. Glenelly
R. Owenkillew
Castlederg
R. Derg
Newtownstewart
Gortin
R. Strule
Ulster American Folk Park
OMAGH
Drumquin
R. Fairy Water
Creggan
TYRONE
Carrickmore
R. Camowen
Beragh
Gortaclare
R. Owenreagh
Dromore
Fintona
Irvinestown
Ballygawley
R. Blackwater
Augher
Clogher
Aughnacloy
FERMANAGH
Tempo
Fivemiletown
ENNISKILLEN
Enniskillen Castle
Brookeborough
Emyvale
Glaslough
Caledon
ARMAGH
Armagh Planetarium
Navan Fort & Centre
Palace Stables Heritage Centre
St. Patrick's Trian Visitor Complex
Benbane Head
White Park Bay
Giant's Causeway
Causeway Head
Portballintrae
Portbradden
Straid
Ramore Head
PORTRUSH
Bushmills
Magilligan Point
PORTSTEWART
Magilligan
Downhill
Articlave
Derrykeighan
COLERAINE
Ballybogy
R. Bush
BALLYMONEY
Agivey
LIMAVADY
Ringsend
Aghadowey
R. Roe
R. Bann
ANTRIM
Garvagh
Kilrea
Rasharkin
Portglenone
MAGHERA
R. Moyola
Moneyneany
Tobermore
Bellaghy
Draperstown
Magherafelt
Toome
R. Ballinderry
COOKSTOWN
Coagh
Newport Trench
Lough Neagh
Ardboe
Tullaghogue
Pomeroy
Stewartstown
Coalisland
Donaghmore
Castlecaulfield
DUNGANNON
Derrytrasna
Moy
Charlemont
PORTADOWN
Benburb
Loughgall
Richhill
Tandragee
Hamiltonsbawn
A2
A29
A26
A37
A40
A5
A6
A54
A42
A31
A53
A505
A45
A4
M1
A3
A28
A32
N13
N14
N15
N2

O
P
Q
R
21
20
19
18
17
Rathlin Island
Mull of Kintyre
Southend
Sanda I.
NORTH CHANNEL
Ballycastle Bay
Benmore or Fair Head
Ballintoy
BALLYCASTLE
Murlough Bay
Runabay Head
Cushendun
Armoy
ANTRIM MOUNTAINS
R. Bush
Cushendall
Red Bay
Glenariff
Garron Point
Cloughmills
Newtown Crommelin
Carnlough
Carnlough Bay
Glenarm
Cairnryan
Stranraer
R. Braid
Ballygalley
Ballygalley Head
Drains Bay
Cullybackey
Broughshane
BALLYMENA
ANTRIM
LARNE
Gracehill
Ahoghill
Moorfields
Mullaghboy
Lough Larne
R. Main
Kells
Ballynure
Black Head
Randalstown
BALLYCLARE
Whitehead
CARRICKFERGUS
Greenisland
Belfast Lough
Douglas (I. of Man)
Templepatrick
NEWTOWNABBEY
BANGOR
Copeland Island
HOLYWOOD
Crawfordsburn
Donaghadee
BELFAST AIRPORT
HARBOUR AIRPORT
Ulster Folk & Transport Museum
Crumlin
Nutt's Corner
Clady
Lough Neagh
BELFAST
DUNDONALD
Mount Stewart
NEWTOWNARDS
Glenavy
Queens University
Somme Heritage Centre
Stonyford
W5 & Ulster Museum
Newtownbreda
COMBER
Greyabbey
Ards Peninsula
Lough Beg
Strangford Lough
LISBURN
Carryduff
Burr Point
LURGAN
Magheralin
Hillsborough
Saintfield
Portavogie
CRAIGAVON
Clogby Bay
PORTADOWN
DROMORE
Crossgar
Killyleagh
R. Lagan
BALLYNAHINCH
R. Quoile
Castle Ward
Strangford
PORTAFERRY Exploris Aquarium
Gilford
Tandragee
BANBRIDGE
DOWN
DOWNPATRICK
Ballyquintin Point
Scarva
Killard Point
Down County Museum
Clough
A2
A44
A43
A42
M2
A36
A26
A6
A8
A57
A5
M5
A6
A2
A52
A21
A48
A20
A55
A30
A501
A26
A23
M1
A3
M1
A20
A2
A22
A49
A21
A7
A1
A26
A50
A24
A25
A2
14
12
15

# 2008 Calendar

## JANUARY

| S | M | T | W | T | F | S |
|---|---|---|---|---|---|---|
| | | 1 | 2 | 3 | 4 | 5 |
| 6 | 7 | 8 | 9 | 10 | 11 | 12 |
| 13 | 14 | 15 | 16 | 17 | 18 | 19 |
| 20 | 21 | 22 | 23 | 24 | 25 | 26 |
| 27 | 28 | 29 | 30 | 31 | | |
| | | | | | | |

## FEBRUARY

| S | M | T | W | T | F | S |
|---|---|---|---|---|---|---|
| | | | | | 1 | 2 |
| 3 | 4 | 5 | 6 | 7 | 8 | 9 |
| 10 | 11 | 12 | 13 | 14 | 15 | 16 |
| 17 | 18 | 19 | 20 | 21 | 22 | 23 |
| 24 | 25 | 26 | 27 | 28 | 29 | |
| | | | | | | |

## MARCH

| S | M | T | W | T | F | S |
|---|---|---|---|---|---|---|
| | | | | | | 1 |
| 2 | 3 | 4 | 5 | 6 | 7 | 8 |
| 9 | 10 | 11 | 12 | 13 | 14 | 15 |
| 16 | 17 | 18 | 19 | 20 | 21 | 22 |
| 23 | 24 | 25 | 26 | 27 | 28 | 29 |
| 30 | 31 | | | | | |

## APRIL

| S | M | T | W | T | F | S |
|---|---|---|---|---|---|---|
| | | 1 | 2 | 3 | 4 | 5 |
| 6 | 7 | 8 | 9 | 10 | 11 | 12 |
| 13 | 14 | 15 | 16 | 17 | 18 | 19 |
| 20 | 21 | 22 | 23 | 24 | 25 | 26 |
| 27 | 28 | 29 | 30 | | | |
| | | | | | | |

## MAY

| S | M | T | W | T | F | S |
|---|---|---|---|---|---|---|
| | | | | 1 | 2 | 3 |
| 4 | 5 | 6 | 7 | 8 | 9 | 10 |
| 11 | 12 | 13 | 14 | 15 | 16 | 17 |
| 18 | 19 | 20 | 21 | 22 | 23 | 24 |
| 25 | 26 | 27 | 28 | 29 | 30 | 31 |
| | | | | | | |

## JUNE

| S | M | T | W | T | F | S |
|---|---|---|---|---|---|---|
| 1 | 2 | 3 | 4 | 5 | 6 | 7 |
| 8 | 9 | 10 | 11 | 12 | 13 | 14 |
| 15 | 16 | 17 | 18 | 19 | 20 | 21 |
| 22 | 23 | 24 | 25 | 26 | 27 | 28 |
| 29 | 30 | | | | | |
| | | | | | | |

## JULY

| S | M | T | W | T | F | S |
|---|---|---|---|---|---|---|
| | | 1 | 2 | 3 | 4 | 5 |
| 6 | 7 | 8 | 9 | 10 | 11 | 12 |
| 13 | 14 | 15 | 16 | 17 | 18 | 19 |
| 20 | 21 | 22 | 23 | 24 | 25 | 26 |
| 27 | 28 | 29 | 30 | 31 | | |
| | | | | | | |

## AUGUST

| S | M | T | W | T | F | S |
|---|---|---|---|---|---|---|
| | | | | | 1 | 2 |
| 3 | 4 | 5 | 6 | 7 | 8 | 9 |
| 10 | 11 | 12 | 13 | 14 | 15 | 16 |
| 17 | 18 | 19 | 20 | 21 | 22 | 23 |
| 24 | 25 | 26 | 27 | 28 | 29 | 30 |
| 31 | | | | | | |

## SEPTEMBER

| S | M | T | W | T | F | S |
|---|---|---|---|---|---|---|
| | 1 | 2 | 3 | 4 | 5 | 6 |
| 7 | 8 | 9 | 10 | 11 | 12 | 13 |
| 14 | 15 | 16 | 17 | 18 | 19 | 20 |
| 21 | 22 | 23 | 24 | 25 | 26 | 27 |
| 28 | 29 | 30 | | | | |
| | | | | | | |

## OCTOBER

| S | M | T | W | T | F | S |
|---|---|---|---|---|---|---|
| | | | 1 | 2 | 3 | 4 |
| 5 | 6 | 7 | 8 | 9 | 10 | 11 |
| 12 | 13 | 14 | 15 | 16 | 17 | 18 |
| 19 | 20 | 21 | 22 | 23 | 24 | 25 |
| 26 | 27 | 28 | 29 | 30 | 31 | |
| | | | | | | |

## NOVEMBER

| S | M | T | W | T | F | S |
|---|---|---|---|---|---|---|
| | | | | | | 1 |
| 2 | 3 | 4 | 5 | 6 | 7 | 8 |
| 9 | 10 | 11 | 12 | 13 | 14 | 15 |
| 16 | 17 | 18 | 19 | 20 | 21 | 22 |
| 23 | 24 | 25 | 26 | 27 | 28 | 29 |
| 30 | | | | | | |

## DECEMBER

| S | M | T | W | T | F | S |
|---|---|---|---|---|---|---|
| | 1 | 2 | 3 | 4 | 5 | 6 |
| 7 | 8 | 9 | 10 | 11 | 12 | 13 |
| 14 | 15 | 16 | 17 | 18 | 19 | 20 |
| 21 | 22 | 23 | 24 | 25 | 26 | 27 |
| 28 | 29 | 30 | 31 | | | |
| | | | | | | |

**19th Green (The)**
*Killarney, Co. Kerry* ..............192
☎ 064-32868

## A

**Abberley Court Hotel**
*Dublin City, Co. Dublin* ..........278
☎ 01-459 6000

**Abbey Court Hotel, Lodges & Trinity Leisure Spa**
*Nenagh, Co. Tipperary* ..........237
☎ 067-41111

**Abbey Gate Hotel**
*Tralee, Co. Kerry* ..................215
☎ 066-712 9888

**Abbey Hotel**
*Ballyvourney, Co. Cork* ..........144
☎ 026-45324

**Abbey Hotel**
*Dublin City, Co. Dublin* ..........278
☎ 01-872 8188

**Abbey Hotel, Conference and Leisure Centre**
*Roscommon Town, Co. Roscommon* ..129
☎ 090-666 6200

**Abbey House**
*Galway City, Co. Galway*..........79
☎ 091-524394

**Abbey Lodge**
*Killarney, Co. Kerry* ..............192
☎ 064-34193

**Abbeyfield Hotel Conference and Leisure Centre**
*Ballaghaderreen, Co. Roscommon*......128
☎ 094-986 2736

**Abbeyglen Castle Hotel**
*Clifden, Co. Galway* ................73
☎ 095-22832

**Abbeyleix Manor Hotel**
*Abbeyleix, Co. Laois*..............341
☎ 057-873 0111

**Aberdeen Lodge**
*Dublin City, Co. Dublin* ..........279
☎ 01-283 8155

**Abrae Court**
*Dublin City, Co. Dublin* ..........279
☎ 01-492 2242

**AbsoluteHotel.com**
*Limerick City, Co. Limerick*....106
☎ 061-463600

**Ach Na Sheen Guesthouse**
*Tipperary Town, Co. Tipperary* ......238
☎ 062-51298

**Achill Cliff House Hotel**
*Achill Island, Co. Mayo*..........113
☎ 098-43400

**Achill House**
*Cork City, Co. Cork*................154
☎ 021-427 9447

**Actons Hotel**
*Kinsale, Co. Cork*..................166
☎ 021-477 9900

**Adams Trinity Hotel**
*Dublin City, Co. Dublin* ..........279
☎ 01-670 7100

**Adare Guest House**
*Galway City, Co. Galway*..........79
☎ 091-582638

**Adare Manor Hotel & Golf Resort**
*Adare, Co. Limerick*..............104
☎ 061-396566

**Aghadoe Heights Hotel & Spa**
*Killarney, Co. Kerry* ..............193
☎ 064-31766

**Aherlow House Hotel and Lodges**
*Glen of Aherlow, Co. Tipperary* ......235
☎ 062-56153

**Aherne's Townhouse & Seafood Restaurant**
*Youghal, Co. Cork* ................176
☎ 024-92424

**Airport Manor**
*Dublin Airport, Co. Dublin*......274
☎ 01-840 1818

**Airportview Hotel & Spa**
*Blakes Cross, Co. Dublin* ......273
☎ 01-843 8756

**Aisleigh Guest House**
*Carrick-on-Shannon, Co. Leitrim* ..101
☎ 071-962 0313

**Alcock and Brown Hotel**
*Clifden, Co. Galway* ................73
☎ 095-21206

**Alpine House**
*Dingle (An Daingean), Co. Kerry*....181
☎ 066-915 1250

**Ambassador Hotel**
*Cork City, Co. Cork*................154
☎ 021-453 9000

**Amber Springs Hotel and Health Spa**
*Gorey, Co. Wexford* ..............256
☎ 053-948 4000

**An Bothar Guesthouse, Restaurant & Bar**
*Dingle (An Daingean), Co. Kerry*....182
☎ 066-915 5342

**An Chúirt, Gweedore Court Hotel**
*Gweedore, Co. Donegal* ..........61
☎ 074-953 2900

**An Crúiscín Lán Hotel**
*Spiddal, Co. Galway*................99
☎ 091-553148

**An Glen Guesthouse**
*Dublin City, Co. Dublin* ..........280
☎ 01-855 1374

**An Portán**
*Dingle (An Daingean), Co. Kerry*....182
☎ 066-915 6212

**Anchor Guest House**
*Dublin City, Co. Dublin* ..........280
☎ 01-878 6913

**Anchorage Inn (The)**
*Portstewart, Co. Derry* ..........390
☎ 028-7083 2003

**Anglers Rest Hotel**
*Headford, Co. Galway* ............93
☎ 093-35528

**Annaly Hotel**
*Longford Town, Co. Longford*........344
☎ 043-42058

**Annebrook House**
*Mullingar, Co. Westmeath*......368
☎ 044-935 3300

**Anner Hotel & Leisure Centre**
*Thurles, Co. Tipperary* ..........238
☎ 0504-21799

**Anno Santo Hotel**
*Galway City, Co. Galway*..........79
☎ 091-523011

**Aran Islands Hotel**
*Aran Islands, Co. Galway* ........68
☎ 099-61104

**Aran View House Hotel & Restaurant**
*Doolin, Co. Clare* ....................39
☎ 065-707 4061

**Arbutus Hotel**
*Killarney, Co. Kerry* ..............193
☎ 064-31037

**Ard Einne Guesthouse**
*Aran Islands, Co. Galway* ........68
☎ 099-61126

**Ard Na Breátha**
*Donegal Town, Co. Donegal* ....58
☎ 074-972 2288

**Ardagh Hotel & Restaurant**
*Clifden, Co. Galway* ................74
☎ 095-21384

**Ardagh House**
*Killenaule, Co. Tipperary*........236
☎ 052-56224

**Ardagh House**
*Dublin City, Co. Dublin* ..........280
☎ 01-497 7068

**Ardawn House**
*Galway City, Co. Galway*..........80
☎ 091-568833

**Ardboyne Hotel**
*Navan, Co. Meath* ................355
☎ 046-902 3119

**Ardenode Hotel**
*Ballymore Eustace, Co. Kildare* ....333
☎ 045-864198

**Ardilaun Guesthouse**
*Ennis, Co. Clare*......................41
☎ 065-682 2311

**Ardilaun Hotel, Conference Centre & Leisure Club**
*Galway City, Co. Galway*..........80
☎ 091-521433


SEE ALSO INDEX TO LOCATIONS PAGES 12-13

## B





SEE ALSO INDEX TO LOCATIONS PAGES 12-13

**Bayview Hotel**
Bushmills, Co. Antrim............382
☎ 028-2073 4100

**Beach Guest House**
Dunmore East, Co. Waterford........242
☎ 051-383316

**Beach Haven House**
Tramore, Co. Waterford ........244
☎ 051-390208

**Beach Hotel and Leisure Club**
Mullaghmore, Co. Sligo ........132
☎ 071-916 6103

**Beaufort House**
Carlingford, Co. Louth ..........344
☎ 042-937 3879

**Beech Hill Country House Hotel**
Derry City, Co. Derry ...........388
☎ 028-7134 9279

**Bel-Air Hotel**
Ashford, Co. Wicklow...........371
☎ 0404-40109

**Belfry Hotel**
Waterford City, Co. Waterford........247
☎ 051-844800

**Bellbridge House Hotel**
Milltown Malbay, Co. Clare......52
☎ 065-708 4038

**Belleek Castle**
Ballina, Co. Mayo..................114
☎ 096-22400

**Bellingham Castle Hotel**
Castlebellingham, Co. Louth..346
☎ 042-937 2176

**Belmont Hotel**
Knock, Co. Mayo .................121
☎ 094-938 8122

**Ben View House**
Clifden, Co. Galway ................74
☎ 095-21256

**Benners Hotel**
Tralee, Co. Kerry ..................216
☎ 066-712 1877

**Berkeley House**
Kilkenny City, Co. Kilkenny ....221
☎ 056-776 4848

**Best Western Academy Plaza Hotel**
Dublin City, Co. Dublin ..........284
☎ 01-817 4141

**Best Western Eviston House Hotel**
Killarney, Co. Kerry .............194
☎ 064-31640

**Best Western Flannery's Hotel**
Galway City, Co. Galway..........81
☎ 091-755111

**Best Western Hotel Rosslare**
Rosslare Harbour, Co. Wexford ....260
☎ 053-913 3110

**Best Western International**
Killarney, Co. Kerry .............194
☎ 064-31816

**Best Western Pery's Hotel**
Limerick City, Co. Limerick....106
☎ 061-413822

**Best Western White Horse Hotel**
Derry City, Co. Derry ............388
☎ 028-7186 0606

**Bettystown Court Conference & Leisure Hotel**
Bettystown, Co. Meath..........352
☎ 041-981 2900

**Bewley's Hotel Ballsbridge**
Dublin City, Co. Dublin ..........285
☎ 01-668 1111

**Bewley's Hotel Dublin Airport**
Dublin Airport, Co. Dublin......274
☎ 01-871 1000

**Bewley's Hotel Leopardstown**
Dublin City, Co. Dublin ..........286
☎ 01-293 5000

**Bewley's Hotel Newlands Cross**
Dublin City, Co. Dublin ..........286
☎ 01-464 0140

**Bianconi**
Killorglin , Co. Kerry..............212
☎ 066-976 1146

**Blarney Castle Hotel**
Blarney, Co. Cork..................147
☎ 021-438 5116

**Blarney Golf Resort**
Blarney, Co. Cork..................147
☎ 021-438 4477

**Blarney Stone**
Cork City, Co. Cork................155
☎ 021-427 0083

**Blarney Woollen Mills Hotel**
Blarney, Co. Cork..................148
☎ 021-438 5011

**Bloomfield House Hotel**
Mullingar, Co. Westmeath......368
☎ 044-934 0894

**Blooms Hotel**
Dublin City, Co. Dublin ..........286
☎ 01-671 5622

**Blue Haven Kinsale (The)**
Kinsale, Co. Cork..................166
☎ 021-477 2209

**Boffin Lodge**
Westport, Co. Mayo .............124
☎ 098-26092

**Boland's Guesthouse**
Dingle (An Daingean), Co. Kerry....183
☎ 066-915 1426

**Boyne Valley Hotel & Country Club**
Drogheda, Co. Louth ............346
☎ 041-983 7737

**Bracken Court Hotel**
Balbriggan, Co. Dublin ..........273
☎ 01-841 3333

**Brandon Hotel Conference and Leisure Centre**
Tralee, Co. Kerry ..................216
☎ 066-712 3333

**Brandon House Hotel, Health Club & Spa**
New Ross, Co. Wexford ........258
☎ 051-421703

**Breffni Arms Hotel**
Arvagh, Co. Cavan................268
☎ 049-433 5127

**Brehon (The)**
Killarney, Co. Kerry .............194
☎ 064-30700

**Bridge Hotel**
Arklow, Co. Wicklow..............370
☎ 0402-31666

**Bridge House Hotel, Leisure Club & Spa**
Tullamore, Co. Offaly ............361
☎ 057-932 5600

**Brighton House**
Clonmel, Co. Tipperary..........234
☎ 052-23665

**Broadmeadow Country House & Equestrian Centre**
Ashbourne, Co. Meath ..........351
☎ 01-835 2823

**Brog Maker Hotel**
Kilkenny City, Co. Kilkenny ....221
☎ 056-775 2900

**Brook Lodge Hotel**
Killarney, Co. Kerry .............195
☎ 064-31800

**Brook Manor Lodge**
Tralee, Co. Kerry ..................217
☎ 066-712 0406

**Brookfield Hotel**
Cork City, Co. Cork................155
☎ 021-480 4700

**Brookhaven Country House**
Waterville, Co. Kerry ............219
☎ 066-947 4431

**BrookLodge and Wells Spa**
Aughrim, Co. Wicklow ..........371
☎ 0402-36444

**Brooks Hotel**
Dublin City, Co. Dublin ..........287
☎ 01-670 4000

**Brosna Lodge Hotel**
Banagher , Co. Offaly............359
☎ 057-915 1350

**Brown Trout Golf & Country Inn**
Aghadowey, Co. Derry ..........387
☎ 028-7086 8209

**Brownes Dublin**
Dublin City, Co. Dublin ..........287
☎ 01-638 3939

SEE ALSO INDEX TO LOCATIONS PAGES 12-13

## D





SEE ALSO INDEX TO LOCATIONS PAGES 12-13

GUINNESS

SEE ALSO INDEX TO LOCATIONS PAGES 12-13

SEE ALSO INDEX TO LOCATIONS PAGES 12-13

## I

**IMI Residence**
*Dublin City, Co. Dublin ..........304*
☎ 01-207 5900

**Imperial Hotel with Escape Salon and Spa**
*Cork City, Co. Cork................159*
☎ 021-427 4040

**Inch Beach Guest House**
*Inch Beach, Co. Kerry ..........188*
☎ 066-915 8118

**Inchydoney Island Lodge & Spa**
*Clonakilty, Co. Cork ..............151*
☎ 023-33143

**Inishbofin House Hotel**
*Inishbofin Island, Co. Galway ..93*
☎ 095-45809

**Inishmore Guesthouse**
*Galway City, Co. Galway..........86*
☎ 091-582639

**Inishowen Gateway Hotel**
*Buncrana, Co. Donegal ..........57*
☎ 074-936 1144

**Innishannon House Hotel**
*Innishannon, Co. Cork ..........166*
☎ 021-477 5121

**Inveraray Farm Guesthouse**
*Killarney, Co. Kerry ..............203*
☎ 064-44224

## J

**Jackson's Hotel, Conference & Leisure Centre**
*Ballybofey, Co. Donegal ..........54*
☎ 074-913 1021

**Jim Edwards**
*Kinsale, Co. Cork..................168*
☎ 021-477 2541

**JJ Gannon's Hotel**
*Ballinrobe, Co. Mayo ............116*
☎ 094-954 1008

**Joyces Waterloo House**
*Clifden, Co. Galway ................77*
☎ 095-21688

**Jurys Cork Hotel**
*Cork City, Co. Cork................159*
☎ 021-425 2700

**Jurys Croke Park Hotel**
*Dublin City, Co. Dublin ..........305*
☎ 01-871 4444

**Jurys Inn Belfast**
*Belfast City, Belfast City ........386*
☎ 028-9053 3500

**Jurys Inn Christchurch**
*Dublin City, Co. Dublin ..........305*
☎ 01-454 0000

**Jurys Inn Cork**
*Cork City, Co. Cork................160*
☎ 021-494 3000

**Jurys Inn Custom House**
*Dublin City, Co. Dublin ..........305*
☎ 01-607 5000

**Jurys Inn Galway**
*Galway City, Co. Galway..........86*
☎ 091-566444

**Jurys Inn Limerick**
*Limerick City, Co. Limerick....109*
☎ 061-207000

**Jurys Inn Parnell Street**
*Dublin City, Co. Dublin ..........306*
☎ 01-878 4900

## K

**Kathleens Country House**
*Killarney, Co. Kerry ..............203*
☎ 064-32810

**Keadeen Hotel**
*Newbridge, Co. Kildare..........340*
☎ 045-431666

**Keepers Arms**
*Ballyconnell, Co. Cavan ........268*
☎ 049-952 3318

**Keernaun House**
*Dundalk, Co. Louth ..............349*
☎ 042-932 1795

**Kee's Hotel**
*Ballybofey, Co. Donegal ..........55*
☎ 074-913 1018

**Kelly's Gateway Hotel**
*Swinford, Co. Mayo ..............123*
☎ 094-925 2156

**Kelly's Resort Hotel & Spa**
*Rosslare, Co. Wexford ..........259*
☎ 053-913 2114

**Kennys Guest House**
*Castlebar, Co. Mayo..............118*
☎ 094-902 3091

**Kilbrackan Arms Hotel**
*Carrigallen, Co. Leitrim ........102*
☎ 049-433 9737

**Kilcaw House**
*Kinsale, Co. Cork..................169*
☎ 021-477 4155

**Kilcoran Lodge Hotel, Lodges & Leisure Centre**
*Cahir, Co. Tipperary ..............231*
☎ 052-41288

**Kildare Hotel, Spa and Country Club - The K Club**
*Straffan, Co. Kildare..............341*
☎ 01-601 7200

**Kilford Arms Hotel**
*Kilkenny City, Co. Kilkenny ....224*
☎ 056-776 1018

**Kilkea Castle**
*Castledermot, Co. Kildare......333*
☎ 059-914 5156

**Kilkee Bay Hotel**
*Kilkee, Co. Clare ....................45*
☎ 065-906 0060

**Kilkenny Hibernian Hotel**
*Kilkenny City, Co. Kilkenny ....224*
☎ 056-777 1888

**Kilkenny House Hotel**
*Kilkenny City, Co. Kilkenny ....225*
☎ 056-777 0711

**Kilkenny Inn Hotel**
*Kilkenny City, Co. Kilkenny ....225*
☎ 056-777 2828

**Kilkenny Ormonde Hotel**
*Kilkenny City, Co. Kilkenny ....225*
☎ 056-772 3900

**Kilkenny River Court**
*Kilkenny City, Co. Kilkenny ....226*
☎ 056-772 3388

**Killarney Avenue Hotel**
*Killarney, Co. Kerry ..............204*
☎ 064-32522

**Killarney Guest House**
*Cork City, Co. Cork................160*
☎ 021-427 0290

**Killarney Lodge**
*Killarney, Co. Kerry ..............204*
☎ 064-36499

**Killarney Oaks**
*Killarney, Co. Kerry ..............204*
☎ 064-37600

**Killarney Park Hotel**
*Killarney, Co. Kerry ..............205*
☎ 064-35555

**Killarney Plaza Hotel & Spa**
*Killarney, Co. Kerry ..............205*
☎ 064-21111

**Killarney Royal**
*Killarney, Co. Kerry ..............206*
☎ 064-31853

**Killashee House Hotel & Villa Spa**
*Naas, Co. Kildare..................337*
☎ 045-879277

**Killeen House Hotel**
*Killarney, Co. Kerry ..............206*
☎ 064-31711

**Killeshin (The)**
*Portlaoise, Co. Laois ............342*
☎ 057-863 1200

**Killyhevlin Hotel**
*Enniskillen, Co. Fermanagh ..392*
☎ 028-6632 3481

**Kilmurry Lodge Hotel**
*Limerick City, Co. Limerick....109*
☎ 061-331133

**Kilmurvey House**
*Aran Islands, Co. Galway ........68*
☎ 099-61218

**Kilronan Guesthouse**
*Dublin City, Co. Dublin ..........306*
☎ 01-475 5266

**Kincora House and Art Gallery**
*Lisdoonvarna, Co. Clare ..........50*
☎ 065-707 4300


 SEE ALSO INDEX TO LOCATIONS PAGES 12-13

**King Sitric Fish Restaurant & Accommodation**
*Howth, Co. Dublin ................326*
☎ 01-832 5235

**Kingfisher Lodge Guesthouse**
*Killarney, Co. Kerry .............206*
☎ 064-37131

**Kingsfort Country House**
*Ballintogher, Co. Sligo ..........130*
☎ 071-911 5111

**Kingsley Hotel & Residences**
*Cork City, Co. Cork................160*
☎ 021-480 0500

**Kingston Hotel**
*Dun Laoghaire, Co. Dublin ....325*
☎ 01-280 1810

**Kirby's Lanterns Hotel**
*Tarbert, Co. Kerry ................214*
☎ 068-36210

**Knightsbrook Hotel & Golf Resort**
*Trim, Co. Meath....................357*
☎ 046-948 2110

**Knock House Hotel**
*Knock, Co. Mayo ..................121*
☎ 094-938 8088

**Knockranny House Hotel & Spa**
*Westport, Co. Mayo ..............126*
☎ 098-28600

**Knockranny Lodge**
*Westport, Co. Mayo ..............126*
☎ 098-28595

**Kylemore Pass Hotel**
*Kylemore, Co. Galway ............94*
☎ 095-41141

## L

**La Mon Hotel & Country Club**
*Belfast City, Belfast City ........386*
☎ 028-9044 8631

**La Stampa Hotel**
*Dublin City, Co. Dublin ..........306*
☎ 01-677 4444

**Lacken House**
*Kilkenny City, Co. Kilkenny ....226*
☎ 056-776 1085

**Lady Gregory Hotel, Conference & Leisure Club**
*Gort, Co. Galway ....................92*
☎ 091-632333

**Lahinch Golf & Leisure Hotel**
*Lahinch, Co. Clare ..................48*
☎ 065-708 1100

**Lake Hotel**
*Killarney, Co. Kerry ..............207*
☎ 064-31035

**Lake House Hotel**
*Portnoo, Co. Donegal..............66*
☎ 074-954 5123

**Lakelands Farm Guesthouse**
*Waterville, Co. Kerry ............220*
☎ 066-947 4303

**Lakeside Hotel & Leisure Centre**
*Killaloe, Co. Clare ..................46*
☎ 061-376122

**Lakeside Manor Hotel**
*Virginia, Co. Cavan ..............272*
☎ 049-854 8200

**Lancaster Lodge**
*Cork City, Co. Cork................161*
☎ 021-425 1125

**Langton House Hotel**
*Kilkenny City, Co. Kilkenny ....226*
☎ 056-776 5133

**Lansdowne Arms Hotel**
*Kenmare, Co. Kerry ..............189*
☎ 064-41368

**Lansdowne Hotel**
*Dublin City, Co. Dublin ..........307*
☎ 01-668 2522

**Lantern House**
*Killaloe, Co. Clare ..................46*
☎ 061-923034

**Laragh Guest House**
*Kilkenny City, Co. Kilkenny ....227*
☎ 056-776 4674

**Laurels**
*Kilkenny City, Co. Kilkenny ....227*
☎ 056-776 1501

**Lawlors Hotel**
*Naas, Co. Kildare..................338*
☎ 045-906444

**Leenane Hotel**
*Leenane, Co. Galway ..............94*
☎ 095-42249

**Leeson Inn Downtown**
*Dublin City, Co. Dublin ..........307*
☎ 01-662 2002

**Legends Townhouse & Restaurant**
*Cashel, Co. Tipperary............233*
☎ 062-61292

**Leixlip House Hotel**
*Leixlip, Co. Kildare ................335*
☎ 01-624 2268

**Lemongrove House**
*Enniscorthy, Co. Wexford ......254*
☎ 053-923 6115

**Lime Court**
*Killarney, Co. Kerry ..............207*
☎ 064-34547

**Limerick Marriott Hotel**
*Limerick City, Co. Limerick ....110*
☎ 061-448700

**Lisdonagh House**
*Caherlistrane, Co. Galway ......71*
☎ 093-31163

**Lismar Guesthouse & Serviced Apartments**
*Dundalk, Co. Louth ..............350*
☎ 042-935 7246

**Lismore House Hotel**
*Lismore, Co. Waterford ........244*
☎ 058-72966

**Loch Lein Country House**
*Killarney, Co. Kerry ..............207*
☎ 064-31260

**Lodge (The)**
*Kenmare, Co. Kerry ..............190*
☎ 064-41512

**Londonderry Arms Hotel**
*Carnlough, Co. Antrim ..........383*
☎ 028-2888 5255

**Long Quay House**
*Kinsale, Co. Cork..................169*
☎ 021-477 4563

**Longford Arms Hotel**
*Longford Town, Co. Longford ......344*
☎ 043-46296

**Longueville House Hotel**
*Mallow, Co. Cork ..................172*
☎ 022-47156

**Lord Bagenal Inn**
*Leighlinbridge, Co. Carlow ....142*
☎ 059-977 4000

**Lotamore House**
*Cork City, Co. Cork................161*
☎ 021-482 2344

**Lough Erne Golf Resort**
*Enniskillen, Co. Fermanagh ..392*
☎ 028-6632 0613

**Lough Inagh Lodge**
*Recess, Co. Galway ................98*
☎ 095-34706

**Lough Rynn Castle**
*Mohill, Co. Leitrim ................103*
☎ 071-963 2700

**Lucan Spa Hotel**
*Lucan, Co. Dublin ................328*
☎ 01-628 0494

**Lydons Lodge Hotel**
*Cong, Co. Mayo....................120*
☎ 094-954 6053

**Lynam's Hotel**
*Dublin City, Co. Dublin ..........307*
☎ 01-888 0856

**Lyndon Guesthouse**
*Dublin City, Co. Dublin ..........308*
☎ 01-878 6950

**Lynham's Hotel**
*Glendalough, Co. Wicklow ....375*
☎ 0404-45345

**Lyrath Estate Hotel, Spa & Convention Centre**
*Kilkenny City, Co. Kilkenny ....227*
☎ 056-776 0088

## M

**Ma Dwyers Guesthouse**
*Navan, Co. Meath ................355*
☎ 046-907 7992

**Magowna House Hotel**
*Ennis, Co. Clare......................43*
☎ 065-683 9009

 SEE ALSO INDEX TO LOCATIONS PAGES 12-13

**Mulcahys**
*Clonmel, Co. Tipperary..........235*
☎ 052-25054

**Mullingar Park Hotel**
*Mullingar, Co. Westmeath......369*
☎ 044-933 7500

**Munster Arms Hotel**
*Bandon, Co. Cork ................145*
☎ 023-41562

**Murphy's Hotel**
*Tubbercurry, Co. Sligo ..........135*
☎ 071-918 5598

**Murphys of Killarney**
*Killarney, Co. Kerry ..............209*
☎ 064-31294

**Muskerry Arms**
*Blarney, Co. Cork..................148*
☎ 021-438 5200

## N

**Neptune Beach Hotel & Leisure Club**
*Bettystown, Co. Meath..........352*
☎ 041-982 7107

**Nesbitt Arms Hotel**
*Ardara, Co. Donegal................54*
☎ 074-954 1103

**Newbay Country House**
*Wexford Town, Co. Wexford ..262*
☎ 053-914 2779

**Newgrange Hotel**
*Navan, Co. Meath ................356*
☎ 046-907 4100

**Newgrange Lodge**
*Newgrange, Co. Meath ........356*
☎ 041-988 2478

**Newpark Hotel**
*Kilkenny City, Co. Kilkenny ....228*
☎ 056-776 0500

**Newtown Farm Guesthouse**
*Ardmore, Co. Waterford ........239*
☎ 024-94143

**North Star Hotel**
*Dublin City, Co. Dublin ..........312*
☎ 01-836 3136

**Number 31**
*Dublin City, Co. Dublin ..........312*
☎ 01-676 5011

**Nuremore Hotel & Country Club**
*Carrickmacross, Co. Monaghan....358*
☎ 042-966 1438

## O

**Oakwood Arms Hotel**
*Shannon Airport, Co. Clare......53*
☎ 061-361500

**O'Callaghan Alexander Hotel**
*Dublin City, Co. Dublin ..........312*
☎ 01-607 3700

**O'Callaghan Davenport Hotel**
*Dublin City, Co. Dublin ..........313*
☎ 01-607 3500

**O'Callaghan Mont Clare Hotel**
*Dublin City, Co. Dublin ..........313*
☎ 01-607 3800

**O'Callaghan Stephen's Green Hotel**
*Dublin City, Co. Dublin ..........313*
☎ 01-607 3600

**Ocean Crest House**
*Galway City, Co. Galway..........87*
☎ 091-589028

**Ocean Hotel**
*Dunmore East, Co. Waterford ......243*
☎ 051-383136

**O'Connors Farmhouse**
*Doolin, Co. Clare ....................40*
☎ 065-707 4314

**O'Connor's Guesthouse**
*Cloghane, Co. Kerry..............181*
☎ 066-713 8113

**O'Connors Warwick Hotel**
*Galway City, Co. Galway..........87*
☎ 091-522740

**O'Deas Hotel**
*Loughrea, Co. Galway ............96*
☎ 091-841611

**O'Donnabhain's**
*Kenmare, Co. Kerry ..............190*
☎ 064-42106

**O'Donovan's Hotel**
*Clonakilty, Co. Cork ..............151*
☎ 023-33250

**O'Gara's Royal Hotel**
*Roscommon Town, Co. Roscommon ..130*
☎ 090-662 6317

**Old Bank House**
*Kinsale, Co. Cork..................169*
☎ 021-477 4075

**Old Darnley Lodge Hotel**
*Athboy, Co. Meath ................352*
☎ 046-943 2283

**Old Ground Hotel**
*Ennis, Co. Clare......................43*
☎ 065-682 8127

**Old Inn (The)**
*Crawfordsburn, Co. Down ....391*
☎ 028-9185 3255

**Old Pier, Restaurant and Guesthouse**
*Dingle (An Daingean), Co. Kerry....187*
☎ 066-915 5242

**Old Quarter Lodge**
*Limerick City, Co. Limerick....110*
☎ 061-315320

**Old Weir Lodge**
*Killarney, Co. Kerry ..............209*
☎ 064-35593

**Oldcastle House Hotel**
*Oldcastle, Co. Meath ............356*
☎ 049-854 2400

**O'Loughlins Hotel**
*Portlaoise, Co. Laois ............343*
☎ 057-862 1305

**Oranmore Lodge Hotel, Conference & Leisure Centre**
*Galway City, Co. Galway..........88*
☎ 091-794400

**Oriel House Hotel, Leisure Club & Spa**
*Ballincollig, Co. Cork ............143*
☎ 021-420 8400

**O'Sheas Hotel**
*Dublin City, Co. Dublin ..........314*
☎ 01-836 5670

**O'Shea's Hotel...by the sea**
*Tramore, Co. Waterford ........245*
☎ 051-381246

**Osprey Hotel & Spa**
*Naas, Co. Kildare..................338*
☎ 045-881111

**Óstán Cheann Sibéal**
*Ballyferriter, Co. Kerry ..........178*
☎ 066-915 6433

**Ostan Na Rosann**
*Dungloe, Co. Donegal ............61*
☎ 074-952 2444

**Ostán Oileán Acla**
*Achill Island, Co. Mayo..........114*
☎ 098-45138

**Ostan Radharc Na Mara / Sea View Hotel**
*Bunbeg, Co. Donegal..............57*
☎ 074-953 1159

**Othello House**
*Dublin City, Co. Dublin ..........314*
☎ 01-855 5442

## P

**Palmerstown Lodge**
*Dublin City, Co. Dublin ..........314*
☎ 01-623 5494

**Paramount Hotel**
*Dublin City, Co. Dublin ..........315*
☎ 01-417 9900

**Park Avenue Hotel**
*Belfast City, Belfast City ........387*
☎ 028-9065 6520

**Park Hotel Kenmare**
*Kenmare, Co. Kerry ..............190*
☎ 064-41200

**Park Hotel Kiltimagh**
*Kiltimagh, Co. Mayo..............121*
☎ 094-937 4922

**Park Hotel, Leisure Centre & Holiday Homes**
*Dungarvan, Co. Waterford ....242*
☎ 058-42899

SEE ALSO INDEX TO LOCATIONS PAGES 12-13

SEE ALSO INDEX TO LOCATIONS PAGES 12-13

**Tigh Chualain**
Spiddal, Co. Galway .............100
☎ 091-553609

**Tigh Fitz**
Aran Islands, Co. Galway ........69
☎ 099-61213

**Tinakilly House Hotel**
Rathnew, Co. Wicklow ..........377
☎ 0404-69274

**Tir Gan Ean House Hotel**
Doolin, Co. Clare ....................41
☎ 065-707 5726

**Tower Hotel**
Dublin City, Co. Dublin ..........322
☎ 01-468 5400

**Tower Hotel & Leisure Centre**
Waterford City, Co. Waterford ......251
☎ 051-862300

**Tralee Townhouse**
Tralee, Co. Kerry ..................219
☎ 066-718 1111

**Treacy's Hotel**
Enniscorthy, Co. Wexford ......255
☎ 053-923 7798

**Trident Hotel**
Kinsale, Co. Cork ..................170
☎ 021-477 9300

**Trim Castle Hotel**
Trim, Co. Meath....................358
☎ 046-948 3000

**Trinity Capital Hotel**
Dublin City, Co. Dublin ..........322
☎ 01-648 1000

**Tulip Inn Dublin Airport**
Dublin Airport, Co. Dublin ......278
☎ 01-895 7777

**Tullamore Court Hotel Conference & Leisure Centre**
Tullamore, Co. Offaly ............363
☎ 057-934 6666

**Tullylagan Country House Hotel**
Cookstown, Co. Tyrone..........393
☎ 028-8676 5100

**Twelfth Lock Hotel (The)**
Dublin City, Co. Dublin ..........323
☎ 01-860 7400

**Twelve (The)**
Barna, Co. Galway ..................70
☎ 091-597000

## U

**Uppercross House**
Dublin City, Co. Dublin ..........323
☎ 01-497 5486

## V

**Valley Hotel (The)**
Fivemiletown, Co. Tyrone ......394
☎ 028-8952 1505

**Valley Suites (The)**
Killarney, Co. Kerry .............211
☎ 064-23600

**Vaughan Lodge and Seafood Restaurant**
Lahinch, Co. Clare ..................49
☎ 065-708 1111

**Victoria Hotel**
Cork City, Co. Cork................163
☎ 021-427 8788

**Victoria Hotel**
Galway City, Co. Galway..........90
☎ 091-567433

**Victoria House Hotel**
Killarney, Co. Kerry .............211
☎ 064-35430

**Villa Rose Hotel & V - Spa**
Ballybofey, Co. Donegal ..........55
☎ 074-913 2266

**Virginia's Guesthouse**
Kenmare, Co. Kerry ..............192
☎ 064-41021

## W

**Walter Raleigh Hotel**
Youghal, Co. Cork ................177
☎ 024-92011

**Wards Hotel**
Galway City, Co. Galway..........90
☎ 091-581508

**Waterford Castle Hotel & Golf Club**
Waterford City, Co. Waterford ......251
☎ 051-878203

**Waterford Marina Hotel**
Waterford City, Co. Waterford ......251
☎ 051-856600

**Waterfront (The)**
Baltimore, Co. Cork ..............145
☎ 028-20600

**Waterfront Hotel**
Galway City, Co. Galway..........91
☎ 091-588100

**Waterloo House**
Dublin City, Co. Dublin ..........323
☎ 01-660 1888

**Watermarque Boutique Hotel**
Cahersiveen, Co. Kerry..........179
☎ 066-947 2222

**Waters Edge (The)**
Rathmullan, Co. Donegal ........67
☎ 074-915 8182

**WatersEdge Hotel**
Cobh, Co. Cork ....................152
☎ 021-481 5566

**Waterside**
Graiguenamanagh, Co. Kilkenny ..220
☎ 059-972 4246

**Waterside House Hotel (The)**
Donabate, Co. Dublin............274
☎ 01-843 6153

**Wellington Park Hotel**
Belfast City, Belfast City ........387
☎ 028-9038 1111

**West Cork Hotel**
Skibbereen, Co. Cork............176
☎ 028-21277

**West County Hotel**
Dublin City, Co. Dublin ..........324
☎ 01-626 4011

**Westbrook House**
Ennis, Co. Clare......................44
☎ 065-684 0173

**Westbury (The)**
Dublin City, Co. Dublin ..........324
☎ 01-679 1122

**Westcourt Hotel**
Drogheda, Co. Louth ............347
☎ 041-983 0965

**Western Hotel (The)**
Galway City, Co. Galway..........91
☎ 091-562834

**Western Strands Hotel**
Belmullet, Co. Mayo..............117
☎ 097-81096

**Westfield House**
Killorglin , Co. Kerry..............213
☎ 066-976 1909

**Westgrove Hotel & Conference Centre**
Clane, Co. Kildare ................334
☎ 045-989900

**Westin Dublin**
Dublin City, Co. Dublin ..........324
☎ 01-645 1000

**Westlodge Hotel**
Bantry, Co. Cork ..................146
☎ 027-50360

**Westport Inn Hotel**
Westport, Co. Mayo ..............127
☎ 098-29200

**Westport Plaza Hotel**
Westport, Co. Mayo ..............127
☎ 098-51166

**Westport Woods Hotel & Spa**
Westport, Co. Mayo ..............127
☎ 098-25811

**Westwood (The)**
Galway City, Co. Galway..........91
☎ 091-521442

**Whispering Pines Hotel**
Crosshaven, Co. Cork ..........164
☎ 021-483 1843

**White House**
Kinsale, Co. Cork..................170
☎ 021-477 2125

**White House**
Galway City, Co. Galway..........92
☎ 091-529399

**White Sands Hotel**
Portmarnock, Co. Dublin ......329
☎ 01-866 6000

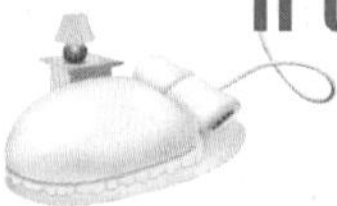